SMS 2003 Recipes

A Problem-Solution Approach

Greg Ramsey
and Warren Byle

Apress®

SMS 2003 Recipes: A Problem-Solution Approach

Copyright © 2006 by Greg Ramsey and Warren Byle

ISBN 978-1-59059-712-5

President and Publisher: Paul Manning
Lead Editor: Jonathan Gennick
Technical Reviewer: Chris Minaugh, Michael Niehaus, Duncan Mcalynn
Editorial Board: Steve Anglin, Mark Beckner, Ewan Buckingham, Gary Cornell, Jonathan Gennick, Jonathan Hassell, Michelle Lowman, James Markham, Matthew Moodie, Jeff Olson, Jeffrey Pepper, Frank Pohlmann, Douglas Pundick, Ben Renow-Clarke, Dominic Shakeshaft, Matt Wade, Tom Welsh
Coordinating Editor: Laura Cheu
Copy Editor: Heather Lang, Nicole LeClerc
Compositor: Kinetic Publishing Services, LLC
Indexer: Present Day Indexing
Artist: Kinetic Publishing Services, LLC
Cover Designer: Anna Ishchenko

Distributed to the book trade worldwide by Springer Science+Business Media, LLC., 233 Spring Street, 6th Floor, New York, NY 10013. Phone 1-800-SPRINGER, fax (201) 348-4505, e-mail orders-ny@springer-sbm.com, or visit www.springeronline.com.

For information on translations, please e-mail rights@apress.com, or visit www.apress.com.

Apress and friends of ED books may be purchased in bulk for academic, corporate, or promotional use. eBook versions and licenses are also available for most titles. For more information, reference our Special Bulk Sales–eBook Licensing web page at www.apress.com/bulk-sales.

Contents at a Glance

Contents

Foreword

Long ago, in a land far, far away, the life of the SMS administrator was lonely indeed! My first exposure to SMS was the Release to Manufacturing (RTM) of version 2.0 (v2.0). My challenge was to design, implement, and administer what was to become a 40-site, worldwide implementation. Much to my chagrin, my only technical resource was the *Administrator's Guide* that accompanied the product—a compelling and informative work, it was not.

As a seasoned IT professional, I have learned that one of the best ways to become familiar (and ultimately proficient) with a new technology is to elicit the experiences of others who have gone before me—the peer community. To my surprise, for SMS there seemed to be none. After a lot of digging, I uncovered something called the SMS Alliance. No, this was not the Alliance we all know and love today. It was a fee-based consortium of SMS administrators, facilitated by Software Spectrum. For $5,000, we joined with high expectations of all the pearls of wisdom that would surely come after paying such an entrance fee. After all, there was a members-only forum space where one could pose a question or a problem, and other members could share their insights. Sure, this fee also included an annual pilgrimage to the Mecca of the SMS world (Redmond, Washington) for meetings with the SMS program team. Unfortunately, my experience with this entire community was painful. A question posted to the forum could go days or even weeks without a response, and often there was no response. To their credit, several of the Software Spectrum engineers who moderated the forum would often step up with some help, but all in all, it was a very lonely place.

Eventually, I found my way to the SMS e-mail list hosted by Steve Wynkoop and known as SWYNK. There, I found what I was looking for: an active e-mail list with many subscribers, most of whom knew much more than I did. This early experience with an SMS community was a godsend. I posted frequently, asking tons of questions and getting many good answers. This resource was a large part of the unqualified success of my first SMS deployment. Throughout this period, however, the amount and quality of published technical information about SMS was still nearly nonexistent. The SWYNK list continued to be my only resource for quality information.

After many months of SWYNK participation, gaining experience of my own along the way, I was finally able to *answer* more and more questions instead of only asking them. I also began to notice a trend: frequently, the same questions were asked repeatedly as more and more newbies joined our ranks over time. About that same time, I also discovered the power of the Outlook e-mail client's Notes feature. I began to save questions and their answer or answers (as there are often more ways than one to solve the same issue). To that end, I started to build up my Notes inventory. I developed a system in which each note was a problem, followed by the contact information for the person with the answer (this system was great for doing one-on-one follow-up after the fact, if needed), and lastly with the answer. This way, when I saw a reprise of a previously discussed problem, a simple search through the Outlook Notes database would reveal the solution. I would then quickly and easily copy and paste the answer into a reply e-mail to the poster, and presto!—another happy administrator. Eventually, I began to preface my replies with an attempt at a witty prelude and a not-so-subtle reference to TechNet by labeling my reply "From EdNet." Eventually, I got ambitious; I compiled my entire database and released it as a commercial technical reference e-book. (If you're curious, you can see it today at http://www.myitforum.com attached as a download to my article "EdNet 2002—The SMS 2.0 Reference Work.")

Eventually, the SWYNK list fell on hard times, and the quantity and quality of published articles began to deteriorate. The e-mail list server became an issue as well. What to do? Rod Trent, one of the more prolific columnists contributing to SWYNK's content, decided to try to pull together a new site and try again. By that time, quite a few folks were enrolled on the SWYNK list. A number of us who had grown to depend on the mutual-support model inherent in that kind of online community joined Rod in what was to become myITForum.com (http://www.myitforum.com). This site has become arguably the preeminent resource outside of Microsoft for the systems administrator who specializes in SMS, Microsoft Operations Manager (MOM), scripting, and myriad other related disciplines.

Why do I provide this history lesson? It's simply to help you understand the power of community and of people helping people. You see, throughout this entire period (we're talking about the life cycle of SMS v2.0; SMS 2003 was still on the drawing board!), the amount and quality of SMS technical documentation from Microsoft was still pretty sparse. Sure, white papers began to appear, and the webcast paradigm was ramping up, as were the annual SMS conferences. But more often than not, when you got into a jam during your daily routine, the myITforum.com SMS forum or the e-mail list was your first stop. Feeding this community was the significant increase in sales in the SMS world following the release of SMS v2.0. Along with those increasing numbers came more and more newbies looking for help. Eventually, they too began answering questions instead of asking them. The end result was an unprecedented growth in expertise within the administrator community. People started tinkering and poking around under the hood, looking for ways to make life easier, to pull more and more information out of the system, to build custom reports, and to modify the SMS_DEF.MOF file to create *very* cool stuff heretofore unknown to even exist. The community flourished and was awash with great information and how-to solutions.

Then it happened: the Microsoft software development project known as Topaz was officially released, and SMS 2003 was born. Along with that event came the beginnings of a flood of technical documentation: guides, white papers, and so on. You see, during all this time, Redmond was not asleep at the switch. They heard the community loud and clear. "We need documentation!" the community said, and documentation is what we got, by the truckload.

It's a good thing we had asked for documentation, because SMS 2003 was an entirely new beast. Sure, the Administrator console still looked pretty much the same, and we still had packages, programs, collections, and advertisements. But the similarities stopped when we looked under the hood. Just look at that LOGS folder! Extending the Active Directory schema? Advanced Security? Signed communications? Advanced Client? Management points? And what the heck am I doing learning about Internet Information Services (IIS)? We clearly weren't in Kansas anymore. The initial transition to SMS 2003 was tough enough on those who migrated from SMS v2.0, but pity the brand-new administrator who had not a *clue* about what was going on.

Well, all I can say is remember the old adage "Be careful what you ask for." Before you could say "SP1," SMS administrators were totally awash in information: monthly webcasts, white papers by the score, Management Summit sessions and a DVD that contained them all, all sorts of new and very cool tools and utilities from the community itself, and more and more articles published on myITForum.com.

Throughout all of this, one significant problem remained. Administrators were still confronted with new problems on a daily basis. Where could they find the answers? Were they in the *SMS 2003 Administrator's Companion*? *SMS 2003 Operations Guide*? *Scenarios and Procedures for SMS 2003*? A forum article? Or wait, was it in someone's download utility? Sure enough, the pendulum had swung to the other extreme—too *much* information. There was so much information that even my ability to keep up with the old Outlook Notes database began to suffer significantly. One just could not keep up.

Enter a couple of guys from within the ranks of the myITForum.com community who apparently said, "Enough is enough!" They tackled this problem. In *SMS 2003 Recipes: A Problem-Solution Approach*, you will find what I consider to be the single document to pull a great deal of information together into a neat, simple, and eminently usable resource. Greg Ramsey and Warren Byle document virtually *every* piece of the *SMS 2003 Operations Guide* and the Administrator console, and they explain every step, feature, function, and setting along the way. Think of this as the *SMS 2003 Operations Guide* on steroids, with a hefty dose of third-party tools and utilities information tossed in for good measure.

This book has valuable information for administrators at every level, from novice to expert. Each recipe is (to me) reminiscent of my crude efforts in EdNet 2002: list a task; explain how it is accomplished using the SMS Administrator console (assuming it *can* be done in the GUI); follow up with an example doing the same thing using VBScript (including the code—talk about a great tutorial on scripting!); follow this up with a discussion of the entire process; and finally, toss in a "See Also" summary of related works. The format of *SMS 2003 Recipes*—the excellent use of the recipe format, the clear and descriptive recipe titles, and the inclusion of numerous URLs—make this book a must have. Here, in one place, you see cross-references to the SDK; the *SMS 2003 Operations Guide*; the *SMS 2003 Administrator's Companion*; *Scenarios and Procedures for SMS 2003*; particular authors' related articles, tools, or utilities on myITForum.com or elsewhere; and on and on. Got a question about or a problem with a particular feature or function? Open *SMS 2003 Recipes* to the table of contents or the index; find the feature, function, or solution you need to implement; and go to the recipe that relates to it. Here, *all in one place*, are details on *how* to get it done and *all* the related references the authors could find that are germane, with a URL to point you directly to resources for further research on the Web. Just type the URL, and you're there! Digging through reams of documentation, Googling terms, searching forums, and the like are history. Odds are good that it's all in here—in one place and in the right context. I found the recipes on security patching alone to be priceless! Toss in the step-by-step summary of how to build your very own SMS lab using Microsoft Virtual PC, and the book pays for itself.

As the world of the SMS administrator becomes more and more complex, and as Microsoft and the SMS community at large continue to put forth their superb supporting materials, the peer community grows in numbers and sophistication, with corresponding demands for more information. This recipe book needs to be in every SMS administrator's kitchen!

Ed Aldrich
SMS and Symantec Antivirus Administrator, Perot Systems
Microsoft MVP, SMS (2003–2006)
myITForum.com Advisory Council member and columnist
TOPAZ Early Adopters Program
Founder and co-chair, New England Area SMS User Group
SMS Industry Expert Speaker (2002–2006)

About the Authors

GREG RAMSEY, a Microsoft Most Valuable Professional (MVP) for SMS, has been working with SMS and desktop deployment since 1998. He currently works for Dell, Inc., in Austin, Texas, as an SMS administrator. He has extensive knowledge in VBScript, WMI, ADSI, SMS Installer, Wise Package Studio, and VB .NET. Prior to 1998, he was a sergeant in the United States Marine Corps. He holds a bachelor's degree in computer sciences and engineering (BSCSE) from The Ohio State University. Greg is a member of the Institute of Electrical and Electronics Engineers (IEEE) and Association for Computing Machinery (ACM), and he is a columnist for myITforum.com. He is also cofounder of the Ohio SMS Users Group (http://www.myitforum.com/blog/osug) and the creator of SMSView (http://www.smsview.com).

WARREN BYLE is a Microsoft Certified Systems Engineer (MCSE) and has been working with SMS for the last seven years. He works at Grange Insurance in Columbus, Ohio, as an SMS engineer. He is cofounder of the Ohio SMS Users Group and serves as chairman.

About the Technical Reviewers

CHRIS MINAUGH graduated with honors from Ohio Dominican University, where he received his bachelor's degree in information science. He has worked for the past 14 years at the Ohio Bureau of Workers Compensation and has been an SMS administrator for the past 5 years. He has extensive knowledge in VBScript, WMI, SMS Installer, Wise Package Studio, and VB .NET. He is a member of the Ohio SMS Users Group, where he serves as head of the state government subcommittee.

MICHAEL NIEHAUS is a systems design engineer for Microsoft, currently working as the developer for the Solution Accelerator for Business Desktop Deployment, creating new tools and guidance for deploying Windows XP, Windows Vista, and Office 2007. Prior to joining Microsoft, Michael spent ten years working as an enterprise IT infrastructure architect, focusing on deploying and operating Microsoft products such as Windows, Office, SMS, Active Directory, and Exchange. Before that, he was a mainframe systems programmer and database analyst.

DUNCAN MCALYNN is a three-time Microsoft MVP award winner with over ten years' experience with SMS. When not acting in his role as managing consultant for Catapult Systems, he and his wife, Amanda, take full advantage of the natural surroundings of Austin, Texas.

Acknowledgments

Books don't write themselves—especially SMS books. First, our hats are off to our editor, Jonathan Gennick, and our project manager, Richard Dal Porto. Jonathan, your keen eye and technical expertise really helped shape this book into a book, rather than just a stack of somewhat organized thoughts. You helped us learn how to improve our writing skills and consistency. Richard, your persistence and organizational skills helped make this book a reality.

To our technical reviewers, Duncan, Michael, and Chris: We were very fortunate to have all three of you. Each of you brought your expertise to the table and did a great job of keeping us on target and concise. Thanks for your hard work and dedication.

To the SMS community: myITforum.com, the SMS e-mail lists, and the Microsoft SMS newsgroups have been our most valuable resources throughout our SMS careers. Without the community interaction over the years, we would all probably be a little less SMS-savvy.

Greg Ramsey and Warren Byle

My fiancée and my sunshine, Tina: Thank you for understanding all the late nights, techie talk, and home-improvement project delays because of this book. Just like working on the car or installing a new garage door, take my estimated time to complete a project and double it. Thank you for your patience, understanding, and love.

Greg Ramsey

I want to thank my wife, Julianne, and daughter, Olivia, for still smiling through the late nights and short weekends that this project demanded. Thanks for loving me through it all.

Warren Byle

Preface

If you're like us, you have always wished to have a handy reference for Microsoft Systems Management Server (SMS). As you are probably aware, SMS is a complex and powerful product, and remembering information about every configuration point would be nearly impossible. That's where this book comes in—to help you quickly get through those unfamiliar configuration tasks. We hope this book will become the reference you keep closest to you.

SMS 2003 Recipes: A Problem-Solution Approach is written in a convenient format for quick reference. As with a cookbook, you browse the detailed table of contents or index to locate a specific task. After navigating to the task, review the problem statement, which is followed by the solution. Many recipes also provide source code for scripted processes to complete the tasks. One more valuable feature you will find in most recipes is the "See Also" section. If you still have questions after reading the solution, the "See Also" section directs you to other recipes in the book, as well as to other documentation (in both print and electronic formats), to help you accomplish the task.

■ ■ ■

CHAPTER 1

Getting Started

Microsoft Systems Management Server (SMS) is likely one of the most challenging and rewarding technologies that you will ever encounter. To help you get started on your quest to master SMS, in this chapter we give you an overview of some key tools you need to succeed with SMS. We look at scripting and packaging tools, along with additional resources that we rely on every day.

Programming Notes for VBScript

The intent of VBScript solutions is to provide you with the minimum amount of code required to allow you focus on the solution to the specific problem. As with all changes being introduced into a production environment, validate your VBScript solutions in a test environment first. If you do not have a test environment, don't worry—we'll show you how to set one up later in Chapter 17. If you're new to VBScripting, we highly recommend you spend some time developing your scripting skills. You'll soon realize the power of scripting in a Windows environment, whether for SMS or for general Windows administrative tasks.

Text Editor

Windows Notepad may be used to edit VBScript scripts. However, if you plan to spend a lot of time editing and testing scripts, we recommend using an editor designed for this purpose. Crimson Editor (http://www.crimsoneditor.com) is a free editor that has syntax highlighting and allows execution of command-line code from within the application. Sapien's PrimalScript (http://www.primalscript.com) is also a good editor.

Replaceable Text

We provide many VBScript examples in this book, a number of which will connect to the SMS site to accomplish a task. Replaceable text is used instead of fictitious names in such cases. Replaceable text is easy to identify, because it is surrounded by brackets (< >) and appears in italics. The following are the most frequently used throughout this book:

    <SMSServer>: The server name of the site to connect (e.g., HQSMSServer)

    <SMSSiteCode>: The SMS site code of the site to connect (e.g., LAB)

Error Checking and Best Practices

Error checking is a very important part of scripting. By implementing error checking, you create more control in your script, because you can identify a problem and initiate appropriate action. Now that we have mentioned how important error checking is, please note that most of the sample code in this book does not include error checking. To include proper error checking would be ideal, but it would also noticeably increase the size of the book.

The code examples that follow in this section accomplish the same task: establishing a connection to an SMS primary site. The first example shows the bare minimum required for the code to function properly. The second example demonstrates how most code in this book will be displayed.

First, let's look at the bare minimum:

```
Set objSMS = GetObject("WinMgmts:\\SMSVPCLAB\root\SMS\site_LAB")
```

As you can see, all it really takes to establish a connection to an SMS primary site (in most cases, anyway) is one line of code. SMSVPCLAB is the server name of the SMS primary site, and LAB is the SMS site code of that primary site. This code is clear and concise, but if you have multiple primary SMS sites or you like to share your code with other SMS administrators, consider using variables, for example:

```
strSMSServer = <SMSServer>
Set objLoc =  CreateObject("WbemScripting.SWbemLocator")
Set objSMS= objLoc.ConnectServer(strSMSServer, "root\sms")
Set Results = objSMS.ExecQuery _
    ("SELECT * From SMS_ProviderLocation WHERE ProviderForLocalSite = true")
For each Loc in Results
    If Loc.ProviderForLocalSite = True Then
        Set objSMS = objLoc.ConnectServer(Loc.Machine, "root\sms\site_" & _
            Loc.SiteCode)
    end if
Next
```

As you can see, the variable strSMSServer has been added and set to the server name of the SMS primary site. After connecting, we query the primary site to obtain the server name and site code to the SMS provider. Although the code appears a little more complex, using variables enables you to modify the code more easily to connect to different servers. For example, if your code requires the SMS server name in four different sections, you can either edit each line every time you want to use a different server or declare a variable, so that you need to change the server name in only one location.

By default in VBScript, the interpreter will display the first error encountered and then exit. To prevent your script from terminating, start with the following declaration at the beginning of the script:

```
On Error Resume Next
```

By adding one line of code, your VBScript will run from start to finish and not report any errors. Errors encountered will be ignored, and the interpreter will continue to attempt to process each line of the script until completion. Using On Error Resume Next in conjunction with error checking maximizes your ability to detect and gracefully handle errors encountered. Use the err object to obtain the error number and description, and to clear the error as follows:

```
On Error Resume Next
strSMSServer = <SMSServer>
Set objLoc =  CreateObject("WbemScripting.SWbemLocator")
Set objSMS= objLoc.ConnectServer(strSMSServer, "root\sms")
Set Results = objSMS.ExecQuery _
    ("SELECT * From SMS_ProviderLocation WHERE ProviderForLocalSite = true")
For each Loc in Results
    If Loc.ProviderForLocalSite = True Then
        Set objSMS = objLoc.ConnectServer(Loc.Machine, "root\sms\site_" & _
            Loc.SiteCode)
    end if
Next
```

```
If Err.Number <> 0 then
    Wscript.echo "An Error Occurred:  Error Number=" & _
    Err.Number & vbCRLF & Err.Description & vbCRLF
    Err.Clear
Else
    Wscript.echo "Successfully connected to " & strSMSSiteCode
End if
```

While testing, you may want to avoid using On Error Resume Next as much as possible, as you will then be able to see all the errors your code encounters.

Another best practice when scripting is to include Option Explicit at the beginning of every script, which forces the declaration of variables before they are used. In VBScript, declare variables using the Dim keyword. In addition to declaring variables, it's good practice to release variables when they are no longer needed, to free up memory for other processes. To release a variable, set it equal to Nothing. Observe the inclusion of Option Explicit, declaration of variables (the Dim statement), and release of variables in the following example:

```
Option Explicit
On Error Resume Next
Dim strSMSServer, strSMSSiteCode, objSMS
strSMSServer = <SMSServer>
Set objLoc = CreateObject("WbemScripting.SWbemLocator")
Set objSMS= objLoc.ConnectServer(strSMSServer, "root\sms")
Set Results = objSMS.ExecQuery _
    ("SELECT * From SMS_ProviderLocation WHERE ProviderForLocalSite = true")
For each Loc in Results
    If Loc.ProviderForLocalSite = True Then
        Set objSMS = objLoc.ConnectServer(Loc.Machine, "root\sms\site_" & _
            Loc.SiteCode)
    end if
Next
If Err.Number <> 0 then
    Wscript.echo "An Error Occurred:  Error Number=" & _
    Err.Number & vbCRLF & Err.Description & vbCRLF
    Err.Clear
Else
    Wscript.echo "Successfully connected to " & strSMSSiteCode
End if
Set strSMSServer = Nothing
Set strSMSSiteCode = Nothing
Set objSMS = Nothing
```

For more information about general programming in VBScript, check out one of O'Reilly's books on VBScript (http://www.oreilly.com/catalog/vbscripting). W3Schools provides a very nice (and free) tutorial for VBScript here: http://www.w3schools.com/vbscript. Microsoft TechNet's Script Center Script Repository (http://www.microsoft.com/technet/scriptcenter/scripts) also contains several tutorials and examples. Note that the Script Center Script Repository now contains a link to VBScript scripts for SMS 2003: http://www.microsoft.com/technet/scriptcenter/scripts. The Code Repository, managed by Ron Crumbaker and Dan Thomson on myITforum.com, offers many sample scripts for SMS and VBScripting in general: http://myitforum.com/articles/1/view.asp?id=8645.

WHICH IS BETTER: ADMINSTUDIO (SMS EDITION) OR SMS INSTALLER?

We're glad you asked! Some say that Macrovision's FLEXnet AdminStudio SMS Edition is the replacement for SMS Installer. While these technologies do overlap, we find that the SMS Edition of AdminStudio is missing some of what we consider "key" features of SMS Installer. Definitely take some time to evaluate each product (after all, they are free with the purchase of SMS), and see how each fits your needs. As alternatives, you may consider Wise Solutions' Wise Package Studio (http://www.wise.com) and Macrovision's FLEXnet Admin-Studio (http://www.macrovision.com/products/flexnet_adminstudio; this is the full version of AdminStudio—we discuss the limitations of the free SMS Edition later in this chapter).

We recommend starting with the free utilities provided by Microsoft. The costs of the other products mentioned here are significant and will probably require advance budgeting for your organization.

SMS Installer

Microsoft SMS Installer is a free tool SMS administrators can use to create installations, repackage installations, and more. On the surface, it may appear to be a basic (and outdated) tool. But as some of the examples in this book demonstrate, you can use SMS Installer to accomplish the difficult tasks SMS administrators encounter often. Because SMS Installer is free (with the purchase of SMS, of course) and fairly intuitive, it is a nice tool for beginners. And as many SMS experts will tell you, SMS Installer is very handy to have around to take care of smaller tasks. SMS Installer also has uninstall support.

Obtaining SMS Installer

You can download SMS Installer from the Microsoft Systems Management Server 2003 Downloads site at http://www.microsoft.com/smserver/downloads/2003. The download's file size is approximately 10MB. Run the executable on an SMS primary site to extract the files to the directory of your choice. Note that the executable must be run on an SMS primary site, as it prevents non–SMS administrators from obtaining this free utility.

SMS Installer Basics

In this section, we cover a few SMS Installer basics.

SMS Installer has two views: Installation Expert and Script Editor. The Installation Expert is used primarily for repackaging installations and testing installations. It offers a wizard-based display for creating an installation, as shown in Figure 1-1.

The Script Editor, shown in Figure 1-2, is not quite as intuitive as the Installation Expert, but it's more flexible and powerful. The Script Editor has several "mini-wizards" that you can use in very creative ways to generate complete installations. Using the Script Editor, you can create very powerful scripts, wrappers, and utilities fairly easily. You can also switch views from the Installation Expert to the Script Editor to see all script actions, and you can customize the installation created in the Installation Expert. Also, after repackaging an application, you can switch to the Script Editor view to inspect and edit the repackaged installation for extraneous data captured during the repackaging that is not part of the installation.

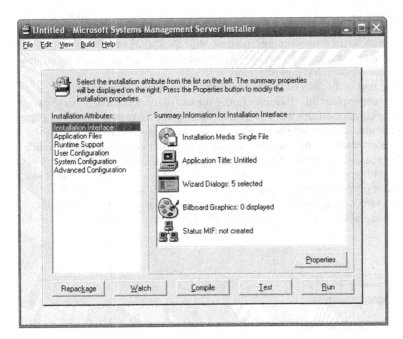

Figure 1-1. *SMS Installer—Installation Expert*

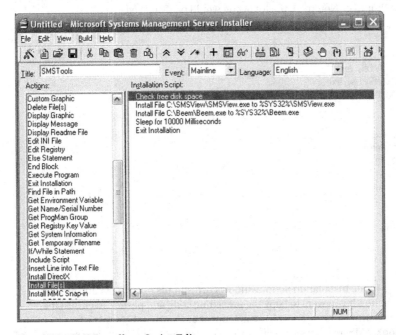

Figure 1-2. *SMS Installer—Script Editor*

SMS Installer Scripting Notes

SMS Installer does not use an actual programming language. Most SMS administrators consider SMS Installer more of a scripting language, driven by several wizards. The examples throughout this book will help you understand how to leverage this utility.

The most challenging part of the SMS Installer Script Editor, for the purposes of this book, is to provide example code. To help explain this challenge, notice the Installation Script window shown in Figure 1-2. Think of the contents of this window as an outline of the tasks to accomplish. For example, to install a file, double-click Install File(s) in the Actions window, select the file source and destination, include any additional information (Replace Always, Register DLL, etc.), and then click OK. After completing these steps, one line of text will appear in the Installation Script window (e.g., Install File C:\SMSView\SMSView.exe to %SYS32%\SMSView.exe). This line briefly details what will occur in that step, but it doesn't give the complete picture.

Figure 1-3 shows an example of installing two files and then "sleeping" for ten seconds before exiting the installation. It displays just the script portion of a larger screen (such as that shown in Figure 1-2).

```
Check free disk space
Install File C:\SMSView\SMSView.exe to %SYS32%\SMSView.exe
Install File C:\Beem\Beem.exe to %SYS32%\Beem.exe
Sleep for 10000 Milliseconds
Exit Installation
```

Figure 1-3. *SMS Installer—Script Editor code*

If you were to highlight all the lines of this script's code, copy them to the clipboard, and then paste them into a text editor (e.g., Notepad), the following would be displayed:

```
item: Check Disk Space
end
item: Install File
  Source=C:\SMSView\SMSView.exe
  Destination=%SYS32%\SMSView.exe
  Flags=0000000000000010
end
item: Install File
  Source=C:\Beem\Beem.exe
  Destination=%SYS32%\Beem.exe
  Flags=0000000000000010
end
item: Sleep
  Sleep=10000
end
item: Exit Installation
  Variable=0
  Flags=0
end
```

Notice that each line in the Installation Script window corresponds to an item: and end tag when pasted into a text editor. If you were to copy the preceding code and paste it back into the SMS Installer Installation Script window, it would again appear as shown in Figure 1-3.

Throughout this book, SMS Installer code will be displayed as code with item: and end tags, which will provide you with complete information for the code. Please note that you can download all of the book's code from the Source Code area of the Apress web site (http://www.apress.com).

Tip For a thorough reference guide with a number of examples, we highly recommend picking up a copy of *Microsoft SMS Installer* by Rod Trent (McGraw-Hill, 2000). Also, Chapter 15 of *Microsoft Systems Management Server 2003 Administrator's Companion* by Steven Kaczmarek (Microsoft Press, 2004) and Chapter 7 of the *SMS 2003 Operations Guide* (http://www.microsoft.com/technet/prodtechnol/sms/sms2003/opsguide) provide additional information about SMS Installer.

Providing Feedback to the SMS Team

There has been a good deal of discussion in the SMS administrator community during the past couple of years surrounding the following question: "Why hasn't Microsoft updated SMS Installer?" Most SMS administrators would like to see an update to this free utility, and if you're in that group, be sure to voice your opinion to the SMS team at Microsoft by sending an e-mail to smswish@microsoft.com. In fact, anytime you would like to see a change in SMS or have suggestions for improvement, send the team an e-mail. There are no guarantees that you will receive a reply, but rest assured that your e-mail will be read and know that functionality has been added to SMS over the years as a result of user feedback.

Once you become familiar with SMS Installer, and you feel you're ready to take it to the next level, we recommend taking some time to evaluate Wise Package Studio (http://www.wise.com) and AdminStudio (http://www.macrovision.com/products/flexnet_adminstudio).

Macrovision's AdminStudio SMS Edition

The following quote is from the FLEXnet AdminStudio SMS Edition download site:[1]

> *AdminStudio provides businesses with the ability to prepare, publish, and distribute software packages via SMS 2003 without ever touching the SMS server console, significantly improving the efficiency of application management efforts.*

So far this sounds really good. Unfortunately, this sentence refers to the full version of AdminStudio, not the SMS Edition. A little more detail helps us see more of the complete picture of AdminStudio SMS Edition:

> *AdminStudio SMS Edition includes the full-featured industry leading InstallShield Repackager that prepares one or more legacy setup.exe packages for deployment by converting it to a Windows Installer .MSI package. The InstallShield Tuner is included to assist in customizing MSI packages by adding files, changing registry settings, adding license keys, removing registration wizards, or making other modifications that will then be compiled in a transform (MST). Finally, a Distribution Wizard and secure SMS Web console are included to assist in handing the packages off for distribution through Systems Management Server 2003.*

While many features are available with this version, it is a not a full-featured product. Macrovision details the differences among AdminStudio versions here: http://www.installshield.com/products/adminstudio/sms.

---

1. See http://www.microsoft.com/smserver/downloads/2003/featurepacks/adminstudio/default.mspx

The most important feature missing in the SMS Edition of AdminStudio is the AdminStudio Editor. The Editor (only available with the full product) allows you to create and edit an MSI package. The SMS Edition only allows you to repackage or create a Windows Installer transform. For example, if your manager instructs you to create a shortcut and make five registry entries on every workstation in your environment, AdminStudio SMS Edition would not do the job for you. Instead, consider using SMS Installer or one of the full-featured products mentioned previously to accomplish this task.

Obtaining AdminStudio SMS Edition

You can download FLEXnet AdminStudio SMS Edition from the Microsoft Systems Management Server 2003 downloads site at http://www.microsoft.com/smserver/downloads/2003. The download is approximately 275MB. Install the software on the workstation or server of your choice. To install AdminStudio SMS Edition, you will need to register with Macrovision to obtain a valid serial number.

AdminStudio SMS Edition Basics

In this section, we cover a few AdminStudio SMS Edition basics. At the time of this writing, no books have been written specifically for AdminStudio SMS Edition. Currently, the only resource available is the help integrated with the product.

The following are the main features of AdminStudio SMS Edition:

Repackager: The Repackager allows you to repackage or convert legacy installations into Windows Installer packages.

Tuner: The Tuner allows you to customize Windows Installer packages by using transforms.

Distribution Wizard: The Distribution Wizard helps you prepare packages created in AdminStudio SMS Edition for deployment.

As you can see, AdminStudio SMS Edition has limited functionality. The full version of AdminStudio provides much more functionality, but it also carries a much larger price tag. One confusing part of the SMS Edition is that all features of the full product are visible, but disabled. As you start to use AdminStudio SMS Edition, be prepared to frequently encounter the dialog box shown in Figure 1-4.

Figure 1-4. *AdminStudio SMS Edition dialog*

Repackager

The Repackager is nice, but it is also missing functionality in our opinion. Using SMS Installer, when you repackage an application, you can add, remove, and edit additional files, registry keys, and shortcuts. With AdminStudio SMS Edition, you can only include or exclude what was captured by the repackaging process. To get around this limitation, you would have to make the modifications manually during the repackaging process, which isn't always practical.

Figure 1-5 shows an example of selecting registry entries to include in an installation after repackaging an application (the lighter folder graphics signify exclusion from installation).

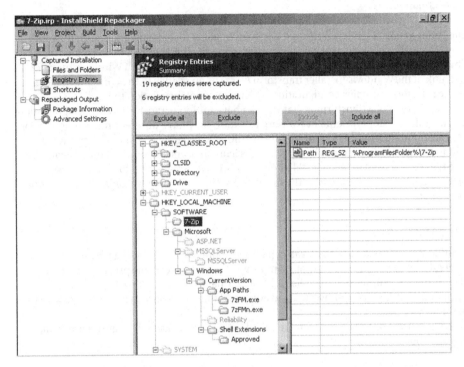

Figure 1-5. *Customization after repackaging an application in AdminStudio SMS Edition*

After including and excluding files, registry entries, and shortcuts, you configure the program information and build the product to generate a Windows Installer application. You can use the Distribution Wizard at this point to copy required files to your SMS package source location and also create a package definition file to easily import the installation into SMS.

Generally speaking, a best practice when repackaging an application is to always use a clean "model" workstation that is representative of the systems on which you intend to deploy the application. You must install the Repackager (in this case, AdminStudio SMS Edition) on the model workstation before you can begin repackaging. AdminStudio SMS Edition is significantly larger than SMS Installer (275MB vs. 10MB), so it requires more time and hard-drive space to prepare to repackage an installation. Also, AdminStudio requires an activation serial number to be entered each time the product is installed. This makes repackaging with AdminStudio more time consuming than with SMS Installer.

Tuner

The most valuable feature (in our opinion) of AdminStudio SMS Edition is the Tuner. The welcome screen of the Tuner says it best:

> *InstallShield Tuner allows Systems Administrators to use task-based views to easily customize third-party Windows Installer-based applications. Tuner contains everything you need to tailor and customize your application—without risking increased support costs from broken installations.*

Use the Tuner to take a vendor-generated Windows Installer installation and tune it for your environment. Generally speaking, you will never want to modify the Windows Installer file (.msi) provided by the vendor. Instead, use Tuner (or Wise InstallTailor) to create a Windows Installer transform. Think of the Windows Installer transform (.mst) as an overlay to the Windows Installer (.msi) file. The transform contains configuration settings to use at installation time.

The greatest benefit of a transform is that you can have multiple transforms for one application installation, as different departments in your organization may have different requirements. For example, the accounting department may require an Adobe Acrobat Reader shortcut on each user's desktop, but the loans department might not want this icon on users' desktops. In this scenario, the same source files can be used for each installation: simply create a transform for each one with the customizations required, and then deploy the installation with the proper transform to the appropriate department.

Distribution Wizard

The Distribution Wizard can be used to create a package definition file, copy to a network location, or launch the AdminStudio SMS web console. Unfortunately, the web console provided with AdminStudio SMS Edition will only allow you to distribute a new package. General package administration (modifying package settings, programs, etc.) and advertisement creation are only available with the full AdminStudio product.

Figure 1-6 displays one screen of several required to create a package, configure a program, and identify distribution points.

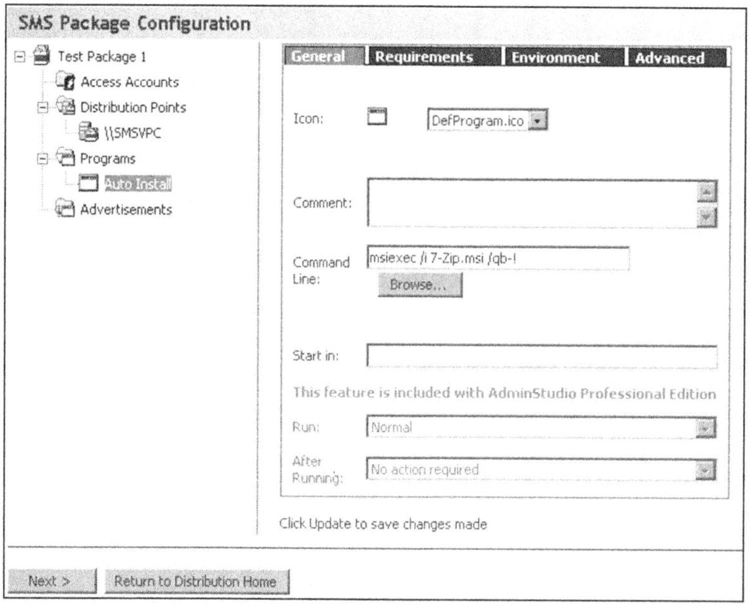

Figure 1-6. *Distributing a new package with the AdminStudio SMS Edition web console*

As the bold text in Figure 1-6 reminds you, not all features are available with the SMS Edition. The full-featured product allows you to set the environment and advanced settings. We feel the SMS Edition of the web console is so limited in functionality that it may not be worth the effort to use on a regular basis. Hopefully, future versions of AdminStudio SMS Edition will allow more functionality in the web console.

Finding More Information

We hope this book will help satisfy your appetite for SMS knowledge, but we know that we cannot cover absolutely everything you might need to manage your SMS environment, so in this section we present a list of the resources we use frequently.

Microsoft Knowledge Base

One of the first questions asked when someone suggests a solution to a Microsoft product problem is "Does Microsoft support that?" If the company does, there's usually a Knowledge Base (KB) article on it, which may or may not be published. You can find all of the published KB articles at http:// support.microsoft.com. KB articles are identified by a six-digit number; for example, KB 892429 covers the cluster support requirements for SMS 2003. If you want to be notified when new KB articles are available, subscribe to the e-mail/RSS feed notifications at http://www.kbalertz.com.

Microsoft Developer Network

Although you may not be a developer, you should be familiar with the Microsoft Developer Network (MSDN) web site (http://msdn.microsoft.com) and the vast amount of information available there. If you are looking to extend the functionality of SMS with another program, then MSDN is your first stop, since the SMS 2003 Software Development Kit (SDK) is maintained there. Information on WMI, error codes, and other hard-to-find answers can also be found on the MSDN site.

Web Sites

Most web sites provide information, but not all of that information is helpful to you as an SMS administrator. The following list contains a selection of web sites that will consistently provide you with good SMS information:

Microsoft Systems Management home page (http://www.microsoft.com/smserver): This site is the jumping-off point for systems management at Microsoft. It contains links to product information, technical resources, downloads, support information, and community resources.

Microsoft SMS Support home page (http://www.microsoft.com/smserver/support): This site is the clearinghouse for SMS support links. Keep it bookmarked.

SMS 2003 Technical FAQs (http://www.microsoft.com/technet/prodtechnol/sms/sms2003/ techfaq/default.mspx): This site contains frequently asked questions concerning updates to SMS, as well as clarification of Microsoft documentation for SMS.

The Blogcast Repository (http://www.blogcastrepository.com): Brian Tucker has over 200 blogcasts on all types of Microsoft technology. If you like to learn by watching, then this site will become a favorite.

Learn Systems Management (http://www.learnsystemsmanagement.com): Chris Urban has put together over 100 video tutorials for specific tasks using Microsoft technologies. If you are new to SMS and would like video training, check with Chris.

Training4sms (http://www.training4sms.com): This is another great site for SMS training material. John Green has online and CD-based courses available.

AppDeploy.com (http://www.appdeploy.com): This site is a great place to find tips and tricks on how to deploy applications in your environment.

Google (http://www.google.com): Google is a great search engine, but it really shines when you use it to search a specific web site such as http://www.microsoft.com. To search for SMS 2003 information on the Microsoft site, use SMS 2003 site:microsoft.com as your search parameters in Google.

Online Communities

As the saying goes, "Misery loves company," and when you are having problems, the best place to go is a community of your peers. The following list has are several very active communities that you should be involved in:

myITforum.com (http://myitforum.com): This is the premier systems management community that boasts over 18,000 members. Here you will find forums, articles, downloads, a daily newsletter, blogs, and regional user groups.

Cliff Hobb's FAQShop (http://faqshop.com): Cliff hosts this great site from the UK, but it has answers for everyone.

Microsoft's SMS Community (http://www.microsoft.com/smserver/community): Microsoft has created a web page that links many of the blogs of its own SMS team members along with MVPs. The site also provides links to Microsoft newsgroups, articles, webcasts, and the other communities just mentioned.

Newsgroups

Newsgroups are excellent forums for exchanging ideas and asking for help. Microsoft has newsgroups on practically every product they sell, including a number for SMS.

Microsoft's SMS Newsgroups (http://www.microsoft.com/technet/community/newsgroups/server/sms.mspx): Eight newsgroups that pertain to different areas of SMS are available at this web site. They are also available as RSS feeds.

Mailing Lists

Mailing lists are similar to newsgroups but are hosted on a different technology. Here is the main SMS e-mail list that we follow closely:

MSSMS (http://www.myitforum.com/Lists.asp): This is the very active SMS e-mail list for the *myITforum.com* community. For many, this e-mail list is a lifeline when they run into problems with SMS, since most posts to this list are answered very quickly.

RSS Feeds

Really Simple Syndication (RSS) and the blogging phenomenon have spread to nearly every corner of the SMS information landscape. If you are new to blogging and RSS, you will need to find an RSS feed reader that suits your needs. They come in all shapes and sizes, so check out the RSS Info web site to get started: http://blogspace.com/rss/readers.

The following is a short list of available RSS feeds that we follow:

myITforum.com RSS feeds (http://myitforum.com/blog): myITforum.com has a long list of SMS bloggers that is available as a main feed or individually. The daily newsletter and general news are also available as RSS feeds.

Microsoft MVP blogs (http://msmvps.com): These are the blogs of the men and women that Microsoft has awarded MVP status for their commitment to helping the user community.

Microsoft SMS team member blogs (http://www.microsoft.com/smserver/community): The Microsoft SMS Community web page provides links to the blogs of many of the SMS team members.

Books

In addition to the Microsoft online documentation, the following books are great sources of information:

Microsoft Systems Management Server 2003 Administrator's Companion by Steven Kaczmarek (Microsoft Press, 2004): If you are new to SMS and want to get a better understanding of the core concepts of SMS along with planning and implementation help, then you will want to check out this book.

Microsoft SMS Installer by Rod Trent (McGraw-Hill, 2000): This book covers all the ins and outs of SMS Installer. It is currently out of print, so grab it if you're lucky enough to find one.

CHAPTER 2

■■■

SMS Site Administration

Once you have successfully installed your first SMS site server, you will encounter myriad configuration options that you will need to evaluate and implement to expose SMS 2003's full potential. The recipes in this chapter are geared toward identifying and explaining the site configuration options available to you, so that you can tune up SMS and start taking advantage of its power.

Once your SMS site is up and running with management points/proxy management points and client access points created, various administration tasks will be required from time to time to extend or enhance SMS in your environment. This chapter will walk you through these configuration changes when required.

2-1. Setting the Parent Site

Problem

You want to set the parent site for a primary SMS site.

Solution

1. Open the SMS Administrator console.
2. From the SMS Administrator console, expand Site Database (*<Site Code>*), expand Site Hierarchy, right-click *<Site Name>*, and select Properties.
3. Select the General tab.
4. Click the Set Parent Site button.
5. Select the Report to Parent Site option and choose the parent site from the drop-down list.
6. Click OK to close the selection dialog box.
7. Click OK to apply the settings.

Discussion

When a secondary site is installed, the parent site is immediately identified. When a primary site is installed, no parent is required. When you install a primary site that is to report to a parent, you must set the parent site. Before setting the parent site (or changing the site's parent), you must ensure the parent-child and child-parent addresses are properly configured.

Note Before identifying the parent site, create an address between the two sites (one from child to parent, and one from parent to child).

See Also

- Recipe 2-17, "Creating an Address," shows how to create an address between two sites.

- Chapter 4 of the *Microsoft Systems Management Server 2003 Administrator's Companion* by Steven Kaczmarek (Microsoft Press, 2004) and Chapter 15 of the *SMS 2003 Concepts, Planning, and Deployment Guide* (part of the SMS 2003 documentation) show how to set a parent site.

2-2. Enabling Advanced Security Mode

Problem

You want to enable Advanced Security mode.

Solution

1. Open the SMS Administrator console.

2. From the SMS Administrator console, expand Site Database (<*Site Code*>), expand Site Hierarchy, right-click <*Site Name*>, and select Properties.

3. Select the General tab.

4. Click the Set Security button.

5. Click Yes on the Warning dialog box.

6. Click OK to apply the settings.

Discussion

In SMS 2003 advanced security mode, the Local System account is used to access local resources, and computer accounts are used to access network resources. Since computer accounts are used to access network resources, credentials (maintained by the operating system) are used that have very strong passwords, thus increasing the security of SMS. Security modes are configured on SMS primary sites and affect all secondary sites

You have the option to upgrade to advanced security on some sites, while leaving other sites in standard security mode if required for your environment. In such a case, the key is that you must have a "top-down" security configuration. To enable advanced security mode on a child site, its parent (and all other parents in its hierarchy) must be configured to use advanced security. So when upgrading to advanced security, you should upgrade the central site first.

Caution Upgrade to advanced security from the top down. A site configured for advanced security cannot report to a parent site configured for standard security.

Ensure the following requirements have been met before upgrading to advanced security:

- You must have SQL Server 2000 SP3 or higher.

- The SMS site server computer account is added to the Administrators group on each site system in the site (such as client access points and Microsoft SQL Server).

- Permissions are granted to the SMS site server computer account on the site servers of parent and child sites.

- The site server computer account rights are assigned to Active Directory.

- The site server is running Windows 2000 SP4 or later and has QFE 325804 applied.

The following are additional requirements:

- The SMS site server and all SMS site systems must be in an Active Directory domain.

- The SMS site database servers must be run in Windows authentication-only mode.

To add computer accounts to a domain group or local group of another computer from the command line, run the following command:

```
net localgroup <group> ➡
<domain name or local computer name>\<remote computer name>$ /add
```

For example, the following adds the YOUNGSTOWN computer to the Administrators group of the system where this command was executed:

```
net localgroup administrators smsvpclab\YOUNGSTOWN$ /add
```

Note Dynamic Host Configuration Protocol (DHCP) network discovery is disabled in advanced security mode. The Local System account does not have the appropriate security credentials to access DHCP data. Review the recipes that describe SMS discovery methods later in this chapter for alternatives to DHCP network discovery.

Caution Be certain you are ready to upgrade to advanced security mode. Once advanced security mode is applied, the only way to return to standard security mode is to reinstall SMS or restore your SMS site (and its registry) from a backup.

See Also

- The SMS 2003 FAQ section titled "Security Frequently Asked Questions" (http://www.microsoft.com/technet/prodtechnol/sms/sms2003/techfaq/tfaq12.mspx) provides answers to several questions concerning the upgrade to advanced security.

- Chapter 17 of the *Microsoft Systems Management Server 2003 Administrator's Companion* by Steve Kaczmarek (Microsoft Press, 2004) and Chapter 5 of the *SMS 2003 Concepts, Planning, and Deployment Guide* show how to upgrade to advanced security.

- The guide titled *Scenarios and Procedures for SMS 2003: Security* (part of the SMS documentation) provides an advanced security checklist to assist you when upgrading to advanced security.

2-3. Modifying SMS Service Accounts

Problem

You want to modify the SMS service and SQL accounts.

Solution

1. Open the SMS Administrator console.

2. From the SMS Administrator console, expand Site Database (*<Site Code>*), expand Site Hierarchy, right-click *<Site Name>*, and select Properties.

3. Select the Accounts tab.

4. Click the Set button for the account you want to modify.

5. Enter the user name and password for the account.

6. Click OK.

7. Click OK to apply the settings.

Tip You can also use the Manage Site Accounts command-line tool (msac.exe) to automate changes to the service accounts on multiple sites.

Discussion

The SMS Service account is the most important account when you are using SMS standard security. The following SMS services running on a site server use this account:

- SMS Executive
- Site Component Manager
- Site Backup
- SQL Monitor
- Client Configuration Manager

Typically, the Service account is a domain administrator, and the default name for it is SMSService. To make this account more secure, you may consider using a name other than SMSService, and you will also want to use a complex password. Another way to increase security is to add the SMS Service account to the local Administrators account of all servers running SMS components (site server, client access point, distribution point, management point, SQL, etc.), and then remove the SMS Service account from the domain administrators group. For the most secure method, eliminate the SMS Service account completely by upgrading to advanced security.

See Also

- Chapter 17 of the *Microsoft Systems Management Server 2003 Administrator's Companion* by Steve Kaczmarek (Microsoft Press, 2004) and Chapter 5 of the *SMS 2003 Concepts, Planning, and Deployment Guide* provide information for accounts specific to standard security.

- Appendix C of *Scenarios and Procedures for SMS 2003: Security* provides specific information on the functions of the SMS Service account.

2-4. Enumerating Site Boundaries

Problem

You want to enumerate all site boundaries for an SMS site.

Solution

Example 2-1 demonstrates how to display SMS site boundaries for a desired site. By querying the SMS_SCI_SiteAssignment class, we're able to identify the site boundary type (IP subnet or Active Directory site) and value.

Example 2-1. *DisplaySiteBoundaries.vbs*

```
Set objArgs = WScript.Arguments
strSMSServer = objArgs(0)
strSiteToDisplay = objArgs(1)

Set objLoc =  CreateObject("WbemScripting.SWbemLocator")
Set objSMS= objLoc.ConnectServer(strSMSServer, "root\sms")
Set Results = objSMS.ExecQuery _
    ("SELECT * From SMS_ProviderLocation WHERE ProviderForLocalSite = true")
For each Loc in Results
    If Loc.ProviderForLocalSite = True Then
        Set objSMS = objLoc.ConnectServer(Loc.Machine, "root\sms\site_" & _
            Loc.SiteCode)
    end if
Next

strInfo = "Site Boundary Information for Site " & _
    strSiteToDisplay & vbCRLF
Set boundaries=objSMS.Get _
    ("SMS_SCI_SiteAssignment.SiteCode='" & _
    strSiteToDisplay & "',Filetype=1,ItemName='" & _
    "Site Assignment',ItemType='Site Assignment'")

For i=0 to ubound(boundaries.AssignDetails)
    strInfo = strInfo & space(len(descr)) & _
        boundaries.AssignTypes(i) & _
        ": " & boundaries.AssignDetails(i) & vbCRLF
Next
wscript.echo strInfo
```

Discussion

Example 2-1 also demonstrates how to use command-line arguments. Save this file as
ShowSiteBoundaries.vbs, and from a command line, enter the following:

```
ShowSiteBoundaries.vbs <Server> <Sub_SiteCode>
```

where *<Server>* is the server name of the SMS primary site and *<Sub_SiteCode>* is the site code of
the site you are querying.

The following example connects to the SMS primary site server SMSVPCLAB and displays the site
boundary information for site CLE:

```
ShowSiteBoundaries.vbs SMSVPCLab CLE
```

Next is an example connecting to the SMS primary site server SMSVPCLAB with a site code of LAB
and displaying the site boundary information for itself:

```
ShowSiteBoundaries.vbs SMSVPCLab LAB
```

The VBScript queries the SMS_SCI_SiteAssignment class for the desired site code, and then displays the contents of the arrays AssignTypes (boundary type) and AssignDetails (boundary data).

See Also

- Recipe 2-5, "Adding IP Subnet Site Boundaries," demonstrates how to add an IP subnet to the SMS site boundaries.

- Recipe 2-7, "Adding Active Directory Sites to Site Boundaries," demonstrates how to add an Active Directory site to the site boundaries.

- The SMS 2003 SDK provides information for managing site boundaries.

- The *SMS 2003 Scripting Guide* also provides an example for how to display site boundaries.

- Recipe 2-10, "Adding Roaming Boundaries," describes how to enumerate roaming boundaries.

2-5. Adding IP Subnet Site Boundaries

Problem

You want to add an IP subnet to an SMS site.

Solution: Using a Graphical Interface

1. Open the SMS Administrator console.

2. From the SMS Administrator console, expand Site Database (*<Site Code>*), expand Site Hierarchy, right-click *<Site Name>*, and select Properties.

3. Select the Site Boundaries tab.

4. Click the New button.

5. For Boundary type, select IP subnet.

6. Enter the subnet in the Subnet ID field.

7. Click OK.

8. From the *<Site Name>* Properties window, click OK.

Solution: Using VBScript

Example 2-2 demonstrates how to add IP subnet site boundaries to the specified SMS site. This example also shows how to make changes to the SMS site control file programmatically.

Example 2-2. *AddIPSiteBoundary.vbs*

```
strSMSServer = <SMSServer>
strSubnet = "10.5.123.0" 'replace with desired subnet
Set objLoc =  CreateObject("WbemScripting.SWbemLocator")
Set objSMS= objLoc.ConnectServer(strSMSServer, "root\sms")
Set Results = objSMS.ExecQuery _
    ("SELECT * From SMS_ProviderLocation WHERE ProviderForLocalSite = true")
For each Loc in Results
    If Loc.ProviderForLocalSite = True Then
        Set objSMS = objLoc.ConnectServer(Loc.Machine, "root\sms\site_" & _
            Loc.SiteCode)
        strSMSSiteCode = Loc.SiteCode
    end if
Next
```

```
Set WbemContext=CreateObject("WbemScripting.SWbemNamedValueSet")
WbemContext.Add "SessionHandle", objSMS.ExecMethod _
    ("SMS_SiteControlFile", "GetSessionHandle").SessionHandle
objSMS.ExecMethod "SMS_SiteControlFile.Filetype=1,SiteCode='" _
    & strSMSSiteCode & "'", "Refresh", , , WbemContext
'retrieve boundary details
Set WbemInst = objSMS.Get _
    ("SMS_SCI_SiteAssignment.Filetype=2,Itemtype='Site Assignment'," _
        & "SiteCode='" & strSMSSiteCode & _
        "',ItemName='Site Assignment'", , WbemContext)
proparray1 = WbemInst.AssignDetails
proparray2 = WbemInst.AssignTypes

onemore = ubound(proparray1) + 1
redim preserve proparray1( onemore ) 'add one to size of array
redim preserve proparray2( onemore )
proparray1( onemore ) = strSubnet
proparray2( onemore ) = "IP Subnet"
WbemInst.AssignDetails = proparray1
WbemInst.AssignTypes = proparray2
WbemInst.Put_ , WbemContext
objSMS.ExecMethod "SMS_SiteControlFile.Filetype=0,SiteCode=""" & _
    strSMSSiteCode & """", "Commit", , , WbemContext
objSMS.Get("SMS_SiteControlFile").ReleaseSessionHandle _
    WbemContext.Item("SessionHandle").Value
```

Discussion

In VBScript, you obtain the current array of site boundaries, and then you enlarge the array by one and add the IP subnet. Make sure you are importing the proper subnet for the desired system. Review the next recipe to learn how to identify the proper subnet.

See Also

- Recipe 2-6, "Computing the IP Subnet," shows how to obtain the IP subnet of a computer.
- Recipe 2-7, "Adding Active Directory Sites to Site Boundaries," shows how to add an Active Directory site.
- The SMS 2003 SDK provides information for managing site boundaries.
- The *SMS 2003 Scripting Guide* has an example of adding IP subnets to an SMS site.

2-6. Computing the IP Subnet

Problem

You want to compute the IP subnet to be able to add it to your site boundaries.

Solution: Using a Graphical Interface

If the system in question has been discovered by SMS, you can find the IP subnet in the system properties in SMS.

1. Open the SMS Administrator console.
2. From the SMS Administrator console, expand Site Database (<*Site Code*>), and then expand the Collections node, followed by All Systems.

3. Locate the computer name in the All Systems collection, right-click it, and then select Properties.

4. View the Discovery Data in the General tab. Scroll until IPSubnets(0) is visible, and record the IP subnet.

Solution: Using VBScript

The VBScript in Example 2-3 is adopted from Appendix C of the *Scenarios and Procedures for SMS 2003* guide. Simply enter an IP address and subnet mask, and the script will display the IP subnet to add to your SMS site boundaries.

Example 2-3. *ComputeIPSubnet.vbs*

```
'adopted from the SMS 2003 Scenarios and Procedures guide
strIPAddress = inputbox("Enter IP Address")
strSubnetMask = inputbox("Enter Subnet Mask")

dim addressbytes(4)
dim subnetmaskbytes(4)
i=0
period = 1
while period<>len( strIPAddress ) + 2
        prevperiod=period
        period = instr( period+1, strIPAddress, "." ) + 1
        if period = 1 then period = len( strIPAddress ) + 2
         addressbyte = _
             mid( strIPAddress, prevperiod, period-prevperiod-1 )
         addressbytes(i)=addressbyte
        i=i+1
wend

i=0
period = 1
while period<>len( strSubnetMask ) + 2
        prevperiod=period
        period = instr( period+1, strSubnetMask, "." ) + 1
        if period = 1 then period = len( strSubnetMask ) + 2
         subnetmaskbyte = _
             mid( strSubnetMask, prevperiod, period-prevperiod-1 )
         subnetmaskbytes(i)=subnetmaskbyte
        i=i+1
wend
for i=0 to 3
        subnet = subnet & _
            (addressbytes(i) AND subnetmaskbytes(i)) & "."
next
subnet = left( subnet, len(subnet)-1 )
msgbox "Subnet: " & subnet
```

Discussion

This script is just one example of how to obtain the subnet of a system. To find other available methods, browse to your favorite search engine and enter **network calculator** or **subnet calculator** as your search string.

See Also

- Recipe 2-5, "Adding IP Subnet Site Boundaries," shows how to add an IP subnet to site boundaries.
- Appendix C of the *Scenarios and Procedures for SMS 2003* guide provides a VBScript script (subnet.vbs) that will calculate the subnet ID for the computer, given the IP address and subnet mask.

2-7. Adding Active Directory Sites to Site Boundaries

Problem

You want to add an Active Directory site boundary to an SMS site.

Solution: Using a Graphical Interface

1. Open the SMS Administrator console.
2. From the SMS Administrator console, expand Site Database (*<Site Code>*), expand Site Hierarchy, right-click *<Site Name>*, and select Properties.
3. Select the Site Boundaries tab.
4. Click the New button.
5. For the Boundary type, select Active Directory site.
6. Enter the Active Directory site in the Site Name field.
7. Click OK.
8. From the *<Site Name>* Properties window, click OK.

Solution: Using VBScript

Example 2-4 demonstrates how to add an Active Directory site boundary to SMS.

Example 2-4. *AddADSiteBoundary.vbs*

```
strSMSServer = <SMSServer>
strADSite = "Cleveland"

Set objLoc =  CreateObject("WbemScripting.SWbemLocator")
Set objSMS= objLoc.ConnectServer(strSMSServer, "root\sms")
Set Results = objSMS.ExecQuery _
    ("SELECT * From SMS_ProviderLocation WHERE ProviderForLocalSite = true")
For each Loc in Results
    If Loc.ProviderForLocalSite = True Then
        Set objSMS = objLoc.ConnectServer(Loc.Machine, "root\sms\site_" & _
            Loc.SiteCode)
            strSMSSiteCode = Loc.SiteCode
    end if
Next

Set WbemContext=CreateObject("WbemScripting.SWbemNamedValueSet")
WbemContext.Add "SessionHandle", objSMS.ExecMethod _
    ("SMS_SiteControlFile", "GetSessionHandle").SessionHandle
objSMS.ExecMethod "SMS_SiteControlFile.Filetype=1,SiteCode='" _
    & strSMSSiteCode & "'", "Refresh", , , WbemContext
```

```
'retrieve boundary details
Set WbemInst = objSMS.Get _
    ("SMS_SCI_SiteAssignment.Filetype=2,Itemtype='Site Assignment'," _
        & "SiteCode='" & strSMSSiteCode & _
        "',ItemName='Site Assignment'", , WbemContext)
proparray1 = WbemInst.AssignDetails
proparray2 = WbemInst.AssignTypes

onemore = ubound(proparray1) + 1
redim preserve proparray1( onemore ) 'add one to size of array
redim preserve proparray2( onemore )
proparray1( onemore ) = strADSite
proparray2( onemore ) = "Active Directory site"
WbemInst.AssignDetails = proparray1
WbemInst.AssignTypes = proparray2
WbemInst.Put_ , WbemContext
objSMS.ExecMethod "SMS_SiteControlFile.Filetype=0,SiteCode=""" & _
    strSMSSiteCode & """", "Commit", , , WbemContext
objSMS.Get("SMS_SiteControlFile").ReleaseSessionHandle _
    WbemContext.Item("SessionHandle").Value
```

Discussion

In VBScript, you obtain the current array of site boundaries. Then you enlarge the array by one and add the Active Directory site. Make sure you enter the Active Directory site name properly; SMS will not generate an error if the Active Directory site name is invalid.

See Also

- Recipe 2-5, "Adding IP Subnet Site Boundaries," shows how to add an IP subnet to site boundaries.

- The SMS 2003 SDK provides information on managing site boundaries.

- The *SMS 2003 Scripting Guide* provides an example of adding Active Directory sites to an SMS site.

2-8. Adding Site Boundaries from the Command Line

Problem

You want to add Active Directory sites and IP subnets to an SMS site from the command line.

Solution

Example 2-5 combines Examples 2-4 and 2-2 to create a script that can be run from the command line to create Active Directory or IP subnet site boundaries.

Example 2-5. *AddSiteBoundaries.vb*

```
Set objArgs = WScript.Arguments
strSMSServer = objArgs(0)
strSiteToConfig= objArgs(1)
strBoundaryType = ucase(objArgs(2))
strBoundaryData = objArgs(3)
'creating 2 arrays of size one
```

```
Dim inputArray1(1)
Dim inputArray2(1)

select case strBoundaryType
    case "SUBNET"
        strBoundaryType = "IP Subnet"
     case "AD"
         strBoundaryType = "Active Directory site"
End Select

inputArray1(0) = trim(strBoundaryData)
inputArray2(0) = trim(strBoundaryType)

Set objLoc =  CreateObject("WbemScripting.SWbemLocator")
Set objSMS= objLoc.ConnectServer(strSMSServer, "root\sms")
Set Results = objSMS.ExecQuery _
    ("SELECT * From SMS_ProviderLocation WHERE ProviderForLocalSite = true")
For each Loc in Results
    If Loc.ProviderForLocalSite = True Then
        Set objSWbemServices = objLoc.ConnectServer _
            (Loc.Machine, "root\sms\site_" & Loc.SiteCode)
    end if
Next

Set objSWbemContext=CreateObject _
    ("WbemScripting.SWbemNamedValueSet")
objSWbemContext.Add "SessionHandle", _
    objSWbemServices.ExecMethod("SMS_SiteControlFile", _
    "GetSessionHandle").SessionHandle
objSWbemServices.ExecMethod _
    "SMS_SiteControlFile.Filetype=1,Sitecode='" & _
    strSiteToConfig & "'", "RefreshSCF", , , objSWbemContext
Set objSWbemInst = objSWbemServices.Get _
    ("SMS_SCI_SiteAssignment.Filetype=2,Itemtype='" & _
    "Site Assignment',Sitecode='" & strSiteToConfig & _
    "',ItemName='Site Assignment'", , objSWbemContext)

'Retrieve the boundary details.
proparray1 = objSWbemInst.AssignDetails
proparray2 = objSWbemInst.AssignTypes

if ubound(objSWbemInst.AssignDetails)=-1 then
    'There are no boundaries so create an array.
    bounds=0
    redim proparray1(0)
    redim proparray2(0)
    proparray1(bounds)=inputArray1(0)
    proparray2(bounds)=inputArray2(0)
Else
    bounds=ubound (objSWbemInst.AssignDetails)+1
    'Increase array for new boundaries
    ReDim Preserve proparray1 (ubound (proparray1) + _
        ubound (inputArray1))
    ReDim Preserve proparray2 (ubound (proparray2) + _
        ubound (inputArray2))
```

```
        for i= 0 to ubound(inputArray1)-1 'Add boundaries
            proparray1(bounds+i)=inputArray1(i)
            proparray2(bounds+i)=inputArray2(i)
        Next
End If

objSWbemInst.AssignDetails = proparray1
objSWbemInst.AssignTypes = proparray2
objSWbemInst.Put_ , objSWbemContext

objSWbemServices.ExecMethod _
    "SMS_SiteControlFile.Filetype=0,Sitecode=""" & _
    strSiteToConfig & """", "Commit", , , objSWbemContext
objSWbemServices.Get("SMS_SiteControlFile"). _
    ReleaseSessionHandle objSWbemContext.Item _
    ("SessionHandle").Value
```

Discussion

To add the NAWLINS Active Directory site to the site boundaries of the JAZ SMS secondary site, whose parent server is SOUTHERNUS, use the following:

AddSiteboundaries.vbs *SOUTHERNUS JAZ ad NAWLINS*

ad is used to add an Active Directory site to the SMS site boundaries. To add an IP subnet instead, replace ad with subnet.

To add the IP subnet 192.168.21.0 to the Biloxi (BIL) site (which has the same parent as the preceding example), execute the following from the command line:

AddSiteboundaries.vbs *SOUTHERNUS BIL subnet 192.168.21.0*

See Also

- Recipes 2-3 through 2-7 provide more information about adding site boundaries, enumerating site boundaries, and calculating subnets.

- The SMS 2003 SDK provides information on managing site boundaries.

- The *SMS 2003 Scripting Guide* provides an example of adding Active Directory sites to an SMS site.

- Recipe 2-10, "Adding Roaming Boundaries," shows how to add roaming boundaries to a given SMS site.

2-9. Enumerating Roaming Boundaries

Problem

You want to enumerate all roaming boundaries for an SMS site.

Solution

Example 2-6 demonstrates how to show roaming site boundaries using VBScript. The script also displays whether site boundaries are to be included in the local roaming boundaries.

Example 2-6. *ShowRoamingSiteBoundaries.vbs*

```
Set objArgs = WScript.Arguments
strSMSServer = objArgs(0)
strSiteToDisplay = ucase(objArgs(1))

Set objLoc =  CreateObject("WbemScripting.SWbemLocator")
Set objSMS= objLoc.ConnectServer(strSMSServer, "root\sms")
Set Results = objSMS.ExecQuery _
    ("SELECT * From SMS_ProviderLocation WHERE ProviderForLocalSite = true")
For each Loc in Results
    If Loc.ProviderForLocalSite = True Then
        Set objSMS = objLoc.ConnectServer(Loc.Machine, "root\sms\site_" & _
            Loc.SiteCode)
    end if
Next

strInfo = "Roaming Site Boundary Information for Site " & _
    strSiteToDisplay & vbCRLF

Set boundaries=objSMS.Get("SMS_SCI_RoamingBoundary." & _
    "SiteCode='" & strSiteToDisplay & "',Filetype=2,ItemName='" & _
    "Roaming Boundary',ItemType='Roaming Boundary'")
if boundaries.IncludeSiteBoundary then
    strInfo = strInfo &  "Site Boundaries are included in the "& _
    "local roaming boundaries." & vbCRLF
else
    strInfo = strInfo &  "Site Boundaries are NOT included in the "& _
    "local roaming boundaries." & vbCRLF
end if
msgbox ubound(boundaries.Details)
For i=0 to ubound(boundaries.Details)
    if boundaries.Flags(i) = 1 then
        strBoundary = "Remote Boundary"
    else
        strBoundary = "Local Boundary"
    end if
    strInfo = strInfo & _
        boundaries.Types(i) & _
        ": " & boundaries.Details(i) & vbTAB & strBoundary & vbCRLF
Next
wscript.echo strInfo
```

Discussion

This VBScript demonstrates how to use command-line arguments. From a command line, enter the following:

```
ShowRoamingSiteBoundaries.vbs <Server> <Sub_SiteCode>
```

where *<Server>* is the server name of the SMS primary site, and *<Sub_SiteCode>* is the site code of the site you are querying.

The following example connects to the SMS primary site server SMSVPCLAB and displays the roaming site boundary information for site CLE:

ShowRoamingSiteBoundaries.vbs *SMSVPCLab CLE*

This next example connects to the SMS primary site server SMSVPCLAB with a site code of LAB and displays the roaming site boundary information for itself:

ShowRoamingSiteBoundaries.vbs *SMSVPCLab LAB*

The VBScript queries the SMS_SCI_RoamingBoundary class for the desired site code, and then displays the contents of the arrays Types (boundary type) and Details (boundary data).

See Also

- Recipe 2-5, "Adding IP Subnet Site Boundaries," demonstrates how to add an IP subnet to the site boundaries.
- Recipe 2-7, "Adding Active Directory Sites to Site Boundaries," demonstrates how to ad an Active Directory site to the site boundaries.
- The SMS 2003 SDK provides information for managing site boundaries.
- The *SMS 2003 Scripting Guide* provides an example of adding Active Directory sites to an SMS site.
- Recipe 2-10, "Adding Roaming Boundaries," describes how to add roaming boundaries.

2-10. Adding Roaming Boundaries

Problem

You want to add roaming boundaries to your SMS site.

Solution: Using a Graphical Interface

1. Open the SMS Administrator console.
2. From the SMS Administrator console, expand Site Database (<*Site Code*>), expand Site Hierarchy, right-click <*Site Name*>, and select Properties.
3. Select the Roaming Boundaries tab.
4. Click the New button.
5. Select the appropriate boundary type.
6. Enter the appropriate boundary data (IP subnet, Active Directory site, or IP address range).
7. Designate this new boundary as a local or roaming boundary.
8. Click OK.
9. From the <*Site Name*> Properties window, click OK.

Solution: Using VBScript

Example 2-7 demonstrates how to add roaming site boundaries to the desired SMS site. This process is very similar to adding regular site boundaries, except that we can also add an IP range, and we have to specify local or remote roaming for each boundary added.

Example 2-7. *AddRoamingSiteBoundaries.vbs*

```
Set objArgs = WScript.Arguments
strSMSServer = objArgs(0)
strSiteToModify = objArgs(1)
strBoundaryType = ucase(objArgs(2))
strBoundaryData = objArgs(3)
strRemote = ucase(objArgs(4))
Dim inputArray1(1)
Dim inputArray2(1)
Dim inputArray3(1)

select case strBoundaryType
    case "SUBNET"
        strBoundaryType = "IP Subnets"
     case "AD"
         strBoundaryType = "AD Site Name"
      case "RANGE"
         strBoundaryType = "IP Ranges"
End Select

select case strRemote
    case "LOCAL"
        strRemote = 0
    case "REMOTE"
        strRemote = 1
end select
inputArray1(0)=strBoundaryData
inputArray2(0)=strRemote
inputArray3(0)=strBoundaryType


Set objLoc =  CreateObject("WbemScripting.SWbemLocator")
Set objSMS= objLoc.ConnectServer(strSMSServer, "root\sms")
Set Results = objSMS.ExecQuery _
    ("SELECT * From SMS_ProviderLocation WHERE ProviderForLocalSite = true")
For each Loc in Results
    If Loc.ProviderForLocalSite = True Then
        Set objSMS = objLoc.ConnectServer(Loc.Machine, "root\sms\site_" & _
            Loc.SiteCode)
    end if
Next

Set objSWbemContext = CreateObject _
    ("WbemScripting.SWbemNamedValueSet")
objSWbemContext.Add "SessionHandle", _
    objSMS.ExecMethod("SMS_SiteControlFile", _
    "GetSessionHandle").SessionHandle
objSMS.ExecMethod _
    "SMS_SiteControlFile.Filetype=1,Sitecode='" & _
    strSiteToModify & "'", "RefreshSCF", , , objSWbemContext
Set objSWbemInst = objSMS.Get _
    ("SMS_SCI_RoamingBoundary.Filetype=2,Itemtype='" & _
    "Roaming Boundary',Sitecode='" & strSiteToModify & _
    "',ItemName='Roaming Boundary'", , objSWbemContext)
```

```
'Retrieve the roaming boundary details.
proparray1 = objSWbemInst.Details
proparray2 = objSWbemInst.Flags
proparray3 = objSWbemInst.Types

if ubound(objSWbemInst.Details)=-1 then
    'There are no boundaries so create an array.
    bounds=0
    redim proparray1(0)
    redim proparray2(0)
    redim proparray3(0)
    proparray1(bounds)=inputArray1(0)
    proparray2(bounds)=inputArray2(0)
    proparray3(bounds)=inputArray3(0)
Else
    bounds=ubound (objSWbemInst.Details)+1
    'Increase array for new boundaries
    ReDim Preserve proparray1 (ubound (proparray1) + _
        ubound (inputArray1))
    ReDim Preserve proparray2 (ubound (proparray2) + _
        ubound (inputArray2))
    ReDim Preserve proparray3 (ubound (proparray3) + _
        ubound (inputArray3))
    for i= 0 to ubound(inputArray1)-1 'Add boundaries
        proparray1(bounds+i)=inputArray1(i)
        proparray2(bounds+i)=inputArray2(i)
        proparray3(bounds+i)=inputArray3(i)
    Next
End If

objSWbemInst.Details = proparray1
objSWbemInst.Flags = proparray2
objSWbemInst.Types = proparray3
objSWbemInst.Put_ , objSWbemContext

objSMS.ExecMethod _
    "SMS_SiteControlFile.Filetype=0,Sitecode=""" & _
    strSiteToModify & """", "Commit", , , objSWbemContext
objSMS.Get("SMS_SiteControlFile"). _
    ReleaseSessionHandle objSWbemContext.Item _
    ("SessionHandle").Value
```

Discussion

Roaming boundaries are used by roaming Advanced Clients to access distribution points that belong to the selected SMS site. Roaming boundaries are defined though Active Directory sites, IP address ranges, and IP subnets.

Roaming boundaries designate how software is distributed to roaming Advanced Clients. When an advertisement is created, one of the properties to configure is how (or whether) an advertisement is executed when no local distribution point is available. At this point, you can decide whether the source files will be downloaded from the distribution point for the advertisement to execute, or whether the files will not be downloaded, with the advertisement not run until the client is in a local site boundary. Roaming boundaries are especially important for mobile systems and systems that do not have a broadband connection. One great benefit to configuring roaming boundaries is that you can specify an IP address range (which is not possible with regular site boundaries). This is beneficial for SMS clients that use remote access or a virtual private network to connect to the network.

The solution's VBScript is very similar to that found in Recipe 2-8, "Adding Site Boundaries from the Command Line." To add the NAWLINS Active Directory site to the local remote site boundaries of the JAZ SMS secondary site, whose parent server is SOUTHERNUS, use the following:

```
AddRoamingSiteBoundaries.vbs SOUTHERNUS JAZ ad NAWLINS local
```

ad is used to denote the type of subnet to add. ad is for adding the Active Directory site, and subnet is for adding a subnet. local is used to denote a local roaming boundary; to denote a remote roaming boundary, you would use remote.

To add the remote roaming boundary IP subnet 192.168.21.0 to the Biloxi (BIL) site (which has the same parent as the example just shown), execute the following from the command line:

```
AddRoamingSiteboundaries.vbs SOUTHERNUS BIL subnet 192.168.21.0 remote
```

To add the remote roaming boundary IP range of 192.168.21.2 to 192.168.21.48 to the Atlanta (ATL) site (which has the same parent as the example just shown), execute the following from the command line:

```
AddRoamingSiteboundaries.vbs SOUTHERNUS ATL range 192.168.21.2-192.168.21.48 remote
```

See Also

- To assist your understanding of Advanced Client roaming, view the demonstration located here: http://www.microsoft.com/smserver/techinfo/productdoc/media/acr.htm.

- Chapter 8 of the *SMS 2003 Concepts, Planning, and Deployment Guide* provides more information about roaming boundaries.

- A Microsoft TechNet webcast called "Understanding SMS 2003 Roaming" is also available (search for event code 1032253115).

- If you need to know the nitty-gritty of Advanced Client roaming, download the "Configuration and Operation of Advanced Client Roaming" white paper from the Microsoft Download Center (http://www.microsoft.com/downloads).

- Recipe 2-8, "Adding Site Boundaries from the Command Line," demonstrates how to add site boundaries for the desired SMS site or IP subnet from the command line.

- The SMS 2003 SDK provides information for managing site boundaries.

- The *SMS 2003 Scripting Guide* provides an example of adding Active Directory sites to an SMS site.

- Recipe 2-9, "Enumerating Roaming Boundaries," demonstrates how to display all roaming boundaries (and local/remote information) for a desired SMS site.

2-11. Configuring HTTP Ports for SMS

Problem

You want to modify the ports that SMS uses for Advanced Client communication.

Solution

1. Open the SMS Administrator console.

2. From the SMS Administrator console, expand Site Database (*<Site Code>*), expand Site Hierarchy, right-click *<Site Name>*, and select Properties.

3. Select the Ports tab.

4. Click the New button to add a port or double-click an existing port to modify it.

5. Enter the port number and a description. Select the Default Client port check box if you want to use the port as the default.

6. Click OK.

7. Click OK to apply the settings.

Discussion

The SMS 2003 Advanced Client uses Hypertext Transfer Protocol (HTTP) and Background Intelligent Transfer Service (BITS) communications to contact its management point and distribution points. With the release of Service Pack 1 for SMS 2003, SMS administrators now have the ability to configure a port other than port 80 for client communications, and they can change the default HTTP port to provide enhanced security. A maximum of two ports can be configured, and one must be set as the default (and by default, that is port 80).

In addition to changing the port on the server, you must change the port that the SMS client uses to communicate to match the server. Be careful when modifying the port—you want to make sure your client maintains contact with your management point and distribution points during this process. We recommend the following procedure:

1. Add a new port to the SMS site (any port from 1 to 65535 is acceptable). Leave the current port (probably port 80) as the default.

2. Create a new SMS package using the source from the SMS Service Pack media (the path in SP2 media is SMS2003SP2Beta_ENU\tools\portconfiguration).

3. Create a program as described in portswitch.vbs. Open this file with Notepad. It provides a proper command line and status Machine Information Format (MIF) matching.

4. Deploy the program to all desired systems (after testing, of course).

5. When you are certain that all targeted systems have run the SMS port configuration installation, you can set your new port as the default, remove port 80 from your ports list, and add a new secondary port if desired.

Note All systems installed with the SMS 2003 SP1 Advanced Clients after the HTTP ports have been reconfigured for your site will have the custom ports configured by default. You only need to modify systems that had SMS installed prior to this configuration change in the SMS site. You can modify SMS_DEF.MOF to obtain the configured port on Advanced Clients during hardware inventory by querying the dword named HttpPort in HKEY_LOCAL_MACHINE\SOFTWARE\Microsoft\CCM.

See Also

As the TCP port modification feature is a post-RTM addition to SMS, you probably won't find much documentation of it (we didn't).

- Matt Tinney published two articles on myITforum.com that provide more insight: "SMS Port Configurations & Considerations" (http://myitforum.com/articles/8/view.asp?id=8284) and "Configuring Ports for Advanced Client Communications: Step by Step" (http://myitforum.com/articles/8/view.asp?id=8285).

- The Microsoft TechNet page titled "What's New in SMS 2003 Service Pack 1" (http://www.microsoft.com/technet/prodtechnol/sms/sms2003/whatsnew.mspx) provides additional information about using a TCP port other than port 80.

2-12. Extending the Active Directory Schema

Problem

You want to extend the Active Directory schema for SMS after installing the SMS site.

Solution

1. Obtain extadsch.exe from the latest service pack for SMS 2003 (located in the \SMSSETUP\BIN\ I386 folder).

2. Log in with the proper user account and execute extadsch.exe.

Caution Extending the Active Directory schema forces the synchronization of all global catalog servers within your forest if you are using Windows 2000 domain controllers. Windows 2003 domain controllers will be forced to send a delta replication.

---

3. View ExtADSch.log in the root of the system drive for the results of running extadsch.exe.

4. With appropriate permissions, create a new container named System Management (notice it's singular "System," not plural "System*s*") under the System container in Active Directory.

5. Set appropriate permissions on the System Management container: read, write, create all child objects, and delete all child objects. These permissions must be set for the current object and all child objects.

Discussion

The solution in this recipe is very simplified. We suggest researching the information described in the "See Also" section of this recipe. Without extending the schema and publishing data to Active Directory, the following features are not available for Advanced Clients in SMS:

- Global roaming
- Automatic site assignment (where no server locator point has been specified)

Extending the schema is not difficult, but proper planning and research are required to ensure a successful extension that SMS can use.

Two requirements must be met before extending the schema:

- The Active Directory schema must allow schema updates to be performed.
- The account used to extend the schema must have proper permissions to extend the schema; specifically, it must be a member of the Schema Administrators group.

To create the System Management container, you must use the Active Directory Services Interface (ADSI) Editor. ADSI Editor is included with the Windows Support Tools for Windows 2000 Server and Windows Server 2003 CD (in the Support folder). Once you have the support tools installed, perform the following steps:

1. Execute adsiedit.msc (e.g., select Start ➤ Run c:\Program Files\Support Tools\adsiedit.msc).

2. Expand Domain until CN=System appears, then right-click CN=System and select New ➤ Object.

3. Select Container from the list of classes, and enter a value of **System Management**.

Note An alternative method for creating the System Management container is discussed in the white paper mentioned in the "See Also" section of this recipe.

To configure proper permissions, if advanced security is enabled, grant the SMS site computer account Full Control of the System Management container. If standard security is enabled, grant the SMS Service account Full Control of the System Management container. Many SMS administrators create a new Security group that contains all SMS servers (or all SMS Service accounts if possible), and then grant this group the appropriate permissions to the System Management container, instead of individual servers or user accounts.

The Microsoft white paper for extending the schema, referenced in this recipe's "See Also" section, provides a nice paragraph about the replication that occurs when extending the schema:

> *When you extend the Active Directory schema, you add several classes and attributes that any SMS 2003 site in the SMS hierarchy can use later. These attributes are added to the global catalog and allow the clients to locate the information quickly. After the schema is extended, the global catalog servers must complete a full replication. In domains hosted by Windows 2000 domain controllers, a full replication takes place immediately after the schema extensions have been applied. In domains hosted by Windows 2003 domain controllers, replication occurs in the background, and may take longer for a full replication cycle to complete. The schema extension process does not publish any SMS site-specific information to Active Directory.[1]*

Now that you have extended the schema, you must publish identity data to Active Directory. Refer to the next recipe for this process.

See Also

- Recipe 2-13, "Modifying Active Directory Publishing Configuration," demonstrates how to modify the Active Directory publishing in SMS.

- Dave Randall has published an article titled "Active Directory Schema Modification and Publishing for Systems Management Server 2003" on myITforum.com that may be helpful to you: http://myitforum.com/articles/8/view.asp?id=6324.

- The Microsoft white paper titled "Active Directory Schema Modification and Publishing for Systems Management Server 2003" can be downloaded from the Systems Management Server 2003 Product Documentation web page (http://www.microsoft.com/smserver/techinfo/productdoc).

2-13. Modifying Active Directory Publishing Configuration
Problem

You want to modify the Active Directory publishing in SMS.

---

1. See http://www.microsoft.com/smserver/techinfo/administration.

Solution

1. Open the SMS Administrator console.

2. From the SMS Administrator console, expand Site Database (*<Site Code>*), expand Site Hierarchy, right-click *<Site Name>*, and select Properties.

3. Select the Advanced tab.

4. Change the "Publish identity data to Active Directory" check box to match your objective.

5. Click OK to apply the settings.

Discussion

Obviously, before you can enable SMS to publish identity information into Active Directory, you must be in an Active Directory environment, and the schema must be extended for SMS. You must extend the schema to publish objects to Active Directory. Without extending the schema and publishing data to Active Directory, the following features are not available for Advanced Clients in SMS:

- Global roaming

- Automatic site assignment (where no server locator point has been specified)

The following requirements must be met before successfully publishing data to Active Directory:

- The Active Directory schema must already be successfully extended.

- The site properties must be configured to publish identity data to Active Directory.

- The System Management container must exist under the System container in Active Directory.

- The account(s) that publish the data must have appropriate permissions to publish to the System Management container. If you are using standard security, the SMS Service account is used. If you are using advanced security, the site server's computer account is used. See Recipe 2-12, "Extending the Active Directory Schema," for more information about permissions for the System Management container.

If you have enabled the "Publish identity data to Active Directory" check box and later decide to no longer publish identity data to Active Directory (which means you disabled the check box), manual cleanup is required.

Caution Note the following warning from the SMS help in the Administrator console:

"After Microsoft Systems Management Server (SMS) data is published in Active Directory, the published data persists in Active Directory unless it is manually removed. If Active Directory publishing is disabled and the default management point is changed, existing Advanced Clients continue contacting the previously defined management point until SMS data is deleted from Active Directory."

To manually remove the data in the System Management container from Active Directory, perform these steps:

1. Open Active Directory Users and Computers.

2. From the Toolbar, select View ➤ Advanced Features to show the System container.

3. Expand *<Domain>*, System, and then System Management.

4. Delete all contents in the System Management container.

5. Close Active Directory Users and Computers.

See Also

- Recipe 2-12, "Extending the Active Directory Schema," demonstrates how to extend the schema for SMS.

- Dave Randall has published an article titled "Active Directory Schema Modification and Publishing for Systems Management Server 2003" on myITforum.com that may be helpful to you: http://myitforum.com/articles/8/view.asp?id=6324.

- The Microsoft white paper titled "Active Directory Schema Modification and Publishing for Systems Management Server 2003" can be downloaded from the Systems Management Server 2003 Product Documentation web page (http://www.microsoft.com/smserver/techinfo/productdoc).

2-14. Modifying Site-to-Site Connection Security

Problem

You want to modify the site-to-site connection security.

Solution

1. Open the SMS Administrator console.

2. From the SMS Administrator console, expand Site Database (*<Site Code>*), expand Site Hierarchy, right-click *<Site Name>*, and select Properties.

3. Select the Advanced tab.

4. Change the settings in the site connection frame to match your objective.

5. Click OK to apply the settings.

Discussion

The following is a brief description of each site connection option:

Do not accept unsigned data from sites running SMS 2.0 SP4 and earlier: Prior to SMS 2.0 SP5, SMS sites were unable to sign data. By enabling this option, you will prevent SMS 2.0 SP4 and earlier versions from communicating with this site. If all of your SMS sites are SMS 2.0 SP5 or SMS 2003, enabling this option will reduce the risk of an attacker sending a bogus site control file from a nonexistent parent or child site.

Require secure key exchange between sites: When enabled, communication between this site and all child sites will only occur when secure keys are exchanged. Pre–SMS 2.0 SP5 systems will be unable to communicate with SMS 2.0 SP5 and newer systems with this option enabled. As the previous point in this recipe states, if all of your SMS sites are SMS 2.0 SP5 or SMS 2003, enabling this option will reduce the risk of an attacker sending a bogus site control file from a nonexistent parent or child site. If the schema has been extended and SMS has proper permissions to publish to the schema, SMS will exchange keys through Active Directory. If the schema has not been extended, or if SMS does not have the proper permissions to publish in Active Directory, the SMS administrator must exchange the keys through a manual process described in the *Scenarios and Procedures for SMS 2003: Security* guide in the section titled "Manually Transferring Site Keys."

Note A newly created secondary site will be unable to connect to its primary site until you manually perform the initial key exchange between the new secondary site and its parent, regardless of whether you have extended the Active Directory schema. Once the secondary is communicating properly with its parent, enable the Require Secure Key Exchange option on the secondary site.

See Also

- The section "Securing SMS Communications" in the *Scenarios and Procedures for SMS 2003: Security* guide provides specific information on the functions of the SMS Service account.

2-15. Modifying Inventory Data Protection

Problem

You want to modify the inventory data protection options.

Solution

1. Open the SMS Administrator console.
2. From the SMS Administrator console, expand Site Database (*<Site Code>*), expand Site Hierarchy, right-click *<Site Name>*, and select Properties.
3. Select the Advanced tab.
4. Change the settings in the inventory protection frame to match your objective.
5. Click OK to apply the settings.

Discussion

By default, the SMS 2003 Advanced Client does not sign or encrypt messages. SMS 2003 SP1 introduces the options described in this recipe. Both the management point and the Advanced Client must have at least Service Pack 1 installed on SMS 2003 for proper functionality. The following options are then available.

Enable the *Sign data before sending to management point* option to sign inventory messages sent from the Advanced Client to a management point. As described in the Microsoft TechNet page titled "What's New in SMS 2003 Service Pack 1," the flow of signed messages from the Advanced Client to its management point is as follows:

1. The client retrieves the trusted root key and management point keys from the site server and management point.
2. The client sends its identity key in a discovery data record.
3. The Discovery Data Manager on the site server inserts the key as Client Identity in the SMS site database.
4. The SMS 2003 SP1 client signs only inventory messages.
5. When a signed message arrives from the client, the management point determines whether the public key of the client is in the SMS site database.

   - If the key cannot be found, the message is marked as not verified.
   - If the client's public key is found in the database, the signature of the message is validated.
   - If the signature is valid, the message is marked as verified and the message is processed.
   - If the signature is not valid, the message is discarded and an error message is logged.

Enable the *Encrypt data before sending to management point* option to encrypt inventory messages sent from the Advanced Client to its management point. Encryption is recommended for software, hardware, and discovery data record messages. As described in the Microsoft Tech-Net page titled "What's New in SMS 2003 Service Pack 1," the flow of signed messages from the Advanced Client to its management point is as follows:

1. The client generates inventory and encrypts it using its symmetrical encryption key. The client also signs the inventory by using the client identity key.

2. The inventory contains the encryption key signed by using the management point key.

3. The management point retrieves the encryption key from the inventory message by using its own key.

4. The management point decrypts the message.

   - If the management point fails to decrypt the message, the message is discarded and a status message is generated.

   - If the decryption succeeds, the message is sent to the site server for client identity verification and message processing.

See Also

- The Microsoft TechNet page titled "What's New in SMS 2003 Service Pack 1" (http://www.microsoft.com/technet/prodtechnol/sms/sms2003/whatsnew.mspx) provides additional information about Advanced Client authentication and encryption.

2-16. Modifying Security of Site Properties

Problem

You want to modify access to your SMS site properties.

Solution

1. Open the SMS Administrator console.

2. From the SMS Administrator console, expand Site Database (*<Site Code>*), expand Site Hierarchy, right-click *<Site Name>*, and select Properties.

3. Select the Security tab.

4. Click the New or Delete button to add or remove class or instance security rights. You can also double-click any existing class or instance rights to modify them.

5. Click OK to apply the settings.

Discussion

Managing site properties is the heart and soul of SMS; proper management can make or break your SMS implementation. Use extreme caution when delegating privileges.

For example, say you go out of town for the weekend and leave your teenaged son your car keys so he can drive your 1987 Ford Crown Victoria LTD station wagon to the store to pick up some snacks for the weekend. Of course, your key ring also contains the keys to your brand-new Dodge Viper. You obviously have a son that you trust, but it may be in your best interest to remove the keys for the Viper from the key ring, just to make sure your son doesn't *accidentally* take the wrong vehicle for a drive. Similarly, with SMS, you want to make sure that proper permissions are granted to a user or group for SMS site settings—nothing more and nothing less. Two types of permissions can be granted:

Class security rights: Class security rights apply to the entire class. In this case, the class is the SMS site. By granting class security rights to a user or group, all site settings within the site will be available for the user or group.

Instance security rights: Instance security rights modify permissions for a specific instance of a class. For example, to give your help desk the capability to manage a specific collection, grant them the appropriate instance rights.

The following note is from Chapter 5 of the *SMS 2003 Concepts, Planning, and Deployment Guide*:

Because SMS rights are cumulative, if you grant a user class security rights to an SMS security object and conflicting instance security rights to a specific SMS security object, SMS reconciles the class and instance security rights to grant the highest level of permissions. The exception to this rule is no permissions. For example, if you grant the user full permissions to all packages at the class level and Read permission to a specific package at the instance level, the user's effective permissions are full permissions to all packages including that one specific package set with read permission. If you grant the user full permissions to all packages at the class level and no permissions to a specific package at the instance level, the user's effective permissions are full permissions to all packages except the one specific package set with no permissions. Similarly, if you grant a user no permissions to all packages at the class level, and full permissions to a specific package at the instance level, the user's effective permissions are no permissions to any packages except the one specific package set with full permissions.

See Also

- Chapter 5 of the *SMS 2003 Concepts, Planning, and Deployment Guide* provides additional information about SMS security.
- The *Scenarios and Procedures Guide for SMS 2003: Security* guide provides additional information about SMS security.

2-17. Creating an Address

Problem

You want to create an address to a new site.

Solution

1. Open the SMS Administrator console.
2. From the SMS Administrator console, expand Site Database (*<Site Code>*), and then expand Site Hierarchy, *<Site Name>*, Site Settings, and Addresses.
3. Right-click Addresses and select New ➤ Standard Sender Address.
4. On the General tab, choose the destination site code from the drop-down list.
5. Enter the destination site server name.
6. Click the Set button to enter an account that the address will use for communication.

7. On the Schedule tab, set the communication weekly time schedule for the address.

8. On the Rate Limits tab, set any bandwidth restrictions for the address.

9. Click OK to create the address.

Discussion

Proper site-to-site communications depend on properly configured senders, and senders depend on properly configured addresses. The example solution demonstrates how to create a standard sender address. Use the same process to create other sender addresses, with the exception of special properties for each one.

Note Both the parent and the child need the same type of address.

You can define more than one address to a site. For example, you could have a standard sender address that uses your T1 line to connect to the remote site, and you could use a Remote Access Service (RAS) sender address as a backup in case your T1 line is unavailable. You could set the standard sender address a higher priority than the RAS sender address, so that the standard sender address will always be used when available.

You can also create addresses between a primary site and a grandchild site to establish a direct connection.

See Also

- Recipe 2-47, "Creating a Sender," shows how to create a sender.

- Recipe 2-18, "Modifying the Sending Schedule of an Address," describes how to control network load during critical time periods.

- Recipe 2-19, "Modifying the Rate Limits of an Address," describes how to prevent SMS from consuming all available bandwidth on the connection.

- Table E.6 in the *Scenarios and Procedures for SMS 2003: Planning and Deployment* guide shows how to determine which senders (and thus addresses) are required for different types of communications links.

- Chapter 4 of the *Microsoft Systems Management Server 2003 Administrator's Companion* by Steven Kaczmarek (Microsoft Press, 2004) describes how to create an address.

2-18. Modifying the Sending Schedule of an Address

Problem

You want to modify the sending schedule of an address.

Solution

1. Open the SMS Administrator console.

2. From the SMS Administrator console, expand Site Database (<*Site Code*>), and then expand Site Hierarchy, <*Site Name*>, Site Settings, and Addresses.

3. Double-click an address in the right pane to open the Address Properties dialog box.

4. On the Schedule tab, select the weekly time blocks for which you would like to restrict the data transfers to this address.

5. Choose your level of availability from the drop-down box and indicate whether this address can be used if another address becomes inoperative.

6. Click OK to apply the settings.

Discussion

The sending schedule allows you to specify when the address can be used to transfer data between sites. By default, the sender is available for all priorities at all times. The Schedule tab allows you to set availability times (down to the hour of the week) for allowing network traffic produced by SMS. If, for example, you know that your T1 line is heavily used on weekdays from 8:00 a.m. to 9:00 a.m., you may consider allowing only high-priority communications during that time. SMS packages can be configured to a specific priority on a per-package basis. For example, you could set your virus definitions package to a high priority so that the package source will still successfully update during times that you only allow high priorities.

Note If you specify time(s) that are closed, you will prevent transfer of standard site-to-site communications between the child site and its parent.

You may need to prevent an address from being used as a substitute for another address that isn't working properly during a specified time period. To do so, highlight the desired hours in the schedule grid and check the "Unavailable to substitute for inoperative addresses" box.

See Also

- Recipe 2-17, "Creating an Address," describes how to create or modify an address.

- Recipe 2-19, "Modifying the Rate Limits of an Address," describes how to prevent SMS from consuming all available bandwidth on the connection.

- Table E.6 in the *Scenarios and Procedures for SMS 2003: Planning and Deployment* guide shows how to determine which senders (and thus addresses) are required for different types of communications links.

- Chapter 4 of the *Microsoft Systems Management Server 2003 Administrator's Companion* by Steven Kaczmarek (Microsoft Press, 2004) describes how to create an address.

- Appendix G of the *Scenarios and Procedures for SMS 2003: Planning and Deployment* guide provides additional information about senders and addresses.

2-19. Modifying the Rate Limits of an Address

Problem

You want to modify the rate limits of an address.

Solution

1. Open the SMS Administrator console.

2. From the SMS Administrator console, expand Site Database (*<Site Code>*), and then expand Site Hierarchy, *<Site Name>*, Site Settings, and Addresses.

3. Double-click an address in the right pane to open the Address Properties dialog box.

4. On the Rate Limits tab, select either pulse mode or bandwidth limiting.

5. If you selected pulse mode, set your data block size and time delay between data blocks. If you selected bandwidth limiting, select the daily hour range that is to be restricted and set the amount of bandwidth that is available for SMS to use.

6. Click OK to apply the settings.

Discussion

The previous recipe described how to control network load based on priorities used by SMS. This recipe discusses transfer rate limits and pulse mode for standard sender addresses. Think of the following options for transferring a large amount of data from a parent site to one or more child sites across a wide area network (WAN) link. For our example, consider adding the latest version of Microsoft Office Professional (approximately 600MB) to a remote distribution point. This example also assumes the package has the proper priority that allows the process to continue at this time.

Here is a list of options available in the Rate Limits tab for an SMS sender address:

Unlimited when sending to this address: Selecting this option allows unlimited data transfer. By leaving the option set to unlimited, the WAN link can be consumed entirely by SMS while pushing the Office package to the distribution point.

Pulse mode: This option can be useful when you're dealing with a very low-bandwidth connection. Enabling this option allows you to set the specific amount of data that can be transferred, followed by a specific amount of time before the next transfer. For example, you can set pulse mode to send data in a cycle of 3KB of data, followed by a five-second delay, then another 3KB of data, then another five-second delay, and continue in this manner until all data has been transferred. This process could be used to transfer the data very slowly to a remote site, with minimal impact on other systems that use the WAN to access resources.

Limited to specified maximum transfer rates by hour: This option allows you to specify the percentage of maximum transfer rate allowed for a specific time period. For example, you can use this setting to allow SMS to use only 50 percent of the bandwidth from 7:00 a.m. to 5:00 p.m., and 75 percent otherwise.

Note Setting a rate limit will limit the SMS site to single-thread communication with the other site. If you do not set a rate limit (unlimited), SMS will use multiple threads to communicate with the other site.

See Also

- Recipe 2-17, "Creating an Address," describes how to create or modify an address.

- Recipe 2-18, "Modifying the Sending Schedule of an Address," describes how to control network load during critical time periods.

- Table E.6 in the *Scenarios and Procedures for SMS 2003: Planning and Deployment* guide shows how to determine which senders (and thus addresses) are required for different types of communications links.

- Chapter 4 of the *Microsoft Systems Management Server 2003 Administrator's Companion* by Steven Kaczmarek (Microsoft Press, 2004) describes how to create an address.

- Appendix G of the *Scenarios and Procedures for SMS 2003: Planning and Deployment* guide provides additional information about senders and addresses.

2-20. Configuring Hardware Inventory

Problem

You want to enable hardware inventory.

Solution

1. Open the SMS Administrator console.
2. From the SMS Administrator console, expand Site Database (*<Site Code>*), and then expand Site Hierarchy, *<Site Name>*, Site Settings, and Client Agents.
3. Right-click Hardware Inventory Client Agent and select Properties.
4. Select the "Enable hardware inventory on clients" check box.
5. In the Inventory schedule frame, select Simple schedule, and change the interval if needed.
6. On the MIF Collection tab, enable IDMIF and NOIDMIF file collection only as needed for your environment.
7. Click OK to save changes.

Discussion

SMS hardware inventory collects detailed hardware information from the SMS client. Information such as memory, operating system, services, and process information are collected during hardware inventory. Hardware inventory information is obtained from the client by querying Windows Management Instrumentation (WMI) and the registry. Approximately 1,500 hardware properties are included in WMI, but SMS does not query all of these by default.

MIF collection is a technology used more frequently in SMS 2.0, but it is also available in SMS 2003. See Chapter 11 for more information.

See Also

- Chapter 11 provides detailed information for configuring and extending hardware inventory.
- A sidebar in Chapter 11 titled "What Is a MIF File?" describes MIF and NOIDMIF files in more detail.
- Chapter 9 of the *Microsoft Systems Management Server 2003 Administrator's Companion* by Steven Kaczmarek (Microsoft Press, 2004) provides additional information about hardware inventory.
- Chapter 2 of the *SMS 2003 Operations Guide* provides an in-depth look at hardware inventory.

2-21. Configuring Software Inventory

Problem

You want to enable software inventory.

Solution

1. Open the SMS Administrator console.
2. From the SMS Administrator console, expand Site Database (*<Site Code>*), and then expand Site Hierarchy, *<Site Name>*, Site Settings, and Client Agents.

3. Right-click Software Inventory Client Agent and select Properties.

4. Select the "Enable software inventory on clients" check box.

5. In the Inventory and File Collection schedule frame, select Simple schedule and change the interval if needed.

6. On the Inventory Collection tab, add additional file names and/or file types as needed.

7. On the File Collection tab, add names of files to collect if desired.

8. Click OK to save the changes.

Discussion

Software inventory collects the file name, file description, file version, and file size from the file properties. In addition to these properties, the path to the file is also recorded. By default, when software inventory is enabled, information for each executable (`.exe`) will be added to the database. You can add specific file names (e.g., `myApp.dll`) and/or specific file paths (e.g., `C:\program files\foo\myApp.dll`).

See Also

- Chapter 10 provides detailed information for configuring and extending software inventory.

- Chapter 9 of the *Microsoft Systems Management Server 2003 Administrator's Companion* by Steven Kaczmarek (Microsoft Press, 2004) provides additional information for software inventory.

- Chapter 2 of the *SMS 2003 Operations Guide* provides an in-depth look at software inventory.

2-22. Configuring Remote Tools

Problem

You want to enable and configure remote tools.

Solution

1. Open the SMS Administrator console.

2. From the SMS Administrator console, expand Site Database (*<Site Code>*), and then expand Site Hierarchy, *<Site Name>*, Site Settings, and Client Agents.

3. Right-click Remote Tools Client Agent and select Properties.

4. On the Advanced tab, verify that the settings are configured as desired (modify these settings before enabling remote tools).

5. On the General tab, select the "Enable remote tools on clients" check box.

6. On the Security tab, add users or groups to the list of permitted viewers.

7. On the Policy tab, configure permissions for SMS Remote Tools and Remote Assistance as required for your environment.

8. Click OK to save the changes.

Discussion

Remote Tools is an SMS agent that allows you to remotely control systems. The configuration options available in this section determine how Remote Control will be configured for all clients in this SMS site. Remote Assistance is a technology built into Windows XP and Windows Server 2003 (and future operating systems). Review Chapter 12 for information about the differences between Remote Control and Remote Assistance.

See Also

- Chapter 12 provides complete configuration of the SMS Remote Tools Client Agent.
- Chapter 10 of the *Microsoft Systems Management Server 2003 Administrator's Companion* by Steven Kaczmarek (Microsoft Press, 2004) provides additional information on the Remote Tools Client Agent.
- Chapter 9 of the *SMS 2003 Operations Guide* provides an in-depth look at Remote Tools.

2-23. Configuring the Advertised Programs Client Agent

Problem

You want to enable and configure the Advertised Programs Client Agent.

Solution

1. Open the SMS Administrator console.
2. From the SMS Administrator console, expand Site Database (*<Site Code>*), and then expand Site Hierarchy, *<Site Name>*, Site Settings, and Client Agents.
3. Right-click Advertised Programs Client Agent and select Properties.
4. On the General tab, select the "Enable software distribution to clients" check box.
5. Modify the Legacy and Advanced Client settings as desired.
6. Click OK to save the changes.

Discussion

One of the most powerful features of SMS is software distribution. Enable the Advertised Programs Client Agent so you can install software throughout your enterprise.

For Legacy Client settings, select the "Clients cannot change agent settings" check box to prevent users from modifying the polling interval and notification settings for the Legacy Client. The program polling interval (a default of 60 minutes) specifies how often the SMS Legacy Client checks its client access point for new (or modified) advertisements. Software distribution (located under Component Configuration) must also be properly configured with the Legacy Client software installation account. For Legacy Clients, this account is used during software installation and network connectivity.

For Advanced Client settings, the policy polling interval (a default of 60 minutes) specifies how often the SMS Advanced Client checks its management point or proxy management point for new (or modified) advertisements. You can also enable the check box to display notifications for new programs in Add or Remove Programs (in the Windows Control Panel) if desired. The network access account (located under Component Configuration) must also be properly configured for the Advanced Client to access some network resources during installations, if required.

See Also

- Recipe 2-28, "Configuring the Advanced Client Network Access Account," shows how to configure the Advanced Client network access account.

- Many chapters of this book are geared toward advertised programs (software distribution). Chapters 3, 4, 5, and 6 are all used with advertised programs.

- Chapter 5 of the *SMS 2003 Operations Guide* explains the software distribution process.

- Chapter 12 of the *Microsoft Systems Management Server 2003 Administrator's Companion* by Steven Kaczmarek (Microsoft Press, 2004) provides additional information for Advertised Programs Client Agent configuration.

2-24. Configuring the Software Metering Client Agent

Problem

You want to enable and configure the Software Metering Client Agent.

Solution

1. Open the SMS Administrator console.

2. From the SMS Administrator console, expand Site Database (*<Site Code>*), and then expand Site Hierarchy, *<Site Name>*, Site Settings, and Client Agents.

3. Right-click Software Metering Client Agent and select Properties.

4. On the General tab, select the "Enable software metering on clients" check box.

5. On the Schedule tab, modify the data collection schedule and metering rules download schedule as desired.

6. Click OK to save the changes.

Discussion

For all you SMS 2.0 veterans out there, don't be afraid. SMS 2003 software metering is completely different from SMS 2.0 software metering. Software metering in SMS 2003 does not require a separate database or separate servers, and it is not resource intensive. The following list describes the two scheduling actions used with software metering:

Data collection schedule: This option specifies when the client collects the data on metered applications. Once the data is collected, it is forwarded to the SMS site. The default schedule is every seven days.

Metering rules download schedule: This option specifies the frequency with which the Legacy Client downloads an updated list of monitored applications. The default schedule is every seven days. The Advanced Client downloads software-metering rules based on the polling schedule configured in the Advertised Programs Client Agent.

Here's an important note from the *Scenarios and Procedures for SMS 2003: Planning and Deployment* guide:

Be aware that, as the number of software programs monitored by software metering increases, the load on the network increases. Network traffic also depends on how you configure the software metering data collection schedule and the software metering rules download schedule.

See Also

- Chapter 7 provides detailed information on configuring software metering and metering rules.

- Chapter 8 of the *SMS 2003 Operations Guide* discusses software metering.

- Chapter 15 of the *Microsoft Systems Management Server 2003 Administrator's Companion* by Steven Kaczmarek (Microsoft Press, 2004) discusses software metering.

- The *Scenarios and Procedures for SMS 2003: Planning and Deployment* guide provides information on how to calculate the amount of network traffic used by each client agent.

2-25. Configuring Client Push Installation

Problem

You want to configure client push installation.

Solution

1. Open the SMS Administrator console.

2. From the SMS Administrator console, expand Site Hierarchy, *<Site Name>*, Site Settings, and Client Installation Methods.

3. Right-click Client Push Installation and select Properties

4. Select the first check box to enable Client Push Installation to automatically push to assigned resources that do not currently have the SMS client installed. (See the "Discussion" section for an important note about this.)

5. For System types, determine which systems to allow Client Push Installation to initiate client installation.

6. Select "Enable Client Push Installation to site systems" to allow the client to be installed on SMS site systems in your environment.

7. For client types, select Platform Dependent for the installation to automatically determine which client to install, or you can force a specific client type. (The Legacy Client will only install on legacy systems, so if you push a Legacy Client install to a Windows 2000 system, the installation will not succeed.)

8. On the Accounts tab, add the account or accounts that have administrator privileges on the clients to be installed.

9. On the Advanced Client tab, add any additional installation properties required for your environment (e.g., SMSSITECODE=Auto to autodetect the SMS site code, and SMSCACHESIZE=800 to set the cache size to 800MB).

10. Click OK to apply the settings.

Discussion

As the Client Push Installation dialog states, you must configure the Advanced Client network access account before you can use the client push installation method to deploy the SMS 2003 Advanced Client on computers that are not in an Active Directory environment. This account is used to access network resources. The network access account serves a similar purpose on the SMS 2003 Advanced Client as the client connection account serves for Legacy Clients (and similarly, SMS 2.0 clients in an SMS 2.0 environment).

Note Client Push Installation does not need to be enabled to use manually. Use the Client Push Installation Wizard to push the SMS client to desired systems or collections of systems.

Tip For redundancy of accounts, you can use %MACHINENAME%\Administrator if you have a standardized local administrator account password.

It is important to realize that checking the box for "Enable Client Push Installation to assigned resources" will automatically push to all non-SMS clients that are assigned. Many SMS administrators do not want client push to automatically occur. If you configure everything else, but leave this box unchecked, you will be able to use the Client Push Installation Wizard (available when you right-click a collection or computer in a collection) to direct client installations to specific collections or systems.

Here are a few of the more popular installation properties that you can use with Client Push Installation:

SMSSITECODE=<SMSSITE>: Depending on your environment, you may not be able to use the default setting of AUTO. You may need to specify the site code for the client to connect.

SMSCACHESIZE=800: In this example, 800MB will be set for the size of the SMS cache on the client instead of the default cache size of 250MB.

CCMLOGMAXSIZE=20000: This would be the maximum size (in bytes) for each log on the client.

CCMSTARTSERVICES=FALSE: With this option configured, the Advanced Client installs, but the service does not start until the next reboot of the system.

DISABLESITEOPT=TRUE: This setting prevents end users with administrative credentials on the client computer from changing the SMS assigned site code for the Advanced Client by using the Systems Management icon in the Control Panel.

DISABLECACHEOPT=TRUE: This setting prevents end users with administrative credentials on the client computer from changing the cache settings for the Advanced Client by using the Systems Management icon in the Control Panel.

From the examples provided, the installation properties for Client Push Installation could be similar to the following:

SMSSITECODE=LAB SMSCACHESIZE=800 DISABLECACHEOPT=TRUE

This would force the SMS client to connect to the LAB site, set the local cache maximum size to 800MB, and prevent administrators from changing the cache size from the Systems Management applet.

See Also

- Recipe 2-28, "Configuring the Advanced Client Network Access Account," demonstrates how to configure the Advanced Client Network Access account.

- Chapter 8 of the *Microsoft Systems Management Server 2003 Administrator's Companion* by Steven Kaczmarek (Microsoft Press, 2004) provides additional information on enabling and configuring Client Push Installation.

- Microsoft Knowledge Base article 838436, "How to prepare the Systems Management 2003 site for a Client Push Installation," available at http://support.microsoft.com/?kbid=838436, shows how to configure Client Push Installation for both Advanced Clients and Legacy Clients.

- Appendix I of the *Scenarios and Procedures for SMS 2003: Planning and Deployment* guide describes how to install and configure SMS clients.

2-26. Modifying the Default Location for Software Packages

Problem

You want to modify the location for storage of compressed software packages.

Solution

1. Open the SMS Administrator console.

2. From the SMS Administrator console, expand Site Database (*<Site Code>*), and then expand Site Hierarchy, *<Site Name>*, Site Settings, and Component Configuration.

3. In the right pane, double-click Software Distribution.

4. On the General tab, enter the local drive on the site server that is to be used for storing packages.

5. Click OK to apply the settings.

Discussion

The "Location of stored packages" option is used to specify where compressed packages are stored on site servers; C: is the default location. To determine if a package is configured to use a compressed copy, browse to the desired package, right-click it, and select Properties. On the Data Source tab, observe whether or not the "Use a compressed copy of the source directory" option is enabled.

Caution Modifying the storage location for compressed packages will not move compressed packages that are already on the site. All compressed packages that are sent to the site after this change has been made will be stored in the new location.

See Also

- Microsoft Knowledge Base article 829839, "Distribution Manager cannot decompress a package onto a FAT drive if the package source files reside on an NTFS drive," provides important information for when your package source directory contains a different file system (e.g., FAT) than the site server stored packages file system (e.g., NTFS).

2-27. Configuring the Legacy Client Software Installation Account

Problem

You want to modify the Legacy Client software installation account.

Solution

1. Open the SMS Administrator console.

2. From the SMS Administrator console, expand Site Database (*<Site Code>*), and then expand Site Hierarchy, *<Site Name>*, Site Settings, and Component Configuration.

3. In the right pane, double-click Software Distribution.

4. On the General tab, under the Legacy Client Software Installation Account section, click Set to modify the current account.

5. If you do not want to specify an account, click Clear.

6. Click OK to apply the settings.

Discussion

The name "Legacy Client Software Installation Account" is somewhat misleading. It is used by SMS for connecting to network resources (other than the package distribution point) in addition to launching local installations of software on Legacy Clients. According to the *SMS 2003 Operations Guide*, this account is required when the advertised program meets all of the following conditions:

- The program must access network resources other than the distribution point from which it is run.

- The program is not an application coded to use SMS or other explicit connection mechanisms.

- The program requires administrative rights.

Note If a domain name is not specified with the account name, SMS will use the client computer's domain.

If possible, avoid using the Legacy Client Software Installation account. Also, avoid using the SMS Service account as the Legacy Client Software Installation account. Use the lowest possible permissions to access required resources. According to the *Scenarios and Procedures for SMS 2003: Security* guide, the Legacy Client Software Installation account should never have higher rights than the domain user. Remove the Legacy Client Software Installation account from your environment if it's no longer needed.

See Also

- Recipe 2-28, "Configuring the Advanced Client Network Access Account," demonstrates how to configure the Advanced Client Network Access account.

- The *Scenarios and Procedures for SMS 2003: Security* guide provides best practices for managing SMS accounts.

- Chapter 5 of the *SMS 2003 Concepts, Planning, and Deployment Guide* provides additional information about SMS 2003 security.

- Chapter 5 of the *SMS 2003 Operations Guide* provides more information about the Legacy Client Software Installation account.

2-28. Configuring the Advanced Client Network Access Account

Problem

You want to modify the Advanced Client Network Access account.

Solution

1. Open the SMS Administrator console.

2. From the SMS Administrator console, expand Site Database (*<Site Code>*), and then expand Site Hierarchy, *<Site Name>*, Site Settings, and Component Configuration.

3. In the right pane, double-click Software Distribution.

4. On the General tab, under the Advanced Client Network Access Account section, click Set to modify the current account.

5. If you do not want to specify an account, click Clear.

6. Click OK to apply the settings.

Discussion

The Advanced Client Network Access account serves a similar purpose on the Advanced Client that the Legacy Client Software Installation account serves on the Legacy Client, except that it does not provide administrative credentials. According to the *SMS 2003 Operations Guide*, this account is required when the advertised program meets the following conditions:

- The program must access network resources other than the distribution point from which it is run.

- The program is not an application coded to use SMS or other explicit connection mechanisms.

Client Push Installation may also use the Advanced Client Network Access account when the computer account does not have access to the content for installation.

See Also

- The *Scenarios and Procedures for SMS 2003: Security* guide provides best practices for managing SMS accounts.

- Chapter 5 of the *SMS 2003 Concepts, Planning, and Deployment Guide* provides additional information about SMS 2003 security.

- Chapter 5 of the *SMS 2003 Operations Guide* provides more information about the Legacy Client Software Installation account.

- Microsoft Knowledge Base article 829869, "How to configure the Systems Management Server 2003 Advanced Client Network Access account," provides information about configuring the Advanced Client Network Access account.

2-29. Modifying Distribution Point Communication Settings

Problem

You want to modify the communication setting used for updating distribution points.

Solution

1. Open the SMS Administrator console.

2. From the SMS Administrator console, expand Site Database (*<Site Code>*), and then expand Site Hierarchy, *<Site Name>*, Site Settings, and Component Configuration.

3. In the right pane, double-click Software Distribution.

4. Select the Distribution Point tab.

5. Under "Concurrent distribution settings," set the maximum number of packages and threads per package that can be used at the same time during distribution point replication.

6. Under Retry settings, set the number of retry attempts and the retry delay that will be used during package distribution.

7. If you have a site that is closer to the distribution point, you can check the box to have it source the packages from the nearest site in the hierarchy.

8. Click OK to apply the settings.

Discussion

Prior to SP1 for SMS 2003, distribution points were updated in a single-threaded manner. For example, when sending the latest version of Microsoft Office to all distribution points, they would update one at a time until completion. If a distribution point encountered a problem, the process would not continue until the problem was resolved. So because of one distribution point encountering a problem, many other distribution points would not be updated.

Since SP1, SMS now copies package to multiple distribution points at the same time. This change reduces the total time required to update all distribution points in a site, and it also allows you to effectively manage more child sites under one parent.

The "Concurrent distribution settings" options are as follows:

Maximum number of packages: This is the total number of packages that SMS may copy in parallel.

Maximum threads per package: This option determines how many threads each package can use.

These two options for concurrent distribution settings are related. Say, for example, you have 20 child sites with distribution points attached to your parent site. On the parent site, you set "Maximum number of packages" to 3 and "Maximum threads per package" to 5. This means that you may have as many as 15 (3 * 5 = 15) threads running for updating distribution points at any given time. Now when you add/update distribution points for your Office package, five distribution points will be updated in parallel because of the maximum of five per package. While this process occurs, two additional packages may be processed to distribution points, with five threads each.

The Retry Settings options are as follows:

Number of retries: This is the number of times the Distribution Manager attempts to distribute the software. Choose from 1 to 1,000 retry attempts.

Retry delay: This is the interval between retry attempts. Choose from 1 to 1,440 minutes (24 hours).

Select the "Send package from the nearest site in the hierarchy" check box to reduce WAN traffic. Before SP1, source packages were always sent from the top site that contained the source files, to all child sites. If you have a two-tiered environment, this works fine for you. If you have an SMS environment with three or more tiers, getting from the parent to the grandchild (or great-grandchild, etc.) could take quite a bit of time depending on all the network links of the sites in between the parent and its grandchildren. Enabling this option will allow a grandchild site to obtain package source (or compressed package source) faster if another site in its hierarchy already has the source files. According to the *Scenarios and Procedures for SMS 2003: Planning and Deployment* guide, enabling this option affects package distribution in the following ways:

- When compressed package source files with the correct version are available at a parent site that is near the requesting site, the source site instructs the closest parent site to send content to the requesting site.

- When a site's distribution point is targeted to receive a new package, the source files are retrieved from the closest higher-level parent site in the hierarchy.

- When a new distribution point is created, the site where the package was originally created identifies the parent site that has the correct package contents and version that is closest to the target site. That parent site then updates the newly created distribution point.

See Also

- The SMS 2003 Administrator console Help Library (press F1 while in the SMS console) provides definitions for each setting.

- The Microsoft TechNet page titled "What's New in SMS 2003 Service Pack 1" (http://www.microsoft.com/technet/prodtechnol/sms/sms2003/whatsnew.mspx) provides additional information about distribution point improvements.

- Appendix F of the *Scenarios and Procedures for SMS 2003: Planning and Deployment* guide provides more information about the Distribution Point tab of the Software Distribution dialog box.

2-30. Modifying Client Access Point Retry Settings

Problem

You want to modify the client access point retry settings.

Solution: Using a Graphical Interface

1. Open the SMS Administrator console.

2. From the SMS Administrator console, expand Site Database (*<Site Code>*), and then expand Site Hierarchy, *<Site Name>*, Site Settings, and Component Configuration.

3. In the right pane, double-click Software Distribution.

4. Click the Client Access Point tab.

5. Under Retry Settings, set the number of retry attempts and the retry delay that will be used during package distribution.

6. Click OK to apply the settings.

Discussion

Similar to the distribution point settings, you can configure how the SMS site server retries the package update process for client access points if it is unable to update on the first attempt.

See Also

- Recipe 2-55, "Creating a Client Access Point," demonstrates how to create a client access point.

2-31. Modifying Status Reporting Properties

Problem

You want to modify the status reporting properties.

Solution: Using a Graphical Interface

1. Open the SMS Administrator console.
2. From the SMS Administrator console, expand Site Database (*<Site Code>*), and then expand Site Hierarchy, *<Site Name>*, Site Settings, and Component Configuration.
3. In the right pane, double-click Status Reporting.
4. Enable or disable the status reporting and logging of both the server and client components by selecting the appropriate check boxes.
5. Limit the type of status reporting by selecting from the drop-down lists.
6. Click OK to apply the settings.

Discussion

If you find that the default settings for status reporting and event logging are inadequate, you can increase or decrease them in the Status Reporting Properties dialog box. However, these settings apply to all site components or all clients, so any changes made will have a significant impact on the amount of data returned. Increasing the reporting to include all details could impact your network with the increased data. Decreasing the reporting could eliminate essential status messages and limit the effectiveness of the status summarizers.

See Also

- Recipe 2-62, "Creating Status Filter Rules," demonstrates how to create new status filter rules.
- Recipe 2-63, "Modifying Status Summarizers," demonstrates how to modify the status summarizers.

2-32. Modifying Data Processing and Storage

Problem

You want to modify the data processing and storage settings.

Solution: Using a Graphical Interface

1. Open the SMS Administrator console.
2. From the SMS Administrator console, expand Site Database (*<Site Code>*), and then expand Site Hierarchy, *<Site Name>*, Site Settings, and Component Configuration.
3. In the right pane, double-click Data Processing and Storage.
4. Enable and configure the update intervals of the database statistics.
5. Select whether to have a status message created when the database reaches your specified capacity.
6. Click OK to apply the settings.

Discussion

The SMS Administrator console Help Library states that these settings are for SMS 2.0 only, which explains why the Update Database Statistics option is grayed out. Also, the option to create a status message after the database has reached a specified capacity is not available for SQL 7.0 and is set to automatically send a status message at 80 percent, whether the option is enabled or not. This is probably the only SMS site configuration that you can safely disregard.

2-33. Configuring the Default Management Point

Problem

You want to change the default management point settings.

Solution: Using a Graphical Interface

1. Open the SMS Administrator console.
2. From the SMS Administrator console, expand Site Database (*<Site Code>*), and then expand Site Hierarchy, *<Site Name>*, Site Settings, and Component Configuration.
3. In the right pane, double-click Management Point.
4. If you have multiple management points, you can change the default management point by choosing another server from the drop-down list.
5. If you have load-balanced your management point, choose that option and enter the virtual IP address of the network load balancing (NLB) management point.
6. Click OK to apply the settings.

Discussion

The first time you create a management point, you will be prompted to make it the default so you do not have to set this manually. However, if you have a large site and plan on using network load balancing for your management point, then you will need to define that here. You can also have a backup management point in the case of a failure or downtime for the default management point. In that situation, you will need to manually make it the default, as there is no automatic failover mechanism.

See Also

- Recipe 2-53, "Creating a Management Point," describes how to create a management point.
- Recipe 2-54, "Creating a Proxy Management Point," demonstrates how to create a proxy management point.
- Table 2-1, "Site System Role Requirements," located in Recipe 2-50, shows the required Windows components for each site role.

2-34. Modifying Client Connection Accounts

Problem

You want to create or modify a client connection account.

Solution: Using a Graphical Interface

1. Open the SMS Administrator console.

2. From the SMS Administrator console, expand Site Database (*<Site Code>*), and then expand Site Hierarchy, *<Site Name>*, Site Settings, Connection Accounts, and Client.

3. Right-click Client and select New ➤ Windows User Account.

4. Click the Set button and enter the name and password of the account you would like to use as a client connection account.

5. Click OK to apply the settings.

Discussion

The Client Connection account is used to support Legacy Clients and is created by default during a standard security installation. It is a local account on the site server that allows the Legacy Client to connect to the client access point and distribution points. If you plan on having Legacy Clients in an advanced security site, you will need to manually create this account, as it will not be created if the site is created as an advanced security site.

See Also

- Recipes 2-55, "Creating a Client Access Point," and 2-30, "Modifying Client Access Point Retry Settings," show how to manage client access points.

- Recipe 2-2, "Enabling Advanced Security Mode," provides information on advanced security mode.

2-35. Modifying the Site System Connection Account

Problem

You want to create or modify a site system connection account.

Solution: Using a Graphical Interface

1. Open the SMS Administrator console.

2. From the SMS Administrator console, expand Site Database (*<Site Code>*), and then expand Site Hierarchy, *<Site Name>*, Site Settings, Connection Accounts, and Site System.

3. Right-click Site System and select New ➤ Windows User Account.

4. Click the Set button and enter the name and password of the account you would like to use as a site system connection account.

5. Click OK to apply the settings.

Discussion

This account is optional, as the SMS Service account will be used in its absence. It is recommended that you specify an account for increased security. In advanced security mode, this account is substituted for the site server computer account.

See Also

- Recipe 2-3, "Modifying SMS Service Accounts," demonstrates how to modify the SMS service account.
- Recipe 2-2, "Enabling Advanced Security Mode," demonstrates how to switch to advanced security mode.

2-36. Configuring Active Directory System Discovery

Problem

You want to enable Active Directory System Discovery.

Solution

1. Open the SMS Administrator console.
2. From the SMS Administrator console, expand Site Database (*<Site Code>*), Site Hierarchy, *<Site Name>*, and Site Settings, and then select Discovery Methods.
3. Double-click Active Directory System Discovery in the right pane to open the Active Directory System Discovery Properties dialog box.
4. On the General tab, select the Enable Active Directory System Discovery check box.
5. Click the New button to define your Active Directory container search criteria and search options.
6. On the Polling Schedule tab, click the Schedule button to define the frequency of the discovery.
7. Click OK to apply the settings.

Discussion

The Active Directory System Discovery method will identify the computer name, Active Directory container name, IP address, and assigned Active Directory site for all systems in the containers that you specified for discovery by querying the nearest domain controller. All systems will be discovered even if they are a disabled account.

See Also

- Recipes 2-45, "Configuring Enhanced System Discovery," and 2-42, "Configuring the Net-Crawler Discovery Service," show how to achieve more granular control of system discovery.

2-37. Configuring Active Directory System Group Discovery

Problem

You want to enable Active Directory System Group Discovery.

Solution

1. Open the SMS Administrator console.
2. From the SMS Administrator console, expand Site Database (*<Site Code>*), Site Hierarchy, *<Site Name>*, and Site Settings, and then select Discovery Methods.

3. Double-click Active Directory System Group Discovery in the right pane to open the Active Directory System Group Discovery Properties dialog box.

4. On the General tab, select the Enable Active Directory System Group Discovery check box.

5. Click the New button to define your Active Directory container search criteria and search options.

6. On the Polling Schedule tab, click the schedule button to define the frequency of the discovery.

7. Click OK to apply the settings.

Discussion

The Active Directory System Group Discovery is a secondary discovery method in that it discovers Active Directory information for existing SMS clients instead of performing an initial discovery. For existing assigned resources, it will discover the organizational unit (OU) and group membership that the resource is associated with in Active Directory, so you have more options for collection creation and software distribution targeting.

See Also

- Recipe 2-45, "Configuring Enhanced System Discovery," shows how to achieve more granular control of system discovery.

2-38. Configuring Active Directory User Discovery

Problem

You want to add or modify Active Directory User Discovery.

Solution

1. Open the SMS Administrator console.

2. From the SMS Administrator console, expand Site Database (<*Site Code*>), Site Hierarchy, <*Site Name*>, and Site Settings, and then select Discovery Methods.

3. Double-click Active Directory User Discovery in the right pane to open the Active Directory User Discovery Properties dialog box.

4. On the General tab, select the Enable Active Directory User Discovery check box.

5. Click the New button to define your Active Directory container search criteria and search options.

6. On the Polling Schedule tab, click the schedule button to define the frequency of the discovery.

7. Click OK to apply the settings.

Discussion

If you would like to create collections based on Active Directory user groups, then this is the discovery method of choice. It will discover the user name, Active Directory domain, Active Directory container name, and User groups from Active Directory for the containers you specify.

See Also

- Recipe 2-46, "Configuring Enhanced User Discovery," demonstrates how to return more data with User Discovery.

2-39. Configuring Active Directory Security Group Discovery

Problem

You want to add or modify Active Directory Security Group Discovery.

Solution

1. Open the SMS Administrator console.
2. From the SMS Administrator console, expand Site Database (*<Site Code>*), Site Hierarchy, *<Site Name>*, and Site Settings, and then select Discovery Methods.
3. Double-click Active Directory Security Group Discovery in the right pane to open the Active Directory Security Group Discovery Properties dialog box.
4. On the General tab, select the Enable Active Directory Security Group Discovery check box.
5. Click the New button to define your Active Directory container search criteria and search options.
6. On the Polling Schedule tab, click the schedule button to define the frequency of the discovery.
7. Click OK to apply the settings.

Discussion

This new discovery method is included with SMS 2003 SP2. It is different from all other discovery methods in that it doesn't discover users or systems—it actually discovers security groups and creates resource records for them. This speeds up software deployments that are targeted at users of those groups since the collection will not have to be refreshed to add the user before the advertisement is detected. Essentially, a collection would contain only one resource: the security group being targeted.

See Also

- Recipe 2-46, "Configuring Enhanced User Discovery," demonstrates how to return more data with User Discovery.

2-40. Configuring Heartbeat Discovery

Problem

You want to enable or modify Heartbeat Discovery.

Solution

1. Open the SMS Administrator console.
2. From the SMS Administrator console, expand Site Database (*<Site Code>*), Site Hierarchy, *<Site Name>*, and Site Settings, and then select Discovery Methods.

3. Double-click Heartbeat Discovery in the right pane to open the Heartbeat Discovery Properties dialog box.

4. On the General tab, select the Enable Heartbeat Discovery check box and set your desired schedule in hours, days, or weeks using the appropriate drop-down menus.

5. Click OK to apply the settings.

Discussion

Heartbeat Discovery is not really a true discovery method, as the system must already be an SMS client for it to work. It is easier to look at this as a rediscovery method since the SMS client is simply refreshing its discovery data on the schedule that you specified.

See Also

- Recipes 2-36, "Configuring Active Directory System Discovery," 2-41, "Configuring Network Discovery," 2-42, "Configuring the NetCrawler Discovery Service," and 2-45, "Configuring Enhanced System Discovery," show methods of discovering systems on your network.

2-41. Configuring Network Discovery

Problem

You want to enable or modify Network Discovery.

Solution

1. Open the SMS Administrator console.

2. From the SMS Administrator console, expand Site Database (<*Site Code*>), Site Hierarchy, <*Site Name*>, and Site Settings, and then select Discovery Methods.

3. Double-click Network Discovery in the right pane to open the Network Discovery Properties dialog box.

4. On the General tab, select the Enable Network Discovery check box, select your discovery type, and indicate whether Network Discovery will be traversing a low-bandwidth link.

5. Use the Subnets, Domains, SNMP, SNMP Devices, and DHCP tabs to define the search criteria for Network Discovery to use.

6. On the Schedule tab, click the New button to schedule a discovery. You can create multiple schedules.

7. Click OK to apply the settings.

Discussion

Network Discovery is very powerful, and it should be configured properly before use; otherwise, it could negatively affect the performance of the network. In a nutshell, Network Discovery will discover any device that has an IP address on your network.

Let's look at each of the tabs available in the Network Discovery Properties dialog box in detail.

General: This is the overall on/off switch for Network Discovery. If you enable Network Discovery and it starts to flood your network, this is where you want to go to fix it. The type of discovery that is most useful is "topology, client, and client operating system," since having the operating system discovered is helpful if you are going to use the Client Push Installation method.

Subnets: In addition to the details of the subnets that you would like to discover, you can also control whether individual subnets are enabled for discovery and in which order they are searched. The "Search local subnets" check box enables all settings for this tab, so if this option isn't selected, the subnets will not be discovered.

Domains: Here you specify the domains that you want Network Discovery to query with Windows Internet Name Service (WINS). However, this tab is not useful by itself, since a correct subnet mask must be identified for each client in order for a discovery data record (DDR) to be created, and the domain discovery alone cannot provide that. Use this tab in conjunction with the DHCP, Subnets, and SNMP tabs. Select the "Search local domain" check box to enable this feature.

SNMP: Enter the SNMP community names that are valid on your network if you want to query SNMP enabled devices. Configure the maximum hops that are allowed in the SNMP discovery.

SNMP Devices: The local router will be used by default, but you can list additional SNMP devices for SMS to use for Network Discovery.

DHCP: This is the most critical feature of Network Discovery, which explains why it is on by default. If you don't specify a DHCP server for Network Discovery to use, you will find out that Network Discovery won't be able to create DDRs from the other discovery data if it doesn't have a DHCP server available. Also, the DHCP server must be a Microsoft DHCP server.

Note The DHCP tab is not available if you are using advanced security because MS-DHCP cannot leverage computer-based security.

Schedule: You can create any type of schedule or group of schedules that you want. You also have the ability to limit how long the discovery cycle can run by setting the duration options. This is very handy the first time you run Network Discovery and you aren't sure how much of an impact it will have on your network.

See Also

- If you do not use Microsoft DHCP, you will want to check out Recipes 2-42, "Configuring the NetCrawler Discovery Service," and 2-45, "Configuring Enhanced System Discovery."

2-42. Configuring the NetCrawler Discovery Service

Problem

You want to install the NetCrawler Discovery service.

Solution

1. Contact your Microsoft Technical Account Manager (TAM) or call Microsoft Product Support Services and request a copy of the SMS NetCrawler tool written by Chris Sugdinis.

2. Unzip the file bundle to your favorite location.

3. Read the extensive help file.

4. Install the NetCrawler Discovery service on your site server with the desired configuration.

Discussion

The NetCrawler tool was written by Chris Sugdinis at Microsoft. At the time of this writing, it is not publicly available for download, but users can request a copy through Microsoft sales and support channels. NetCrawler is a rich and customizable tool similar to Steve Bobosky's discovery tools. If you have a complex network or systems in workgroups that you need to discover, you will want to try the NetCrawler Discovery service.

See Also

- See Steve Bobosky's tools in Recipes 2-45, "Configuring Enhanced System Discovery," and 2-46, "Configuring Enhanced User Discovery."

2-43. Configuring Windows User Account Discovery

Problem

You want to enable or modify Windows User Account Discovery.

Solution

1. Open the SMS Administrator console.

2. From the SMS Administrator console, expand Site Database (<*Site Code*>), Site Hierarchy, <*Site Name*>, and Site Settings, and then select Discovery Methods.

3. Double-click Windows User Account Discovery in the right pane to open the Windows User Account Discovery Properties dialog box.

4. On the General tab, select the Enable Windows User Account Discovery check box.

5. Click the New button to select the domains you would like to discover.

6. On the Polling Schedule tab, click the schedule button to define the frequency of the discovery.

7. Click OK to apply the settings.

Discussion

If you still have any NT 4.0 domains in your environment, then you will need to use this discovery method to discover the users in those domains. It will work with a mixed-mode Active Directory domain, but you will lose this functionality when you move to native mode, so it is better to use Active Directory user discovery for all Active Directory domains.

See Also

- Recipes 2-38, "Configuring Active Directory User Discovery," and 2-46, "Configuring Enhanced User Discovery," demonstrate how to discover user information.

2-44. Configuring Windows User Group Discovery

Problem

You want to enable or modify Windows User Group Discovery.

Solution

1. Open the SMS Administrator console.

2. From the SMS Administrator console, expand Site Database (*<Site Code>*), Site Hierarchy, *<Site Name>*, and Site Settings, and then select Discovery Methods.

3. Double-click Windows User Group Discovery in the right pane to open the Windows User Group Discovery Properties dialog box.

4. On the General tab, select the Enable Windows User Group Discovery check box.

5. Click the New button to select the domains you would like to discover.

6. On the Polling Schedule tab, click the schedule button to define the frequency of the discovery.

7. Click OK to apply the settings.

Discussion

This discovery method has the same constraints as Recipe 2-43, "Configuring Windows User Account Discovery," since it works primarily for NT domains.

See Also

- Recipes 2-38, "Configuring Active Directory User Discovery," and 2-46, "Configuring Enhanced User Discovery," demonstrate how to configure user discovery methods.

2-45. Configuring Enhanced System Discovery

Problem

You want to control your system discovery in ways that are not available with the default discovery methods.

Solution

1. Go to http://www.systemcentertools.com and download the Enhanced System Discovery tool. Extract the .zip file to your location of choice.

2. Run the .msi file on your primary site server to install the tool.

3. Customize the two configuration files.

4. Run the executable manually or schedule it to run periodically using SMS or Windows Scheduler.

Discussion

You might think that seven built-in discovery methods would be sufficient to discover just about anything, but there are some exceptions. For those exceptions, Steve Bobosky created the Enhanced System Discovery tool while he was at Microsoft. Steve continues to support and develop this and other tools at his current position with Centerlogic.

Here are the main features that the Enhanced System Discovery tool provides:

- Combined discovery of systems in NT and Active Directory domains.
- Disabled computer accounts are not discovered by default.
- Computer account password age option. Systems with older passwords than the value you specify in the configuration file will not be discovered.
- Name resolution dependency. You can choose to discover only systems that resolve to an IP or all systems.
- Local site restriction. With this option configured, discovery records will be created only for systems that fall within the site boundaries of the site specified in the configuration file.
- Ping reply option. Discovers only systems that reply to a ping.
- Flexible Active Directory attribute control. There is a specific configuration file for selecting the Active Directory attributes you would like to return to SMS in the discovery record.
- SMS 2003 and SMS 2.0 compatibility.

All of these options are configurable to meet the needs of your environment.

See Also

- Recipes 2-36, "Configuring Active Directory System Discovery," 2-37, "Configuring Active Directory System Group Discovery," 2-41, "Configuring Network Discovery," 2-42, "Configuring the NetCrawler Discovery Service," and 2-46, "Configuring Enhanced User Discovery," demonstrate the many discovery methods available for SMS.

2-46. Configuring Enhanced User Discovery

Problem

You want to discover more user data than is available with the default discovery methods.

Solution

1. Go to http://www.systemcentertools.com and download the Enhanced System Discovery tool. Extract the .zip file to your location of choice.
2. Run the .msi file on your primary site server to install the tool.
3. Customize the two configuration files.
4. Run the executable manually or schedule it to run periodically using SMS or Windows Scheduler.

Discussion

Steve Bobosky created the Enhanced User Discovery tool to complement the Active Directory User Discovery method. With this tool, you have complete flexibility on which Active Directory attributes are returned in the DDR for each user. For example, you can configure it to return e-mail addresses, phone numbers, office locations, titles, or any of the other Active Directory attributes in the user object.

See Also

- Recipes 2-45, "Configuring Enhanced System Discovery," 2-38, "Configuring Active Directory User Discovery," 2-39, "Configuring Active Directory Security Group Discovery," 2-43, "Configuring Windows User Account Discovery," and 2-44, "Configuring Windows User Group Discovery," demonstrate the many discovery methods available in SMS.

2-47. Creating a Sender

Problem

You want to create a sender.

Solution

1. Open the SMS Administrator console.
2. From the SMS Administrator console, expand Site Database (*<Site Code>*), Site Hierarchy, *<Site Name>*, Site Settings, and Senders.
3. Right-click Senders and select New ➤ Standard Sender.
4. On the General tab, enter the name of the site server.
5. On the Advanced tab, set the concurrent sendings limits and retry settings.
6. Click OK to create the sender.

Discussion

Senders work in conjunction with addresses and are responsible for communicating SMS data and packages to the site systems underneath them via their corresponding address type. The standard Sender is installed and configured by default during SMS site server installation. Besides the standard Sender, you can also use a number of Remote Access Services (RAS) senders if your environment is set up that way. The Courier Sender is for delivering large packages that you do not want to send over the WAN.

If you have a deep hierarchy, you may want to add additional senders from a primary site to child sites that are several tiers below. This will speed up the process flow, as the child site will not have to wait for the communication to traverse the hierarchy to reach it.

See Also

- Recipes 2-17, "Creating an Address," 2-18, "Modifying the Sending Schedule of an Address," and 2-19, "Modifying the Rate Limits of an Address," demonstrate how to create and configure sender addresses.

2-48. Modifying Sender Properties

Problem

You want to modify the properties of a sender.

Solution

1. Open the SMS Administrator console.

2. From the SMS Administrator console, expand Site Database (*<Site Code>*), Site Hierarchy, *<Site Name>*, Site Settings, and Senders.

3. In the right pane, double-click a sender.

4. On the Advanced tab, set the concurrent sendings limits and retry settings.

5. Click OK to create the sender.

Discussion

The Sender properties are one of the ways that you can manage the impact that SMS 2003 has on your network. In addition to the Address settings, you can configure how the sender for each SMS site processes its communication. If you want less of an impact on your network, lower your concurrent sendings and increase your retry interval. If you want a more responsive hierarchy, increase your concurrent sendings and decrease your retry interval. Leaving these settings at their defaults may not be a good thing for your environment (as they may be either too restrictive or too intrusive), so we strongly advise that you review and adjust them to meet the needs of your organization.

See Also

- Recipes 2-47, "Creating a Sender," 2-17, "Creating an Address," 2-18, "Modifying the Sending Schedule of an Address," and 2-19, "Modifying the Rate Limits of an Address," demonstrate how to create and configure sender addresses.

2-49. Configuring Site Maintenance Tasks

Problem

You want to configure site maintenance tasks.

Solution

1. Open the SMS Administrator console.

2. From the SMS Administrator console, expand Site Database (*<Site Code>*), Site Hierarchy, *<Site Name>*, Site Settings, Site Maintenance, and Tasks.

3. Select the desired task to configure, right-click it, and select Properties.

4. Modify the desired task.

5. Click OK.

Discussion

The following list describes each task that appears under Tasks in Site Maintenance:

Backup SMS Site Server: This task enables and configures the backup process for the SMS site. View the backup control file located in `sms\inboxes\smsbkup.box\smsbkup.ctl` to see what will be backed up and where. This file is also customizable and well annotated. Chapter 15 of the *SMS 2003 Operations Guide* provides more information on this task.

Rebuild Indexes: This task creates and rebuilds indexes on database columns that are at least 50 percent unique. This task also drops indexes on database columns that are less than 50 percent unique.

Monitor Keys: This task monitors primary keys in the SMS site database and generates a status message if a problem is detected.

Delete Aged Inventory History: By default, all inventory history older than 90 days is deleted when this task executes. The number of days of history to preserve can be modified using this task.

Delete Aged Status Messages: This task by default deletes audit messages more than 180 days old and all other messages older than 30 days. Change these intervals by modifying the existing status filter rules (or create new ones if required).

Delete Aged Discovery Data: This task deletes aged discovery of data resources. This task identifies resources that have not reported any discovery data in more than 90 days by default. Modify this task to retain discovery data more or less than 90 days.

Delete Aged Collected Files: Use this task to remove orphaned software inventory records and to delete collected files that are older than 90 days by default. This task deletes aged collected files from the site server and removes references to these files in the SMS site database.

Delete Aged Software Metering Data: Depending on if and how you are using software metering, SMS may be storing large amounts of software metering data in the site database. Use this task to remove aged software metering data. See Chapter 8 of the *SMS 2003 Operations Guide* for more information.

Delete Aged Software Metering Summary Data: Similar to the preceding task, use this task to remove aged software metering summary data. By default, summary data is kept for 270 days. See Chapter 8 of the *SMS 2003 Operations Guide* for more information.

Summarize Software Metering File Usage Data: As described, this task summarizes software metering data.

Summarize Software Metering Monthly Usage Data: As described, this task summarizes software metering data.

Clear Install Flag: In SMS 2003, when clients are installed, they are flagged by SMS with an *installed* status. The Client Push Installation method looks at this flag, and pushes only to clients that are not flagged as being installed. This task examines each client in the SMS database and checks to make sure that the client has not been recently discovered by Heartbeat Discovery, and that the client is flagged as installed. The task then marks these clients with an *uninstalled* status. This allows the Client Push Installation method to reinstall these clients.

Caution The Clear Install Flag task is only useful if Heartbeat Discovery is running. Also, be sure to set the rediscovery period to be longer than the Heartbeat Discovery interval to ensure that the task switches the client status only for clients that have been uninstalled.

Delete Inactive Client Discovery Data: Use this task to delete clients' aged discovery records even if the clients are rediscovered by Active Directory System Discovery. Also, be sure to run this task at an interval greater than the Heartbeat Discovery schedule. This allows active clients to send a Heartbeat Discovery record, which prevents them from being deleted by this task.

Delete Obsolete Client Discovery Data: As indicated by the task name, clients that are marked obsolete are deleted by this task. A client record is typically marked obsolete if a newer record for the same client is in the database. These usually result from a computer image being restored. Also, be sure to run this task at an interval greater than the Heartbeat Discovery schedule. This allows active clients to send a Heartbeat Discovery record, which prevents them from being deleted by this task.

Research and verify any changes you desire to make to the site maintenance tasks. The settings are not difficult to change, but the results of modifying these tasks can make your database swell or shrink, and they can also cause healthy clients to sporadically disappear and reappear in your SMS environment. Generally speaking, make sure that Heartbeat Discovery is configured to run more frequently than any of the Delete tasks. Many of the Delete tasks rely on Heartbeat Discovery to report accurate data.

See Also

- *Microsoft Systems Management Server 2003 Administrator's Companion* by Steven Kacz-marek (Microsoft Press, 2004) provides more information on many of the tasks listed in this recipe.

- The *SMS 2003 Operations Guide* and the *Scenarios and Procedures for SMS 2003: Planning and Deployment* guide provide information on each of these tasks.

- The SMS interactive help (in the SMS Administrator console) contains information on most of these tasks. Highlight the desired task, and press F1 for help.

2-50. Creating a Reporting Point

Problem

You want to create a reporting point.

Solution

1. Open the SMS Administrator console.

2. From the SMS Administrator console, expand Site Database (*<Site Code>*), Site Hierarchy, *<Site Name>*, Site Settings, and Site Systems.

3. In the right pane, double-click the server to be modified.

4. On the Reporting Point tab, select the "Use this site system as a reporting point" check box.

5. Click OK to create the reporting point.

Discussion

Reporting points can be installed at any level of your SMS hierarchy, but they only communicate with the SMS databases on primary site servers. Some organizations find it useful to create a central SMS site that does not support any clients but is used for reporting on the entire SMS hierarchy. It can also be advantageous to place a reporting point on a primary site server that may be managed by a different group or is used by a separate company within your organization. This will allow them to report on only those SMS clients and servers in their branch of the SMS hierarchy.

The various SMS site system roles have differing requirements for them to function properly. Table 2-1 identifies what those requirements are for each site system. If you plan on combining multiple system roles on a single server, you will need to have the combined requirements met for all site system roles to function properly.

Table 2-1. *SMS 2003 Site System Role Requirements*

Role	NTFS	IIS	BITS	WebDAV	ASP
Reporting point	No (recommended)	Yes	No	No	Yes
Server locator point	No (recommended)	Yes	No	No	No
Management point/proxy management point	No (recommended)	Yes	Yes	Yes	No
Client access point	Yes	No	No	No	No
Distribution point	No (recommended)	No	No	No	No
BITS-enabled distribution point	No (recommended)	Yes	Yes	Yes	No

See Also

- Chapter 8 provides detailed information about SMS web reporting.

2-51. Creating a Server Locator Point

Problem

You want to create a server locator point.

Solution

1. Open the SMS Administrator console.

2. From the SMS Administrator console, expand Site Database (<*Site Code*>), Site Hierarchy, <*Site Name*>, Site Settings, and Site Systems.

3. In the right pane, double-click the server to be modified.

4. On the Server Locator Point tab, select the "Use this site system as a server locator point" check box and choose to use the site database or specify a different database.

5. Click OK to create the server locator point.

Discussion

The server locator point helps SMS clients locate management points or client access points. It also aids in site assignment for Advanced Clients that were installed with their site assignment set to Auto. In most cases, you will need only one server locator point in your entire SMS hierarchy that is usually installed on your central primary site. If you have extended the Active Directory schema and are using only Advanced Clients that aren't being installed with a logon script, then having a server locator point is not necessary.

Note The server locator point requires that a WINS entry be manually added to your WINS database. See Recipe 2-52, "Registering a Server Locator Point in WINS," for details.

See Also

- Recipe 2-12, "Extending the Active Directory Schema," explains how to avoid registering your server locator point in WINS.

- Table 2-1, "Site System Role Requirements," located in Recipe 2-50, shows the required Windows components for each site system role.

2-52. Registering a Server Locator Point in WINS

Problem

You want to register a server locator point in WINS.

Solution: Using a Command-Line Interface

1. At the command line, type **netsh** and press Enter.

2. Type **wins** and press Enter.

3. Type **server** and press Enter.

4. If you are connecting to a remote WINS server, type **<servername>** or the IP address of the WINS server and press Enter.

5. Type **add name Name=SMS_SLP endchar=1A rectype=0 ip={*ip address of the SLP*}** and press Enter (note that the {} brackets are required).

6. You can check your DNS management console or type **show Name name=SMS_SLP endchar=1A** at the previous command line prompt.

Discussion

If you haven't extended your schema yet or are still utilizing an NT domain, you will need to add the SMS_SLP record to WINS for your server locator point to be identified by SMS clients. If you are still using an NT 4.0–based WINS server, you will need to use the wincl.exe tool to register the server locator point.

See Also

- Microsoft Knowledge Base article 137582, "Using WINSCL.EXE," gives more information on registering a server locator point with an NT 4.0–based WINS server.

- Chapter 15 of the *SMS 2003 Concepts, Planning, and Deployment Guide* has more information on registering the WINS entries for the server locator point.

2-53. Creating a Management Point

Problem

You want to create a management point.

Solution: Using a Graphical Interface

1. Open the SMS Administrator console.

2. From the SMS Administrator console, expand Site Database (*<Site Code>*), Site Hierarchy, *<Site Name>*, Site Settings, and Site Systems.

3. In the right pane, double-click the primary site server to be modified.

4. On the Management Point tab, select the "Use this site system as a management point" check box and choose to use the site database or specify a different database.

5. Click OK to create the management point.

Discussion

The management point is the hub of activity for SMS clients. The Advanced Client was redesigned to leverage policies for all actions. These policies are found on the management point, so if a management point is not available, an SMS client cannot retrieve any new advertisements or changes to existing advertisements or configurations.

The installation of the management point has been a sticky point for many, so make sure you have all of the prerequisites in place before attempting an installation.

Note Installing the SMS client before the management point on a server will cause the SMS client and management point to reside in different directories on the server. To have them install in the same directory, install the management point first, so the SMS client install will identify it as a management point and install the SMS client in the same directory as the management point.

See Also

- Recipes 2-33, "Configuring the Default Management Point," and 2-54, "Creating a Proxy Management Point," show how to configure a management point.

- Table 2-1, "Site System Role Requirements," located in Recipe 2-50, shows the required Windows components for each site system role.

- The SMS 2003 Toolkit (available from the Microsoft SMS download site) contains two utilities to help you watch (MP Spy) and troubleshoot (MP Troubleshooter) SMS management points.

2-54. Creating a Proxy Management Point

Problem

You want to create a proxy management point on a secondary site server.

Solution: Using a Graphical Interface

1. Open the SMS Administrator console.

2. From the SMS Administrator console, expand Site Database (*<Site Code>*), Site Hierarchy, *<Site Name>*, Site Settings, and Site Systems.

3. In the right pane, double-click the secondary site server to be modified.

4. On the Management Point tab, select the "Use this site system as a management point" check box and choose to use the site database or specify a different database.

5. Click OK to create the proxy management point.

Discussion

The proxy management point is essentially the same as a management point, except it resides on a secondary site server. Proxy management points help limit communication over slow links since they retrieve and store policies for the Advanced Client so that each client doesn't have to communicate over a slow link to the management point on the primary site every time it checks for new policies (by default every 60 minutes).

See Also

- Recipes 2-33, "Configuring the Default Management Point," and 2-53, "Creating a Management Point," show how to configure a management point.
- Table 2-1, "Site System Role Requirements," located in Recipe 2-50, shows the required Windows components for each site system role.
- The SMS 2003 Toolkit (available from the Microsoft SMS download site) contains two utilities to help you watch (MP Spy) and troubleshoot (MP Troubleshooter) SMS management points.

2-55. Creating a Client Access Point

Problem

You want to create a client access point.

Solution: Using a Graphical Interface

1. Open the SMS Administrator console.
2. From the SMS Administrator console, expand Site Database (<*Site Code*>), Site Hierarchy, <*Site Name*>, Site Settings, and Site Systems.
3. In the right pane, double-click the server to be modified.
4. On the Client Access Point tab, select the "Use this site system as a client access point" check box.
5. Click OK to create the client access point.

Discussion

A client access point is required for every site server, even though it is primarily for support of the Legacy Client. You will not be allowed to delete the last client access point for a site. If you have security concerns that users might use the client access point, you can restrict the access of the client access point to only administrative accounts. The Advanced Client uses the management point for all functions that the Legacy Client uses the client access point.

See Also

- Recipe 2-30, "Modifying Client Access Point Retry Settings," shows how to modify the retry settings for the client access point.
- Table 2-1, "Site System Role Requirements," located in Recipe 2-50, shows the required Windows components for each site system role.

2-56. Creating a Distribution Point

Problem

You want to create a distribution point.

Solution

1. Open the SMS Administrator console.

2. From the SMS Administrator console, expand Site Database (*<Site Code>*), Site Hierarchy, *<Site Name>*, Site Settings, and Site Systems.

3. Right-click Site Systems and select New ➤ Server.

4. Click the Set button and enter the name of the server you would like to use as a distribution point.

5. Click OK.

6. On the Distribution Point tab, select the "Use this site system as a distribution point" check box.

7. Click OK to create the distribution point.

Discussion

The distribution point is a foundational element to software distribution success with SMS. If you have enough distribution points properly configured, you should be able to deploy software at nearly anytime during the day without worrying about impacting the performance of the network.

See Also

- Recipes 2-29, "Modifying Distribution Point Communication Settings," 2-56, "Creating a Distribution Point Share," 2-58, "Creating a BITS-Enabled Distribution Point," 2-59, "Creating a Distribution Point Group," and 2-60, "Creating a Protected Distribution Point," demonstrate more ways to configure your distribution points.

- Table 2-1, "Site System Role Requirements," located in Recipe 2-50, shows the required Windows components for each site system role.

2-57. Creating a Distribution Point Share

Problem

You want to create a distribution point share.

Solution

1. Open the SMS Administrator console.

2. From the SMS Administrator console, expand Site Database (*<Site Code>*), Site Hierarchy, *<Site Name>*, Site Settings, and Site Systems.

3. Right-click Site Systems and select New ➤ Server Share.

4. Click the Set button and enter the name of the server share you would like to use as a distribution point.

5. Click OK.

6. On the Distribution Point tab, select the "Use this site system as a distribution point" check box.

7. Click OK to create the distribution point share.

Discussion

Many SMS administrators overlook using a share for a distribution point, even though it has many benefits. With a standard distribution point on a server, there is the potential for it to put packages on drives that you don't want. Using a share also gives you more control over the permissions and naming of the share.

Caution Windows Server 2003 uses new default share permissions which only give read access to Everyone instead of Full Control. You will need to give Full Control to Everyone on the share you plan on using as a distribution point in order for it to function properly.

See Also

- Recipes 2-29, "Modifying Distribution Point Communication Settings," 2-56, "Creating a Distribution Point," 2-58, "Creating a BITS-Enabled Distribution Point," 2-59, "Creating a Distribution Point Group," and 2-60, "Creating a Protected Distribution Point," show more ways to configure your distribution points.

- Table 2-1, "Site System Role Requirements," located in Recipe 2-50, shows the required Windows components for each site system role.

2-58. Creating a BITS-Enabled Distribution Point

Problem

You want to create a BITS-enabled distribution point.

Solution

1. Open the SMS Administrator console.
2. From the SMS Administrator console, expand Site Database (<*Site Code*>), Site Hierarchy, <*Site Name*>, Site Settings, and Site Systems.
3. In the right pane, double-click the distribution point for which you would like to enable BITS.
4. On the Distribution Point tab, select the "Enable Background Intelligent Transfer Service (BITS)" check box.
5. Click OK to apply the settings.

Discussion

Having a BITS-enabled distribution point allows the Advanced Client to download the package files locally in an incremental fashion without affecting local applications that are in use. BITS also will resume the download from where it left off if the network connection is broken.

Caution IIS is required on a BITS-enabled distribution point server. On Windows 2003 servers, the BITS extension in IIS is not enabled by default and is required for the BITS-enabled distribution point to function.

See Also

- Recipes 2-29, "Modifying Distribution Point Communication Settings," 2-56, "Creating a Distribution Point," 2-57, "Creating a Distribution Point Share," 2-59, "Creating a Distribution Point Group," and 2-60, "Creating a Protected Distribution Point," show more ways to configure your distribution points.

- Table 2-1, "Site System Role Requirements," located in Recipe 2-50, shows the required Windows components for each site system role.

2-59. Creating a Distribution Point Group

Problem

You want to create a distribution point group.

Solution

1. Open the SMS Administrator console.

2. From the SMS Administrator console, expand Site Database (*<Site Code>*), Site Hierarchy, *<Site Name>*, Site Settings, and Site Systems.

3. In the right pane, double-click the distribution point for which you would like to add a distribution point group.

4. On the Distribution Point tab, click the New button to create a new distribution point group.

5. Enter a name for the group, indicate whether this distribution point is a member of the group, and click OK.

6. The new group will be listed in the window. Use the far-right button to toggle the membership in a selected group.

7. Click OK to apply the settings.

Discussion

Distribution point groups are extremely helpful in large environments, as they free you up from having to select individual distribution points out of a long list when copying a package to select distribution points.

See Also

- Recipes 2-29, "Modifying Distribution Point Communication Settings," 2-56, "Creating a Distribution Point," 2-57, "Creating a Distribution Point Share," 2-58, "Creating a BITS-Enabled Distribution Point," and 2-60, "Creating a Protected Distribution Point," show more ways to configure your distribution points.

2-60. Creating a Protected Distribution Point

Problem

You want to create a protected distribution point.

Solution

1. Open the SMS Administrator console.

2. From the SMS Administrator console, expand Site Database (*<Site Code>*), Site Hierarchy, *<Site Name>*, Site Settings, and Site Systems.

3. In the right pane, double-click the distribution point that you would like to protect.

4. On the Distribution Point tab, select the "Enable as a protected distribution point" check box.

5. Click the Configure Boundaries button.

6. Click the New button to display the available site boundaries for that distribution point. Select the site boundaries that you would like to protect and click OK.

7. Click OK to apply the settings.

Discussion

Protected distribution points can be a difficult concept to understand since it isn't obvious who is being protected from whom. When a protected distribution point is created, any client that is not in the boundaries of the protected distribution point cannot download or run software packages from it. This is great for a distribution point that is on the end of a slow WAN link—you don't want a client from the main office reaching out over a low-bandwidth connection to install software. On the other hand, clients within the boundaries of the protected distribution point will always use the protected distribution point unless it is unavailable, which keeps the clients on the far end of the slow WAN link from reaching back to the main office for software updates.

See Also

- Recipes 2-29, "Modifying Distribution Point Communication Settings," 2-56, "Creating a Distribution Point," 2-57, "Creating a Distribution Point Share," 2-58, "Creating a BITS-Enabled Distribution Point," and 2-59, "Creating a Distribution Point Group," show more ways to configure your distribution points.

2-61. Viewing Site System Roles

Problem

You want to view the SMS roles for a site system.

Solution

1. Open the SMS Administrator console.

2. From the SMS Administrator console, expand Site Database (*<Site Code>*), Site Hierarchy, *<Site Name>*, Site Settings, and Site Systems.

3. In the right pane, double-click an existing site system.

4. The System Roles tab lists all of the roles assigned to the site system and a description of each of those roles.

5. Click OK to close the dialog box.

Discussion

Keeping track of all the system roles on all the site systems in your SMS hierarchy can be a difficult task, especially if you are trying to track down a problem. The system roles are also visible in the site systems list, but if a site system has multiple roles, it may be difficult to view them all from the list.

See Also

- Recipes 2-29, "Modifying Distribution Point Communication Settings," 2-50, "Creating a Reporting Point," 2-51, "Creating a Server Locator Point," 2-53, "Creating a Management Point," 2-55, "Creating a Client Access Point," and 2-56, "Creating a Distribution Point," contain more information on site systems roles.

2-62. Creating Status Filter Rules

Problem

You want to create a custom status filter rule.

Solution

The following example shows how to report a status message to the event log of the SMS site. The example creates a filter rule to capture messages from the SMS_DISTRIBUTION_MANAGER component with a message ID of 2330 (successfully installed package to distribution point).

1. Open the SMS Administrator console.
2. From the SMS Administrator console, expand Site Database (*<Site Code>*), Site Hierarchy, *<Site Name>*, Site Settings, and Status Filter Rules.
3. Right-click Status Filter Rules and select New ➤ Status Filter Rule.
4. On the General tab, perform the following steps:
    a. For the Name, enter **Log Event msg 2330 to the event viewer (DP Update Success)**.
    b. Enable Source and select SMS Server.
    c. Enable Component and select SMS_DISTRIBUTION MANAGER.
    d. Enable Message ID and enter a message ID of **2330**.
5. On the Actions tab, select the "Report to the event log" check box.
6. Click OK to save the changes.

The next example shows how to *prevent* a status messages from appearing in the SMS Status Summarizers:

1. Open the SMS Administrator console.
2. From the SMS Administrator console, expand Site Database (*<Site Code>*), Site Hierarchy, *<Site Name>*, Site Settings, and Status Filter Rules.
3. Right-click Status Filter Rules and select New ➤ Status Filter Rule.
4. On the General tab, perform the following steps:
    a. For the Name, enter **Don't forward Message ID 1215 (Time Sync) to status summarizers**.
    b. Enable Source and select SMS Server.
    c. Enable Message ID and enter a message ID of **1215**.

5. On the Actions tab, select the "Do not forward to status summarizers" check box.

6. Click OK to save the changes.

Discussion

The two examples in the solution demonstrate the basics for creating status filter rules. The true power of status filter rules are realized when you use the Run a Program action. Being able to run a program provides many possibilities with status filter rules. For example, you could run a program to perform additional actions or send notifications.

BLAT (http://www.blat.net) is a command-line tool that when configured properly allows you to send e-mail from the command line. For example, blat.exe - -t user@domain.com -s "SMS is Fun!" -body "I hope you like it too!" will send an e-mail to user@domain.com with a subject of "SMS is Fun" and a message body of "I hope you like it too!" BLAT is a great utility that you can use to implement e-mail notification for critical issues within your SMS site. Many pager systems also provide e-mail addresses for their pagers, so you may be able to send e-mail alerts to your pager.

If your environment supports net send to send simple text messages, you could call a batch file from the Run a Program action to issue net send commands to desired systems.

Another option is a program called Beem (http://www.beem-me-up.com). Beem is a notification system that uses the balloon notification technology built into current versions of Microsoft Windows. The Run a Program action can be used to launch Beem on a remote system, creating a visual indicator (the balloon) to alert the SMS administrator of possible issues.

Run a Program runs with Local System privileges. If your program is attempting to connect to network resources, you may need to give your SMS site server proper access permissions to the network resource.

See Also

- Chapter 14 of the *SMS 2003 Operations Guide* provides more information on creating, modifying, and replicating status messages.

- Chapter 5 of the *Microsoft Systems Management Server 2003 Administrator's Companion* by Steven Kaczmarek (Microsoft Press, 2004) provides a real-world example of using status filter rules.

- Recipes 2-32, "Modifying Status Reporting Properties," and 2-63, "Modifying Status Summarizers," demonstrate how to modify status reporting and status summarizer settings.

2-63. Modifying Status Summarizers

Problem

You want to adjust the configuration of one of the status summarizers.

Solution

1. Open the SMS Administrator console.

2. From the SMS Administrator console, expand Site Database (*<Site Code>*), Site Hierarchy, *<Site Name>*, and Site Settings, and then select Status Summarizers.

3. Choose the summarizer that you need to configure and double-click its icon in the right pane to open the Status Summarizer Properties dialog box.

4. On the General tab, choose whether to enable the summarizer, replication, and replication priority. You can also configure the summarization schedule.

5. On the Threshold tab, make the necessary adjustments to change the behavior of the status summarizer.

6. Click OK to apply the settings.

Discussion

Status summarizers are often overlooked as an important part of your tuning strategy for SMS. It's not clear if the reason for this is that most people don't keep a pair of summarizers in their toolbox at home, or because summarizers are at the bottom of the list of site settings in the SMS administrator console. Either way, you should use status summarizers to your advantage since they have complete control over whether your site status is displayed as a happy green check mark or an ugly red dot with an "X" through it. If the site status doesn't match what you think it should be, then you need to make some changes to your status summarizers.

Let's look at each summarizer in more detail:

Component Status Summarizer. This is by far the most important status summarizer, since nearly all of the site status warnings and errors will come from the various site components. The Thresholds tab allows you to set the Warning and Error thresholds for each of the three message types (Informational, Warning, and Error). For example, say in reviewing the site status you notice that your primary site status is being changed to Warning (yellow triangle icon) because you have more than 2,000 informational status messages from the Collection Evaluator component. This may be perfectly normal for your environment, so you will want to change the thresholds for that component so that it does not trigger a site status change.

Site System Status Summarizer. This is the "free disk space" status monitor for all site systems. On the Thresholds tab you can adjust the default setting for free space, which is used for all systems unless a specific threshold is set for an individual site system. A specific threshold is set during the installation of SMS 2003 for the site database and transaction log. You are able to adjust those as necessary and add specific thresholds for the other components of the primary site server.

Advertisement Status Summarizer. There are no thresholds available for this status summarizer, so you can disable it if you do not plan to use software distribution.

See Also

- Recipes 2-31, "Modifying Status Reporting Properties," and 2-62, "Creating Status Filter Rules," demonstrate how to modify reporting properties and create new status filter rules.

2-64. Transferring Site Settings

Problem

You want to transfer or mirror site settings from one site to another.

Solution: Using a Graphical Interface

1. Open the SMS Administrator console.

2. From the SMS Administrator console, expand Site Database (*<Site Code>*), Site Hierarchy, and *<Site Name>*.

3. Right-click one of your site servers and select All Tasks ➤ Transfer Settings to open the Transfer Site Settings Wizard.

4. Select to transfer site settings or package and collection settings and click Next.

5. Select to create a new template or import an existing one and click Next.

6. Select the source site from the list of site servers and click Next.

7. Select the configuration settings that you would like to transfer and click Next.

8. Select the target sites to which you want to transfer the settings and click Next.

9. Select to apply the settings now or save them for future use and click Finish.

10. Click OK to the completion notification.

11. View the transfer log or close the Transfer Site Settings Wizard.

Discussion

Tweaking an SMS site to do exactly what you want may qualify as an art form. You don't have to be an artist to know that trying to replicate a masterpiece is next to impossible. Thankfully, SMS 2003 will do the replicating for you, so you can get back to creating masterpieces and not copying them. Even if you don't have a large environment that mandates that you use the Transfer Site Settings Wizard to implement your site servers, you can still use it with two site servers to guarantee that the settings that need to be the same are copied correctly.

Note The Transfer Site Settings Wizard is included in the Administration Feature Pack.

CHAPTER 3

■■■

Collections

Collections are an integral part of SMS. Without properly defined collections, you run the risk of installing software (and rebooting systems) on systems you did not intend to target. SMS collections may appear to be simple to the novice SMS administrator, but the more you use SMS, the more you will realize the power and complexity of collections.

Collections are primarily used for software distribution and SMS web reports. Collections of systems or users are created using direct membership rules, query membership rules, or a combination of both.

A *direct membership* rule explicitly names a single resource and is a *static* member of the collection. For example, if a request to install Microsoft Office Visio Standard 2003 is approved for computer A, you could add a direct membership rule to add computer A to your VisioStd2003 collection. Provided you already have an advertisement for installing Visio Standard 2003 to that collection, the software would automatically install, minimizing the effort required by the SMS administrator.

A *query membership* rule can contain multiple resources, and it can also be *dynamic*, in that the collection membership can be scheduled to refresh on a defined schedule. Say, for example, that you want to ensure all PCs have the latest version of Adobe Acrobat Reader. You could simply create a query-based collection that contains all systems that do not have the latest version of Adobe Acrobat Reader and advertise the installation to this collection. When software inventory, hardware inventory, or both (depending on how the query-based collection is written) are updated on the client and forwarded to the SMS primary site, the updated data will be available for the next time the collection updates its membership. (By default, collection membership information is updated every 24 hours.) When collection membership has been updated, the collection will no longer contain systems that received the updated installation, provided updated inventory has been received from the client. Eventually, this collection would be reduced to only a few systems that have not yet run the installation (typically, mobile clients take a little longer to run the installations and report updated inventory to the SMS site).

Remember that many collections may never be used for software distribution purposes, but they are equally as important in your SMS environment. Web reports can be created that prompt the user at runtime to select an appropriate collection, which will *filter* the report to only show data related to the selected query. For example, you could create a web report to show all applicable security patches for a specific collection, or you could allow the user to select the desired collection just before executing the report.

3-1. Creating a Collection

Problem

You want to create a collection.

Solution: Using a Graphical Interface

1. Open the SMS Administrator console.

2. From the SMS Administrator console, expand Site Database (<*Site Code*>) and then Collections.

3. Right-click Collections and select New ➤ Collection from the menu.

4. On the General tab, enter the name of the new collection and any comments.

5. Use the Membership rules tab to create query or direct membership rules now, or you can add them later.

6. Click OK to create the new collection.

Solution: Using VBScript

Example 3-1 demonstrates how to create an empty SMS collection and associate it with a parent collection in the tree.

Example 3-1. *CreateCollection.vbs*

```
 strSMSServer = <SMSServer>
strParentCollID = "COLLROOT"
'This example creates the collection in
'the collection root.  Replace COLLROOT with the CollectionID
'of an existing collection to make the new collection a child

strCollectionName = "Systems Without Windows Update Agent"
strCollectionComment = "This collection contains all systems " & _
    "that do not have the Windows Update Agent installed."

Set objLoc =  CreateObject("WbemScripting.SWbemLocator")
Set objSMS= objLoc.ConnectServer(strSMSServer, "root\sms")
Set Results = objSMS.ExecQuery _
    ("SELECT * From SMS_ProviderLocation WHERE ProviderForLocalSite = true")
For each Loc in Results
    If Loc.ProviderForLocalSite = True Then
        Set objSMS = objLoc.ConnectServer(Loc.Machine, "root\sms\site_" & _
            Loc.SiteCode)
    end if
Next

Set newCollection = objSMS.Get("SMS_Collection").SpawnInstance_()

newCollection.Name = strCollectionName
newCollection.OwnedByThisSite = True
newCollection.Comment = strCollectionComment
path=newCollection.Put_

'the following two lines are used to obtain the CollectionID
'of the collection we just created
Set Collection=objSMS.Get(path)
strCollID= Collection.CollectionID
'now we create a relationship between the new collection
'and its parent.
```

```
Set newCollectionRelation = objSMS.Get _
    ( "SMS_CollectToSubCollect" ).SpawnInstance_()
newCollectionRelation.parentCollectionID = strParentCollID
newCollectionRelation.subCollectionID = strCollID
newCollectionRelation.Put_
```

Discussion

Creating a collection is a basic function of the SMS administrator and may be the very first step in every software distribution that you do. Don't think that a collection has to be perfect before you click OK; many of our collections begin as empty "placeholder" collections that have queries added or imported at a later date.

Example 3-1 demonstrates how to create a collection. Granted, the code appears to be a bit bulky, but when you create a collection, more steps are involved than just creating it. First, we set the name and description of the new collection, and then we save the collection (newCollection.Put_). Then we use Get(path) to obtain the CollectionID of the collection we just created. Next, we create a relationship between the new collection and its parent. In Example 3-1, we associate the new collection with the parent CollectionID COLLROOT, which is the root collection. By associating the new collection with COLLROOT, the collection will appear in the root of the Collections node. To make your new collection a subcollection of an existing collection, simply replace COLLROOT in Example 3-1 with the desired CollectionID. The next recipe describes how to obtain the CollectionID of an existing collection.

Caution You must associate each collection you create to a parent. If you do not set a parent, the collection will not appear in the SMS Administrator console and will be unusable.

Note The SMS Administrator console will not allow you to create a duplicate collection name. However, when you create a new collection programmatically, there is no automatic check to verify the collection does not currently exist. You should verify that the collection name does not exist before creating a new collection programmatically.

See Also

- Recipe 3-5, "Creating a Linked Collection," describes how to create a linked collection.
- Recipe 3-7, "Creating a Direct Membership Rule," describes how to create a direct membership collection.
- Recipe 3-8, "Creating a Query-Based Membership Rule," describes how to create a query-based membership rule.
- Recipe 3-9, "Creating a Collection Based on an Existing SMS Query," demonstrates how to import an existing SMS query statement as the criteria for a new query-based collection.
- Recipe 4-1, "Creating a Package," describes how to create a package.
- Recipe 5-1, "Creating a Program," describes how to create a program.
- Recipe 6-1, "Creating an Advertisement," describes how to create an advertisement.

- The *SMS 2003 Operations Guide* and the *Microsoft Systems Management Server 2003 Administrator's Companion* by Steven Kaczmarek (Microsoft Press, 2004) provide additional information on creating a collection.

- Appendix C of the *SMS 2003 Operations Guide* provides an additional example of creating a collection using VBScript.

3-2. Listing Subcollections

Problem

You want to enumerate subcollections of a given `CollectionID` from the command line.

Solution: Using VBScript

Example 3-2 demonstrates how to list all subcollections of the desired collection, given the CollectionID.

Example 3-2. *ListSubcollections.vbs*

```
strSMSServer = <SMSServer>

'If you want to start from the root collection, set
'    strCollID = "COLLROOT"
strCollID = "LAB00080"

Set objLoc =  CreateObject("WbemScripting.SWbemLocator")
Set objSMS= objLoc.ConnectServer(strSMSServer, "root\sms")
Set Results = objSMS.ExecQuery _
    ("SELECT * From SMS_ProviderLocation WHERE ProviderForLocalSite = true")
For each Loc in Results
    If Loc.ProviderForLocalSite = True Then
        Set objSMS = objLoc.ConnectServer(Loc.Machine, "root\sms\site_" & _
            Loc.SiteCode)
    end if
Next

wscript.echo strCollID & vbTAB & GetCollectionName(strCollID)

DisplaySubCollections strCollID, 3

Sub DisplaySubCollections(strCollID, intSpace)

strWQL ="SELECT col.* FROM SMS_Collection as col " & _
        "INNER JOIN SMS_CollectToSubCollect as ctsc " & _
        "ON col.CollectionID = ctsc.subCollectionID " & _
        "WHERE ctsc.parentCollectionID='" & strcollID & "' " & _
        "ORDER by col.Name"

    Set colSubCollections = objSMS.ExecQuery(strWQL) _

    For each objSubCollection in colSubCollections
        wscript.echo space(intSpace) & objSubCollection.CollectionID & _
            vbTAB & objSubCollection.Name
```

```
        DisplaySubCollections strSubCollID, intSpace + 3
    Next
End Sub

Function GetCollectionName(strCollID)
    Set objCollection = objSMS.Get _
    ("SMS_Collection.CollectionID='" & strCollID & "'")
    GetCollectionName = objCollection.Name
End Function
```

Discussion

By default, when creating an SMS advertisement and selecting a collection for deployment, all sub-collections of the selected collection are also targeted. Example 3-2 demonstrates how to list all subcollections for a specified collection. This VBScript is a good example of using *recursion*. We start by displaying the base collection defined in strCollID, and then call DisplaySubCollections, passing the base collection of interest. In DisplaySubCollections, we query SMS_CollectToSubCollect to identify all collections, of which the base collection is the parent. And for each subcollection identified, we display the CollectionID and collection name, and then call the DisplaySubCollections subroutine again, but this time pass the CollectionID of the subcollection. By calling it this way, we can use the same subroutine to find all subcollections. The GetCollectionName function is used to display the collection name for each CollectionID displayed.

Recursion is a great tool for situations like this—where you know that you will reach an ending to the "loop." When you work with collections, the number of subcollections will eventually come to an end. SMS doesn't allow for endless loops of CollectionA referring to CollectionB, which refers to CollectionC, which refers to CollectionA, which refers to . . . well, you get the idea.

Caution When programming, only use recursion when you are certain that your basis for recursion will come to an end. Otherwise, your code may recurse infinitely, causing much the same problem as an endless loop.

See Also

- Recipe 4-3, "Enumerating Package and Package-Folder Structure," describes how to list all SMS packages.

- Recipe 5-3, "Viewing All Programs in a Package," describes how to list all programs for a package.

- Recipe 6-3, "Viewing All Advertisements," describes how to list all advertisements.

3-3. Identifying the CollectionID of a Collection

Problem

You want to identify the CollectionID of a collection.

Solution: Using a Graphical Interface

1. Open the SMS administrator console.

2. From the SMS Administrator console, expand Site Database (*<Site Code>*) and then Collections.

3. In the right pane, you will see the CollectionID listed next to the collection name.

Solution: Using VBScript

Example 3-3 demonstrates how to list all SMS collections in an SMS site.

Example 3-3. *ListCollectionIDs.vbs*

```
strSMSServer = <SMSServer>

Set objLoc =  CreateObject("WbemScripting.SWbemLocator")
Set objSMS= objLoc.ConnectServer(strSMSServer, "root\sms")
Set Results = objSMS.ExecQuery _
    ("SELECT * From SMS_ProviderLocation WHERE ProviderForLocalSite = true")
For each Loc in Results
    If Loc.ProviderForLocalSite = True Then
        Set objSMS = objLoc.ConnectServer(Loc.Machine, "root\sms\site_" & _
            Loc.SiteCode)
    end if
Next

Set colCollections = objSMS.ExecQuery _
("select * from SMS_Collection order by Name")
for each objCollection in colCollections
    wscript.echo objCollection.Name & vbTAB & _
        objCollection.CollectionID
next
```

Discussion

If you're managing SMS from only the SMS Administrator console, the CollectionID may be of little use to you. If, however, you are ready to extend SMS by leveraging some of the VBScript scripts in this book, then the SMS CollectionID will be one of your best friends. Most of the scripts in this book that require a CollectionID will assume that you know it. You can use either method described in this recipe to obtain the CollectionID you need. If you plan to be a frequent scripter, we suggest paying attention to the following hot tip.

Note The easiest way to find an object ID is to modify the shortcut for your SMS Administrator console. For example, instead of the shortcut launching C:\SMSAdmin\bin\i386\sms.msc, have it launch C:\SMSAdmin\bin\i386\sms.msc /sms:nodeinfo=1. Now when you launch your SMS Administrator console, you can right-click any node, select Properties, and view the Node Information tab. For example, when you view the Node Information tab on a Collection, look for CollectionID="LAB0001F", where "LAB0001F" is the CollectionID you would use. As an example, consider the following figure.

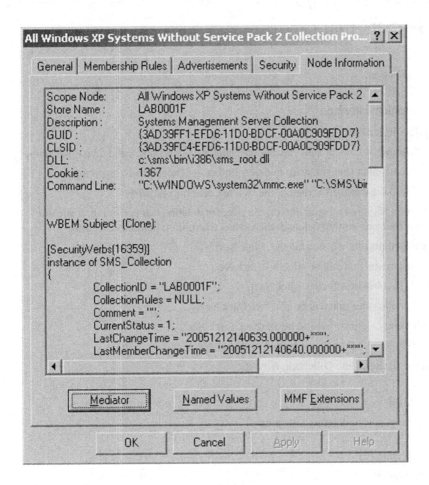

Example 3-3 is a good example of querying a class in the SMS database. In this solution, we display all collections in alphabetical order by name, and we also display the CollectionID. Other properties (such as LastChangeTime, LastRefreshTime, ReplicateToSubSites, etc.) are also available for display from the SMS_Collection class.

See Also

- Recipe 4-2, "Determining a Package's PackageID," describes how to identify the PackageID for a package.

3-4. Deleting a Collection

Problem

You want to delete a collection.

Solution: Using a Graphical Interface

1. Open the SMS Administrator console.

2. From the SMS Administrator console, expand Site Database (<*Site Code*>) and then Collections.

3. Right-click the collection that you want to delete and select Delete from the menu.

4. Click Next to go to the welcome screen of the Delete Collection Wizard.

5. Click Next to see additional information on the effect of deleting this collection. If you are absolutely sure that you want to delete it, then select that option before proceeding.

6. Review subcollections that will be affected. Click Next

7. Review advertisements that will be affected. Click Next.

8. Review queries that will be affected. Click Next.

9. Review membership rules that will be affected. Click Next.

10. Review administrative rights that will be affected. Click Next.

11. Confirm your choice to delete the collection and click Next.

12. Click Finish to exit the Delete Collection Wizard.

Solution: Using VBScript

Example 3-4 demonstrates how to delete a collection.

Example 3-4. *DeleteCollection.vbs*

```
strSMSServer = <SMSServer>

strCollID = "LAB001A7"

Set objLoc =  CreateObject("WbemScripting.SWbemLocator")
Set objSMS= objLoc.ConnectServer(strSMSServer, "root\sms")
Set Results = objSMS.ExecQuery _
    ("SELECT * From SMS_ProviderLocation WHERE ProviderForLocalSite = true")
For each Loc in Results
    If Loc.ProviderForLocalSite = True Then
        Set objSMS = objLoc.ConnectServer(Loc.Machine, "root\sms\site_" & _
            Loc.SiteCode)
    end if
Next

    Set col = objSMS.Get _
    ("SMS_Collection.CollectionID='" & strCollID & "'")
Col.Delete_
```

Discussion

Deleting collections should not be an afterthought in your understanding of SMS. The Delete Collection Wizard does an excellent job of showing you exactly what components of SMS will be impacted by the deletion of a collection. Also remember that some items will be deleted automatically if you choose to delete a collection, so don't move too quickly through the seemingly endless Next, Next, Next button-clicking of the Delete Collection Wizard.

Example 3-4 demonstrates how to delete a collection programmatically using VBScript. If you delete a collection that is directly targeted from an advertisement, SMS automatically deletes the advertisement too.

Caution When deleting a collection programmatically, be sure to delete all subcollections for the collection and all parent-child relationships for that collection. Otherwise, those objects will become *orphaned* and not accessible from the SMS Administrator console.

See Also

- Recipe 3-6, "Deleting a Linked Collection," describes how to delete a linked collection.
- Recipe 3-14, "Removing Direct Members from a Collection," describes how to remove direct members from a collection.
- Recipe 3-15, "Deleting Resources from SMS," describes how to permanently remove resources (computers and users) from SMS.
- Recipe 6-2, "Deleting an Advertisement," describes how to delete an advertisement.
- Recipe 5-2, "Deleting a Program," describes how to delete a program.
- Recipe 4-4, "Deleting a Package," describes how to delete a package.

3-5. Creating a Linked Collection

Problem

You want to create a collection linked under an existing collection.

Solution: Using a Graphical Interface

1. Open the SMS Administrator console.
2. From the SMS Administrator console, expand Site Database (*<Site Code>*), expand Collections, and then select a collection you want to link to another collection underneath it.
3. Right-click the collection and select New ➤ Link to collection from the menu.
4. Select the collection that you want to link under your initial collection and click OK. The linked collection should show up underneath the first collection if you expand it.

Solution: Using VBScript

Example 3-5 demonstrates how to create a linked collection.

Example 3-5. *CreateCollectionLink.vbs*

```
strSMSServer = <SMSServer>

strParentColl = "LAB0000D" 'parent collection ID
strSubColl = "LAB0000E"   'collection ID to link
```

```
Set objLoc =  CreateObject("WbemScripting.SWbemLocator")
Set objSMS= objLoc.ConnectServer(strSMSServer, "root\sms")
Set Results = objSMS.ExecQuery _
    ("SELECT * From SMS_ProviderLocation WHERE ProviderForLocalSite = true")
For each Loc in Results
    If Loc.ProviderForLocalSite = True Then
        Set objSMS = objLoc.ConnectServer(Loc.Machine, "root\sms\site_" & _
            Loc.SiteCode)
    end if
Next

Set ColSvcs = objSMS.Get("SMS_Collection")
    ColSvcs.VerifyNoLoops "SMS_Collection.CollectionID=""" & _
    strParentColl & """", "SMS_Collection.CollectionID=""" & _
    strSubColl & """", Result

if Result = 0 then
    wscript.echo "Link would cause looping condition, exiting"
else
    Set objCol = objSMS.Get _
        ("SMS_CollectToSubCollect").SpawnInstance_()
    objCol.parentCollectionID = strParentColl
    objCol.subCollectionID = strSubColl
    objCol.Put_
    wscript.echo "Created Collection Link!"
end if
```

Discussion

Linked collections are a very handy feature of SMS. When advertising a new product or patch, you can start by sending the advertisement to a small group, and next to a beta group, followed by your desired distribution process. If you have an advertisement advertised to a collection (and the advertisement is also configured to include members of subcollections), use collection linking to easily add various groups to your advertisement.

Example 3-5 programmatically creates a parent-child relationship between two collections. Notice that we call the VerifyNoLoops method to verify that the relationship will not create an infinite parent-child relationship. If you later decide to remove this specific linked collection, you may do so safely with VBScript since this parent-child relationship is unique.

See Also

- Recipe 3-1, "Creating a Collection," describes how to create a collection.

- Recipe 3-7, "Creating a Direct Membership Rule," describes how to create a direct membership collection.

- Recipe 3-8, "Creating a Query-Based Membership Rule," describes how to create a query-based membership collection rule.

- Chapter 4 of the *SMS 2003 Operations Guide* demonstrates how to create a linked collection.

- Chapter 11 of the *Microsoft Systems Management Server 2003 Administrator's Companion* by Steven Kaczmarek (Microsoft Press, 2004) details linking collections.

3-6. Deleting a Linked Collection

Problem

You want to delete a linked collection.

Solution

1. Open the SMS Administrator console.

2. From the SMS Administrator console, expand Site Database (<*Site Code*>), expand Collections, and then expand the collection that contains the linked collection.

3. Right-click the linked collection that you want to delete and select Delete from the menu.

4. Click Next to go to the welcome screen of the Delete Collection Wizard.

5. Confirm your choice to delete the linked instance of the collection and click Next.

6. Click Finish to exit the Delete Collection Wizard.

Discussion

The process for deleting a linked collection may be a little confusing since you are not actually deleting the linked collection at all—more accurately, you are removing the link between the two collections. This also explains why you don't have to go through numerous screens in the Delete Collections Wizard, because nothing else is affected when you break the link between the collections except what was happening as a result of the link.

See Also

- Recipe 3-4, "Deleting a Collection," describes how to delete a collection.

3-7. Creating a Direct Membership Rule

Problem

You want to add a system to a collection using direct membership.

Solution: Using a Graphical Interface

1. Open the SMS Administrator console.

2. From the SMS Administrator console, expand Site Database (<*Site Code*>), expand Collections, and then select a collection to add a system by direct membership rule.

3. Right-click the collection, select Properties from the menu, and select the Membership Rules tab in the Collection Properties dialog box.

4. Click the New Direct Membership button (the icon of a computer with a sunburst) to create a new direct membership. This action opens the Create Direct Membership Rule Wizard.

5. Click Next.

6. Select a resource class, attribute name, and value for your search criteria. For example, to search for PC1234, you could select the System Resource class, Name attribute, and PC1234 for a search value. You can also use wildcard characters to expand your search. Click Next.

7. Click Next if you have access to all resources; otherwise, select a collection to limit your search and click Next.

8. Select the check box next to the resource that you want added to the collection. If no available resources are presented to you, go back and expand your search criteria until your desired resources are found. Then click Next.

9. Click Finish to exit the wizard. Your direct membership rule will now be in the membership rules list.

10. Click OK to apply the settings.

Solution: Using Free Tools

1. Open the SMS Administrator console.

2. From the SMS Administrator console, expand Site Database (<*Site Code*>), expand Collections, and then select a collection to add a system by direct membership.

3. Right-click the collection and select SMS Tools ➤ Add PCs to this Collection.

4. Enter the PC names or copy and paste them from another source, and then click Add PCs to Collection.

5. The tool will process the list and return any systems that could not be added.

6. If you need to add more systems, click Reset Form; otherwise, click Exit.

Solution: Using VBScript

Example 3-6 demonstrates how to create a direct membership rule.

Example 3-6. *CreateDirectMembership.vbs*

```
strSMSServer = <SMSServer>

strCollID = "LAB0000F" 'ID of the collection
strComputerName = "2kPro" 'computer name to add

Set objLoc =  CreateObject("WbemScripting.SWbemLocator")
Set objSMS= objLoc.ConnectServer(strSMSServer, "root\sms")
Set Results = objSMS.ExecQuery _
    ("SELECT * From SMS_ProviderLocation WHERE ProviderForLocalSite = true")
For each Loc in Results
    If Loc.ProviderForLocalSite = True Then
        Set objSMS = objLoc.ConnectServer(Loc.Machine, "root\sms\site_" & _
            Loc.SiteCode)
    end if
Next

'obtain the ResourceID for strComputerName
Set colResourceIDs=objSMS.ExecQuery _
    ("SELECT ResourceId FROM SMS_R_System WHERE NetbiosName ='" & _
        strComputerName & "'")
For each insResource in colResourceIDs
        strNewResourceID = insResource.ResourceID
```

```
Next
'add the ResourceID to the collection
Set instColl = objSMS.Get _
    ("SMS_Collection.CollectionID=""" & strCollID & """")
Set instDirectRule = objSMS.Get _
    ("SMS_CollectionRuleDirect").SpawnInstance_ ()
instDirectRule.ResourceClassName = "SMS_R_System"
instDirectRule.ResourceID = strNewResourceID
instDirectRule.RuleName = strComputerName
instColl.AddMembershipRule instDirectRule
```

Discussion

If the graphical interface method seems to be rather involved for adding a single system to a collection, don't worry. Members of the SMS community have created tools that make the process much easier. For example, Greg Ramsey has created one of these tools specifically to add a single system to a collection. You can get a free copy of his "Right-Click, Add PCs to Collection" tool at myITforum.com (http://www.myitforum.com/articles/1/view.asp?id=7609). The steps to use it are described in the "Right-click Tools" section of Appendix A. All of the free tools discussed in this book are listed in Appendix A, along with a brief description.

Example 3-6 assumes that you know the CollectionID of the affected collection. Review Recipe 3-3, "Identifying the CollectionID of a Collection," for more information. When you know the CollectionID of the affected collection, you can proceed through the script. Collections in SMS use ResourceIDs to identify membership, so first obtain the ResourceID for the computer to add to the collection. Next, create a new instance of a direct membership rule (("SMS_CollectionRuleDirect").SpawnInstance_ ()) and set the appropriate properties for the rule.

See Also

- Recipe 3-1, "Creating a Collection," describes how to create a collection.
- Recipe 3-8, "Creating a Query-Based Membership Rule," describes how to create a query-based collection rule.
- The SMS 2003 SDK provides more information about adding members to a collection.
- Appendix C of the *SMS 2003 Operations Guide* provides an additional example of creating a collection using VBScript.

3-8. Creating a Query-Based Membership Rule

Problem

You want to create a query-based rule for a collection based on dynamic data, such as a program listed in Add or Remove Programs.

Solution: Using a Graphical Interface

The solution is to add a new query rule to the query-based collection, ensuring that the new rule encompasses the new systems or users that you wish to add. Here are the steps to follow:

1. Open the SMS Administrator console.
2. From the SMS Administrator console, expand Site Database (*<Site Code>*), expand Collections, and then select a collection in preparation for adding a query-based membership rule.

3. Right-click the collection, select Properties from the menu, and select the Membership Rules tab in the Collection Properties dialog box.

4. Click the New Query-based Membership button (the icon of a database with a sunburst) to create a new query rule. This will open the Query Rule Properties dialog box.

5. Enter a name for your query rule and click Edit Query Statement to open the Query Statement Properties dialog box.

6. Click the New button to open the Criterion Properties dialog box.

7. Select your criterion type and click the Select button to open the Select Attribute dialog box.

8. Select an attribute class and attribute to use in your query criteria and click OK. For example, if you want to query for systems with WinZip installed, you could select the Add/Remove Programs attribute class and Display name attribute.

9. In the Criterion Properties dialog box, select your operator and enter a search value or click the Values button to return real values from the SMS database for you to choose from and click OK. Continuing our previous example, use the "is equal to" operator and enter WinZip in the value string box.

10. You will now see your search selection in the criteria box. You can now add additional search criteria or click OK.

11. Click OK to the Query Rules properties box after you have named the query rule and defined your query limitations.

12. Your query will now appear in the list of membership rules. Click OK for the settings to be applied.

Solution: Using VBScript

Example 3-7 demonstrates how to create a query-based membership rule to encompass new systems or users that you wish to add.

Example 3-7. *CreateQueryMembershipRule.vbs*

```
strSMSServer = <SMSServer>

strCollID = "LAB0000F"
strQuery = "select * from SMS_R_System inner join " & _
    "SMS_G_System_ADD_REMOVE_PROGRAMS on " & _
    "SMS_G_System_ADD_REMOVE_PROGRAMS.ResourceID = " & _
    "SMS_R_System.ResourceId where " & _
    "SMS_G_System_ADD_REMOVE_PROGRAMS.DisplayName = 'SMS View'"
strQueryName = "Systems that have SMSView Installed"

Set objLoc =  CreateObject("WbemScripting.SWbemLocator")
Set objSMS= objLoc.ConnectServer(strSMSServer, "root\sms")
Set Results = objSMS.ExecQuery _
    ("SELECT * From SMS_ProviderLocation WHERE ProviderForLocalSite = true")
For each Loc in Results
    If Loc.ProviderForLocalSite = True Then
        Set objSMS = objLoc.ConnectServer(Loc.Machine, "root\sms\site_" & _
            Loc.SiteCode)
    end if
Next
```

```
    Set instCollection = objSMS.Get _
    ("SMS_Collection.CollectionID='" & strCollID & "'")
Set clsQueryRule = objSMS.Get _
    ("SMS_CollectionRuleQuery")

'next we need to validate the query
ValidQuery = clsQueryRule.ValidateQuery(strQuery)

If ValidQuery Then
    Set instQueryRule = clsQueryRule.SpawnInstance_
    instQueryRule.QueryExpression = strQuery
    instQueryRule.RuleName = strQueryName
    instCollection.AddMembershipRule instQueryRule
End If
```

Discussion

The full power of SMS is not unleashed until you begin to use collections based on queries. We attempt to use query-based collections whenever possible purely for the dynamic nature that they provide. If a new SMS client is placed on your network, it will be added to the appropriate collections (based on client inventory information) and receive the associated advertisements without requiring any administrative intervention. That powerful automation may seem scary at first, but you will quickly see how dependable and trouble-free it is. Just be careful how you wield that power by creating your collections first, before you advertise a package to them. You want to make sure that you are targeting correctly before you pull the trigger!

Example 3-7 assumes you know the CollectionID of the affected collection. Review Recipe 3-3, "Identifying the CollectionID of a Collection," for more information. StrQuery contains a WBEM Query Language (WQL) query to identify all systems that have the program DisplayName of SMSView in Add or Remove Programs (use the GUI to create proper queries with the wizard). You can then obtain the desired collection (using the CollectionID), and verify that the query is valid by calling ValidateQuery(strQuery). Provided the query is valid, create a new instance of a query rule, and add the membership rule.

See Also

- Recipe 3-1, "Creating a Collection," describes how to create a new collection.

- Recipe 3-7, "Creating a Direct Membership Rule," describes how to create a direct membership rule for a collection.

- The SMS 2003 SDK provides more information about adding members to a collection.

- Appendix C of the *SMS 2003 Operations Guide* provides an additional example of creating a collection using VBScript.

3-9. Creating a Collection Based on an Existing SMS Query

Problem

You want to create a collection based on an existing SMS query.

Solution: Using a Graphical Interface

1. Open the SMS Administrator console.

2. From the SMS Administrator console, expand Site Database (*<Site Code>*), expand Collections, and then select a collection to add a query-based membership rule.

3. Right-click the collection, select Properties from the menu, and select the Membership Rules tab in the Collection Properties dialog box.

4. Click the New Query-based Membership button (the icon of a database with a sunburst) to create a new query rule. This action opens the Query Rule Properties dialog box.

5. Enter a name for your query rule and click Import Query Statement. Browse the existing queries and select the one that you would like to import, and then click OK.

6. Click OK to the Query Rules properties box after you have named the query rule and defined your query limitations.

7. Your query will now appear in the list of membership rules. Click OK to apply the settings.

Discussion

You may find it easier to build your query first so you can fine-tune it before using it in a collection, or you may have a basic query that you plan on using for a number of collections with only minor modifications. In both situations, building the query first will save you some time when you get around to building your collections. However, the SMS query and the imported query are not linked in any way. If you make a change in the SMS query, you will have to re-import it, as the import function simply copies the query attributes.

See Also

- Recipe 3-1, "Creating a Collection," describes how to create a new collection.

- Recipe 3-7, "Creating a Direct Membership Rule," describes how to create a direct membership rule for a collection.

- Recipe 3-8, "Creating a Query-Based Membership Rule," describes how to create a query-based membership rule.

- The SMS 2003 SDK provides more information about the SMS_Collection class.

- Appendix C of the *SMS 2003 Operations Guide* provides an additional example of creating a collection using VBScript.

3-10. Creating a Collection That Uses a Subselect Query

Problem

You want to create a collection that uses a subselect query.

Solution: Using a Graphical Interface

Use a subselect query when you want to query for objects that are missing something. For example, the query in Example 3-8 displays all systems that do not have the Windows Update file wuauclt.exe in the system32 directory of the system. Here are the steps to follow:

1. Open the SMS Administrator console.

2. From the SMS Administrator console, expand Site Database (*<Site Code>*), expand Collections, and then select a collection to add a query-based membership rule.

3. Right-click the collection, select Properties from the menu, and select the Membership Rules tab in the Collection Properties dialog box.

4. Click the New Query-based Membership button (the icon of a database with a sunburst) to create a new query rule. This action opens the Query Rule Properties dialog box.

5. Enter a name for your query rule and click Edit Query Statement to open the Query Statement Properties dialog box.

6. Click the New button to open the Criterion Properties dialog box.

7. Select Sub-selected values for your Criterion type and click the Select button to open the Select Attribute dialog box.

8. Select an attribute class and attribute to use in your query criteria and click OK.

9. In the Criterion Properties dialog box, select your operator and enter a subselect query, or click the Browse button to select an existing query. Click OK to close the Criterion Properties dialog box.

10. You will now see your search selection in the criteria box. You can add additional search criteria or click OK.

11. Click OK on the Query Rules properties box after you have named the query rule and defined your query limitations.

12. Your query will now appear in the list of membership rules. Click OK to apply the settings.

Solution: Using VBScript

Example 3-8 demonstrates how to create a subselect query rule.

Example 3-8. *CreateSubSelectQueryRule.vbs*

```
strSMSServer = <SMSServer>

strCollID = "LAB0002B"

strQuery = "select SMS_R_System.ResourceID," & _
    "SMS_R_System.ResourceType,SMS_R_System.Name," & _
    "SMS_R_System.SMSUniqueIdentifier," & _
    "SMS_R_System.ResourceDomainORWorkgroup," & _
    "SMS_R_System.Client from SMS_R_System inner join " & _
    "SMS_G_System_SYSTEM on " & _
    "SMS_G_System_SYSTEM.ResourceID = " & _
    "SMS_R_System.ResourceId where " & _
    "SMS_G_System_SYSTEM.Name not in (select " & _
    "SMS_G_System_SYSTEM.Name from SMS_R_System inner " & _
    "join SMS_G_System_SoftwareFile on " & _
    "SMS_G_System_SoftwareFile.ResourceID = " & _
    "SMS_R_System.ResourceId inner join " & _
    "SMS_G_System_SYSTEM on " & _
    "SMS_G_System_SYSTEM.ResourceID =" & _
    "SMS_R_System.ResourceId where " & _
    "SMS_G_System_SoftwareFile.FileName = 'wuauclt.exe' " & _
    "and SMS_G_System_SoftwareFile.FilePath like '%system32\\%')"
strQueryName = "Systems That Need Windows Update Agent"
```

```
Set objLoc =  CreateObject("WbemScripting.SWbemLocator")
Set objSMS= objLoc.ConnectServer(strSMSServer, "root\sms")
Set Results = objSMS.ExecQuery _
    ("SELECT * From SMS_ProviderLocation WHERE ProviderForLocalSite = true")
For each Loc in Results
    If Loc.ProviderForLocalSite = True Then
        Set objSMS = objLoc.ConnectServer(Loc.Machine, "root\sms\site_" & _
            Loc.SiteCode)
    end if
Next

Set instCollection = objSMS.Get _
    ("SMS_Collection.CollectionID='" & strCollID & "'")
Set clsQueryRule = objSMS.Get _
    ("SMS_CollectionRuleQuery")
'make sure we have a valid query
ValidQuery = clsQueryRule.ValidateQuery(strQuery)
If ValidQuery Then
    Set instQueryRule = clsQueryRule.SpawnInstance_
    instQueryRule.QueryExpression = strQuery
    instQueryRule.RuleName = strQueryName
    instCollection.AddMembershipRule instQueryRule
End If
```

Discussion

There are some things a simple query can't do, and for everything else there's a subselect query (sorry, MasterCard!). As you spend more time building queries, you may hit the simple query wall. For example, you may need to find all systems that have application A and not application B, and a simple query just won't do. If you aren't a programmer, the term "subselect" may not be in your vocabulary, and it may be easier to understand subselect as "select then select," for example:

> Select all systems with application B and then select all systems with application A that aren't in the group with application B.

If you are wondering where to get the subselect query to paste into the subselect window, try to create the subselect portion of your query as a simple query first. For example, begin with a query to select all systems with application B. Then open the Show SQL query window and copy and paste the query into the subselect window. Finally, apply the Not in operator.

Note Example 3-8 is the same as Recipe 3-8, "Creating a Query-Based Membership Rule." The only difference is the WQL query.

See Also

- Recipe 3-1, "Creating a Collection," describes how to create a collection.

- Recipe 3-7, "Creating a Direct Membership Rule," describes how to create a direct membership rule for a collection.

- Recipe 3-8, "Creating a Query-Based Membership Rule," describes how to create a query-based membership rule.

- The SMS 2003 SDK provides more information about the SMS_Collection class.

- Appendix C of the *SMS 2003 Operations Guide* provides an additional example of creating a collection using VBScript.

3-11. Updating Collection Membership

Problem

You want to immediately update the query-based membership of a collection.

Solution: Using a Graphical Interface

1. Open the SMS Administrator console.

2. From the SMS Administrator console, expand Site Database (*<Site Code>*) and then Collections.

3. Right-click the collection you want to update the membership of and select All Tasks ➤ Update Collection Membership.

4. Choose whether to update subcollections and click OK.

Solution: Using VBScript

Example 3-9 demonstrates how to update collection membership.

Example 3-9. *UpdateCollectionMembeship.vbs*

```
strSMSServer = <SMSServer>
strSMSServer = <SMSServer>

strCollID = "LAB00017"

Set objLoc =  CreateObject("WbemScripting.SWbemLocator")
Set objSMS= objLoc.ConnectServer(strSMSServer, "root\sms")
Set Results = objSMS.ExecQuery _
    ("SELECT * From SMS_ProviderLocation WHERE ProviderForLocalSite = true")
For each Loc in Results
    If Loc.ProviderForLocalSite = True Then

            strSMSSiteCode = Loc.Sitecode
    end if
Next

Set objCollection = GetObject( "WinMgmts:!\\" & strSMSServer & _
    "\root\SMS\site_" & strSMSSiteCode & _
    ":SMS_Collection.CollectionID='" & strCollID & "'")
objCollection.RequestRefresh False
```

Discussion

Most likely, you do not have your collections set to update every 15 minutes (as it is not that practical), but you may have the need on occasion to update query-based collection memberships faster than defined by your refresh schedule. For example, immediately updating collection membership becomes very important when a new system is being built and you need to have all of the advertisements run in a short amount of time. By updating query-based memberships, new systems that meet the query-based criteria will be added to the collection (and, of course, systems that were in the collection that no longer meet the criteria will be removed from the collection). New clients that appear in the collection will obtain advertisement policy that is targeted to the collection on the next client-polling interval. At this time, the client will execute any mandatory advertisements that are past the mandatory start time, but have not yet expired.

Updating the collection membership is not the same as updating the current view in the console. After you update the collection membership, you will see a small hourglass next to the collection icon, and you won't see the new members in the right pane. The small hourglass indicates that the collection membership is being updated but the view is not current. Refresh the collection view by either using the refresh button or pressing F5. If the collection is large or has an intricate query, it may take a while for the update to process. Refresh the collection view until the small hourglass goes away; then you can be sure that the console is displaying the current membership.

Example 3-9 is straightforward. We connect to the appropriate collection in SMS and refresh the collection. Notice the last line of the script:

```
objCollection.RequestRefresh False
```

This code refreshes the current collection membership, but does not refresh the collection membership of subcollections. To refresh collection membership of all subcollections, change False to True.

See Also

- Recipe 3-8, "Creating a Query-Based Membership Rule," describes how to create a query-based membership rule.

- Recipe 3-12, "Setting the Update Collection Interval," describes how to set the collection refresh interval.

- The SMS 2003 SDK contains a section titled "Adding, Deleting, and Refreshing Members of a Collection."

- Appendix C of the *SMS 2003 Operations Guide* provides an additional example of creating a collection using VBScript.

3-12. Setting the Update Collection Interval

Problem

You want to set the interval for a collection to evaluate its membership.

Solution: Using a Graphical Interface

1. Open the SMS Administrator console.

2. From the SMS Administrator console, expand Site Database (*<Site Code>*), expand Collections, and then select a collection to modify its update schedule.

3. Right-click the collection, select Properties from the menu, and select the Membership Rules tab in the Collection Properties dialog box.

4. Click the Schedule button to adjust the frequency with which the collection updates its membership.

5. Click OK. The new settings appear in the Collection Properties dialog box.

6. Click OK to apply the settings.

Solution: Using VBScript

Example 3-10 demonstrates how to set the collection membership to update daily (Token.DaySpan=1). Token.StartTime is a WMI date string.

Example 3-10. *SetUpdateCollInterval.vbs*

```
strSMSServer = <SMSServer>
strCollID = "LAB0002B"

Set objLoc = CreateObject("WbemScripting.SWbemLocator")
Set objSMS= objLoc.ConnectServer(strSMSServer, "root\sms")
Set Results = objSMS.ExecQuery _
    ("SELECT * From SMS_ProviderLocation WHERE ProviderForLocalSite = true")
For each Loc in Results
    If Loc.ProviderForLocalSite = True Then
        Set objSMS = objLoc.ConnectServer(Loc.Machine, "root\sms\site_" & _
            Loc.SiteCode)
    end if
Next

Set Token = objSMS.Get("SMS_ST_RecurInterval")
Token.DaySpan = 1
Token.StartTime = "20051202103000.000000+***" 'wmi date-string
'If omitted, StartTime = Jan 1, 1990 - this shouldn't
'cause any issues
Set objCollection = objSMS.Get _
    ("SMS_Collection.CollectionID='"  & strCollID & "'")
objCollection.RefreshSchedule = Array(Token)
objCollection.RefreshType = 2  'Periodic refresh
objCollection.Put_
```

Discussion

You can use the collection update interval to your advantage, and it does not need to stay at the default 24 hours. You may have some query-based collections that you don't use on a regular basis. For example, perhaps you only use them at the end of the month for reporting purposes. In this situation, you may configure the collection interval to update at the end of every month (instead of the default of 24 hours). Conversely, if you have an important advertisement that needs to be delivered in a timely manner, then you may want to shrink the associated collection refresh interval to an hour or so to give you a swifter response. New clients that appear in the collection after a collection update refresh will obtain an advertisement policy targeted to the collection on the next client-polling interval. At this time, the client will execute any mandatory advertisements past the mandatory start time, but not yet expired.

Note If you have a collection that is made of only direct memberships, then you do not need to refresh the collection at all.

Example 3-11 demonstrates how to convert a normal date-time into a WMI date-time.

Example 3-11. *ConvertToWMIDate.vbs*

```
wscript.echo ConvertToWMIDate(Now())

Function ConvertToWMIDate(strDate)
    strYear = year(strDate)
    strMonth = month(strDate)
    strDay = day(strDate)
    strHour = hour(strDate)
    strMinute = minute(strDate)
    'pad date appropriately
    if len(strmonth) = 1 then strMonth = "0" & strMonth
    if len(strDay) = 1 then strDay = "0" & strDay
    if len(strHour) = 1 then strHour = "0" & strHour
    if len(strMinute) = 1 then strMinute = "0" & strMinute
    ConvertToWMIDate = strYear & strMonth & strDay & strHour & _
        strMinute & "00.000000+***"
end function
```

In Example 3-11, the date function Now() is used to obtain the current date and time on the system. Any valid date and time can be used. For example, 12/02/2007 2:43 AM will be converted to 20071202024300.000000+***.

See Also

- Recipe 3-11, "Updating Collection Membership," demonstrates how to manually update collection membership.

- The SMS 2003 SDK provides additional information about SMS_ST_RecurInterval.

- Recipe 6-8, "Configuring a Recurring Advertisement," provides a solution that uses SMS_ST_RecurWeekly so you can configure a weekly update schedule.

3-13. Limiting Collection Membership to Another Collection

Problem

You want to limit a query-based collection's membership to only members of another collection.

Solution: Using a Graphical Interface

1. Open the SMS Administrator console.

2. From the SMS Administrator console, expand Site Database (*<Site Code>*), expand Collections, and then select a query-based collection to limit the membership by another collection.

3. Right-click the collection, select Properties from the menu, and select the Membership Rules tab in the Collection Properties dialog box.

4. Double-click the query membership rule that you would like to limit to another collection.

5. On the Query Rule Properties dialog box, change Collection Limiting from Not Collection Limited to Limit to Collection and enter the collection name or use the Browse button to identify the collection for limiting the query.

6. Click OK and you will see the collection limit associated with your query rule in the "Limit to" column of the Membership Rules tab of the Collection Properties dialog box.

7. Click OK to apply the settings.

Solution: Using VBScript

Example 3-12 demonstrates how to limit collection membership to another collection.

Example 3-12. *LimitCollectionMembership.vbs*

```
strSMSServer = <SMSServer>

strCollID = "LAB0002B" 'this is the collection to modify
strCollLimit = "SMS000GS" 'this is the limiting collection

Set objLoc =  CreateObject("WbemScripting.SWbemLocator")
Set objSMS= objLoc.ConnectServer(strSMSServer, "root\sms")
Set Results = objSMS.ExecQuery _
    ("SELECT * From SMS_ProviderLocation WHERE ProviderForLocalSite = true")
For each Loc in Results
    If Loc.ProviderForLocalSite = True Then
        Set objSMS = objLoc.ConnectServer(Loc.Machine, "root\sms\site_" & _
            Loc.SiteCode)
    end if
Next

Set objCollection=objSMS.Get("SMS_Collection='" & _
    strCollID & "'" )
'Get the array of embedded SMS_CollectionRule objects.
RuleSet = objCollection.CollectionRules
For Each Rule In RuleSet
    if Rule.Path_.Class = "SMS_CollectionRuleQuery" then
        Rule.LimitToCollectionID = strCollLimit
    end if
Next
objCollection.Put_
```

Discussion

Limiting collection membership to members of another collection is a great way to easily step into an application deployment. You don't have to create several different queries for each group of your deployment as long as you already have collections for them. For example, say you are going to deploy version 6.0 of an application to all systems with version 5.0 or earlier. First, create your base query of all systems that have version 5.0 or earlier. Import the query into your "Version 6.0" collection but limit it to your "Test systems" collection. Advertise the package to the "Version 6.0" collection. When the systems from the "Test systems" collection have successfully installed the application, you can change the "Version 6.0" collection to limit the query to a collection for a floor or a department, but less than the entire target group. Once you feel comfortable with the deployment, you can remove the collection limit and all systems that meet the query criteria will be targeted.

In Example 3-12, we enumerate all query-based rules for the collection and add the collection limit to each one. After we have modified all query rules, we use the Put_ method to save the changes to the SMS_Collection object. This script could be modified to display current collection limiting information for auditing purposes also.

See Also

- Recipe 3-5, "Creating a Linked Collection," describes how to create a linked collection.
- Recipe 3-11, "Updating Collection Membership," describes how to update collection membership.

- The SMS 2003 SDK contains a section titled "Adding, Deleting, and Refreshing Members of a Collection."
- Appendix C of the *SMS 2003 Operations Guide* provides an additional example of creating a collection using VBScript.

3-14. Removing Direct Members from a Collection

Problem

You want to remove direct members from a collection.

Solution: Using a Graphical Interface

1. Open the SMS Administrator console.
2. From the SMS Administrator console, expand Site Database (<*Site Code*>), expand Collections, and then select a collection from which to delete a direct membership rule.
3. Right-click the collection, select Properties from the menu, and select the Membership Rules tab in the Collection Properties dialog box.
4. Select the direct membership rule that you would like to remove and click the Delete Direct Membership button (black "X") to remove it.
5. Click OK to apply the settings.

Solution: Using VBScript

Example 3-13 demonstrates how to delete all direct membership rules from a collection.

Example 3-13. *DelDirectMembership.vbs*

```
strSMSServer = <SMSServer>

strCollID = "LAB0002B"

Set objLoc =  CreateObject("WbemScripting.SWbemLocator")
Set objSMS= objLoc.ConnectServer(strSMSServer, "root\sms")
Set Results = objSMS.ExecQuery _
    ("SELECT * From SMS_ProviderLocation WHERE ProviderForLocalSite = true")
For each Loc in Results
    If Loc.ProviderForLocalSite = True Then
        Set objSMS = objLoc.ConnectServer(Loc.Machine, "root\sms\site_" & _
            Loc.SiteCode)
    end if
Next

Set objCollection=objSMS.Get("SMS_Collection='" & strCollID & "'" )
'Get the array of embedded SMS_CollectionRule objects.
RuleSet = objCollection.CollectionRules
For Each Rule In RuleSet
    if Rule.Path_.Class = "SMS_CollectionRuleDirect" then
        objCollection.DeleteMembershipRule Rule
    end if
Next
```

Discussion

A common mistake among SMS administrators is deleting a resource from SMS entirely when they actually wanted to only delete the membership of a resource from a collection. You will want to heed the warning that is displayed when you attempt to delete a resource, as it may be the only reminder that you are about to delete the wrong thing. This is one of the main reasons we try to avoid direct memberships in collections whenever possible; managing those direct memberships can become a difficult task. It's an especially difficult task if one of those systems is rebuilt or replaced, because then you will have to add another direct membership for the new system.

Each direct membership is a membership rule for the collection in question. So in Example 3-13, we enumerate and delete all direct membership rules. This script could be modified to remove a specific rule, but you would also be required to identify the ResourceID (or RuleName) for the specific rule to be deleted.

See Also

- Recipe 3-4, "Deleting a Collection," describes how to delete a collection.

- Recipe 3-15, "Deleting Resources from SMS," describes how to delete resources from SMS.

- Appendix C of the *SMS 2003 Operations Guide* provides an additional example of using DeleteMembershipRule.

3-15. Deleting Resources from SMS

Problem

You want to delete members of a collection. Unlike the case in Recipe 3-14, "Removing Direct Members from a Collection," this time you really do want to delete the resources (representing the members) from SMS.

Caution Be aware that the solutions in this recipe will delete resources from SMS. Deleting is different from removing a member from a collection—review the "Discussion" section of this recipe for more information. Be sure that you fully understand what you are doing before executing this recipe.

Solution: Using a Graphical Interface

Deleting One Resource from SMS

1. Open the SMS Administrator console.

2. From the SMS Administrator console, expand Site Database (*<Site Code>*), expand Collections, and then select a collection that contains the member to delete.

3. Right-click the appropriate resource and select Delete.

4. Click Yes to confirm deletion.

Deleting Multiple Resources from SMS

1. Open the SMS Administrator console.

2. From the SMS Administrator console, expand Site Database (*<Site Code>*), expand Collections, and then select a collection that contains all members to be deleted.

3. Right-click the collection and select Delete Special.

4. Click Yes to confirm deletion of *all* resources in a specified collection.

Solution: Using VBScript

Example 3-14 demonstrates how to delete a resource from SMS.

Example 3-14. *DelResource.vbs*

```
strSMSServer = <SMSServer>

strComputer = "Computer1"

Set objLoc =  CreateObject("WbemScripting.SWbemLocator")
Set objSMS= objLoc.ConnectServer(strSMSServer, "root\sms")
Set Results = objSMS.ExecQuery _
    ("SELECT * From SMS_ProviderLocation WHERE ProviderForLocalSite = true")
For each Loc in Results
    If Loc.ProviderForLocalSite = True Then
        Set objSMS = objLoc.ConnectServer(Loc.Machine, "root\sms\site_" & _
            Loc.SiteCode)
        strSMSSiteCode = Loc.SiteCode
    end if
Next

'get the resource ID of the computer
intResourceID = GetResourceID(strComputer)

'Remove ResourceID
Set objResource = GetObject( "WinMgmts:\\" & strSMSServer & _
    "\root\SMS\site_" & strSMSSiteCode & _
    ":SMS_R_System.ResourceID=" & cint(intResourceID))
objResource.Delete_
wscript.echo "Deleted " & strComputer & "(" & intResourceID & ")"

Function GetResourceID(strComputerName)
    Set colResourceIDs = objSMS.ExecQuery _
        ("select ResourceID from SMS_R_System where Name = '" & _
            strComputer & "'")
    for each objResID in colResourceIDs
        GetResourceID = objResID.ResourceID
    next
End Function
```

Discussion

When you delete a resource from SMS, that resource will disappear from all collections, web reports, and everywhere else within SMS. This recipe shows how to delete resources when you no longer need them. If you wish to simply remove a resource from a direct membership collection while retaining that resource for possible use in other collections, then refer to Recipe 3-14, "Removing Direct Members from a Collection." If you wish to remove a resource from a query-based collection, then you need to modify the query to exclude the resource that's no longer desired.

Rather than delete just one resource, you may find you need to delete multiple resources from SMS. Say, for example, you have replaced all systems in the human resources department, and you see the "old" PCs in SMS (these PCs will remain there by default for 90 days). If for some reason you want to remove these systems from SMS before SMS purges them automatically, you could create a collection of all systems in the HR organizational unit that have not processed a hardware inventory within the past 30 days. Once you have this collection, you could perform a "delete special" to permanently remove these resources from SMS.

Keep in mind that when you delete resources from SMS you lose all inventory information, including all inventory history information. For license audits, these "extra" systems in SMS can skew the license counts, so that may be a driver to remove the inventory information. On the other hand, by having the old inventory data available, you have an additional avenue to research when Joe User says, "Hey, I had Visio 2003 Professional on my old PC, but I don't have it installed on my new one. Please install ASAP." By keeping the inventory of the old systems, you may be able to determine whether Joe is being honest, or if he's trying to obtain software without paying for it.

If you happen to delete a resource by mistake, the good news is the resource will reappear within SMS the next time a discovery record is generated for the resource. The bad news is that if the resource was a member of any collections by direct membership, those memberships will not, of course, be restored (because you deleted them, implicitly, when you deleted the resource). Membership in query-based collections will be restored the next time those collection memberships are updated. And, when the resource is brought back into a query-based collection, any advertisements that the client has already run will not rerun (unless, of course, the advertisement is set to rerun on a schedule).

In Example 3-14, we obtain the ResourceID of the computer resource, and then delete it from SMS_R_System. To perform the same actions as a "delete special," you could enumerate all resources in a collection and call the Delete_ method on each.

See Also

- Recipe 3-4, "Deleting a Collection," describes how to delete a collection.

- Recipe 3-6, "Deleting a Linked Collection," describes how to delete a linked collection.

- Recipe 3-14, "Removing Direct Members from a Collection," describes how to remove members from a collection.

- The *SMS 2003 Scripting Guide* demonstrates how to delete objects from SMS.

3-16. Modifying Permissions of a Collection

Problem

You want to modify permissions to a specific collection.

Solution: Using a Graphical Interface

1. Open the SMS Administrator console.

2. From the SMS Administrator console, expand Site Database (*<Site Code>*), expand Collections, and then select a collection to modify.

3. Right-click the collection, select Properties from the menu, and select the Permissions tab in the Collection Properties dialog box.

4. Click the New or Delete button to add or remove class or instance security rights. You can also double-click any existing classes or instance rights to modify them.

5. Click OK to apply the settings.

Solution: Using VBScript

Example 3-15 demonstrates how to modify access permissions to a collection.

Example 3-15. *ModCollPerms.vbs*

```
'This script will grant the group "SMSVPC\Help Desk" read and
    ' modify permissions to collection ID "LAB00159".
strSMSServer = <SMSServer>
strHelpDesk="LAB\SMSHelpDesk" 'Domain\Group or username
strCollID = "LAB00159"  'ID of the collection

Set objLoc =  CreateObject("WbemScripting.SWbemLocator")
Set objSMS= objLoc.ConnectServer(strSMSServer, "root\sms")
Set Results = objSMS.ExecQuery _
    ("SELECT * From SMS_ProviderLocation WHERE ProviderForLocalSite = true")
For each Loc in Results
    If Loc.ProviderForLocalSite = True Then
        Set objSMS = objLoc.ConnectServer(Loc.Machine, "root\sms\site_" & _
            Loc.SiteCode)
    end if
Next

Set objNewRight = objSMS.Get _
  ("SMS_UserInstancePermissions").SpawnInstance_()
objNewRight.UserName = strHelpDesk
objNewRight.ObjectKey = 1 '1=collection
objNewRight.InstanceKey = strCollID
objNewRight.InstancePermissions = 1+2'grant Read and Modify
objNewRight.Put_
```

Discussion

Proper collection permissions are essential if you will be delegating any SMS tasks to other users in your environment and want to make sure that they can only impact those systems they are responsible for. If you haven't looked into delegating any SMS tasks, you should try it. You will find that you can safely give access to people to perform functions (such as adding a computer to a collection), which will allow for faster service from SMS.

Be very careful when modifying permissions, or you may lock yourself out of a collection! Especially when you modify permissions programmatically, be sure to test your code in a test environment before running it in production.

See Also

- Recipe 4-9, "Modifying Permissions of a Package," describes how to modify the permissions of a package.

- Recipe 6-17, "Modifying the Permissions of an Advertisement," describes how to modify the permissions of an advertisement.

- The *SMS 2003 Scripting Guide* provides more information about setting security rights for an SMS object.

- The SMS 2003 SDK describes SMS_UserInstancePermissions.

- The *SMS 2003 Scripting Guide* also describes SMS_UserInstancePermissions.

3-17. Viewing Advertisements Assigned to a Collection

Problem

You want to show all advertisements that apply to a specific collection.

Solution: Using a Graphical Interface

1. Open the SMS Administrator console.

2. From the SMS Administrator console, expand Site Database (*<Site Code>*), expand Collections, and then select a collection to view the advertisements for that collection.

3. Right-click the collection, select Properties from the menu, and select the Advertisements tab in the Collection Properties dialog box to view the advertisements.

4. Click OK or Cancel to close the dialog box.

Solution: Using VBScript

Example 3-16 demonstrates how to view advertisements assigned to a collection.

Example 3-16. *ListAdvertsToColl.vbs*

```
strSMSServer = <SMSServer>
strCollID = "LAB000FE"

Set objLoc = CreateObject("WbemScripting.SWbemLocator")
Set objSMS= objLoc.ConnectServer(strSMSServer, "root\sms")
Set Results = objSMS.ExecQuery _
    ("SELECT * From SMS_ProviderLocation WHERE ProviderForLocalSite = true")
For each Loc in Results
    If Loc.ProviderForLocalSite = True Then
        Set objSMS = objLoc.ConnectServer(Loc.Machine, "root\sms\site_" & _
            Loc.SiteCode)
    end if
Next

ListAdverts strCollID, False
CheckParent strCollID

Sub ListAdverts(strCollID,blnSubCollect)
    If blnSubCollect then
        'This is to check all parent questions of the
        'collection in question. We can only look at
        'parent collections that are set to "Include
        'members of subcollections"
        Set colAdverts = objSMS.ExecQuery _
        ("select * from SMS_Advertisement where " & _
        "CollectionID = '" & strCollID & "' and " & _
        "IncludeSubCollection = 1")
    Else
        'This is for the first check; it will look for
        'advertisements assigned directly to the collection
        Set colAdverts = objSMS.ExecQuery _
        ("select * from SMS_Advertisement where " & _
        "CollectionID = '" & strCollID & "'")
    end if
    for each objAdvert in colAdverts
        wscript.echo "Advertisement: " & _
            objAdvert.AdvertisementName
        wscript.echo "    Collection: " & _
            GetCollectionName(objAdvert.CollectionID) & _
            " (" & objAdvert.CollectionID  & ")" & VbCRLF
    next
End Sub
```

```
Function GetCollectionName(strCollID)
    Set instColl = objSMS.Get _
    ("SMS_Collection.CollectionID=""" & strCollID & """")
    GetCollectionName = instColl.Name
End Function

Sub CheckParent(strCollID)
    Set colParents = objSMS.ExecQuery _
    ("select * from SMS_CollectToSubCollect where subCollectionID = '" & _
    strCollID & "'")
    for each objParent in colParents
        if not objParent.ParentCollectionID = "COLLROOT" then
            ListAdverts objParent.ParentCollectionID , True
            CheckParent objParent.ParentCollectionID
        end if
    next
End Sub
```

Discussion

Using the techniques shown in this recipe is a great way of keeping track of current advertisements and planning the impact of adding new systems to current collections. The list of advertisements displayed by this recipe's solution include not only the advertisements targeted directly at the collection in question, but also the advertisements targeted to the collection through links. The collection value listed with each advertisement tells you which collection is the base collection, but it won't show you how the current collection is linked to it.

Example 3-16 is a good example of the use of subroutines, functions, and recursion. If SMS did not contain the functionality to "Include Members of SubCollections," the recipe solution would be much easier to code. We would simply need to look at all advertisements, and see if any of them are assigned to the collection in question. However, since the collection in question could be a subcollection to a collection that is receiving the advertisement, we need to dig a little deeper.

In Example 3-16, we start by taking the collection in question and seeing whether there are any advertisements directly assigned to that collection (Sub ListAdverts handles this task). We then check to see if the collection in question has a parent collection. If the collection does have a parent, we check that parent collection for advertisements that are set to include subcollections. This process continues until we run out of parent collections to check.

See Also

- Recipe 3-18, "Viewing Advertisements Assigned to a Computer," demonstrates how to display all advertisements for a computer.

- The SMS 2003 SDK describes SMS_Advertisement, SMS_Collection, and SMS_CollectToSubCollect in detail.

3-18. Viewing Advertisements Assigned to a Computer

Problem

You want to show all advertisements that apply to a specific client computer in a collection.

Solution: Using a Graphical Interface

1. Open the SMS Administrator console.

2. From the SMS Administrator console, expand Site Database (*<Site Code>*), expand Collections, and then select a collection to view the advertisements for a system in that collection.

3. Right-click a system in the right pane, select Properties from the menu, and select the Advertisements tab in the Resource Properties dialog box to view the advertisements for that system.

4. Click OK or Cancel to close the dialog box.

Solution: Using VBScript

Example 3-17 demonstrates how to view advertisements assigned to a computer.

Example 3-17. *ViewAdvertsAssignedToMachine.vbs*

```
strSMSServer = <SMSServer>

strComputer = "Computer1"

Set objLoc = CreateObject("WbemScripting.SWbemLocator")
Set objSMS= objLoc.ConnectServer(strSMSServer, "root\sms")
Set Results = objSMS.ExecQuery _
    ("SELECT * From SMS_ProviderLocation WHERE ProviderForLocalSite = true")
For each Loc in Results
    If Loc.ProviderForLocalSite = True Then
        Set objSMS = objLoc.ConnectServer(Loc.Machine, "root\sms\site_" & _
            Loc.SiteCode)
    end if
Next

'first, get the resource ID of the computer
intResourceID = GetResourceID(strComputer)

Set colAdverts = objSMS.ExecQuery _
("select * from SMS_ClientAdvertisementStatus where ResourceID = " & _
    intResourceID)
for each strAdvert in colAdverts 'enumerate all adverts for client
    wscript.echo GetAdvertisementName(strAdvert.AdvertisementID) & _
        "(" & strAdvert.AdvertisementID & ")" & vbTAB  & _
    strAdvert.LastStateName & vbTAB & strAdvert.LastStatusTime & _
    vbTAB & GetCollectionName(strAdvert.AdvertisementID)
next

'used to obtain the Advertisement Name
Function GetAdvertisementName(strAdvertID)
    Set instAdvert = objSMS.Get _
        ("SMS_Advertisement.AdvertisementID='" & strAdvertID & "'")
    GetAdvertisementName = instAdvert.AdvertisementName
End Function
```

```
'used to obtain the Collection Name
Function GetCollectionName(strAdvertID)
    'first, get advert based on advert ID
    Set instAdvert = objSMS.Get _
        ("SMS_Advertisement.AdvertisementID='" & strAdvertID & "'")
    'then, get collection name based on collectionID from advert
    Set instCollection = objSMS.Get _
        ("SMS_Collection.CollectionID='" & instAdvert.CollectionID & "'")
    GetCollectionName = instCollection.Name
End Function

'used to obtain the SMS resource ID
Function GetResourceID(strComputerName)
    Set colResourceIDs = objSMS.ExecQuery _
        ("select ResourceID from SMS_R_System where Name = '" & _
            strComputer & "'")
    for each objResID in colResourceIDs
        GetResourceID = objResID.ResourceID
    next
End Function
```

Discussion

We would direct help desk personnel and department managers to the SMS web reports to get information on advertisements assigned to a specific computer. For the SMS administrator who is working in the SMS Administrator console, the solution in this recipe can be very helpful when taking inventory of which advertisements are currently being targeted at a specific SMS client. Maybe you have been asked to make sure that Suzy's computer has the same applications as Jack's PC. In such a case, you can easily discover which applications may need to be added and which collections to change.

In Example 3-17, we first obtain the ResourceID of the computer, and then check the class SMS_ClientAdvertisementStatus to obtain all advertisements assigned to that client. Finally, we display the advertisement name, the advertisement ID, and the last reported state for the advertisement for the client in question.

See Also

- The SMS web report titled "All advertisements for a specific computer" displays all advertisements assigned to a specific computer.

- Recipe 3-17, "Viewing Advertisements Assigned to a Collection," details how to obtain a list of all advertisements advertised to a specific collection.

- The SMS 2003 SDK describes SMS_ClientAdvertisementStatus, SMS_Advertisement, SMS_Collection, and SMS_R_System in detail.

3-19. Viewing Resources for a Member of a Collection

Problem

You want to view hardware and software resources for a specific client in a collection.

Solution: Using a Graphical Interface

1. Open the SMS Administrator console.

2. From the SMS Administrator console, expand Site Database (*<Site Code>*), expand Collections, and then select a collection that contains the computer you wish to analyze.

3. Locate the computer resource in the right pane, right-click it, and select All Tasks ➤ Start Resource Explorer.

4. From Resource Explorer, expand *<Computer Name>*.

5. Then expand and browse Hardware, Hardware History, and Software as desired.

6. Close Resource Explorer when you've finished.

Solution: From the Command Line

1. Create a batch file called ResExplorer.bat and save it in %windir%\System32.

2. Enter the following text into ResExplorer.bat:

```
set strSMSServer = <SMSServer>
set strSMSSiteCode = <SMSSiteCode>
rem ***The next three lines are actually one line!
start mmc C:\SMSAdmin\bin\i386\explore.msc -s -sms:ResExplrQuery=
"Select ResourceID From SMS_R_SYSTEM Where Name = ""%1""" -
sms:connection=\\%strSMSServer%\root\sms\site_%strSMSSiteCode%
```

3. Enter the appropriate site code and SMS server name, and verify the proper path to explore.msc for your environment.

4. Ensure the last three lines in the example are all on the same line.

5. Save ResExplorer.bat.

6. Click Start ➤ Run, enter **ResExplorer** *Computer1* (where *Computer1* is the name of the computer to observe), and click OK.

7. Resource Explorer will launch and display data for *Computer1*.

8. Close Resource Explorer when you've finished.

Discussion

Resource Explorer is a great tool for viewing hardware and software inventory information on a specific system. Hardware history is also available in Resource Explorer. The following is a brief explanation of each major node in Resource Explorer:

Hardware: This displays all data collected through hardware inventory. The majority of this information appears because of settings in the SMS_DEF.MOF file. Other sources for hardware inventory include IDMIF and NOIDMIF files (if enabled). Review Chapter 11 for more information about the sources for hardware inventory.

Hardware History: Think of Hardware History as a "paper trail" of changes that have occurred (as far as hardware inventory is concerned) over the past 90 days (by default). Modify the Delete Aged Inventory History task to reduce or extend the amount of time to keep this history. The history data can be helpful in determining when hardware was installed, when the amount of memory in a system has changed, and when a disk drive(s) free space is below a predetermined amount, among many other possibilities.

Software: Software inventory displays properties for inventoried files (by default, *.exe) and helps to associate product names to files. If you utilize the file collection feature of SMS, the file data is also available here.

Resource Explorer allows SMS administrators to see the data available for use when creating query-based collections and SMS queries.

WHY IS ADD/REMOVE PROGRAMS LISTED IN HARDWARE INVENTORY WHEN THE PROGRAMS ARE ACTUALLY SOFTWARE?

Good question. *Every* new SMS administrator asks that question. Think of Software inventory as querying only specific files (e.g., msxml3.dll) or files with wildcards (e.g., *.exe). Hardware inventory queries Windows Management Instrumentation (WMI) to obtain processor information, disk information, and more. Hardware inventory is also used to obtain data from the Windows registry (using WMI). Add/Remove Programs data is stored in HKEY_LOCAL_MACHINE\Software\Microsoft\Windows\CurrentVersion\Uninstall, which explains why this data is included in Hardware inventory. Review Chapter 11 for more information about inventorying registry data using SMS and WMI.

See Also

- Recipe 3-17, "Viewing Advertisements Assigned to a Collection," describes how to view advertisements assigned to a collection.

- Recipe 3-18, "Viewing Advertisements Assigned to a Computer," describes how to view advertisements assigned to a client.

- Chapter 9 of the *Microsoft Systems Management Server 2003 Administrator's Companion* by Steven Kaczmarek (Microsoft Press, 2004) provides some detail about Resource Explorer.

- Chapter 2 of the *SMS 2003 Operations Guide* provides additional information on SMS Resource Explorer.

- The *SMS 2003 Operations Guide*, Table 3-1 (titled "Inventory Data Type and Classification in SMS") provides more information about which inventory component is used for various system properties.

3-20. Adding a Right-click Option to Affect a Member of a Collection

Problem

You want to add an action to the right-click functionality in the SMS Administrator console that affects a specific client.

Note Two solutions are provided in this recipe. The first demonstrates the basic process using a batch file, and the second provides a more advanced solution using VBScript. You will likely find that both are valuable for your environment.

Solution: Displaying the Logs Directory of an SMS Advanced Client

The following example solution uses a batch file to add a right-click menu option allowing you to display the logs directory of an SMS Advanced Client. You can adapt the solution to other tasks by following the same process while using a different batch file name and script.

1. From the system that has the SMS Administrator console installed, browse to `C:\SMSAdmin\` (or `SMSAdmin` or `SMS`, depending on SMS components installed).

2. Create a new directory called `SMSTools` and open it for viewing.

3. Create a batch file called `ShowClientLogs.bat`.

4. Edit `ShowClientLogs.bat` in Notepad, and enter the following text:

```
if not exist \\%1\admin$\system32\ccm\logs goto notexist
explorer \\%1\admin$\system32\ccm\logs
exit

:notexist
echo "\\%1\admin$\system32\ccm\logs does not exist."
echo "  Verify admin$ and SMS Adv Client Installed"
pause
exit
```

5. Save `ShowClientLogs.bat`.

6. Open the Windows registry editor by selecting Start ➤ Run, entering **Regedit.exe**, and then clicking OK.

7. Browse to `HKEY_LOCAL_MACHINE\SOFTWARE\Microsoft\MMC\NodeTypes\{4D26C0D4-A8A8-11D1-9BD9-00C04FBBD480}\Extensions`.

8. From the `Extensions` key, create a new key named `SMS_Tools`.

9. From the `SMS_Tools` key, create a new key named `ShowClientLogs`. It's a good idea to have this registry key name match your batch file name; doing so can help you keep things straight.

10. From the `ShowClientLogs` key, create a new string value called `Name`, and for the data, enter **Show Client Logs Folder**.

11. From the `ShowClientLogs` key, create a new string value called `CommandLine`, and for the data, enter **C:\SMSAdmin\SMSTools\ShowClientLogs.bat ##SUB:Name##**.

12. To verify functionality, right-click a system in any collection and select SMSTools ➤ Show Client Logs Folder.

Solution: Requesting Machine Policy for an SMS Advanced Client

The following example solution uses a VBScript file to add a right-click menu option allowing you to refresh machine policy of an SMS Advanced Client. You can adapt the solution to other tasks by following the same process while using a different file name, script, and registry entries.

1. From the system that has the SMS Administrator console installed, browse to `C:\SMSAdmin\` (or `SMSAdmin` or `SMS`, depending on SMS components installed).

2. Create a new directory called `SMSTools` and open it for viewing.

3. Create a batch file called `RefreshMachinePolicy.vbs`.

4. Edit `RefreshMachinePolicy.vbs` in Notepad, and enter the following text:

```
Set objArgs = WScript.Arguments
strComputerName = objArgs(0)
Set smsClient = GetObject("winmgmts:\\" & strComputerName & _
    "\root\ccm:SMS_Client")
smsClient.RequestMachinePolicy(0)
wscript.echo "Machine Policy Refreshed on " & strComputerName
wscript.sleep 5000
```

5. Save RefreshMachinePolicy.vbs.

6. Open the Windows registry editor by selecting Start ➤ Run, entering **Regedit.exe**, and then clicking OK.

7. Browse to HKEY_LOCAL_MACHINE\SOFTWARE\Microsoft\MMC\NodeTypes\{4D26C0D4-A8A8-11D1-9BD9-00C04FBBD480}\Extensions.

8. From the Extensions key, create a new key named SMS_Tools.

9. From the SMS_Tools key, create a new key named RequestMachinePolicy.

10. From the RequestMachinePolicy key, create a new string value called Name, and for the data, enter **Request Machine Policy**.

11. From the RequestMachinePolicy key, create a new string value called CommandLine, and for the data, enter **cscript.exe C:\SMSAdmin\SMSTools\RefreshMachinePolicy.vbs ##SUB:Name##**.

12. To verify functionality, right-click a system in any collection and select SMSTools ➤ Request Machine Policy.

Discussion

The process demonstrated in this recipe is called *context menu integration*, and it is a very powerful tool to extend the SMS Administrator console. Any node in the SMS Administrator console can be extended in this fashion. The SMS 2003 SDK provides more information regarding how to determine the location in the registry required to use other nodes.

The basic structure of the two recipe solutions may be used for several tasks to make your job easier. Keep in mind that anything that can be executed from a command line (.exe, .mdb, etc.) can be used in right-click functionality in the SMS Administrator console. SMSView (http://www.smsview.com) is an example of an application that can be launched by performing a right-click of a client in a collection. Also, there is no requirement for the external application to execute an SMS function. For example, if you often find yourself viewing an internal (or external) web site when managing collections, you could change your command line to launch your favorite web browser, passing a command-line argument giving the desired web site.

Review step 11 from this recipe and note that ##SUB:Name## is the variable used for the computer name when executing from a right-click tool in the Administrator console. Additional discovery data can be obtained by replacing Name with the data name (e.g., ADSiteName, ClientVersion, ResourceDomainOrWorkgroup, etc.). Data can also be passed to the external program by inserting multiples in the CommandLine field (e.g., ##SUB:Name## ##SUB:ADSITENAME## ##SUB:ClientVerision##). Here are a few constants also available with context menu integration:

##SUB:__SERVER##: This is the name of the SMS server.

##SUB:__NAMESpace##: This is the namespace name for SMS. It's often used to connect to WMI on the server.

Arrays are also available for discovery data of type array (e.g., IPAddresses, MACAddresses, SMSAssignedSites, etc.). Refer to the SMS 2003 SDK for more information about using arrays with context menu integration.

Both solutions provided assume the user who initiates the actions has proper permissions to perform the actions. In both solutions, the remote system must be powered on and connected to the network. In the first solution, the user must have permissions to the admin$ share. In the second solution, proper permissions to WMI are required. Notice the strComputerName = objArgs(0) in the preceding VBScript example. This is used to obtain the first argument (zero-indexed) on the command line (in this case, the computer name). To create and capture a second argument, simply modify your CommandLine in the registry (e.g., ##SUB:ADSiteName##), and add a line to the VBScript to capture the second argument (strADSiteName = objArgs(1)).

This solution only scratches the surface of this functionality's possibilities. Other solutions throughout this book also leverage context menu integration.

CORY BECHT'S RIGHT-CLICK TOOL

One of the best right-click utilities you'll find for SMS is a tool by Cory Becht to initiate SMS Advanced Client actions remotely. You can find this tool at myITforum.com: `http://www.myitforum.com/articles/8/view.asp?id=7099`. Once you've downloaded and installed the tool, you can initiate the following actions by right-clicking a collection or a computer object in the SMS Administrator console:

- Reassign the SMS site code
- Restart the SMS Agent host service
- Regenerate the SMS client GUID
- Rerun advertisements without modifying the advertisement
- Discovery
- Perform software inventory: delta and full
- Perform hardware inventory: delta and full
- Perform file collection
- Check software metering usage
- Refresh machine policies
- Evaluate policies
- Update Windows Installer sources
- Change port number
- Change cache size

See Also

- Recipe 3-21, "Adding a Right-click Option to Affect All Members of a Collection," shows how to use these functions on all members of a collection.

- Cory Becht's right-click tool at `http://www.myitforum.com/articles/8/view.asp?id=7099` enables you to remotely manage one or multiple SMS clients, as described in this recipe.

- The SMS 2003 SDK details the context menu integration process in a section titled "Implementing Context Menu Integration."

3-21. Adding a Right-click Option to Affect All Members of a Collection

Problem

You want to add an action to the right-click functionality in the SMS Administrator console that affects *all* systems in a specific collection.

Solution

This recipe's solution is an improvement on the previous recipe's VBScript solution. This solution provides right-click functionality for both a single system and multiple systems in a collection. Here are the steps to follow:

1. From the system that has the SMS Administrator console installed, browse to C:\SMSAdmin\ (or SMSAdmin or SMS, depending on SMS components installed).

2. Create a new directory called SMSTools and open it for viewing.

3. Create a batch file called RefreshMachinePolicy.vbs.

4. Edit RefreshMachinePolicy.vbs in Notepad, and enter the following text:

```
if wscript.arguments(0) = "S" then
    strComputerName = wscript.arguments(1)
    Set smsClient = GetObject("winmgmts:\\" & strComputerName & _
        "\root\ccm:SMS_Client")
    smsClient.RequestMachinePolicy(0)
    wscript.echo "Machine Policy Refreshed on " & strComputerName
    wscript.sleep 5000
else
    strSMSServer =  wscript.arguments(1)
    strSMSNameSpace = wscript.arguments(2)
    strSMSCollectionID = wscript.arguments(3)
    Set loc = CreateObject("WbemScripting.SWbemLocator")
    Set objSMS = loc.ConnectServer(strSMSServer, strSMSNameSpace)
    set ColMembers=objSMS.ExecQuery _
        ("select Name from SMS_CM_RES_COLL_" & strSMSCollectionID)
    for Each Member in ColMembers
        wscript.echo "Refreshing Machine Policy on " & Member.Name
        Set smsClient = GetObject("winmgmts:\\" & Member.Name & _
            "\root\ccm:SMS_Client")
        smsClient.RequestMachinePolicy(0)
    next
    wscript.sleep 5000
end if
```

5. Save RefreshMachinePolicy.vbs.

6. Open the Windows registry editor by selecting Start ➤ Run, entering **Regedit.exe**, and then clicking OK.

7. Browse to HKEY_LOCAL_MACHINE\SOFTWARE\Microsoft\MMC\NodeTypes\{4D26C0D4-A8A8-11D1-9BD9-00C04FBBD480}\Extensions.

8. From the Extensions key, create a new key named SMS_Tools.

9. From the SMS_Tools key, create a new key named RequestMachinePolicy.

10. From the RequestMachinePolicy key, create a new string value called Name, and for the data, enter **Request Machine Policy**.

11. From the RequestMachinePolicy key, create a new string value called CommandLine, and for the data, enter **cscript.exe C:\SMSAdmin\SMSTools\RefreshMachinePolicy.vbs S ##SUB:Name##**.

12. Browse to HKEY_LOCAL_MACHINE\SOFTWARE\Microsoft\MMC\NodeTypes\ {3AD39FF1-EFD6-11D0-BDCF-00A0C909FDD7}\Extensions.

13. From the Extensions key, create a new key named SMS_Tools.

14. From the SMS_Tools key, create a new key named RequestMachinePolicy.

15. From the `RequestMachinePolicy` key, create a new string value called `Name`, and for the data, enter **Request Machine Policy**.

16. From the `RequestMachinePolicy` key, create a new string value called `CommandLine`, and for the data, enter **cscript.exe C:\SMSAdmin\SMSTools\RefreshMachinePolicy.vbs M ##SUB:__SERVER## ##SUB:__Namespace## ##SUB:COLLECTIONID##**.

17. To verify single system functionality, right-click a system in any collection and select SMSTools ➤ Request Machine Policy.

18. To verify multiple system functionality, right-click any collection and select SMSTools ➤ Request Machine Policy.

Discussion

The discussion in the previous recipe's solution explains most of what you see in this solution. Here we will describe the differences and provide additional required information.

First, an `if-else` statement is included to allow functionality from one script for initiating on both a single system and a collection. Notice that in step 11 an "S" is added for "single" computer, while in step 16 an "M" was added to signify "multiple" computers. By adding an "S" or "M" to the command line, we can determine which part of the VBScript to execute at runtime. The first section of the script (under the `if` statement) is identical to the previous solution. The second section of the script (under the `else` statement) is the code that pertains directly to performing functions on multiple systems.

If, for example, an "M" is passed to the script, we capture the arguments into variables for clarity, and then connect to the SMS namespace. After connecting to the SMS namespace on the SMS site, we execute a query to obtain all members of the desired collection. During the `for-each` loop, we perform the actual process of refreshing the machine policy on the system. Finally, the script sleeps for five seconds to allow the administrator a moment to view the results. Before implementing this code into production, be sure to add error handling (or at least an `On Error Resume Next` at the beginning of the script). If you attempt to connect to a system that is not currently on the network, the script will fail *very slowly*. Later in this book, we provide an example to demonstrate how to verify a system is on the network before attempting to connect to it via WMI.

Also in Recipe 3-20, "Adding a Right-click Option to Affect a Member of a Collection," we discuss Cory Becht's right-click tool. This tool can be used on both a collection and a specific member of a collection. Don't reinvent the wheel! Download and install Cory's application, and then review the VBScript to learn how to extend and customize to your needs.

See Also

- Recipe 3-21, "Adding a Right-click Option to Affect all Members of a Collection," describes how to use these functions on all members of a collection.

- Cory Becht's right-click tool at `http://www.myitforum.com/articles/8/view.asp?id=7099` enables you to remotely manage one or multiple SMS clients, as described in this recipe.

- The SMS 2003 SDK details the context menu integration process in a section titled "Implementing Context Menu Integration."

CHAPTER 4

■■■

Packages

The term "package" is used in many different ways in general software distribution discussions. For example, it can refer to what SMS delivers to the SMS client. It can also refer to the application that is being installed. And it can be used to refer to the process of rebuilding an application (i.e., repackaging). This overloading of the term can cause confusion in any discussion on SMS packages, so we would like to clarify its use.

If software distribution is like mailing a birthday present to a friend, the SMS package is the cardboard box, packing material, and tape. It isn't the present itself, nor is it the address label on the box. It isn't the mail carrier either, for that matter. Proper packaging may seem like an unimportant piece of the "mail a birthday present" process, but if you've ever had something damaged during shipping, you know how important the packing material is. Likewise, you should take care in how you create your SMS packages, as they are a critical part of successful software distribution.

Think of a SMS package as the foundation for SMS programs and advertisements. Without a properly configured SMS package, SMS programs and advertisements are useless. The SMS package is where you configure access to the source files (if any) required for software distribution. *Package source files should contain the minimum amount of files (in terms of both number and size) possible.* This same source will be "mirrored" to all distribution points you select, and it can also be configured to be downloaded to each advanced client (depending on how you configure the advertisement).

SMS package size will vary greatly depending on how you leverage SMS in your environment. For example, if you write an SMS Installer script to create a shortcut on clients' desktops, that package source will (or at least should) be less than 1MB. But if you're installing Office Professional, your package size may be 600MB or more. And in an extreme case, if you're using the SMS 2003 Operating System Deployment (OSD) Feature Pack, the package size could be 1, 2, or even 5GB or more depending on the size of your image! Both available hard drive space and available bandwidth are directly impacted when package source files are copied to child sites and to the SMS Advanced Client (when using download & execute). Generally speaking, the larger the package, the longer it takes to copy the package source.

Also, within one SMS package, you can create multiple SMS programs for flexibility. If, for example, you have different customization requirements for installing Office Professional for members of the human resources department than for executive staff, you can configure different programs and have both use the same package source. We discuss this aspect of packaging in more detail in the next chapter. This chapter focuses on managing your SMS packages: creating, modifying, and removing packages. We also discuss managing package distribution points in detail.

4-1. Creating a Package

Problem

You want to create a new SMS package.

Solution: Using a Graphical Interface

1. Open the SMS Administrator console.

2. From the SMS Administrator console, expand Site Database (<*Site Code*>), and then expand Packages.

3. Right-click Packages and select New ➤ Package from the menu to open the Package Properties dialog box.

4. On the General tab, enter at least the name of the new package.

5. Specify any of the additional parameters.

6. Click OK to create the new package.

Solution: Using VBScript

Example 4-1 creates a package to distribute Visual Studio .NET Framework 1.1, Service Pack 1. The example illustrates the basic pattern to follow when creating any package.

Example 4-1. *CreatePackage.vbs*

```
strSMSServer = <SMSServer>
'Specify package attributes one time. From here on out
'we reference these variables.
pkgName = "Visual Studio .NET Framework 1.1 SP1"
pkgSource = "\\smsvpc\source\KB867460"
pkgDesc = "This Package Installs .NET 1.1 SP1"
pkgManufacturer = "Microsoft"

Set objLoc =  CreateObject("WbemScripting.SWbemLocator")
Set objSMS= objLoc.ConnectServer(strSMSServer, "root\sms")
Set Results = objSMS.ExecQuery _
    ("SELECT * From SMS_ProviderLocation WHERE ProviderForLocalSite = true")
For each Loc in Results
    If Loc.ProviderForLocalSite = True Then
        Set objSMS = objLoc.ConnectServer(Loc.Machine, "root\sms\site_" & _
            Loc.SiteCode)
    end if
Next

'Define package attributes such as name, source for the files, etc.
Set newPackage = objSMS.Get("SMS_Package").SpawnInstance_()
newPackage.Name = pkgName
newPackage.Description = pkgDesc
newPackage.Manufacturer = pkgManufacturer
newPackage.PkgSourceFlag = 2
'2=direct, 1=no source 3=use compressed source
newPackage.PkgSourcePath = pkgSource
Set path=newPackage.Put_

'the following three lines are used to obtain the PackageID
'of the package we just created
Set Package=objSMS.Get(path)
PackageID= Package.PackageID
wscript.echo PackageID & " = " & pkgName
```

Discussion

It may appear that a package can have a dizzying number of options applied to it, but the only requirement is a name. You may find it easier to give a new package a name and then save the package before configuring it and adding programs to it. We look at the array of package options individually in the following recipes.

In Example 4-1, we first set a couple variables for clarity. After connecting to the SMS namespace, we create a new instance of SMS_Package, set package properties (name, description, source, etc.), and save it (newPackage.Put_). The last three lines of the code are not required for creating a package, but if you are planning to perform additional functions to the package immediately after creating it (such as creating a program, moving the package to another folder, etc.), these lines demonstrate how to obtain the PackageID of the package you just created.

See Also

- Recipe 4-2, "Determining a Package's PackageID," demonstrates how to enumerate all packages by package name and PackageID.

- Recipe 4-4, "Deleting a Package," presents an example of how to delete a package.

- Recipe 4-11, "Adding a Package to Distribution Points," demonstrates how to add a newly created package to distribution points.

- Recipe 4-16, "Creating a Package from a Package Definition File," demonstrates how to create a package based on a package definition file (.pdf or .sms).

- Refer to the SMS 2003 Software Development Kit (SDK) for more information about the properties available for creating a package.

- Chapter 5 of the *SMS 2003 Operations Guide* details creating and managing packages.

- Sample C.20 in Appendix C of the *SMS 2003 Operations Guide* demonstrates how to create a package and program using VBScript and also provides more information about the PkgSourceFlag property.

4-2. Determining a Package's PackageID

Problem

You want to determine the ID of a package.

Solution: Using a Graphical Interface

1. Open the SMS Administrator console.

2. From the SMS Administrator console, expand Site Database (<*Site Code*>), and then expand Packages.

3. Expand any folders that contain the package for which you need the PackageID.

4. The right pane will display the PackageID next to the package name.

Solution: Using VBScript

Example 4-2 generates a report showing the identifier for each package that you have defined.

Example 4-2. *ShowPackageIDs.vbs*

```
strSMSServer = <SMSServer>

Set objLoc =  CreateObject("WbemScripting.SWbemLocator")
Set objSMS= objLoc.ConnectServer(strSMSServer, "root\sms")
Set Results = objSMS.ExecQuery _
    ("SELECT * From SMS_ProviderLocation WHERE ProviderForLocalSite = true")
For each Loc in Results
    If Loc.ProviderForLocalSite = True Then
        Set objSMS = objLoc.ConnectServer(Loc.Machine, "root\sms\site_" & _
            Loc.SiteCode)
    end if
Next

Set Packages = objSMS.ExecQuery _
    ("Select * From SMS_Package order by Name")
For each objPackage in Packages
    wscript.echo objPackage.Name & vbTAB & objPackage.PackageID
Next
```

Discussion

It's very important to be able to find the PackageID for a given package, when you plan to access the package programmatically. SMS by default stores all packages on the distribution point in folders that are named by only their PackageID. If you are ready to extend SMS by leveraging some of the VBScript scripts in this book, the SMS PackageID will be one of your best friends. Most of the scripts in this book that require a PackageID assume you know it. You can use either method described in this recipe to obtain the PackageID for a given package.

▬**Tip** If you plan to make heavy use of scripting, be aware that adding the /sms:nodeinfo=1 switch to the command line of the shortcut to the SMS Administrator console will add the Node Information tab to the Properties dialog box of any node in the SMS Administrator console. This tab offers a great way to see the inner workings of SMS.

The VBScript in Example 4-2 is a good example of querying a class in the SMS database. The script displays all packages in alphabetical order by name, and it also displays each package's PackageID. Other properties (such as LastRefreshTime, SourceVersion, PkgSourcePath, etc.) are also available for display from the SMS_Package class.

▬**Note** You may want to consider adding a where clause to the Windows Management Instrumentation Query Language (WQL) query Select * From SMS_Package order by Name. Instead, use Select * From SMS_Package where ActionInProgress <> 3 order by Name. If ActionInProgress=3, this package is in a "pending deletion" state. A package that you attempt to delete will be in this state until all dependencies (advertisements, distribution points, etc.) are removed.

See Also

- Recipe 4-3, "Enumerating Package and Package-Folder Structure," shows how to display package and package folders.

- Appendix C of the *SMS 2003 Operations Guide* demonstrates how to create a new package and program.

- The *SMS 2003 Scripting Guide* uses SMS_Package in some examples.

4-3. Enumerating Package and Package-Folder Structure

Problem

You want to enumerate the package and package-folder structure for packages in SMS.

Solution

In this case, to generate a report showing your package and package-folder structure, you'll want to use VBScript, as shown in Example 4-3.

Example 4-3. *EnumPackagesAndFolders.vbs*

```
strSMSServer = <SMSServer>

Set objLoc =  CreateObject("WbemScripting.SWbemLocator")
Set objSMS= objLoc.ConnectServer(strSMSServer, "root\sms")
Set Results = objSMS.ExecQuery _
    ("SELECT * From SMS_ProviderLocation WHERE ProviderForLocalSite = true")
For each Loc in Results
    If Loc.ProviderForLocalSite = True Then
        Set objSMS = objLoc.ConnectServer(Loc.Machine, "root\sms\site_" & _
            Loc.SiteCode)
            strSMSSiteCode = Loc.Sitecode
    end if
Next

'for intPackageFolder=0 enumerate from the root package node
' to enumerate from a subfolder, replace the 0 with
' the proper ContainerNodeID
intPackageFolder = 0
intSpace = 0
'First, display packages in current folder (as defined
' by intPackageFolder
ListPkgsInFolder "", intPackageFolder, intSpace
'Then enumerate all subfolders of the current folder
DisplaySubFolders intPackageFolder, intSpace + 3

Sub DisplaySubFolders(intPackageFolder, intSpace)
        Set colItems = objSMS.ExecQuery _
            ("select * from SMS_ObjectContainerNode where " & _
            "ObjectType = 2 and " & _
            "ParentContainerNodeID = " & cint(intPackageFolder))
```

```
            For each objContainerItem in colItems
                ListPkgsInFolder objContainerItem.Name, _
                    objContainerItem.ContainerNodeID,intSpace + 3
                DisplaySubFolders objContainerItem.ContainerNodeID, _
                    intSpace + 3
            Next
    End Sub

    Sub ListPkgsInFolder(strContainerName, intPkgFolder, intSpace)
        If intPkgFolder = 0 then    'we're looking at the root node here

            strSQL = "Select PackageID From SMS_Package where " & _
                "PackageID not in (select InstanceKey " & _
                "from SMS_ObjectContainerItem where ObjectType=2) " & _
                "and ImageFlags = 0"
            'ImageFlags = 0 is used to make sure we don't pick up
            'any image packages from the Operating System Deployment
            'Feature Pack (OSD FP)
            Set colPkgs = objSMS.ExecQuery(strSQL)
            wscript.echo space(intSpace) & "----" & vbCRLF & _
                space(intSpace) & "Root Collection"
            For each objPkg in colPkgs
                wscript.echo objPkg.PackageID & vbTAB & _
                    GetPackageName(objPkg.PackageID)
            Next
        Else
            Set colItems = objSMS.ExecQuery _
                ("select * from SMS_ObjectContainerItem where " & _
                "ObjectType = 2 and " & _
                "ContainerNodeID = " & cint(intPkgFolder))
            wscript.echo space(intSpace) & "----" & vbCRLF & _
                space(intSpace) &   strContainerName
            For each objContainerItem in colItems
                strPackageID = objContainerItem.InstanceKey
                wscript.echo space(intSpace) & strPackageID & vbTAB & _
                    GetPackageName(strPackageID)
            Next
        End If
    End Sub

    Function GetPackageName(strPckID)
        Set objPackage = GetObject( "WinMgmts:\\" & strSMSServer & _
            "\root\SMS\site_" & strSMSSiteCode & _
            ":SMS_Package.PackageID='" & strPckID & "'")
        GetPackageName =  objPackage.Name & vbTAB & objPackage.Version
    End Function
```

Discussion

In Example 4-3, we enumerate the package and package-folder structure in the SMS environment.
intPackageFolder is set to the desired folder to begin enumeration. Setting intPackageFolder to
zero will start enumeration from the root of packages. If you only want to enumerate the information of a subfolder, enter the package folder number (ContainerNodeID) for intPackageFolder.
intSpace is used to allow for indentation to display the tree structure. We first call ListPkgsInFolder

to list all packages in the desired base folder. We then call `DisplaySubFolders` to start the recursive process of enumerating subfolders and the contents of the subfolders.

The `DisplayFolders` subroutine is used to enumerate all subfolders of the desired folder. Here are the basic steps of `DisplayFolders`:

1. Performs a query for all subfolders of type package (`ObjectType=2`)

2. For each subfolder,

    - Calls `ListPkgsInFolder` to display the packages in each subfolder

    - Calls `DisplaySubFolders` (recursive call) to repeat the same process for the subfolder

The `ListPkgsInFolder` subroutine is used to enumerate all nonimage packages in a folder. A special case is created for when we're querying for the root node (`intPkgFolder=0`). Our WQL query is for all packages in `SMS_Package` that do not have a subfolder associated with them and are not an Operating System Deployment (OSD) package (`ImageFlags=0`). If `intPkgFolder` does not equal zero, we perform a WQL query to display all packages (`ObjectType=2`) that belong to the specified folder (`ContainerNodeID`). The `GetPackageName` subroutine is used to obtain the package name, given the `PackageID`.

See Also

- Recipe 4-1, "Creating a Package," shows how to create a package.

- Recipe 4-2, "Determining a Package's PackageID," demonstrates how to enumerate all packages by package name and `PackageID`.

- Recipes 4-17 and 4-18 demonstrate how to create package folders and move packages between folders.

- The SMS 2003 SDK provides more detail about the SMS classes used in this example.

4-4. Deleting a Package

Problem

You want to delete a package.

Solution: Using a Graphical Interface

1. Open the SMS Administrator console.

2. From the SMS Administrator console, expand Site Database (*<Site Code>*), and then expand Packages.

3. Expand any folders that contain the package you need to delete.

4. Right-click the package and select Delete from the menu to launch the Delete Package Wizard.

5. Click Next on the welcome screen of the Delete Package Wizard.

6. Click Next to see additional information on the effect of deleting this collection. If you are absolutely sure that you want to delete it, then select that option before proceeding.

7. Review programs that will be affected. Click Next.

8. Review advertisements that will be affected. Click Next.

9. Review distribution points that will be affected. Click Next.

10. Review access accounts that will be affected. Click Next.

11. Review administrative rights that will be affected. Click Next.

12. Confirm your choice to delete the package. Click Next.

13. Click Finish to exit the Delete Package Wizard.

Solution: Using VBScript

Example 4-4 demonstrates how to delete a package using VBScript.

Example 4-4. *DeletePackage.vbs*

```
strSMSServer = <SMSServer>

strPackageID = "LAB000CC"

Set objLoc =  CreateObject("WbemScripting.SWbemLocator")
Set objSMS= objLoc.ConnectServer(strSMSServer, "root\sms")
Set Results = objSMS.ExecQuery _
    ("SELECT * From SMS_ProviderLocation WHERE ProviderForLocalSite = true")
For each Loc in Results
    If Loc.ProviderForLocalSite = True Then
        Set objSMS = objLoc.ConnectServer(Loc.Machine, "root\sms\site_" & _
            Loc.SiteCode)
            strSMSSiteCode = Loc.Sitecode
    end if
Next

'Remove Package
Set objPackage = GetObject( "WinMgmts:\\" & strSMSServer & _
    "\root\SMS\site_" & strSMSSiteCode & _
    ":SMS_Package.PackageID='" & strPackageID & "'")
objPackage.Delete_
wscript.echo "Deleted " & strPackageID
```

Discussion

The Delete Package Wizard provides an efficient way to keep your SMS environment and Adminis-trator console neat and tidy. If you have a package that is no longer needed, deleting it will clean up the console by removing the package from all distribution points along with the associated adver-tisements, programs, and security rights. Deleting a package using VBScript as shown in Example 4-4 also automatically removes all package dependencies.

See Also

- Recipe 4-1, "Creating a Package," demonstrates how to create a package.

- The *SMS 2003 Scripting Guide* provides more information about deleting objects from SMS.

- The SMS 2003 SDK provides more detail about SMS _Package and property information for SMS _Package.

4-5. Changing Package Source Location

Problem

You want to change the source location of a package. For example, perhaps you have added a new disk to your distribution system, and you want to move several package sources to that new drive (to free up space on your first drive).

Solution: Using a Graphical Interface

1. Open the SMS Administrator console.

2. From the SMS Administrator console, expand Site Database (<*Site Code*>), and then expand Packages.

3. Expand any folders that contain the package you need to modify.

4. Right-click the package and select Properties.

5. Select the Data Source tab in the Package Properties dialog box.

6. Click the Set button to change the location of the package source files.

7. Click OK to apply the settings.

Solution: Using VBScript

Example 4-5 demonstrates how to modify the package source location using VBScript.

Example 4-5. *ModPkgSourceLocation.vbs*

```
strSMSServer = <SMSServer>

strPackageID = "LAB0000A"
strSourcePath = "\\smsvpc\Source\867460_1.1SP1"

Set objLoc =  CreateObject("WbemScripting.SWbemLocator")
Set objSMS= objLoc.ConnectServer(strSMSServer, "root\sms")
Set Results = objSMS.ExecQuery _
    ("SELECT * From SMS_ProviderLocation WHERE ProviderForLocalSite = true")
For each Loc in Results
    If Loc.ProviderForLocalSite = True Then
        Set objSMS = objLoc.ConnectServer(Loc.Machine, "root\sms\site_" & _
            Loc.SiteCode)
            strSMSSiteCode = Loc.Sitecode
    end if
Next

Set objPackage = GetObject( "WinMgmts:!\\" & strSMSServer & _
    "\root\SMS\site_" & strSMSSiteCode & _
    ":SMS_Package.PackageID='" & strPackageID & "'")
objPackage.PkgSourceFlag = 2 ' specifies direct source
objPackage.PkgSourcePath = strSourcePath
objPackage.Put_
```

Discussion

SMS doesn't manage source data for you, so if you find that you need to clean up your source data structure, you need to change locations for the affected packages. However, when you change the source location of a package, SMS will automatically refresh the package on all distribution points.

Caution Changing the package source location will cause an automatic update of distribution points for the package. Depending on your network and bandwidth throttling (discussed in Chapter 2 and Recipe 4-7), you may want to avoid modifying the package source during peak network utilization periods.

Example 4-5 obtains the package from SMS_Package and ensures that PkgSourceFlag=2 (which specifies the files are taken directly from the source without compression), and then it sets the new source path. Options for PkgSourceFlag are as follows:

- 1: No source files are required for this package.
- 2: Source files are taken directly from the source without compression.
- 3: Source files are compressed and copied to the site server.

See Also

- Recipe 4-11, "Adding a Package to Distribution Points," demonstrates how to add a package to a distribution point.
- The SMS 2003 SDK provides details for the SMS_Package class.
- Appendix C of the *SMS 2003 Operations Guide* provides an example of setting the package source during package creation.

4-6. Modifying How the Package Is Accessed

Problem

You want to modify how a package is accessed on the distribution point.

Solution: Using a Graphical Interface

1. Open the SMS Administrator console.
2. From the SMS Administrator console, expand Site Database (*<Site Code>*), and then expand Packages.
3. Expand any folders that contain the package you need to modify.
4. Right-click the package and select Properties.
5. Select the Data Access tab in the Package Properties dialog box.
6. Choose either the common SMS package or share, or specify your own.
7. Select the "Disconnect users from distribution points" check box if you want to control the time limit and retries of the SMS client.
8. Click OK to apply the settings.

Solution: Using VBScript

Example 4-6 demonstrates how to modify package properties using VBScript.

Example 4-6. *ModPkgProps.vbs*

```
strSMSServer = <SMSServer>

strPackageID = "LAB0000A"
intDisconnectDelay = 5
blnDisconnectEnabled = True
intDisconnectNumRetries = 2

Set objLoc = CreateObject("WbemScripting.SWbemLocator")
Set objSMS= objLoc.ConnectServer(strSMSServer, "root\sms")
Set Results = objSMS.ExecQuery _
    ("SELECT * From SMS_ProviderLocation WHERE ProviderForLocalSite = true")
For each Loc in Results
    If Loc.ProviderForLocalSite = True Then
        Set objSMS = objLoc.ConnectServer(Loc.Machine, "root\sms\site_" & _
            Loc.SiteCode)
            strSMSSiteCode = Loc.Sitecode
    end if
Next

Set objPackage = GetObject( "WinMgmts:!\\" & strSMSServer & _
    "\root\SMS\site_" & strSMSSiteCode & _
    ":SMS_Package.PackageID='" & strPackageID & "'")
objPackage.ForcedDisconnectDelay = intDisconnectDelay
objPackage.ForcedDisconnectEnabled = blnDisconnectEnabled
objPackage.ForcedDisconnectNumRetries = intDisconnectNumRetries
objPackage.Put_
```

Discussion

If you don't like the way SMS stores packages on the distribution points, you can create your own structure. However, understand that doing so adds an extra step to every package you create.

You may experience difficulty updating distribution points for packages that update frequently and for packages whose programs are run frequently (i.e., antivirus updates). For such packages, you will want to set the disconnection limits in the package that gets updated even if it means that some clients fail to run the program because they were disconnected. This ensures that the latest version of the package is available as soon as possible.

The VBScript in Example 4-6 demonstrates how to add or modify the Package Update settings on the Data Access tab of the package properties. You can also configure these settings when programmatically creating a new package.

See Also

- Recipe 4-1, "Creating a Package," demonstrates how to create a package.
- The SMS 2003 SDK provides additional information for SMS_Package.

4-7. Modifying the Distribution Settings of a Package

Problem

You want to modify the distribution settings of a package.

Solution: Using a Graphical Interface

1. Open the SMS Administrator console.

2. From the SMS Administrator console, expand Site Database (<*Site Code*>), and then expand Packages.

3. Expand any folders that contain the package that you need to modify.

4. Right-click the package and select Properties.

5. Select the Distribution Settings tab in the Package Properties dialog box.

6. Select a sending priority from the drop-down list.

7. Select a preferred sender from the drop-down list.

8. Click OK to apply the settings.

Solution: Using VBScript

Example 4-7 demonstrates how to modify package distribution settings using VBScript.

Example 4-7. *ModPkg-DPSettings.vbs*

```
strSMSServer = <SMSServer>

strPackageID = "LAB000CE"
strPreferredAddressType = "SMS_LAN_SENDER"
intPriority = 1

Set objLoc =  CreateObject("WbemScripting.SWbemLocator")
Set objSMS= objLoc.ConnectServer(strSMSServer, "root\sms")
Set Results = objSMS.ExecQuery _
    ("SELECT * From SMS_ProviderLocation WHERE ProviderForLocalSite = true")
For each Loc in Results
    If Loc.ProviderForLocalSite = True Then
        Set objSMS = objLoc.ConnectServer(Loc.Machine, "root\sms\site_" & _
            Loc.SiteCode)
            strSMSSiteCode = Loc.Sitecode
    end if
Next

Set objPackage = objSMS.Get("SMS_Package.PackageID='" & strPackageID & "'")
objPackage.PreferredAddressType = strPreferredAddressType
objPackage.Priority = intPriority
objPackage.Put_
```

Discussion

If you have a number of slow links that you need to traverse with your SMS hierarchy, then the package distribution settings will be vital to your software distribution strategy. For those slow link sites, you can set the address to only send medium- or high-priority communication during business hours. This procedure is helpful only if you change your packages to use a sending priority of "low." If the priorities are set correctly, those low-priority packages will be delivered automatically after business hours, when the network is not being used heavily.

Example 4-7 shows another basic modification to the package. The following are the available values for `PreferredAddressType`:

- `SMS_ASYNC_RAS_SENDER`
- `SMS_COURIER_SENDER`
- `SMS_ISDN_RAS_SENDER`
- `SMS_LAN_SENDER`
- `SMS_SNA_RAS_SENDER`
- `SMS_X25_RAS_SENDER`

Three values are available for priority: High (1), Normal (2), and Low (3).

You can also configure address type and priority settings when programmatically creating a new package.

See Also

- Recipe 4-1, "Creating a Package," demonstrates how to create a package.
- The SMS 2003 SDK provides additional information for `SMS_Package`.

4-8. Modifying the Management Information Format Settings of a Package

Problem

You want to modify the Management Information Format (MIF) settings of a package.

Solution: Using a Graphical Interface

1. Open the SMS Administrator console.
2. From the SMS Administrator console, expand Site Database (<*Site Code*>), and then expand Packages.
3. Expand any folders that contain the package you need to modify.
4. Right-click the package and select Properties.
5. Select the Reporting tab in the Package Properties dialog box.
6. Choose whether to use the package properties for status MIF matching or supply your own.
7. Click OK to apply the settings.

Discussion

Status MIF files are created after every program is run for a package. These MIF files are used to report the success or failure of the program and are identified by the associated package information during processing. If you have a number of similarly named packages, you may run into a problem with conflicting MIF file names. It is best to provide as much information as possible in a package, or to provide specific MIF data for the package. Doing so will eliminate the possibility of conflicting status MIFs. Also, too little information may cause a MIF to not get matched to a package, causing it to be discarded and the status of the program to be unknown.

MIF settings for a package can also be created or modified programmatically. Review the SMS_Package class for more information about the package properties MIFFileName, MIFName, MIFPublisher, and MIFVersion.

See Also

- Chapter 5 of the *SMS 2003 Operations Guide* provides information on using status MIFs.

- Appendix B of the *Scenarios and Procedures for Microsoft SMS 2003: Software Distribution and Patch Management* guide provides additional details for status MIFs.

4-9. Modifying Permissions of a Package

Problem

You want to modify a package's permissions.

Solution: Using a Graphical Interface

1. Open the SMS Administrator console.

2. From the SMS Administrator console, expand Site Database (*<Site Code>*), and then expand Packages.

3. Expand any folders that contain the package you need to modify.

4. Right-click the package and select Properties.

5. Select the Security tab in the Package Properties dialog box.

6. Click the New or Delete button to add or remove class or instance security rights. You can also double-click any existing class or instance rights to modify them.

7. Click OK to apply the settings.

Solution: Using VBScript

Example 4-8 demonstrates how to grant the help desk Read, Modify, and Distribute permissions to PackageID = LAB00007.

Example 4-8. *ModPkgPerms.vbs*

```
strSMSServer = <SMSServer>

strHelpDesk="SMSVPC\Help Desk"
strPackageID="LAB00007"

Set objLoc =  CreateObject("WbemScripting.SWbemLocator")
Set objSMS= objLoc.ConnectServer(strSMSServer, "root\sms")
Set Results = objSMS.ExecQuery _
    ("SELECT * From SMS_ProviderLocation WHERE ProviderForLocalSite = true")
For each Loc in Results
    If Loc.ProviderForLocalSite = True Then
        Set objSMS = objLoc.ConnectServer(Loc.Machine, "root\sms\site_" & _
            Loc.SiteCode)
```

```
            strSMSSiteCode = Loc.Sitecode
    end if
Next

Set objPackage = objSMS.Get("SMS_Package.PackageID='" & strPackageID & "'")
wscript.echo objPackage.PackageID
Set objNewRight = objSMS.Get _
    ("SMS_UserInstancePermissions").SpawnInstance_()
objNewRight.UserName = strHelpDesk
objNewRight.ObjectKey = 2 'package
objNewRight.InstanceKey = objPackage.PackageID
objNewRight.InstancePermissions = 11
    '0000000000001011 (read, modify, distribute)
objNewRight.Put_
```

Discussion

Package permissions allow you to control exactly who has access to manage a package's properties. This control is important if you have distributed your SMS administration among several people or departments. Leveraging package permissions along with enforcing stringent security of your distribution points can make your packages virtually bulletproof.

In Example 4-8, we obtain a new object to the package, create a new instance of SMS_UserInstancePermissions, and set appropriate permissions for a user or group. We set ObjectKey to 2 because we're modifying instance rights to a package. Notice that InstancePermissions is equal to 11.

Table 4-1 describes the bit fields for the InstancePermissions property for the SMS_UserInstanacePermissions class. You can see that a permissions value of 11 translates to Read, Modify, and Distribute permissions.

Table 4-1. *Bit Fields for the InstancePermissions Property*

Permission	Bit Position	Binary Representation (Integer Value)
Read	0	0000000000000001 (1)
Modify	1	0000000000000010 (2)
Delete	2	0000000000000100 (4)
Distribute	3	0000000000001000 (8)
Create Child	4	0000000000010000 (16)
Remote Control	5	0000000000100000 (32)
Advertise	6	0000000001000000 (64)
Modify Resource	7	0000000010000000 (128)
Administer	8	0000000100000000 (256)
Delete Resource	9	0000001000000000 (512)
Create	10	0000010000000000 (1024)
View Collected Files	11	0000100000000000 (2048)
Read Resource	12	0001000000000000 (4096)
Delegate	13	0010000000000000 (8192)
Meter	14	0100000000000000 (16384)
Manage SQL Command	15	01000000000000000 (32768)
Manage Status Filters	16	10000000000000000 (65536)

As you can see from the Integer Value column in Table 4-1, each bit position represents a specific permission. Table 4-2 lists the three bit positions required for the permissions we desire.

Table 4-2. *Bit Field Values for the Read, Modify, and Distribute Permissions*

Permission	Bit Position
Read	00000000000000001 (1)
Modify	00000000000000010 (2)
Distribute	00000000000001000 (8)

Example 4-8 uses *bit ORing* (pronounced *OR-ring*) to create one binary number with all three bit positions set. The number we obtain is 00000000000001011, which when translated to decimal equals 11. If, instead of Read, Modify, and Distribute permissions, we wanted to grant Delete, Distribute, Modify, and Read, we would use bit ORing to obtain a binary number of 00000000000001111, which is 15 in decimal. Then we would set InstancePermissions = 15 to grant the help desk Delete, Distribute, Modify, and Read permissions.

Not all of the permission settings shown in Table 4-1 work on all objects. For example, if you try to set the Meter permissions for a package, your code will fail.

See Also

- Recipe 3-16, "Modifying Permissions of a Collection," provides an example of setting instance permissions on a collection.

- The *SMS 2003 Operations Guide* provides example VBScript for setting instance permissions.

- The SMS 2003 SDK provides details for the SMS_UserInstancePermissions class.

4-10. Updating Distribution Points on a Schedule

Problem

You want to automatically update distribution points on a schedule.

Solution: Using a Graphical Interface

1. Open the SMS Administrator console.

2. From the SMS Administrator console, expand Site Database (*<Site Code>*), and then expand Packages.

3. Expand any folders that contain the package you need to modify.

4. Right-click the package and select Properties.

5. Select the Data Source tab in the Package Properties dialog box.

6. Select the "Update distribution points on a schedule" check box.

7. Click the Schedule button to set the frequency with which the package is updated on the distribution points.

8. Click OK. The new schedule will be shown in the Package Properties dialog box.

9. Click OK to apply the settings.

Solution: Using VBScript

Example 4-9 demonstrates how to create a schedule to update distribution points for a given package on a weekly schedule.

Example 4-9. *UpdateDP_Sched.vbs*

```
Const STORAGE_DIRECT=2
strSMSServer = <SMSServer>
strPackageID = "LAB0000A"

Set objLoc =  CreateObject("WbemScripting.SWbemLocator")
Set objSMS= objLoc.ConnectServer(strSMSServer, "root\sms")
Set Results = objSMS.ExecQuery _
    ("SELECT * From SMS_ProviderLocation WHERE ProviderForLocalSite = true")
For each Loc in Results
    If Loc.ProviderForLocalSite = True Then
        Set objSMS = objLoc.ConnectServer(Loc.Machine, "root\sms\site_" & _
            Loc.SiteCode)
            strSMSSiteCode = Loc.Sitecode
    end if
Next

Set Token = objSMS.Get("SMS_ST_RecurWeekly")
Token.Day = 5 'Thursday
Token.DayDuration = 0 'recur indefinitely
Token.ForNumberOfWeeks = 1 'recur every 1 week
Token.StartTime = "20061202103000.000000+***" 'wmi date-string
'If omitted, StartTime = Jan 1, 1990 - this shouldn't
'cause any issues

Set objPackage = objSMS.Get _
    ("SMS_Package.PackageID='" & strPackageID & "'")
'Make sure package is set to "Always obtain files
' from source directory, then add schedule.
if objPackage.PkgSourceFlag=STORAGE_DIRECT then
    objPackage.RefreshSchedule = Array(Token)
    objPackage.Put_
end if
```

Discussion

The option to update the distribution points on a schedule can greatly reduce your administrative load for those packages that get updated frequently. If you deploy an update to an application every Thursday night, for example, you can schedule the update of the distribution points to happen before the advertisement is scheduled to run. This means you only have to ensure the source file is updated—the rest is automatic.

The VBScript in Example 4-9 demonstrates how to set a recurring interval of once daily deployment (beginning on December 2, 2006, at 10:30 a.m.) for a package. We create an SMS_ST_RecurWeekly token of Day=5 (Thursday), DayDuration=0 (recur indefinitely), and ForNumberOfWeeks=1 (recur every week), and then set the StartTime. Next, we verify that the package is set to "Always obtain files from source directory" because the recurring package refresh only works with this option. We then modify the package, inserting the refresh schedule.

Notice that the start time is December 2, 2006, at 10:30 a.m. (equivalent to the WMI date string 20061202103000). Since December 2, 2006, is a Saturday, the first package refresh on the schedule will be the following Thursday, December 7, 2006, at 10:30 a.m., because we specified the refresh to occur every Thursday.

Token.StartTime is a Windows Management Instrumentation (WMI) date string. The following function converts a standard date to a WMI date string:

```
wscript.echo ConvertToWMIDate(Now())

Function ConvertToWMIDate(strDate)
    strYear = year(strDate)
    strMonth = month(strDate)
    strDay = day(strDate)
    strHour = hour(strDate)
    strMinute = minute(strDate)
    'pad date appropriately
    if len(strmonth) = 1 then strMonth = "0" & strMonth
    if len(strDay) = 1 then strDay = "0" & strDay
    if len(strHour) = 1 then strHour = "0" & strHour
    if len(strMinute) = 1 then strMinute = "0" & strMinute
    ConvertToWMIDate = strYear & strMonth & strDay & strHour & _
        strMinute & "00.000000+***"
end function
```

See Also

- Recipe 4-14, "Updating Distribution Points," shows how to force an immediate update of distribution points for a package.

- Recipe 4-15, "Refreshing Distribution Points," demonstrates how to refresh a possibly corrupted distribution point.

- Recipe 3-12, "Setting the Update Collection Interval," provides a solution that uses SMS_ST_RecurInterval so that you can configure a daily update schedule.

- The SMS 2003 SDK provides additional information about SMS_ST_RecurWeekly.

4-11. Adding a Package to Distribution Points

Problem

You want to add a package to a distribution point.

Solution: Using a Graphical Interface

1. Open the SMS Administrator console.

2. From the SMS Administrator console, expand Site Database (<*Site Code*>), and then expand Packages.

3. Expand any folders that contain the package that you need to modify.

4. Right-click the package you want to add to distribution points and select All Tasks ➤ Manage Distribution Points.

5. Click Next on the welcome screen of the Manage Distribution Points Wizard.

6. Choose the "Copy the package to new distribution points" radio button. Click Next.

7. Check the box next to each of the distribution points that you would like to copy to the package. Click Next.

8. Click Finish to exit the Manage Distribution Points Wizard.

Solution: Using VBScript

Two VBScript examples are provided in this recipe. Example 4-10 demonstrates how to add a package to all distribution points that belong to a specific site code. Example 4-11 demonstrates how to add a package to all distribution points (similar to choosing Select All in the Administrator console when you select distribution points).

Example 4-10. *LoadDPs_OneSite.vbs*

```
strSMSServer = <SMSServer>

strSiteCode = "BLO" 'this is the site code of the DP to add
PackageID = "LAB0000A"

Set objLoc =  CreateObject("WbemScripting.SWbemLocator")
Set objSMS= objLoc.ConnectServer(strSMSServer, "root\sms")
Set Results = objSMS.ExecQuery _
    ("SELECT * From SMS_ProviderLocation WHERE ProviderForLocalSite = true")
For each Loc in Results
    If Loc.ProviderForLocalSite = True Then
        Set objSMS = objLoc.ConnectServer(Loc.Machine, "root\sms\site_" & _
            Loc.SiteCode)
            strSMSSiteCode = Loc.Sitecode
    end if
Next

Set AllDPs = objSMS.ExecQuery _
    ("Select * From SMS_SystemResourceList WHERE " & _
    "RoleName='SMS Distribution Point' and " & _
    "SiteCode='" & strSiteCode & "'")
For Each DP In AllDPs
    Wscript.echo DP.SiteCode & vbTAB & DP.ServerName
    Set Site = objSMS.Get("SMS_Site='" & DP.SiteCode & "'")
    Set newDP = objSMS.Get _
        ("SMS_DistributionPoint").SpawnInstance_()
    newDP.ServerNALPath = DP.NALPath
    newDP.PackageID = PackageID
    newDP.SiteCode = DP.SiteCode
    newDP.SiteName = Site.SiteName
    newDP.Put_
Next
```

Example 4-11. *LoadDPs_All.vbs*

```
strSMSServer = <SMSServer>

PackageID = "LAB0000A"

Set objLoc =  CreateObject("WbemScripting.SWbemLocator")
Set objSMS= objLoc.ConnectServer(strSMSServer, "root\sms")
Set Results = objSMS.ExecQuery _
    ("SELECT * From SMS_ProviderLocation WHERE ProviderForLocalSite = true")
For each Loc in Results
    If Loc.ProviderForLocalSite = True Then
        Set objSMS = objLoc.ConnectServer(Loc.Machine, "root\sms\site_" & _
            Loc.SiteCode)
```

```
            strSMSSiteCode = Loc.Sitecode
    end if
Next

Set AllDPs = objSMS.ExecQuery _
    ("Select * From SMS_SystemResourceList WHERE " & _
    "RoleName='SMS Distribution Point'")
For Each DP In AllDPs
    Wscript.echo DP.SiteCode & vbTAB & DP.ServerName
    Set Site = objSMS.Get("SMS_Site='" & DP.SiteCode & "'")
    Set newDP = objSMS.Get _
        ("SMS_DistributionPoint").SpawnInstance_()
    newDP.ServerNALPath = DP.NALPath
    newDP.PackageID = PackageID
    newDP.SiteCode = DP.SiteCode
    newDP.SiteName = Site.SiteName
    newDP.Put_
Next
```

Discussion

Packages are worthless if they do not get copied to distribution points (unless, of course, no package source files are required). If you are in a hurry to deploy an application and forget to copy it to a distribution point, SMS will kindly remind you of this before you are able to create an advertisement.

Example 4-10's solution targets all distribution points for a specific site, because the WQL query contains criteria for the SiteCode. The script then enumerates all distribution points in that site and adds the PackageID to the distribution point. The second VBScript solution, in Example 4-11, targets all distribution points for the site and all child sites.

See Also

- Recipe 4-1, "Creating a Package," demonstrates how to create a package.

- Recipe 4-12, "Removing a Package from Distribution Points," shows how to remove one package from all distribution points.

- Recipe 4-13, "Removing All Packages from a Distribution Point," demonstrates how to remove all packages from a distribution point.

- The SMS 2003 SDK provides additional information about SMS_DistributionPoint.

- Appendix C of the *SMS 2003 Operations Guide* demonstrates how to add a package to all distribution points.

4-12. Removing a Package from Distribution Points

Problem

You want to remove a package from distribution points.

Solution: Using a Graphical Interface

1. Open the SMS Administrator console.

2. From the SMS Administrator console, expand Site Database (*<Site Code>*), and then expand Packages.

3. Expand any folders that contain the package you need to modify.

4. Right-click the package you want to delete to distribution points and select All Tasks ➤ Manage Distribution Points.

5. Click Next on the welcome screen of the Manage Distribution Points Wizard.

6. Choose the "Remove the package from selected distribution points" radio button. Click Next.

7. Check the box next to each of the distribution points you would like to remove from the package. Click Next.

8. Click Finish to exit the Manage Distribution Points Wizard.

Solution: Using VBScript

Two examples are provided in this recipe. Example 4-12 demonstrates how to remove a package from all distribution points for one SMS site. Example 4-13 demonstrates how to remove a package from all distribution points for the current site and all child sites.

Example 4-12. *RemoveFromDPs_OneSite.vbs*

```
strSMSServer = <SMSServer>

strSiteCode="BLO"
strPackageID = "LABOOOOA"

Set objLoc = CreateObject("WbemScripting.SWbemLocator")
Set objSMS= objLoc.ConnectServer(strSMSServer, "root\sms")
Set Results = objSMS.ExecQuery _
    ("SELECT * From SMS_ProviderLocation WHERE ProviderForLocalSite = true")
For each Loc in Results
    If Loc.ProviderForLocalSite = True Then
        Set objSMS = objLoc.ConnectServer(Loc.Machine, "root\sms\site_" & _
            Loc.SiteCode)
            strSMSSiteCode = Loc.Sitecode
    end if
Next

Set AllDPs = objSMS.ExecQuery _
    ("Select * From SMS_DistributionPoint where " & _
    "PackageID = '" & strPackageID & "'")
for each DP in AllDPs
    if DP.SiteCode = strSiteCode then
        wscript.echo DP.ServerNALPath
        DP.Delete_
    end if
next
```

Example 4-13. *RemoveFromAllDPs.vbs*

```
strSMSServer = <SMSServer>

strPackageID = "LABOOOOA"

Set objLoc = CreateObject("WbemScripting.SWbemLocator")
Set objSMS = objLoc.ConnectServer(strSMSServer, "root\sms")
Set Results = objSMS.ExecQuery _
```

```
    ("SELECT * From SMS_ProviderLocation WHERE ProviderForLocalSite = true")
For each Loc in Results
    If Loc.ProviderForLocalSite = True Then
        Set objSMS = objLoc.ConnectServer(Loc.Machine, "root\sms\site_" & _
            Loc.SiteCode)
            strSMSSiteCode = Loc.Sitecode
    end if
Next

Set AllDPs = objSMS.ExecQuery _
    ("Select * From SMS_DistributionPoint where " & _
    "PackageID = '" & strPackageID & "'")
for each DP in AllDPs
        wscript.echo "Removing " & DP.ServerNALPath
        DP.Delete_
next
```

Discussion

If you have a distribution point that is running out of disk space, the easiest way to free some space is to remove packages that you no longer need. You will be able to select only the distribution package that needs space, leaving all others intact.

The first VBScript solution (Example 4-12) targets all distribution points for a specific site, and the second VBScript solution (Example 4-13) targets all distribution points for this site and all child sites. Use caution when running these scripts in your production environment. *Triple-check* the PackageID to ensure you're removing only what you intend to remove.

See Also

- Recipe 4-11, "Adding a Package to Distribution Points," demonstrates how to add a package to all distribution points.

- Recipe 4-13, "Removing All Packages from a Distribution Point," demonstrates how to remove all packages from a distribution point.

- The SMS 2003 SDK provides additional information about SMS_DistributionPoint.

- Appendix C of the *SMS 2003 Operations Guide* provides some information about managing distribution points using VBScript.

4-13. Removing All Packages from a Distribution Point

Problem

You want to remove all packages from a distribution point.

Solution

Example 4-14 demonstrates how to remove all packages from a distribution point using VBScript. To accomplish this task using the graphical user interface would require you to navigate through each package and use the Manage Distribution Points Wizard to remove a specific distribution point for a package.

Example 4-14. *UnloadOneDP.vbs*

```
strSMSServer = <SMSServer>'primary site server

strSMSSiteCodeforDP = <SMSDPSiteCode>'site code that
                        ' contains packages to remove
strServerSharePath = "\\sms-testgmr\smspkgd$"
                        'partial package path

Set objLoc =  CreateObject("WbemScripting.SWbemLocator")
Set objSMS= objLoc.ConnectServer(strSMSServer, "root\sms")
Set Results = objSMS.ExecQuery _
    ("SELECT * From SMS_ProviderLocation WHERE ProviderForLocalSite = true")
For each Loc in Results
    If Loc.ProviderForLocalSite = True Then
        Set objSMS = objLoc.ConnectServer(Loc.Machine, "root\sms\site_" & _
            Loc.SiteCode)
            strSMSSiteCode = Loc.Sitecode
    end if
Next

Set objDPs = objSMS.ExecQuery("select * from " & _
    "SMS_DistributionPoint where SiteCode = '" & _
    strSMSSiteCodeforDP & "'")

For each objDP in objDPs
    if instr(ucase(objDP.ServerNALPath), _
        ucase(strServerSharePath)) then
          wscript.echo "Removing " & objDP.PackageID & _
              vbTAB & objDP.ServerNALPath
          objDP.Delete_
    end if
Next
```

Discussion

In Example 4-14, we connect to the primary site and query it for all distribution points. Our code uses the placeholder <*SMSDPSiteCode*> to represent the site code. (Replace <*SMSDPSiteCode*> with the code number identifying your site.) We then enumerate each package on the distribution point, and look for distribution points that contain the ServerNALPath of strServerSharePath and delete them. By adding the filter for the correct share path, we prevent removing all distribution points for a site. If you desire to remove all distribution points from a site, simply remove the if-end if in the for-each loop.

Caution Be very careful when using Example 4-14! Accidentally inserting the wrong site codes into this script may cause you to have a really bad day.

Always test a script such as Example 4-14 before running it in production. In fact, when we're ready to run something like that in production, we comment out the action line (in this case, objDP.Delete_) to first see what is going to be removed. Once we're positive of the action, and of the consequences, we then uncomment the action line and proceed with caution.

See Also

- Recipe 4-11, "Adding a Package to Distribution Points," demonstrates how to add a package to all distribution points.

- Recipe 4-13, "Removing All Packages from a Distribution Point," demonstrates how to remove all packages from a distribution point.

- The SMS 2003 SDK contains detailed information about the SMS_DistributionPoint class.

- Appendix C of the *SMS 2003 Operations Guide* provides information about managing distribution points using VBScript.

4-14. Updating Distribution Points

Problem

You want to update distribution points for a specific package.

Solution: Using a Graphical Interface

1. Open the SMS Administrator console.

2. From the SMS Administrator console, expand Site Database (<*Site Code*>), and then expand Packages.

3. Expand any folders that contain the package you need to modify.

4. Right-click the package for which you want to update the distribution points and select All Tasks ➤ Update Distribution Points.

5. Click Yes in response to the warning that this will update all distribution points and may take some time.

Solution: Using VBScript

Example 4-15 demonstrates how to manually initiate the update distribution points task using VBScript.

Example 4-15. *UpdateDPs.vbs*

```
strSMSServer = <SMSServer>
strPackageID = "LAB000BD"

Set objLoc =  CreateObject("WbemScripting.SWbemLocator")
Set objSMS= objLoc.ConnectServer(strSMSServer, "root\sms")
Set Results = objSMS.ExecQuery _
  ("SELECT * From SMS_ProviderLocation WHERE ProviderForLocalSite = true")
For each Loc in Results
  If Loc.ProviderForLocalSite = True Then
    Set objSMS = objLoc.ConnectServer(Loc.Machine, "root\sms\site_" & _
        Loc.SiteCode)
    strSMSSiteCode = Loc.SiteCode
  end if
Next


Set objPkg = objSMS.Get _
    ("SMS_Package.PackageID=""" & strPackageID & """")
objPkg.RefreshPkgSource(0)
```

Discussion

Updating distribution points is a simple but powerful task. If you are working on a 2GB package of a client image, you want to be careful when you update your distribution points with a new version of the package, as moving that much data could have a dramatic impact on your network. This recipe's solution always updates all distribution points that contain the package in question. You can't select a subset of distribution points to update; it's all or nothing. However, with SMS 2003, some of the pain of updating distribution points has been alleviated by delta updates. When you add files to a package source, SMS will only copy the new files to the distribution point, instead of copying the entire package again. This is known as *delta replication*—only the files that have changed are copied.

Example 4-15 does the exact same thing using VBScript that the GUI solution does. It updates distribution points for all distribution points configured for a package. If the package is configured to use compressed source files, then those source files (CD, flash drive, etc.) *must* be in a ready state when the RefreshPkgSource method is executed.

See Also

- Recipe 4-10, "Updating Distribution Points on a Schedule," demonstrates how to configure the package to automatically update distribution points on the schedule you desire.

- Recipe 4-15, "Refreshing Distribution Points," shows how to refresh a single distribution point or multiple distribution points.

- Recipes 4-12, "Removing a Package from Distribution Points," and 4-13, "Removing All Packages from a Distribution Point," show how to remove one or more packages from multiple distribution points.

- Recipe 4-11, "Adding a Package to Distribution Points," demonstrates how to add a package to all distribution points.

- The SMS 2003 SDK provides additional information about the method RefreshPkgSource.

- Chapter 5 of the *SMS 2003 Operations Guide* provides more information about the differences between updating and refreshing distribution points.

- Appendix C of the *SMS 2003 Operations Guide* provides information about managing distribution points using VBScript.

4-15. Refreshing Distribution Points

Problem

You want to refresh specific distribution points for a certain package.

Solution: Using a Graphical Interface

1. Open the SMS Administrator console.

2. From the SMS Administrator console, expand Site Database (<*Site Code*>), and then expand Packages.

3. Expand any folders that contain the package you need to modify.

4. Right-click the package to which you want to refresh distribution points and select All Tasks ➤ Manage Distribution Points.

5. Click Next on the welcome screen of the Manage Distribution Points Wizard.

6. Choose the "Refresh the package on selected distribution points" radio button. Click Next.

7. Check the box next to each of the distribution points that you would like to refresh with a new copy of the package. Click Next.

8. Click Finish to exit the Manage Distribution Points Wizard.

Solution: Using VBScript

The VBScript in Example 4-16 refreshes all distribution points that are part of the CLE site.

Example 4-16. *RefreshDPs.vbs*

```
strSMSServer = <SMSServer>

strPackageID = "LAB0000A"
StrSiteCode = "CLE"

Set objLoc =  CreateObject("WbemScripting.SWbemLocator")
Set objSMS= objLoc.ConnectServer(strSMSServer, "root\sms")
Set Results = objSMS.ExecQuery _
  ("SELECT * From SMS_ProviderLocation WHERE ProviderForLocalSite = true")
For each Loc in Results
  If Loc.ProviderForLocalSite = True Then
    Set objSMS = objLoc.ConnectServer(Loc.Machine, "root\sms\site_" & _
        Loc.SiteCode)
    strSMSSiteCode = Loc.SiteCode
  end if
Next


Set DPs = objSMS.ExecQuery _
    ("Select * From SMS_DistributionPoint " & _
    "WHERE SiteCode='" & strSiteCode & _
    "' AND PackageID='" & strPackageID & "'")
For Each DP In DPs
    DP.RefreshNow = True
    DP.Put_
Next
```

Discussion

Refreshing a distribution point would seem at first glance to be just like updating a distribution point, but the two tasks are not the same. Refreshing a distribution point recopies the compressed package source to the selected distribution point. If a compressed version of the package source does not exist, the package source is used.

Tip Use the Refresh Distribution Points option if one or more distribution points become corrupted, or if you want to manually force copying the current package source version to a distribution point. When you want to update distribution points with a new version of the package source, follow the instructions in Recipe 4-14.

See Also

- Recipe 4-14, "Updating Distribution Points," demonstrates how to update distribution points.

- The SMS 2003 SDK provides additional information about SMS_DistributionPoint.

- Chapter 5 of the *SMS 2003 Operations Guide* provides more information about the differences between updating and refreshing distribution points.

- Appendix C of the *SMS 2003 Operations Guide* demonstrates how to add a package to all distribution points.

4-16. Creating a Package from a Package Definition File

Problem

You want to create a package from a package definition file.

Solution

1. Open the SMS Administrator console.

2. From the SMS Administrator console, expand Site Database (*<Site Code>*), and then expand Packages.

3. Right-click Packages and select New ➤ Package from Definition.

4. Click Next on the welcome screen of the Create Package from Definition Wizard.

5. Choose an existing package definition or click Browse to locate your .pdf, .sms, or .msi file. Click Next.

6. Choose how SMS should handle the source files. Click Next.

7. If your package contains source files, specify the source directory. Click Next.

8. Click Finish to exit the Create Packages from Definition Wizard.

Discussion

Many manufacturers include package definition files for their applications. The package definition files create the package and any programs that are necessary for a given application. It's a good practice to use package definition files when they are supplied, as they should already contain everything you need to deploy an application successfully with SMS. Package definition files will have either a .pdf or an .sms extension.

Windows Installer (.msi) files can also be imported using the process described in this recipe. When importing a Windows Installer file, the package data (name, version, publisher, etc.) is imported from the data in the Windows Installer file. MIF matching information is also automatically imported. In addition, a default set of programs is created that will execute the application in different environments, and on a user- or system-based environment.

See Also

- Recipe 4-1, "Creating a Package," demonstrates how to create a package.

- Recipes 4-17, "Creating a Folder to Group Packages," and 4-18, "Moving Packages Between Folders," show how to manage packages in package folders.

- Chapter 5 of the *SMS 2003 Operations Guide* details how to import a package definition file.

4-17. Creating a Folder to Group Packages

Problem

You want to create package folders to organize packages.

Solution: Using a Graphical Interface

1. Open the SMS Administrator console.

2. From the SMS Administrator console, expand Site Database (*<Site Code>*), and then expand Packages.

3. Right-click Packages and select New ➤ Folder.

4. Provide a name for the folder.

5. Click OK to create the new folder.

Solution: Using VBScript

Example 4-17 demonstrates how to create a package folder in the SMS Administrator console.

Example 4-17. *CreatePackageFolder.vbs*

```
strSMSServer = <SMSServer>

strNewFolderName = "Security Patches"

Set objLoc =  CreateObject("WbemScripting.SWbemLocator")
Set objSMS= objLoc.ConnectServer(strSMSServer, "root\sms")
Set Results = objSMS.ExecQuery _
  ("SELECT * From SMS_ProviderLocation WHERE ProviderForLocalSite = true")
For each Loc in Results
  If Loc.ProviderForLocalSite = True Then
    Set objSMS = objLoc.ConnectServer(Loc.Machine, "root\sms\site_" & _
        Loc.SiteCode)
    strSMSSiteCode = Loc.SiteCode
  end if
Next


Set newFolder = objSMS.Get("SMS_ObjectContainerNode") _
    .SpawnInstance_()
newFolder.Name = strNewFolderName
newFolder.ObjectType = 2  'package
newFolder.ParentContainerNodeId = 0
newFolder.Put_
```

Discussion

Folders for packages have long been sought after by SMS administrators. Thankfully, Microsoft included that functionality in Service Pack 1 of SMS 2003. Not only do folders allow you to easily group your packages, but they also cut down on the time it takes for the SMS Administrator console to display those packages, as the console doesn't have to enumerate them all—only the ones in the current folder.

In Example 4-17, we create a folder called Security Patches in the root of the Packages folder. By setting the `ParentContainerNodeId` to zero, we create this folder in the root of the Packages node. If we wanted to make Security Patches a subfolder of an existing folder, we would add the appropriate `ParentContainerNodeID`.

Note As described in Recipe 4-2, "Determining a Package's PackageID," the easiest way to find the `ParentContainerNodeID` (and most other object IDs, for that matter) is to modify the shortcut to launch your SMS Administrator console. For example, instead of the shortcut launching `C:\SMSAdmin\bin\i386\sms.msc`, have it launch `C:\SMSAdmin\bin\i386\sms.msc /sms:nodeinfo=1`. Now, when you launch your SMS Administrator console, you can right-click any node, select Properties, and view the Node Information tab. When you view the Node Information tab on a folder, look for `ContainerNodeID=x`, where x is the ID you would use in this script.

See Also

- Recipe 4-18, "Moving Packages Between Folders," shows how to move packages between folders and from the root folder.
- The SMS Script Center Script Repository contains scripts that demonstrate managing console folders in SMS.
- The SMS 2003 SDK has a topic titled "Creating a Console Folder."

4-18. Moving Packages Between Folders

Problem

You want to move a package from one package folder to another.

Solution: Using a Graphical Interface

1. Open the SMS Administrator console.
2. From the SMS Administrator console, expand Site Database (*<Site Code>*), and then expand Packages.
3. Expand any folders that contain the packages you need to move.
4. Right-click the folder and select Move Folder items.
5. Select the packages you want to move.
6. Click Browse to select the destination folder.
7. Click OK to move the packages.

Solution: Using VBScript

Example 4-18 demonstrates how to move multiple SMS packages to a new package folder.

Example 4-18. *MovePackagesBtwnFolder.vbs*

```
strSMSServer = <SMSServer>

strPackageIDs = "LAB00004,LAB00001"
'to move more than one, separate with commas
intSourceFolder=0 'Source Folder (root node in this case)
```

```
intDestFolder=4 'Destination Folder
intObjectType=2 '2=Package for type of object

Set objLoc =  CreateObject("WbemScripting.SWbemLocator")
Set objSMS= objLoc.ConnectServer(strSMSServer, "root\sms")
Set Results = objSMS.ExecQuery _
  ("SELECT * From SMS_ProviderLocation WHERE ProviderForLocalSite = true")
For each Loc in Results
  If Loc.ProviderForLocalSite = True Then
    Set objSMS = objLoc.ConnectServer(Loc.Machine, "root\sms\site_" & _
        Loc.SiteCode)
    strSMSSiteCode = Loc.SiteCode
  end if
Next


Set objFolder = objSMS.Get("SMS_ObjectContainerItem")
arrPackageIDs = split(strPackageIDs, ",")
retval = objFolder.MoveMembers _
    (arrPackageIDs, intSourceFolder , intDestFolder , intObjectType)
```

Discussion

With the organizational capabilities of folders, you should be able to structure your packages in a logical and easy-to-find way. You aren't restricted to moving packages; you can move folders into other folders to create a structure that works for you. Don't hesitate to leverage folders, as moving packages between folders doesn't change their source locations or the locations of the packages on the distribution points.

Tip Use the Shift or Ctrl key to select multiple packages or folders before you move them.

Example 4-18 demonstrates how to move multiple packages from the root Packages node to the subfolder of your choice. To move one package, list only one PackageID in the value for strPackageIDs. To move more than one package, simply separate the IDs with commas (not spaces). Since the packages moved by Example 4-18 are presumed to currently exist in the root Packages node, intSourceFolder is set to zero. If the packages are in a subfolder, replace the zero with the appropriate ContainerNodeID. Moving packages between folders does not affect any aspect of the package other than where it is organized in the Packages node of the SMS Administrator console. All advertisements, distribution points, programs, and so forth that are associated with the package will not be affected.

Note As described in Recipe 4-2, "Determining a Package's PackageID," the easiest way to find the ParentContainerNodeID (and most other object IDs, for that matter) is to modify the shortcut to launch your SMS Administrator console. For example, instead of the shortcut launching C:\SMSAdmin\bin\i386\sms.msc, have it launch C:\SMSAdmin\bin\i386\sms.msc /sms:nodeinfo=1. Now when you launch your SMS Administrator console, you can right-click any node, select Properties, and view the Node Information tab. When you view the Node Information tab on a folder, look for ContainerNodeID=x, where x is the ID you would use in this script.

See Also

- Recipe 4-18, "Creating a Folder to Group Packages," demonstrates how to create package folders.

- The SMS 2003 SDK provides details about `SMS_ObjectContainerNodeItem` and the `MoveMembers` method.

- The SMS Script Center Script Repository contains scripts that demonstrate managing console folders in SMS.

C H A P T E R 5

■■■

Programs

The lowly program may not have its own node in the SMS administrator console like advertisements, collections, and packages, but it is no less important—it is the driving force behind every software distribution. The SMS programs for a package are the objects that specify much of the *how* the software will be installed.

Why aren't packages the same as programs? Good question. SMS packages contain the source files, distribution settings, and all programs associated with the package. An SMS program is an object that belongs to a package that provides specific information for launching a desired type of installation. One package may have several programs.

For example, say you are charged with deploying the latest version of Microsoft Office. The human resources (HR) department supervisor requires shortcuts for each Office application to be installed on the users' desktops in the HR department. Unfortunately, the finance department supervisor requires that *no* shortcuts be installed on users' desktops in the finance department. Now you're in a pickle. Fortunately, you have spent quite a bit of time checking out the forums on http://www.appdeploy.com and have become savvy enough with Office installations to know you can create two transforms to take care of this problem. You create one transform that does not install shortcuts on the desktop (let's call it finance.mst) and a second transform that does install shortcuts on the desktop (let's call it hr.mst).

Since the only difference between the two installations is the Windows Installer transform, place both transforms in one Microsoft Office source directory. Create one package that uses those source files, and two programs where the only difference is the transform used on the command line. (This book's appendix describes how to create a transform.) Now you can create two collections: one to target finance and the other to target HR. Finally, create two advertisements: one using the program that has finance.mst in the command line to target finance systems and the other using hr.mst to target HR systems.

The scenario we've just presented is just one example of using multiple programs with the same package to reduce administration and package duplication. Many other powerful options that you can leverage are tucked into SMS programs. Here are a few of our favorite program options:

Program Dependencies: If, for example, you have several patches for an application that require they be installed in a specific order (e.g., Adobe Acrobat Reader), you can create multiple programs with dependencies on each other to ensure they're run in the proper order.

Suppress Program Notifications: Use this option to hide advertisement notifications from the user.

Disable a Program: This option prevents a program from running on any system (kind of like hitting the emergency stop button on an elevator—everything stops that uses the program).

This chapter will help you tackle the various tasks associated with managing programs.

5-1. Creating a Program

Problem

You want to create a program.

Solution: Using a Graphical Interface

1. Open the SMS Administrator console.

2. From the SMS Administrator console, expand Site Database (*<Site Code>*), and expand Packages.

3. Expand any folders necessary, and expand the package that will contain the new program.

4. Right-click Programs and select New ➤ Program from the menu to open the Program Properties dialog box.

5. On the General tab, enter at least the name of the new program and a command line parameter.

6. Specify any additional parameters.

7. Click OK to create the new program.

Solution: Using VBScript

Example 5-1 demonstrates how to create a basic program.

Example 5-1. *CreateProgram.vbs*

```
strSMSServer = <SMSServer>
strPackageID = "LAB0000A"
strProgramName = "NET Framework 1.1 SP1"
strProgramCMDLine = _
    "NDP1.1sp1-KB867460-X86.exe /I /Q /L:%temp%\NetFW1.1.sp1.log"

Set objLoc =  CreateObject("WbemScripting.SWbemLocator")
Set objSMS= objLoc.ConnectServer(strSMSServer, "root\sms")
Set Results = objSMS.ExecQuery _
    ("SELECT * From SMS_ProviderLocation WHERE ProviderForLocalSite = true")
For each Loc in Results
    If Loc.ProviderForLocalSite = True Then
        Set objSMS = objLoc.ConnectServer(Loc.Machine, "root\sms\site_" & _
            Loc.SiteCode)
            strSMSSiteCode = Loc.Sitecode
    end if
Next

Set newProgram = objSMS.Get("SMS_Program").SpawnInstance_()
newProgram.PackageID = strPackageID
newProgram.ProgramName = strProgramName
newProgram.CommandLine = strProgramCMDLine
newProgram.Put_
```

Discussion

In its most basic form, a program contains a name for the program and a command. Those are the only requirements to create a program using the SMS Administrator console. In addition to the basic command, you have plenty of optional configurations that you can use to create flexible and powerful programs.

In Example 5-1, we connect to the SMS primary site where the package resides, and then we create a new instance of SMS_Program. Next, we set the three required fields to create a package using VBScript:

PackageID: Each program must be related to a package, and the PackageID must exist at the time of creating the program.

Caution To associate a program with a different package, you must delete and re-create the program—it cannot be moved.

ProgramName: The name of the program. The program name must be unique to the package.

CommandLine: The command line to be executed by SMS. Enter the command line exactly as you want the program executed. Do not include a drive letter or Universal Naming Convention (UNC) path—only include the relative path to the executable from the package source directory (which is defined in the package properties).

Finally, in Example 5-1, we save the program using the Put_ method.

Note A program name must be unique within a package. A best practice when creating a new program programmatically is to enumerate all the program names associated to the package to verify the program name doesn't currently exist.

Caution If the program name is already in use for a package, and you programmatically create a new program with the same name, the original program will be overwritten (not modified).

See Also

- Recipe 3-1, "Creating a Collection," demonstrates how to create a collection.
- Recipe 4-1, "Creating a Package," demonstrates how to create a package.
- Recipe 6-1, "Creating an Advertisement," demonstrates how to create an advertisement.
- MSDN, the SMS 2003 SDK, and the *SMS 2003 Scripting Guide* provide additional information about the SMS_Program class.
- Appendix C of the *SMS 2003 Operations Guide* provides more information about using VBScript with SMS_Program.

5-2. Deleting a Program

Problem

You want to delete a program.

Solution: Using a Graphical Interface

1. Open the SMS Administrator console.

2. From the SMS Administrator console, expand Site Database (*<Site Code>*), and expand Packages.

3. Expand any folders necessary, and expand the package that contains the program you want to delete.

4. Select Programs to display the existing programs in the right pane.

5. In the right pane, select the program and open the Delete Program Wizard by either pressing the Delete key, clicking the Delete button on the toolbar in the SMS Administrator console, or right-clicking the program and selecting Delete from the menu.

6. Click Next on the welcome screen of the Delete Program Wizard.

7. Click Next to see additional information on the effect of deleting this program. If you are absolutely sure that you want to delete it, then select that option before proceeding.

8. Review advertisements that will be affected. Click Next.

9. Confirm your choice to delete the program. Click Next.

10. Click Finish to exit the Delete Collection Wizard.

Solution: Using VBScript

Example 5-2 demonstrates how to delete a specific program from a package.

Example 5-2. *DeleteProgram.vbs*

```
strSMSServer = <SMSServer>

strPackageID = "LAB0000B"
strProgramName = "NET Framework 1.1 SP1"

Set objLoc =  CreateObject("WbemScripting.SWbemLocator")
Set objSMS= objLoc.ConnectServer(strSMSServer, "root\sms")
Set Results = objSMS.ExecQuery _
    ("SELECT * From SMS_ProviderLocation WHERE ProviderForLocalSite = true")
For each Loc in Results
    If Loc.ProviderForLocalSite = True Then
        Set objSMS = objLoc.ConnectServer(Loc.Machine, "root\sms\site_" & _
            Loc.SiteCode)
            strSMSSiteCode = Loc.Sitecode
    end if
Next

Set objProgram=objSMS.Get("SMS_Program.PackageID='" & _
    strPackageID & "',ProgramName='" & strProgramName & "'")
wscript.echo "Deleting " & objProgram.ProgramName
objProgram.Delete_
```

Example 5-3 demonstrates how to delete all programs from a package.

Example 5-3. *DeletePrograms.vbs*

```
strSMSServer = <SMSServer>
strPackageID = "LAB0000B"

Set objLoc = CreateObject("WbemScripting.SWbemLocator")
Set objSMS= objLoc.ConnectServer(strSMSServer, "root\sms")
Set Results = objSMS.ExecQuery _
    ("SELECT * From SMS_ProviderLocation WHERE ProviderForLocalSite = true")
For each Loc in Results
    If Loc.ProviderForLocalSite = True Then
        Set objSMS = objLoc.ConnectServer(Loc.Machine, "root\sms\site_" & _
            Loc.SiteCode)
            strSMSSiteCode = Loc.Sitecode
    end if
Next

Set colPrograms = objSMS.ExecQuery("Select * From SMS_Program " & _
    "WHERE PackageID='" & strPackageID & "'")
For Each objProgram In colPrograms
    wscript.echo "Deleting " & objProgram.ProgramName
    objProgram.Delete_
Next
```

Discussion

You don't have to worry about deleting programs if you plan to delete the package itself. Deleting a package with a script or the Delete Package Wizard will delete all associated programs and advertisements for you.

Two VBScript scripts are provided in this recipe, to demonstrate two different ways to obtain and delete a program object. Example 5-2 uses the Get method to obtain a single instance of an object—a specific program associated to a specific package. Example 5-3 uses a select statement to query all programs associated with a specific package. By using the for-each loop, we are able to enumerate all programs for a particular package and perform an action on each one. In this example, we delete each program associated to a specific package.

See Also

- Recipe 3-4, "Deleting a Collection," demonstrates how to delete a collection.

- Recipe 4-4, "Deleting a Package," demonstrates how to delete a package.

- Recipe 6-2, "Deleting an Advertisement," demonstrates how to delete an advertisement.

- Recipe 5-18, "Disabling a Program," shows an alternative to deleting a program.

- MSDN, the SMS 2003 SDK, and the *SMS 2003 Scripting Guide* provide additional information about the SMS_Program class.

- Appendix C of the *SMS 2003 Operations Guide* provides more information about using VBScript with SMS_Program.

5-3. Viewing All Programs in a Package

Problem

You want to view all programs for a given package.

Solution: Using a Graphical Interface

1. Open the SMS Administrator console.

2. From the SMS Administrator console, expand Site Database (*<Site Code>*), and expand Packages.

3. Expand any folders necessary, and expand the package that contains the program you want to modify.

4. Select Programs to display the existing programs for the package in the right pane.

Solution: Using VBScript

Example 5-4 demonstrates how to display all programs for a given package.

Example 5-4. *ViewingAllProgramsInAPackage.vbs*

```
strSMSServer = <SMSServer>
strPackageID = "LAB0000C"

Set objLoc =  CreateObject("WbemScripting.SWbemLocator")
Set objSMS= objLoc.ConnectServer(strSMSServer, "root\sms")
Set Results = objSMS.ExecQuery _
    ("SELECT * From SMS_ProviderLocation WHERE ProviderForLocalSite = true")
For each Loc in Results
    If Loc.ProviderForLocalSite = True Then
        Set objSMS = objLoc.ConnectServer(Loc.Machine, "root\sms\site_" & _
            Loc.SiteCode)
            strSMSSiteCode = Loc.Sitecode
    end if
Next

Set colPrograms = objSMS.ExecQuery("Select * From SMS_Program " & _
    "WHERE PackageID='" & strPackageID & "' order by ProgramName")
wscript.echo "All Programs for " & _
    GetPackageName(strPackageID) & " (" & strPackageID & ")"
For Each objProgram In colPrograms
    wscript.echo vbTAB & objProgram.ProgramName
Next

Function GetPackageName(strPckID)
    Set objPackage=objSMS.Get("SMS_Package.PackageID='" & strPckID & "'")
    GetPackageName = objPackage.Name
End Function
```

Discussion

In Example 5-4, we first query the SMS_Program class for all programs associated with a PackageID. Next, we call the function GetPackageName to obtain the package name for the specified PackageID. Finally, we display each program name. Properties such as CommandLine, Comment, and others could be displayed if desired. Review the properties of the SMS_Program class for a complete list of program properties.

See Also

- Recipe 5-4, "Viewing All Packages and Programs," demonstrates how to display all packages and programs in your SMS site using VBScript.

- Recipe 4-2, "Determining a Package's PackageID," shows how to determine the PackageID for a package.

- MSDN, the SMS 2003 SDK, and the *SMS 2003 Scripting Guide* provide additional information about the SMS_Program class.

- Appendix C of the *SMS 2003 Operations Guide* provides more information about using VBScript with SMS_Program.

5-4. Viewing All Packages and Programs

Problem

You want to view all packages and their associated programs.

Solution: Using a Graphical Interface

The SMS Administrator console is not capable of showing all packages and associated programs at the same time.

Solution: Using VBScript

Example 5-5 demonstrates how to view all packages with associated programs.

Example 5-5. *ViewingAllPackagesWithPrograms.vbs*

```
strSMSServer = <SMSServer>

Set objLoc =  CreateObject("WbemScripting.SWbemLocator")
Set objSMS= objLoc.ConnectServer(strSMSServer, "root\sms")
Set Results = objSMS.ExecQuery _
    ("SELECT * From SMS_ProviderLocation WHERE ProviderForLocalSite = true")
For each Loc in Results
    If Loc.ProviderForLocalSite = True Then
        Set objSMS = objLoc.ConnectServer(Loc.Machine, "root\sms\site_" & _
            Loc.SiteCode)
            strSMSSiteCode = Loc.Sitecode
    end if
Next

Set colPackages = objSMS.ExecQuery("Select * From SMS_Package where " & _
    "ImageFlags = 0 order by Name")

For each objPackage in ColPackages
    wscript.echo objPackage.Name & " (" & objPackage.PackageID & ")"
    ListPrograms(objPackage.PackageID)
Next
```

```
Sub ListPrograms(strPackageID)
    Set colPrograms = objSMS.ExecQuery("Select * From SMS_Program " & _
        "WHERE PackageID='" & strPackageID & "' order by ProgramName")
    For Each objProgram In colPrograms
        wscript.echo vbTAB & objProgram.ProgramName
    Next
End Sub
```

Discussion

Example 5-5 enumerates all packages in the SMS_Package class that are not Operating System Deployment (OSD) image packages (where ImageFlags=0). For each package, the package Name and PackageID are displayed, and then the subroutine ListPrograms is called to display the programs for each package. As explained in Recipe 5-3, "Viewing All Programs in a Package," additional program properties can be displayed using the properties of the SMS_Program class.

See Also

- Recipe 5-3, "Viewing All Programs in a Package," demonstrates how to display all programs for a specific package using VBScript.

- MSDN, the SMS 2003 SDK, and the *SMS 2003 Scripting Guide* provide additional information about the SMS_Program class.

- Appendix C of the *SMS 2003 Operations Guide* provides more information about using VBScript with SMS_Program.

5-5. Modifying a Program

Problem

You want to modify the properties of a program.

Solution: Using a Graphical Interface

1. Open the SMS Administrator console.

2. From the SMS Administrator console, expand Site Database (*<Site Code>*), and expand Packages.

3. Expand any folders necessary, and expand the package that contains the program you want to modify.

4. Select Programs to display the existing programs in the right pane.

5. In the right pane, double-click the program to open the Program Properties dialog box.

6. Make the modifications that you require.

7. Click OK to apply the settings.

Solution: Using VBScript

Example 5-6 demonstrates how to modify the comment property of a program.

Example 5-6. *ModifyProgram.vbs*

```
strSMSServer = <SMSServer>

strPackageID = "LAB0000A"
strProgramName = "NET Framework 1.1 SP1"
strComment = "This program installs SP1 for the .NET Framework"

Set objLoc =  CreateObject("WbemScripting.SWbemLocator")
Set objSMS= objLoc.ConnectServer(strSMSServer, "root\sms")
Set Results = objSMS.ExecQuery _
    ("SELECT * From SMS_ProviderLocation WHERE ProviderForLocalSite = true")
For each Loc in Results
    If Loc.ProviderForLocalSite = True Then
        Set objSMS = objLoc.ConnectServer(Loc.Machine, "root\sms\site_" & _
            Loc.SiteCode)
            strSMSSiteCode = Loc.Sitecode
    end if
Next

Set objProgram=objSMS.Get("SMS_Program.PackageID='" & _
    strPackageID & "',ProgramName='" & strProgramName & "'")
objProgram.Comment = strComment
objProgram.Put_
```

Discussion

You are able to modify over 25 options in a program. Some of these options have dependencies on other settings, and others do not. Your understanding of these optional components of a program will greatly increase your software deployments' chances for success.

Tip When testing the behavior of a program, limit the number of program modifications made between testing cycles. This will allow you to quickly identify which configuration changes are beneficial and which are not.

Example 5-6 demonstrates how to add a comment to an existing SMS program using VBScript. We obtain the program object by using the Get_ method, passing the specific PackageID and ProgramName. We then add (or replace) the comment and save the change using the Put_ method.

See Also

- Many recipes in this chapter provide examples of more complex modification of program properties.

- Recipe 5-11, "Configuring Program Environment Settings," provides an advanced example of modifying program properties.

- MSDN, the SMS 2003 SDK, and the *SMS 2003 Scripting Guide* provide additional information about the SMS_Program class.

- Appendix C of the *SMS 2003 Operations Guide* provides more information about using VBScript with SMS_Program.

5-6. Configuring Command-Line Properties

Problem

You want to configure the command-line properties of a program.

Solution: Using a Graphical Interface

1. Open the SMS Administrator console.

2. From the SMS Administrator console, expand Site Database (*<Site Code>*), and expand Packages.

3. Expand any folders necessary, and expand the package that contains the program you want to modify.

4. Select Programs to display the existing programs in the right pane.

5. In the right pane, double-click the program to open the Program Properties dialog box.

6. Select the General tab if it isn't already visible.

7. If you do not require any special command-line parameters besides the name of the executable, click Browse to select one of the executables contained in the package.

8. If your package root folder contains the executable, you do not need to provide a value for the "Start in" property.

9. Select the Run mode that you would like SMS to use to execute the program by selecting from the drop-down list. Normal is the default.

10. Select an "After running" action from the drop-down list. "No action required" is the default.

11. If you want to group this program into a category, enter the category or select it from the dialog box if it has already been created.

12. Click OK to apply the settings.

Solution: Using VBScript

The technique for modifying the `CommandLine` string is very similar to the technique shown in Recipe 5-5, "Modifying a Program," for basic modification of a program. Simply replace `objProgram.Comment = strComment` with `objProgram.CommandLine = strCommandLine`, where `strCommandLine` contains the desired command-line information.

Discussion

Many problems with a program can be resolved by adjusting the command-line parameter. To establish a correct command line, you need to understand the options available to you for the file you are executing. Command-line switches vary widely depending on the application.

To identify the available switches, open a command window and type the executable name followed by the help switch (e.g., `setup.exe /?`). If this does not give you the information you need, then you may need to consult the documentation that came with the application.

The "Start in" property allows you to select the working directory that a program is run from. The package directory is the default directory, and any directories added will be appended to the package directory. You can also add a full path to a separate source, but this is not recommended, as you lose the functionality of the distributed hierarchy of SMS. Also, when connecting to network resources other than the package source on the distribution point, you will need to configure the Legacy Client Software Installation account (for Legacy Clients) and/or the

Advanced Client Network Access account (for Advanced Clients) in the SMS site hierarchy, and also grant proper permissions for the account(s) to the desired network resource.

The Run option sets the visibility of any command windows that would normally be visible to the end user.

The "After running" option allows you to specify any actions that will help complete the installation. The following are your action choices:

No action required: SMS does nothing after the program completes.

SMS restarts computer: When the program is complete, SMS will restart the computer. If a user is logged on, SMS will notify him or her that a restart is necessary and proceed to restart the computer (as long as the "Suppress program notifications" check box on the Advanced tab is not enabled).

Program restarts computer: SMS will prepare for a restart event that is initiated by the application and log the success of the program upon restart.

SMS logs user off: SMS will log off any logged-on users upon completion of the program. (Users will be notified prior to being logged off as long as the "Suppress program notifications" check box on the Advanced tab is not enabled.)

The Category option will enable you to organize programs in both the Add or Remove Programs applet and the Run Advertised Programs applet into logical groups. This will allow the end user to sort the available programs by those categories.

See Also

- Chapter 13 provides additional information about silent switches and unattended installations.

- Recipe 5-7, "Modifying the Program Category for All Programs in Multiple Packages," describes how to modify the program category using VBScript.

- Recipe 2-27, "Configuring the Legacy Client Software Installation Account," provides information on configuring the Legacy Client Software Installation account and the Advanced Client Network Access account.

- MSDN, the SMS 2003 SDK, and the *SMS 2003 Scripting Guide* provide additional information about the SMS_Program class.

- Appendix C of the *SMS 2003 Operations Guide* provides more information about using VBScript with SMS_Program.

5-7. Modifying the Program Category for All Programs in Multiple Packages

Problem

You want to modify the program category for every program in a list of packages.

Solution: Using a Graphical Interface

The SMS Administrator console is not capable of modifying multiple programs in multiple packages.

Solution: Using VBScript

Example 5-7 demonstrates how to modify the Category property for each program on multiple packages, given the PackageID.

Example 5-7. *ModifyCategoryOnMultiplePrograms.vbs*

```
strSMSServer = <SMSServer>

strCategory = "SMS Admin"

strPkgList = "LAB00002,LAB00006,LAB00003,LAB00005"
arrPackages = split(strPkgList,",")

Set objLoc =  CreateObject("WbemScripting.SWbemLocator")
Set objSMS= objLoc.ConnectServer(strSMSServer, "root\sms")
Set Results = objSMS.ExecQuery _
    ("SELECT * From SMS_ProviderLocation WHERE ProviderForLocalSite = true")
For each Loc in Results
    If Loc.ProviderForLocalSite = True Then
        Set objSMS = objLoc.ConnectServer(Loc.Machine, "root\sms\site_" & _
            Loc.SiteCode)
            strSMSSiteCode = Loc.Sitecode
    end if
Next

For each strPackageID in arrPackages
    Set colPrograms = objSMS.ExecQuery _
        ("Select * From SMS_Program " & _
        "WHERE PackageID='" & strPackageID & "'")
    For Each objProgram In colPrograms
        wscript.echo "Modifying category for:" & _
            objProgram.ProgramName
        objProgram.Description = strCategory
        objProgram.Put_
    Next
Next
```

Discussion

Example 5-7 takes a comma-separated list of PackageIDs and creates an array using the Split function. For each PackageID, a query is performed on the SMS_Program class to obtain every program associated with the desired PackageID. Finally, the objProgram.Description is set to strCategory and Put_ is called to save the category modification.

See Also

- Recipe 5-5, "Modifying a Program," demonstrates how to modify program properties for a single program.

- Recipe 5-11, "Configuring Program Environment Settings," provides a more advanced example of modifying program properties.

- MSDN, the SMS 2003 SDK, and the *SMS 2003 Scripting Guide* provide additional information about the SMS_Program class.

- Appendix C of the *SMS 2003 Operations Guide* provides more information about using VBScript with SMS_Program.

5-8. Configuring Program Requirements

Problem

You want to configure the requirements for a program to run.

Solution: Using a Graphical Interface

1. Open the SMS Administrator console.

2. From the SMS Administrator console, expand Site Database (*<Site Code>*), and expand Packages.

3. Expand any folders necessary, and expand the package that contains the program you want to modify.

4. Select Programs to display the existing programs in the right pane.

5. In the right pane, double-click the program to open the Program Properties dialog box.

6. Select the Requirements tab if it isn't already visible.

7. Enter an estimated disk space or leave it as the default, Unknown. If you entered a value, choose the unit of measure to be coupled with your value.

8. Enter a maximum allowed runtime if you would like to limit how long SMS monitors the program or leave it as the default, Unknown.

9. If the program requires a specific platform, choose the "This program can run only on specified client platforms" option and select the check box next to each platform or platform group that is allowed.

10. You can specify additional requirements that will be displayed to the end user if the program is initiated by the end user.

11. Click OK to apply the settings.

Solution: Using VBScript

Configure program requirements using the basic technique shown in Recipe 5-5, "Modifying a Program." To modify estimated disk space, simply set objProgram.DiskSpaceReq to a string such as "874 KB", "40 MB", or "2 GB". DiskSpaceReq is a string data type, with a space between the number and the type. To change a program's maximum allowed runtime, simply set objProgram.Duration to a positive integer in minutes (e.g., objProgram.Duration = 93 for 1 hour, 33 minutes).

The task of specifying a list of client platforms is a little more challenging. You will have to create (or modify) an array of SMS_OS_Details to correctly create or modify such a list. Recipe 5-9, "Viewing Supported Platforms for a Specific Program," provides more information on displaying supported platform information. To display additional program requirements to the user, simply set objProgram.Requirements to a text string describing those requirements. As we explain in the "Discussion" section, text entered for objProgram.Requirements is simply displayed to the user while running Run Advertised Programs—no actual requirements are enforced using this property.

Discussion

The options on the Requirements tab of the Program Properties dialog box may introduce some confusion, and some of that confusion may start with the title of this tab: Requirements. None of the options is required to create the program, so you might assume that they are requirements that must be met for the program to run. That is not exactly true either. Let's look at the Requirements tab options in closer detail:

Estimated disk space: This option does not cause SMS to check whether there is the specified amount of disk space available before running the program; it simply transfers the information to the user, so that the user can see how much disk space will be consumed by the program should he or she choose to manually initiate the install. If you will be deploying an application with a mandatory advertisement, you don't need to specify the estimated disk space.

Maximum allowed run time: It might appear that after the maximum runtime is exceeded, the program is not allowed to run anymore and will be forced to exit, but that is not the case. This option is similar to the previous one in that it provides information to the end user who is manually initiating an install so that he or she will know approximately how long the install will take. SMS will monitor the program for the time specified and then "walk away," leaving the program to complete successfully or fail without any further status. If you leave this setting at the default of Unknown, then SMS will monitor the program for 12 hours.

This program can run only on specified client platforms: This setting is actually a requirement that will be checked before the program is executed. If the client is not one of the checked operating systems, it will not execute the program.

Additional requirements: This is simply a place to put text that you want the end user to see if he or she runs the program for the Run Advertised Programs applet in the Control Panel. Again, if you plan on using a mandatory advertisement, this option will be of little use to you.

See Also

- Recipe 5-9, "Viewing Supported Platforms for a Specific Program," provides information on displaying supported platform information.

- Recipe 5-23, "Controlling Microsoft Operations Manager Alerts," provides information about how the maximum allowed runtime ties in to disabling Microsoft Operations Manager (MOM) alerts.

- MSDN, the SMS 2003 SDK, and the *SMS 2003 Scripting* Guide provide additional information about the SMS_Program class.

- Appendix C of the *SMS 2003 Operations Guide* provides more information about using VBScript with SMS_Program.

- MSDN and the SMS 2003 SDK provide additional information about SMS_OS_Details.

5-9. Viewing Supported Platforms for a Specific Program

Problem

You want to show all supported Windows platforms that apply to a specific program using VBScript.

Solution: Using VBScript

Example 5-8 demonstrates how to show all supported platforms configured for a specific program.

Example 5-8. *ShowSupportedPlatforms.vbs*

```
strSMSServer = <SMSServer>

ANY_PLATFORM = 2^(27)  'sms doc incorrect

strPackageID = "LAB00086"
strProgramName = "Microsoft Updates"
```

```
Set objLoc =  CreateObject("WbemScripting.SWbemLocator")
Set objSMS= objLoc.ConnectServer(strSMSServer, "root\sms")
Set Results = objSMS.ExecQuery _
    ("SELECT * From SMS_ProviderLocation WHERE ProviderForLocalSite = true")
For each Loc in Results
    If Loc.ProviderForLocalSite = True Then
        Set objSMS = objLoc.ConnectServer(Loc.Machine, "root\sms\site_" & _
            Loc.SiteCode)
            strSMSSiteCode = Loc.Sitecode
    end if
Next

Set objProgram=objSMS.Get("SMS_Program.PackageID='" & _
    strPackageID & "',ProgramName='" & strProgramName & "'")

'Check for "Any Platform in ProgramFlags first
if (objProgram.ProgramFlags and ANY_PLATFORM) then
    wscript.echo "This program is configured to run " & _
        "on any platform"
else
    for i = 0 to ubound(objProgram.SupportedOperatingSystems)
        strInfo = _
            objProgram.SupportedOperatingSystems(i).Name & vbTAB
        strInfo = strInfo & _
            objProgram.SupportedOperatingSystems(i).Platform & _
                vbTAB
        strInfo = strInfo & _
            objProgram.SupportedOperatingSystems(i). _
                MinVersion & vbTAB
        strInfo = strInfo & objProgram. _
            SupportedOperatingSystems(i).MaxVersion
        wscript.echo strInfo
    next
end if
```

Discussion

The VBScript in Example 5-8 queries SMS_Program for a specific PackageID and ProgramName, and then evaluates objProgram.ProgramFlags and ANY_PLATFORM to see if bit 27 of ProgramFlags is enabled. If bit 27 is not enabled, the script proceeds to display the operating system name, platform, and minimum and maximum versions.

Caution If bit 27 of ProgramFlags is enabled (which means this program can run on any platform), all information in the SupportedOperatingSystems array is ignored.

ProgramFlags is interesting and also sometimes confusing. Each bit in the unsigned integer ProgramFlags represents a specific setting. In this example, bit 27 means that the program in question runs on any platform and to ignore any information in the SupportedOperatingSystems field. We use bit ANDing to compare a specific bit in the objProgram.ProgramFlags field to a desired bit. In our example, by testing for objProgram.ProgramFlags and ANY_PLATFORM, we're basically saying

"If the 27th bit is enabled, continue in the `if` statement." Several recipes that follow in this chapter use bit ANDing and bit ORing to check and/or set various `ProgramFlags`.

See Also

- Recipe 5-8, "Configuring Program Requirements," contains a brief discussion about supported platforms.

- Recipe 5-10, "Viewing All Programs That Apply to a Specific Platform," demonstrates how to view all programs that apply to a specific platform.

- MSDN, the SMS 2003 SDK, and the *SMS 2003 Scripting Guide* provide additional information about the `SMS_Program` class.

- Appendix C of the *SMS 2003 Operations Guide* provides more information about using VBScript with `SMS_Program`.

- MSDN and the SMS 2003 SDK provide additional information about `SMS_OS_Details`.

5-10. Viewing All Programs That Apply to a Specific Platform

Problem

You want to display all programs configured to install on a specific platform (e.g., Windows 2000).

Solution: Using a Graphical Interface

The SMS Administrator console is not capable of displaying all programs that apply to a specific platform.

Solution: Using VBScript

Example 5-9 demonstrates how to display all programs that are configured to apply to Windows 2000.

Example 5-9. *ShowAllExplicitPlatformsWO2K.vbs*

```
strSMSServer = <SMSServer>

strWindowsVersion = "5.00" 'looking for Windows 2000 here
ANY_PLATFORM = 2^(27)

Set objLoc =  CreateObject("WbemScripting.SWbemLocator")
Set objSMS= objLoc.ConnectServer(strSMSServer, "root\sms")
Set Results = objSMS.ExecQuery _
    ("SELECT * From SMS_ProviderLocation WHERE ProviderForLocalSite = true")
For each Loc in Results
    If Loc.ProviderForLocalSite = True Then
        Set objSMS = objLoc.ConnectServer(Loc.Machine, "root\sms\site_" & _
            Loc.SiteCode)
            strSMSSiteCode = Loc.Sitecode
    end if
Next
```

```
Set colPrograms = objSMS.ExecQuery _
    ("Select * From SMS_Program order by PackageID")
For Each objProgram In colPrograms
    if (objProgram.ProgramFlags and ANY_PLATFORM) then
        'program is set to "any platform" - don't check further
    else
        ListFilteredPrograms objProgram.ProgramName, objProgram.PackageID, _
            trWindowsVersion
    end if
Next

Sub ListFilteredPrograms(strProgramName, strPackageID, strWinVer)
    Set objProgram=objSMS.Get _
        ("SMS_Program.PackageID='" & _
        strPackageID & "',ProgramName='" & _
        strProgramName & "'")
    for i = 0 to ubound(objProgram.SupportedOperatingSystems)
        if instr(objProgram.SupportedOperatingSystems(i). _
            MaxVersion, strWinVer) then
            blnFoundOne = true
        end if
    next
    if blnFoundOne then
        wscript.echo "Package Name:" & _
            GetPackageName(strPackageID) & vbTAB & _
            "Program Name:" & strProgramName
    else
        'this would capture all programs that had supported
        'platforms configured that did not contain strWinVer
    end if
End Sub

Function GetPackageName(strPckID)
    Set objPackage=objSMS.Get("SMS_Package.PackageID='" & _
        strPckID & "'")
    GetPackageName = objPackage.Name
End Function
```

Discussion

In Example 5-9, we are searching for all programs set to run on Windows 2000 platforms (Windows version 5.00) as defined on the Requirements tab of the Program Properties dialog box.

For each program in the SMS_Program class, we check to see if bit 27 of the ProgramFlags property is enabled. If this bit is enabled, the specified platforms array is ignored.

If bit 27 of ProgramFlags is not enabled, we call the subroutine CheckFilteredPrograms. CheckFilteredPrograms looks at each element of the array objProgram.SupportedOperatingSystems to see if the MaxVersion property contains strWinVer (in our example, strWinVer = "5.00"). If the MaxVersion contains strWinVer, we then call the function GetPackageName to display the package name, followed by the program name.

See Also

- Recipe 5-8, "Configuring Program Requirements," contains a brief discussion about supported platforms.

- Recipe 5-9, "Viewing Supported Platforms for a Specific Program," demonstrates how to view supported platforms for a specific program.

- MSDN, the SMS 2003 SDK, and the *SMS 2003 Scripting Guide* provide additional information about the SMS_Program class.

- Appendix C of the *SMS 2003 Operations Guide* provides more information about using VBScript with SMS_Program.

- MSDN and the SMS 2003 SDK provide additional information about SMS_OS_Details.

5-11. Configuring Program Environment Settings

Problem

You want to configure the user environment that a program needs in order to run.

Solution: Using a Graphical Interface

1. Open the SMS Administrator console.

2. From the SMS Administrator console, expand Site Database (*<Site Code>*), and expand Packages.

3. Expand any folders necessary, and expand the package that contains the program you want to modify.

4. Select Programs to display the existing programs in the right pane.

5. In the right pane, double-click the program to open the Program Properties dialog box.

6. Select the Environment tab if it isn't already visible.

7. Specify the user environment that must be present for the program to run.

8. Specify in the Run mode area the security context in which the program will be run.

9. Specify in the Drive mode area the network environment that must be present for the program to run.

10. Click OK to apply the settings.

Solution: Using VBScript

The ProgramFlags property of the program provides all the settings required to programmatically configure the program environment settings. The key to setting these values programmatically is that you must properly configure the run modes as described in Table 5-1 in the "Discussion" section. In addition to examining Table 5-1 in this recipe, review the ProgramFlags property of the SMS_Program class in the SMS 2003 SDK.

Discussion

Executing a program in the proper user environment is not a step you should overlook. Some programs will only run properly in a specific user environment, so you need to be careful to test a given program in the environment you would like to run it in.

Caution Running a program with administrative rights will cause the program to not be visible to any users, unless the program is configured to "Allow users to interact with this program." Make sure the program does not require input of any kind, since there will not be a way for a user to enter that input.

Table 5-1 shows the run modes available for the different environments. It is very possible that the exact same program configuration will succeed in one environment and fail in another, so you will want to test your programs in all environments you intend to use them in.

Table 5-1. *Available Run Modes*

Run Mode	Only When a User Is Logged On	Whether or Not a User Is Logged On	Only When No User Is Logged On
Run with user's rights	Available	Not available	Not available
Run with administrative rights	Available	Available	Available
Use software installation account	Not available	Available	Available
Allow users to interact with this program	Available	Available	Not available

Caution By running a program using administrative rights and selecting the "Allow users to interact with this program" check box, you give a connected user the ability to interact with the program in an administrative security context. For example, if your program inadvertently launched a command prompt window that the user could see, the user may be able to perform administrative functions on the local system (e.g., browse other user profiles, modify system permissions, etc.). If you use this option, triple-check your work to ensure the user doesn't have an opportunity for mischief.

Some applications require that the installation source files be available as a mapped drive. In those cases, you will want to change from the default drive mode of "Runs with UNC name" to one of the mapped drive options that will work with your application.

See Also

- Chapter 12 of the *Microsoft Systems Management Server 2003 Administrator's Companion* by Steven Kaczmarek (Microsoft Press, 2004) details how to create a program.
- MSDN, the SMS 2003 SDK, and the *SMS 2003 Scripting Guide* provide additional information about SMS_Program.
- Appendix C of the *SMS 2003 Operations Guide* provides more information about VBScript with SMS_Program.

5-12. Viewing All Programs with User Logon Requirements

Problem

You want to display the logon requirement for each package and program in your SMS environment.

Solution: Using a Graphical Interface

The SMS Administrator console is not capable of displaying the user logon requirements for all programs in one display.

Solution: Using VBScript

Example 5-10 demonstrates how to display each package with programs, and program environment requirements.

Example 5-10. *DisplayAllPackagesWithPrograms_andProgramEnvironment.vbs*

```
strSMSServer = <SMSServer>

Set objLoc =  CreateObject("WbemScripting.SWbemLocator")
Set objSMS= objLoc.ConnectServer(strSMSServer, "root\sms")
Set Results = objSMS.ExecQuery _
    ("SELECT * From SMS_ProviderLocation WHERE ProviderForLocalSite = true")
For each Loc in Results
    If Loc.ProviderForLocalSite = True Then
        Set objSMS = objLoc.ConnectServer(Loc.Machine, "root\sms\site_" & _
            Loc.SiteCode)
            strSMSSiteCode = Loc.Sitecode
    end if
Next

Set colPackages = objSMS.ExecQuery("Select * From SMS_Package where " & _
    "ImageFlags = 0 order by Name")

For each objPackage in ColPackages
    wscript.echo objPackage.Name & " (" & objPackage.PackageID & ")"
    ListPrograms(objPackage.PackageID)
Next

Sub ListPrograms(strPackageID)
    Set objSWbemLocator =  CreateObject _
        ("WbemScripting.SWbemLocator")
    Set objSMS = objSWbemLocator.ConnectServer _
        (strSMSServer, "root\sms\site_" & strSMSSiteCode )
    Set colPrograms = objSMS.ExecQuery _
        ("Select * From SMS_Program " & _
        "WHERE PackageID='" & strPackageID & _
        "' order by ProgramName")
    For Each objProgram In colPrograms
        wscript.echo vbTAB & objProgram.ProgramName & vbTAB & _
            GetUserLogonRequirement(strPackageID, _
                objProgram.ProgramName)
    Next
End Sub

Function GetUserLogonRequirement(strPackageID, strProgramName)
    USER_LOGGED_ON = 2^(14-1)
    WHETHER_OR_NOT_USER_LOGGED_ON = 2^(15-1)
    NO_USER_LOGGED_ON = 2^(17-1)

    Set objProgram=objSMS.Get _
        ("SMS_Program.PackageID='" & strPackageID & "',ProgramName='" & _
        strProgramName & "'")

    intProgramFlags = objProgram.ProgramFlags
```

```
    if (intProgramFlags and USER_LOGGED_ON) then
        strInfo = "Only when a user is logged on."
    elseif _
    (intProgramFlags and WHETHER_OR_NOT_USER_LOGGED_ON) then
        strInfo = "Whether or not a user is logged on."
    elseif (intProgramFlags and NO_USER_LOGGED_ON) then
        strInfo = "Only when no user is logged on."
    else

    end if
    GetUserLogonRequirement = strInfo
End Function
```

Discussion

Example 5-10 enumerates all packages in the SMS_Package class. We only want to look at non–operating system image packages, so we create a criterion for our query where ImageFlags = 0.

For each package returned in our query, we call the subroutine ListPrograms, which lists each program for the desired package and its logon requirement according to the GetUserLogonRequirement function. GetUserLogonRequirement uses bit ANDing to determine which of the three logon requirement flags are set ("Only when a user is logged on," "Whether or not a user is logged on," or "Only when no user is logged on").

Example 5-10 displays information for all packages and programs, which may appear to be a bit much at first, but you can easily customize the script to fit your needs. For example, you may need to identify all programs configured to run "Only when a user is logged on." You could take the information obtained from GetUserLogonRequirement and create an if statement to display only data pertaining to that specific setting.

See Also

- Recipe 5-9, "Viewing Supported Platforms for a Specific Program," provides additional detail about bit ANDing and bit ORing.

- MSDN, the SMS 2003 SDK, and the *SMS 2003 Scripting Guide* provide additional information about the SMS_Program class.

- Appendix C of the *SMS 2003 Operations Guide* provides more information about using VBScript with SMS_Program.

5-13. Creating Program Dependencies

Problem

You want to ensure program A is executed before program B.

Solution: Using a Graphical Interface

1. Open the SMS Administrator console.

2. From the SMS Administrator console, expand Site Database (*<Site Code>*), and expand Packages.

3. Expand any folders necessary, and expand the package that contains the program you want to modify.

4. Select Programs to display the existing programs in the right pane.

5. In the right pane, double-click the program to open the Program Properties dialog box.

6. Select the Advanced tab if it isn't already visible.

7. Select the "Run another program first" check box to allow you to choose an additional program.

8. Choose the package that contains the program you want to run first from the drop-down menu.

9. Choose the program that you want to run first from the drop-down menu.

10. Specify whether you want to run this program every time by selecting the check box.

11. Click OK to apply the settings.

Solution: Using VBScript

The technique for modifying the `DependentProgram` string is similar to that shown in Recipe 5-5, "Modifying a Program," for basic modification of a program. Simply replace `objProgram.Comment = strComment` with `objProgram.DependentProgram = strDependentProgram`, where `strDependentProgram` contains the properly formatted string for the dependent program. If the desired dependent program is in the same package, set `strDependentProgram` to `;;<ProgramName>`. If the desired dependent program is part of a different package, set `strDependentProgram` to `<PackageID>;;<ProgramName>`.

Discussion

Don't be afraid of the features accessible from the Advanced tab of the Program Properties dialog box. Especially useful is the capability to run another program first. This very powerful and effective feature is easy to leverage.

For instance, say you have an application that you need to install, and it has a `setup.exe` file for installation. However, it also has a service pack, which is another `setup.exe`, and both `.exe` files need to be installed in succession: application first and then service pack. Create two programs: one for the application and one for the service pack. In the program for the service pack, specify that it should "Run another program first" and select the program for the application. Advertise the program for the service pack. Before the service pack application runs, SMS will automatically run the program to install the application.

See Also

- Chapter 13 includes recipes that describe chained installs in more detail.

- Chapter 12 of the *Microsoft Systems Management Server 2003 Administrator's Companion* by Steven Kaczmarek (Microsoft Press, 2004) details how to create a program.

- MSDN, the SMS 2003 SDK, and the *SMS 2003 Scripting Guide* provide additional information about the `SMS_Program` class.

- Recipe 5-14, "Viewing All Program Dependencies," provides an example for viewing all program dependencies.

5-14. Viewing All Program Dependencies

Problem

You want to view all programs that have a program dependency.

Solution: Using a Graphical Interface

The SMS Administrator console is not capable of showing all program dependencies for all packages at the same time.

Solution: Using VBScript

Example 5-11 demonstrates how to display all programs (and associated package information) with dependencies.

Example 5-11. *ShowAllProgramsWithDependencies.vbs*

```
strSMSServer = <SMSServer>

Set objLoc = CreateObject("WbemScripting.SWbemLocator")
Set objSMS= objLoc.ConnectServer(strSMSServer, "root\sms")
Set Results = objSMS.ExecQuery _
    ("SELECT * From SMS_ProviderLocation WHERE ProviderForLocalSite = true")
For each Loc in Results
    If Loc.ProviderForLocalSite = True Then
        Set objSMS = objLoc.ConnectServer(Loc.Machine, "root\sms\site_" & _
            Loc.SiteCode)
            strSMSSiteCode = Loc.Sitecode
    end if
Next

    Set colPrograms = objSMS.ExecQuery("Select * From SMS_Program " & _
    "WHERE DependentProgram <> '' order by PackageID")

for each objProgram in colPrograms
    wscript.echo "Package Name: " & GetPackageName _
        (objProgram.PackageID) & "(" & objProgram.PackageID & ")"
    wscript.echo vbTAB & "Program Name: " & _
        objProgram.ProgramName
    wscript.echo vbTAB & vbTAB & _
        "Dependent PackageID;;Program: " & _
        objProgram.DependentProgram
next

Function GetPackageName(strPckID)
    Set objPackage=objSMS.Get("SMS_Package.PackageID='" & strPckID & "'")
    GetPackageName = objPackage.Name
End Function
```

Discussion

Example 5-11 enumerates all programs that have a dependent program, in PackageID order. Since the programs are in PackageID order, we're able to keep the list in a somewhat ordered state. We then display the package name using the GetPackageName function, followed by the program name and the dependent program information. To display the package name for the dependent program, you could parse the objProgram.DependentProgram property and call GetPackageName for the PackageID found for the dependent program (if any).

See Also

- MSDN, the SMS 2003 SDK, and the *SMS 2003 Scripting Guide* provide additional information about the SMS_Program class.

- Recipe 5-13, "Creating Program Dependencies," describes how to create a program dependency.

5-15. Configuring the Run Frequency of a Program

Problem

You want to configure a program to run once for every user who logs on.

Solution: Using a Graphical Interface

1. Open the SMS Administrator console.

2. From the SMS Administrator console, expand Site Database (*<Site Code>*), and expand Packages.

3. Expand any folders necessary, and expand the package that contains the program you want to modify.

4. Select Programs to display the existing programs in the right pane.

5. In the right pane, double-click the program to open the Program Properties dialog box.

6. Select the Advanced tab if it isn't already visible.

7. Select "Run once for every user who logs on" from the "When this program is assigned to a computer" option.

8. Click OK to apply the settings.

Solution: Using VBScript

Example 5-12 demonstrates how to configure the program to run once for every user who logs on.

Example 5-12. *ConfigRunFrequency.vbs*

```
EVERYUSER = 2^(16)

strSMSServer = <SMSServer>

strPackageID = "LAB0000A"
strProgramName = "NET Framework 1.1 SP1"

Set objLoc =  CreateObject("WbemScripting.SWbemLocator")
Set objSMS= objLoc.ConnectServer(strSMSServer, "root\sms")
Set Results = objSMS.ExecQuery _
    ("SELECT * From SMS_ProviderLocation WHERE ProviderForLocalSite = true")
For each Loc in Results
    If Loc.ProviderForLocalSite = True Then
        Set objSMS = objLoc.ConnectServer(Loc.Machine, "root\sms\site_" & _
            Loc.SiteCode)
            strSMSSiteCode = Loc.Sitecode
    end if
Next
```

```
Set objProgram=objSMS.Get("SMS_Program.PackageID='" & _
    strPackageID & "',ProgramName='" & strProgramName & "'")

intProgramFlags = objProgram.ProgramFlags
intProgramFlags = intProgramFlags or EVERYUSER
objProgram.ProgramFlags = intProgramFlags
objProgram.Put_
```

Discussion

For most applications, you will want SMS to install the application only once on each computer. However, there may be instances where you are trying to make adjustments to a user's environment and you need an installer or other application to run for every user who logs on to a given system. Changing the run frequency setting will allow that to happen.

Example 5-12 obtains the program object from the SMS_Program class and uses bit ANDing to see if the ProgramFlags property has bit 16 (EVERYUSER) enabled. If bit 16 is not enabled, the example uses bit ORing (intProgramFlags = intProgramFlags or EVERYUSER) to set the flag and then saves the flag using the Put_ method.

To set a program back to the default setting of "Run once for every computer," simply replace the if statement from the previous paragraph with the following:

```
intProgramFlags = intProgramFlags and not EVERYUSER
```

By using the and not, you remove the ProgramFlags property to "Run once for every user who logs on" and return it to the "Run once for every computer" default setting.

See Also

- Chapter 12 of the *Microsoft Systems Management Server 2003 Administrator's Companion* by Steven Kaczmarek (Microsoft Press, 2004) details how to create a program.

- MSDN, the SMS 2003 SDK, and the *SMS 2003 Scripting Guide* provide additional information about the SMS_Program class.

- Recipe 5-12, "Viewing All Programs with User Logon Requirements," can be modified to enumerate all programs set to run for every user that logs on.

5-16. Suppressing Program Notifications

Problem

You want to ensure users receive no indication that an SMS advertisement is about to run on their system.

Solution: Using a Graphical Interface

1. Open the SMS Administrator console.

2. From the SMS Administrator console, expand Site Database (*<Site Code>*), and expand Packages.

3. Expand any folders necessary, and expand the package that contains the program you want to modify.

4. Select Programs to display the existing programs in the right pane.

5. In the right pane, double-click the program to open the Program Properties dialog box.

6. Select the Advanced tab if it isn't already visible.

7. Select the "Suppress program notifications" check box.

8. Click OK to apply the settings.

Solution: Using VBScript

Similar to the process shown in Recipe 5-15, "Configuring the Run Frequency of a Program," enable bit 10 to suppress program notifications.

Discussion

SMS can communicate its actions to the end user very efficiently through its notification process. But sometimes you would rather have an install be unknown to the end user; choosing to suppress notifications will accomplish this.

See Also

- Recipe 5-15, "Configuring the Run Frequency of a Program," provides a similar VBScript example.

- Recipe 5-17, "Viewing All Programs Configured to Suppress Notification," provides an example script to show all programs currently configured to suppress program notification.

- MSDN, the SMS 2003 SDK, and the *SMS 2003 Scripting Guide* provide additional information about the SMS_Program class.

5-17. Viewing All Programs Configured to Suppress Notification

Problem

You want to view all programs that have the check box "Suppress program notifications" enabled.

Solution: Using a Graphical Interface

The SMS Administrator console is not capable of displaying information for all programs at the same time.

Solution: Using VBScript

Example 5-13 demonstrates how to display all programs that are configured to suppress user notification.

Example 5-13. *ShowAllProgramsWithNotificationsSet.vbs*

```
SUPPRESS_NOTIFICATIONS = 2^(10)

strSMSServer = <SMSServer>

Set objLoc =  CreateObject("WbemScripting.SWbemLocator")
Set objSMS= objLoc.ConnectServer(strSMSServer, "root\sms")
Set Results = objSMS.ExecQuery _
    ("SELECT * From SMS_ProviderLocation WHERE ProviderForLocalSite = true")
For each Loc in Results
    If Loc.ProviderForLocalSite = True Then
```

```
            Set objSMS = objLoc.ConnectServer(Loc.Machine, "root\sms\site_" & _
                Loc.SiteCode)
                strSMSSiteCode = Loc.Sitecode
        end if
Next

Set colPrograms = objSMS.ExecQuery _
    ("Select * From SMS_Program order by PackageID")

wscript.echo "All Programs with 'Suppress Program " & _
    "Notifications' configured."
for each objProgram in colPrograms
    if (objProgram.ProgramFlags and SUPPRESS_NOTIFICATIONS) then
        wscript.echo objProgram.ProgramName & vbTAB & _
            GetPackageName(objProgram.PackageID) & "(" & _
            objProgram.PackageID & ")"
    end if
next

Function GetPackageName(strPckID)
    Set objPackage=objSMS.Get _
        ("SMS_Package.PackageID='" & _
        strPckID & "'")
    GetPackageName = objPackage.Name
End Function
```

Discussion

Similar to previous VBScript scripts in this chapter, Example 5-13 enumerates all programs, displaying the program and package names for each program that has the "Suppress program notifications" check box enabled.

See Also

- Recipe 5-16, "Suppressing Program Notifications," details how to suppress program notifications for a program.

- MSDN, the SMS 2003 SDK, and the *SMS 2003 Scripting Guide* provide additional information about SMS_Program.

5-18. Disabling a Program

Problem

You want to prevent a program from executing on any client.

Solution: Using a Graphical Interface

1. Open the SMS Administrator console.

2. From the SMS Administrator console, expand Site Database (*<Site Code>*), and expand Packages.

3. Expand any folders necessary, and expand the package that contains the program you want to modify.

4. Select Programs to display the existing programs in the right pane.

5. In the right pane, double-click the program to open the Program Properties dialog box.

6. Select the Advanced tab if it isn't already visible.

7. Select the "Disable this program on computers where it is advertised" check box.

8. Click OK to apply the settings.

Solution: Using VBScript

Example 5-14 demonstrates how to disable an SMS program for all advertisements.

Example 5-14. *DisableProgram.vbs*

```
DISABLE_PROGRAM = 2^(12)

strSMSServer = <SMSServer>

strPackageID = "LAB0000A"
strProgramName = "NET Framework 1.1 SP1"

Set objLoc =  CreateObject("WbemScripting.SWbemLocator")
Set objSMS= objLoc.ConnectServer(strSMSServer, "root\sms")
Set Results = objSMS.ExecQuery _
    ("SELECT * From SMS_ProviderLocation WHERE ProviderForLocalSite = true")
For each Loc in Results
    If Loc.ProviderForLocalSite = True Then
        Set objSMS = objLoc.ConnectServer(Loc.Machine, "root\sms\site_" & _
            Loc.SiteCode)
            strSMSSiteCode = Loc.Sitecode
    end if
Next

Set objProgram=objSMS.Get("SMS_Program.PackageID='" & _
    strPackageID & "',ProgramName='" & strProgramName & "'")

intProgramFlags = objProgram.ProgramFlags

if (intProgramFlags and DISABLE_PROGRAM) then
    wscript.echo "DISABLE_PROGRAM flag " & _
        "already set!"
else
    wscript.echo "Setting DISABLE_PROGRAM flag"
    intProgramFlags = intProgramFlags or _
        DISABLE_PROGRAM
end if
objProgram.ProgramFlags = intProgramFlags
objProgram.Put_
```

Discussion

We know that you would never deploy an application that has not been fully tested, so we don't really need to cover this topic. For argument's sake, however, we'll discuss it.

Hypothetically speaking, say you didn't fully test an application, but you deployed it and found out that it was not installing correctly and was interrupting the user environment. Your first action should be to disable the program. This will stop the program from running on systems that have not received the advertisement or have not started the program.

If the problem is something you can fix, then all you need to do is re-enable the program (after fixing it, of course), and it will continue to install on systems that have not run it yet. You can get the same "disabling" effect by deleting the advertisement, but this method is not recommended. Disabling the programs is the preferred method, since it is easy to accomplish when you are in a hurry and allows you to re-enable the program just as easily after you have corrected any issues with the package or program.

Caution Advanced Clients will need to obtain the new policy that includes the disabled program information. This could take a while depending on your site settings, which could cause some systems to run the program that you have disabled.

The VBScript in Example 5-14 is similar to that in Recipe 5-15, "Configuring the Run Frequency of a Program." The only difference is that we set the disable program flag by using `intProgramFlags = intProgramFlags or DISABLE_PROGRAM`, where `DISABLE_PROGRAM = 2^(12)`.

See Also

- Recipe 5-20, "Re-enabling a Disabled Program," explains how to re-enable a disabled program using VBScript.

- The *SMS 2003 Operations Guide* provides additional information about disabling a program.

- MSDN, the SMS 2003 SDK, and the *SMS 2003 Scripting Guide* provide additional information about the `SMS_Program` class.

5-19. Viewing Disabled Programs

Problem

You want to view all disabled programs.

Solution: Using a Graphical Interface

The SMS Administrator console is not capable of displaying all disabled programs. However, you can view whether the program associated with an advertisement is disabled or not. See Recipe 6-21, "Viewing the Status of an Advertisement."

Solution: Using VBScript

Example 5-15 demonstrates how to display all disabled programs in your SMS site.

Example 5-15. *ShowAllDisabledPrograms.vbs*

```
strSMSServer = <SMSServer>

DISABLE_PROGRAM = 2^(12)

Set objLoc =  CreateObject("WbemScripting.SWbemLocator")
Set objSMS= objLoc.ConnectServer(strSMSServer, "root\sms")
Set Results = objSMS.ExecQuery _
    ("SELECT * From SMS_ProviderLocation WHERE ProviderForLocalSite = true")
```

```
For each Loc in Results
    If Loc.ProviderForLocalSite = True Then
        Set objSMS = objLoc.ConnectServer(Loc.Machine, "root\sms\site_" & _
            Loc.SiteCode)
            strSMSSiteCode = Loc.Sitecode
    end if
Next

Set colPrograms = objSMS.ExecQuery _
    ("Select * From SMS_Program order by PackageID")
For Each objProgram In colPrograms
    if (objProgram.ProgramFlags and DISABLE_PROGRAM) then
        wscript.echo "Program Name: " & _
            objProgram.ProgramName & vbTAB & _
            "Package Name: " & _
            GetPackageName(objProgram.PackageID) & " (" & _
            objProgram.PackageID & ")"
    end if
Next

Function GetPackageName(strPckID)
    Set objSWbemLocator = CreateObject _
        ("WbemScripting.SWbemLocator")
    Set objSMS = objSWbemLocator.ConnectServer _
        (strSMSServer, "root\sms\site_" & strSMSSiteCode )
    Set objPackage=objSMS.Get _
        ("SMS_Package.PackageID='" & _
        strPckID & "'")
    GetPackageName = objPackage.Name
End Function
```

Discussion

Example 5-15 enumerates all programs found in the SMS_Program class. For each program, if objProgram.ProgramFlags and DISABLE_PROGRAM is true, the script displays the program name and package name.

See Also

- Recipe 5-18, "Disabling a Program," explains how to disable a program, and Recipe 5-20, "Re-enabling a Disabled Program," explains how to re-enable a disabled program.

- MSDN, the SMS 2003 SDK, and the *SMS 2003 Scripting Guide* provide additional information about the SMS_Program class.

5-20. Re-enabling a Disabled Program

Problem

You want to re-enable a disabled program using VBScript.

Solution: Using VBScript

Example 5-16 demonstrates how to re-enable a program using VBScript.

Example 5-16. *Re-EnableProgram.vbs*

```
DISABLE_PROGRAM = 2^(12)

strSMSServer = <SMSServer>

strPackageID = "LAB0000C"
strProgramName = "NET Framework 1.1 SP1"

Set objLoc = CreateObject("WbemScripting.SWbemLocator")
Set objSMS= objLoc.ConnectServer(strSMSServer, "root\sms")
Set Results = objSMS.ExecQuery _
    ("SELECT * From SMS_ProviderLocation WHERE ProviderForLocalSite = true")
For each Loc in Results
    If Loc.ProviderForLocalSite = True Then
        Set objSMS = objLoc.ConnectServer(Loc.Machine, "root\sms\site_" & _
            Loc.SiteCode)
            strSMSSiteCode = Loc.Sitecode
    end if
Next

Set objProgram=objSMS.Get("SMS_Program.PackageID='" & _
    strPackageID & "',ProgramName='" & strProgramName & "'")

intProgramFlags = objProgram.ProgramFlags

if (intProgramFlags and DISABLE_PROGRAM) then
    wscript.echo "Re-enabling disabled program"
    intProgramFlags = intProgramFlags and not _
        DISABLE_PROGRAM
else
    wscript.echo "DISABLE_PROGRAM flag not set"
end if

objProgram.ProgramFlags = intProgramFlags
objProgram.Put_
```

Discussion

Example 5-16 shows an example of how to go about programmatically re-enabling a disabled program. After obtaining the program flags, we check to see if the program is disabled using bit ANDing: `intProgramFlags and DISABLE_PROGRAM`. If it is set, we then clear the `DISABLE_PROGRAM` bit using the following line of code:

```
intProgramFlags = intProgramFlags and not DISABLE_PROGRAM
```

See Also

- Recipe 5-18, "Disabling a Program," explains how to disable a program using VBScript.
- Recipe 5-19, "Viewing Disabled Programs," shows how to view all disabled programs.
- The *SMS 2003 Operations Guide* provides additional information about disabling a program.
- MSDN, the SMS 2003 SDK, and the *SMS 2003 Scripting Guide* provide additional information about the SMS_Program class.

5-21. Managing Sources of Windows Installer Products

Problem

You want to manage installation source locations for Windows Installer applications (so an application can perform self-healing).

Solution: Using a Graphical Interface

1. Open the SMS Administrator console.

2. From the SMS Administrator console, expand Site Database (<*Site Code*>), and expand Packages.

3. Expand any folders necessary, and expand the package that contains the program you want to modify.

4. Select Programs to display the existing programs in the right pane.

5. In the right pane, double-click the program to open the Program Properties dialog box.

6. Select the Windows Installer tab if it isn't already visible.

7. Click the Import button.

8. Double-click the file or click Open to select the Windows Installer file (.msi) to be maintained.

9. Click the Clear button if you do not want SMS to maintain the Windows Installer installation source.

10. Click OK to apply the settings.

Solution: Using VBScript

The SMS_Program properties MSIFilePath and MSIProductID can be used to set the Windows Installer file and the product code. Before setting these properties for a program, you must ensure the product code is not already configured for a different program for this package. The product code may be used only one time per package.

Discussion

The repair and self-healing capabilities of Windows Installer applications are effective for maintaining and configuring applications. However, by default, Windows Installer only wants to remember the original installation source file location. This can be problematic if you have roaming clients and you regularly update an application by using the Windows Installer repair function, as your remote clients will attempt to locate the original source files instead of those that might be closer and easier to access. Fortunately, SMS is now able to maintain that local installation source so that repairs of Windows Installer applications will use the local distribution point instead of the distribution point that originally installed the software, which may now be across a wide area network (WAN) link for a roaming client.

See Also

- Recipe 5-5, "Modifying a Program," provides a simple VBScript script for modifying an SMS program. It can also be used to modify MSIFilePath and MSIProductID, which are described in this recipe.

- MSDN, the SMS 2003 SDK, and the *SMS 2003 Scripting Guide* provide additional information about SMS_Program.

- Chapter 5 of the *SMS 2003 Operations Guide* describes the Windows Installer tab.

- Chapter 12 of the *Microsoft Systems Management Server 2003 Administrator's Companion* by Steven Kaczmarek (Microsoft Press, 2004) shows an example of modifying the Windows Installer tab.

- Review the "Windows Installer Source Location Manager" white paper from Microsoft: http://www.microsoft.com/smserver/techinfo/productdoc/default.mspx.

5-22. Viewing All Programs That Contain Windows Installer Source Locations

Problem

You want to view all programs that have a Windows Installer source location configured.

Solution: Using a Graphical Interface

No GUI solution is possible.

Solution: Using VBScript

Example 5-17 demonstrates how to display all programs that contain Windows Installer source locations.

Example 5-17. *ShowAllPackagesProgramsWithWindowsInstallerSourcesConfigured.vbs*

```
strSMSServer = <SMSServer>

Set objLoc =  CreateObject("WbemScripting.SWbemLocator")
Set objSMS= objLoc.ConnectServer(strSMSServer, "root\sms")
Set Results = objSMS.ExecQuery _
    ("SELECT * From SMS_ProviderLocation WHERE ProviderForLocalSite = true")
For each Loc in Results
    If Loc.ProviderForLocalSite = True Then
        Set objSMS = objLoc.ConnectServer(Loc.Machine, "root\sms\site_" & _
            Loc.SiteCode)
            strSMSSiteCode = Loc.Sitecode
    end if
Next

Set colPrograms = objSMS.ExecQuery _
    ("Select * From SMS_Program " & _
    "WHERE MSIProductID <> '' order by PackageID")
```

```
for each objProgram in colPrograms
    wscript.echo "Package Name: " & GetPackageName _
        (objProgram.PackageID) & "(" & objProgram.PackageID & ")"
    wscript.echo vbTAB & "Program Name: " & _
        objProgram.ProgramName
    wscript.echo vbTAB & vbTAB & "MSIFilePath MSIProductID: " & _
        objProgram.MSIFilePath & " " & objProgram.MSIProductID
next

Function GetPackageName(strPckID)
    Set objPackage=objSMS.Get("SMS_Package.PackageID='" & strPckID & "'")
    GetPackageName = objPackage.Name
End Function
```

Discussion

Example 5-17 displays all programs that have a Windows Installer product code configured. First, we query SMS_Program for all programs that have data in the MSIProductID field. Then we display the package name, program name, and Windows Installer information.

See Also

- Recipe 5-21, "Managing Sources of Windows Installer Products," demonstrates how to add a Windows Installer product to an SMS program.

- Chapter 12 of the *Microsoft Systems Management Server 2003 Administrator's Companion* by Steven Kaczmarek (Microsoft Press, 2004) shows an example of the modifying the Windows Installer tab.

- Chapter 5 of the *SMS 2003 Operations Guide* also describes the Windows Installer tab.

- Review the "Windows Installer Source Location Manager" white paper from Microsoft: http://www.microsoft.com/smserver/techinfo/productdoc/default.mspx.

5-23. Controlling Microsoft Operations Manager Alerts

Problem

You want to disable Microsoft Operations Manager (MOM) alerts when a program runs, and you also want to generate a MOM alert if a program fails.

Solution: Using a Graphical Interface

1. Open the SMS Administrator console.

2. From the SMS Administrator console, expand Site Database (*<Site Code>*), and expand Packages.

3. Expand any folders necessary, and expand the package that contains the program you want to modify.

4. Select Programs to display the existing programs in the right pane.

5. In the right pane, double-click the program to open the Program Properties dialog box.

6. Select the MOM tab if it isn't already visible.

7. Select the "Disable MOM alerts while this program runs" check box.

8. Select the "Generate MOM alert if this program fails" check box.

9. Click OK to apply the settings.

Solution: Using VBScript

Example 5-18 demonstrates how to configure MOM alerts during SMS application installation.

Example 5-18. *EnableMOMAlerts.vbs*

```
DISABLE_MOM_ALERT_WHILE_RUNNING = 2^(5)
GENERATE_MOM_ALERT_IF_FAILURE = 2^(6)

strSMSServer = <SMSServer>

strPackageID = "LAB0000A"
strProgramName = "NET Framework 1.1 SP1"

Set objLoc = CreateObject("WbemScripting.SWbemLocator")
Set objSMS= objLoc.ConnectServer(strSMSServer, "root\sms")
Set Results = objSMS.ExecQuery _
    ("SELECT * From SMS_ProviderLocation WHERE ProviderForLocalSite = true")
For each Loc in Results
    If Loc.ProviderForLocalSite = True Then
        Set objSMS = objLoc.ConnectServer(Loc.Machine, "root\sms\site_" & _
            Loc.SiteCode)
            strSMSSiteCode = Loc.Sitecode
    end if
Next

Set objProgram=objSMS.Get("SMS_Program.PackageID='" & _
    strPackageID & "',ProgramName='" & strProgramName & "'")

intProgramFlags = objProgram.ProgramFlags

if (intProgramFlags and DISABLE_MOM_ALERT_WHILE_RUNNING) then
    wscript.echo "DISABLE_MOM_ALERT_WHILE_RUNNING flag " & _
        "already set!"
else
    wscript.echo "Setting DISABLE_MOM_ALERT_WHILE_RUNNING flag"
    intProgramFlags = intProgramFlags or _
        DISABLE_MOM_ALERT_WHILE_RUNNING
end if

if (intProgramFlags and GENERATE_MOM_ALERT_IF_FAILURE) then
    wscript.echo "GENERATE_MOM_ALERT_IF_FAILURE flag " & _
        "already set!"
else
    wscript.echo "Setting GENERATE_MOM_ALERT_IF_FAILURE flag"
    intProgramFlags = intProgramFlags or _
        GENERATE_MOM_ALERT_IF_FAILURE
end if
objProgram.ProgramFlags = intProgramFlags
objProgram.Put_
```

Discussion

If you use MOM in your environment, then the MOM alert settings will make your life easier. One of the alerts that MOM can generate is in response to a reboot event on a client. If one of your SMS programs requires a reboot, as SMS programs sometimes do, and you are currently monitoring systems with MOM, then you will receive an alert for every system that runs the program and then subsequently reboots. To avoid that flood of alerts, you can set the configuration of the program to disable MOM alerts when the program runs.

Note Setting the option "Disable MOM alerts while a program runs" will disable MOM alerts for the time specified in the "Maximum allowed run time" program property. If the value for "Maximum allowed run time" is greater than 12 hours, or if the default value of Unknown is used, MOM alerts will be disabled for 15 minutes.

If you are concerned about failed executions of a program, you can use MOM to alert you of those also. MOM will create an alert if the program fails, so that personnel who are monitoring the MOM alerts can address any issues that result from the failed program.

In Example 5-18, we obtain the program object. If the MOM alerts are not already enabled, we enable them using bit ORing.

See Also

- Several examples in this chapter (such as Recipes 5-20, "Re-enabling a Disabled Program Using VBScript," and 5-12, "Viewing All Programs with User Logon Requirements") describe how to use bit ANDing and bit ORing to modify the `ProgramFlags` property of an SMS program.

- MSDN, the SMS 2003 SDK, and the *SMS 2003 Scripting Guide* provide additional information about `SMS_Program`.

- The SMS 2003 integrated help feature provides additional information about controlling MOM alerts.

5-24. Exporting Packages and Associated Programs

Problem

You want to export packages and associated programs from one SMS site and then import them to a different SMS site.

Solution: Using a Graphical Interface

No GUI solution is possible.

Solution: Using VBScript

Example 5-19 demonstrates how to extract one package and all associated programs to a Managed Object Format (MOF) file using VBScript.

Example 5-19. *ExportingPackageProgramtoMOF.vbs*

```
Const ForWriting = 2
Set fso = CreateObject("Scripting.FileSystemObject")
strSMSServer = "SMSVPC"
strNEWSMSServer = "MYPRODSMSSERVER"
strNewSMSSiteCode = "PRD"
strPackageID = "LAB0000B"
strExportFolder = "C:\Scripts\Packages\"

Set objLoc =  CreateObject("WbemScripting.SWbemLocator")
```

```
Set objSMS= objLoc.ConnectServer(strSMSServer, "root\sms")
Set Results = objSMS.ExecQuery _
    ("SELECT * From SMS_ProviderLocation WHERE ProviderForLocalSite = true")
For each Loc in Results
    If Loc.ProviderForLocalSite = True Then
        Set objSMS = objLoc.ConnectServer(Loc.Machine, "root\sms\site_" & _
            Loc.SiteCode)
    end if
Next


Set colPkgs = objSMS.ExecQuery _
    ("select * from SMS_Package where PackageID = '" & strPackageID & "'")

for each objPkg in colPkgs
'wscript.echo objPkg.GetObjectText_
'wscript.echo objPkg.GetText_(2) 'output to xml
    wscript.echo "Exporting " & objPkg.Name & vbTAB & _
        objPkg.PackageID
    Set fout = fso.OpenTextFile(strExportFolder & _
        objPkg.Name & " (" & objPkg.PackageID & ")" & _
        ".MOF", ForWriting, True)
    fout.writeline "//*******************************"
    fout.writeline "//Created by VBScript" & vbTAB & Now()
    fout.writeline "//*******************************"
    fout.writeline vbCRLF
    'only use the following line if planning to import MOF
    'from the command line
    fout.writeline "#pragma namespace(" & chr(34) & "\\\\" & _
        strNEWSMSServer & "\\root\\SMS\\site_" & _
        strnewSMSSiteCode & chr(34) & ")"

    'Write the package info
    fout.writeline vbCRLF
    fout.writeline "// **** Class : SMS_Package ****"

    for each strLine in split(objPkg.GetObjectText_, chr(10))
        if instr(strLine, "PackageID =") then
            fout.writeline(vbTAB & "PackageID = " & chr(34) & _
                chr(34)) & ";"
        elseif instr(strLine, "instance of SMS_Package") then
            strLine = "instance of SMS_Package as $pID"
            fout.writeline cstr(strLine)
        elseif instr(strLine, "SourceDate") then
            strLine = "SourceDate = " & Chr(34) & Chr(34)
        elseif instr(strLine, "SourceSite") then
            strLine = "SourceSite = " & Chr(34) & Chr(34)
        elseif instr(strLine, "StoredPackagePath ") then
            strLine = "StoredPackagePath = " & Chr(34) & Chr(34)
        elseif instr(strLine, "SourceVersion") then
            strLine = "SourceVersion = " & Chr(34) & Chr(34)        else
            fout.writeline cstr(strLine)
        end if
    next

    'now write program info
    fout.writeline vbCRLF
```

```
        fout.writeline "// **** Class : SMS_Program ****"

        Set colPrograms = objSMS.ExecQuery _
        ("select * from SMS_Program where PackageID = '" & _
            objPkg.PackageID & "'")

        for each objProgram in colPrograms
            for each strLine in split(objProgram.GetObjectText_, chr(10))
                if instr(strLine, "PackageID =") then
                    fout.writeline(vbTAB & "PackageID = $pID;")
                elseif instr(strLine, "DependentProgram") then
                    if len(strLine) = 23 then
                        fout.writeline strLine
                    else
                        fout.writeline vbTAB & "//" & strLine
                        fout.writeline vbTAB & "DependentProgram = " & _
                            Chr(34) & Chr(34) & ";"
                    end if
                else
                    fout.writeline cstr(strLine)
                end if
            next
        next
    next
    fout.writeline "// **** End ****"
    fout.close
next
```

Example 5-20 demonstrates how to extract *all* packages and associated programs to a MOF file using VBScript. Example 5-21 shows an example of the output from executing Example 5-20.

Example 5-20. *ExportingALLPackageProgramtoMOFs.vbs*

```
Const ForWriting = 2
Set fso = CreateObject("Scripting.FileSystemObject")
strSMSServer = "SMSVPC"
strNEWSMSServer = "MYPRODSMSSERVER"
strNewSMSSiteCode = "PRD"
strExportFolder = "C:\Scripts\Packages\"

Set objLoc =  CreateObject("WbemScripting.SWbemLocator")
Set objSMS= objLoc.ConnectServer(strSMSServer, "root\sms")
Set Results = objSMS.ExecQuery _
    ("SELECT * From SMS_ProviderLocation WHERE ProviderForLocalSite = true")
For each Loc in Results
    If Loc.ProviderForLocalSite = True Then
        Set objSMS = objLoc.ConnectServer(Loc.Machine, "root\sms\site_" & _
            Loc.SiteCode)
    end if
Next

Set colPkgs = objSMS.ExecQuery _
("select * from SMS_Package")

for each objPkg in colPkgs
'wscript.echo objPkg.GetObjectText_
'wscript.echo objPkg.GetText_(2) 'output to xml
    wscript.echo "Exporting " & objPkg.Name & vbTAB & _
```

```
            objPkg.PackageID
    Set fout = fso.OpenTextFile(strExportFolder & _
        objPkg.Name & " (" & objPkg.PackageID & ")" & ".MOF", ForWriting, True)
    fout.writeline "//*******************************"
    fout.writeline "//Created by VBScript" & vbTAB & Now()
    fout.writeline "//*******************************"
    fout.writeline vbCRLF
    'only use the following line if planning to import MOF
    'from the command line
    fout.writeline "#pragma namespace(" & chr(34) & "\\\\" & _
        strNEWSMSServer & "\\root\\SMS\\site_" & _
        strnewSMSSiteCode & chr(34) & ")"

    'Write the package info
    fout.writeline vbCRLF
    fout.writeline "// **** Class : SMS_Package ****"

    for each strLine in split(objPkg.GetObjectText_, chr(10))
        if instr(strLine, "PackageID =") then
            fout.writeline(vbTAB & "PackageID = " & chr(34) & _
                chr(34)) & ";"
        elseif instr(strLine, "instance of SMS_Package") then
            strLine = "instance of SMS_Package as $pID"
            fout.writeline cstr(strLine)
        elseif instr(strLine, "SourceDate") then
            strLine = "SourceDate = " & Chr(34) & Chr(34)
elseif instr(strLine, "SourceSite") then
            strLine = "SourceSite = " & Chr(34) & Chr(34)
        elseif instr(strLine, "StoredPackagePath ") then
            strLine = "StoredPackagePath = " & Chr(34) & Chr(34)
elseif instr(strLine, "SourceVersion") then
            strLine = "SourceVersion = " & Chr(34) & Chr(34)
        else
            fout.writeline cstr(strLine)
        end if
    next

    'now write program info
    fout.writeline vbCRLF
    fout.writeline "// **** Class : SMS_Program ****"

    Set colPrograms = objSMS.ExecQuery _
    ("select * from SMS_Program where PackageID = '" & _
        objPkg.PackageID & "'")

    for each objProgram in colPrograms
        for each strLine in split(objProgram.GetObjectText_, chr(10))
            if instr(strLine, "PackageID =") then
                fout.writeline(vbTAB & "PackageID = $pID;")
            elseif instr(strLine, "DependentProgram") then
                if len(strLine) = 23 then
                    fout.writeline strLine
                else
                    fout.writeline vbTAB & "//" & strLine
                    fout.writeline vbTAB & "DependentProgram = " & _
                        Chr(34) & Chr(34) & ";"
                end if
```

```
                else
                    fout.writeline cstr(strLine)
                end if
            next
        next
        fout.writeline "// **** End ****"
        fout.close
next
```

Example 5-21. *Sample MOF File with Package and Programs*

```
//*******************************
//Created by VBScript    4/19/2006 10:40:24 AM
//*******************************

#pragma namespace("\\\\PRODSERVER\\root\\SMS\\site_PRD")

// **** Class : SMS_Package ****

instance of SMS_Package as $pID
{
    ActionInProgress = 0;
    Description = "";
    ForcedDisconnectDelay = 5;
    ForcedDisconnectEnabled = TRUE;
    ForcedDisconnectNumRetries = 2;
    IgnoreAddressSchedule = FALSE;
    ImageFlags = 0;
    Language = "";
    LastRefreshTime = "";
    Manufacturer = "";
    MIFFilename = "PIAStat";
    MIFName = "Software Updates Installation Agent";
    MIFPublisher = "Microsoft";
    MIFVersion = "";
    Name = "MBSA - April 2006 Security Patches";
    PackageID = "";
    PkgFlags = 536870912;
    PkgSourceFlag = 2;
    PkgSourcePath = "\\\\SMSSOURCE\\C$\\MBSA - April 2006 Security Patches";
    PreferredAddressType = "";
    Priority = 2;
    ShareName = "";
    ShareType = 1;
    Version = "";
};


// **** Class : SMS_Program ****

instance of SMS_Program
{
    ActionInProgress = 0;
    ApplicationHierarchy = "";
    CommandLine = ➡
        "PatchInstall.exe /g:0 /n /f /s /c:5 /t:30 /m:\"PatchAuthorize.xml\"";
```

```
    Comment = "";
    DependentProgram = "";
    Description = "";
    DeviceFlags = 0;
    DiskSpaceReq = "57 MB";
    DriveLetter = "";
    Duration = 0;
    MSIFilePath = "";
    MSIProductID = "";
    PackageID = $pID;
    ProgramFlags = 2148574208;
    ProgramName = "MBSA - April 2006 Security Patches";
    RemovalKey = "";
    Requirements = "";
    WorkingDirectory = "";
};

// **** End ****
```

Discussion

Have you ever dreamed of exporting SMS packages and programs from your test site and importing them into your production site? Examples 5-19 and 5-20 are great examples of how to accomplish this task. Granted, at first glance, the code is a little long. Take your time and examine it, though; once you see the process, you may find many ways to expand upon this idea for your environment.

Example 5-19 demonstrates how to export one package and its programs to a MOF file. In this example, the test server is "SMSVPC", and strPackageID is set to the desired PackageID in the test site. strNEWSMSServer contains the server name of the SMS provider for the production server, and strNEWSMSSiteCode is the site code of the production site. Last but not least, strExportFolder is the path to where you want the MOF file(s) to be saved.

After connecting to the SMS site, we perform a WMI Query Language (WQL) query to obtain the instance of the SMS package. Next, we create a file named by package name and PackageID, and then we begin writing data to the file. Notice the for-each loop that contains the following code:

```
split(objPkg.GetObjectText_, chr(10))
```

We use the GetObjectText_ method on the objPkg object, which displays the data in MOF format. We use the split function to create an array to enumerate. chr(10) is a linefeed character. In this for-each loop, we look for specific lines (PackageID, SourceDate, SourceSite, etc.), and set them to "". These properties are important for the current SMS server, but have no meaning in the new SMS server. After enumerating each line returned from the GetObjectText_ method on the package object, we then perform another WQL query to enumerate all programs associated with the package.

Enumerating each program, we write the proper data to the file. If dependent program information is identified, we preserve the data but comment out the line. A dependent program can cause this process to be a bit trickier if the dependent program is part of a different package. So in this example, we simply comment the line.

Review Example 5-21 for a sample MOF file created by the VBScript. You will notice that the namespace has the path to your production SMS provider. Also, notice the following line:

```
instance of SMS_Package as $pID
```

$pID is a variable that will contain the PackageID at compile time. Because of this variable, we're able to include one or more programs in the same MOF file, and simply set PackageID to $pID.

Then at compile time, the proper PackageID will be included to associate the program to the proper package. To create the package and program in your production site, execute the following from the command line:

```
mofcomp WinZipInstall.MOF
```

where WinZipInstall.MOF is the name of the desired MOF file. Example 5-20 is similar to 5-19, except that we enumerate each instance of SMS_Package and write an MOF file for each package. With proper testing and configuration, this could be a great way to archive packages that are no longer needed.

See Also

- Chapter 9 provides additional information about leveraging MOF files to import and export data.

CHAPTER 6

■■■■

Advertisements

Before you push that big red button on your software deployment machine, let's explore what is going to happen. We covered collections, packages, and programs in earlier chapters so you have a clear understanding of what will happen after you create an advertisement. All components of software distribution in SMS 2003 are equally important, but the advertisement can get you into the most trouble. If you enjoy having all of your bosses descend upon your desk like hungry wolves, then you can skip this chapter. If not, then jump into the following recipes and learn how to press that big red button with confidence.

6-1. Creating an Advertisement

Problem

You want to create an advertisement.

Solution: Using a Graphical Interface

1. Open the SMS Administrator console.

2. From the SMS Administrator console, expand Site Database (*<Site Code>*), and expand Advertisements.

3. Right-click Advertisements and select New ➤ Advertisement from the menu to open the Advertisement Properties dialog box.

4. On the General tab, enter at least the name of the new advertisement and select a package, program, and collection.

5. Specify any of the additional parameters.

6. Click OK to create the new advertisement.

Solution: Using VBScript

Example 6-1 demonstrates how to create a nonmandatory advertisement.

Example 6-1. *CreateAdvert.vbs*

```
strSMSServer = <SMSServer>
advName = "Microsoft .NET Framework 1.1 SP1"
advCollection = "SMS000GS"
advPackageID = "LAB0000A"
advProgramName = "NET Framework 1.1 SP1"
```

```
Set objLoc = CreateObject("WbemScripting.SWbemLocator")
Set objSMS= objLoc.ConnectServer(strSMSServer, "root\sms")
Set Results = objSMS.ExecQuery _
    ("SELECT * From SMS_ProviderLocation WHERE ProviderForLocalSite = true")
For each Loc in Results
    If Loc.ProviderForLocalSite = True Then
        Set objSMS = objLoc.ConnectServer(Loc.Machine, "root\sms\site_" & _
            Loc.SiteCode)
            strSMSSiteCode = Loc.Sitecode
    end if
Next

Set newAdvert = objSMS.Get("SMS_Advertisement").SpawnInstance_()
newAdvert.AdvertisementName = advName
newAdvert.CollectionID = advCollection
newAdvert.PackageID = advPackageID
newAdvert.ProgramName = advProgramName
newAdvert.Put_
```

Discussion

By now you should feel pretty comfortable creating the various components in SMS required for software distribution, and creating an advertisement is similar. The one major difference is that an advertisement starts an action. Collections, packages, and programs are completely benign without an advertisement.

Example 6-1 shows the most basic advertisement you can create. All properties in the example script are required. PresentTime, which is the date and time the advertisement is made available to the clients, is also required. When creating an advertisement, if you do not include a PresentTime, SMS sets a default PresentTime of January 1, 1990, 12:00 a.m. for you. SMS also sets PresentTimeEnabled to True by default to enable the advertisement. This makes the nonmandatory advertisement available immediately to the client. If you want to ensure the advertisement isn't available to users immediately, be sure to set PresentTime to a date and time in the future.

Use newAdvert.Put_ to "save" (create) the new advertisement. The following are the required properties of an advertisement:

AdvertisementName: The unique name for the advertisement. A best practice is to first verify that the desired advertisement name does not exist.

CollectionID: The ID of the collection to advertise.

PackageID: The ID of the package to advertise.

ProgramName: The *exact* program name of the program to advertise.

By default, a new advertisement is configured to include members of subcollections. This isn't as obvious when creating an advertisement programmatically. To not include subcollections, be sure to set IncludeSubCollection to False when creating the advertisement. See Recipe 6-6, "Configuring a Voluntary Advertisement," for an example.

Note When creating an advertisement programmatically, a best practice is to first verify that the CollectionID, PackageID, and ProgramName exist.

Caution If an advertisement is created with incorrect properties, SMS may still attempt to create the advertisement, but unexpected results may occur.

See Also

- Recipe 6-6, "Configuring a Voluntary Advertisement," demonstrates how to create a non-mandatory advertisement.

- Recipe 6-7, "Configuring a Mandatory Advertisement," demonstrates how to add a mandatory assignment to an existing advertisement.

- Recipe 6-8, "Configuring a Recurring Advertisement," demonstrates how to create a schedule for an advertisement to recur.

- Recipe 6-9, "Configuring an Event-Triggered Advertisement," demonstrates how to create an advertisement to run as soon as possible.

- Recipe 6-2, "Deleting an Advertisement," demonstrates how to delete an existing advertisement.

- Recipe 6-11, "Expiring an Advertisement," demonstrates how to set an expiration time on an existing advertisement.

- The SMS 2003 SDK provides more information about the SMS_Advertisement class.

- Chapter 5 of the *SMS 2003 Operations Guide* details how to create an advertisement.

- Chapter 12 of the *Microsoft Systems Management Server 2003 Administrator's Companion* by Steven Kaczmarek (Microsoft Press, 2004) discusses how to create an advertisement.

- Sample C.17 of Appendix C of the *SMS 2003 Operations Guide* demonstrates how to programmatically create an advertisement using VBScript.

6-2. Deleting an Advertisement

Problem

You want to delete an advertisement.

Solution: Using a Graphical Interface

1. Open the SMS Administrator console.

2. From the SMS Administrator console, expand Site Database (*<Site Code>*), and expand Advertisements.

3. Expand any folders that contain the advertisement you want to delete.

4. In the right pane, select the advertisement and delete it by either pressing the Delete key, clicking the Delete button on the SMS Administrator console toolbar, or right-clicking the advertisement and selecting Delete from the menu.

5. Click Yes to confirm your choice to delete the advertisement.

Solution: Using VBScript

Example 6-2 demonstrates how to delete a specific advertisement, given the AdvertisementID.

Example 6-2. *DeleteAdvert.vbs*

```
strSMSServer = <SMSServer>

strAdvertID = "LAB20007"

Set objLoc =  CreateObject("WbemScripting.SWbemLocator")
Set objSMS= objLoc.ConnectServer(strSMSServer, "root\sms")
Set Results = objSMS.ExecQuery _
    ("SELECT * From SMS_ProviderLocation WHERE ProviderForLocalSite = true")
For each Loc in Results
    If Loc.ProviderForLocalSite = True Then
        Set objSMS = objLoc.ConnectServer(Loc.Machine, "root\sms\site_" & _
            Loc.SiteCode)
            strSMSSiteCode = Loc.Sitecode
    end if
Next

Set objAdvert=objSMS.Get _
    ("SMS_Advertisement.AdvertisementID='" & strAdvertID & "'")
wscript.echo "Deleting " & objAdvert.AdvertisementName
objAdvert.Delete_
```

Example 6-3 demonstrates how to delete all advertisements associated to a specific PackageID.

Example 6-3. *DeleteMultipleAdverts_SamePackage.vbs*

```
strSMSServer = <SMSServer>
strPackageID = "LAB00002"

Set objLoc =  CreateObject("WbemScripting.SWbemLocator")
Set objSMS= objLoc.ConnectServer(strSMSServer, "root\sms")
Set Results = objSMS.ExecQuery _
    ("SELECT * From SMS_ProviderLocation WHERE ProviderForLocalSite = true")
For each Loc in Results
    If Loc.ProviderForLocalSite = True Then
        Set objSMS = objLoc.ConnectServer(Loc.Machine, "root\sms\site_" & _
            Loc.SiteCode)
            strSMSSiteCode = Loc.Sitecode
    end if
Next

Set colAdverts = objSMS.ExecQuery("Select * From SMS_Advertisement " & _
    "WHERE PackageID='" & strPackageID & "'")
For Each objAdvert In colAdverts
    wscript.echo "Deleting " & objAdvert.AdvertisementName
    objAdvert.Delete_
Next
```

Discussion

The first time you create an advertisement incorrectly, you will immediately want to delete it and hope that the program doesn't run on any systems. However, disabling the advertisement is the preferred method, as it takes less time to disable the program than to delete an advertisement, and doing so allows you to re-enable the advertisement after you have corrected your problem. Deleting advertisements is best for removing advertisements that have completed and are no longer needed.

This recipe provides two VBScript examples for deleting an advertisement. Example 6-2 demonstrates how to remove a specific advertisement using the objSMS.Get method. This method can be used to retrieve only one unique advertisement.

Example 6-3 demonstrates how to remove all advertisements associated with a specific package ID. For example, when deploying the latest version of Microsoft Office, you may have several advertisements that are all associated to the same Microsoft Office package. Example 6-3's VBScript could remove all advertisements associated with the Microsoft Office PackageID.

Tip The easiest way to find the AdvertisementID (and most other object IDs, for that matter) is to modify the shortcut to launch your SMS Administrator console. For example, instead of the shortcut launching C:\SMSAdmin\bin\i386\sms.msc, have it launch this: C:\SMSAdmin\bin\i386\sms.msc /sms:nodeinfo=1. Now when you launch your SMS Administrator console, you can right-click any node, select Properties, and view the Node Information tab. When you view the Node Information tab for an advertisement, look for AdvertisementID=x, where x is the ID you use in this script.

See Also

- Recipe 6-20, "Disabling an Advertisement," describes how to disable an advertisement by disabling the program associated to the advertisement.

- The SMS 2003 SDK provides more information about the SMS_Advertisement class.

6-3. Viewing All Advertisements

Problem

You want to view all advertisements.

Solution: Using a Graphical Interface

1. Open the SMS Administrator console.

2. From the SMS Administrator console, expand Site Database (<*Site Code*>), System Status, and Advertisement Status.

3. In the right pane you will see all advertisements listed.

Solution: Using VBScript

Example 6-4 demonstrates how to display all advertisements.

Example 6-4. *ListAdverts.vbs*

```
strSMSServer = <SMSServer>

Set objLoc =  CreateObject("WbemScripting.SWbemLocator")
Set objSMS= objLoc.ConnectServer(strSMSServer, "root\sms")
Set Results = objSMS.ExecQuery _
    ("SELECT * From SMS_ProviderLocation WHERE ProviderForLocalSite = true")
For each Loc in Results
    If Loc.ProviderForLocalSite = True Then
        Set objSMS = objLoc.ConnectServer(Loc.Machine, "root\sms\site_" & _
            Loc.SiteCode)
            strSMSSiteCode = Loc.Sitecode
```

```
    end if
Next

Set colAdverts = objSMS.ExecQuery _
    ("Select * From SMS_Advertisement order by " & _
        " AdvertisementName")
For Each objAdvert In colAdverts
    wscript.echo objAdvert.AdvertisementName & vbTAB & _
        objAdvert.PresentTime & objAdvert.AssignedSchedule
Next
```

Discussion

Advertisements are like rabbits. One day you have 5 of them, and the next day you have 50. It can be quite difficult to keep track of them all; some companies have tens of thousands of advertisements they have to manage. Viewing the advertisement status will give you the best overview of all of your advertisements.

Example 6-4 enumerates all advertisements (in order by AdvertisementName), and then displays each advertisement name (AdvertisementName), the date and time the advertisement was created (PresentTime), and the date and time the advertisement was made available (nonmandatory) to clients (AssignedSchedule). The example does not show mandatory assignments, which are a bit more difficult to calculate programmatically; we discuss these in greater detail later in this chapter.

See Also

- The SMS 2003 SDK provides more information about the SMS_Advertisement class.

- Recipe 6-10, "Listing Mandatory Assignments for an Advertisement," describes how to list mandatory assignments for an advertisement using VBScript.

6-4. Changing an Advertisement's Package and Program

Problem

You want to change the package or program being advertised.

Solution: Using a Graphical Interface

1. Open the SMS Administrator console.

2. From the SMS Administrator console, expand Site Database (<*Site Code*>), and expand Advertisements.

3. Expand any folders necessary to view the advertisement you want to modify.

4. Double-click the advertisement to open the Advertisement Properties dialog box.

5. On the General tab, choose a different package and program from the drop-down menus.

6. Click OK to apply the settings.

Solution: Using VBScript

Example 6-5 demonstrates how to select a new package and program for an advertisement.

Example 6-5. *Modifying Advertisement Program Information*

```
strSMSServer = <SMSServer>

strAdvertID = "LAB20015"
strNewPackageID = "LAB00006"
strNewProgramName = "Microsoft Updates Tool"

Set objLoc =  CreateObject("WbemScripting.SWbemLocator")
Set objSMS= objLoc.ConnectServer(strSMSServer, "root\sms")
Set Results = objSMS.ExecQuery _
    ("SELECT * From SMS_ProviderLocation WHERE ProviderForLocalSite = true")
For each Loc in Results
    If Loc.ProviderForLocalSite = True Then
        Set objSMS = objLoc.ConnectServer(Loc.Machine, "root\sms\site_" & _
            Loc.SiteCode)
            strSMSSiteCode = Loc.Sitecode
    end if
Next

Set objAdvert=objSMS.Get _
    ("SMS_Advertisement.AdvertisementID='" & strAdvertID & "'")
objAdvert.PackageID = strNewPackageID
objAdvert.ProgramName = strNewProgramName
objAdvert.Put_
```

Discussion

Making changes to an active advertisement should be done very carefully or avoided altogether, as those changes may cause a program to run immediately on your clients, whether or not you intend that to happen. Remember, advertisements are like rabbits, so you can just make another one instead of changing one that is active.

Caution Changing the package or program in an advertisement that is active that has a mandatory start time in the past will cause the SMS client to execute the new program immediately after it receives the updated advertisement.

Example 6-5 demonstrates how to modify an advertisement to use a new program in the same package. We use the Get method to obtain the specific advertisement and set the new program name, and we use Put_ to save the change.

See Also

- Recipe 6-5, "Changing the Target Collection," demonstrates how to change the collection for an advertisement.
- The SMS 2003 SDK describes how to modify advertisement properties.

6-5. Changing the Target Collection

Problem

You want to change the collection being targeted by an advertisement.

Solution: Using a Graphical Interface

1. Open the SMS Administrator console.

2. From the SMS Administrator console, expand Site Database (<*Site Code*>), and expand Advertisements.

3. Expand any folders necessary to view the advertisement you want to modify.

4. Double-click the advertisement to open the Advertisement Properties dialog box.

5. On the General tab, enter a new collection or click Browse to select it from the list.

6. Deselect the "Include members of sub-collections" check box if you would like to exclude subcollections.

7. Click OK to apply the settings.

Solution: Using VBScript

Example 6-6 demonstrates how to change the target collection for an advertisement.

Example 6-6. *ModifyAdvert_Coll.vbs*

```
strSMSServer = <SMSServer>

strAdvertID = "LAB20015"
strNewCollectionID = "LAB00011"

Set objLoc =  CreateObject("WbemScripting.SWbemLocator")
Set objSMS= objLoc.ConnectServer(strSMSServer, "root\sms")
Set Results = objSMS.ExecQuery _
    ("SELECT * From SMS_ProviderLocation WHERE ProviderForLocalSite = true")
For each Loc in Results
    If Loc.ProviderForLocalSite = True Then
        Set objSMS = objLoc.ConnectServer(Loc.Machine, "root\sms\site_" & _
            Loc.SiteCode)
            strSMSSiteCode = Loc.Sitecode
    end if
Next

Set objAdvert=objSMS.Get _
    ("SMS_Advertisement.AdvertisementID='" & strAdvertID & "'")
objAdvert.CollectionID = strNewCollectionID
objAdvert.Put_
```

Discussion

Changing the target collection of an advertisement is one task that you may do quite frequently. You may, for instance, choose to configure one advertisement to target a specific collection and then link collections to the target collection to expand your deployment scope. For example, say you have a Microsoft Office collection, and then you link the Purchasing collection to the Microsoft Office collection to deploy Office to the purchasing department.

Another approach you might take in the same situation is to change the target collection to an existing collection that properly defines your target scope. For example, say you have a Microsoft Office Test collection, and after successfully deploying Office to the test collection, you change the target collection to the Purchasing collection to deploy Office to the purchasing department. Both methods achieve the same result.

Example 6-6 is very similar to Example 6-5. Instead of modifying the program name, we modify the CollectionID. As with other examples, a best practice is to ensure the CollectionID exists before assigning the CollectionID to the advertisement.

See Also

- Recipe 6-4, "Changing an Advertisement's Package and Program," demonstrates how to modify the package and program associated with an advertisement.

- Recipe 3-5, "Creating a Linked Collection," demonstrates how to link collections.

- The SMS 2003 SDK provides more information about the SMS_Advertisement class.

6-6. Configuring a Voluntary Advertisement

Problem

You want to configure an advertisement that is user initiated.

Solution: Using a Graphical Interface

1. Open the SMS Administrator console.

2. From the SMS Administrator console, expand Site Database (<*Site Code*>), and expand Advertisements.

3. Expand any folders necessary to view the advertisement you want to modify.

4. Double-click the advertisement to open the Advertisement Properties dialog box.

5. On the Schedule tab, configure the start time for the advertisement by selecting a date and time from the drop-down menus.

6. Select the Greenwich Mean Time check box if you would not like the start time to use the local time of the client.

7. Select the "Allow users to run the program independently of assignments" check box so the program will be visible to the user in the Advertised Programs Control Panel applet or Add/Remove Programs.

8. Click OK to apply the settings.

Solution: Using VBScript

Example 6-7 demonstrates how to configure an advertisement to allow a user to run the program independent of mandatory assignments.

Example 6-7. *ModAdvert_Voluntary.vbs*

```
NO_DISPLAY = 2^(25)

strSMSServer = <SMSServer>

strAdvertID = "LAB20153"

Set objLoc =  CreateObject("WbemScripting.SWbemLocator")
Set objSMS= objLoc.ConnectServer(strSMSServer, "root\sms")
Set Results = objSMS.ExecQuery _
    ("SELECT * From SMS_ProviderLocation WHERE ProviderForLocalSite = true")
For each Loc in Results
    If Loc.ProviderForLocalSite = True Then
        Set objSMS = objLoc.ConnectServer(Loc.Machine, "root\sms\site_" & _
            Loc.SiteCode)
            strSMSSiteCode = Loc.Sitecode
    end if
Next

Set objAdvertisement = objSMS.Get _
    ("SMS_Advertisement.AdvertisementID='" & strAdvertID & "'")

objAdvertisement.AdvertFlags = objAdvertisement.AdvertFlags _
    and not NO_DISPLAY
objAdvertisement.Put_
```

Discussion

We generally prefer to use mandatory advertisements because it gives us greater control over a deployment. But you may have some deployments that are better suited to being initiated by the end user. A good example of this may be an operating system upgrade like XP SP2. This is an extensive deployment, and for laptop users who travel frequently, it may be a better option to give them control over when that upgrade happens.

If you are an extremely nice SMS administrator (we're not), you can use voluntary advertisements to give your end users a grace period for installing a package. Simply create a mandatory assignment in the future and enable notifications so SMS will let them know that they can run the program at their leisure until the mandatory assignment time. This is particularly useful for groups of users like sales executives who may not want to have an XP SP2 upgrade happen in the middle of a customer demonstration. Though this may effectively demonstrate your company's vigor for a managed environment, it does little to further sales efforts for those employees!

Example 6-7 demonstrates how to modify an advertisement to allow a user to run the program independent of assignments. After connecting to the SMS provider, we use the Get method to obtain the instance of the desired advertisement. We then use bit ANDing (specifically, and not) to clear the NO_DISPLAY flag. Finally, we use the Put_ method to save the change to the advertisement.

See Also

- Recipe 6-7, "Configuring a Mandatory Advertisement," describes how to create a mandatory advertisement.
- Recipe 6-8, "Configuring a Recurring Advertisement," describes how to create a recurring advertisement.
- Recipe 6-9, "Configuring an Event-Triggered Advertisement," describes how to configure an event-triggered advertisement (e.g., user logon, user logoff, etc.).

- The SMS 2003 SDK provides more information about the SMS_Advertisement class and the AdvertFlags property.

- Chapter 5 of the *SMS 2003 Operations Guide* details how to create an advertisement.

- Chapter 12 of the *Microsoft Systems Management Server 2003 Administrator's Companion* by Steven Kaczmarek (Microsoft Press, 2004) discusses how to create an advertisement.

6-7. Configuring a Mandatory Advertisement

Problem

You want to configure an advertisement that will execute at a specific time.

Solution: Using a Graphical Interface

1. Open the SMS Administrator console.

2. From the SMS Administrator console, expand Site Database (*<Site Code>*), and expand Advertisements.

3. Expand any folders necessary to view the advertisement you want to modify.

4. Double-click the advertisement to open the Advertisement Properties dialog box.

5. On the Schedule tab, click the New button (the icon with the sunburst) to open the Assignment Schedule dialog box.

6. Click the Schedule button and select a date and time for the mandatory assignment.

7. Select the Greenwich Mean Time check box if you would not like the mandatory assignment time to use the local time of the client.

8. Click OK.

9. The new mandatory assignment will be visible in the mandatory assignment list.

10. Click OK to apply the settings.

Solution: Using VBScript

Example 6-8 demonstrates how to add a mandatory assignment to a given advertisement.

Example 6-8. *ModAdvert_Mandatory.vbs*

```
strSMSServer = <SMSServer>

strAdvertID = "LAB20016"
'For advAssignedSchedule, 'Now()' is used to get the current
'date/time of the system. A properly formatted date/time would be
'just fine here also: e.g., "12/02/2006 12:59 AM"
advAssignedSchedule = Now()

Set objLoc = CreateObject("WbemScripting.SWbemLocator")
Set objSMS= objLoc.ConnectServer(strSMSServer, "root\sms")
Set Results = objSMS.ExecQuery _
    ("SELECT * From SMS_ProviderLocation WHERE ProviderForLocalSite = true")
For each Loc in Results
    If Loc.ProviderForLocalSite = True Then
        Set objSMS = objLoc.ConnectServer(Loc.Machine, "root\sms\site_" & _
            Loc.SiteCode)
```

```
            strSMSSiteCode = Loc.Sitecode
    end if
Next

'create a nonrecurring schedule token
Set instToken = objSMS.Get("SMS_ST_NonRecurring"). _
        SpawnInstance_()
instToken.StartTime = ConvertToWMIDate(advAssignedSchedule)
retval = AddSchedToken(instToken, strAdvertID)

Function AddSchedToken(objSchedToken, strAdvertID)
    'enlarge the current schedule array by 1
    Set objAdvert=objSMS.Get _
        ("SMS_Advertisement.AdvertisementID='" & strAdvertID & "'")
    advertArray = objAdvert.AssignedSchedule
    onemore = ubound(advertArray) + 1
    redim preserve advertArray(onemore)
    objAdvert.AssignedSchedule = advertArray
    'add the new assignment
    objAdvert.AssignedSchedule(onemore) = objSchedToken
    objadvert.AssignedScheduleEnabled = True
    AddSchedToken = objAdvert.Put_
End Function

Function ConvertToWMIDate(strDate)
    'Convert from a standard date time to wmi date
    '4/18/2005 11:30:00 AM = 2005041811300.000000+***
    strYear = year(strDate):strMonth = month(strDate)
    strDay = day(strDate):strHour = hour(strDate)
    strMinute = minute(strDate)
    'Pad single digits with a leading zero
    if len(strmonth) = 1 then strMonth = "0" & strMonth
    if len(strDay) = 1 then strDay = "0" & strDay
    if len(strHour) = 1 then strHour = "0" & strHour
    if len(strMinute) = 1 then strMinute = "0" & strMinute
    ConvertToWMIDate = strYear & strMonth & strDay & strHour _
        & strMinute & "00.000000+***"
end function
```

Discussion

If you have been called a control freak at some time in your life (as we both have), you will probably fall in love with the mandatory advertisement. The mandatory advertisement does not require any intervention from the end user to initiate the execution of the program being advertised. If you have built your packages and programs correctly, you can deploy software without a single user knowing what you're doing . . . sorry—that is, without a single user being interrupted.

Example 6-8 demonstrates how to add a mandatory assignment to an existing advertisement. As you can see, we set advAssignedSchedule to Now() in this example, but any properly formatted (and valid) date will suffice. For example, if you set advAssignedSchedule = "12/02/2006 2:48 PM", the mandatory assignment will be configured to execute at that time.

As you can see, we create a new instance in Example 6-8 of an SMS_ST_NonRecurring schedule token, and we set the StartTime equal to the date and time contained in advAssignedSchedule (and call ConvertToWMIDate to get the date and time properly formatted). Then we call AddSchedToken to add the scheduled token to the token array for this advertisement.

In the function AddSchedToken, we first obtain the specified advertisement object. Next, we obtain the advertisement schedule array (objAdvert.AssignedSchedule). We redimension the array, adding one more element that contains the desired schedule token. Then we ensure the mandatory schedule is enabled (AssignedScheduleEnabled = True). Finally, we save the changes.

See Also

- Recipe 6-6, "Configuring a Voluntary Advertisement," describes how to configure a voluntary advertisement.

- Recipe 6-8, "Configuring a Recurring Advertisement," describes how to configure a recurring advertisement.

- Recipe 6-9, "Configuring an Event-Triggered Advertisement," describes how to configure an event-triggered advertisement (e.g., user logon, user logoff, etc.).

- The SMS 2003 SDK provides more information about the SMS_Advertisement class.

- Chapter 5 of the *SMS 2003 Operations Guide* details how to create an advertisement.

- Chapter 12 of the *Microsoft Systems Management Server 2003 Administrator's Companion* by Steven Kaczmarek (Microsoft Press, 2004) discusses how to create an advertisement.

6-8. Configuring a Recurring Advertisement

Problem

You want to configure an advertisement that runs more than one time.

Solution: Using a Graphical Interface

1. Open the SMS Administrator console.

2. From the SMS Administrator console, expand Site Database (*<Site Code>*), and expand Advertisements.

3. Expand any folders necessary to view the advertisement you want to modify.

4. Double-click the advertisement to open the Advertisement Properties dialog box.

5. On the Schedule tab, click the New button (the icon with the sunburst) to open the Assignment Schedule dialog box.

6. Click the Schedule button and select a recurrence pattern of minutes, hours, days, weeks, or months that meets your requirements.

7. Click OK.

8. The new recurring mandatory assignment will be visible in the mandatory assignment list.

9. Click OK to apply the settings.

Solution: Using VBScript

Example 6-9 demonstrates how to configure a recurring advertisement using SMS_ST_ RecurInterval. Examples 6-10 through 6-12 demonstrate how to use other schedule tokens for various recurring schedules.

Example 6-9. *ModAdvert_RecurringSMS_ST_RecurInterval.vbs*

```
strSMSServer = <SMSServer>

strAdvertID = "LAB20016"
'"Occurs every ten minutes beginning now()"
'For advStartTime, 'Now()' is used to get the current
'date/time of the system. A properly formatted date/time would be
'just fine here also:  e.g., "12/02/2006 12:59 AM"
advStartTime = Now()

Set objLoc =  CreateObject("WbemScripting.SWbemLocator")
Set objSMS= objLoc.ConnectServer(strSMSServer, "root\sms")
Set Results = objSMS.ExecQuery _
    ("SELECT * From SMS_ProviderLocation WHERE ProviderForLocalSite = true")
For each Loc in Results
    If Loc.ProviderForLocalSite = True Then
        Set objSMS = objLoc.ConnectServer(Loc.Machine, "root\sms\site_" & _
            Loc.SiteCode)
            strSMSSiteCode = Loc.Sitecode
    end if
Next

'''''''''''''Schedule Token Information
'Create a new instance of SMS_ST_RecurInterval
Set advNewRecurToken = objSMS.Get("SMS_ST_RecurInterval"). _
    SpawnInstance_()
advNewRecurToken.MinuteSpan=10
advNewRecurToken.StartTime = ConvertToWMIDate(advStartTime)
'''''''''''''END Schedule Token Information

retval = AddSchedToken(advNewRecurToken,strAdvertID)

Function AddSchedToken(objSchedToken, strAdvertID)
    'enlarge the current schedule array by 1
    Set objAdvert=objSMS.Get _
        ("SMS_Advertisement.AdvertisementID='" & strAdvertID & "'")
    advertArray = objAdvert.AssignedSchedule
    onemore = ubound(advertArray) + 1
    redim preserve advertArray(onemore)
    objAdvert.AssignedSchedule = advertArray
    'add the new assignment
    objAdvert.AssignedSchedule(onemore) = objSchedToken
    objadvert.AssignedScheduleEnabled = True
    AddSchedToken = objAdvert.Put_
End Function

Function ConvertToWMIDate(strDate)
    'Convert from a standard date time to wmi date
    '4/18/2005 11:30:00 AM = 2005041811300.000000+***
    strYear = year(strDate):strMonth = month(strDate)
    strDay = day(strDate):strHour = hour(strDate)
    strMinute = minute(strDate)
    'Pad single digits with a leading zero
    if len(strmonth) = 1 then strMonth = "0" & strMonth
    if len(strDay) = 1 then strDay = "0" & strDay
    if len(strHour) = 1 then strHour = "0" & strHour
```

```
        if len(strMinute) = 1 then strMinute = "0" & strMinute
        ConvertToWMIDate = strYear & strMonth & strDay & strHour _
            & strMinute & "00.000000+***"
end function
```

Example 6-10. *ModAdvert_RecurringSMS_ST_RecurMonthlyByDate.vbs*

```
'''''''''''''Schedule Token Information
'"Occurs on the fifth day every two months
'    beginning at mm/dd/yyyy hh:mm am/pm"
'Create a new instance of SMS_ST_RecurInterval
Set advNewRecurToken = objSMS.Get("SMS_ST_RecurMonthlyByDate"). _
    SpawnInstance_()
advNewRecurToken.ForNumberOfMonths = 2
advNewRecurToken.MonthDay = 5 'set to zero for last day of month
advNewRecurToken.StartTime = ConvertToWMIDate(advStartTime)
'''''''''''''END Schedule Token Information
```

Example 6-11. *ModAdvert_RecurringSMS_ST_RecurMonthlyByWeekDay.vbs*

```
'''''''''''''Schedule Token Information
'"Occurs the second Monday every four months
'    beginning at mm/dd/yyyy hh:mm am/pm"
'Create a new instance of SMS_ST_RecurInterval
Set advNewRecurToken = objSMS.Get("SMS_ST_RecurMonthlyByWeekday"). _
    SpawnInstance_()
advNewRecurToken.ForNumberOfMonths = 4
advNewRecurToken.Day = 2 '2=Monday
advNewRecurToken.WeekOrder = 2 '2=Second week of month
advNewRecurToken.StartTime = ConvertToWMIDate(advStartTime)
'''''''''''''END Schedule Token Information
```

Example 6-12. *ModAdvert_RecurringSMS_ST_RecurWeekly.vbs*

```
'''''''''''''Schedule Token Information
'"Occurs every two weeks on Monday
'    beginning at mm/dd/yyyy hh:mm am/pm"
'Create a new instance of SMS_ST_RecurInterval
Set advNewRecurToken = objSMS.Get("SMS_ST_RecurWeekly"). _
    SpawnInstance_()
advNewRecurToken.Day = 2 '2=Monday
advNewRecurToken.ForNumberOfWeeks = 2
advNewRecurToken.StartTime = ConvertToWMIDate(advStartTime)
'''''''''''''END Schedule Token Information
```

Discussion

Next to mandatory advertisements, recurring advertisements are a favorite among SMS administrators. Leveraging recurring advertisements is like getting paid to turn on the automatic sprinklers at the local golf course. A perfect example of the need for a recurring advertisement is virus signature updates. You get them every day and update your package with the latest files. A recurring advertisement then instructs the SMS client to rerun the program every day. Recurring advertisements can turn daily chores into zero-effort productivity gains.

Most of the code in Example 6-9 is very similar to that in Example 6-8. The only difference is what appears between the `'''''''Schedule Token Information` and `''''''''END Schedule Token Information` sections. In Example 6-9, we create a recurring schedule that "Occurs every ten minutes beginning at mm/dd/yyyy hh:mm am/pm." As you can see, first we create a new instance of `SMS_ST_RecurInterval`. Next, we set `MinuteSpan=10`, which gives us the "every ten minutes" part. Then we set `StartTime` to specify when this schedule is to begin. In our example, we set `AdvStartTime = Now()`, which makes this schedule effective immediately. Finally, we call the `AddSchedToken` function to add the new schedule to the advertisement schedule array. See Example 6-8 for more information about the `AddSchedToken` function.

Here is a list of properties available for `SMS_ST_RecurInterval`:

`DaySpan`: Days between schedule intervals. Values are in the range 0 to 31.

`HourSpan`: Hours between schedule intervals. Values are in the range 0 to 23.

`MinuteSpan`: Minutes between schedule intervals. Values are in the range 0 to 59.

`IsGMT`: Configure to `True` to indicate the time is Greenwich Mean Time (GMT). A value of `FALSE` means that local time is used. The default is local time.

`StartTime`: Date and time when the scheduled action takes place. (The default is January 1, 1990, 12:00 a.m.)

Only one of `DaySpan`, `HourSpan`, and `MinuteSpan` can be used per schedule. If no start time is specified, then the default of January 1, 1990, 12:00 a.m. is used, and your advertisement will more than likely run immediately after the client receives the advertisement information.

Example 6-10 demonstrates how to create an advertisement that occurs at designated monthly intervals, such as every two months on the fifth day of the month. The framework of Example 6-9 can be used to create a fully functional script for Example 6-10.

Here is a list of properties available for `SMS_ST_RecurMonthlyByDate`:

`ForNumberOfMonths`: Months between events. Values are in the range 1 to 12. The default is 1 (every month).

`MonthDay`: Day of the month on which the action occurs. Zero specifies the last day of the month, regardless of its date. Values are in the range 0 to 31. The default is 0 (last day of the month).

`IsGMT`: Configure to `True` to indicate the time is in GMT. A value of `False` means that local time is used. The default is local time.

`StartTime`: Date and time when the scheduled action takes place. (The default is January 1, 1990, 12:00 a.m.)

Example 6-11 demonstrates how to create an advertisement that occurs for a specific day of the week, on a given week of the month, or at a given monthly interval. The VBScript in Example 6-11 creates an advertisement that runs on the second Monday every four months. The framework of Example 6-9 can be used to create a fully functional script for Example 6-11.

Here is a list of properties available for `SMS_ST_RecurMonthlyByWeekday`:

`Day`: Scheduled day of the week that the event is to occur. The default is 1, Sunday. Values for each day of the week are as follows: 1, Sunday; 2, Monday; 3, Tuesday; 4, Wednesday; 5, Thursday; 6, Friday; and 7, Saturday.

`ForNumberOfMonths`: Months between events. Values are in the range 1 to 12. The default is 1 (every month).

WeekOrder: Scheduled week of the month that the event is to occur. The default is 0 (the last week of the month). Values for each week of the month are as follows: 0, last week of the month; 1, first week of the month; 2, second week of the month; 3, third week of the month; and 4, fourth week of the month.

IsGMT: Configure to True to indicate the time is in GMT. A value of False means that local time is used. The default is local time.

StartTime: Date and time when the scheduled action takes place. (The default is January 1, 1990, 12:00 a.m.)

Only one of Day and WeekOrder can be used per schedule.

Example 6-12 demonstrates how to create an advertisement scheduled to occur at weekly intervals. For example, you can create an advertisement that occurs every two weeks on Monday. The framework of Example 6-9 can be used to create a fully functional script for this example.

From the SMS 2003 SDK (and MSDN), here is a list of properties available for SMS_ST_RecurWeekly:

Day: Scheduled day of the week that the event is to occur. The default is 1, Sunday. Values for each day of the week are as follows: 1, Sunday; 2, Monday; 3, Tuesday; 4, Wednesday; 5, Thursday; 6, Friday; and 7, Saturday.

ForNumberOfWeeks: Number of months between events. Values are in the range 1 to 4. The default is 1 (every week).

IsGMT: Configure to True to indicate the time is in GMT. A value of False means that local time is used. The default is local time.

StartTime: Date and time when the scheduled action takes place. (The default is January 1, 1990, 12:00 a.m.)

Note You may notice three additional properties in the SDK for the recurring intervals described in this recipe: DayDuration, HourDuration, and MinuteDuration. Please note that these properties are not used when creating advertisements; they are only used when configuring schedules for network discovery.

See Also

- Recipe 6-6, "Configuring a Voluntary Advertisement," describes how to configure a voluntary advertisement.

- Recipe 6-7, "Configuring a Mandatory Advertisement," describes how to configure a mandatory advertisement.

- Recipe 6-9, "Configuring an Event-Triggered Advertisement," describes how to configure an event-triggered advertisement (e.g., user logon, user logoff, etc.).

- The SMS 2003 SDK provides more information about the SMS_Advertisement class and recurring interval classes.

- Chapter 5 of the *SMS 2003 Operations Guide* details how to create an advertisement.

- Chapter 12 of the *Microsoft Systems Management Server 2003 Administrator's Companion* by Steven Kaczmarek (Microsoft Press, 2004) also discusses how to create an advertisement.

6-9. Configuring an Event-Triggered Advertisement

Problem

You want to configure an advertisement that runs after an event condition is met.

Solution: Using a Graphical Interface

1. Open the SMS Administrator console.

2. From the SMS Administrator console, expand Site Database (*<Site Code>*), and expand Advertisements.

3. Expand any folders necessary to view the advertisement you want to modify.

4. Double-click the advertisement to open the Advertisement Properties dialog box.

5. On the Schedule tab, click the New button (the icon with the sunburst) to open the Assignment Schedule dialog box.

6. Choose the "Assign immediately after this event" radio button, and select the appropriate event from the drop-down menu.

7. Click OK.

8. The new mandatory assignment will be visible in the mandatory assignment list.

9. Click OK to apply the settings.

Solution: Using VBScript

Example 6-13 demonstrates how to create a mandatory assignment to run as soon as possible.

Example 6-13. *ModAdvert_AssignImmediately.vbs*

```
IMMEDIATE = 2^(5)
strSMSServer = <SMSServer>

strAdvertID = "LAB20016"

Set objLoc = CreateObject("WbemScripting.SWbemLocator")
Set objSMS= objLoc.ConnectServer(strSMSServer, "root\sms")
Set Results = objSMS.ExecQuery _
    ("SELECT * From SMS_ProviderLocation WHERE ProviderForLocalSite = true")
For each Loc in Results
    If Loc.ProviderForLocalSite = True Then
        Set objSMS = objLoc.ConnectServer(Loc.Machine, "root\sms\site_" & _
            Loc.SiteCode)
            strSMSSiteCode = Loc.Sitecode
    end if
Next

Set objAdvertisement = objSMS.Get _
    ("SMS_Advertisement.AdvertisementID='" & strAdvertID & "'")

intAdvertFlags = objAdvertisement.AdvertFlags
if (intAdvertFlags and IMMEDIATE) then
    wscript.echo "IMMEDIATE flag " & _
        "already set!"
```

```
else
    wscript.echo "Setting IMMEDIATE flag"
    intAdvertFlags = intAdvertFlags or _
        IMMEDIATE
end if
objAdvertisement.AdvertFlags = intAdvertFlags
objAdvertisement.Put_
```

Discussion

You can choose one of the following three events to trigger an advertisement:

As soon as possible: This is more of a point in time than an event, but it is useful for immediate deployments. In Example 6-13, we used IMMEDIATE = 2^(5) to set the bit flag so that the advertisement runs as soon as possible.

Logon: The advertisement will run after someone has logged on to the computer. To modify Example 6-13 so that the advertisement runs after logon, you need to do two things. First, replace IMMEDIATE = 2^(5) with ONUSERLOGON = 2^(9). Second, change all subsequent occurrences of IMMEDIATE to ONUSERLOGON. For the logon to properly function, the program flag must also be set to run "Only when a user is logged on."

Logoff: The advertisement will run after the user has logged off. To get this behavior, change the flag setting in Example 6-13 to ONUSERLOGOFF = 2^(10), and then specify ONUSERLOGOFF in place of IMMEDIATE throughout the example. For the logoff flag to properly function, the program flag must also be set to run "Only when no user is logged on."

Example 6-13 demonstrates how to set the advertisement flag (AdvertFlags) for the advertisement to execute "As soon as possible." To clear the "As soon as possible" flag, use the and not operators as follows:

```
intAdvertFlags = intAdvertFlags and not IMMEDIATE
```

Clearing the "As soon as possible" flag will produce the same results as removing a mandatory assignment. One additional AdvertFlag worth mentioning is NO_DISPLAY = 2^(25). NO_DISPLAY is used to configure or determine if a user is able to run the program independent of the assignment(s). If the NO_DISPLAY flag is enabled, the user will not be able to run the program independently.

See Also

- Recipe 6-6, "Configuring a Voluntary Advertisement," describes how to configure a voluntary advertisement.

- Recipe 6-7, "Configuring a Mandatory Advertisement," describes how to configure a mandatory advertisement.

- Recipe 6-8, "Configuring a Recurring Advertisement," describes how to configure a recurring advertisement.

- The SMS 2003 SDK provides more information about the SMS_Advertisement class.

- Chapter 5 of the *SMS 2003 Operations Guide* details how to create an advertisement.

- Chapter 12 of the *Microsoft Systems Management Server 2003 Administrator's Companion* by Steven Kaczmarek (Microsoft Press, 2004) also discusses how to create an advertisement.

6-10. Listing Mandatory Assignments for an Advertisement

Problem

You want to display all mandatory assignments for an advertisement from the command line.

Solution: Using a Graphical Interface

No GUI solution is available.

Solution: Using VBScript

Example 6-14 demonstrates how to display all mandatory assignments for a given advertisement.

Example 6-14. *ShowMandatoryAssignments.vbs*

```
IMMEDIATE = 2^(5)
ONUSERLOGON = 2^(9)
ONUSERLOGOFF = 2^(10)

strSMSServer = <SMSServer>

strAdvertID = "LAB20015"

Set objLoc =  CreateObject("WbemScripting.SWbemLocator")
Set objSMS= objLoc.ConnectServer(strSMSServer, "root\sms")
Set Results = objSMS.ExecQuery _
    ("SELECT * From SMS_ProviderLocation WHERE ProviderForLocalSite = true")
For each Loc in Results
    If Loc.ProviderForLocalSite = True Then
        Set objSMS = objLoc.ConnectServer(Loc.Machine, "root\sms\site_" & _
            Loc.SiteCode)
            strSMSSiteCode = Loc.Sitecode
    end if
Next

Set objAdvert=objSMS.Get _
    ("SMS_Advertisement.AdvertisementID='" & strAdvertID & "'")

wscript.echo "Mandatory Assignment(s) for " & chr(34) & _
    objAdvert.AdvertisementName & " (" & strAdvertID & ")" & _
        chr(34)

intAdvertFlags = objAdvert.AdvertFlags
if (intAdvertFlags and IMMEDIATE) then
    wscript.echo "Event Assignment to run IMMEDIATELY."
end if
if (intAdvertFlags and ONUSERLOGON) then
    wscript.echo "Event Assignment to run On User Logon."
end if
if (intAdvertFlags and ONUSERLOGOFF) then
    wscript.echo "Event Assignment to run On User Logoff."
end if

for each objSched in objAdvert.AssignedSchedule
    'for a 'quick and dirty', instead of the case statement
```

```
'below, you could just display the information in the object
'by using objSched.GetObjectText_
'wscript.echo objSched.GetObjectText_
wscript.echo objSched.Path_.Class
select case objSched.Path_.Class
    case "SMS_ST_NonRecurring"
        strInfo = vbTAB & "Non-Recurring Assignment: "
        strInfo = strInfo & "Occurs at " & _
            WMIDateStringToDate(objSched.StartTime)
        if objSched.IsGMT then
            strInfo = strInfo & " GMT"
        end if


    case "SMS_ST_RecurInterval"
        strInfo = vbTAB & "Recurring Interval Assignment: "
        strInfo = strInfo & "Every " & objSched.DaySpan & _
            " days, " & objSched.MinuteSpan & " minutes, "
        strInfo = strInfo & "beginning on " & _
            WMIDateStringToDate(objSched.StartTime)
        if objSched.IsGMT then
            strInfo = strInfo & " GMT"
        end if


    case "SMS_ST_RecurMonthlyByDate"
        strInfo = vbTAB & "Recurring Monthly By Date: "
        strInfo = strInfo & "Occurs on the " & _
            objSched.MonthDay & " day, every " & _
            objSched.ForNumberOfMonths & " months, "
        strInfo = strInfo & "beginning on " & _
            WMIDateStringToDate(objSched.StartTime)
        if objSched.IsGMT then
            strInfo = strInfo & " GMT"
        end if


    case "SMS_ST_RecurMonthlyByWeekday"
        strInfo = vbTAB & "Recurring Monthly By Weekday: "
        strInfo = strInfo & "Occurs on the " & _
            objSched.Day & " day, every " & _
            objSched.ForNumberOfMonths & " months, " & _
            "for week order " & objSched.WeekOrder & ","
        strInfo = strInfo & "beginning on " & _
            WMIDateStringToDate(objSched.StartTime)
        if objSched.IsGMT then
            strInfo = strInfo & " GMT"
        end if


    case "SMS_ST_RecurWeekly"
        strInfo = vbTAB & "Recurring Monthly By Weekday: "
        strInfo = strInfo & "Occurs on the " & _
            objSched.Day & " day, every " & _
            objSched.ForNumberOfWeeks & " weeks, "
        strInfo = strInfo & "beginning on " & _
            WMIDateStringToDate(objSched.StartTime)
        if objSched.IsGMT then
            strInfo = strInfo & " GMT"
        end if
```

```
        end select
        wscript.echo strInfo
next

Function WMIDateStringToDate(dtmInstallDate)
WMIDateStringToDate = CDate(Mid(dtmInstallDate, 5, 2) & "/" & _
    Mid(dtmInstallDate, 7, 2) & "/" & Left(dtmInstallDate, 4) _
        & " " & Mid (dtmInstallDate, 9, 2) & ":" & _
            Mid(dtmInstallDate, 11, 2) & ":" & _
            Mid(dtmInstallDate, 13, 2))
End Function
```

Discussion

Example 6-14 demonstrates how to display all mandatory assignments for an advertisement. Both scheduled assignments and event-triggered assignments create mandatory assignments, so we must look at both types to identify all mandatory assignments. After obtaining the advertisement object, we first check AdvertFlags to see if IMMEDIATE, ONUSERLOGON, or ONUSERLOGOFF is enabled. If so, we display that information. Next, we enumerate each mandatory schedule (from AssignedSchedule). ObjSched.Path_Class is used to obtain the type of schedule (SMS_ST_NonRecurring, SMS_ST_RecurInterval, SMS_ST_RecurMonthlyByDate, SMS_ST_RecurMonthlyByWeekday, and SMS_ST_RecurWeekly). Finally, we use a case statement to display the appropriate schedule information for the identified type of class.

If you intend to use this schedule information to gather mandatory assignment information for advertisements, remember that other factors, including the following, may prevent the mandatory assignments from executing:

- If ExpirationTimeEnabled is set to True, and the ExpirationTime has passed, the advertisement will not run.

- If AssignedScheduleEnabled is set to False, the advertisement will not run.

- If the program used by the advertisement has been disabled (through the SMS_Program class), the advertisement will not run.

See Also

- Recipe 6-7, "Configuring a Mandatory Advertisement," describes how to configure a mandatory advertisement.

- Recipe 6-8, "Configuring a Recurring Advertisement," describes how to configure a recurring advertisement.

- Recipe 6-9, "Configuring an Event-Triggered Advertisement," describes how to configure an event-triggered advertisement (e.g., user logon, user logoff, etc.).

- Recipe 6-11, "Expiring an Advertisement," shows how to expire an advertisement.

- Recipe 6-12, "Listing Advertisements That Have an Expiration Time Enabled," offers information on how to list advertisements that have an expiration time enabled.

- The SMS 2003 SDK provides more information about the SMS_Advertisement class. It also provides more information about the SMS_ScheduleToken class. (This is the parent class of the SMS_ST_ schedule token classes used in this recipe.)

6-11. Expiring an Advertisement

Problem

You want to cancel an advertisement at a specific time.

Solution: Using a Graphical Interface

1. Open the SMS Administrator console.

2. From the SMS Administrator console, expand Site Database (*<Site Code>*), and expand Advertisements.

3. Expand any folders necessary to view the advertisement you want to modify.

4. Double-click the advertisement to open the Advertisement Properties dialog box.

5. On the Schedule tab, select the "Advertisement will expire" check box.

6. Choose the date and time to expire the advertisement from the drop-down menus.

7. Check the Greenwich Mean Time check box if you would not like the advertisement expiration time to use the local time of the client.

8. Click OK to apply the settings.

Solution: Using VBScript

Example 6-15 demonstrates how to create an expiration time for an advertisement.

Example 6-15. *ExpireAdvert.vbs*

```
strSMSServer = <SMSServer>

strAdvertID = "LAB20016"
'For advExpTime, 'Now()' is used to get the current
'date/time of the system. A properly formatted date/time would be
'just fine here also:  e.g., "12/02/2006 12:59 AM"
' and in this example, we're adding 5 days to the current date
' to calculate the expire time
dtmExpireDateTime = dateadd("d",5,Now())

Set objLoc =  CreateObject("WbemScripting.SWbemLocator")
Set objSMS= objLoc.ConnectServer(strSMSServer, "root\sms")
Set Results = objSMS.ExecQuery _
    ("SELECT * From SMS_ProviderLocation WHERE ProviderForLocalSite = true")
For each Loc in Results
    If Loc.ProviderForLocalSite = True Then
        Set objSMS = objLoc.ConnectServer(Loc.Machine, "root\sms\site_" & _
            Loc.SiteCode)
            strSMSSiteCode = Loc.Sitecode
    end if
Next

Set objAdvert=objSMS.Get _
    ("SMS_Advertisement.AdvertisementID='" & strAdvertID & "'")
objAdvert.ExpirationTime = ConvertToWMIDate(dtmExpireDateTime)
objAdvert.ExpirationTimeEnabled = True
'objAdvert.ExpirationTimeIsGMT = True  'if using GMT
objAdvert.Put_
```

```
Function ConvertToWMIDate(strDate)
    'Convert from a standard date time to wmi date
    '4/18/2005 11:30:00 AM = 2005041811300.000000+***
    strYear = year(strDate):strMonth = month(strDate)
    strDay = day(strDate):strHour = hour(strDate)
    strMinute = minute(strDate)
    'Pad single digits with leading zero
    if len(strmonth) = 1 then strMonth = "0" & strMonth
    if len(strDay) = 1 then strDay = "0" & strDay
    if len(strHour) = 1 then strHour = "0" & strHour
    if len(strMinute) = 1 then strMinute = "0" & strMinute
    ConvertToWMIDate = strYear & strMonth & strDay & strHour _
        & strMinute & "00.000000+***"
end function
```

Discussion

Expiring an advertisement is very helpful when you are concerned that an advertisement targeted for after-hours deployment may cause issues with end users if it runs during business hours. Setting the expiration on the advertisement will cause the SMS client to disregard the advertisement if it is attempting to run after the expiration timestamp.

The drawback to expiring an advertisement is that you probably will want to create a new advertisement to catch those systems that did not run the program before its advertisement expired. Disabling the advertisement may be a better option than expiring, but that approach has its drawbacks also, such as you will have to enable the advertisement again.

Example 6-15 demonstrates how to set an expiration time for an advertisement. First, we use the Get method to obtain the advertisement object, and we set the ExpirationTime using a WMI date-time string. Next, we set ExpirationTimeEnabled = True to enable the setting. If you have sites in multiple time zones, and you want the advertisement to expire across all time zones at the same time, use a GMT date and time for your ExpirationTime, and set ExpirationTimeIsGMT = True. Finally, we use the Put_ method to save the settings.

See Also

- Recipe 6-20, "Disabling an Advertisement," demonstrates how to disable an advertisement.

- The SMS 2003 SDK provides more information about the SMS_Advertisement class.

- Chapter 5 of the *SMS 2003 Operations Guide* details how to create an advertisement.

- Chapter 12 of the *Microsoft Systems Management Server 2003 Administrator's Companion* by Steven Kaczmarek (Microsoft Press, 2004) discusses how to create an advertisement.

6-12. Listing Advertisements That Have an Expiration Time Enabled

Problem

You want to display all advertisements that have an expiration time enabled.

Solution: Using a Graphical Interface

If you are using a folder structure for advertisements, the SMS Administrator console is not capable of showing all packages and expiration times at the same time.

Solution: Using VBScript

Example 6-16 demonstrates how to display all advertisements that have an enabled expiration time.

Example 6-16. *ShowAllAdverts_Expired.vbs*

```
strSMSServer = <SMSServer>

Set objLoc = CreateObject("WbemScripting.SWbemLocator")
Set objSMS= objLoc.ConnectServer(strSMSServer, "root\sms")
Set Results = objSMS.ExecQuery _
    ("SELECT * From SMS_ProviderLocation WHERE ProviderForLocalSite = true")
For each Loc in Results
    If Loc.ProviderForLocalSite = True Then
        Set objSMS = objLoc.ConnectServer(Loc.Machine, "root\sms\site_" & _
            Loc.SiteCode)
            strSMSSiteCode = Loc.Sitecode
    end if
Next

Set colAdverts = objSMS.ExecQuery _
    ("Select * From SMS_Advertisement order by " & _
        " AdvertisementName")
For Each objAdvert In colAdverts
    strExpireTime = GetExpirationDateTimeString _
        (objAdvert.AdvertisementID)
    if (not strExpireTime = "") then
        wscript.echo objAdvert.AdvertisementID & vbTAB & _
            objAdvert.AdvertisementName & vbTAB & strExpireTime
    end if
Next

Function GetExpirationDateTimeString(strAdvertID)
    Set objAdvert=objSMS.Get _
        ("SMS_Advertisement.AdvertisementID='" & _
        strAdvertID & "'")
    if objAdvert.ExpirationTimeEnabled = True then
        GetExpirationDateTimeString = _
            WMIDateStringToDate(objAdvert.ExpirationTime)
        if (objAdvert.ExpirationTimeIsGMT) Then
            GetExpirationDateTimeString = _
                GetExpirationDateTimeString & " GMT"
        end if
    end if
End Function

'Utility function to convert WMI Date string to a real date
Function WMIDateStringToDate(dtmInstallDate)
    '4/12/2005 3:46:04 AM = 20050412034604.000000-000
    WMIDateStringToDate = CDate(Mid(dtmInstallDate, 5, 2) & _
        "/" & Mid(dtmInstallDate, 7, 2) & "/" & _
        Left(dtmInstallDate, 4) & " " & _
        Mid (dtmInstallDate, 9, 2) & ":" & _
        Mid(dtmInstallDate, 11, 2) & ":" & _
        Mid(dtmInstallDate,13, 2))
End Function
```

Discussion

Example 6-16 demonstrates how to list advertisements that have an expiration time enabled. First, we execute a WMI Query Language (WQL) query to obtain all advertisements. Next, for each advertisement, we call GetExpirationDateTimeString to obtain the expiration date and time, if enabled (ExpirationTimeEnabled = True). If an expiration date and time are enabled, we display the information.

The function GetExpirationDateTimeString is required since some of the expiration time properties (ExpirationTimeIsGMT, ExpirationTimeEnabled) are *lazy properties* (see the sidebar titled "What Are Lazy Properties?" for more information). The SMS 2003 SDK provides more information about lazy properties.

WHAT ARE LAZY PROPERTIES?

Some data for SMS objects is not returned using a standard WQL query; these objects are described as "lazy." For example, in the SMS_Advertisement class, AssignedSchedule, AssignedScheduleEnabled, and AssignedScheduleIsGMT are all lazy properties. If you were to use WQL to query the SMS_Advertisement class, these properties would appear to have no data when enumerating the instances returned from the query. To obtain the properties' data, you must explicitly call the Get (or GetInstance) method, as demonstrated in the GetExpirationDateTimeString function in this recipe.

Review the class properties in the SMS 2003 SDK to identify lazy properties for a particular class.

See Also

- Review the sidebar titled "What Is WQL?" in Recipe 9-2, "Listing All Queries from the Command Line."

- Recipe 6-11, "Expiring an Advertisement," demonstrates how to set an expiration date and time on an advertisement.

- The SMS 2003 SDK provides more information about the SMS_Advertisement class and lazy properties.

6-13. Changing the Advertisement Priority

Problem

You want to change the priority of an advertisement.

Solution: Using a Graphical Interface

1. Open the SMS Administrator console.

2. From the SMS Administrator console, expand Site Database (*<Site Code>*), and expand Advertisements.

3. Expand any folders necessary to view the advertisement you want to modify.

4. Double-click the advertisement to open the Advertisement Properties dialog box.

5. On the Schedule tab, choose the appropriate priority for the advertisement from the drop-down menu.

6. Click OK to apply the settings.

Solution: Using VBScript

Example 6-17 demonstrates how to change the priority of the advertisement.

Example 6-17. *ChangeAdvertPriority.vbs*

```
strSMSServer = <SMSServer>

strAdvertID = "LAB20016"

Set objLoc =  CreateObject("WbemScripting.SWbemLocator")
Set objSMS= objLoc.ConnectServer(strSMSServer, "root\sms")
Set Results = objSMS.ExecQuery _
    ("SELECT * From SMS_ProviderLocation WHERE ProviderForLocalSite = true")
For each Loc in Results
    If Loc.ProviderForLocalSite = True Then
        Set objSMS = objLoc.ConnectServer(Loc.Machine, "root\sms\site_" & _
            Loc.SiteCode)
            strSMSSiteCode = Loc.Sitecode
    end if
Next

Set objAdvert=objSMS.Get _
    ("SMS_Advertisement.AdvertisementID='" & strAdvertID & "'")
objAdvert.Priority = 1 '1=high, 2=normal, 3=low
objAdvert.Put_
```

Discussion

The advertisement priority is used to control when the advertisement is replicated to other SMS sites. Typically this is more important with packages, as they contain a much larger amount of data than do advertisements, but the functionality is the same. If your site only sends high-priority data to its child sites during business hours, and your advertisement is set to medium, then the child sites will not receive the advertisement until after business hours.

Example 6-17 describes how to set the advertisement priority to high by setting the Priority flag to 1. Available settings for Priority are high (1), normal (2), and low (3). The default is normal.

See Also

- The SMS 2003 SDK provides more information about the SMS_Advertisement class.

6-14. Configuring an Advertisement to Run Only from a Distribution Point

Problem

You want to configure an advertisement to run from either a local or remote distribution point.

Solution: Using a Graphical Interface

1. Open the SMS Administrator console.

2. From the SMS Administrator console, expand Site Database (<*Site Code*>), and expand Advertisements.

3. Expand any folders necessary to view the advertisement you want to modify.

4. Double-click the advertisement to open the Advertisement Properties dialog box.

5. Select the Advanced Client tab.

6. Choose the "Run program from distribution point" radio button for the "When a distribution point is available locally" option.

7. Choose the "Run program from a remote distribution point" radio button for the "When no distribution point is available locally" option if you want to allow your Advanced Clients to run the program from distribution points that may not be on their local area network (LAN). Otherwise, choose the "Do not run program" radio button to limit the advertisement to only execute from local distribution points.

8. Click OK to apply the settings.

Solution: Using VBScript

Example 6-18 demonstrates how to change the advertisement properties to allow the client to only run the advertisement from a local or remote distribution point.

Example 6-18. *RemoteClientFlagsFromDP.vbs*

```
RUN_FROM_LOCAL_DISPPOINT = 2^(3)
RUN_FROM_REMOTE_DISPPOINT = 2^(7)

strSMSServer = <SMSServer>

strAdvertID = "LAB20016"

Set objLoc =  CreateObject("WbemScripting.SWbemLocator")
Set objSMS= objLoc.ConnectServer(strSMSServer, "root\sms")
Set Results = objSMS.ExecQuery _
    ("SELECT * From SMS_ProviderLocation WHERE ProviderForLocalSite = true")
For each Loc in Results
    If Loc.ProviderForLocalSite = True Then
        Set objSMS = objLoc.ConnectServer(Loc.Machine, "root\sms\site_" & _
            Loc.SiteCode)
            strSMSSiteCode = Loc.Sitecode
    end if
Next

Set objAdvertisement = objSMS.Get _
    ("SMS_Advertisement.AdvertisementID='" & strAdvertID & "'")

objAdvertisement.RemoteClientFlags = _
    RUN_FROM_LOCAL_DISPPOINT + RUN_FROM_REMOTE_DISPPOINT
objAdvertisement.Put_
```

Discussion

If you are familiar with SMS 2.0, then configuring an advertisement to run the program from a distribution point will make you feel right at home. When running the program to install the application being advertised, the SMS client will access the package files directly from the distribution point. This is a very effective way of distributing software on highly available systems like servers or PCs on a corporate LAN.

Example 6-18 shows how to modify the Advanced Client properties of an advertisement. In the example, we get the advertisement object and set RemoteClientFlags = RUN_FROM_LOCAL_DISPPOINT + RUN_FROM_REMOTE_DISPPOINT. Additional remote client flags are defined in Table 6-1.

Table 6-1. *Remote Client Flags*

Action	Value
RUN_FROM_LOCAL_DISPPOINT	2^3
DOWNLOAD_FROM_LOCAL_DISPPOINT	2^4
DONT_RUN_NO_LOCAL_DISPPOINT	2^5
DOWNLOAD_FROM_REMOTE_DISPPOINT	2^6
RUN_FROM_REMOTE_DISPPOINT	2^7

Two and only two remote client flags must be used at a time (no more, no less), and not all flags can be used together. Here are the valid combinations:

- RUN_FROM_LOCAL_DISPPOINT + DONT_RUN_NO_LOCAL_DISPPOINT
- RUN_FROM_LOCAL_DISPPOINT + DOWNLOAD_FROM_REMOTE_DISPPOINT
- RUN_FROM_LOCAL_DISPPOINT + RUN_FROM_REMOTE_DISPPOINT
- DOWNLOAD_FROM_LOCAL_DISPPOINT + DONT_RUN_NO_LOCAL_DISPPOINT
- DOWNLOAD_FROM_LOCAL_DISPPOINT + DOWNLOAD_FROM_REMOTE_DISPPOINT

See Also

- Recipe 6-15, "Configuring an Advertisement to Download and Execute," describes how to configure an advertisement to download package source and execute.
- Recipe 6-16, "Listing All Advertisements Configured to Download," demonstrates how to list all advertisements that are configured to download installation files.

6-15. Configuring an Advertisement to Download and Execute

Problem

You want to create an advertisement that downloads the package source and executes the program from the local cache.

Solution: Using a Graphical Interface

1. Open the SMS Administrator console.

2. From the SMS Administrator console, expand Site Database (<*Site Code*>), and expand Advertisements.

3. Expand any folders necessary to view the advertisement you want to modify.

4. Double-click the advertisement to open the Advertisement Properties dialog box.

5. Select the Advanced Client tab.

6. Choose the "Download program from distribution point" radio button for the "When a distribution point is available locally" option.

7. Choose the "Download program from a remote distribution point" radio button for the "When no distribution point is available locally" option if you want to allow Advanced Clients to download the program from distribution points that may not be on their local LAN. Otherwise, choose the "Do not run program" radio button to limit the advertisement to only execute from local distribution points.

8. Click OK to apply the settings.

Solution: Using VBScript

Example 6-19 demonstrates how to change the advertisement properties so that the client always downloads the package source from the local or remote distribution point.

Example 6-19. *RemoteClientFlagsDLFromDP.vbs*

```
DOWNLOAD_FROM_LOCAL_DISPPOINT = 2^(4)
DOWNLOAD_FROM_REMOTE_DISPPOINT = 2^(6)

strSMSServer = <SMSServer>

strAdvertID = "LAB20016"

Set objLoc =  CreateObject("WbemScripting.SWbemLocator")
Set objSMS= objLoc.ConnectServer(strSMSServer, "root\sms")
Set Results = objSMS.ExecQuery _
    ("SELECT * From SMS_ProviderLocation WHERE ProviderForLocalSite = true")
For each Loc in Results
    If Loc.ProviderForLocalSite = True Then
        Set objSMS = objLoc.ConnectServer(Loc.Machine, "root\sms\site_" & _
            Loc.SiteCode)
            strSMSSiteCode = Loc.Sitecode
    end if
Next

Set objAdvertisement = objSMS.Get _
    ("SMS_Advertisement.AdvertisementID='" & strAdvertID & "'")

objAdvertisement.RemoteClientFlags = _
    DOWNLOAD_FROM_LOCAL_DISPPOINT + _
        DOWNLOAD_FROM_REMOTE_DISPPOINT
objAdvertisement.Put_
```

Discussion

To help solve the problem of deploying software to moving targets like traveling laptops, Microsoft incorporated download and execute functionality into the SMS 2003 Advanced Client. Configuring an advertisement to download and execute will cause the SMS client to copy the package source files to a local cache using Background Intelligent Transfer Service (BITS). Once the download is complete, the client will execute the program from the local cache. The ability of the Advanced Client to download and execute an advertisement significantly increases your success of deployment to roaming computers, as they can move around while they are downloading the package data, stopping and restarting the download from where it left off and executing the install locally after the download is completed.

Example 6-19 is very similar to Example 6-18. The only difference is that we're setting `RemoteClientFlags = DOWNLOAD_FROM_LOCAL_DISPPOINT + DOWNLOAD_FROM_REMOTE_DISSPOINT`. Recipe 6-14, "Configuring an Advertisement to Run Only from a Distribution Point," provides more information about `RemoteClientFlags`.

Note The SMS client will begin to download the package source when the advertisement becomes available (`PresentedTime` in VBScript), but won't execute the program until the scheduled mandatory time.

WHAT IS BITS?

Binary Intelligent Transfer Service (BITS) is a file-transfer technology used to transfer files. In the SMS world, BITS is used by the SMS Advanced Client to download package source files from a BITS-enabled distribution point to the local SMS client cache. The SMS Advanced Client also uses BITS to pass data to the management point. The primary benefits to using BITS are as follows:

- *HTTP usage:* BITS downloads files using Hypertext Transfer Protocol (HTTP). HTTP packets pass more easily through firewalls.

- *Checkpoint restart:* If a connection to the distribution point becomes severed during the package source download, the download state will be preserved and will restart upon successful connection to the network.

- *Automatic network throttling:* BITS will slow its transfer rate depending on other network adapter activity, causing minimal effect to the end user's response time when accessing resources over the network.

Review Chapter 5 of the *SMS 2003 Operations Guide* and Chapter 15 of the *SMS 2003 Concepts, Planning, and Deployment Guide* for more information about how SMS uses BITS.

See Also

- Recipe 6-14, "Configuring an Advertisement to Run Only from a Distribution Point," describes how to configure an advertisement to run only from a distribution point.

- Review the sidebar in this recipe titled "What Is BITS?" for more information about SMS and BITS.

- Recipe 6-16, "Listing All Advertisements Configured to Download," demonstrates how to list all advertisements that are configured to download.

6-16. Listing All Advertisements Configured to Download

Problem

You want to display all advertisements that are configured to download.

Solution: Using a Graphical Interface

The SMS Administrator console is not capable of showing all advertisements configured to download at the same time.

Solution: Using VBScript

Example 6-20 demonstrates how to display all advertisements that are configured to download the package before executing the installation.

Example 6-20. *ShowAdvertsConfiguredtoDandE_RemClientFlags.vbs*

```
RUN_FROM_LOCAL_DISPPOINT = 2^(3)
DOWNLOAD_FROM_LOCAL_DISPPOINT = 2^(4)
DONT_RUN_NO_LOCAL_DISPPOINT = 2^(5)
DOWNLOAD_FROM_REMOTE_DISPPOINT = 2^(6)
RUN_FROM_REMOTE_DISPPOINT = 2^(7)

RunFromLocalDP_DownloadIfRemoteDP = _
    RUN_FROM_LOCAL_DISPPOINT + DOWNLOAD_FROM_REMOTE_DISPPOINT
DownloadFromLocal_DontRunNoLocal = _
    DOWNLOAD_FROM_LOCAL_DISPPOINT + DONT_RUN_NO_LOCAL_DISPPOINT
DownloadFromLocalDP_DownloadIfRemoteDP = _
    DOWNLOAD_FROM_LOCAL_DISPPOINT + _
        DOWNLOAD_FROM_REMOTE_DISPPOINT


strSMSServer = <SMSServer>

Set objLoc =  CreateObject("WbemScripting.SWbemLocator")
Set objSMS= objLoc.ConnectServer(strSMSServer, "root\sms")
Set Results = objSMS.ExecQuery _
    ("SELECT * From SMS_ProviderLocation WHERE ProviderForLocalSite = true")
For each Loc in Results
    If Loc.ProviderForLocalSite = True Then
        Set objSMS = objLoc.ConnectServer(Loc.Machine, "root\sms\site_" & _
            Loc.SiteCode)
            strSMSSiteCode = Loc.Sitecode
    end if
Next

Set colAdverts = objSMS.ExecQuery _
    ("Select * From SMS_Advertisement where " & _
    "RemoteClientFlags = " & _
    RunFromLocalDP_DownloadIfRemoteDP & _
    " or RemoteClientFlags = " & _
    DownloadFromLocal_DontRunNoLocal & _
    " or RemoteClientFlags = " & _
    DownloadFromLocalDP_DownloadIfRemoteDP & " order by " & _
    " AdvertisementName")
```

```
For Each objAdvert In colAdverts
    Select Case objAdvert.RemoteclientFlags

        Case RunFromLocalDP_DownloadIfRemoteDP
            wscript.echo objAdvert.AdvertisementName & vbTAB & _
                "(RunFromLocalDP_DownloadIfRemoteDP)"

        Case DownloadFromLocal_DontRunNoLocal
            wscript.echo objAdvert.AdvertisementName & vbTAB & _
                "(DownloadFromLocal_DontRunNoLocal)"

        Case DownloadFromLocalDP_DownloadIfRemoteDP
            wscript.echo objAdvert.AdvertisementName & vbTAB & _
                "(DownloadFromLocalDP_DownloadIfRemoteDP)"

        Case Else
            'neither remote or local are configured to
            ' download from DP
    End Select
Next
```

Discussion

There are three different valid combinations for downloading from the distribution points. In our script, we set each equal to a new variable for ease of use in our WQL script:

```
RunFromLocalDP_DownloadIfRemoteDP = _
    RUN_FROM_LOCAL_DISPPOINT + DOWNLOAD_FROM_REMOTE_DISPPOINT
DownloadFromLocal_DontRunNoLocal = _
    DOWNLOAD_FROM_LOCAL_DISPPOINT + DONT_RUN_NO_LOCAL_DISPPOINT
DownloadFromLocalDP_DownloadIfRemoteDP = _
    DOWNLOAD_FROM_LOCAL_DISPPOINT + _
        DOWNLOAD_FROM_REMOTE_DISPPOINT
```

Then, we use a WQL query to locate all advertisements that have one of these flag combinations present, and then we use a case statement to display the proper information.

See Also

- Recipe 6-14, "Configuring an Advertisement to Run Only from a Distribution Point," demonstrates how to configure an advertisement to run only from a distribution point.

- Recipe 6-15, "Configuring an Advertisement to Download and Execute," demonstrates how to configure an advertisement to download source files and execute.

6-17. Modifying the Permissions of an Advertisement

Problem

You want to modify the permissions of an advertisement.

Solution

1. Open the SMS Administrator console.
2. From the SMS Administrator console, expand Site Database (*<Site Code>*), and expand Advertisements.
3. Expand any folders that contain the advertisement you need to modify.
4. Right-click the advertisement and select Properties.
5. Select the Security tab in the Advertisement Properties dialog box.
6. Click the New or Delete button to add or remove class or instance security rights. You can also double-click any existing class or instance rights to modify them.
7. Click OK to apply the settings.

Discussion

The permissions of an advertisement are somewhat more important than those of other components due to the action factor that is inherent in all advertisements. You don't want someone to change the target collection of an advertisement without knowing what he's doing, as the consequences could severely affect your career (not his)!

See Also

- Recipe 4-9, "Modifying Permissions of a Package," describes how to modify permissions for an SMS package. The same process can be used to modify permissions of an advertisement.
- Chapter 3 of the *SMS 2003 Operations Guide* discusses SMS security in detail.

6-18. Creating an Advertisement Folder

Problem

You want to create an advertisement folder.

Solution: Using a Graphical Interface

1. Open the SMS Administrator console.
2. From the SMS Administrator console, expand Site Database (*<Site Code>*), and expand Advertisements.
3. Right-click Advertisements and select New ➤ Folder.
4. Provide a name for the folder.
5. Click OK to create the new folder.

Solution: Using VBScript

Example 6-21 demonstrates how to create an advertisement folder.

Example 6-21. *CreateAdvertFolder.vbs*

```
strSMSServer = <SMSServer>

strNewFolderName = "Security Patches"
```

```
Set objLoc =  CreateObject("WbemScripting.SWbemLocator")
Set objSMS= objLoc.ConnectServer(strSMSServer, "root\sms")
Set Results = objSMS.ExecQuery _
    ("SELECT * From SMS_ProviderLocation WHERE ProviderForLocalSite = true")
For each Loc in Results
    If Loc.ProviderForLocalSite = True Then
        Set objSMS = objLoc.ConnectServer(Loc.Machine, "root\sms\site_" & _
            Loc.SiteCode)
            strSMSSiteCode = Loc.Sitecode
    end if
Next

Set newFolder = objSMS.Get("SMS_ObjectContainerNode") _
    .SpawnInstance_()
newFolder.Name = strNewFolderName
newFolder.ObjectType = 3  'advertisement
newFolder.ParentContainerNodeId = 0
newFolder.Put_
```

Discussion

Folders are great for keeping similar advertisements together. For example, you can keep all of your security update advertisements in one folder so they are easy to find.

In Example 6-21, we create a folder in the root of the Advertisements folder titled Security Patches. By setting the ParentContainerNodeId to 0, we create this folder in the root of the Advertisements node. If we wanted to make Security Patches a subfolder of an existing folder, we would insert the appropriate ParentContainerNodeID.

The easiest way to find the ParentContainerNodeID (and most other object IDs, for that matter) is to modify the shortcut to launch your SMS administrator console. For example, instead of the shortcut launching C:\SMSAdmin\bin\i386\sms.msc, have it launch C:\SMSAdmin\bin\i386\sms.msc/ sms:nodeinfo=1. Now when you launch your SMS Administrator console, you can right-click any node, select Properties, and view the Node Information tab. When you view the Node Information tab on a folder, look for ContainerNodeID=x, where x is the ID you would use in this script. Recipe 4-2, "Determining a Package's PackageID," describes how to identify the PackageID for a package. The same process can be used to identify an AdvertisementID. Simply view the properties of an advertisement.

See Also

- Recipe 6-19, "Moving Advertisements Between Folders," shows how to move advertisements between folders.

- Chris Rees's blog contains example scripts for creating folders: http://spaces.msn.com/members/cheekysimian. (Chris Rees is one of the Microsoft SMS SDK gurus.)

- The SMS Script Repository also contains scripts that demonstrate managing console folders in SMS.

- The SMS 2003 SDK contains a topic titled "Creating a Console Folder."

6-19. Moving Advertisements Between Folders

Problem

You want to organize advertisements in folders and move advertisements from one folder to another.

Solution: Using a Graphical Interface

1. Open the SMS Administrator console.

2. From the SMS Administrator console, expand Site Database (*<Site Code>*), and expand Advertisements.

3. Expand any folders that contain the advertisements you need to move.

4. Right-click the folder and select Move Folder items.

5. Select the advertisements that you want to move.

6. Click Browse to select the destination folder.

7. Click OK to move the advertisements.

Solution: Using VBScript

Example 6-22 demonstrates how to move advertisements to another advertisement folder.

Example 6-22. *MoveAdvertsBetweenFolders.vbs*

```
strSMSServer = <SMSServer>

strAdvertIDs = "LAB20013,LAB20014"

'to move more than one, separate with commas
intSourceFolder=0 'Source Folder (root node in this case)
intDestFolder=7 'Destination Folder ID
intObjectType=3 '3=Advertisement for type of object

Set objLoc =  CreateObject("WbemScripting.SWbemLocator")
Set objSMS= objLoc.ConnectServer(strSMSServer, "root\sms")
Set Results = objSMS.ExecQuery _
    ("SELECT * From SMS_ProviderLocation WHERE ProviderForLocalSite = true")
For each Loc in Results
    If Loc.ProviderForLocalSite = True Then
        Set objSMS = objLoc.ConnectServer(Loc.Machine, "root\sms\site_" & _
            Loc.SiteCode)
            strSMSSiteCode = Loc.Sitecode
    end if
Next

Set objFolder = objSMS.Get("SMS_ObjectContainerItem")
arrAdvertIDs = split(strAdvertIDs, ",")
retval = objFolder.MoveMembers _
    (arrAdvertIDs, intSourceFolder, intDestFolder , intObjectType)
```

Discussion

It is best to create package and advertisement folders that are similar so that both a package and corresponding advertisements will be easy to locate. You can also use folders to separate advertisements that are created by different SMS administrators.

Note Use the Shift or Ctrl key to select multiple packages or folders before you move them.

Example 6-22 demonstrates how to move multiple advertisements from the root Advertisement node to the subfolder of your choice. To move one advertisement, insert only one AdvertisementID into strAdvertIDs. To move more than one, simply separate their IDs with commas (no spaces). The example assumes that the advertisements to be moved currently exist in the root Advertisements node, so intSourceFolder is set to 0. To move the advertisements from a subfolder, replace the zero with the appropriate ContainerNodeID. Moving advertisements between folders does not affect any aspect of those advertisements other than where they are organized in the Advertisements node of the SMS Administrator console.

The easiest way to find the ParentContainerNodeID (and most other object IDs, for that matter) is to modify the shortcut to launch your SMS Administrator console. For example, instead of the shortcut launching C:\SMSAdmin\bin\i386\sms.msc, have it launch this: C:\SMSAdmin\bin\i386\sms.msc /sms:nodeinfo=1. Now when you launch your SMS Administrator console, you can right-click any node, select Properties, and view the Node Information tab. When you view the Node Information tab on a folder, look for ContainerNodeID=x, where x is the ID you would use in this script. Recipe 4-2, "Determining a Package's PackageID," describes how to identify the PackageID for a package. The same process can be used to identify an AdvertisementID. Simply view the properties of an advertisement.

See Also

- Recipe 6-18, "Creating an Advertisement Folder," demonstrates how to create an advertisement folder.

- Chris Rees's blog contains example scripts for creating folders: http://spaces.msn.com/members/cheekysimian. (Chris Rees is one of the Microsoft SMS SDK gurus.)

- The SMS Script Repository also contains scripts that demonstrate managing console folders in SMS.

- The SMS 2003 SDK contains a topic titled "Creating a Console Folder."

6-20. Disabling an Advertisement

Problem

You want to disable an advertisement.

Solution: Using a Graphical Interface

1. Open the SMS Administrator console.

2. From the SMS Administrator console, expand Site Database (*<Site Code>*), and expand Advertisements.

3. Expand any folders that contain the advertisement that you need to disable.

4. Right-click the advertisement and select All Tasks ➤ Disable Program.

5. Click Yes on the warning dialog box.

6. The status column will now indicate that the advertisement is disabled.

Solution: Using VBScript

Example 6-23 demonstrates how to disable a program. By disabling the program, all advertisements associated to that program will not execute.

Example 6-23. *DisableProgram_Advert.vbs*

```
strSMSServer = <SMSServer>

strPackageID = "LAB00006"
strProgramName = "Microsoft Updates Tool"
DISABLE_PROGRAM = 2^(12)

Set objLoc =  CreateObject("WbemScripting.SWbemLocator")
Set objSMS= objLoc.ConnectServer(strSMSServer, "root\sms")
Set Results = objSMS.ExecQuery _
    ("SELECT * From SMS_ProviderLocation WHERE ProviderForLocalSite = true")
For each Loc in Results
    If Loc.ProviderForLocalSite = True Then
        Set objSMS = objLoc.ConnectServer(Loc.Machine, "root\sms\site_" & _
            Loc.SiteCode)
            strSMSSiteCode = Loc.Sitecode
    end if
Next

Set objProgram=objSMS.Get("SMS_Program.PackageID='" & _
    strPackageID & "',ProgramName='" & strProgramName & "'")
intProgramFlags = objProgram.ProgramFlags

if (intProgramFlags and DISABLE_PROGRAM) then
    wscript.echo "Disable Program Flag already set!"
    'intProgramFlags = intProgramFlags and not _
        'DISABLE_PROGRAM
else
    wscript.echo "Disabling program now."
    intProgramFlags = intProgramFlags or DISABLE_PROGRAM
end if
objProgram.ProgramFlags = intProgramFlags
objProgram.Put_
```

Discussion

Disabling an advertisement is probably the quickest way to kill an advertisement that isn't working properly. However, disabling an advertisement actually disables the program being advertised and will cause any other advertisements associated with that program to be disabled.

Example 6-23 demonstrates how to disable a program, which is the fastest way to disable an advertisement. First, we obtain the package object, and then we examine the `ProgramFlags` to see if the `DisableProgram` flag is already enabled. If it is, we simply display that the flag is already set, and exit. If it is not set, we set `intProgramFlags = intProgramFlags or DISABLE_PROGRAM` to enable the flag. Finally, we save the change using the `Put_` method.

The process for re-enabling a program is the same as we've just described, except for the flag setting. To clear the `DisableProgram` flag, and thus re-enable the program, we would set `intProgramFlags = intProgramFlags and not DISABLE_PROGRAM` in the `if` statement (before the `else` statement).

Caution Use caution when running a script to re-enable a program. As soon as clients "see" the program is available, all advertisements with mandatory start times that have passed will execute.

See Also

- Recipe 6-2, "Deleting an Advertisement," describes how to delete an advertisement.
- Recipe 6-11, "Expiring an Advertisement," describes how to expire an advertisement.

6-21. Viewing the Status of an Advertisement

Problem

You want to view the status of an advertisement.

Solution: Using a Graphical Interface

1. Open the SMS Administrator console.

2. From the SMS Administrator console, expand Site Database (<*Site Code*>), and expand Advertisements.

3. Expand any folders that contain the advertisement for which you need to view the status.

4. The right pane will list the advertisement and the status will indicate whether it is enabled or disabled.

Solution: Using VBScript

Example 6-24 demonstrates how to display the advertisement status summary for a given advertisement.

Example 6-24. *ShowAdvertStatus.vbs*

```
CONST SINCE_ADVERTISED = "0001128000080008"

strSMSServer = <SMSServer>

strAdvertID = "LAB20014"

Set objLoc =  CreateObject("WbemScripting.SWbemLocator")
Set objSMS= objLoc.ConnectServer(strSMSServer, "root\sms")
Set Results = objSMS.ExecQuery _
    ("SELECT * From SMS_ProviderLocation WHERE ProviderForLocalSite = true")
For each Loc in Results
    If Loc.ProviderForLocalSite = True Then
        Set objSMS = objLoc.ConnectServer(Loc.Machine, "root\sms\site_" & _
            Loc.SiteCode)
            strSMSSiteCode = Loc.Sitecode
    end if
Next

Set colAdvertStatus = objSMS.ExecQuery _
    ("Select * From SMS_AdvertisementStatusSummarizer where" & _
        " AdvertisementID = '" & strAdvertID & _
        "' and DisplaySchedule = '" & SINCE_ADVERTISED &  "'")
 for each objAS in colAdvertStatus
    wscript.echo objAS.SiteCode  & vbTAB & _
        objAS.AdvertisementsReceived & vbTAB & _
        objAS.AdvertisementsFailed & vbTAB & _
        objAS.ProgramsStarted & vbTAB & _
        objAS.ProgramsFailed & vbTAB & _
        objAS.ProgramsSucceeded & vbTAB & _
        objAS.ProgramsFailedMIF & vbTAB & _
        objAS.ProgramsSucceededMIF
 next
```

Discussion

Understanding the status of an advertisement is very important, since the SMS client still processes the policies for disabled advertisements, even when not executing them.

Example 6-24 demonstrates how to display the status (by SMS site code) of an advertisement using SMS_AdvertisementStatusSummarizer. First, we execute a WQL query to obtain the status summarizer information for a specific AdvertisementID, and also specify to obtain only Since Advertised status. Next, we enumerate each advertisement returned in our query and display status information. Right-clicking in the SMS Administrator console and selecting Display Interval can also be completed programmatically. Table 6-2 lists the available DisplaySchedule values for SMS_AdvertisementStatusSummarizer.

Table 6-2. *Display Schedule String Values*

DisplaySchedule Variable	Value
SINCE_ADVERTISED	0001128000080008
SINCE12_00_AM	0001128000100008
SINCE06_00AM	00C1128000100008
SINCE12_00_PM	0181128000100008
SINCE06_00_PM	0241128000100008
SINCE_SUNDAY	0001128000192000
SINCE_MONDAY	00011280001A2000
SINCE_TUESDAY	00011280001B2000
SINCE_WEDNESDAY	00011280001C2000
SINCE_THURSDAY	00011280001D2000
SINCE_FRIDAY	00011280001E2000
SINCE_SATURDAY	00011280001F2000
SINCE_1ST_OF_MONTH	000A470000284400
SINCE_15TH_OF_MONTH	000A4700002BC400

See Also

- The SMS 2003 SDK provides additional information about the SMS_AdvertisementStatusSummarizer class.

CHAPTER 7

■■■

Software Metering

Software metering in SMS 2003 does exactly what it intends to do—meter software usage on SMS clients. The previous version of software metering attempted to do much more than track program usage, but it was very difficult to implement. Microsoft went back to the drawing board and completely rebuilt it for SMS 2003, improving the product tremendously. Metering no longer has the capability to restrict the use of software that doesn't have a license, as in the previous version, but it does an excellent job of tracking when and how long an application is used, including Terminal Server application usage.

If you aren't familiar with software metering, you may be wondering how it can be helpful to your organization. There are a couple great reasons to use software metering. The first is license management. If you have a very clear picture of how everyone in your enterprise uses specific software, then you will be able to properly budget, purchase, or reallocate licenses to reflect the actual needs of your company. The more covert reason for using software metering is tracking user productivity. The value in this tracking becomes immediately obvious if you meter a game program, like solitaire, for example.

Software metering collects and summarizes usage data for you, but getting complete, usable data takes a month or more. Jump into the recipes in this chapter to get started today, so you will have plenty of software metering data to use when you need it.

7-1. Creating a Software Metering Rule

Problem

You want to create a software metering rule.

Solution: Using a Graphical Interface

1. Open the SMS Administrator console.

2. From the SMS Administrator console, expand Site Database (*<Site Code>*) and Software Metering Rules.

3. Right-click Software Metering Rules, and select New ➤ Software Metering Rule from the menu to open the Software Metering Rule Properties dialog box.

4. On the General tab, enter at least the name of the new software metering rule, and enter the software executable file name to be metered.

5. Specify any of the additional parameters.

6. Click OK to create the new advertisement.

Solution: Using VBScript

Example 7-1 demonstrates how to create a software metering rule for WinZip. This rule will meter all WinZip versions (which have an executable by the name of WinZip32.exe) and all language types.

Example 7-1. *CreatingMeteringRule.vbs*

```
strSMSServer = <SMSServer>

strProdcutName = "WinZip"
strFileName = "WinZip32.exe"
strFileVersion = "*"
strLanguageID = 65535 '65535 = 'any language'

Set objLoc =  CreateObject("WbemScripting.SWbemLocator")
Set objSMS= objLoc.ConnectServer(strSMSServer, "root\sms")
Set Results = objSMS.ExecQuery _
    ("SELECT * From SMS_ProviderLocation WHERE ProviderForLocalSite = true")
For each Loc in Results
    If Loc.ProviderForLocalSite = True Then
        Set objSMS = objLoc.ConnectServer(Loc.Machine, "root\sms\site_" & _
            Loc.SiteCode)
    end if
Next

Set newMTRRule = _
    objSMS.Get("SMS_MeteredProductRule").SpawnInstance_()

newMTRRule.ProductName = strProdcutName
newMTRRule.FileName = strFileName
newMTRRule.FileVersion = strFileVersion
newMTRRule.LanguageID = strLanguageID
newMTRRule.SiteCode = ucase(strSMSSiteCode)
newMTRRule.ApplyToChildSites = TRUE
newMTRRule.Enabled = TRUE
newMTRRule.Put_
```

Discussion

Software metering tracks the usage of an executable that you specify in the properties of a software metering rule. You can use software inventory to identify the exact executable to select, so that the appropriate application is monitored properly.

Use the OriginalFileName property to enter the true file name of the executable. The FileName property of an executable may be easily renamed from within Windows, but the OriginalFileName is embedded in the executable (and viewable through file properties), which makes it difficult for your average user to modify. If, for instance, you're metering usage of solitaire, you may want to consider inserting sol.exe for both the FileName and the OriginalFileName, just in case Sally User modified the file name to MyImportantWork.exe. The OriginalFileName will still be metered to accurately detect usage of solitaire.

If you want to meter a group of applications together, like Office, you can create a rule for each executable but use the same name for each rule.

Caution Choosing an incorrect version or language option will cause the application to not be metered. If you select the executable by browsing, the proper version and language will be populated for you. Or use the asterisk (*) as a wildcard for the version and ANY for the language to widen your scope.

Example 7-1 demonstrates how to create a software metering rule using VBScript. While creating one metering rule programmatically may not be worth the effort, this example can be extended to read and insert multiple rules from a file.

After connecting to the SMS site, we create a new instance of SMS_MeteredProductRule, and set the following required properties, as defined in the SMS 2003 SDK:

ProductName: Name of the product being metered. This is the display name of the rule and is not used in matching.

FileName: Name of the file to be metered. This property is used for matching.

FileVersion: Version of the file being metered. This property is used for matching and matches to the FileVersion property stored in the file's version information. It can contain wildcards, such as * (match multiple characters) and ? (match a single character). An empty FileVersion property only matches to those executable files that have no version.

LanguageID: Language identifier of the rule being metered. This property matches the Language property stored in the file's version information. If it is set to 65535, it matches any language.

SiteCode: Site code of the SMS site on which the rule runs. The rule applies to clients of this site and to the clients of child sites if ApplyToChildSites is True.

ApplyTochildSites: Determines whether the rule should be applied to child sites. If the rule is applied to child sites, the value is True. If the rule is not applied to child sites, the value is False.

Enabled: Determines whether the rule is enabled. Data is only collected by the client if the rule is enabled. If the rule is enabled, the value is True. If the rule is not enabled, the value is False.

An additional (and optional) property to consider is OriginalFileName. From the SMS 2003 SDK, this property is used for matching and matches the OriginalFileName property stored in the file's version information. Because FileName is the Resource Explorer name of the file and might be changed by users, OriginalFileName is used to ensure that the file is metered.

See Also

- Recipe 7-2, "Deleting a Software Metering Rule," demonstrates how to delete a software metering rule.

- Recipe 7-3, "Viewing All Software Metering Rules," demonstrates how to view a summary of all software metering rules.

- Recipe 7-10, "Viewing the Status of a Software Metering Rule," demonstrates how to view the status (enabled or disabled) of the rule.

- Chapter 8 of the *SMS 2003 Operations Guide* provides more information about creating software metering rules.

- Chapter 15 of the *Microsoft Systems Management Server 2003 Administrator's Companion* by Steven Kaczmarek (Microsoft Press, 2004) also provides more information about creating software metering rules.

- The SMS 2003 SDK provides more information about SMS_MeteredProductRule.

7-2. Deleting a Software Metering Rule

Problem

You want to delete a software metering rule.

Solution: Using a Graphical Interface

1. Open the SMS Administrator console.

2. From the SMS Administrator console, expand Site Database (*<Site Code>*) and Software Metering Rules.

3. Expand the folder that contains the rule you want to delete.

4. In the right pane, select the rule, and delete it by either pressing the Delete key, clicking the Delete button on the SMS Administrator console toolbar, or right-clicking the rule and selecting Delete from the menu.

5. Click Yes to confirm your choice to delete the rule.

Solution: Using VBScript

Example 7-2 demonstrates how to delete a software metering rule based on the product name.

Example 7-2. *DeletingASoftwareMeteringRule.vbs*

```
strSMSServer = <SMSServer>

strProductName = "WinZip"

Set objLoc =  CreateObject("WbemScripting.SWbemLocator")
Set objSMS= objLoc.ConnectServer(strSMSServer, "root\sms")
Set Results = objSMS.ExecQuery _
    ("SELECT * From SMS_ProviderLocation WHERE ProviderForLocalSite = true")
For each Loc in Results
    If Loc.ProviderForLocalSite = True Then
        Set objSMS = objLoc.ConnectServer(Loc.Machine, "root\sms\site_" & _
            Loc.SiteCode)
    end if
Next

Set colMTRRules = objSMS.ExecQuery _
    ("Select * From SMS_MeteredProductRule where " & _
        "ProductName = '" & strProductName & "'")
For Each objMTRRule In colMTRRules
    wscript.echo "Deleting " & objMTRRule.ProductName
    objMTRRule.Delete_
Next
```

Discussion

Since software metering takes time to collect enough data to be usable, you should think twice before deleting a software metering rule. However, having lots of enabled rules that are no longer needed can cause performance problems, so if a rule has served its purpose or the software being metered is retired, go ahead and delete the rule.

Example 7-2 demonstrates how to delete a software metering rule using VBScript. After connecting to the SMS provider, execute a WMI Query Language (WQL) query to find all `SMS_MeteredProductRule` objects that have a `ProductName` of `WinZip`. Then, for each rule that is found, use the `Delete_` method to delete the rule.

See Also

- Recipe 7-5, "Disabling a Software Metering Rule," demonstrates how to disable a rule.

- Chapter 8 of the *SMS 2003 Operations Guide* provides more information about deleting software metering rules.

- Chapter 15 of the *Microsoft Systems Management Server 2003 Administrator's Companion* by Steven Kaczmarek (Microsoft Press, 2004) also provides more information about creating software metering rules.

- The SMS 2003 SDK provides more information about `SMS_MeteredProductRule`.

7-3. Viewing All Software Metering Rules

Problem

You want to view a summary of all software metering rules for your SMS site.

Solution: Using a Graphical Interface

1. Open the SMS Administrator console.

2. From the SMS Administrator console, expand Site Database (*<Site Code>*), System Status, and then Software Metering Rules.

3. In the right pane, you will see all rules listed.

Solution: Using VBScript

Example 7-3 demonstrates how to show a summary of all software metering rules for your SMS site.

Example 7-3. *ViewingAllSoftwareMeteringRules.vbs*

```
strSMSServer = <SMSServer>

Set objLoc =  CreateObject("WbemScripting.SWbemLocator")
Set objSMS= objLoc.ConnectServer(strSMSServer, "root\sms")
Set Results = objSMS.ExecQuery _
    ("SELECT * From SMS_ProviderLocation WHERE ProviderForLocalSite = true")
For each Loc in Results
    If Loc.ProviderForLocalSite = True Then
        Set objSMS = objLoc.ConnectServer(Loc.Machine, "root\sms\site_" & _
            Loc.SiteCode)
    end if
Next

Set colMTRs = objSMS.ExecQuery _
    ("Select * From SMS_MeteredProductRule order by " & _
        " ProductName")
for each objMTRRule in colMTRS
    wscript.echo objMTRRule.ProductName & vbTAB & _
```

```
        objMTRRule.FileName & vbTAB & objMTRRule.FileVersion & _
        vbTAB & objMTRRule.SiteCode & vbTAB & _
        objMTRRule.ApplyToChildSites & vbTAB & objMTRRule.Enabled
next
```

Discussion

Software metering collects a large amount of data. It is best to keep track of the rules that you have enabled and disable or delete those that you no longer need.

Note If you have several people creating software metering rules, make sure there aren't any duplicate rules, which create extra overhead without providing any value.

Example 7-3 demonstrates how to display all software metering rules using VBScript. After connecting to the SMS provider, we execute a WQL query to find all SMS_MeteredProductRule objects. Then, for each rule that is found, details about the rule are displayed. The Enabled property may be of specific interest to you. If you're only looking for enabled rules, modify your WQL query as follows:

```
("Select * From SMS_MeteredProductRule where Enabled = 'true'" & _
" order by  ProductName")
```

See Also

- Chapter 8 of the *SMS 2003 Operations Guide* provides more information about software metering rules.

- Chapter 15 of the *Microsoft Systems Management Server 2003 Administrator's Companion* by Steven Kaczmarek (Microsoft Press, 2004) also provides more information about creating software metering rules.

- The SMS 2003 SDK provides more information about SMS_MeteredProductRule.

7-4. Modifying a Software Metering Rule

Problem

You want to change a software metering rule.

Solution: Using a Graphical Interface

1. Open the SMS Administrator console.

2. From the SMS Administrator console, expand Site Database (<*Site Code*>) and Software Metering Rules.

3. Expand the folder that contains the rule you want to modify.

4. In the right pane, double-click the rule to open the Software Metering Rule Properties dialog box.

5. Edit the name of the rule, select a different file to meter, or change the language, version, or site code parameters to meet your specifications.

6. Click OK to apply the settings.

Solution: Using VBScript

Example 7-4 demonstrates how to modify the ProductName property for a software metering rule.

Example 7-4. *ModifyMeteringRule.vbs*

```
strSMSServer = <SMSServer>

strProductName = "Sol"
strNewProductName = "Solitaire"

Set objLoc = CreateObject("WbemScripting.SWbemLocator")
Set objSMS= objLoc.ConnectServer(strSMSServer, "root\sms")
Set Results = objSMS.ExecQuery _
    ("SELECT * From SMS_ProviderLocation WHERE ProviderForLocalSite = true")
For each Loc in Results
    If Loc.ProviderForLocalSite = True Then
        Set objSMS = objLoc.ConnectServer(Loc.Machine, "root\sms\site_" & _
            Loc.SiteCode)
    end if
Next

Set colMTRs = objSMS.ExecQuery _
    ("Select * From SMS_MeteredProductRule where " & _
        "ProductName = '" & strProductName & "'")
for each objMTRRule in colMTRS
    objMTRRule.ProductName = strNewProductName
    objMTRRule.Put_
next
```

Discussion

Try to configure your software metering rule correctly when you first create it, as future changes can affect the collected data and give you a skewed picture of software usage. For example, you wouldn't want to meter an application with a specific version and then change the version being metered after collecting several months of data. That would most likely show a sharp increase or decrease in the usage, which would make it look like you had a drastic change in usage, instead of reflecting a change in the rule itself.

Note Creating a new rule is better than making a major modification to an existing rule if you plan to use the existing collected usage data.

See Also

- Recipe 7-6, "Enabling a Software Metering Rule," demonstrates how to enable a disabled metering rule.
- Chapter 8 of the *SMS 2003 Operations Guide* provides more information about software metering rules.
- Chapter 15 of the *Microsoft Systems Management Server 2003 Administrator's Companion* by Steven Kaczmarek (Microsoft Press, 2004) also provides more information about creating software metering rules.

7-5. Disabling a Software Metering Rule

Problem

You want to disable a software metering rule.

Solution: Using a Graphical Interface

1. Open the SMS Administrator console.

2. From the SMS Administrator console, expand Site Database (*<Site Code>*) and Software Metering Rules.

3. Expand the folder that contains the rule you want to disable.

4. In the right pane, right-click the rule, and select All Tasks ➤ Disable.

5. The rule will now display a status of Disabled in the right pane.

Solution: Using VBScript

Example 7-5 demonstrates how to disable a software metering rule.

Example 7-5. *DisableMeteringRule.vbs*

```
strSMSServer = <SMSServer>

strProductName = "Sol"

Set objLoc =  CreateObject("WbemScripting.SWbemLocator")
Set objSMS= objLoc.ConnectServer(strSMSServer, "root\sms")
Set Results = objSMS.ExecQuery _
    ("SELECT * From SMS_ProviderLocation WHERE ProviderForLocalSite = true")
For each Loc in Results
    If Loc.ProviderForLocalSite = True Then
        Set objSMS = objLoc.ConnectServer(Loc.Machine, "root\sms\site_" & _
            Loc.SiteCode)
    end if
Next

Set colMTRs = objSMS.ExecQuery _
    ("Select * From SMS_MeteredProductRule where " & _
        "ProductName = '" & strProductName & "'")
for each objMTRRule in colMTRS
        objMTRRule.Enabled = False
        objMTRRule.Put_
next
```

Discussion

Disabling a rule is appropriate if you aren't absolutely sure that you won't need the rule again. This recipe will stop the collection of metering information, but it won't delete the current data that has been collected. Simply enable the rule again if you need to meter the application at a later date.

See Also

- Recipe 7-6, "Enabling a Software Metering Rule," demonstrates how to enable a software metering rule.

- Chapter 8 of the *SMS 2003 Operations Guide* provides more information about software metering rules.

- Chapter 15 of the *Microsoft Systems Management Server 2003 Administrator's Companion* by Steven Kaczmarek (Microsoft Press, 2004) also provides more information about creating software metering rules.

7-6. Enabling a Software Metering Rule

Problem

You want to enable a disabled software metering rule.

Solution: Using a Graphical Interface

1. Open the SMS Administrator console.

2. From the SMS Administrator console, expand Site Database (*<Site Code>*) and Software Metering Rules.

3. Expand the folder that contains the rule you want to enable.

4. In the right pane, right-click the rule, and select All Tasks ➤ Enable.

5. The rule will now display a status of Enabled in the right pane.

Solution: Using VBScript

Example 7-6 demonstrates how to enable a software metering rule.

Example 7-6. *EnableMeteringRule.vbs*

```
strSMSServer = <SMSServer>

strProductName = "Sol"

Set objLoc =  CreateObject("WbemScripting.SWbemLocator")
Set objSMS= objLoc.ConnectServer(strSMSServer, "root\sms")
Set Results = objSMS.ExecQuery _
    ("SELECT * From SMS_ProviderLocation WHERE ProviderForLocalSite = true")
For each Loc in Results
    If Loc.ProviderForLocalSite = True Then
        Set objSMS = objLoc.ConnectServer(Loc.Machine, "root\sms\site_" & _
            Loc.SiteCode)
    end if
Next

Set colMTRs = objSMS.ExecQuery _
    ("Select * From SMS_MeteredProductRule where " & _
        "ProductName = '" & strProductName & "'")
for each objMTRRule in colMTRS
    if not (objMTRRule.Enabled) then
        wscript.echo "Enabling Rule " & strProductName
        objMTRRule.Enabled = True
```

```
        objMTRRule.Put_
    else
        wscript.echo "Rule " & strProductName & " aready " & _
            "enabled!"
    end if
next
```

Discussion

If you have disabled a rule and need to resume collecting data on the application, simply enable the rule again.

Note Software metering rules are enabled by default when they are created.

Example 7-6 demonstrates how to enable a software metering rule using VBScript. After connecting to the SMS site, we perform a WQL query to find all metering rules that have a specific product name (e.g., solitaire). Next, we enumerate each rule that is returned from the query. If each rule is not currently enabled, we enable it, and save the changes.

See Also

- Recipe 7-5, "Disabling a Software Metering Rule," describes how to disable a software metering rule.

- Recipe 7-3, "Viewing All Software Metering Rules," demonstrates how to list each rule and its current status (enabled or disabled).

- Chapter 8 of the *SMS 2003 Operations Guide* provides more information about software metering rules.

- Chapter 15 of the *Microsoft Systems Management Server 2003 Administrator's Companion* by Steven Kaczmarek (Microsoft Press, 2004) also provides more information about creating software metering rules.

7-7. Modifying the Permissions of a Software Metering Rule

Problem

You want to modify the permissions of a software metering rule.

Solution

1. Open the SMS Administrator console.
2. From the SMS Administrator console, expand Site Database (*<Site Code>*) and Software Metering Rules.
3. Expand the folder that contains the rule that you need to modify.
4. Right-click the rule, and select Properties.
5. Select the Security tab in the Software Metering Rule Properties dialog box.
6. Click the New or Delete button to add or remove class or instance security rights. You can also double-click any existing class or instance rights to modify them.
7. Click OK for the settings to be applied.

Discussion

Modify the class rights to grant or restrict permissions for other SMS administrators to create or delete rules. Also, if you have a business reason to monitor an application that may be affecting productivity, you might want to check the instance rights security of the metering rule to make sure that only the appropriate people have access to view the data from the metering rule.

If possible, consider removing the nonbusiness application from client systems. You can write software and hardware inventory queries to identify the software and (depending on the application) create an SMS advertisement to uninstall that application.

See Also

- Chapter 8 of the *SMS 2003 Operations Guide* provides more information about managing software metering rules.

- Chapter 15 of the *Microsoft Systems Management Server 2003 Administrator's Companion* by Steven Kaczmarek (Microsoft Press, 2004) also provides more information about creating software metering rules.

7-8. Creating a Software Metering Rule Folder

Problem

You want to create a software metering rule folder.

Solution: Using a Graphical Interface

1. Open the SMS Administrator console.

2. From the SMS Administrator console, expand Site Database (*<Site Code>*) and Software Metering Rules.

3. Right-click Software Metering Rules, and select New ➤ Folder.

4. Provide a name for the folder.

5. Click OK to create the new folder.

Solution: Using VBScript

Example 7-7 demonstrates how to create a folder to contain software metering rules.

Example 7-7. *CreateMeteringFolder.vbs*

```
strSMSServer = <SMSServer>

strNewFolderName = "InBit Software"

Set objLoc = CreateObject("WbemScripting.SWbemLocator")
Set objSMS= objLoc.ConnectServer(strSMSServer, "root\sms")
Set Results = objSMS.ExecQuery _
    ("SELECT * From SMS_ProviderLocation WHERE ProviderForLocalSite = true")
For each Loc in Results
    If Loc.ProviderForLocalSite = True Then
        Set objSMS = objLoc.ConnectServer(Loc.Machine, "root\sms\site_" & _
            Loc.SiteCode)
    end if
Next
```

```
Set newFolder = objSMS.Get("SMS_ObjectContainerNode") _
    .SpawnInstance_()
newFolder.Name = strNewFolderName
newFolder.ObjectType = 9  'metering Folder
newFolder.ParentContainerNodeId = 0 'root folder
newFolder.Put_
```

Discussion

Creating folders is a quick and easy task. Use them to group your rules by business unit, cost center, application department, or other logical grouping.

Example 7-7 is very similar to examples of how to create folders for other SMS objects. In this case, we're creating a folder for software metering rules. After connecting to the SMS provider, we create a new instance of SMS_ObjectContainerNode. Next, we set the Name of the folder, the ObjectType to 9 (which is a metering folder), and the ParentContainerNodeID to 0 to create this folder in the root of the Software Metering Rules node. If we want to make this folder a subfolder of an existing folder, we add the appropriate ParentContainerNodeID.

Note The easiest way to find the ParentContainerNodeID (and most other object IDs, for that matter) is to modify the shortcut to launch your SMS Administrator console. For example, instead of the shortcut launching C:\SMSAdmin\bin\i386\sms.msc, have it launch this: C:\SMSAdmin\bin\i386\sms.msc /sms:nodeinfo=1. Now, when you launch your SMS Administrator console, you can right-click any node, select Properties, and view the Node Information tab. When you view a folder's Node Information tab, look for ContainerNodeID=x, where x is the ID you use in this script.

See Also

- Recipe 7-9, "Moving Software Metering Rules Between Folders," describes how to move metering rules to a new folder.

- Chris Rees's blog contains example scripts for creating folders: http://spaces.msn.com/members/cheekysimian. (Chris Rees is one of the Microsoft SMS SDK gurus.)

- The SMS Script Repository also contains scripts that demonstrate managing console folders in SMS.

- The SMS 2003 SDK also has a topic titled "Creating a Console Folder."

7-9. Moving Software Metering Rules Between Folders

Problem

You want to move software metering rules between folders.

Solution: Using a Graphical Interface

1. Open the SMS Administrator console.

2. From the SMS Administrator console, expand Site Database (*<Site Code>*) and Software Metering Rules.

3. Expand any folders that contain the rules that you need to move.

4. Right-click the folder, and select Move Folder items.

5. Select the rules that you want to move (hold down the Ctrl key to select multiple rules).

6. Click Browse to select the destination folder.

7. Click OK to move the software metering rules.

Solution: Using VBScript

Example 7-8 demonstrates how to move software metering rules between folders.

Example 7-8. *MoveMeteringRulesBetweenFolders.vbs*

```
strSMSServer = <SMSServer>

strMeteringIDs = "LAB00008,LAB00009"
'to move more than one, separate with commas
intSourceFolder = 0 'Source Folder (root node in this case)
intDestFolder = 8 'Destination Folder
intObjectType = 9 '9=Metering Rule for type of object

Set objLoc = CreateObject("WbemScripting.SWbemLocator")
Set objSMS= objLoc.ConnectServer(strSMSServer, "root\sms")
Set Results = objSMS.ExecQuery _
    ("SELECT * From SMS_ProviderLocation WHERE ProviderForLocalSite = true")
For each Loc in Results
    If Loc.ProviderForLocalSite = True Then
        Set objSMS = objLoc.ConnectServer(Loc.Machine, "root\sms\site_" & _
            Loc.SiteCode)
    end if
Next

Set objFolder = objSMS.Get("SMS_ObjectContainerItem")
arrMeteringIDs = split(strMeteringIDs, ",")
retval = objFolder.MoveMembers _
(arrMeteringIDs, intSourceFolder, intDestFolder , intObjectType)
```

Discussion

Example 7-6 demonstrates how to move one or more metering rules to a new metering rule folder. In the example, we move multiple metering rules from the root package node to a subfolder of your choice. To move one package, insert only one SecurityKey into strMeteringIDs. To move more than one rule, simply separate multiple SecurityKeys with commas (no spaces). Since the example assumes that the metering rules to be moved are currently found in the root Software Metering Rules node, the example sets intSourceFolder to 0. If the rules you are moving are in a subfolder, replace the 0 with the appropriate ContainerNodeID. Also, the destination folder (intDestFolder) must exist and be set to the proper ContainerNodeID. Moving metering rules between folders does not affect any aspect of the rules other than where they are organized in the Software Metering Rules node of the SMS Administrator console. All permissions, rules data, and options that are associated with the metering rule will be unaffected.

Note The easiest way to find the `ParentContainerNodeID` (and most other object IDs, for that matter) is to modify the shortcut to launch your SMS Administrator console. For example, instead of the shortcut launching `C:\SMSAdmin\bin\i386\sms.msc`, have it launch `C:\SMSAdmin\bin\i386\sms.msc /sms:nodeinfo=1`. Now, when you launch your SMS Administrator console, you can right-click any node, select Properties, and view the Node Information tab. When you view the Node Information tab on a folder, look for `ContainerNodeID=x`, where x is the ID you use in this script.

To locate the `SecurityKey` for a metering rule right-click the metering rule, select Properties, and view the Node Information tab. When you view the Node Information tab on a metering rule, look for `SecurityKey="LAB00005"`, where `LAB00005` is one of the `strMeteringIDs` you use in this script.

See Also

- Recipe 7-8, "Creating a Software Metering Rule Folder," describes how to create a new software metering folder.

- Chris Rees's blog contains example scripts for creating folders: `http://spaces.msn.com/members/cheekysimian`. (Chris Rees is one of the Microsoft SMS SDK gurus.)

- The SMS Script Repository also contains scripts that demonstrate managing console folders in SMS.

- The SMS 2003 SDK describes the `MoveMembers` method.

7-10. Viewing the Status of a Software Metering Rule

Problem

You want to view the status of a software metering rule.

Solution: Using a Graphical Interface

1. Open the SMS Administrator console.

2. From the SMS Administrator console, expand Site Database (*<Site Code>*) and Software Metering Rules.

3. In the right pane, you will see all metering rules listed with a Status column that indicates whether the rule is enabled or disabled.

Solution: Using VBScript

Example 7-3 in Recipe 7-3, "Viewing All Software Metering Rules," includes the current status of each rule with its output.

Discussion

If you have organized your software metering rules into folders, you will not be able to see the status of all rules at a glance using the GUI. Example 7-3 demonstrates how to display all rules with their current status using VBScript.

See Also

- Recipe 7-6, "Enabling a Software Metering Rule," describes how to enable a software metering rule.

- Recipe 7-5, "Disabling a Software Metering Rule," describes how to disable a software metering rule.

- Example 7-3 demonstrates how to display all rules with current status using VBScript.

- Chapter 8 of the *SMS 2003 Operations Guide* provides more information about software metering rules.

- Chapter 15 of the *Microsoft Systems Management Server 2003 Administrator's Companion* by Steven Kaczmarek (Microsoft Press, 2004) also provides more information about creating software metering rules.

7-11. Displaying Metered Summary Data for a Specific User Using VBScript

Problem

You want to display summarized metering data for a specific user for the past 180 days.

Solution

Example 7-9 demonstrates how to display software metering summary data for a specific user.

Example 7-9. *DisplayMonthlySummaryData.vbs*

```
strSMSServer = <SMSServer>

strUserName = "ramseyg"
intDays = 180

Set objLoc = CreateObject("WbemScripting.SWbemLocator")
Set objSMS= objLoc.ConnectServer(strSMSServer, "root\sms")
Set Results = objSMS.ExecQuery _
    ("SELECT * From SMS_ProviderLocation WHERE ProviderForLocalSite = true")
For each Loc in Results
    If Loc.ProviderForLocalSite = True Then
        Set objSMS = objLoc.ConnectServer(Loc.Machine, "root\sms\site_" & _
            Loc.SiteCode)
    end if
Next

strWQL = "SELECT SMS_MeteredFiles.ProductName, " & _
    "SMS_MeteredUser.FullName, SMS_MonthlyUsageSummary.UsageCount, " & _
    "SMS_MonthlyUsageSummary.TSUsageCount, " & _
    "SMS_MonthlyUsageSummary.LastUsage, SMS_R_System.Name " & _
  "FROM SMS_MonthlyUsageSummary INNER JOIN " & _
    "SMS_R_System ON SMS_MonthlyUsageSummary.ResourceID = " & _
    "SMS_R_System.ResourceID INNER JOIN " & _
    "SMS_MeteredUser ON SMS_MonthlyUsageSummary.MeteredUserID = " & _
    "SMS_MeteredUser.MeteredUserID INNER JOIN " & _
    "SMS_MeteredFiles ON SMS_MonthlyUsageSummary.FileID = " & _
    "SMS_MeteredFiles.MeteredFileID " & _
```

```
"WHERE (SMS_MeteredUser.UserName = '" & strUserName & "') " & _
    "and datediff" & _
    "(day, SMS_MonthlyUsageSummary.LastUsage, getdate()) <= " & _
    intDays & "ORDER BY SMS_MonthlyUsageSummary.LastUsage"

wscript.echo "Product Name" & vbTAB & "Domain\UserName" & vbTAB & _
    "Usage Count" & vbTAB & "TSUsage Count" & vbTAB & _
    "ComputerName" & vbTAB & "LastUsageRecordedForMonth"

Set colMTRResults = objSMS.ExecQuery(strWQL)
for each objMTRResult in colMTRResults
    wscript.echo objMTRResult.SMS_MeteredFiles.ProductName & vbTAB & _
    objMTRResult.SMS_MeteredUser.FullName & vbTAB & _
    objMTRResult.SMS_MonthlyUsageSummary.UsageCount & vbTAB & _
    objMTRResult.SMS_MonthlyUsageSummary.TSUsageCount & vbTAB & _
    objMTRResult.SMS_R_System.Name & vbTAB & _
        WMIDateStringToDate(objMTRResult.SMS_MonthlyUsageSummary.LastUsage)
next

Function WMIDateStringToDate(dtmInstallDate)
    WMIDateStringToDate = CDate(Mid(dtmInstallDate, 5, 2) & "/" & _
        Mid(dtmInstallDate, 7, 2) & "/" & Left(dtmInstallDate, 4) _
            & " " & Mid (dtmInstallDate, 9, 2) & ":" & _
                Mid(dtmInstallDate, 11, 2) & ":" & Mid(dtmInstallDate, _
                    13, 2))
End Function
```

Discussion

Example 7-9 demonstrates how to summarize and display meter data from the past 180 days for a given user. The script may appear a bit intimidating—in fact, it's a little intimidating to us also. If you want to get a little more out of software metering, the example is worth a second look. Let's take it piece by piece.

First, we declare our variables and connect to the SMS provider. Next comes a very long WQL query statement. This WQL query appears much clearer on the screen, where you can format and indent it as you like. You can see from the query that we're using the following four classes:

SMS_MeteredFiles: Displays the ProductName in our example. Some of the other properties available are FileName, OriginalFileName, FileVersion, and SiteCode.

SMS_MeteredUser: Obtains the FullName (domain\user name) of the user. Domain and UserName are also available properties if you need to separate the domain and user name.

SMS_MonthlyUsageSummary: Obtains the summary data (UsageCount, TSUsageCount, LastUsage). UsageTime may also be of benefit to you—it provides the total amount of time (in seconds) the file was used during the month.

SMS_R_System:SMS_R_System: Contains discovery data for all discovered system resources. For our example, we use it to display the Name (computer name).

Notice the use of the DateDiff and GetDate functions in the WQL query. These two functions (and the DateAdd function) are now supported in the WHERE clause when executing WQL queries against SMS. Review the SMS 2003 SDK for more information.

Next, after initializing the variables, we display the column headings and execute the WQL query. Finally, we use a for-each loop to display the information. The utility WMIDateStringToDate is used to convert a WMI date-time string to a "standard" date-time string.

See Also

- Several software metering web reports are also available to you when you enable web reporting. See Chapter 8 for more information.

- Recipe 7-11, "Displaying Metered Summary Data for a Specific User Using VBScript," demonstrates how to display metered file usage summary data using VBScript.

- The SMS 2003 SDK provides additional information about the SMS classes used in this example (SMS_MeteredFiles, SMS_MeteredUser, SMS_MonthlyUsageSummary, and SMS_R_System).

- The *SMS 2003 Scripting Guide* provides an example titled "How to Get Monthly Summary Data for Metered Files in SMS."

7-12. Displaying Metered File Usage Summary Data Using VBScript

Problem

You want to display metered file usage summary data and identify usage peaks using VBScript.

Solution

Example 7-10 displays software metering file usage summary data for a specific metered file for the past ten days.

Example 7-10. *DisplayMeteredFileUsageSummaryData.vbs*

```
strSMSServer = <SMSServer>

intDays = 10
strProductName = "sol"

Set objLoc = CreateObject("WbemScripting.SWbemLocator")
Set objSMS= objLoc.ConnectServer(strSMSServer, "root\sms")
Set Results = objSMS.ExecQuery _
    ("SELECT * From SMS_ProviderLocation WHERE ProviderForLocalSite = true")
For each Loc in Results
    If Loc.ProviderForLocalSite = True Then
        Set objSMS = objLoc.ConnectServer(Loc.Machine, "root\sms\site_" & _
            Loc.SiteCode)
    end if
Next

strWQL = "SELECT SMS_MeteredFiles.ProductName, " & _
    "SMS_FileUsageSummary.DistinctUserCount, " & _
    "SMS_FileUsageSummary.IntervalStart, " & _
    "SMS_FileUsageSummary.IntervalWidth, " & _
    "SMS_FileUsageSummary.SiteCode " & _
  "FROM SMS_MeteredFiles INNER JOIN SMS_FileUsageSummary " & _
    "ON SMS_MeteredFiles.MeteredFileID = " & _
    "SMS_FileUsageSummary.FileID WHERE " & _
    "datediff(day,SMS_FileUsageSummary.IntervalStart, getdate()) " & _
    "<= " & intDays & " AND " & _
    "(SMS_FileUsageSummary.IntervalWidth = 15) AND " & _
    "(SMS_MeteredFiles.ProductName = '" & strProductName & "')"
```

```
wscript.echo "Product Name" & vbTAB & "Metered Interval" & vbTAB & _
    "Distinct Users" & vbTAB & "Site Code"
Set colMTRResults = objSMS.ExecQuery(strWQL)
for each objMTRResult in colMTRResults
    wscript.echo objMTRResult.SMS_MeteredFiles.ProductName & _
        vbTAB & WMIDateStringToDate(objMTRResult. _
        SMS_FileUsageSummary.IntervalStart) & _
        vbTAB & objMTRResult.SMS_FileUsageSummary.DistinctUserCount & _
        vbTAB & objMTRResult.SMS_FileUsageSummary.SiteCode
    if intPeak < objMTRResult.SMS_FileUsageSummary.DistinctUserCount then
        intPeak = objMTRResult.SMS_FileUsageSummary.DistinctUserCount
        strPeakInfo = WMIDateStringToDate(objMTRResult. _
            SMS_FileUsageSummary.IntervalStart)  & vbTAB & _
            objMTRResult.SMS_FileUsageSummary.DistinctUserCount _
            & vbTAB & objMTRResult.SMS_FileUsageSummary.SiteCode _
            & vbCRLF
    elseif intPeak = _
        objMTRResult.SMS_FileUsageSummary.DistinctUserCount then
            strPeakInfo = strPeakInfo & WMIDateStringToDate(objMTRResult. _
            SMS_FileUsageSummary.IntervalStart)  & vbTAB & _
            objMTRResult.SMS_FileUsageSummary.DistinctUserCount _
            & vbTAB & objMTRResult.SMS_FileUsageSummary.SiteCode _
            & vbCRLF
    end if
next

wscript.echo vbCRLF & vbCRLF
wscript.echo "Peak concurrentusage over the past " & intDays & _
    " days of metering data:" & vbCRLF & strPeakInfo

Function WMIDateStringToDate(dtmInstallDate)
    WMIDateStringToDate = CDate(Mid(dtmInstallDate, 5, 2) & "/" & _
        Mid(dtmInstallDate, 7, 2) & "/" & Left(dtmInstallDate, 4) _
            & " " & Mid (dtmInstallDate, 9, 2) & ":" & _
                Mid(dtmInstallDate, 11, 2) & ":" & Mid(dtmInstallDate, _
                    13, 2))
End Function
```

Discussion

Example 7-10 demonstrates how to display metered file usage summary data and identify the peak concurrent usage over a specified interval. Similar to Example 7-7, this script may appear a bit intimidating, but take the code section by section, and you will see that it's not too difficult.

First, we declare our variables and connect to the SMS site. Next, we execute a very long WQL query statement. This WQL query appears much clearer on the screen, where you can format and indent it as you would like. You can see from the query that we're using the following two classes:

SMS_MeteredFiles: Displays the ProductName in our example. Some of the other properties available are FileName, OriginalFileName, FileVersion, and SiteCode.

SMS_FileUsageSummary: Displays the DistinctUserCount, IntervalStart, and SiteCode in our example. We also use the IntervalWidth of 15, so that we see concurrent usage based on a 15-minute window. Any use identified during the 15-minute window is considered concurrent, even if it's not exactly concurrent. The alternative value for IntervalWidth is 60, so any use identified during a 60-minute window would be considered concurrent.

Notice the use of the DateDiff and GetDate functions in the WQL query. These two functions (and the DateAdd function) are now supported in the WHERE clause when executing WQL queries against SMS. Review the SMS 2003 SDK for more information.

Next, we display the column headings, and then execute the WQL query. Finally, we display the data using a for-each loop. The utility WMIDateStringToDate is used to convert a WMI date-time string to a standard date-time string.

See Also

- Review the standard web reports for SMS. The "Software Metering" category contains several reports to help make your job easier.

- Recipe 7-11, "Displaying Metered Summary Data for a Specific User Using VBScript," demonstrates how to display metered summary data for a specific user using VBScript.

- The SMS 2003 SDK provides additional information about the SMS classes used in this example (SMS_MeteredFiles and SMS_FileUsageSummary).

- The *SMS 2003 Scripting Guide* provides an example titled "How to Get Metered File Usage Summary Data in SMS."

CHAPTER 8

■■■

Reporting

SMS web reporting is the SMS administrator's chance for peace and harmony.

"Johnson, I need a list of all systems that have less than 1GB of RAM."

"Johnson, how many systems have SCSI cards installed?"

"Johnson, I need a list of all computers on the 192.168.2.0 subnet."

"Johnson, I need a list of all Windows operating systems with service packs in our environment."

"Johnson, I need to know what systems have foo.exe installed."

"Johnson . . . Johnson . . . JOHNSON!"

You get the picture. Often your manager, colleagues, the IT security officer, or maybe even someone from the building maintenance department will benefit from one of the reports available in SMS. More than 160 web reports are installed out of the box that will help make your job easier.

If your supervisor is trainable, spend some time with him or her in web reporting. Show your supervisor how to navigate the SMS reporting web site and click those new things called hyperlinks to get reports. We must caution you—one administrator's manager may be more trainable than another's; some managers may require a more heavy-handed approach to succeed. This is where patience and the skills you've learned from using SMS come into play. You may even have to create a new node (category) in web reporting to make the job easier.

Seriously, though, web reporting can be your (and maybe even your manager's) best friend. In our experience, most people have no idea the amount of data regularly collected by SMS. The more your colleagues know about the data available in SMS, the more they will appreciate and accept SMS in your environment. Take the time to become an expert at web reporting, and take the time to ensure that your colleagues are aware of the power of it.

And the best part (in our humble opinion) is that web reports are similar to the Ronco Showtime rotisserie—"Just set it and forget it!" You configure a new report, grant appropriate personnel access to the report, send them a link, and voilà! They can run reports at any time without your assistance.

Another great benefit of web reporting is that it can be extended to display custom information that SMS may be collecting for you. For example, most data located in the Windows registry can be obtained through SMS and configured to be available through SMS web reporting—data such as virus data definition updates and custom user or business information.

To become an SMS web reporting expert, you may want to consider becoming a SQL expert. The biggest challenges to custom web reporting are determining the tables and fields to join and developing the ability to create the proper query to return accurate information in a *manager-friendly* and efficient format. In this chapter, we're going to show you how to create, modify, link, and extend reports. We will talk a little about SQL but not enough to make you an expert. To learn more, take a look at some free resources on the Web, for example, http://www.w3schools.com/sql and http://sqlcourse.com, or invest in a good SQL book, such as *SQL: Access to SQL Server* by Susan Sales Harkins and Martin Reid (Apress, 2002).

One final introduction note—you will not find many code samples in this chapter, not because code examples are impossible, but because we feel they're impractical. Creating web reports using

VBScript is possible (using the SMS_REPORT class). However, unless you plan to mirror several SMS sites with custom web reports, we feel the time and effort required to create a custom web report programmatically is much greater than that involved in manually exporting a report from one site and importing it to another.

8-1. Creating a Report

Problem

You want to create a report.

Solution

1. Open the SMS Administrator console.

2. From the SMS Administrator console, expand Site Database (*<Site Code>*), Reporting, and Reports.

3. Right-click Reports, and select New ➤ Report from the menu to open the Report Properties dialog box.

4. On the General tab, enter at least the name of the new report and a category that the report will be associated with.

5. Specify any of the additional parameters.

6. Click OK to create the new report.

Discussion

Well, there you have it—the most basic report you can create. If you run this report by only entering the report name and category, no data will be returned (unless, of course, you have a system in SMS named computer_name). To modify this report to return *real* information, simply replace computer_name in the SQL statement with a valid computer name in your environment. The report will display SMS discovery data information from the SQL view v_R_System. Later in this chapter, we'll discuss various SQL views that you may find helpful in creating and modifying queries.

We find ourselves cloning a report almost as often as creating a new report. Check out the next recipe for more information about cloning a report.

See Also

- Recipe 8-2, "Cloning a Report," describes how to clone a report.

- Recipe 8-3, "Deleting a Report," demonstrates how to delete a report.

- Recipe 8-20, "Categorizing Reports," helps you logically group reports.

- Chapter 11 of the *SMS 2003 Operations Guide* provides additional detail about creating SMS web reports.

- Chapter 16 of the *Microsoft Systems Management Server 2003 Administrator's Companion* by Steven Kaczmarek (Microsoft Press, 2004) also provides additional detail about creating SMS web reports.

8-2. Cloning a Report

Problem

You want to create a report based on an existing report.

Solution

1. Open the SMS Administrator console.

2. From the SMS Administrator console, expand Site Database (*<Site Code>*), Reporting, and Reports.

3. Expand any folders that contain the report you want to clone.

4. Right-click the report, and select All Tasks ➤ Clone from the menu to open the Clone Report dialog box.

5. Enter a name for the new report.

6. Click OK to create the cloned report.

Discussion

You may find occasionally that a canned report contains 90 percent of the information you're looking for but is missing just that column or two that your supervisor requested. Instead of creating a brand-new report, take the report that is most like what you desire, clone it, and then modify it to meet your needs.

Caution Avoid tweaking the SMS 2003 canned reports. Clone the desired report, and then modify it, in order to preserve the integrity of the SMS 2003 canned reports.

See Also

- Recipe 8-1, "Creating a Report" demonstrates how to create a basic report.

- Recipe 8-3, "Deleting a Report," demonstrates how to delete a report.

- Chapter 11 of the *SMS 2003 Operations Guide* provides additional detail about cloning SMS web reports.

- Chapter 16 of the *Microsoft Systems Management Server 2003 Administrator's Companion* by Steven Kaczmarek (Microsoft Press, 2004) also provides additional detail about cloning SMS web reports.

8-3. Deleting a Report

Problem

You want to delete a report.

Solution

1. Open the SMS Administrator console.

2. From the SMS Administrator console, expand Site Database (<*Site Code*>), Reporting, and Reports.

3. Expand any folders that contain the report you want to delete.

4. In the right pane, select the report, and delete it by either pressing the Delete key on your keyboard, clicking the Delete button on the toolbar in the SMS Administrator console, or right-clicking the report and selecting Delete from the menu.

5. Click Yes to confirm your choice to delete the report.

Discussion

As with all other actions in the SMS Administrator console, this deletion is impossible to undo, so be sure you no longer need that web report before deleting it. You should consider modifying a report's category as an alternative to deleting the report. For example, modify the category to something like "archive." Another alternative might be to export the report to a MOF file and then delete it. You could always reimport the MOF file if you need the report later.

See Also

- Recipe 8-9, "Exporting a Report," demonstrates how to export a report.

- Chapter 11 of the *SMS 2003 Operations Guide* provides additional detail about deleting SMS web reports.

- Chapter 16 of the *Microsoft Systems Management Server 2003 Administrator's Companion* by Steven Kaczmarek (Microsoft Press, 2004) also provides additional detail about deleting SMS web reports.

8-4. Listing All Reports from the Command Line

Problem

You want to display all reports (with various report properties) from the command line.

Solution

Example 8-1 uses VBScript to generate a listing of all reports. The listing includes some of the more useful report properties. It demonstrates how to display each SMS report (using SQL query) from the command line.

Example 8-1. *ListAllReports.vbs*

```
strSMSServer = <SMSServer>

Set objLoc = CreateObject("WbemScripting.SWbemLocator")
Set objSMS= objLoc.ConnectServer(strSMSServer, "root\sms")
Set Results = objSMS.ExecQuery _
    ("SELECT * From SMS_ProviderLocation WHERE ProviderForLocalSite = true")
For each Loc in Results
    If Loc.ProviderForLocalSite = True Then
        Set objSMS = objLoc.ConnectServer(Loc.Machine, "root\sms\site_" & _
            Loc.SiteCode)
    end if
Next

Set colReports = objSMS.ExecQuery _
    ("Select * From SMS_Report order by " & _
        " ReportID")

For Each objReport In colReports
    DisplayRptInfo(objReport.ReportID)
Next

Sub DisplayRptInfo(intReportID)
    'SQLQuery is a lazy property, so we need to use the
    'Get method to retrieve the information
    Set objRpt = objSMS.Get("SMS_Report.ReportID=" & intReportID)
    wscript.echo objRpt.ReportID & vbTAB & objRpt.Name & _
        vbTAB & objRpt.DrillThroughReportID & _
        objRpt.SecurityKey & vbTAB & objRpt.MachineDetail & _
        vbCRLF & vbCRLF & objRpt.SQLQuery & vbCRLF & vbCRLF
End Sub
```

Discussion

Example 8-1 displays all reports in your SMS site and can be invoked from the command line. After connecting to the SMS site, we perform a WMI Query Language (WQL) query to obtain all web reports (from the SMS_Report class). For each report, we call the subroutine DispalyRptInfo and pass the ReportID. We use this subroutine to display the data, because SQLQuery is a lazy property. To display the data in a lazy property, we use the Get method to obtain the specific instance of the report. We can then display all data for the report. Calling the Get method on each report adds a lot of overhead, but you must call Get to obtain the lazy data. If we were only interested in properties that are lazy, we could display the data for each report in the for-each loop, significantly decreasing the time required to display the report information.

Review the SMS 2003 SDK to identify lazy properties. Use the SMS_Report class as an example, and search the SDK documentation for SMS_Report. Review each property of SMS_Report, searching for the Lazy qualifier. The following are lazy properties in the SMS_Report class: SQLQuery, DrillThroughReportID, DrillThroughReportPath, MachineDetail, and MachineSource.

■**Note** The easiest way to find the ReportID (and most other object IDs, for that matter) is to modify the shortcut to launch your SMS Administrator console. For example, instead of using the shortcut to launch C:\SMSAdmin\bin\ i386\sms.msc, have it launch this: C:\SMSAdmin\bin\i386\sms.msc /sms:nodeinfo=1. Now when you launch your SMS Administrator console, you can right-click any node, select Properties, and view the Node Information tab. When you view the Node Information tab for a report, look for ReportID=x, where x is the ID you would use in this script.

WHAT IS A LAZY PROPERTY?

Some SMS properties are time consuming to retrieve. Retrieving these properties for many instances of a class could cause a significant degradation of performance. By design, these lazy properties are not returned when executing a WQL query.

"Lazy" is a pretty good term for this type of property. To understand this concept a little more, let's examine Example 8-1. If we look at the WQL query, you can see that we're querying for all instances and all properties in the SMS_Report class:

```
Select * From SMS_Report order by ReportID
```

Now, replace the current line in the for-each loop with the following lines of code:

```
Wscript.echo objReport.Name
Wscript.echo objReport.SQLQuery
```

When you run the modified VBScript, you will see the Name displayed properly, but the SQLQuery property will display a value of null. Results are returned quickly, but as you can see, the lazy properties in SMS_Report cannot be reached using only this basic WQL query. Therefore, we call the DisplayRptInfo method in the example. In DisplayRptInfo, we use the Get method to obtain all properties (including lazy ones). This increases the time to complete the script significantly but is the only way to display the desired data.

See Also

- The *SMS 2003 Scripting Guide* provides more information about lazy properties.
- The SMS 2003 SDK provides more information about the SMS_Report class.

8-5. Running a Report

Problem

You want to run a report.

Solution

1. Open the SMS Administrator console.
2. From the SMS Administrator console, expand Site Database (*<Site Code>*), Reporting, and Reports.
3. Expand any folders that contain the report you want to run.
4. Right-click the report, and select All Tasks ➤ Run ➤ *<Reporting Point Server>* from the menu to open the report in a web browser.
5. Enter any variables that may be required by the report, and click Display.
6. Close your browser to close the report.

Discussion

This recipe shows one of many ways to run a report. If you're in the Reports section of the Administrator console, the method we show is probably the easiest way to launch a web report. Otherwise,

consider using the SMS web reporting home page (`http://<reportingpointServer>/SMSReporting_`
`<SiteCode>/`) or a direct link to the desired report. And of course, to launch a web report, you must
have proper permissions.

See Also

- Recipe 8-23, "Modifying the Permissions of a Report," shows how to modify permissions to
  a web report.
- Chapter 11 of the *SMS 2003 Operations Guide* provides additional detail about running SMS
  web reports.
- Chapter 16 of the *Microsoft Systems Management Server 2003 Administrator's Companion* by
  Steven Kaczmarek (Microsoft Press, 2004) also provides additional detail about running SMS
  web reports.

8-6. Modifying a Report

Problem

You want to change an existing report.

Solution

1. Open the SMS Administrator console.
2. From the SMS Administrator console, expand Site Database (*<Site Code>*), Reporting, and
   Reports.
3. Expand any folders that contain the report you want to modify.
4. Double-click the report to open the Report Properties dialog box.
5. Make your modifications using the tabs in the dialog box.
6. Click OK to apply the changes to the report.

Discussion

Be sure to close all instances of the web report you intend to modify. Refreshing a web report may
not include the change(s) you just saved. Relaunch the web report to ensure new changes are
included.

Caution Avoid tweaking the SMS 2003 canned reports. Clone the desired report, and then tweak it, in order to
preserve the integrity of the SMS 2003 canned reports.

See Also

- Chapter 11 of the *SMS 2003 Operations Guide* provides additional detail about changing SMS
  web reports.
- Chapter 16 of the *Microsoft Systems Management Server 2003 Administrator's Companion* by
  Steven Kaczmarek (Microsoft Press, 2004) also provides additional detail about changing
  SMS web reports.

8-7. Importing a Report

Problem

You want to import a report.

Solution

1. Open the SMS Administrator console.
2. From the SMS Administrator console, expand Site Database (<*Site Code*>), Reporting, and Reports.
3. Right-click the Reports node, and select All Tasks ➤ Import Objects to open the Import Objects Wizard.
4. Click Next at the Welcome screen.
5. Browse for the MOF file that contains the objects you want to import.
6. Click Next.
7. Review the objects that you plan to import.
8. Click Next.
9. Review the comments associated with the objects to be imported.
10. Click Next.
11. Review the status of the imported objects.
12. Click Finish to exit the Import Objects Wizard.

Discussion

Sharing web reports is a wonderful thing, and SMS 2003 helps you share them easily. Basic web reports are very simple to import. Web reports that rely on linked reports or statically defined data (such as a CollectionID or a custom file name) may require additional actions on your part after you import them to make them function properly. Hopefully, whoever provided the MOF file will provide you with the required information to successfully configure the web report after you import it.

Note Review other recipes in this chapter for assistance in creating linked reports and prompted queries. The easiest way to find the object ID of the report you want to import is to modify the shortcut to launch your SMS Administrator console. For example, instead of using the shortcut to launch C:\SMSAdmin\bin\i386\sms.msc, have it launch C:\SMSAdmin\bin\i386\sms.msc /sms:nodeinfo=1. Now when you launch your SMS Administrator console, you can right-click any node, select Properties, and view the Node Information tab. For example, when you view the Node Information tab on a collection, look for CollectionID="LAB00023", where "LAB00023" is the CollectionID you would use.

Spend some time in the online SMS communities (such as http://www.myITforum.com. Many SMS administrators have posted web reports to share with others. Avoid reinventing the wheel by performing a little research on the Web.

See Also

- Recipe 8-8, "Importing a Report from the Command Line," describes how to import a report from the command line and defines a MOF file.

- Recipe 8-9, "Exporting a Report," describes how to export a report.

- Recipe 8-16, "Creating Prompts in a Report," describes how to create a prompted query at runtime for a report.

- Recipe 8-22, "Linking Reports," demonstrates how to link a report.

- Chapter 11 of the *SMS 2003 Operations Guide* provides additional detail about importing SMS web reports.

- Chapter 16 of the *Microsoft Systems Management Server 2003 Administrator's Companion* by Steven Kaczmarek (Microsoft Press, 2004) also provides additional detail about importing SMS web reports.

8-8. Importing a Report from the Command Line

Problem

You want to import a web report from the command line.

Solution

1. Using a text editor, edit the MOF file you intend to import.

2. Just below the comments section (indicated by //), insert the following line (replace SMSVPC with the SMS server, and LAB with the SMS site code):

   ```
   #pragma namespace("\\\\SMSVPC\\root\\SMS\\site_LAB")
   ```

3. Save the changes, and close the MOF file.

4. From a command line, browse to the directory that contains the MOF file you just modified, and execute the following (replace myNewWebReport with the proper file name):

   ```
   Mofcomp myNewWebReport.MOF
   ```

5. Back in the SMS Administrator console, refresh the Reports node to see the new web report.

Discussion

When you export a web report to a MOF file, it is created with the assumption that you will import it using the SMS Administrator console. The procedure in this recipe adds a line to declare the namespace, allowing you to import the report from the command line instead. If you like, you can even import multiple web reports from the command line using a simple batch file.

■Caution Use extreme care when modifying a MOF file. Improper modification may cause unexpected results.

WHAT IS A MOF FILE?

MOF is an abbreviation for Managed Object Format. According to the Microsoft Developer Network, Managed Object Format is a language based on Interface Definition Language (IDL) that describes management information. The MOF syntax is a way to describe object definitions in textual form. The MOF compiler processes a MOF file and adds the required object definitions to the CIM repository.

   View and edit a MOF file using a text editor, such as Microsoft Notepad. Lines of text that start with // are comment lines. Lines that start with #pragma namespace are used to set the Windows Management Instrumentation (WMI) namespace.

   In SMS, MOF files are used for many purposes:

- *SMS setup*. Many MOF files are used by the installer during SMS setup to configure your primary (and secondary) site.

- *Hardware inventory*. SMS_DEF.MOF is used by SMS to configure the hardware inventory collection.

- *Web report and SMS query objects*. SMS creates MOF files when you export and import these types of objects.

See Also

- Recipe 8-7, "Importing a Report," shows how to manually import a report.

- Recipe 8-9, "Exporting a Report," demonstrates how to export a report.

- In the Windows Platform SDK, the "WMI Utilities" section provides additional information about mofcomp.exe.

8-9. Exporting a Report

Problem

You want to export a report.

Solution

1. Open the SMS Administrator console.

2. From the SMS Administrator console, expand Site Database (*<Site Code>*), Reporting, and Reports.

3. Right-click the desired report node, and select All Tasks ➤ Export Objects to open the Export Object Wizard.

4. Click Next at the Welcome screen.

5. Select the desired report(s) to export.

6. Click Next.

7. Enter a valid path and file name (with a MOF extension).

8. Add comments in the Comment section that will be beneficial to you or any other SMS administrator that may attempt to import at a later date.

9. Click Next.

10. Review the Completing the Export Object Wizard dialog, and click Finish.

Discussion

If you've created great web reports, do yourself and your fellow SMS administrators a favor by making your custom web reports available to other administrators (provided, of course, that the reports aren't highly customized to your environment). One other favor you can do for yourself and your fellow SMS administrators is to *comment your report*. When exporting a web report, add comments to help other SMS administrators import the report. Detail any manual steps that are required after the import (e.g., linking to other reports or entering static data into the SQL statement). Also, consider using the import and export features of SMS web reporting to move tested reports from your SMS test lab to your SMS production environment.

See Also

- Recipe 8-7, "Importing a Report," demonstrates how to import a report.

- Chapter 11 of the *SMS 2003 Operations Guide* provides additional detail about exporting SMS web reports.

- Chapter 16 of the *Microsoft Systems Management Server 2003 Administrator's Companion* by Steven Kaczmarek (Microsoft Press, 2004) also provides additional detail about exporting SMS web reports.

8-10. Automatically Exporting Report Results

Problem

You want to automatically export report results to a comma-separated values file.

Solution

1. View the desired web report.

2. Copy the URL in the address bar (e.g., `http://SMSVPC/SMSReporting%5FGHQ/Report.asp?ReportID=229&AdvertID=LAB20127`), and paste it into Microsoft Notepad temporarily.

3. In Microsoft Notepad, append the following to the URL: `&ExportTo=\\`**`<yourserver>\`**
   `ReportExport\patchstat.csv`, replacing `<yourserver>` with the reporting point server name and `ReportExport` with the name of a Windows share on the reporting server.

4. In Windows, click Start ➤ Run, and paste the new URL into the text box. The URL should look similar to the following:

   `http://SMSVPC/SMSReporting%5FGHQ/Report.asp?ReportID=229&`➡
   `AdvertID=LAB20127&ExportTo=\\SMSVPC\ReportExport\patchstat.csv`

5. Click OK to execute the export.

6. Click Yes to close the Internet browsing window.

Discussion

If you have a standard web report that you're always exporting to a `.csv` file, the method in this recipe may help make your job a little easier. By using `&ExportTo=`, you can export a report directly instead of loading the report and then exporting. You can use any file extension for the export file that you desire (e.g., `.txt`, `.csv`, etc.), but the data will always be exported as a comma-delimited text file.

The path to export can be a UNC (e.g., \\SMSVPC\ReportExport\patchstat.csv) or a drive letter (e.g., C:\ReportExport\patchstat.csv). Whichever path you choose, the destination *must* be on the reporting point, and the user running the report must have Modify permissions to the target.

There are a few important limitations to the &ExportTo method used in this recipe:

- Because of the security context in which SMS web reporting is executed, the destination must be on the reporting point server (whether you use a drive letter or a UNC path doesn't matter—in our experience, the only place the data can be written is to a local drive on the reporting point server).

- The user who launches the URL must have Modify permissions to the destination.

- When exporting a report using this method, the Internet browser window still appears while the data is being exported and attempts to close programmatically afterward. Depending on your browser settings, you may be prompted to confirm closure of the results page.

See Also

- Chapter 11 of the *SMS 2003 Operations Guide* provides additional detail about exporting the results of SMS web reports.

- Chapter 16 of the *Microsoft Systems Management Server 2003 Administrator's Companion* by Steven Kaczmarek (Microsoft Press, 2004) also provides additional detail about exporting the results of SMS web reports.

8-11. Displaying More Than 10,000 Rows in Web Report Results

Problem

You want to display more than 10,000 rows in the results of a web report.

Solution

1. Navigate to the following registry key on the SMS reporting server:

   HKEY_LOCAL_MACHINE\Software\Microsoft\SMS\Reporting

2. In the Reporting key, add the DWORD value Rowcount, and assign it the maximum desired number of records to return.

Discussion

For performance reasons, 10,000 rows is the default maximum row count for results returned in a web report. The maximum explicit row count you can assign is 32,767. If you want to return all rows (even if the row count is greater than 32,767), assign Rowcount the hexadecimal value of 0xffffffff. However, if you are frequently running return reports with high row counts, you should consider modifying your reports to target subsets of the data to limit the performance degradation that results from processing high-row-count reports.

See Also

- Recipe 8-12, "Displaying More Than 1,000 Values in a Prompted Query," shows how to display more than 1,000 values in a prompted query.

- Chapter 11 of the *SMS 2003 Operations Guide* provides additional detail about formatting SMS web reports.

- Chapter 16 of the *Microsoft Systems Management Server 2003 Administrator's Companion* by Steven Kaczmarek (Microsoft Press, 2004) also provides additional detail about formatting SMS web reports.

8-12. Displaying More Than 1,000 Values in a Prompted Query

Problem

You want to display more than 1,000 values in the results from a prompted query.

Solution

1. Navigate to the following registry key on the SMS reporting server:

    `HKEY_LOCAL_MACHINE\Software\Microsoft\SMS\Reporting`

2. In the `Reporting` key, add the `DWORD` value `Values Rowcount`, and assign it the maximum desired number of values to return.

Discussion

The default maximum value row count for results returned when clicking the Values button in a web report is 1,000. If you want to return all, assign `Values Rowcount` the hexadecimal value of `0xffffffff`. However, if you frequently return values with high row counts, you should consider modifying your reports to use the `LIKE` clause and wildcards (e.g., abc%) when returning values, so that you limit the performance degradation that results from processing high-row-count queries.

See Also

- Recipe 8-1, "Creating a Report," shows how to create a new web report.

- Recipe 8-11, "Displaying More Than 10,000 Rows in Web Report Results," demonstrates how to display more than 10,000 rows in a web report result.

- Chapter 11 of the *SMS 2003 Operations Guide* provides additional detail about displaying values in prompted queries of SMS web reports.

- Chapter 16 of the *Microsoft Systems Management Server 2003 Administrator's Companion* by Steven Kaczmarek (Microsoft Press, 2004) also provides additional detail about displaying values in prompted queries of SMS web reports.

8-13. Editing the SQL Statement of a Report

Problem

You want to modify the SQL statement of a report.

Solution

1. Open the SMS Administrator console.
2. From the SMS Administrator console, expand Site Database (<*Site Code*>), Reporting, and Reports.
3. Expand any folders that contain the report you want to modify.
4. Double-click the report to open the Report Properties dialog box.
5. On the General tab, click Edit SQL Statement to open the Report SQL Statement dialog box.
6. If you have a new SQL query to use with the report, paste it into the SQL statement box. Otherwise, manually modify the SQL statement using the Views and Columns areas for reference.
7. Click OK to close the Report SQL Statement dialog box.
8. Click OK to apply the changes to the report.

Discussion

SQL statement editing is a very broad topic. Not only is it broad, but it's also the meat and potatoes of using SMS web reporting. Without a proper SQL statement, web reports are of not much value to you. *Only use SQL views for web reporting SQL query statements.* By default, you can only use views, and we strongly suggest only using views instead of accessing tables directly.

How Do I Build a SQL Query Statement?

There are many possibilities for building a query statement. Some of the most popular ways follow:

Using the Report SQL Statement dialog in SMS reports: This is the method you may think to use most frequently. The benefit to this method is that all the views you see are available to you in web reports. You can simply browse through the views, select the desired columns, and build a query manually. This can be a difficult task, unless of course you are a SQL expert and are familiar with the SMS schema. Only views that begin with v_ are visible in the Report SQL Statement dialog.

Using a SQL query builder tool (such as Microsoft SQL Query Builder): Using a query builder tool makes the process more visual, allowing you to create proper joins and select data more easily than with the manual method. The biggest drawback we see is that *all* SQL views are visible using this method, but not all views have proper permissions to be used in web reporting. Only views that have granted Select permission to webreport_approle and smsschm_users are available in SMS web reporting.

Learning by example: Check out other web reports in your Administrator console, or download them from SMS sites on the Web, such as http://www.myitforum.com.

Using SMS queries: SMS queries are easier to build than SQL queries, because the SMS Query Builder automatically creates the joins between database tables for you. The SMS Query Builder uses WBEM Query Language (also called WQL) instead of SQL. To convert a WQL query to a SQL query, review the SMS 2003 SDK section titled "SMS Schema View Mapping." In addition to SMS Schema View Mapping, you can use the Microsoft SQL Profiler and watch for SQL:BatchCompleted events. This shows you the SQL equivalent of the WQL query, except that it calls the SQL tables and not the views. You then transpose from the table name to the view name, which typically isn't very difficult.

Phoning a friend: Well, OK, don't use this one all the time, or your friends might stop returning your calls. But when you get stumped, don't hesitate to post to online SMS resources, such as Microsoft SMS newsgroups, online SMS forums, or a Microsoft SMS e-mail list (see Chapter 1). You will almost always find someone willing to help you there.

Which SQL Views May I Use for Web Reporting?

By default, all SQL views that begin with v_ in the SMS database are accessible through SMS web reporting. In order to use views in the SMS database, you must grant Select permission to webreport_approle and smsschm_users.

Even after granting Select permissions to webreport_approle, the view may not appear in the Report SQL Statement dialog if it doesn't start with v_, but SMS web reporting will be able to use the view without issue.

Table 8-1 provides a brief overview of different types of views (by view name) that you may want to use in SMS web reporting. While not all-inclusive, this list provides the most frequently used views in SMS web reporting.

Table 8-1. *Overview of SQL Views for SMS Web Reporting*

Table Prefix	Description
v_CM_RES_COLL_	Collections in your SMS environment. The last eight characters of the view name are the collection ID of the collection. Depending on your task, v_FullCollectionMembership may be a more flexible alternative. Recipe 8-16, "Creating Prompts in a Report," uses v_FullCollectionMembership in an example.
v_GS_	Current inventory information. Generally speaking, this is the data you find under Resource Explorer for a system (e.g., v_GS_COMPUTER_SYSTEM ➤ Computer System, v_GS_LOGICALDISK ➤ Logical Disk, etc.).
v_HS_	Historical inventory information. This is the data that you find under the Hardware History node in Resource Explorer.
v_R_ and v_RA	Discovery data views, such as v_R_System and v_RA_System_IPAddresses (RA means it's an array).

Some views that only have a v_ prefix will also be of interest to you. A few of them follow, with brief descriptions:

v_Advertisement: Displays the contents of the SMS_Advertisement class in WMI as described in Chapter 6. This view tells you the CollectionID of the collection being advertised, whether or not subcollections are included, if there is an assigned schedule, and more.

v_ApplicableUpdatesSummaryEx: Provides an overview of applicable and installed software updates.

v_ClientAdvertisementStatus: Provides the last status message for each client for each advertisement.

v_Collection: Provides information about each collection in your site, such as whether or not the collection is replicated to child sites and the last member change date and time.

v_DistributionPoint: Displays each distribution point in your site and the status of each package on each distribution point.

v_FullCollectionMembership: Contains all the members of all the collections in your site.

Many other views are also available. Spend some time in your test environment to familiarize yourself with the views that are available to you for web reporting.

Which Fields Should I Use to Create Joins?

Deciding which fields to use can sometimes be the most challenging aspect of creating joins. Your most successful option is to learn by example. Take a look at the canned SMS reports to see which views are called, and use those as much as possible. Once you have exhausted your search for examples, we recommend the following joins:

Computer name: Often you will find yourself querying data in the system resource (v_GS_) views. Use the ResourceID field to map to ResourceID in v_R_System to obtain the computer name.

Collection name: Map CollectionID from views such as v_Advertisement to CollectionID in v_Collection. v_Collection contains the collection name.

Package name: Map PackageID from views such as v_Advertisement to PackageID in v_Package to obtain the package name.

These are methods to create a SQL statement—the *proper* part still falls on your shoulders. As stated earlier in this recipe, *learn by example*. Use canned reports to learn proper joins, and do your homework to become a better SQL guru.

See Also

- Recipe 8-1, "Creating a Report," shows how to create a web report.
- Recipe 8-2, "Cloning a Report," shows how to clone a web report.
- Chapter 11 of the *SMS 2003 Operations Guide* provides additional detail about working with SMS web reports.
- Chapter 16 of the *Microsoft Systems Management Server 2003 Administrator's Companion* by Steven Kaczmarek (Microsoft Press, 2004) also provides additional detail about working with SMS web reports.

8-14. Displaying Last Hardware Inventory Information

Problem

You want to generate a report of all systems that have not reported hardware inventory during the past 30 days.

Solution

Create a new web report using the following SQL statement:

```
SELECT v_R_System.Name0, v_R_System.Resource_Domain_OR_Workgr0,
    v_GS_WORKSTATION_STATUS.LastHWScan, DATEDIFF([day],
    v_GS_WORKSTATION_STATUS.LastHWScan, GETDATE())
    AS [Days Since Last HW Scan]
FROM v_R_System
    INNER JOIN v_GS_WORKSTATION_STATUS ON v_R_System.ResourceID =
    v_GS_WORKSTATION_STATUS.ResourceID
WHERE (v_R_System.Client0 = 1) AND (DATEDIFF([day],
    v_GS_WORKSTATION_STATUS.LastHWScan, GETDATE()) > 30)
ORDER BY v_GS_WORKSTATION_STATUS.LastHWScan
```

Discussion

This recipe's SQL query displays all SMS clients that have not reported a hardware inventory within the past 30 days. The following example shows how to use the DateDiff function to calculate the number of days between the current date (GETDATE()) and the last hardware scan (LastHWScan):

```
DATEDIFF([day],v_GS_WORKSTATION_STATUS.LastHWScan, GETDATE()) > 30
```

Depending on the frequency of hardware inventory (if enabled) in your environment, this recipe's report may help you identify systems that have SMS client issues or systems that have not connected to SMS for an extended period of time.

See Also

- Recipe 8-1, "Creating a Report," shows how to create a report.

- Chapter 11 of the *SMS 2003 Operations Guide* provides additional detail about displaying hardware information in SMS web reports.

- Chapter 16 of the *Microsoft Systems Management Server 2003 Administrator's Companion* by Steven Kaczmarek (Microsoft Press, 2004) also provides additional detail about displaying hardware information in SMS web reports.

8-15. Querying for Laptops

Problem

You want to display a report of all laptops in your environment.

Solution

Create a new web report using the following SQL statement:

```
SELECT v_R_System.Name0, v_R_System.Operating_System_Name_and0,
    v_R_System.Resource_Domain_OR_Workgr0,
    (CASE WHEN v_GS_SYSTEM_ENCLOSURE.ChassisTypes0 = 8 THEN 'Portable'
    WHEN v_GS_SYSTEM_ENCLOSURE.ChassisTypes0 = 9 THEN 'Laptop'
    WHEN v_GS_SYSTEM_ENCLOSURE.ChassisTypes0 = 10 THEN 'Notebook'
    WHEN v_GS_SYSTEM_ENCLOSURE.ChassisTypes0 = 14 THEN 'Sub Notebook'
    END) AS [Chassis Type]
FROM v_R_System INNER JOIN
```

```
    v_GS_SYSTEM_ENCLOSURE ON v_R_System.ResourceID =
    v_GS_SYSTEM_ENCLOSURE.ResourceID
WHERE (v_GS_SYSTEM_ENCLOSURE.ChassisTypes0 IN (8, 9, 10, 14))
ORDER BY [Chassis Type]
```

Discussion

This recipe's SQL query displays all systems in SMS that have a chassis type of 8 (portable), 9 (laptop), 10 (notebook), and 14 (subnotebook). These are all the currently known chassis types for laptops. Notice that we use CASE statement to make the display data user-friendly. Also, in the WHERE clause, we use IN (8, 9, 10, 14) instead of four OR conditions. For your viewing pleasure, Table 8-2 provides a list of all known chassis types at this time (data obtained from Microsoft TechNet).

Table 8-2. *Known Chassis Types*

Chassis Type	Description
1	Other
2	Unknown
3	Desktop
4	Low-profile desktop
5	Pizza box
6	Mini tower
7	Tower
8	Portable
9	Laptop
10	Notebook
11	Hand-held
12	Docking station
13	All-in-one
14	Subnotebook
15	Space-saving
16	Lunch box
17	Main system chassis
18	Expansion chassis
19	Subchassis
20	Bus-expansion chassis
21	Peripheral chassis
22	Storage chassis
23	Rack-mounted chassis
24	Sealed-case PC

See Also

- To learn more about chassis types, review the Microsoft TechNet article titled "New Application Installation Using Microsoft Systems Management Server" (http://www.microsoft.com/technet/itsolutions/cits/dsd/naisms/naismsag.mspx).

8-16. Creating Prompts in a Report

Problem

You want to prompt for information before generating a report.

Solution

1. Open the SMS Administrator console.

2. From the SMS Administrator console, expand Site Database (<*Site Code*>), Reporting, and Reports.

3. Expand any folders that contain the report you want to modify.

4. Double-click the report to open the Report Properties dialog box.

5. On the General tab, click Edit SQL Statement to open the Report SQL Statement dialog box.

6. Click the Prompts button to open the Prompts dialog box.

8. Click the New button (the yellow starburst icon), or double-click an existing prompt to open the Prompt Properties dialog box.

9. Enter at least a prompt name and prompt text. A SQL statement is not required, but it is best to use one to help the user select the proper data for the prompt.

10. Click OK to close the Prompt Properties dialog box.

11. Click OK to close the Prompts dialog box.

12. Click OK to close the Report SQL Statement dialog box.

13. Click OK to apply the changes to the report.

Discussion

Prompted reports are a great way to make SMS web reports flexible. For example, you could create a customized web report to display a specific set of hardware information for all systems in your SMS database, or you may only want to see a specific set of systems, like systems in a specific collection. Instead of hard-coding this information into the SQL query, you can create a prompted query, so the user can select criteria (in this case, the collection) at the time the report is run.

You can create a prompted query for any criteria you desire. We use prompts for collections more than anything else, but you could prompt for computer model numbers, network card models, software companies—the list is as long as the data that's available in the SMS database.

As an example, suppose your manager asks you for a report that displays the computer name and operating system for every SMS client. You can create a report using the following SQL statement:

```
select Name0, Operating_System_Name_and0
from v_R_System
where Client0 = 1
```

Now suppose that the following Tuesday your manager asks you for a report that lists every system on the eighth floor. You may have multiple avenues for providing the data to your manager. You may be able to query for systems on a specific subnet or query on a custom field that has been added to SMS for your environment. But you realize that you already have a collection that includes all systems on the eighth floor, so why not tie this web report to only display the systems that are in the "eighth floor" collection? That sounds like a good idea, so you obtain the CollectionID of the collection (by following the note in Recipe 8-7, "Importing a Report"). You insert the following SQL statement into a new web report (replacing LAB00023 with the desired CollectionID):

```
SELECT v_R_System.Name0, v_R_System.Operating_System_Name_and0,
    v_FullCollectionMembership.Name,
    v_FullCollectionMembership.CollectionID
FROM v_R_System INNER JOIN
    v_FullCollectionMembership ON v_R_System.ResourceID =
    v_FullCollectionMembership.ResourceID
WHERE (v_R_System.Client0 = 1) AND
    (v_FullCollectionMembership.CollectionID = 'LAB00023')
```

Now you have two web reports displaying the same information for two different sets of systems. And if you're asked for a report of systems on the seventh floor, you might either modify the report you just created or create a new report. Instead, let's create a query that prompts your boss to select a collection at runtime.

Create a new report titled something like "Operating System Information by Collection," and enter the following SQL statement for the report:

```
SELECT v_R_System.Name0, v_R_System.Operating_System_Name_and0
FROM v_R_System INNER JOIN
    v_FullCollectionMembership ON v_R_System.ResourceID =
    v_FullCollectionMembership.ResourceID
WHERE (v_R_System.Client0 = 1) AND
    (v_FullCollectionMembership.CollectionID = @CollectionID)
```

Notice the @CollectionID variable. That is a SQL variable that will be replaced with a collection ID at runtime. Next, click the Prompts button to display the Prompts dialog. Click the New Button (the yellow starburst icon) to create a new prompt. For Name, enter **CollectionID**. For Prompt Text, type **Enter a CollectionID** or **Filter with Collection Name**. Enable the "Provide a SQL statement" check box, and click the Edit SQL Statement button. Enter the following statement into the Prompt SQL Statement dialog:

```
begin
 if (@__filterwildcard = '')
  select CollectionID, Name from v_Collection order by Name
 else
  select CollectionID, Name from v_Collection
  WHERE Name like @__filterwildcard
  order by Name
end
```

When creating a prompted query, make sure the first column returned by the prompted query SQL statement contains the appropriate data to be used as criteria for the report SQL statement. Only data in the first column is used by the prompt when the report is run.

Notice in the prompt SQL statement that if @__filterwildcard = '', we show all collections. Otherwise, we use the like operator along with wildcards (e.g., WHERE Name like '%Windows XP%') to display only collections that contain a user-entered string.

Now that you have the prompt query in place, click the series of OK buttons to save the new report. Then, run the new report. When you run the report, you have two options for submitting criteria for the collection:

- Enter the exact CollectionID, and select Display.
- Select from a list using the Values button (which, in turn, uses your prompted query).

Typically your manager won't know the CollectionID. Most of the time when SMS administrators use web reports, we don't know the CollectionID of the collection we would like to query either. That's why option 2 is very popular. Because of the if-else statement in our Prompt SQL Statement section, option 2 (selecting from a list) also has two options:

- Click the Values button to display all collections.

- Enter a partial collection name, with wildcards for the like operator in SQL, to display a filtered list of collections to select from.

The following are examples of SQL wildcard usage:

like 'XP%': Returns every collection that begins with "XP" (e.g., "XP Systems", "XP Upgrade", "XP (extreme programming) Programmers", but not "Microsoft XP").

like '%XP%': Returns every collection that contains the string "XP" (e.g., "XP SP 2 Systems", "Windows XP Hotfixes", "Microsoft XP", "Office XP", "FaxPress", and "DB2 FixPack").

like '%XP': Returns every collection that ends with "XP" (e.g., "Office XP", "IloveXP", "Hello World XP", but not "XP Tools").

like 'a__ Systems' (two underscores after the "a"): Returns every collection that begins with "a", followed by any two characters (letters, numbers, spaces, etc.), a space, and "Systems" (e.g., "All Systems", "ATT Systems", but not "Arch Systems").

like 'All Systems_%': Returns every collection that begins with "All Systems" and has at least one more character (e.g., "All Systems with Office Installed", "All Systems 1", "All Systems " [note the space at the end of the string], but not "All Systems").

As the examples demonstrate, the underscore (_) matches any *single* character. The percent symbol (%) matches *zero or more characters*. We often know part of a collection name, so we'll use the percent sign around the part we know to filter the collections to a more manageable size. For example, when searching for collections that contain the string "Project", simply enter %Project% in the text box on the web report, and select Values to choose from a filtered list.

Notice when you run the report that the prompt parameters are included in the URL on the results page. You can copy this URL, paste it into an e-mail, and send it to your manager, so the report can be run without prompting for data. The report is still flexible, but you're able to forward specific data to others simply by forwarding the URL.

See Also

- Recipe 8-1, "Creating a Report," shows how to create a web report.

- Chapter 11 of the *SMS 2003 Operations Guide* provides additional detail about creating prompts in SMS web reports.

- Chapter 16 of the *Microsoft Systems Management Server 2003 Administrator's Companion* by Steven Kaczmarek (Microsoft Press, 2004) also provides additional detail about creating prompts in SMS web reports.

- SQL.org provides some basic tutorials for performing basic SQL queries and more information about using the like operator (http://www.sql.org).

8-17. Displaying Patch Installation Progress

Problem

You want to display a report of authorized, attempted, and failed security patches that were deployed from an advertisement that used a program created by the Distribute Software Updates Wizard (DSUW).

Solution

1. Create a new web report using the following SQL statement.

```
SELECT msg.MachineName AS [Computer Name], msg.SiteCode AS
    [Site Code], DATEADD(ss,@__timezoneoffset,msg.[Time]) AS
    [Status Time], att.AttributeValue AS [Advertisement ID],
    auth.InsStrValue AS Authorized, attemp.InsStrValue AS Attempted,
    fail.InsStrValue AS Failed
FROM v_StatusMessage msg
    INNER JOIN    v_StatMsgAttributes att ON msg.RecordID =
    att.RecordID AND msg.[Time] = att.AttributeTime
    INNER JOIN v_StatMsgInsStrings auth ON msg.RecordID =
    auth.RecordID AND auth.InsStrIndex = 0
    INNER JOIN v_StatMsgInsStrings attemp ON msg.RecordID =
    attemp.RecordID AND attemp.InsStrIndex = 1
    inner JOIN v_StatMsgInsStrings fail ON msg.RecordID =
    fail.RecordID AND fail.InsStrIndex = 2
WHERE (msg.MessageID = 11255) AND (att.AttributeID = 401) AND
    (att.AttributeValue = @advertid)
ORDER BY msg.[Time] DESC
```

2. Add a prompt. Give it the name AdvertID. Enter **Advertisement ID** as the prompt text, and add the following SQL statement for the prompt query:

```
begin
 if (@__filterwildcard = '')
  select AdvertisementID, AdvertisementName,
    Comment from v_Advertisement order by AdvertisementName
  else
   select AdvertisementID, AdvertisementName,
    Comment from v_Advertisement
   WHERE AdvertisementID like @__filterwildcard
   order by AdvertisementName
end
```

Discussion

First, let's describe the problem statement in a little more detail. If you're using SMS 2003 for patch management, chances are you are using the SMS scanning and deployment tools provided by Microsoft. The most recent scanning tool is the Inventory Tool for Microsoft Updates (ITMU). When deploying patches using the Distribute Software Updates Wizard (DSUW), a special package and program are created to deploy the selected security patches. The status messages that you see in SMS, by default, labels each patch as one of the following: Received, Running, Reboot Pending, and Success.

Buried in the status messages returned from the client is a message that describes how many patches were authorized, attempted, and failed. It is possible for an advertisement to return a Success status message when, say, three out of five patch installations failed. The only way (by default) to see the information about how many patches failed is to query for status message 11255 for each client in an advertisement. You can do that by viewing all advertisement status messages for a specific advertisement and filtering for message status 11255.

An alternative to the rather tedious default approach of searching for message status 11255 is to write a SQL query to display patch statistics. That's what the query in the solution does. It displays patch statistics for each client, given the AdvertisementID.

Notice DATEADD(ss,@__timezoneoffset, msg.[Time]) in the SQL statement. We are using the DATEADD function to convert the status message timestamp (which is in GMT) to the local time on the server.

Only the following three SQL views are required for this query:

v_StatusMessage: This SQL view contains each status message in the SMS environment. In our query, we obtain the MachineName, SiteCode, timestamp, and most important, MessageID.

v_StatMsgAttributes: This SQL view contains optional data associated with a status message. We use AdvertisementID as criteria for our query.

v_StatMsgInsStrings: This SQL view contains insertion strings that are inserted into the status message. This is where we obtain the attempted, authorized, and failed numbers. Using join clauses, we restrict query results to the following cases:

- auth (authorized) is equal to InstrValue when InsStrIndex = 0.
- attemp (attempted) is equal to InstrValue when InsStrIndex = 1.
- fail (failed) is equal to InsStrValue when InsStrIndex = 2.

Our second query is the prompt query, and we use it to allow the person running the report to select the desired DSUW advertisement at runtime.

See Also

- The solution query is loosely based on an example from a Microsoft TechNet article titled "Patch Management Using Systems Management Server 2003" (http://www.microsoft.com/technet/security/prodtech/sms/secmod199.mspx).

8-18. Displaying a Report in Computer Details

Problem

You want to view a report in the Computer Details section of the web reports.

Solution

1. Open the SMS Administrator console.
2. From the SMS Administrator console, expand Site Database (*<Site Code>*), Reporting, and Reports.
3. Expand any folders that contain the report you want to modify.
4. Double-click the report to open the Report Properties dialog box.
5. On the General tab, check the Display in Computer Details check box.
6. Click OK to apply the changes to the report.

Discussion

You can think of the Computer Details page as similar to Resource Explorer in the SMS Administrator console. On the Computer Details page, you enter the computer name in the text box, and select any report you desire; the results will be displayed in the right-hand frame. During this discussion, we'll add a report to the Computer Details page to show all collections of which the computer is a member and display whether the membership is a direct or query-based membership.

Create a new SMS web report, and enter the following SQL for the report:

```
SELECT v_R_System.Name0 AS [Computer Name],
    v_FullCollectionMembership.CollectionID AS [Collection ID],
```

```
    v_Collection.Name AS [Collection Name],
    v_FullCollectionMembership.SiteCode AS [Site Code],
    (CASE WHEN v_FullCollectionMembership.IsDirect = 1 THEN
    'Direct' ELSE 'Query' END) AS [Membership Type]
FROM v_FullCollectionMembership INNER JOIN
    v_R_System ON v_FullCollectionMembership.ResourceID
    = v_R_System.ResourceID INNER JOIN
    v_Collection ON v_FullCollectionMembership.CollectionID =
    v_Collection.CollectionID
WHERE      (v_R_System.Name0 = @ComputerName)
ORDER BY v_Collection.Name
```

Before we continue, we'd like to make a few comments on the SQL query. We will display the computer name, collection ID, collection name, site code, and the membership type (Direct or Query) in order by Collection Name. For membership type, notice the following CASE statement:

```
(CASE WHEN v_FullCollectionMembership.IsDirect = 1 THEN
    'Direct' ELSE 'Query' END)
```

We use the CASE statement to indicate that when the value of IsDirect equals 1 (which is true), the word "Direct" will be displayed. Otherwise, the word "Query" will be displayed.

The WHERE clause uses the variable @ComputerName, which is defined by a prompted query. This prompted query is different than the prompted query described in Recipe 8-16, "Creating Prompts in a Report"—no SQL is used for this query. Simply enter **ComputerName** for the Name property and **Enter Computer Name** for the Prompt text property, and click OK twice to save the changes.

Run the report from the SMS Administrator console, and you will see the prompt for the computer name. Confirm that the report functions properly by entering a valid computer name and selecting Display. After success, close the results page, and click the Computer Details node on the web reporting home page (you may need to click the Show Tree link to redisplay the available reports first).

From the Computer Details page, enter the computer name in the Computer Name text box, and select the report you just created. It should display the information for the specified computer without prompting.

A report displayed in the Computer Details page can only have one variable in the SQL statement prompt. However, the variable may be used more than once in the SQL statement.

The most common use of the Computer Details page is to display computer details (yes, that's pretty obvious). However, any query that prompts for one value could be added to the Computer Details page (we're not sure why you would do this, but we think it's worth mentioning). For example, you could have a report that displays CollectionID and Name from v_Collection, with a prompt on the CollectionID. Selecting your new query in the Computer Details screen would then request that you enter the CollectionID to display proper information.

See Also

- Chapter 11 of the *SMS 2003 Operations Guide* provides additional detail about working with the Computer Details page for SMS web reports.

- Chapter 16 of the *Microsoft Systems Management Server 2003 Administrator's Companion* by Steven Kaczmarek (Microsoft Press, 2004) also provides additional detail about working with the Computer Details page for SMS web reports.

8-19. Running Multiple SQL Queries in a Web Report

Problem

You want to run multiple SQL queries in one web report.

Solution

1. Create a new web report using the following SQL statements exactly:

```
SELECT v_R_System.Name0 AS [Computer Name],
    v_R_System.Operating_System_Name_and0 AS OS,
    v_GS_OPERATING_SYSTEM.CSDVersion0 as [Service Pack],
    v_GS_OPERATING_SYSTEM.LastBootUpTime0 as [Last Boot Time]
FROM v_R_System
    INNER JOIN v_GS_OPERATING_SYSTEM ON v_R_System.ResourceID =
    v_GS_OPERATING_SYSTEM.ResourceID
WHERE(v_R_System.Name0 = @ComputerName)

SELECT v_GS_ADD_REMOVE_PROGRAMS.DisplayName0 AS [Display Name],
    CONVERT(datetime, v_GS_ADD_REMOVE_PROGRAMS.InstallDate0)
    AS [Install Date], v_GS_ADD_REMOVE_PROGRAMS.ProdID0 AS
    [Product ID], v_GS_ADD_REMOVE_PROGRAMS.Publisher0 AS Publisher,
    v_GS_ADD_REMOVE_PROGRAMS.Version0 AS Version
FROM v_R_System
    INNER JOIN v_GS_ADD_REMOVE_PROGRAMS ON v_R_System.ResourceID =
    v_GS_ADD_REMOVE_PROGRAMS.ResourceID
WHERE (v_R_System.Name0 = @ComputerName)
ORDER BY v_GS_ADD_REMOVE_PROGRAMS.DisplayName0
```

2. Enable the Display in the Computer Details check box.

3. Create a prompt with the name ComputerName and the prompt text **Computer Name**.

Discussion

Our solution to this recipe is an example that simply demonstrates how to use two SQL statements to display data on one web report. The first SQL statement displays the computer name, operating system (with the service pack level), and last boot-up time. The second SQL statement displays Add Remove Programs data. Also in this second SQL statement, we use the CONVERT method to convert InstallDate0 to a more familiar-looking date and time (if it exists for the date row).

See also

- Recipe 8-1, "Creating a Report," shows how to create a new web report.

- Chapter 11 of the *SMS 2003 Operations Guide* provides additional detail about SQL queries in SMS web reports.

- Chapter 16 of the *Microsoft Systems Management Server 2003 Administrator's Companion* by Steven Kaczmarek (Microsoft Press, 2004) also provides additional detail about SQL queries in SMS web reports.

8-20. Categorizing Reports

Problem

You want to change the category that a report is associated with.

Solution

1. Open the SMS Administrator console.
2. From the SMS Administrator console, expand Site Database (<*Site Code*>), Reporting, and Reports.
3. Expand any folders that contain the report you want to modify.
4. Double-click the report to open the Report Properties dialog box.
5. On the General tab, select a category from the drop-down list, or enter a new category to use.
6. Click OK to apply the changes to the report.

Discussion

Report categories are used to create separate nodes in the main page of the SMS Report Viewer. Using categories effectively can greatly increase the value of your web reports. On many occasions, we have been asked for reports that already existed in a different category. After cloning such a report and placing it within a more recognizable category like "CIO Reports," the report gets used more frequently.

See Also

- Recipe 8-2, "Cloning a Report," explains how to clone a report.
- Recipe 8-1, "Creating a Report," demonstrates how to create a report.

8-21. Modifying the Refresh Interval of a Report

Problem

You want to change a report, so that it automatically refreshes.

Solution

1. Open the SMS Administrator console.
2. From the SMS Administrator console, expand Site Database (<*Site Code*>), Reporting, and Reports.
3. Expand any folders that contain the report you want to modify.
4. Double-click the report to open the Report Properties dialog box.
5. On the Display tab, check the "Refresh the report automatically" check box.
6. Select how often you would like the report to refresh (in minutes).
7. Click OK to apply the changes to the report.

Discussion

Automatically refreshing reports works well with dashboards or summary reports that are being viewed regularly, since the report data will be kept up-to-date automatically. Also, if members of your IT management team have taken a keen interest in following SMS deployments, modifying those reports to automatically refresh will save managers the hassle of clicking the refresh button or pressing F5 every time they want to view the latest data.

See Also

- Recipe 8-28, "Creating a Dashboard," explains how to create a dashboard.
- Chapter 11 of the *SMS 2003 Operations Guide* provides additional detail about refresh intervals for SMS web reports.
- Chapter 16 of the *Microsoft Systems Management Server 2003 Administrator's Companion* by Steven Kaczmarek (Microsoft Press, 2004) also provides additional detail about refresh intervals for SMS web reports.

8-22. Linking Reports

Problem

You want to link a report to another report.

Solution

1. Open the SMS Administrator console.
2. From the SMS Administrator console, expand Site Database (*<Site Code>*), Reporting, and Reports.
3. Expand any folders that contain the report you want to modify.
4. Double-click the report to open the Report Properties dialog box.
5. On the Links tab, choose a link type from the drop-down box.
6. If you are linking to another report, select the report to link to, and select which columns of your report will provide prompt data for the linked report.
7. If you are linking to Computer Details, select the column that contains the computer name.
8. If you are linking to Status Message Details, select the column that contains the status message RecordID.
9. If you are linking to an external URL, enter the URL in the space provided.
10. Click OK to apply the changes to the report.

Discussion

Linking reports provides the perfect answer to the question "How do I get more information?" in a single click. Each row in a linked report has a small arrow button on the far left of the report. Clicking the button passes the data from that row into the prompts in the linked report and opens the linked report in a new window. The more reports you have linked, the more a user can drill down into the data.

A great use for linked reports is patch compliance. You start with an enterprise-wide report that shows counts of systems by patches applicable. Click the row for "two patches applicable" to open a report that lists the systems falling into that category. Click a single system in that linked report to open another linked report that shows precisely which two patches are applicable to that particular system.

See Also

- Recipe 8-14, "Displaying Last Hardware Inventory Information," explains report prompts.
- Chapter 11 of the *SMS 2003 Operations Guide* provides additional detail about linking SMS web reports.
- Chapter 16 of the *Microsoft Systems Management Server 2003 Administrator's Companion* by Steven Kaczmarek (Microsoft Press, 2004) also provides additional detail about linking SMS web reports.

8-23. Modifying the Permissions of a Report

Problem

You want to modify the permissions of a report.

Solution

1. Open the SMS Administrator console.
2. From the SMS Administrator console, expand Site Database (*<Site Code>*), Reporting, and Reports.
3. Expand any folders that contain the report you want to modify.
4. Double-click the report to open the Report Properties dialog box.
5. On the Security tab, modify the class or instance security rights.
6. Click OK to apply the changes to the report.

Discussion

In our experience, permissions of web reports are either tightly controlled or wide open. If you feel that your SMS data is beneficial to all, giving read rights to your domain users is the easy way to let everybody run reports on that data. If you have reason to limit access to the web reports, changing the permissions will do the trick.

The same granular control that you have grown to love in SMS for advertisements, packages, and so forth is available for web reports. You can be very granular and specific in granting different users access to different sets of reports.

See Also

- Chapter 11 of the *SMS 2003 Operations Guide* provides additional detail about modifying permissions of SMS web reports.
- Chapter 16 of the *Microsoft Systems Management Server 2003 Administrator's Companion* by Steven Kaczmarek (Microsoft Press, 2004) also provides additional detail about modifying permissions of SMS web reports.

8-24. Creating a Chart

Problem

You want to create a chart in an SMS web report.

Solution

1. Open the SMS Administrator console.
2. From the SMS Administrator console, expand Site Database (*<Site Code>*), Reporting, and Reports.
3. Expand any folders that contain the report you want to modify.
4. Double-click the report to open the Report Properties dialog box.
5. On the Display tab, check the "Provide a chart for the report" check box.
6. Select a chart type and title along with the columns and titles for the x and y axes.
7. Click OK to apply the changes to the report.

Discussion

If your web reports only receive a yawn from your managers, then it is time to bring out the charts. Not only will your managers be impressed by the clarity of information that is inherent with charts, but they will love the fact that they can play with them too.

Charts are especially useful for providing a graphical picture for enterprise-wide reports like patch compliance or operating system versions.

Note You must install Office Web Components on your reporting point server for charts to work properly.

See Also

- Chapter 11 of the *SMS 2003 Operations Guide* provides additional detail about creating charts for SMS web reports.
- Chapter 16 of the *Microsoft Systems Management Server 2003 Administrator's Companion* by Steven Kaczmarek (Microsoft Press, 2004) also provides additional detail about creating charts for SMS web reports.

8-25. Filtering Reports

Problem

You want to filter the reports that are viewed in the SMS Administrator console.

Solution

1. Open the SMS Administrator console.
2. From the SMS Administrator console, expand Site Database (*<Site Code>*), Reporting, and Reports.

3. Right-click the Reports node, and select All Tasks ➤ Filter Reports to open the Filter Reports dialog box.

4. Select a category or multiple categories (by holding down the Shift or Ctrl key while selecting) that you would like to filter out, and use the toggle buttons (red and green arrows) to change the display status to No.

5. Click OK to apply the filter changes.

Discussion

If you find that the built-in reports get in your way when creating new reports in the SMS Administrator console, simply filter them out.

Caution Filtering reports does not hide the built-in reports from display in your web browser. It only hides them in the SMS Administrator console.

See Also

- Chapter 11 of the *SMS 2003 Operations Guide* provides additional detail about filtering SMS web reports.

- Chapter 16 of the *Microsoft Systems Management Server 2003 Administrator's Companion* by Steven Kaczmarek (Microsoft Press, 2004) also provides additional detail about filtering SMS web reports.

8-26. Creating a Report Folder

Problem

You want to create a report folder.

Solution: Using a Graphical Interface

1. Open the SMS Administrator console.

2. From the SMS Administrator console, expand Site Database (*<Site Code>*), Reporting, and Reports.

3. Right-click the Reports node, and select New ➤ Folder to open the Folder Properties dialog box.

4. Enter a name for the folder.

5. Click OK to apply the filter changes.

Solution: Using VBScript

Example 8-2 demonstrates how to create a folder in the reporting node of the SMS Administrator console.

Example 8-2. *CreateReportFolder.vbs*

```
strSMSServer = <SMSServer>
strNewFoldername = "Securit"

Set objLoc = CreateObject("WbemScripting.SWbemLocator")
Set objSMS= objLoc.ConnectServer(strSMSServer, "root\sms")
Set Results = objSMS.ExecQuery _
    ("SELECT * From SMS_ProviderLocation WHERE ProviderForLocalSite = true")
For each Loc in Results
    If Loc.ProviderForLocalSite = True Then
        Set objSMS = objLoc.ConnectServer(Loc.Machine, "root\sms\site_" & _
            Loc.SiteCode)
    end if
Next

Set newFolder = objSMS.Get("SMS_ObjectContainerNode") _
    .SpawnInstance_()
newFolder.Name = strNewFolderName
newFolder.ObjectType = 8    'Report
newFolder.ParentContainerNodeId = 0
newFolder.Put_
```

Discussion

Reports already use categories, so you may not need to use folders to organize them. However, as your report-building skills increase so will the number of reports that you need to keep track of, so organizing them by folder can be useful.

In Example 8-2, we create a folder in the root of the Reporting folder titled Admin Reports. By setting the ParentContainerNodeId to 0, we create the new folder in the root of the Reporting Node. If we wanted to make Admin Reports a subfolder of an existing folder, we would set the appropriate ParentContainerNodeID.

The easiest way to find the ParentContainerNodeID (and most other object IDs, for that matter) is to modify the shortcut to launch your SMS Administrator console. For example, instead of using the shortcut to launch C:\SMSAdmin\bin\i386\sms.msc, have it launch this: C:\SMSAdmin\bin\i386\ sms.msc /sms:nodeinfo=1. Now when you launch your SMS Administrator console, you can right-click any node, select Properties, and view the Node Information tab. When you view the Node Information tab on a folder, look for ContainerNodeID=x, where x is the ID you would use in this script.

See Also

- Recipe 8-27, "Moving Reports Between Folders," shows how to move web reporting objects between folders.

- Chapter 11 of the *SMS 2003 Operations Guide* provides additional detail about creating folders for SMS web reports.

- Chapter 16 of the *Microsoft Systems Management Server 2003 Administrator's Companion* by Steven Kaczmarek (Microsoft Press, 2004) also provides additional detail about creating folders for SMS web reports.

- Chris Rees's blog contains example scripts for creating folders: http://spaces.msn.com/members/ cheekysimian. (Chris Rees is one of the Microsoft SMS SDK gurus.)

- The SMS Script Repository contains scripts that demonstrate managing console folders in SMS.

- The SMS 2003 SDK has a topic titled "Creating a Console Folder."

8-27. Moving Reports Between Folders
Problem

You want to move reports between folders.

Solution: Using a Graphical Interface

1. Open the SMS Administrator console.

2. From the SMS Administrator console, expand Site Database (*<Site Code>*), Reporting, and Reports.

3. Expand any folders that contain the reports that you need to move.

4. Right-click the folder, and select Move Folder Items.

5. Select the reports that you want to move.

6. Click Browse to select the destination folder.

7. Click OK to move the reports.

Solution: Using VBScript

Example 8-3 demonstrates how to move reports between folders in the reporting node of the SMS Administrator console.

Example 8-3. *MoveReportsBetweenFolders.vbs*

```
strSMSServer = <SMSServer>

Set objLoc =  CreateObject("WbemScripting.SWbemLocator")
Set objSMS= objLoc.ConnectServer(strSMSServer, "root\sms")
Set Results = objSMS.ExecQuery _
    ("SELECT * From SMS_ProviderLocation WHERE ProviderForLocalSite = true")
For each Loc in Results
    If Loc.ProviderForLocalSite = True Then
        Set objSMS = objLoc.ConnectServer(Loc.Machine, "root\sms\site_" & _
            Loc.SiteCode)
    end if
Next
'Use the "SecuirtyKey" ID as the Report ID
strReportIDs = "LAB00001,LAB00002,LAB00004,LAB00005,LAB00023"
'to move more than one, separate with commas
intSourceFolder=0 'Source Folder (root node in this case)
intDestFolder=9 'Destination Folder
intObjectType=8 '8=Report for type of object

Set objFolder = objSMS.Get("SMS_ObjectContainerItem")
arrReportIDs = split(strReportIDs, ",")
retval = objFolder.MoveMembers _
(arrReportIDs, intSourceFolder, intDestFolder , intObjectType)
wscript.echo retval
```

Discussion

Example 8-3 demonstrates how you can use VBScript to move multiple reports from the root Reporting node to the subfolder of your choice. To move one web report, specify only one SecurityKey for strReportIDs. To move more than one, specify a list of SecurityKeys and separate them by commas (no spaces). Example 8-3 assumes that the web reports currently exist in the root Reporting node, and thus sets intSourceFolder to 0. If the web reports to be moved are in a subfolder, replace the 0 with the appropriate ContainerNodeID. Moving web reports between folders does not affect any aspect of the web reports other than where they are organized in the Reporting node of the SMS Administrator console.

Note The easiest way to find the SecurityKey (and most other object IDs, for that matter) is to modify the shortcut to launch your SMS Administrator console. For example, instead of using the shortcut to launch C:\SMSAdmin\bin\i386\sms.msc, have it launch this: C:\SMSAdmin\bin\i386\sms.msc /sms:nodeinfo=1. Now when you launch your SMS Administrator console, you can right-click any node, select Properties, and view the Node Information tab. When you view the Node Information tab on a folder, look for SecurityKey=x, where x is the Report ID you would use in this script.

See Also

- Recipe 8-26, "Creating a Report Folder," shows how to create a web report folder.
- Chapter 11 of the *SMS 2003 Operations Guide* provides additional detail about moving SMS web reports.
- Chapter 16 of the *Microsoft Systems Management Server 2003 Administrator's Companion* by Steven Kaczmarek (Microsoft Press, 2004) also provides additional detail about moving SMS web reports.
- Chris Rees's blog contains example scripts for creating folders: http://spaces.msn.com/members/cheekysimian. (Chris Rees is one of the Microsoft SMS SDK gurus.)
- The SMS Script Repository also contains scripts that demonstrate managing console folders in SMS.
- The SMS 2003 SDK also has a topic titled "Creating a Console Folder."

8-28. Creating a Dashboard

Problem

You want to create a dashboard.

Solution

1. Open the SMS Administrator console.
2. From the SMS Administrator console, expand Site Database (*<Site Code>*), Reporting, and Dashboards.
3. Right-click Dashboards, and select New ➤ Dashboard from the menu to open the Dashboard Properties dialog box.
4. On the General tab, enter at least the name of the new dashboard.

5. Specify any of the additional parameters.

6. Click OK to create the new report.

Discussion

If your IT management team likes your web reports and charts, then they will think that dashboards are candy. Creating dashboards is very easy, and they provide a rich, multilayered experience for tracking SMS information. You might want to customize a dashboard for specific roles (e.g., CIO dashboard, Help Desk dashboard, Server Team dashboard, etc.) to provide different managers with critical reports without forcing them to wade through reports that they may deem unimportant. Configure reports in a dashboard to refresh automatically to make a real-time heads-up display for your call center or network operations.

Caution Dashboards are designed for reports that do not require input in order to be displayed. If you have a report that requires input and you would like to include it in a dashboard, clone the report, remove the prompts, and replace the variables in the SQL statement with static values.

See Also

- Chapter 11 of the *SMS 2003 Operations Guide* provides additional detail about working with SMS dashboards.

- Chapter 16 of the *Microsoft Systems Management Server 2003 Administrator's Companion* by Steven Kaczmarek (Microsoft Press, 2004) also provides additional detail about working with SMS dashboards.

CHAPTER 9

■ ■ ■

Queries

Queries may appear near the bottom of your SMS Administrator console, but that doesn't make them unimportant. Despite being one of the most powerful features in SMS, they tend to be misunderstood. In this chapter we'll try to demystify queries, so you can put them right to work for your enterprise.

A query is simply a question that is presented to a data source. However, you do need to know the language involved. If you don't know the local language, simple questions that are frequent in our daily lives can be quite difficult, while complex questions can seem impossible. Likewise, with SMS, you need to understand the query language—WBEM Query Language (WQL) in this case—to be able to leverage queries. However, SMS is able to help you create queries even if you don't know the language by presenting you with a Query Builder to guide you. Those of you with Transact-SQL (T-SQL) or other database programming backgrounds should find WQL queries particularly easy to grasp, since WQL and T-SQL have some similarities. Also, you may be able to skip the dialog boxes in the Query Builder and edit your queries directly if you like.

In case queries are completely new to you, we've included some sidebars in this chapter to explain some of the core terminology and provide additional resources for you to explore.

9-1. Creating a Query

Problem

You want to create a query.

Solution: Using a Graphical Interface

1. Open the SMS Administrator console.

2. From the SMS Administrator console, expand Site Database (*<Site Code>*) and Queries.

3. Right-click Queries, and select New ➤ Query from the menu to open the Query Properties dialog box.

4. On the General tab, enter at least the name of the new query.

5. Specify any of the additional parameters.

6. Click OK to create the new query.

7. Click Yes to the warning dialog box that informs you that you will be returning all resources, which may take awhile.

Solution: Using VBScript

Example 9-1 demonstrates how to create a basic query to show all systems in SMS.

Example 9-1. *CreateAQuery.vbs*

```
strSMSServer = <SMSServer>
strQueryName = "Basic Query"

Set objLoc =  CreateObject("WbemScripting.SWbemLocator")
Set objSMS= objLoc.ConnectServer(strSMSServer, "root\sms")
Set Results = objSMS.ExecQuery _
    ("SELECT * From SMS_ProviderLocation WHERE ProviderForLocalSite = true")
For each Loc in Results
    If Loc.ProviderForLocalSite = True Then
        Set objSMS = objLoc.ConnectServer(Loc.Machine, "root\sms\site_" & _
            Loc.SiteCode)
    end if
Next

Set newQuery = objSMS.Get("SMS_Query").SpawnInstance_()
newQuery.Name = strQueryName
newQuery.Expression = "select * from SMS_R_System"
newQuery.TargetClassName = "SMS_R_System"
newQuery.Put_
```

Example 9-2 demonstrates how to create a basic query, but it first verifies that the query name doesn't currently exist in your SMS site.

Example 9-2. *CreateQuery-VerifyName.vbs*

```
strSMSServer = <SMSServer>
strQueryName = "Basic Query"

Set objLoc =  CreateObject("WbemScripting.SWbemLocator")
Set objSMS= objLoc.ConnectServer(strSMSServer, "root\sms")
Set Results = objSMS.ExecQuery _
    ("SELECT * From SMS_ProviderLocation WHERE ProviderForLocalSite = true")
For each Loc in Results
    If Loc.ProviderForLocalSite = True Then
        Set objSMS = objLoc.ConnectServer(Loc.Machine, "root\sms\site_" & _
            Loc.SiteCode)
    end if
Next

if QueryDoesntExist(strQueryname) then
    Set newQuery = objSMS.Get("SMS_Query").SpawnInstance_()
    newQuery.Name = strQueryName
    newQuery.Expression = "select *  from  SMS_R_System"
    newQuery.TargetClassName = "SMS_R_System"
    newQuery.Put_
else
    wscript.echo "Query named " & chr(34) & strQueryname & _
        chr(34) & " already exists!"
end if
```

```
'function used to verify query name doesn't exist
Function QueryDoesntExist(strName)
    Set colQueries = objSMS.ExecQuery _
    ("select * from SMS_Query where TargetClassName <> '" & _
    "SMS_StatusMessage" & "' and Name = '" & strName & "'")
    if colQueries.Count > 0 then
        QueryDoesntExist = False
    else
        QueryDoesntExist = True
    end if
End Function
```

Discussion

Now that you've created a very basic query, we'll further explain some of the components before we move on. The query that you created using the graphical interface translates to Select * from SMS_R_System in the WQL language. The results from this query contain data from all of the columns in the SMS_R_System table (the * indicates "all"). From here you can refine your query by using the WHERE clause.

Tip If you need to build a collection based on a complex query, first create the query, and modify it to your specifications. Once you have the query completed, you can import it into your collection. However, the SMS query is only imported; it is not linked to your collection. Subsequent changes to the SMS query will not be replicated to the collection.

Examples 9-1 and 9-2 both demonstrate how to create a basic SMS query, the same query that is created when using the SMS Administrator console. You're only specifying the name of the query (and not entering any criteria). Select * from SMS_R_System will return discovery data for all discovered system resources.

Example 9-1 demonstrates the most basic VBScript script to create a query. After connecting to the site, we create a new instance of SMS_Query and set the Name, Expression, and TargetClassName variables. Finally, we save the new query using the Put_ method.

Example 9-2 uses the same basic code as Example 9-1, except that it uses the function QueryDoesntExist to verify that the desired name of the query is not currently used in the SMS site.

Here is a brief description of the fields used to create a basic query:

Name: The query identifier that will be visible in the SMS Administrator console. This name must be unique.

Expression: The WQL statement used by the SMS query.

TargetClassName: The class name used by SMS queries for displaying data in the SMS Administrator console.

See Also

- Recipe 9-14, "Limiting a Query to a Collection," describes how to limit a query to a collection.
- Recipe 9-2, "Listing All Queries from the Command Line," describes how to display all queries and query statements using VBScript.
- SMS_Query is described in the SMS 2003 SDK.

- Chapter 16 of the *Microsoft Systems Management Server 2003 Administrator's Companion* by Steven Kaczmarek (Microsoft Press, 2004) provides additional information about creating SMS queries.

- Chapter 4 of the *SMS 2003 Operations Guide* also provides additional information about creating SMS queries.

WHAT IS WMI?

We consider Windows Management Instrumentation (WMI) one of Windows's best-kept secrets. We don't mean there was any attempt to keep WMI secret—it's just one of those features that you don't see unless you look for it. WMI has been embedded in the Windows operating system since Windows 2000 (and Windows ME) and was installable for Windows NT and Windows 98.

All recent versions of SMS depend on WMI as a key component. WMI is Microsoft's implementation of the Web-Based Enterprise Management (WBEM) standard. It's a standardized repository for information on Windows-based computers, specifically management data. WMI data can be leveraged through common interfaces by applications as well as being remotely accessible. SMS capitalizes on all of this rich management data by collecting and consolidating it, so that it can be utilized. The WMI data is made available through the SMS Provider.

On a very basic level, you can think of WMI as a database of information about your hardware, operating system, and other applications. You can query this database for information using a query language that is very similar to SQL. You can also modify many (but not all) settings for a particular piece of hardware or software through WMI. For example, using the SMS Provider, you can list all advertisements in SMS. You can use the SMS Provider to modify settings for a specific advertisement (or all advertisements) as well. You can also use WMI to list all processes currently running on a system and terminate a process if desired.

Both SMS clients and servers use WMI constantly. SMS clients use WMI to obtain hardware inventory, software inventory, SMS client settings, SMS advertisement information, and more. SMS servers use it to display the data you see in the SMS Administrator console and to create, modify, and delete objects in SMS, just to name a few.

There is much more to WMI than just getting and setting values. You can use WMI to monitor events on a system, such as a registry change, a process start or finish, event log entries, and more. For further information, search your favorite bookstore for WMI books or visit some of the following web sites:

- Windows Management Instrumentation (an Overview): `http://msdn.microsoft.com/library/en-us/wmisdk/wmi/wmi_start_page.asp`

- WMI: Introduction to Windows Management Instrumentation: `http://www.microsoft.com/whdc/system/pnppwr/wmi/WMI-intro.mspx`

- Introduction to WMI: `http://www.computerperformance.co.uk/vbscript/wmi.htm`

- Microsoft TechNet's Windows Script Center: `http://www.microsoft.com/technet/scriptcenter` Review the section of the *SMS 2003 Scripting Guide* titled "How SMS Uses WMI."

9-2. Listing All Queries from the Command Line

Problem

You want to list all SMS queries from the command line.

Solution

Example 9-3 demonstrates how to display all queries in your SMS site.

Example 9-3. *ListQueries.vbs*

```
strSMSServer = <SMSServer>

Set objLoc = CreateObject("WbemScripting.SWbemLocator")
Set objSMS= objLoc.ConnectServer(strSMSServer, "root\sms")
Set Results = objSMS.ExecQuery _
    ("SELECT * From SMS_ProviderLocation WHERE ProviderForLocalSite = true")
For each Loc in Results
    If Loc.ProviderForLocalSite = True Then
        Set objSMS = objLoc.ConnectServer(Loc.Machine, "root\sms\site_" & _
            Loc.SiteCode)
    end if
Next

Set colQueries = objSMS.ExecQuery _
    ("select * from SMS_Query where TargetClassName <> " & _
    "'SMS_StatusMessage' order by Name")
for each objQuery in colQueries
    wscript.echo objQuery.Name & "(" & _
        objQuery.QueryID & ")" & vbTAB & objQuery.Expression
next
```

Discussion

Example 9-3 demonstrates how to display all SMS queries through the use of a query expression (WQL statement). After connecting to the site, we execute the following WQL query:

```
select * from SMS_Query where TargetClassName <> " & _
"'SMS_StatusMessage' order by Name"
```

This WQL statement queries the SMS_Query class for all instances that do not have a TargetClassName of SMS_StatusMessage.

Caution The SMS_Query class contains instances for both SMS queries and for SMS status message queries. Use where TargetClassName <> 'SMS_StatusMessage' to ensure that you are only listing SMS queries.

The VBScript script displays Name, QueryID, and Expression (WQL statement) properties.

See Also

- Review the topic titled "How to Enumerate Available Queries on an SMS Site" from the *SMS 2003 Scripting Guide*.

- Recipe 9-24, "Exporting Multiple Query Objects from the Command Line," demonstrates how to export multiple queries from the command line.

- SMS_Query and SMS_StatusMessage are described in the SMS 2003 SDK.

WHAT IS WQL?

Think of WQL as SQL for WMI. This is not a stretch of the imagination, since WQL is based on the American National Standards Institute Structured Query Language (ANSI SQL) with only some minor changes required by WMI.

WQL is very similar to SQL. If you are familiar with SQL, you should be able to work with WQL without much difficulty. For example, to query all properties of the Win32_Processor class, you would use SELECT * FROM Win32_Processor.

The most important difference between SQL and WQL is that WQL only supports read-only queries. Review the section of the MSDN Windows Platform SDK titled "Querying with WQL" for more information about WQL and the differences between WQL and SQL. More information about WQL is also available on the following web pages:

- WQL (SQL for WMI): http://msdn.microsoft.com/library/en-us/wmisdk/wmi/wql_sql_for_wmi.asp
- Querying with WQL: http://msdn.microsoft.com/library/en-us/wmisdk/wmi/querying_with_wql.asp
- WQL Operators: http://msdn.microsoft.com/library/en-us/wmisdk/wmi/wql_operators.asp

9-3. Deleting a Query

Problem

You want to delete a query.

Solution: Using a Graphical Interface

1. Open the SMS Administrator console.
2. From the SMS Administrator console, expand Site Database (*<Site Code>*) and Queries.
3. Expand any folders that contain the query you want to delete.
4. In the left pane, select the query, and delete it by pressing the Delete key, clicking the Delete button on the toolbar in the SMS Administrator console, or right-clicking the query and selecting Delete from the menu.
5. Click Yes to confirm your choice to delete the query.

Solution: Using VBScript

Example 9-4 demonstrates how to delete an SMS query by query name using VBScript. After connecting to the site, we perform a WQL query to obtain all instances in the SMS_Query class that have a name of "Basic Query" and use a for-each loop to delete them.

Example 9-4. *DeleteQuery.vbs*
```
strSMSServer = <SMSServer>
strQueryName = "Basic Query"

Set objLoc =  CreateObject("WbemScripting.SWbemLocator")
Set objSMS= objLoc.ConnectServer(strSMSServer, "root\sms")
Set Results = objSMS.ExecQuery _
    ("SELECT * From SMS_ProviderLocation WHERE ProviderForLocalSite = true")
For each Loc in Results
    If Loc.ProviderForLocalSite = True Then
```

```
        Set objSMS = objLoc.ConnectServer(Loc.Machine, "root\sms\site_" & _
            Loc.SiteCode)
    end if
Next

Set colQueries = objSMS.ExecQuery _
    ("select * from SMS_Query where Name = '" & strQueryName & "'")
for each objQuery in colQueries
    wscript.echo "Deleting " & objQuery.Name & "(" & _
        objQuery.QueryID & ")"
    objQuery.Delete_
next
```

Discussion

Sooner or later, no matter how organized you are, you'll need to delete some queries that you no longer use. You can delete them with either of the methods shown in this recipe.

Caution Use caution when deleting queries programmatically. The SMS_Query class also contains SMS_StatusMessage queries. If you have a status message query with the same name as a regular query, you will delete it by mistake, so verify that your queries have unique names.

See Also

- Recipe 9-4, "Deleting Multiple Queries," describes how to delete multiple queries using VBScript. The VBScript script can also be used to delete single queries, given the QueryID.

- Chapter 16 of the *Microsoft Systems Management Server 2003 Administrator's Companion* by Steven Kaczmarek (Microsoft Press, 2004) provides additional information about deleting SMS queries.

- Chapter 4 of the *SMS 2003 Operations Guide* also provides additional information about deleting SMS queries.

9-4. Deleting Multiple Queries

Problem

You want to delete multiple SMS queries from the command line.

Solution

Example 9-5 demonstrates how to delete multiple queries using VBScript.

Example 9-5. *DeleteMultipleQueries.vbs*

```
strSMSServer = <SMSServer>
'to delete more than one, separate with commas as shown below
strQueryIDs = "LAB00001,LAB00002,LAB00014"
arrQueryIDs = split(strQueryIDs, ",")
```

```
Set objLoc =  CreateObject("WbemScripting.SWbemLocator")
Set objSMS= objLoc.ConnectServer(strSMSServer, "root\sms")
Set Results = objSMS.ExecQuery _
    ("SELECT * From SMS_ProviderLocation WHERE ProviderForLocalSite = true")
For each Loc in Results
    If Loc.ProviderForLocalSite = True Then
        Set objSMS = objLoc.ConnectServer(Loc.Machine, "root\sms\site_" & _
            Loc.SiteCode)
    end if
Next

for each strQueryID in arrQueryIDs
    Set objQuery = objSMS.Get ("SMS_Query.QueryID='" & strQueryID & "'")
    objQuery.Delete_
next
```

Discussion

Notice the following line from Example 9-5:

```
strQueryIDs = "LAB00001,LAB00002,LAB00014"
```

LAB00001, LAB00002, and LAB00014 are the QueryIDs of three SMS queries. Notice that commas, and no spaces, separate them. We use the comma-delimited format so that we can use the Split function in VBScript to create an array of QueryIDs. If you want to delete only one query, simply enter one QueryID, with no commas or spaces.

We use the Split function to split strQueryIDs on the commas to create an array of QueryIDs. After connecting to the site, we use a for-each loop to delete each query (by QueryID) in the array.

Note The easiest way to find an object ID is to modify the shortcut to launch your SMS Administrator console. For example, instead of using the shortcut to launch C:\SMSAdmin\bin\i386\sms.msc, have it launch this: C:\SMSAdmin\bin\i386\sms.msc /sms:nodeinfo=1. Now when you launch your SMS Administrator console, you can right-click any node, select Properties, and view the Node Information tab. For example, when you view the Node Information tab on a query, look for QueryID="LAB00023", where "LAB00023" is the QueryID you use.

See Also

- Recipe 9-3, "Deleting a Query," describes how to delete a single query. It also describes how to delete a single query by name using VBScript.

- Chapter 16 of the *Microsoft Systems Management Server 2003 Administrator's Companion* by Steven Kaczmarek (Microsoft Press, 2004) provides additional information about deleting SMS queries.

- Chapter 4 of the *SMS 2003 Operations Guide* also provides additional information about deleting SMS queries.

9-5. Modifying a Query

Problem

You want to modify a query.

Solution: Using a Graphical Interface

1. Open the SMS Administrator console.

2. From the SMS Administrator console, expand Site Database (<*Site Code*>) and Queries.

3. Expand any folders that contain the query you want to modify.

4. In the right pane, right-click the query, and select Properties to open the Query Properties dialog box.

5. Edit the name of the query, add comments, edit or import a query statement, limit the query to a collection, or change the security of the query to meet your specifications.

6. Click OK to apply the settings.

7. Click Yes to any warning dialog boxes (after you've read them!).

Solution: Using VBScript

Example 9-6 demonstrates how to modify the Comments property of a query.

Example 9-6. *ModifyQuery.vbs*

```
strSMSServer = <SMSServer>
strQueryID = "LAB0001D"

Set objLoc =  CreateObject("WbemScripting.SWbemLocator")
Set objSMS= objLoc.ConnectServer(strSMSServer, "root\sms")
Set Results = objSMS.ExecQuery _
    ("SELECT * From SMS_ProviderLocation WHERE ProviderForLocalSite = true")
For each Loc in Results
    If Loc.ProviderForLocalSite = True Then
        Set objSMS = objLoc.ConnectServer(Loc.Machine, "root\sms\site_" & _
            Loc.SiteCode)
    end if
Next

Set objQuery = objSMS.Get("SMS_Query.QueryID='" & _
    strQueryID & "'")
objQuery.Comments = "Use this query to display all systems " & _
    "in the SMS_R_System class"
objQuery.Put_
```

Discussion

The solution using a graphical interface gives the basic steps to modify a query. We will cover the individual modification options in subsequent recipes. For now, get comfortable with the various dialog boxes to avoid confusion later, because there are lots of them.

Note The bundle of dialog boxes used to create queries in SMS is also affectionately known as the SMS Query Builder. It isn't labeled as such, but that name is a good way to describe it.

Example 9-6 shows how to modify a query programmatically. After connecting to the SMS site, we use the Get method to obtain the query. We can then modify the query by setting any of the desired properties (e.g., Name, Comments, Expression, TargetClassName, and LimitToCollectionID). In Example 9-6, we modify the property Comments. Finally, we save the modified query using the Put_ method.

See Also

- Recipe 9-14, "Limiting a Query to a Collection," shows how to modify a query to be limited to a specific collection.

- Chapter 16 of the *Microsoft Systems Management Server 2003 Administrator's Companion* by Steven Kaczmarek (Microsoft Press, 2004) provides additional information about modifying SMS queries.

- Chapter 4 of the *SMS 2003 Operations Guide* also provides additional information about modifying SMS queries.

9-6. Importing a Query Statement

Problem

You want to import a query statement from another query.

Solution

1. Open the SMS Administrator console.
2. From the SMS Administrator console, expand Site Database (*<Site Code>*) and Queries.
3. Expand any folders that contain the query you want to modify.
4. In the right pane, right-click the query, and select Properties to open the Query Properties dialog box.
5. On the General tab, click the Import Query Statement button.
6. Select a query to import from the list or enter the name of the query to import.
7. Click OK to make your selection.
8. Click OK for your setting to be applied.

Discussion

Importing an existing query statement for the purpose of modifying it is not considered cheating—it's being smart! Plenty of good query examples ship with SMS 2003, so many that you should rarely have to build one completely from scratch. Besides, if you look at all your existing queries before creating a new one, you might find that you already have one that does most of what you need, or you may learn a better way to query the data than you originally planned.

Note The difference between a query and a query statement can be a little confusing, so we'll try to clear it up. An SMS query is an object in the SMS Administrator console that displays the results of the query statement associated with it. A query statement is the actual request for data. In SMS, you can create a query statement using the Query Builder or by manually writing it out.

Importing a query statement using VBScript is possible, but there are generally too many unknowns that would have to be resolved before such an import would be practical. For example, you would need to know the QueryID of the model query to import. Once you knew that, you could use code from Example 9-3 (or another example that uses the Get method) to obtain the Expression value (the WQL statement) for the desired query. You could then use the Expression value from the known query as the Expression value for the new query.

However, if you have the WQL statement and want to modify an existing query, see Recipe 9-11, "Modifying the Criteria for a Query Statement," for how to modify the criteria for a query statement.

See Also

- Recipe 9-5, "Modifying a Query," provides more information about modifying a query.
- Chapter 16 of the *Microsoft Systems Management Server 2003 Administrator's Companion* by Steven Kaczmarek (Microsoft Press, 2004) provides additional information about modifying SMS queries.
- Chapter 4 of the *SMS 2003 Operations Guide* also provides additional information about modifying SMS queries.

9-7. Using Different Object Types in Your Queries

Problem

You want to base your query on different object types.

Solution

1. Open the SMS Administrator console.
2. From the SMS Administrator console, expand Site Database (*<Site Code>*) and Queries.
3. Expand any folders that contain the query you want to modify.
4. In the right pane, right-click the query, and select Properties to open the Query Properties dialog box.
5. On the General tab, select an object type from the drop-down list.
6. Click Yes to the dialog box that warns you that your current query statement will be discarded.
7. Click OK to apply the settings.

Discussion

SMS includes the following object types that can be used to base your query. The object type you choose to use will specify which classes of data are available. In the following list, interpret the word "class" as if it were the name of a table in the database:

<unspecified>: Gives you access to data from all object types and is useful when you need to query multiple object types. You will have to manually create the query, and you will not be able to use the collection limiting options, but you can limit by collection in your query statement.

Advertisement: Limits your query to the SMS_Advertisement class. Also, you will not be able to use the collection limiting options, but you can limit by collection in your query statement.

IP Network Resource: Allows you to query for network resources that are not SMS clients. You will have to manually create the query. Collection limiting options are available.

Package: Limits your query to the SMS_Package class. You will not be able to use the collection limiting options, but you can limit by collection in your query statement.

Program: Limits your query to the SMS_Program class. You will not be able to use the collection limiting options, but you can limit by collection in your query statement.

Site: Limits your query to the SMS_Site class. You will not be able to use the collection limiting options, but you can limit by collection in your query statement.

Software Metering Rule: Limits your query to the SMS_MeteredProductRule class. You will not be able to use the collection limiting options, but you can limit by collection in your query statement.

Software Product Compliance: Limits your query to the SMS_SoftwareProductCompliance class. You will not be able to use the collection limiting options, but you can limit by collection in your query statement.

System Resource: Limits your query to the SMS_R_System class. This is by far the most popular object type, because you have access to almost all of the rest of the classes. You also are able to use the collection limiting options.

User Group Resource: Limits your query to the SMS_R_UserGroup class. Collection limiting options are available.

User Resource: Limits your query to the SMS_R_User class. Collection limiting options are available.

See Also

- Chapter 16 of the *Microsoft Systems Management Server 2003 Administrator's Companion* by Steven Kaczmarek (Microsoft Press, 2004) provides additional information about creating SMS queries and using different SMS objects (attribute classes) in SMS queries.

- Chapter 4 of the *SMS 2003 Operations Guide* also provides additional information about using SMS object types in SMS queries.

9-8. Editing a Query Statement

Problem

You want to edit the statement in an SMS query.

Solution: Using a Graphical Interface

1. Open the SMS Administrator console.
2. From the SMS Administrator console, expand Site Database (*<Site Code>*) and Queries.
3. Expand any folders that contain the query you want to modify.
4. In the right pane, right-click the query, and select Properties to open the Query Properties dialog box.

5. On the General tab, click the Edit Query Statement button to open the Query Statement Properties dialog box.

6. Edit your results attributes, criteria, or joins, and click OK to close the Query Statement Properties dialog box.

7. Click OK to apply the settings.

Solution: Using VBScript

Editing a query statement using VBScript is possible, but it can be quite a challenge. If, however, you have WQL experience and want to modify an existing query, simply use Example 9-6, remove the line modifying the `Comments` property (if desired), and insert the following two lines in its place:

```
objQuery.TargetClassName = "SMS_Advertisement"
objQuery.Expression = "select * from SMS_Advertisement"
```

Recipe 9-1, "Creating a Query," provides more information about `TargetClassName` and `Expression`.

Discussion

The query statement is the heart and soul of any SMS query. Without a query statement an SMS query is nothing—really! We will cover the components of a query statement in more detail in subsequent recipes.

Caution The difference between a query and a query statement can be a little confusing, so we'll try to clear it up. An SMS query is an object in the SMS Administrator console that displays the results of the query statement associated with it. A query statement is the actual request for data. In SMS, the query statement is built using the Query Builder or created manually.

See Also

- Recipe 9-5, "Modifying a Query," provides more information about modifying a query.

- Chapter 16 of the *Microsoft Systems Management Server 2003 Administrator's Companion* by Steven Kaczmarek (Microsoft Press, 2004) provides additional information about editing SMS queries.

- Chapter 4 of the *SMS 2003 Operations Guide* also provides additional information about editing SMS queries.

9-9. Omitting Duplicate Rows in Your SMS Query Results

Problem

You want to omit duplicate rows in the results of your SMS query.

Solution

1. Open the SMS Administrator console.

2. From the SMS Administrator console, expand Site Database (*<Site Code>*) and Queries.

3. Expand any folders that contain the query you want to modify.

4. In the right pane, right-click the query, and select Properties to open the Query Properties dialog box.

5. On the General tab, click the Edit Query Statement button to open the Query Statement Properties dialog box.

6. Check the "Omit duplicate rows (select distinct)" check box.

7. Click OK to close the Query Statement Properties dialog box.

8. Click OK to apply the settings.

Discussion

Sometimes when you are building a query statement, it will return multiple results for a single system. If you are trying to return only a single result for each system, use this option (also known as *select distinct*) to disregard any duplicates when the query is run.

After checking the "Omit duplicate rows (select distinct)" check box, click the Show Query Language button, and observe that the WQL query now contains the distinct operator.

See Also

- Chapter 16 of the *Microsoft Systems Management Server 2003 Administrator's Companion* by Steven Kaczmarek (Microsoft Press, 2004) provides additional information about SMS query results.

- Chapter 4 of the *SMS 2003 Operations Guide* also provides additional information about SMS query results.

9-10. Modifying the Results Attributes in a Query Statement

Problem

You want to choose which attributes will be returned in the results of the query.

Solution

1. Open the SMS Administrator console.

2. From the SMS Administrator console, expand Site Database (*<Site Code>*) and Queries.

3. Expand any folders that contain the query you want to modify.

4. In the right pane, right-click the query, and select Properties to open the Query Properties dialog box.

5. On the General tab, click the Edit Query Statement button to open the Query Statement Properties dialog box.

6. On the General tab of the Query Statement Properties dialog box, click the New button (the yellow starburst icon) or double-click an existing result attribute to open the Result Properties dialog box.

7. Click the Select button to open the Select Attribute dialog box.

8. Select an attribute class from the drop-down menu.

9. Select an attribute from the drop-down menu.

10. Click OK to close the Select Attribute dialog box. The chosen class and attribute will now be listed in the Result Properties dialog box.

11. Select a sort order for the result properties, or leave them unsorted, and click OK to close the Result Properties dialog box.

12. Your chosen attribute, attribute class, and sort order will be listed in the Results pane.

13. Click OK to close the Query Statement Properties dialog box.

14. Click OK to apply the settings.

Discussion

The results attributes define what data is returned by the query. If you are looking for a list of systems that have a processor that is less than 500MHz and a hard drive that is smaller than 10GB, then you might specify `SMS_G_System_SYSTEM.Name` for a results attribute. You need to identify the memory and drive space attributes, but those will only be used in the criteria, not in the results.

Note An attribute class can be thought of like the name of a table in a database. An attribute can be thought of like a column name in that table. Therefore, specifying `SMS_G_System_SYSTEM.Name` for a result attribute returns the name of an SMS client system.

When you examine the WQL statement in Example 9-7, take note of where the results attributes are listed in the statement.

Example 9-7. *Basic WQL Query Statement*

```
SELECT
SMS_G_System_SYSTEM.Name

FROM
SMS_R_System
inner join SMS_G_System_SYSTEM
on SMS_G_System_SYSTEM.ResourceID = SMS_R_System.ResourceId
inner join SMS_G_System_PROCESSOR
on SMS_G_System_PROCESSOR.ResourceID = SMS_R_System.ResourceId
inner join SMS_G_System_DISK
on SMS_G_System_DISK.ResourceID = SMS_R_System.ResourceId

WHERE
SMS_G_System_PROCESSOR.MaxClockSpeed < 500
AND
SMS_G_System_DISK.Size < 10000
```

You will notice that the result attribute `SMS_G_System_SYSTEM.Name` comes between `SELECT` and `FROM` in the query statement. The result attribute class `SMS_R_System` follows `FROM`. Lastly, the criteria classes and attributes are included in the statement using joins. The actual data returned by the query is a list of system names and nothing else.

See Also

- Chapter 16 of the *Microsoft Systems Management Server 2003 Administrator's Companion* by Steven Kaczmarek (Microsoft Press, 2004) provides additional information about modifying SMS query statements.

- Chapter 4 of the *SMS 2003 Operations Guide* also provides additional information about modifying SMS query statements.

9-11. Modifying the Criteria for a Query Statement

Problem

You want to select or modify the criteria for a query statement.

Solution

1. Open the SMS Administrator console.

2. From the SMS Administrator console, expand Site Database (<*Site Code*>) and Queries.

3. Expand any folders that contain the query you want to modify.

4. In the right pane, right-click the query, and select Properties to open the Query Properties dialog box.

5. On the General tab, click the Edit Query Statement button to open the Query Statement Properties dialog box.

6. On the Criteria tab, click the New button (the yellow starburst icon) or double-click an existing criterion to open the Criterion Properties dialog box.

7. Select a criterion type from the drop-down menu.

8. Click the Select button to open the Select Attribute dialog box.

9. Select an attribute class from the drop-down menu.

10. Select an attribute from the drop-down menu.

11. Click OK to close the Select Attribute dialog box. The chosen attribute class and attribute will now be listed in the Criterion Properties dialog box.

12. Select an operator from the drop-down menu.

13. Enter a value to use with the operator, or click the Values button to browse for an existing value from the database.

14. Click OK to close the Criterion Properties dialog box. Your selected criterion will be listed in the Criteria pane of the Query Statement Properties dialog box.

15. Click OK to close the Query Statement Properties dialog box.

16. Click OK to apply the setting. (Whew!)

Discussion

The criteria attribute is probably the most important part of the query statement, since it defines the criteria for which data should be returned by the query. If a query returned all rows of data from the desired classes, you would still have to manually dig through them to find the information you need. The criteria attribute does that digging for you.

Note An attribute class can be thought of as the name of a table in a database. An attribute can be thought of as a column name in that table.

Look at Example 9-7 to see where the criteria attributes appear. The criteria attributes are SMS_G_System_PROCESSOR.MaxClockSpeed and SMS_G_System_DISK.Size, which are further refined by the < operator and values. The criteria attributes always follow the WHERE clause.

See Also

- Chapter 16 of the *Microsoft Systems Management Server 2003 Administrator's Companion* by Steven Kaczmarek (Microsoft Press, 2004) provides additional information about modifying SMS query statements.

- Chapter 4 of the *SMS 2003 Operations Guide* also provides additional information about modifying SMS query statements.

9-12. Modifying the Joins in a Query Statement

Problem

You want to change the joins in a query statement.

Solution

1. Open the SMS Administrator console.

2. From the SMS Administrator console, expand Site Database (*<Site Code>*) and Queries.

3. Expand any folders that contain the query you want to modify.

4. In the right pane, right-click the query, and select Properties to open the Query Properties dialog box.

5. On the General tab, click the Edit Query Statement button to open the Query Statement Properties dialog box.

6. On the Joins tab, click the New button (the yellow starburst icon), or right-click an existing join and select properties to open the Attribute Class Join Properties dialog box.

7. Select a join type from the drop-down menu.

8. Click the Select button to open the Select Attribute dialog box.

9. Select an attribute class from the drop-down menu.

10. Select an attribute from the drop-down menu.

11. Click OK to close the Select Attribute dialog box. The chosen attribute class and attribute will now be listed in the Attribute Class Join Properties dialog box.

12. Choose an operator from the drop-down menu.

13. Select the Base attribute by clicking the corresponding Select button.

14. Click OK to close the Select Attribute dialog box for the Base attribute.

15. Click OK to close the Attribute Class Join Properties dialog box. The new join will be listed in the Attribute Class Joins pane.

16. Click OK to close the Query Statement Properties dialog box.

17. Click OK to apply the settings.

Discussion

Joins link two attribute classes together by matching a common attribute found in both classes. By joining the classes together, you can return data from one class that corresponds to data from another.

Note An attribute class can be thought of as the name of a table in a database. An attribute can be thought of as a column name in that table.

There are several types of joins, but the inner join is the default type used by the Query Builder. *Inner joins* will return data only when matching data can be found on both sides of the join, while *outer joins* will return all the data from one class and matching data from the other. Full joins will return all data from both classes.

Look at the joins in Example 9-7 (see Recipe 9-10) to see how they work in a WQL query statement. The second join is based on the `ResourceID` of the first class matching the `ResourceID` of the second (`SMS_G_System_PROCESSOR.ResourceID = SMS_R_System.ResourceId`). Joins are placed after the `FROM` clause and before the `WHERE` clause in the query statement.

See Also

- Chapter 16 of the *Microsoft Systems Management Server 2003 Administrator's Companion* by Steven Kaczmarek (Microsoft Press, 2004) provides additional information about modifying joins SMS query statements.

- Chapter 4 of the *SMS 2003 Operations Guide* also provides additional information about modifying joins SMS query statements.

9-13. Viewing a Query Statement

Problem

You want to edit the query statement for a query.

Solution: Using a Graphical Interface

1. Open the SMS Administrator console.
2. From the SMS Administrator console, expand Site Database (*<Site Code>*) and Queries.
3. Expand any folders that contain the query you want to modify.
4. In the right pane, right-click the query, and select Properties to open the Query Properties dialog box.
5. On the General tab, click the Edit Query Statement button to open the Query Statement Properties dialog box.
6. On the General tab of the Query Statement Properties dialog box, click the Show Query Language button.
7. Make manual edits to the query statement if necessary.
8. Click the Show Query Design button to return to the previous view.
9. Click OK to close the Query Statement Properties dialog box.
10. Click OK to apply the settings.

Solution: Using VBScript

Example 9-8 demonstrates how to display the WQL query for a given collection.

Example 9-8. *DisplayWQL.vbs*

```
strSMSServer = <SMSServer>
strQueryID = "LAB0001D"

Set objLoc =  CreateObject("WbemScripting.SWbemLocator")
Set objSMS= objLoc.ConnectServer(strSMSServer, "root\sms")
Set Results = objSMS.ExecQuery _
    ("SELECT * From SMS_ProviderLocation WHERE ProviderForLocalSite = true")
For each Loc in Results
    If Loc.ProviderForLocalSite = True Then
        Set objSMS = objLoc.ConnectServer(Loc.Machine, "root\sms\site_" & _
            Loc.SiteCode)
    end if
Next

Set objQuery = objSMS.Get("SMS_Query.QueryID='" & strQueryID & "'")
wscript.echo objQuery.Expression
```

Discussion

The more you learn about WQL, the easier it will be to edit query statements directly. Editing statements directly will make it faster for you to create queries and will give you greater flexibility, as complex queries can only be created with a WQL query statement. Studying WQL statements, such as the one in Example 9-7 that was used in the last several recipes, will give you a better understanding of how WQL works. You may eventually find that manually entering a WQL statement is easier than using the Query Builder dialog boxes.

Example 9-8 displays the WQL statement from the query with an ID of LAB0001D. The Expression property of the query contains the WQL statement. To display all query properties in the query object, you could replace the wscript.echo line with the following:

```
wscript.echo objQuery.GetObjectText_
```

to display the class definition formatted in MOF syntax.

If you're running Windows XP or a newer operating system, you can display all data from the query object in XML format with the following line of code:

```
wscript.echo objQuery.GetText_(2)
```

See Also

- SMS_Query is described in the SMS 2003 SDK.

- The topic titled "How to Run an SMS Scripting Query" from the *SMS 2003 Scripting Guide* provides additional information for how to query SMS using VBScript.

- "Representing Objects in XML" from the WMI SDK provides more information about the GetObjectText_ and GetText_(2) methods.

- Chapter 16 of the *Microsoft Systems Management Server 2003 Administrator's Companion* by Steven Kaczmarek (Microsoft Press, 2004) provides additional information about viewing SMS query statements.

- Chapter 4 of the *SMS 2003 Operations Guide* also provides additional information about viewing SMS query statements.

9-14. Limiting a Query to a Collection

Problem

You want to limit a query to a collection.

Solution: Using a Graphical Interface

1. Open the SMS Administrator console.

2. From the SMS Administrator console, expand Site Database (<*Site Code*>) and Queries.

3. Expand any folders that contain the query you want to modify.

4. In the right pane, right-click the query, and select Properties to open the Query Properties dialog box.

5. On the General tab, select the Limit to Collection radio button in the Collection Limiting section.

6. Enter the name of the collection, or click the Browse button to select the collection from a list of all collections.

7. Click OK to apply the settings.

Solution: Using VBScript

Example 9-9 demonstrates how to limit query results to a collection (also called *collection limiting*).

Example 9-9. *CollectionLimitQuery.vbs*

```
strSMSServer = <SMSServer>
strQueryID = "LAB0001E"
strCollLimitID = "LAB00017" 'the collection to limit to

Set objLoc =  CreateObject("WbemScripting.SWbemLocator")
Set objSMS= objLoc.ConnectServer(strSMSServer, "root\sms")
Set Results = objSMS.ExecQuery _
    ("SELECT * From SMS_ProviderLocation WHERE ProviderForLocalSite = true")
For each Loc in Results
    If Loc.ProviderForLocalSite = True Then
        Set objSMS = objLoc.ConnectServer(Loc.Machine, "root\sms\site_" & _
            Loc.SiteCode)
    end if
Next

Set objQuery = objSMS.Get("SMS_Query.QueryID='" & _
    strQueryID & "'")
objQuery.LimitToCollectionID = strCollLimitID
objQuery.Put_
```

Example 9-10 demonstrates how to list all queries that are limited to a specified collection or are prompted for a limiting collection at runtime.

Example 9-10. *ListAllCollLimitQueries.vbs*

```
strSMSServer = <SMSServer>

Set objLoc =  CreateObject("WbemScripting.SWbemLocator")
Set objSMS= objLoc.ConnectServer(strSMSServer, "root\sms")
Set Results = objSMS.ExecQuery _
    ("SELECT * From SMS_ProviderLocation WHERE ProviderForLocalSite = true")
For each Loc in Results
    If Loc.ProviderForLocalSite = True Then
        Set objSMS = objLoc.ConnectServer(Loc.Machine, "root\sms\site_" & _
            Loc.SiteCode)
    end if
Next

Set colQueries = objSMS.ExecQuery _
    ("select * from SMS_Query where TargetClassName <> " & _
    "'SMS_StatusMessage' and LimitToCollectionID <> '' order by Name")
for each objQuery in colQueries
    wscript.echo objQuery.Name & "(" & _
        objQuery.QueryID & ")" & objQuery.LimitToCollectionID
next
```

Discussion

You can limit query results to a collection, thus filtering the results, so that only data related to the systems in the collection will be displayed. If such a query may be useful when filtered on other collections, consider using a prompted query, as described in the next recipe.

Note A query can only be limited to a specified collection. Subcollections of the limiting collection do not affect any results from the query.

Example 9-9 demonstrates how to limit a query to a collection from VBScript. After connecting to the site, we use the Get method to obtain the query object. Next, we set the LimitToCollectionID property to the desired CollectionID. Finally, we use the Put_ method to save the change.

Caution Even when you do not specify collection limiting when creating a query, SMS applies collection limiting whenever you are not authorized to view all resources.

See Also

- Recipe 3-3, "Identifying the CollectionID of a Collection," describes how to obtain the CollectionID of a collection.

- Recipe 9-15, "Creating a Prompted Query," describes how to make a prompted query.

- SMS_Query is described in the SMS 2003 SDK.

- The note in Recipe 9-4, "Deleting Multiple Queries," describes how to obtain the QueryID.

- Chapter 16 of the *Microsoft Systems Management Server 2003 Administrator's Companion* by Steven Kaczmarek (Microsoft Press, 2004) provides additional information about limiting SMS queries.

- Chapter 4 of the *SMS 2003 Operations Guide* also provides additional information about limiting SMS queries.

9-15. Creating a Prompted Query

Problem

You want to create a query that prompts for collection-limiting information.

Solution: Using a Graphical Interface

1. Open the SMS Administrator console.
2. From the SMS Administrator console, expand Site Database (*<Site Code>*) and Queries.
3. Expand any folders that contain the query you want to modify.
4. In the right pane, right-click the query, and select Properties to open the Query Properties dialog box.
5. On the General tab, select the Prompt for Collection radio button in the Collection Limiting section.
6. Click OK to apply the settings.

Solution: Using VBScript

Example 9-11 demonstrates how to create a query that prompts at execution time.

Example 9-11. *CreatePromptedQuery.vbs*

```
strSMSServer = <SMSServer>
strQueryID = "LAB0001E"
strCollLimitID = "<Prompt>"

Set objLoc =  CreateObject("WbemScripting.SWbemLocator")
Set objSMS= objLoc.ConnectServer(strSMSServer, "root\sms")
Set Results = objSMS.ExecQuery _
    ("SELECT * From SMS_ProviderLocation WHERE ProviderForLocalSite = true")
For each Loc in Results
    If Loc.ProviderForLocalSite = True Then
        Set objSMS = objLoc.ConnectServer(Loc.Machine, "root\sms\site_" & _
            Loc.SiteCode)
    end if
Next

Set objQuery = objSMS.Get("SMS_Query.QueryID='" & strQueryID & "'")
objQuery.LimitToCollectionID = strCollLimitID
objQuery.Put_
```

Discussion

A prompted query gives you additional flexibility at runtime. Each time you run the query, you will be given the option to limit your query to a collection. Simply select "Not collection limited", or select "Limit to collection" and browse to select the desired collection name.

Consider the example query in Recipe 9-27, "Creating a Date-Based Query." The purpose of the query is to generate a list of all systems that have not submitted a hardware inventory to SMS within the past 30 days. This is a great query, and it gives you a great overview of your entire SMS site. However, the next step after generating the list is to work through the list to determine why these systems haven't returned a hardware inventory.

If the query returns 25 systems, you can probably work through that list yourself (or assign it to your favorite intern). However, if the query returns 500 systems, and you have 150 different locations, you may want to consider breaking the list down into smaller chunks. Let's say you already have query-based collections that you use to deploy software to various regions of North America (e.g., East Coast, Midwest, West Coast, Texas, Canada), and you have computer support technicians in each region. You can use the prompted query to filter the results of the query based on each of those collections. You can then export the filtered results corresponding to each collection to a text file and forward the file to the desired colleague.

If you rarely need to provide collection-limited information, an SMS query may be the perfect option for this task. If this is a weekly or monthly task however, consider creating an SMS web report and granting appropriate colleagues the proper permissions to execute the report. This can reduce the amount of cyclical work you do.

Note A query can only be limited to a specified collection. Subcollections of the limiting collection do not affect any results of the query.

Example 9-11 is very similar to Example 9-9. The only difference is that we set `strCollLimitID` to `<Prompt>`, which causes the query to prompt for the collection name when executed.

Caution Even when the user does not specify collection limiting when creating a query, SMS applies collection limiting if the user is not authorized to view all resources.

See Also

- Recipe 3-3, "Identifying the CollectionID of a Collection," describes how to obtain the `Collection-ID` of a collection.

- Recipe 9-14, "Limiting a Query to a Collection," describes how to limit a query to a specific collection.

- See Chapter 8 for more information on creating SMS web reports.

- `SMS_Query` is described in the SMS 2003 SDK.

- Chapter 16 of the *Microsoft Systems Management Server 2003 Administrator's Companion* by Steven Kaczmarek (Microsoft Press, 2004) provides additional information about creating prompted SMS queries.

- Chapter 4 of the *SMS 2003 Operations Guide* also provides additional information about creating prompted SMS queries.

9-16. Modifying Permissions of a Query

Problem

You want to modify the permissions of a query to change who is able to run it, modify it, and so forth.

Solution: Using a Graphical Interface

1. Open the SMS Administrator console.

2. From the SMS Administrator console, expand Site Database (<*Site Code*>) and Queries.

3. Expand any folders that contain the query you want to modify.

4. In the right pane, right-click the query, and select Properties to open the Query Properties dialog box.

5. Select the Security tab in the Query Properties dialog box.

6. Click the New or Delete button to add or remove class or instance security rights. You can also double-click any existing class or instance rights to modify them.

7. Click OK to apply the settings.

Solution: Using VBScript

Example 9-12 demonstrates how to grant read permissions to the SMSVPC\Help Desk security group.

Example 9-12. *ModifyQueryPerms.vbs*

```
'This script will grant the group "SMSVPC\Help Desk" read
    ' permissions to Query ID "LAB00040".
strSMSServer = <SMSServer>
strHelpDesk="SMSVPC\Help Desk" 'Domain\Group or username
strQueryID = "LAB00040"  'ID of the Query


Set objLoc =  CreateObject("WbemScripting.SWbemLocator")
Set objSMS= objLoc.ConnectServer(strSMSServer, "root\sms")
Set Results = objSMS.ExecQuery _
    ("SELECT * From SMS_ProviderLocation WHERE ProviderForLocalSite = true")
For each Loc in Results
    If Loc.ProviderForLocalSite = True Then
        Set objSMS = objLoc.ConnectServer(Loc.Machine, "root\sms\site_" & _
            Loc.SiteCode)
    end if
Next

Set colQueries = objSMS.ExecQuery _
    ("Select * From SMS_Query where QueryID = '" & _
    strQueryID & "'")
For Each objQuery In colQueries
  Set objNewRight = objSMS.Get _
      ("SMS_UserInstancePermissions").SpawnInstance_()
  objNewRight.UserName = strHelpDesk
  objNewRight.ObjectKey = 1 '1=collection
  objNewRight.InstanceKey = objQuery.QueryID
```

```
    objNewRight.InstancePermissions = 1 'grant Read
    objNewRight.Put_
Next
```

Discussion

Be very careful when modifying permissions, or you may lock yourself out of a query! Especially when modifying permissions programmatically, be sure to test your code in a test environment before running in production.

See Also

- The *SMS 2003 Scripting Guide* provides more information about setting security rights for an SMS object. It also describes SMS_UserInstancePermissions.

- The SMS 2003 SDK describes SMS_UserInstancePermissions.

- Appendix A of the Microsoft TechNet article titled "Scenarios and Procedures for Microsoft Systems Management Server 2003: Security" provides additional information about modifying permissions for queries.

- Chapter 4 of the *SMS 2003 Operations Guide* also provides additional information about security rights for SMS queries.

9-17. Running a Query

Problem

You want to run a query.

Solution: Using a Graphical Interface

1. Open the SMS Administrator console.

2. From the SMS Administrator console, expand Site Database (<*Site Code*>) and Queries.

3. Expand any folders that contain the query you want to run and select (highlight) the query in the left pane.

4. Right-click the query, and select Run Query.

5. The results of the query will appear in the right pane.

Solution: Using VBScript

Example 9-13 demonstrates how to execute a query and display the results in MOF syntax.

Example 9-13. *DisplayQueryInstanceInfo_MOF.vbs*

```
strSMSServer = <SMSServer>
strQueryID = "LAB0001E"

Set objLoc = CreateObject("WbemScripting.SWbemLocator")
Set objSMS= objLoc.ConnectServer(strSMSServer, "root\sms")
Set Results = objSMS.ExecQuery _
    ("SELECT * From SMS_ProviderLocation WHERE ProviderForLocalSite = true")
```

```
For each Loc in Results
    If Loc.ProviderForLocalSite = True Then
        Set objSMS = objLoc.ConnectServer(Loc.Machine, "root\sms\site_" & _
            Loc.SiteCode)
    end if
Next

Set objQuery = objSMS.Get("SMS_Query.QueryID='" & strQueryID & "'")

Set colQueryResults = objSMS.ExecQuery(objQuery.Expression)
For Each objResult In colQueryResults
    'use the following line to display all instance information
    wscript.echo objResult.GetObjectText_
Next
```

Example 9-14 demonstrates how to execute a query and display the results in XML syntax.

Example 9-14. *DisplayQueryInstance_XML.vbs*

```
Const wbemObjectTextFormatWMIDTD20 = 2
strSMSServer = <SMSServer>
strQueryID = "SMS012"

Set objLoc =  CreateObject("WbemScripting.SWbemLocator")
Set objSMS= objLoc.ConnectServer(strSMSServer, "root\sms")
Set Results = objSMS.ExecQuery _
    ("SELECT * From SMS_ProviderLocation WHERE ProviderForLocalSite = true")
For each Loc in Results
    If Loc.ProviderForLocalSite = True Then
        Set objSMS = objLoc.ConnectServer(Loc.Machine, "root\sms\site_" & _
            Loc.SiteCode)
    end if
Next

Set objQuery = objSMS.Get("SMS_Query.QueryID='" & strQueryID & "'")

Set colQueryResults = objSMS.ExecQuery(objQuery.Expression)
For Each objResult In colQueryResults
    wscript.echo objResult.GetText_(wbemObjectTextFormatWMIDTD20)
Next
```

Discussion

Example 9-13 demonstrates how to run a nonprompted query from the command line, given the QueryID. After connecting to the SMS site, we use the Get method to obtain the specified query. Next, we execute the query using the WQL in the Expression property and return the results to colQueryResults. Finally, we use a for-each loop to display the results of the query. Displaying the results can be a challenge, unless you know the proper field names to specify in your code (or you can perform some additional magic with VBScript). In Example 9-13, we use the GetObjectText_ function to display a textual rendering of the object. This rendering will display each attribute and value(s) for the object.

Example 9-14 is very similar to Example 9-13, except that the output is in XML. The GetText_ method is available only on Windows XP and newer operating systems.

See Also

- SMS_Query is described in the SMS 2003 SDK.

- The topic titled "How to Run an SMS Scripting Query" in the *SMS 2003 Scripting Guide* describes how to run a scripting query.

- The topic "Representing Objects in XML" in the WMI SDK provides information about representing objects in XML.

- Chapter 16 of the *Microsoft Systems Management Server 2003 Administrator's Companion* by Steven Kaczmarek (Microsoft Press, 2004) provides additional information about running SMS queries.

- Chapter 4 of the *SMS 2003 Operations Guide* also provides additional information about creating and running SMS queries.

9-18. Limiting Query Results for All Queries

Problem

You want to limit the query results to a specific number of rows.

Solution

1. Open the SMS Administrator console.
2. From the SMS Administrator console, expand Site Database (*<Site Code>*), and select Queries.
3. Right-click the Queries node, and select Properties from the menu.
4. On the General tab, check the "Limit number of query results" check box.
5. Enter the number of result rows to which you want to limit all queries.
6. Click OK to apply the settings.

Discussion

This recipe allows you to define a default limit for the number of rows returned from *all* queries in your site. By running a query in this manner, you are truncating the results of the query to the number of rows that you define as the limit. The query will run normally until the row count meets the limit you've defined; then it stops. Limiting query results in this manner is similar to using the Select Top SQL statement.

See Also

- Recipe 9-19, "Limiting Query Results for a Specific Query," describes how to temporarily limit results for a specific query.

- Chapter 16 of the *Microsoft Systems Management Server 2003 Administrator's Companion* by Steven Kaczmarek (Microsoft Press, 2004) provides additional information about limiting SMS query results.

- Chapter 4 of the *SMS 2003 Operations Guide* also provides additional information about limiting SMS query results.

9-19. Limiting Query Results for a Specific Query

Problem

You want to limit the number of rows returned by a specific query.

Solution

1. Open the SMS Administrator console.

2. From the SMS Administrator console, expand Site Database (*<Site Code>*), and select Queries.

3. Expand any folders that contain the query you want to run with limited results, and select (highlight) the query in the left pane.

4. Right-click the query, and select All Tasks ➤ Run Query Special.

5. Check the "Limit the number of query result items" check box.

6. Enter the row limit, and click OK to run the query.

7. The results of the limited query will appear in the right pane.

Discussion

By running a query in the manner shown in this recipe, you are truncating the results of the query to the number of rows that you define as the limit (see step 6). The query will run normally until the row count meets the limit you've defined; then it stops. The effect is similar to that from using the `Select Top` SQL statement when using SQL.

See Also

- Recipe 9-18, "Limiting Query Results for all Queries," describes how to limit query results for all queries by default.

- The SMS 2003 Help file provides additional information about the Run Query Special dialog box.

- Chapter 16 of the *Microsoft Systems Management Server 2003 Administrator's Companion* by Steven Kaczmarek (Microsoft Press, 2004) provides additional information about limiting SMS query results.

- Chapter 4 of the *SMS 2003 Operations Guide* also provides additional information about limiting SMS query results.

9-20. Importing Query Objects

Problem

You want to import a query.

Solution

1. Open the SMS Administrator console.

2. From the SMS Administrator console, expand Site Database (*<Site Code>*) and Queries.

3. Right-click the Queries node, and select All Tasks ➤ Import Objects to open the Import Object Wizard.

4. Click next on the Welcome screen.

5. Enter the location and name of the MOF file that contains the objects you want to import, or click the Browse button to search for the file.

6. Click Next.

7. Review the objects that you plan to import.

8. Click Next.

9. Review the comments associated with the objects to be imported.

10. Click Next.

11. Review the status of the imported objects.

12. Click Finish to exit the Import Object Wizard.

Discussion

Queries are simple to import. Some queries may rely on custom or static data. Be sure to view a query's MOF file using a text editor before importing it to look for comments that specify requirements to run the report successfully.

You must have Create permission for the queries' security object class to import queries.

Sharing SMS queries is a wonderful thing, and SMS 2003 helps you share them easily. Spend some time in the online SMS communities (such as http://www.myITforum.com). Many SMS administrators have posted SMS queries to share with other administrators. Avoid reinventing the wheel by first performing a little research on the Internet.

Caution Use caution when importing a query. Ensure that none of the queries in your environment have the same name as the query you desire to import. Duplicate query names will be created, which will cause errors when attempting to modify either of the duplicate queries.

See Also

- Chapter 16 of the *Microsoft Systems Management Server 2003 Administrator's Companion* by Steven Kaczmarek (Microsoft Press, 2004) provides additional information about importing SMS queries.

- Chapter 4 of the *SMS 2003 Operations Guide* also provides additional information about importing SMS queries.

9-21. Importing a Query from the Command Line

Problem

You want to import a query from the command line.

Solution

1. Using a text editor, edit the MOF file you intend to import.

2. Just below the comments section (noted by //), insert the following line (replace SMSVPC with the SMS server, and LAB with the SMS site code):

   ```
   #pragma namespace("\\\\SMSVPC\\root\\SMS\\site_LAB")
   ```

3. Save changes and close the MOF file.

4. From a command line, browse to the directory that contains the MOF you just modified, and execute the following (replace myNewQuery with the proper file name):

   ```
   Mofcomp myNewQuery.MOF
   ```

5. Back in the SMS Administrator console, refresh the Queries node to see the new SMS query.

Discussion

When you export a query to a MOF file, the file is created with the assumption that you will import the query using the SMS Administrator console and not from the command line. This recipe shows that by adding the line to declare the namespace, you can import multiple web reports from the command line using a simple batch file if desired.

Caution   Use extreme care when modifying a MOF file. Improper modification may cause unexpected results.

See Also

- Review the sidebar in Recipe 8-8, "Importing a Report from the Command Line," titled "What Is a MOF File?"

- Recipe 9-22, "Importing Multiple Queries from the Command Line," describes how to import multiple queries from the command line.

- Recipe 9-20, "Importing Query Objects," demonstrates how to manually import an SMS Query.

- Recipe 9-23, "Exporting Queries," shows how to manually export an SMS query.

- In the MSDN Windows Platform SDK, the "WMI Utilities" section provides additional information about mofcomp.exe.

9-22. Importing Multiple Queries from the Command Line

Problem

You want to import multiple queries from the command line.

Solution

1. Create a temporary directory, and place all query export MOF files in it (e.g., `C:\MOFQUERIES`).
2. Insert the proper namespace into each query MOF as described in Recipe 9-21, "Importing a Query from the Command Line."
3. Open a command prompt, and navigate to the temporary directory (e.g., `C:\MOFQUERIES`).
4. From the command prompt, execute the following line:

   ```
   for %f in (*.mof) do mofcomp %f
   ```

5. Refresh the Queries node in the SMS Administrator console.

Discussion

After modifying each MOF file, so that it contains the proper namespace information (as described in Recipe 9-21, "Importing a Query from the Command Line"), a simple `for` loop in the command shell will enumerate each MOF file in the directory and execute a `mofcomp` on each one.

See Also

- The Windows Help topic "Command Shell Reference" gives information on the `for` command.
- Recipe 9-23, "Exporting Queries," describes how to export query objects.
- Recipe 9-24, "Exporting Multiple Query Objects from the Command Line," describes how to export multiple query objects from the command line.
- Review the sidebar in Recipe 8-8, "Importing a Report from the Command Line," titled "What Is a MOF File?"

9-23. Exporting Queries

Problem

You want to export a query.

Solution

1. Open the SMS Administrator console.
2. From the SMS Administrator console, expand Site Database (<*Site Code*>) and Queries.
3. Right-click the Queries node, and select All Tasks ➤ Export Objects to open the Export Object Wizard.
4. Click Next at the Welcome screen.

5. Place a check mark next to the objects you want to export.

6. Click Next.

7. Enter the name of the MOF file you want to create and any comments for this export.

8. Click Next.

9. Review the information of the exported objects.

10. Click Finish to exit the Export Objects Wizard.

Discussion

Share the wealth! Do yourself and your fellow SMS administrators a favor by making your custom SMS queries available to other administrators (provided, of course, that the queries are not highly customized to your environment). And do one other favor for yourself and your fellow SMS administrators: *comment your queries.* When exporting a query, add comments that will help you and other SMS administrators understand how to leverage the data, and note any special requirements. Detail any manual steps that are required after the import (e.g., entering static data into the SQL statement).

Note To export a query, you must have Read permission for the query's security object or instance.

Also, consider using the import and export features of SMS queries to move your tested queries from your SMS test lab to your SMS production environment, which is much easier to do than rebuilding the queries manually.

See Also

- Recipe 9-24, "Exporting Multiple Query Objects from the Command Line," demonstrates how to export multiple queries from the command line.

- Chapter 16 of the *Microsoft Systems Management Server 2003 Administrator's Companion* by Steven Kaczmarek (Microsoft Press, 2004) provides additional information about creating and exporting SMS queries.

- Chapter 4 of the *SMS 2003 Operations Guide* also provides additional information about creating and exporting SMS queries.

9-24. Exporting Multiple Query Objects from the Command Line

Problem

You want to export multiple queries from the command line to separate MOF files.

Solution

Example 9-15 demonstrates how to export all custom queries to MOF files using VBScript.

Example 9-15. *ExportCustomQueries.vbs*

```
Const ForWriting = 2
Set fso = CreateObject("Scripting.FileSystemObject")
Set objFolder = objFSO.CreateFolder("C:\TEMP")

strSMSServer = <SMSServer>

strNEWSMSServer = "MOFSMSSERVER"
strNewSMSSiteCode = "MOFSMSSITECODE"

Set objLoc = CreateObject("WbemScripting.SWbemLocator")
Set objSMS= objLoc.ConnectServer(strSMSServer, "root\sms")
Set Results = objSMS.ExecQuery _
    ("SELECT * From SMS_ProviderLocation WHERE ProviderForLocalSite = true")
For each Loc in Results
    If Loc.ProviderForLocalSite = True Then
        Set objSMS = objLoc.ConnectServer(Loc.Machine, "root\sms\site_" & _
            Loc.SiteCode)
    end if
Next

Set colQueries = objSMS.ExecQuery _
("select * from SMS_Query where TargetClassName <> '" & _
"SMS_StatusMessage' and QueryID not like 'SMS%'")

for each objQuery in colQueries
    wscript.echo "Exporting " & objQuery.Name & vbTAB & _
        objQuery.QueryID
    Set fout = fso.OpenTextFile("C:\TEMP\" & _
        objQuery.QueryID & ".MOF", ForWriting, True)
    fout.writeline "//*******************************"
    fout.writeline "//Created by SMS Recipes Exporter"
    fout.writeline "//*******************************"
    fout.writeline vbCRLF
    'only use the following line if planning to import MOF
    'from the command line
    fout.writeline "#pragma namespace(" & chr(34) & "\\\\" & _
        strNEWSMSServer & "\\root\\SMS\\site_" & _
        strnewSMSSiteCode & chr(34) & ")"
    fout.writeline vbCRLF
    fout.writeline "// **** Class : SMS_Query ****"
    for each strLine in split(objQuery.GetObjectText_, chr(10))
        if instr(strLine, "QueryID =") then
            fout.writeline(vbTAB & "QueryID = " & chr(34) & _
                chr(34)) & ";"
        else
            fout.writeline cstr(strLine)
        end if
    next
    fout.writeline "// **** End ****"
    fout.close
next
```

Discussion

Example 9-15 may become a very handy utility for you. It demonstrates how to export all noncanned SMS queries into individual MOF files using VBScript. At the beginning of the script, we use a couple new variables: strNEWSMSServer and strNewSMSSiteCode. You'll need to set these variables to the SMS server name and site code corresponding to the site in which you plan to import the reports.

After connecting to the SMS site, we perform a query to obtain all query objects that aren't status message queries and do not start with SMS% (canned SMS queries). Next, we begin the for-each loop, where all the action happens.

The for-each loop is used to enumerate all noncanned SMS queries. First, we display the query Name and QueryID. Next, we create (or overwrite) a text file named the same as the QueryID, with a .mof extension. We then write a few comment lines (lines that start with // are comments). Next, we add the namespace line.

Note If you plan to import queries using the Import Object Wizard (as in Recipe 9-20, "Importing Query Objects"), re-mark the three lines of code that are used to write the #pragma namespace line.

After writing a couple more lines of information, we use the Split function in a for-each loop to split data obtained from GetObjectText_. GetObjectText_ contains the query instance information that we need to save—unfortunately, the formatting is a little off for what we need. We use the Split function to split the instance information into an array of strings (one string represents one line of instance data). Notice, we split on chr(10), which is a linefeed character—*usually* we split on a carriage return and linefeed (vbCRLF) combination. Finally, we write each line to the MOF file, using carriage return/linefeed at the end of each line. When writing the instance information to the MOF file, we do modify the line that contains QueryID. In the MOF file, we want the QueryID to be equal to "", so that a new query is created when it is imported into a site. Example 9-16 shows a MOF file created using this VBScript.

Example 9-16. *SampleQuery_MOF.mof*

```
//*******************************
//Created by SMS Recipes Exporter
//*******************************


#pragma namespace("\\\\MOFSMSSERVER\\root\\SMS\\site_MOFSMSSITECODE")


// **** Class : SMS_Query ****

instance of SMS_Query
{
    Comments = "";
    Expression = "select MACAddresses, Name from  SMS_R_System ➥
      order by MACAddresses";
    LimitToCollectionID = "";
    Name = "All Systems with MAC addresses";
    QueryID = "";
    TargetClassName = "SMS_R_System";
};


// **** End ****
```

The query that was exported to generate Example 9-16 displays all Media Access Control (MAC) address information for all discovered systems, which you can see from the query text, or expression, in the example.

Remember from previous recipes that MOF files to be imported from the Administrator console differ from those to be imported from the command line. The difference is in the declaration of a namespace, which you saw in Example 9-16 as follows:

```
#pragma namespace("\\\\SMSSERVER\\root\\SMS\\site_SMSSITECODE")
```

This line enables you to import the query from the command line using mofcomp (as described in Recipe 9-21, "Importing a Query from the Command Line"). If you want to import the query using the Import Object Wizard in the SMS Administrator console, simply comment this line by typing // at the beginning of the line.

See Also

- SMS_Query is described in the SMS 2003 SDK.

- Review the topic titled "How to Run an SMS Scripting Query" in the *SMS 2003 Scripting Guide*.

- The topic "Representing Objects in XML" in the WMI SDK provides information about representing objects in XML.

9-25. Creating a Subselect Query

Problem

You want to create a subselect query.

Solution

1. Open the SMS Administrator console.

2. From the SMS Administrator console, expand Site Database (*<Site Code>*) and Queries.

3. Expand any folders that contain the query you want to modify.

4. In the right pane, right-click the query, and select Properties to open the Query Properties dialog box.

5. On the General tab, click the Edit Query Statement button to open the Query Statement Properties dialog box.

6. On the Criteria tab, click the New button (the yellow starburst icon) or double-click an existing criterion to open the Criterion Properties dialog box.

7. Select the "Subselected values" criterion type from the drop-down menu.

8. Click the Select button to open the Select Attribute dialog box.

9. Select an attribute class from the drop-down menu.

10. Select an attribute from the drop-down menu.

11. Click OK to close the Select Attribute dialog box. The chosen attribute class and attribute will now be listed in the Criterion Properties dialog box.

12. Select an operator from the drop-down menu.

13. Enter a query statement to use with the operator as the subselect statement, or click the Browse button to browse for a statement from an existing query.

14. Click OK to close the Criterion Properties dialog box. Your selected criterion will be listed in the criteria pane of the Query Statement Properties dialog box.

15. Click OK to close the Query Statement Properties dialog box.

16. Click OK for the setting to be applied.

Discussion

Writing a subselect query is one of the most-asked-about tasks in online forums that relate to queries. A classic example of the need for a subselect query occurs when you want to identify all systems that do not have a specific piece of software. Example 9-17 shows a WQL query to obtain a list of all systems that do not have the full version of Adobe Acrobat installed.

Example 9-17. *SampleSubSelect_SystemsWithoutAdobeAcrobat.txt*

```
select SMS_G_System_SYSTEM.Name

from SMS_R_System inner join
    SMS_G_System_SYSTEM on SMS_G_System_SYSTEM.ResourceID =
    SMS_R_System.ResourceId

where SMS_G_System_SYSTEM.Name not in
    (select SMS_G_System_SYSTEM.Name from
    SMS_R_System inner join SMS_G_System_SYSTEM on
    SMS_G_System_SYSTEM.ResourceID = SMS_R_System.ResourceId
    inner join SMS_G_System_SoftwareFile on
    SMS_G_System_SoftwareFile.ResourceID = SMS_R_System.ResourceId
    where SMS_G_System_SoftwareFile.FileName = "Acrobat.exe")
```

As you can see, Example 9-17 begins as a familiar WQL statement. But if you examine the WHERE clause, you notice we're only looking for systems that are not in the list returned by the subselect statement. And upon inspection of the subselect statement, you can see that it's querying for all systems that have the file name Acrobat.exe (which is inventoried using software inventory).

Caution You cannot use the ORDER BY clause in a subselect query.

See Also

- Rod Trent's article titled "Using the Subselect (NOT) Query" provides a very good step-by-step example of how to create a subselect query (http://www.myitforum.com/articles/1/view.asp?id=179).

- Many resources are available on the Internet that describe SQL subselect queries (you might search on the terms "sub queries" or "subselect queries").

9-26. Creating a Query with Multiple Object Types

Problem

You want use multiple object types within a query.

Solution

1. Open the SMS Administrator console.

2. From the SMS Administrator console, expand Site Database (*<Site Code>*) and Queries.

3. Expand any folders that contain the query you want to modify.

4. In the right pane, right-click the query, and select Properties to open the Query Properties dialog box.

5. On the General tab, select the <unspecified> object type from the drop-down list.

6. Click Yes to the dialog box that warns you that your current query statement will be discarded.

7. Click the Edit Query Statement button to open the Query Statement Properties dialog box.

8. Since the object type was not specified, you only have access to the Show Query Language window.

9. Copy and paste multiple queries into this box.

10. Click OK to close the Query Statement Properties dialog box.

11. Click OK to apply the settings.

Discussion

The Query Builder does a good job of helping you build your queries, but it does have limitations. One of those limitations is apparent when you need to query from different object types. In this situation, the Query Builder will present you with an empty Show Query Language window to say, in essence, "Knock yourself out, because I can't help you."

If you find yourself in that situation, it is best to separate the different object types into their own queries to test whether those queries are returning the results that you want; then, copy and paste the objects' WQL statements into a new query with an unspecified object type. After pasting the WQL statements into the new query, you will need to edit the statements to combine them into a single statement that joins the disparate object types.

Example 9-18 demonstrates a complex query that displays the advertisement Name, AdvertisementID, PackageName, ProgramName, and CollectionName, and indicates whether or not subcollections are targeted by the advertisement (IncludeSubCollection).

Example 9-18. *Inner join advertisement, package, and collection*

```
SELECT SMS_Advertisement.AdvertisementName,
    SMS_Advertisement.AdvertisementID, SMS_Package.Name,
    SMS_Advertisement.ProgramName, SMS_Collection.Name,
    SMS_Advertisement.IncludeSubCollection
FROM SMS_Advertisement INNER JOIN
    SMS_Package ON SMS_Advertisement.PackageID =
    SMS_Package.PackageID INNER JOIN SMS_Collection ON
    SMS_Advertisement.CollectionID =
    SMS_Collection.CollectionID
```

9-27. Creating a Date-Based Query

Problem

You want to create a query that returns data for a specific date range.

Solution

1. Open the SMS Administrator console.

2. From the SMS Administrator console, expand Site Database (*<Site Code>*) and Queries.

3. Expand any folders that contain the query you want to modify. The query must contain a date value in the result set:

   ```
   SMS_G_System_WORKSTATION_STATUS.LastHardwareScan
   ```

4. In the right pane, right-click the query, and select Properties to open the Query Properties dialog box.

5. On the General tab, click the Edit Query Statement button to open the Query Statement Properties dialog box.

6. On the General tab of the Query Statement Properties dialog box, click the Show Query Language button.

7. Make manual edits to the query statement to include a date-dependent WHERE clause:

   ```
   where datediff(day,SMS_G_System_WORKSTATION_STATUS.LastHardwareScan, ➡
   getdate()) >= 30
   ```

8. Click OK to close the Query Statement Properties dialog box.

9. Click OK to apply the settings.

Discussion

Date-based queries help you create queries based on a date window. The Query Builder will regard a date-based query as a complex query once it is completed, so you will only be able to edit the query statement manually once you are finished.

Observe the WQL statement in Example 9-19. If you create a new query and enter the WQL query from Example 9-19 as the query statement, you will have a query that displays all systems that have not reported a hardware inventory within the last 30 days. Notice the WHERE clause:

```
(datediff(day,
SMS_G_System_WORKSTATION_STATUS.LastHardwareScan,
getdate()) >= 30)
```

Use DateDiff is to find the day difference between the last hardware scan and the current date (GetDate()). The result of the call to DateDiff is the number of days between the two dates. If the difference is greater than or equal to 30, the system in question has not reported an inventory within the past 30 days, so that system is included in the query results.

Example 9-19 demonstrates how to query for all systems that have reported a hardware scan within the past 30 days.

Example 9-19. *SampleWQLWithGetDate.txt*

```
select
    SMS_G_System_SYSTEM.Name,
    SMS_G_System_WORKSTATION_STATUS.LastHardwareScan
from  SMS_R_System inner join SMS_G_System_SYSTEM on
    SMS_G_System_SYSTEM.ResourceID = SMS_R_System.ResourceId
    inner join SMS_G_System_WORKSTATION_STATUS on
    SMS_G_System_WORKSTATION_STATUS.ResourceID =
    SMS_R_System.ResourceId
WHERE
    (datediff(day,
    SMS_G_System_WORKSTATION_STATUS.LastHardwareScan,
    getdate()) >= 30)
Order by SMS_G_System_WORKSTATION_STATUS.LastHardwareScan DESC
```

When you begin writing date-based queries, you will notice that once you add one of the date functions to a query, you can no longer switch to the query design view, because the date functions are not supported in the design view of the SMS Query Builder.

Note When creating a query that uses the date functions in the WHERE clause, first use the SMS Query Builder to create the query, data, and criteria you desire without the date function. Once you have verified the output is accurate, then add your date function to the WHERE clause of the WQL statement.

SMS 2003 supports the following date functions in the WHERE clause of WQL queries.

GetDate(): This function will return the current date and time on the system. The data is returned in date-time format (e.g., 12:56 AM 12/02/2006).

DateDiff(): This function will return the difference between two date-time values in the increment that you specify (e.g., minute, hour, day). In our testing, the DateParts listed in Table 9-1 are supported when using DateDiff in a WHERE clause in SMS WQL.

- DateDiff (DatePart, StartDate, EndDate)

- DatePart is the part of the date you want to calculate (e.g., minute, day, month, etc.). In our example, the DatePart is day.

- StartDate is the begin date. In our example, LastHardwareScan in the start date.

- EndDate is the ending date. In our example, GetDate() is the end date.

DateAdd(): Returns a new date-time value based on adding an interval to the specified date. In our testing, the DateParts listed in Table 9-1 are supported when using DateAdd in a WHERE clause in SMS WQL.

The proper syntax for DateAdd follows:

- DateAdd (DatePart, Number, Date)

- DatePart is the part of the date you want to calculate (e.g., minute, day, month, etc.).

- Number is the value to increment DatePart.

- Date is a valid date-time value that will be used to calculate the new date.

Table 9-1. *DateParts and Abbreviations Supported by SMS WQL Queries*

DatePart	Abbreviations
Year	year, yy
Month	month, mm
Day	day, dd
Hour	hour, hh
Minute	minute, mi
Second	second, ss

Note In SMS WQL queries, never put the abbreviation in quotes—this is different than when using DateParts with date functions in VBScript.

See Also

- The SQL 2000 SDK and SQL 2005 SDK provide information about using the date functions.
- The SMS 2003 SDK documents the supported date functions in the WHERE clause for SMS.

9-28. Exporting Query Results

Problem

You want to export query results to a file.

Solution

1. Open the SMS Administrator console.
2. From the SMS Administrator console, expand Site Database (*<Site Code>*) and Queries.
3. Expand any folders that contain the query you want to execute.
4. In the right pane, left-click the desired query to select it, right-click the query, and select Run Query.
5. When the query has completed, right-click the query name, and select Export List.
6. Browse to the desired location, and enter the desired name.
7. Modify the file type as desired (e.g., Tab Delimited, Comma Delimited).
8. Click Save to save data results to a file.

Discussion

Having the ability to export query results from the SMS Administrator console is a great feature. After executing a query, you can export it to a tab- or command-delimited file and then import it into your favorite spreadsheet, database, or anything else you desire.

See Also

- Recipe 9-17, "Running a Query," describes how to run a query.

9-29. Creating a Query Folder

Problem

You want to create a folder for your queries.

Solution: Using a Graphical Interface

1. Open the SMS Administrator console.

2. From the SMS Administrator console, expand Site Database (<*Site Code*>) and Queries.

3. Right-click Queries, and select New ➤ Folder.

4. Provide a name for the folder.

5. Click OK to create the new folder.

Solution: Using VBScript

Example 9-20 demonstrates how to create a query folder.

Example 9-20. *CreateQueryFolder.vbs*

```
strSMSServer = <SMSServer>

Set objLoc = CreateObject("WbemScripting.SWbemLocator")
Set objSMS= objLoc.ConnectServer(strSMSServer, "root\sms")
Set Results = objSMS.ExecQuery _
    ("SELECT * From SMS_ProviderLocation WHERE ProviderForLocalSite = true")
For each Loc in Results
    If Loc.ProviderForLocalSite = True Then
        Set objSMS = objLoc.ConnectServer(Loc.Machine, "root\sms\site_" & _
            Loc.SiteCode)
    end if
Next

strNewFolderName = "Admin Queries"

Set newFolder = objSMS.Get("SMS_ObjectContainerNode") _
    .SpawnInstance_()
newFolder.Name = strNewFolderName
newFolder.ObjectType = 7 'Query
newFolder.ParentContainerNodeId = 0
newFolder.Put_
```

Discussion

As your query-building skills improve so will the number of queries that you need to keep track of, so organizing them by folder can be useful. You can create folders from the GUI or using VBScript.

In Example 9-20, we create a folder in the root of the Queries folder titled Admin Queries. By setting the ParentContainerNodeId to zero, we create the new folder in the root of the Queries node. If we wanted to make Admin Reports a subfolder of an existing folder, we would insert the appropriate ParentContainerNodeID.

Note The easiest way to find the `ParentContainerNodeID` (and most other object IDs, for that matter) is to modify the shortcut to launch your SMS Administrator console. For example, instead of using the shortcut to launch `C:\SMSAdmin\bin\i386\sms.msc`, have it launch this: `C:\SMSAdmin\bin\i386\sms.msc /sms:nodeinfo=1`. Now, when you launch your SMS Administrator console, you can right-click any node, select Properties, and view the Node Information tab. When you view the Node Information tab on a folder, look for `ContainerNodeID=x`, where `x` is the ID you use in this script.

See Also

- Recipe 9-30, "Moving Queries Between Folders," demonstrates how to move one or more queries between query folders.

- Chris Rees's blog contains example scripts for creating folders: `http://spaces.msn.com/members/cheekysimian`. (Chris Rees is one of the Microsoft SMS SDK gurus.)

- The SMS Script Repository also contains scripts that demonstrate managing console folders in SMS.

- Review the SMS 2003 SDK topic titled "Creating a Console Folder" for more information about creating console folders in SMS.

- Chapter 16 of the *Microsoft Systems Management Server 2003 Administrator's Companion* by Steven Kaczmarek (Microsoft Press, 2004) provides additional information about creating folders for SMS queries.

- Chapter 4 of the *SMS 2003 Operations Guide* also provides additional information about creating folders for SMS queries.

9-30. Moving Queries Between Folders

Problem

You want to organize your queries in folders.

Solution: Using a Graphical Interface

1. Open the SMS Administrator console.

2. From the SMS Administrator console, expand Site Database (*<Site Code>*) and Queries.

3. Expand any folders that contain the queries that you want to move.

4. Right-click the folder, and select Move Folder items.

5. Select the queries that you want to move.

6. Click Browse to select the destination folder.

7. Click OK to move the queries to the folder.

Solution: Using VBScript

Example 9-21 demonstrates how to move queries between folders.

Example 9-21. *MovingQueriesBetweenFolders.vbs*

```
strSMSServer = <SMSServer>
strQueryIDs = "LAB0001E,LAB0001F,LAB0002E"
'to move more than one, separate with commas

Set objLoc =  CreateObject("WbemScripting.SWbemLocator")
Set objSMS= objLoc.ConnectServer(strSMSServer, "root\sms")
Set Results = objSMS.ExecQuery _
    ("SELECT * From SMS_ProviderLocation WHERE ProviderForLocalSite = true")
For each Loc in Results
    If Loc.ProviderForLocalSite = True Then
        Set objSMS = objLoc.ConnectServer(Loc.Machine, "root\sms\site_" & _
            Loc.SiteCode)
    end if
Next


intSourceFolder=0 'Source Folder (root node in this case)
intDestFolder=10 'Destination Folder
intObjectType=7 '7=Query for type of object

Set objFolder = objSMS.Get("SMS_ObjectContainerItem")
arrQueryIDs = split(strQueryIDs, ",")
retval = objFolder.MoveMembers _
(arrQueryIDs, intSourceFolder, intDestFolder , intObjectType)
wscript.echo retval
```

Discussion

Besides creating categories for your custom queries, you may want to create a folder to organize queries. This is also simplifies exporting your custom queries.

▓**Note** Press the Shift or Ctrl key to select multiple web reports or folders before you move them.

Example 9-21 demonstrates how to move multiple queries from the root Queries node to the subfolder of your choice. To move one query, insert only one QueryID for strQueryIDs. To move more than one, simply separate the QueryIDs with commas (no spaces). Since the queries currently exist in the root Queries node, intSourceFolder is set to 0. If the queries were in a subfolder, replace the 0 with the appropriate ContainerNodeID. Moving queries between folders does not affect any aspect of the queries other than where they are organized in the Queries node of the SMS Administrator console.

▓**Note** The easiest way to find the QueryID (and most other object IDs, for that matter) is to modify the shortcut to launch your SMS Administrator console. For example, instead of using the shortcut to launch C:\SMSAdmin\bin\i386\sms.msc, have it launch this: C:\SMSAdmin\bin\i386\sms.msc /sms:nodeinfo=1. Now, when you launch your SMS Administrator console, you can right-click any node, select Properties, and view the Node Information tab. When you view the Node Information tab on a folder, look for QueryID=x, where x is the QueryID you use in this script.

See Also

- Recipe 9-29, "Creating a Query Folder," demonstrates how to create a query folder.

- Chris Rees's blog contains example scripts for creating folders: `http://spaces.msn.com/members/cheekysimian`. (Chris Rees is one of the Microsoft SMS SDK gurus.)

- The SMS Script Repository also contains scripts that demonstrate managing console folders in SMS.

- Review the SMS 2003 SDK topic titled "Creating a Console Folder" for more information about creating console folders in SMS.

- Chapter 16 of the *Microsoft Systems Management Server 2003 Administrator's Companion* by Steven Kaczmarek (Microsoft Press, 2004) provides additional information about creating SMS queries and folders.

- Chapter 4 of the *SMS 2003 Operations Guide* also provides additional information about creating SMS queries and folders.

CHAPTER 10

■■■

Software Inventory

If you're a seasoned SMS administrator, you may cringe when you read the words "software inventory." Keep reading, though, because you don't want to miss out on the improved version of software inventory in SMS 2003.

The most significant enhancement allows for the use of wildcards to specify files to be inventoried. The performance of software inventory has also been improved on both the SMS server and client. With a little planning, you should be able to leverage software inventory without negatively impacting your network with increased inventory traffic.

Some of the most difficult applications to manage are business applications developed in-house. Both of us, on many occasions, have been tasked with identifying systems by the date or version of a single file. Using software inventory makes that job very easy.

If you're looking for recipes on Add/Remove Programs information, go to the next chapter on hardware inventory. We understand that at first glance it doesn't make sense to have software information being collected by hardware inventory, but as you explore the recipes in this chapter and the next, you will see how inventory is divided between software and hardware inventory.

10-1. Enabling Software Inventory

Problem

You want to enable software inventory.

Solution

1. Open the SMS Administrator console.
2. From the SMS Administrator console, expand Site Database (*<Site Code>*), Site Hierarchy, *<Site Name>*, Site Settings, and Client Agents.
3. Right-click Software Inventory Client Agent, and select Properties.
4. Select the "Enable software inventory on clients" check box.
5. Click OK to apply the settings.

Discussion

Software inventory collects the file name, description, version, and size from the file properties. In addition to these properties, the path to the file is recorded. By default, when software inventory is enabled, information for each executable (*.exe) will be added to the database. You can add specific file names (e.g., myApp.dll) and/or specific file paths (e.g., C:\program files\foo\myApp.dll).

When you enable software inventory as described in this recipe, the software inventory component of the Advanced Client is enabled automatically through a policy change and reports the software inventory using the schedule you defined.

Caution The initial full inventory will be approximately 500KB per client. Subsequent delta inventories are approximately 10KB per client.

Use caution when enabling software inventory. Using the default setting (inventory *.exe files only), a full software inventory will occur on each client, according to the schedule specified. The initial full inventory will be approximately 500KB per client. Subsequent delta inventories are approximately 10KB per client. Multiply these amounts by the total number of systems that report to one SMS site, and you'll get an idea of the amount of data transferred for software inventory.

The software inventory cycle on the Advanced Client can be initiated outside of the schedule. We'll cover that in Chapter 16.

See Also

- Recipe 2-21, "Configuring Software Inventory," also describes how to enable software inventory.

- Recipe 10-2, "Modifying the Inventory and File Collection Schedule," describes how to modify the inventory schedule.

- Recipe 10-3, "Creating a New Software Inventory Rule," describes how to create a new software inventory rule.

- Recipe 16-4, "Initiating Software Inventory," demonstrates how to initiate software inventory both locally and remotely.

- SMS Help in the SMS Administrator console provides additional information for properly configuring software inventory.

- *Scenarios and Procedures for Microsoft SMS 2003: Planning and Deployment* guide provides detailed information about client inventory analysis, including examples for calculating load on an SMS server.

- The SMS 2003 Capacity Planner Tool helps you plan and verify your site configuration (http://www.microsoft.com/smserver/techinfo/deployment).

- Chapter 2 of the *SMS 2003 Operations Guide* also contains more information about enabling software inventory.

- Chapter 9 of the *Microsoft Systems Management Server 2003 Administrator's Companion* by Steven Kaczmarek (Microsoft Press, 2004) also discusses how to enable software inventory.

ENABLING SOFTWARE INVENTORY ON A SITE WITH MANY CLIENTS

You're the SMS administrator, and you've been running your healthy SMS 2003 site for over a year now—without SMS software inventory enabled. All of the sudden, your boss sends you the following e-mail:

Johnson, you know that homegrown claims application we've been using for years? Claims is having trouble with it, and we need to identify each system that has the application installed and the file version of the main executable, `claims.exe`. *If you can't do this with SMS, we're going to have to send the desktop team around to each of our 5,000 systems to obtain the data. I need to know by the end of the month.*

Well, of course we can do this with SMS. Luckily, the end of the month is three weeks away. You could simply enable software inventory to inventory that one file (`claim.exe`), but you have the suspicion that you'll receive more requests for other file information in the near future. And since you have your trusty SMS recipes book by your side, you have a plethora of knowledge (and links to more knowledge) at your fingertips to get this inventory rolling safely.

From your SMS recipes book, you know that when you enable software inventory, the first inventory received from the client is a full inventory and will be approximately 500KB per client. Since all but a few of your clients are SMS Advanced Clients, you know they all report to your one and only primary site, which means that when you enable software inventory on your primary site, all your clients will soon be ready to report that initial full inventory. Your goal is to stagger out that first inventory a bit to reduce the initial hit of a full inventory from each client in your enterprise.

If you enable a simple schedule, all of your clients are going to see that schedule at the next machine policy refresh cycle (also know as the *polling interval*) and immediately initiate the full inventory. Even if your ultimate goal is a simple inventory schedule, you may want to consider enabling a full schedule first.

Enable a full schedule, and create a schedule like the following: "Occurs every 30 days effective 7:00 p.m. on Wednesday, December 2, 2009." That's right, the year *2009*. (Hopefully, 2009 is still in the future by the time you read this book—if not, adjust accordingly.) Now that you have enabled software inventory, your clients will see that it's enabled but will not initiate any actions until 7:00 p.m. on December 2, 2009. This gives you plenty of time to initiate software inventory manually on systems. Believe us, not all manual methods are alike! You can use the two following methods to initiate software inventory manually:

- *From the client control panel*: Initiate the software inventory cycle from the Actions tab of the Systems Management applet in the Control Panel on the client.

- *Programmatically (in our example, with VBScript)*: Remotely initiate the software on one or multiple computers (even by collection) with a couple of simple mouse clicks. Alternatively, you could even send an SMS advertisement to a collection of systems to trigger a software inventory. (Yep, SMS is way cool!)

See Chapter 16 for instructions for initiating software inventory on one or more systems in a collection. You'll find a lot of valuable information in that chapter for completing some of those mundane tasks with more ease than in the past.

Now that you have slowly initiated software inventory on all (or at least a great majority of) your systems, you can go back and configure your software inventory schedule as desired.

This entire process can be accomplished in a matter of days and will help keep the local area network (LAN), wide area network (WAN), and network monitoring guys off of your back. It will make your SMS site server happy too.

10-2. Modifying the Inventory and File Collection Schedule

Problem

You want to modify the software inventory and file collection schedule.

Solution

1. Open the SMS Administrator console.

2. From the SMS Administrator console, expand Site Database (*<Site Code>*), Site Hierarchy, *<Site Name>*, Site Settings, and Client Agents.

3. Right-click Software Inventory Client Agent, and select Properties.

4. On the General tab, select the Simple Schedule radio button if you want to use an interval of hours, days, or weeks as your software inventory collection schedule.

5. If you want the collection to happen at specific times (e.g., only Tuesdays and Thursdays), select the Full Schedule radio button, and click the Schedule button to set the specific schedule for the collection.

6. Click OK to apply the settings.

Discussion

Software inventory has a more drastic impact on the performance of a system than hardware inventory. The default schedule of seven days is not a bad place to start, but don't crank it down to every hour unless you have your resume up to date! The reason for the higher performance drain is that software inventory is disk intensive, as it searches all local drives for the files specified.

Notice the title of this recipe, "Modifying the Inventory and File Collection Schedule." This schedule controls both software inventory *and* file collection. At the scheduled time, software inventory is executed, followed by file collection.

Thankfully, SMS 2003 Advanced Clients send delta updates of only the new software inventory changes after the first full inventory, which makes the process easier on your systems and network.

Caution The initial full inventory will be approximately 500KB per client. Subsequent delta inventories are approximately 10KB per client.

See Also

- *Scenarios and Procedures for Microsoft SMS 2003: Planning and Deployment* guide provides detailed information about client inventory analysis, including examples for calculating load on an SMS server.

- The SMS 2003 Capacity Planner Tool helps you plan and verify your site configuration (http://www.microsoft.com/smserver/techinfo/deployment).

- Chapter 2 of the *SMS 2003 Operations Guide* also contains more information about enabling software inventory and considerations for configuring the software inventory schedule.

- Chapter 9 of the *Microsoft Systems Management Server 2003 Administrator's Companion* by Steven Kaczmarek (Microsoft Press, 2004) also discusses how to enable software inventory.

SOFTWARE INVENTORY SCHEDULING: SIMPLE OR FULL SCHEDULE?

There are many options to consider when configuring your schedule for software inventory. When you enable software inventory, a simple schedule is the default schedule. In our opinion, this is a good place to start. Let's compare a simple schedule to a full schedule.

A *simple schedule* is one that allows you to determine on what interval software inventory is executed, but not the specific time. You can specify hours (1–23), days (1–31), or weeks (1–4). For example, configuring a simple schedule of "Every ten days" will execute software inventory exactly ten days from the last software inventory, to the second. The greatest benefit of the simple schedule is that it recurs based on the previous software inventory time. This creates a randomization in your environment, so that not all systems are executing software inventory at the same time. A few more points about the simple schedule:

- If a client misses its inventory cycle because of being powered off, the inventory cycle will initiate a software inventory as soon as the system is powered back on, and the SMS service realizes it owes the SMS site a software inventory. Whether or not the client missed more than one interval, only one software inventory will be run. The interval begins from this most recent software inventory.

- A similar situation occurs when a client is powered on, but unable to contact a valid SMS site. Once the client contacts the SMS site, inventory will be forwarded. And once again, the interval begins from the most recent software inventory.

- A simple schedule allows you to specify how frequently software inventory is initiated, but it does not allow you to specify the time. So it is possible that a client will complain because of slowness in the system, and upon inspection, you'll see that an SMS software inventory was running at the time of the reported slowness (and, sooner or later, we're sure it will happen).

A *full schedule* is a schedule that allows you to determine the interval and the time for software inventory to run. Since software inventory can noticeably affect a system while running, you may consider creating a full schedule, so that the inventory runs at a specific time (e.g., 9:00 p.m.) while users are away. Of course, there are caveats (or benefits, depending on your environment) to remember when using a full schedule:

- A full schedule is just that—a *full* schedule. When you configure a full schedule for software inventory, every client within the site will run software inventory at the same time, which means that each client will be passing data back to its site at approximately the same time. This may have a significant impact on your network and on your SMS site.

- Missed scans can occur if the system is powered off at the scheduled scan time or the system is unable to report inventory to the server. The scan will occur at the next possible opportunity, and data will be forwarded to the SMS site. The next scheduled scan will occur at the scheduled time (provided the client is powered on). This allows for the possibility of a client running two scans back-to-back (the catch-up scan followed by the scheduled scan).

Caution The initial software inventory occurs within 30 minutes of SMS client installation. Remember, this is a *full* software inventory.

When creating either a simple or full schedule, keep in mind that if the client is powered off when the scan is scheduled to occur, software inventory will start shortly after the system is powered on. For example, if you schedule software inventory to occur "Every 4 hours" and your users generally power off their system at night, when these users arrive the next morning and power on their computer, software inventory will begin. This can be a reason for slow computers first thing in the morning, in addition to a taxed site server for accepting all the inventories.

See the previous sidebar in this chapter titled "Enabling Software Inventory on a Site with Many Clients" for a strategy to enable software inventory in your environment that reduces the potential of bringing your network (and your SMS site server) to its knees.

10-3. Creating a New Software Inventory Rule

Problem

You want to create a new inventory collection rule for software inventory.

Solution

1. Open the SMS Administrator console.

2. From the SMS Administrator console, expand Site Database (<*Site Code*>), Site Hierarchy, <*Site Name*>, Site Settings, and Client Agents.

3. Right-click Software Inventory Client Agent, and select Properties.

4. On the Inventory Collection tab, click the New button (the yellow starburst icon) to open the Inventoried File Properties dialog box.

5. Enter the name of the file or use wildcards to select more than one file to be inventoried (e.g., *.mp3 would inventory all files with an .mp3 file extension).

6. In the Path section, click the Set button to open the Path Properties dialog box.

7. Limit the search to a specific drive or directory. Also, choose to search subdirectories by checking the appropriate check box.

8. Click OK to close the Path Properties dialog box.

9. You can exclude encrypted files, compressed files, or files in the Windows directory by checking the appropriate check boxes.

10. Click OK to close the Inventoried File Properties dialog box.

11. Click OK to apply the settings.

Discussion

In addition to the default rule for all executables, you can create new rules for other files or file types. Software inventory may appear to have limited use until someone asks for all systems with a configuration file from January 14. Without the configurable rules of software inventory, it would be quite difficult to determine which systems have that configuration file.

Caution Use the narrowest possible scope for your software inventory rules. Creating a rule that inventories more files than needed will increase the software inventory cycle time, which decreases performance on the client system without any added benefit.

According to SMS Help, the following properties for the Inventoried File Properties dialog are used to create a new rule:

Name: Specify a file name or a file name with proper wildcards. Two examples of wildcards follow:

- Hello*.dll: Queries for all file names that begin with Hello and end with .dll. Examples of files that would be queried are HelloWorld.dll, Hello World.dll, Hello.dll, and HelloMyNameIsGreg.dll.

- HelloWorld.??e: Queries for all file names that begin with HelloWorld followed by any two valid characters and that end with e. Examples of files that would be queried are HelloWorld.exe, HelloWorld.sle, and HelloWorld.bae.

Path: The client hard disk location where files are inventoried. The path property also determines whether subdirectories are searched. Click Set to open the Path Properties dialog box, so you can update the following file path settings:

- *Location*: Displays inventoried file locations. The location can be all client hard disks, a single path variable (e.g., %ProgramFiles%\SMSView\), or a path name (e.g., D:\UserData\, assuming D: is a local hard disk).

- *Search subdirectories*: Indicates whether the Location subdirectories are searched.

Exclude encrypted and compressed files: Indicates whether to search for encrypted and/or compressed files.

Exclude files in the Windows directory: Indicates whether to search for files in the Windows directory. If you select this option, the search subdirectories option is ignored.

We're stating the obvious here, but it's important to remember that the broader the wildcard, the greater potential for massive amounts of data to be retrieved by SMS. For example, if you create a new software inventory rule to inventory *.dll, the next inventory cycle will have an impact on your site and network as great as (and possibly greater than) the default software inventory of *.exe.

See Also

- Recipe 10-4, "Modifying a Software Inventory Rule," describes how to modify an existing software inventory rule.

- SMS 2003 Help provides more information about creating a new software inventory rule.

- *Scenarios and Procedures for Microsoft SMS 2003: Planning and Deployment* guide provides detailed information about client inventory analysis, including examples for calculating load on an SMS server.

- Chapter 2 of the *SMS 2003 Operations Guide* also contains more information about creating new software inventory rules.

- Chapter 9 of the *Microsoft Systems Management Server 2003 Administrator's Companion* by Steven Kaczmarek (Microsoft Press, 2004) also discusses how to create new software inventory rules.

10-4. Modifying a Software Inventory Rule

Problem

You want to modify an inventory collection rule for software inventory.

Solution

1. Open the SMS Administrator console.

2. From the SMS Administrator console, expand Site Database (*<Site Code>*), Site Hierarchy, *<Site Name>*, Site Settings, and Client Agents.

3. Right-click Software Inventory Client Agent, and select Properties.

4. On the Inventory Collection tab, double-click the inventory rule to open the Inventoried File Properties dialog box.

5. Change the name of the file or use wildcards to select more than one file to be inventoried (e.g., *.mp3 would inventory all files with an .mp3 file extension).

6. In the Path section, click the Set button to open the Path Properties dialog box.

7. Limit the search to a specific drive or directory. Also, choose to search subdirectories by checking the appropriate check box.

8. Click OK to close the Path Properties dialog box.

9. You can exclude encrypted and compressed files or files in the Windows directory by checking the appropriate check boxes.

10. Click OK to close the Inventoried File Properties dialog box.

11. Click OK to apply the settings.

Discussion

So you skipped the previous recipe and popped in a rule that inventories all DLL files. Yikes! No problem, change the rule to narrow the scope and you're done. You also might want to consolidate rules, if possible, so that the number of rules being processed is kept to a minimum.

Note When you remove or modify a software inventory rule, the SMS Advanced Client will obtain the rule changes on its next Machine Policy Retrieval and Evaluation Cycle (polling cycle), and use the modified rules at the next scheduled inventory. When the new inventory is received at the SMS site, the old inventory data is purged and replaced with the new data.

As stated in Recipe 10-3, "Creating a New Software Inventory Rule," it's important to remember that the broader the wildcard, the greater the potential for massive amounts of data to be retrieved by SMS. For example, if you create a new software inventory rule to inventory `*.dll`, the next inventory cycle will have as great an impact on your site and network (and possibly greater) as the default software inventory of `*.exe`.

See Also

- Recipe 10-3, "Creating a New Software Inventory Rule," shows how to create a new software inventory rule.

- Chapter 9 of the *Microsoft Systems Management Server 2003 Administrator's Companion* by Steven Kaczmarek (Microsoft Press, 2004) also discusses how to modify software inventory rules.

- *Scenarios and Procedures for Microsoft SMS 2003: Planning and Deployment* guide provides detailed information about client inventory analysis, including examples for calculating load on an SMS server.

- Chapter 2 of the *SMS 2003 Operations Guide* also contains more information about configuring software inventory rules.

10-5. Querying Software Inventory Data from the Command Line

Problem

You want to query software inventory data in SMS from the command line.

Solution

Example 10-1 demonstrates how to query software inventory from the command line. This query will display all systems that have Adobe Acrobat installed (based on `Acrobat.exe` in software inventory).

Example 10-1. *SWInvQuery.vbs*

```
strSMSServer = <SMSServer>

strFileName = "Acrobat.exe"

Set objLoc = CreateObject("WbemScripting.SWbemLocator")
Set objSMS= objLoc.ConnectServer(strSMSServer, "root\sms")
Set Results = objSMS.ExecQuery _
    ("SELECT * From SMS_ProviderLocation WHERE ProviderForLocalSite = true")
For each Loc in Results
    If Loc.ProviderForLocalSite = True Then
        Set objSMS = objLoc.ConnectServer(Loc.Machine, "root\sms\site_" & _
            Loc.SiteCode)
    end if
Next

strSQL = "select SMS_R_System.Name, " & _
    "SMS_G_System_SoftwareFile.FileName, " & _
    "SMS_G_System_SoftwareFile.FileDescription, " & _
    "SMS_G_System_SoftwareFile.FileVersion from " & _
    "SMS_R_System inner join SMS_G_System_SoftwareFile on " & _
    "SMS_G_System_SoftwareFile.ResourceID = " & _
    "SMS_R_System.ResourceId where " & _
    "SMS_G_System_SoftwareFile.FileName = '" & strFileName & "'"

Set colSystems = objSMS.ExecQuery(strSQL)

for each objSystem in colSystems
    wscript.echo objSystem.SMS_R_System.Name & vbTAB & _
        objSystem.SMS_G_System_SoftwareFile.FileName & vbTAB & _
        objSystem.SMS_G_System_SoftwareFile.FileDescription & vbTAB & _
        objSystem.SMS_G_System_SoftwareFile.FileVersion
next
```

Discussion

In most instances, you will use SMS web reporting to obtain software inventory data. In other instances, you will use SMS queries to obtain the data. But there may be an occasion when you want to pull that data from SMS on a regular basis and do something magical with it. Example 10-1 is a basic VBScript that displays the Name (computer name), FileName, FileDescription, and FileVersion for each instance of Acrobat.exe (this of course assumes that you have software inventory enabled and have a software inventory rule that will inventory Acrobat.exe).

After connecting to the site, we build our WMI Query Language (WQL) query (by the way, this same query could be used as an SMS query). We then use ExecQuery to execute the query. Finally, we use a basic for-each loop to display the information.

The following is an excerpt from the SMS 2003 SDK (with our additional comments) explaining some of the more popular software inventory fields obtained from the SMS_G_System_SoftwareFile class:

`FileName`: The name of the file.

`FileSize`: The size of the file, in bytes.

`FileVersion`: The file version from the file version resource string. In our adventures as SMS administrators, we have discovered that this is a wonderful property to distinguish multiple file versions for retail products. Unfortunately, we have found many instances of in-house applications where the version number was not properly modified before the file was recompiled. When the file version information looks shady, spend some time looking at the `FileModifiedDate` and the `FileSize` to help distinguish versions.

`ModifiedDate`: The time the record in the database was last modified. For example, this date would change if a file on the client that was already being inventoried was modified. The next software inventory would identify that file as changed and update SMS appropriately.

`FileModifiedDate`: The time the file was last modified. This is often helpful in determining different versions of a file.

`ProductID`: This is an SMS-specific property. The `ProductID` property in the `SMS_G_System_SoftwareFile` class is used to map the entry to the `ProductID` property in the `SMS_G_System_SoftwareProduct` class.

`ResourceID`: The `ResourceID` of the client. We generally join this with `SMS_R_System.ResourceID`. `SMS_R_System` contains discovery data for all discovered system resources. In our example, we join to this class to obtain the computer name (`Name`) property.

`FilePath`: The path to the file on the client computer. This can be very handy when determining valid installations (based on install standards) and for filtering out source files that are sitting on a share, compared to the application actually being installed on the system.

See Also

- The SMS 2003 SDK provides additional information about the `SMS_G_System_SoftwareFile` and `SMS_R_System` classes.

10-6. Creating a New File Collection Rule

Problem

You want to create a new file collection rule for software inventory.

Solution

1. Open the SMS Administrator console.
2. From the SMS Administrator console, expand Site Database (*<Site Code>*), Site Hierarchy, *<Site Name>*, Site Settings, and Client Agents.
3. Right-click Software Inventory Client Agent, and select Properties.
4. On the File Collection tab, click the New button (the yellow starburst icon) to open the Collected File Properties dialog box.
5. Enter the name of the file you want to collect or use wildcards to select more than one file to be inventoried (e.g., `*.ini` would inventory all files with the `.ini` extension).
6. In the Path section, click the Set button to open the Path Properties dialog box.
7. Limit the search to a specific drive or directory. Also, choose to search subdirectories by checking the appropriate check box.

8. Click OK to close the Path Properties dialog box.

9. You can exclude encrypted and compressed files by checking the appropriate check box.

10. Specify the maximum size that is allowed to be collected.

11. Click OK to close the Collected File Properties dialog box.

12. Click OK to apply the settings.

Discussion

Don't confuse software inventory rules and file collection rules. The software inventory rules inventory file information only. The file collection rules collect the actual file and copy it to the SMS site server.

Caution File collection should be thoroughly evaluated and tested before you implement it in your environment. The potential for negatively impacting your network performance or site server is very real. However, if you use it wisely to solve a specific problem, it may be the perfect solution.

Let's discuss the available configuration options for SMS file collection in detail:

Name: Similar to software inventory, this can be a complete file name or a partial file name with the * or ? wildcards. Recipe 10-3, "Creating a New Software Inventory Rule," provides more information about using wildcards.

Path: The Path setting allows you to narrow the scope of file collection. This is where you can specify where to look for the file. You can enter a specific path and select whether or not to search subdirectories. For example, if you have an in-house claims application for which you know the program requires the .ini file to be in a specific location, you can explicitly state that location, which will make the file collection more efficient and help prevent you from receiving bogus files (think of those developers who insist on having 20 different versions of that .ini file in their backup folders).

Exclude encrypted and compressed files: This one is pretty self-explanatory. Unchecking this box will cause file collection to collect encrypted and compressed files.

Maximum Size (KB): This option can be confusing. This is the maximum size, in kilobytes, that SMS will collect for this *rule*. Notice this size is per rule, not per file. By default, 128KB is the maximum size. Say, for example, you have a rule that collects *.ini files, and you left the default maximum size at 128KB. When the next software inventory cycle runs (remember, the file collection cycle occurs on the same schedule as the software inventory cycle), file collection on the SMS Advanced Client will start caching all of the files to a temporary location on the client (%WINDIR%\system32\ccm\inventory\temp\FileColl). The SMS client then verifies that the total size of files collected for this rule is less than the maximum size of the rule. If the total size is greater than the maximum size, all collected files are cleared from the temporary location, and no data will be forwarded to the SMS site. If the SMS client determines that the total size of collected files is acceptable, the data is forwarded to the primary site.

The keys to file collection are to use it conservatively and to narrow your collection scope as much as possible.

Note For scheduling purposes, the file collection cycle uses the software inventory schedule to determine the appropriate start time.

As you can see from this recipe, file collection is a very powerful feature of SMS. And of course, with power comes danger. As the warning in this recipe states, use extreme caution to ensure you're only collecting specific files of interest to you.

Collected files are stored in an organized, yet unintuitive, manner. If you have file collection enabled and browse to `\sms\inboxes\sinv.box\FileCol` on the drive of the SMS primary site, you will see many folders. Each folder begins with a number. This number represents the `ResourceID` of the system. If needed, you can map this `ResourceID` to the `v_GS_System` SQL view (or the `SMS_R_System` WMI class on the SMS primary site). When you drill down into one of these `ResourceID` folders, you will see the files collected for that system. Unfortunately, the file names are not the original file names (but the extensions are accurate). We will discuss how to determine the correct file name in Recipe 10-8, "Listing Collected Files for a Specific System from the Command Line."

Note The SMS site retains the files collected until the Delete Aged Collected Files task purges them, and then the task purges them. By default, this setting is configured at "Every 90 days." To adjust this setting, navigate to Site Database ➤ *<Site Name>* ➤ Site Settings ➤ Site Maintenance ➤ Tasks, and modify it to meet your needs.

See Also

- Chapter 2 of the *SMS 2003 Operations Guide* provides additional information about configuring file collection.

- Chapter 9 of the *Microsoft Systems Management Server 2003 Administrator's Companion* by Steven Kaczmarek (Microsoft Press, 2004) also discusses how create and modify file collection rules.

WHY USE FILE COLLECTION?

You might be asking yourself, Why use file collection? Say, for instance, you have an in-house application that uses a `configdb.ini` file that contains connection server names. One of your servers hosting this application has a warranty that will expire soon and must be replaced. Unfortunately, you're unable to remove the old system and implement a new system with the same computer name. You need to identify all systems that have the old server name in the `configdb.ini` file, and either coordinate with your desktop team to have the `.ini` file modified or use SMS to deploy an updated `configdb.ini` file to the identified systems.

To accomplish this task, you could implement file collection to collect `configdb.ini` from all SMS-managed systems. You could then view these files individually or use the example scripts (found later in this chapter) to search each file for a specific string. In this case, you would search for files that contain the old server name in `configdb.ini`.

10-7. Viewing and Saving Collected Files for a Specific System

Problem

You want to view the files that are collected for a specific system by software inventory.

Solution

1. Open the SMS Administrator console.

2. From the SMS Administrator console, expand Site Database (*<Site Code>*) and Collections, and select a collection that contains the system you want to review.

3. In the right pane, right-click the system, and select All Tasks ➤ Start Resource Explorer.

4. In Resource Explorer, expand Software and Collected Files.

5. In the right pane, right-click the collected file you want to view, and select All Tasks ➤ View File.

6. The file will open for you to view.

7. To save the file to a different location, right-click the collected file you want to view, and select All Tasks ➤ Save File.

8. Enter a location and file name for saving the file.

Discussion

If you are going to collect files, you will need to view them, right? The SMS design team thought of that and has included that capability in Resource Explorer, along with the ability to save the collected files to another location. Of course, if you want to save these files for all systems that have reported the collected file inventory, it could be a bit of a challenge to extract each file manually. The next two recipes will help you get the collected files data out of SMS, so you can analyze it for multiple systems, instead of one at a time.

See Also

- Recipe 10-8, "Listing Collected Files for a Specific System from the Command Line," demonstrates how to list collected files for a specific system from the command line.

- Recipe 10-9, "Listing a Specific Collected File for All Systems," demonstrates how to list a specific collected file for all systems.

- Recipe 10-10, "Copying a Specific Collected File for All Systems," demonstrates how to extract a specific collected file for each system.

- Chapter 2 of the *SMS 2003 Operations Guide* provides additional information about viewing and saving collected files.

- Chapter 9 of the *Microsoft Systems Management Server 2003 Administrator's Companion* by Steven Kaczmarek (Microsoft Press, 2004) also discusses viewing and saving collected files.

10-8. Listing Collected Files for a Specific System from the Command Line

Problem

You want list the files that are collected for a specific system by software inventory.

Solution

Example 10-2 demonstrates how to display all collected files for a specific SMS client.

Example 10-2. *ListCollectedFilesForSpecificSystem.vbs*

```
strSMSServer = <SMSServer>

strComputer = "2kPro"

Set objLoc = CreateObject("WbemScripting.SWbemLocator")
Set objSMS= objLoc.ConnectServer(strSMSServer, "root\sms")
Set Results = objSMS.ExecQuery _
    ("SELECT * From SMS_ProviderLocation WHERE ProviderForLocalSite = true")
```

```
For each Loc in Results
    If Loc.ProviderForLocalSite = True Then
        Set objSMS = objLoc.ConnectServer(Loc.Machine, "root\sms\site_" & _
            Loc.SiteCode)
    end if
Next

strSQL = "SELECT sys.Name, colFil.FileName, " & _
    "colFil.FileSize, colFil.ModifiedDate, colFil.FilePath, " & _
    "colFil.LocalFilePath, colFil.CollectionDate " & _
    "FROM SMS_G_System_CollectedFile colFil INNER JOIN " & _
        "SMS_R_System sys ON " & _
         "colFil.ResourceID = sys.ResourceID " & _
    "WHERE sys.Name = '" & strComputer & "'"

Set colFiles = objSMS.ExecQuery(strSQL)
for each objFile in colFiles
    wscript.echo objFile.sys.Name & vbTAB & _
        objFile.colFil.FileName & vbTAB & _
        objFile.colFil.FileSize & vbTAB & _
        WMIDateStringToDate(objFile.colFil.ModifiedDate) & _
        vbTAB & objFile.colFil.FilePath & vbTAB & _
        objFile.colFil.LocalFilePath & vbTAB & _
        WMIDateStringToDate(objFile.colFil.CollectionDate)
next

Function WMIDateStringToDate(dtmInstallDate)
    WMIDateStringToDate = CDate(Mid(dtmInstallDate, 5, 2) & _
        "/" & Mid(dtmInstallDate, 7, 2) & "/" & _
        Left(dtmInstallDate, 4) & " " & _
        Mid (dtmInstallDate, 9, 2) & ":" & _
        Mid(dtmInstallDate, 11, 2) & ":" & Mid(dtmInstallDate, _
        13, 2))
End Function
```

Discussion

You can use SMS Resource Explorer to list the collected files for a system. Example 10-2 demonstrates how to list all collected files for a specific system. But if you have a large number of collected files, this could become stressful when you only want to look at a subset.

After connecting to the site, we build and execute our WQL query. Next, we use a for-each loop to display the file collection data. WMIDateStringToDate is used to convert WMI date-time values to a more user-friendly date.

SMS_G_System_CollectedFile contains the file collection data and is joined to SMS_R_System by ResourceID to obtain the computer name. The WQL used in this example could also be used to create an SMS query in the Administrator console. Also, the v_GS_CollectedFile SQL view can be used to display the data in SMS web reporting. A brief overview of the properties of the SMS_G_System_CollectedFile class follows (from the SMS 2003 SDK with some additional comments from us):

CollectionDate: The date and time the file was collected from the client.

FileName: The name and file extension of the file.

FilePath: The path to the file on the client computer.

LocalFilePath: The path and file name to the file on the site server. The collected file does not keep its original name. By inspecting the LocalFilePath property for a record, you will see that the collected files are stored in sms\sinv.box\filecol\ResourceID, where ResourceID is the resource ID for a unique system. You will notice that the file names do not look familiar in these directories. The file extension looks correct, but the name appears to be a random string of characters (including numbers). By modifying the file names, SMS is able to store all collected files for each computer in one directory. Also, since each file name is unique, multiple revisions of the same file can be stored in the same directory. SMS uses the RevisionID property to keep track of multiple revisions of the same file. The next two recipes demonstrate how to use this information to expand your abilities with file collection. The data found in SMS_G_System_CollectedFile provides everything you need to identify specific files outside of the SMS Administrator console.

ModifiedDate: The date and time the file was last modified.

ResourceID: The property joined to ResourceID in the SMS_R_System table.

RevisionID: The revision of the file. The value increments each time an inventory is taken to identify the number of times this object has been inventoried. *The file is inventoried only when it has changed.*

See Also

- Recipe 10-7, "Viewing and Saving Collected Files for a Specific System," demonstrates how to view and save collected file information for a specific system.

- The SMS 2003 SDK provides additional information about SMS_G_System_CollectedFile and SMS_R_System.

10-9. Listing a Specific Collected File for All Systems

Problem

You want to list all systems that have a specific collected file on the SMS site.

Solution

Example 10-3 lists information for a collected file for all systems.

Example 10-3. *ListSpecificFileForAllSystems.vbs*

```
strSMSServer = <SMSServer>

strFileName = "dbcfg.ini"

Set objLoc =  CreateObject("WbemScripting.SWbemLocator")
Set objSMS= objLoc.ConnectServer(strSMSServer, "root\sms")
Set Results = objSMS.ExecQuery _
    ("SELECT * From SMS_ProviderLocation WHERE ProviderForLocalSite = true")
For each Loc in Results
    If Loc.ProviderForLocalSite = True Then
        Set objSMS = objLoc.ConnectServer(Loc.Machine, "root\sms\site_" & _
            Loc.SiteCode)
    end if
Next
```

```
strSQL = "SELECT sys.Name, colFil.FileName, " & _
    "colFil.LocalFilePath, colFil.RevisionID " & _
    "FROM SMS_G_System_CollectedFile colFil INNER JOIN " & _
        "SMS_R_System sys ON " & _
          "colFil.ResourceID = sys.ResourceID " & _
    "WHERE colFil.FileName = '" & strFileName & "'"

Set colFiles = objSMS.ExecQuery(strSQL)

for each objFile in colFiles
    wscript.echo objFile.sys.Name & vbTAB & _
        objfile.colFil.FileName & vbTAB & _
        objFile.colFil.LocalFilePath
next
```

Discussion

In Example 10-3, we execute a WQL query to obtain all instances in the SMS_G_System_CollectedFile where FileName is dbcfg.ini. We then display the results of the query. This script may not appear to be very exciting. In fact, you could obtain this information using an SMS query or SMS web reporting, but you can extend this script to perform more actions on the files, as we will do in the following two recipes.

See Also

- Recipe 10-7, "Viewing and Saving Collected Files for a Specific System," demonstrates how to view and save collected file information for a specific system.

- Recipe 10-8, "Listing Collected Files for a Specific System from the Command Line," demonstrates how to list all collected files for a specific system from the command line.

- Recipe 10-10, "Copying a Specific Collected File for All Systems," demonstrates how to copy a specific collected file for each system to a specific directory outside of the SMS collected files directory.

- The SMS 2003 SDK provides additional information about SMS_G_System_CollectedFile and SMS_R_System.

10-10. Copying a Specific Collected File for All Systems

Problem

You want to extract a specific file from file collection for each system.

Solution

Example 10-4 demonstrates how to extract the collected file for each system and copy it to a server share.

Example 10-4. *ExtractCollectedFilesForAllSystems.vbs*

```
Const OverwriteExisting = TRUE

strSMSServer = <SMSServer>

strFileName = "dbcfg.ini"
strTargetPath = "\\smsvpc\fileanalysis"
```

```
Set objLoc =  CreateObject("WbemScripting.SWbemLocator")
Set objSMS= objLoc.ConnectServer(strSMSServer, "root\sms")
Set Results = objSMS.ExecQuery _
    ("SELECT * From SMS_ProviderLocation WHERE ProviderForLocalSite = true")
For each Loc in Results
    If Loc.ProviderForLocalSite = True Then
        Set objSMS = objLoc.ConnectServer(Loc.Machine, "root\sms\site_" & _
            Loc.SiteCode)
    end if
Next

strSQL = "SELECT sys.Name, colFil.FileName, " & _
    "colFil.LocalFilePath, colFil.RevisionID " & _
    "FROM SMS_G_System_CollectedFile colFil INNER JOIN " & _
        "SMS_R_System sys ON " & _
        "colFil.ResourceID = sys.ResourceID " & _
    "WHERE colFil.FileName = '" & strFileName & "'"

Set colFiles = objSMS.ExecQuery(strSQL)

for each objFile in colFiles
    wscript.echo objFile.sys.Name & vbTAB & _
        objfile.colFil.FileName & vbTAB & _
        objFile.colFil.LocalFilePath
    Set objFSO = CreateObject("Scripting.FileSystemObject")
    objFSO.CopyFile objFile.colFil.LocalFilePath , _
        strTargetPath & "\" & objFile.sys.Name & "_" & _
        objfile.colFil.RevisionID & "_" & _
        objfile.colFil.FileName, OverwriteExisting
next
```

Discussion

This is one of the handy solutions that cannot be accomplished in the SMS Administrator console. Say, for example, the members of your development team want to get an idea of the type of data stored in an .ini file on each client for a homegrown application. Rather than give them access to SMS Resource Explorer or permissions to the path where the collected files are stored (which means you would probably need to give them access to the database in order to cross-reference to obtain the computer name), you can modify the script in Example 10-4 to fit your needs and copy a collected file (or multiple files) for each system to a common directory outside of your SMS infrastructure.

Notice in Example 10-4 that we specify the file name (strFileName) of the collected file to query and then specify the target path (strTargetPath). Next, we execute a WQL query to obtain all records of files that meet the criteria. Finally, in the for-each loop, we perform a CopyFile to copy the file with its unique name to strTargetPath. We also modify the file name to help identify the computer name and revision of the file (because you can have multiple revisions of the same file in your SMS site for the same system at the same time). The file name will begin with the computer name, followed by the RevisionID number, followed by the real file name.

Note The SMS site retains the files collected until the Delete Aged Collected Files task purges them. By default, this setting is configured for "Every 90 days." To adjust this setting, navigate to Site Database ➤ *<Site Name>* ➤ Site Settings ➤ Site Maintenance ➤ Tasks, and modify it to meet your needs.

See Also

- Recipe 10-7, "Viewing and Saving Collected Files for a Specific System," demonstrates how to view and save collected file information for a specific system.

- The SMS 2003 SDK provides additional information about SMS_G_System_CollectedFile and SMS_R_System.

10-11. Searching Collected Files for Specific Data

Problem

You want to search all collected files for specific data within a specific file.

Solution

Example 10-5 demonstrates how to search a specific collected file for each system, for a specific line of text.

Example 10-5. *SearchINIForSpecificData.vbs*

```
Const ForReading = 1
strSMSServer = <SMSServer>

strFileName = "dbcfg.ini"
strDataToCheck = "DBServername=MYPRODSERVER"
intCount = 0
Set objFSO = CreateObject("Scripting.FileSystemObject")

Set objLoc =  CreateObject("WbemScripting.SWbemLocator")
Set objSMS= objLoc.ConnectServer(strSMSServer, "root\sms")
Set Results = objSMS.ExecQuery _
    ("SELECT * From SMS_ProviderLocation WHERE ProviderForLocalSite = true")
For each Loc in Results
    If Loc.ProviderForLocalSite = True Then
        Set objSMS = objLoc.ConnectServer(Loc.Machine, "root\sms\site_" & _
            Loc.SiteCode)
    end if
Next

strSQL = "SELECT sys.Name, colFil.FileName, " & _
    "colFil.LocalFilePath, colFil.RevisionID " & _
    "FROM SMS_G_System_CollectedFile colFil INNER JOIN " & _
        "SMS_R_System sys ON " & _
         "colFil.ResourceID = sys.ResourceID " & _
    "WHERE colFil.FileName = '" & strFileName & "' " & _
    "ORDER BY colFil.CollectionDate"

Set colFiles = objSMS.ExecQuery(strSQL)

for each objFile in colFiles
    intCount = intCount + 1
    wscript.echo "Checking " & objFile.sys.Name & ". . ."
    Set objReadFile = objFSO.OpenTextFile _
        (objFile.colFil.LocalFilePath, ForReading)
    strContents = objReadFile.ReadAll
```

```
    if instr(ucase(strContents), ucase(strDataToCheck)) = 0 then
        strInfo = strInfo & objFile.sys.Name &  vbTAB & _
            objFile.colFil.RevisionID & vbCRLF
    end if
next

wscript.echo vbCRLF & intCount & " Files Checked" & vbCRLF
wscript.echo "The following computers do not have " & _
    strServerName & "in the file " & strFileName
wscript.echo strInfo
```

Discussion

Example 10-5 shows the basic approach to determining whether all of your systems have the same configuration (i.e., ensure all systems are using MYPRODSERVER). The process in Example 10-5 is very similar to the example in the previous recipe; it's another one of those handy tasks that cannot be accomplished in the SMS Administrator console.

In this example, we query the SMS_G_System_CollectedFile class to identify all systems for which SMS has collected a file by the name of strFileName (in our example, dbcfg.ini). Next, we enumerate each file from the query result and check to see if the string strDataToCheck exists (in our example, DBServername=MYPRODSERVER). If that string does not exist (suggesting that possibly DBServername is equal to something other than MYPRODSERVER, e.g., MYTESTSERVER), we append that information into strInfo, which is displayed at the end of the script.

Again, Example 10-5 is very basic. Use your magical VBScript scripting skills to improve upon it.

Note The SMS site retains the files collected until the Delete Aged Collected Files task purges them. By default, this setting is configured for "Every 90 days." To modify this setting, navigate to Site Database ➤ <Site Name> ➤ Site Settings ➤ Site Maintenance ➤ Tasks, and modify it to meet your needs.

As the preceding note illustrates, there is one caveat in particular worth mentioning in Example 10-5: If your collected file is modified on the client, file collection inventory will pick it up on the next software inventory, but it won't remove any previous revisions of the file until the Delete Aged Collected Files task purges them. Therefore, if you're running a special query as we have in this example, you may need to apply some additional VBScript magic to ensure you're using the latest version of the file, by comparing either the CollectionDate or RevisionID property.

See Also

- Recipe 10-7, "Viewing and Saving Collected Files for a Specific System," demonstrates how to view and save collected file information for a specific system.

- Recipe 10-9, "Listing a Specific Collected File for All Systems," describes how to display all systems that have had a specific file collected.

- The SMS 2003 SDK provides additional information about SMS_G_System_CollectedFile and SMS_R_System.

10-12. Consolidating Manufacturer or Product Names

Problem

You want to consolidate manufacturer or product names that have more than one instance.

Solution

1. Open the SMS Administrator console.

2. From the SMS Administrator console, expand Site Database (*<Site Code>*), Site Hierarchy, *<Site Name>*, Site Settings, and Client Agents.

3. Right-click Software Inventory Client Agent, and select Properties.

4. On the Inventory Names tab, select Manufacturer or Product from the drop-down list.

5. In the Display Name section, click the New button (the yellow starburst icon) to open the Display Name Properties dialog box.

6. Enter the correct name that you want to be displayed for that manufacturer or product.

7. Click OK to close the Display Name Properties dialog box. The new display name should be listed and highlighted.

8. In the Inventoried Names section, click the New button (the yellow starburst icon) to open the Inventoried Name Properties dialog box.

9. Enter an inventoried name of the manufacturer or product, or use wildcards to select more than one name, and click OK.

10. Enter as many inventoried names as necessary to consolidate all of the names used by the manufacturer or product.

11. Click OK to apply the settings.

Discussion

We have heard many SMS administrators grumble about how software manufacturers can't make up their minds on the naming conventions for their companies or products. That isn't a problem with SMS 2003. You can create your own custom mapping of manufacturer and product names to eliminate confusion.

Microsoft has included a couple default rules that correct some of their own naming issues. On the Inventory Names tab, select the Name type of Manufacturer. Notice the "Display name" of Microsoft Corporation. Now notice the lower box titled "Inventoried names." In this box, you will see all the *ugly names* that are collected in inventory that will be displayed as the *pretty name* in the Display name box. If you switch the Name type to Product, you will see similar information.

You may also use wildcards in the Inventoried Name field. According to the SMS 2003 Help, you can use the wildcards listed in Table 10-1.

Table 10-1. *Using Wildcard Characters with Inventoried Names for Software Inventory*

Wildcard	Searches For
% (percent sign)	Any string of zero or more characters. For example, **mo%** searches for all names that begin with the letters "mo" (e.g., mom, Morgan); **%mo** searches for all names that end with "mo" (e.g., Satchmo); and **%mo%** searches for all names that include "mo" (e.g., mom, Satchmo, tomorrow).
_ (underscore)	Any single character. For example, **_ill** searches for any four-letter names ending with the letters "ill" (e.g., mill, will).
[ ] (brackets)	Any single character within the specified range. For example, **[HD]ans[eo]n** searches for all names that begin with "H" or D," followed by "ans," then "e" or "o," and ending with "n" (e.g., Hanson, Hansen, Danson, Dansen), and **[B-K]enson** searches for all names ending with "enson" that begin with any single letter from "B" through "K" (e.g., Benson, Jenson).

Wildcard	Searches For
[^] (caret)	Any single character not within the specified range. For example, **M[^c]%** searches for all names beginning with the letter "M" that do not have the letter "c" as the second letter (e.g., MacPherson).

By mapping several variations of a name to one name, you will see a significant improvement in the data that is displayed in SMS web reports as well as SMS queries. To take this idea to the next level, be sure to check out the next recipe.

See Also

- Recipe 10-13, "Consolidating Manufacturer or Product Names en Masse," describes how to create multiple SMS software inventory manufacturer and product conversion rules in your SMS site with just a little effort.

- Chapter 9 of the *Microsoft Systems Management Server 2003 Administrator's Companion* by Steven Kaczmarek (Microsoft Press, 2004) also discusses how to add and modify inventory names.

- Chapter 2 of the *SMS 2003 Operations Guide* also provides more information about managing inventory names.

10-13. Consolidating Manufacturer or Product Names en Masse

Problem

You want to consolidate a group of manufacturer and product names to improve software inventory data.

Solution

1. Browse to the Synergon Group's Infinity web site (http://www.infinity.cz/view.asp?ID=384), and download SMS Conversion Rules (SMS ConvRules M1 Guide.doc). (As this site is primarily written in Czech, you might find it easier to use the direct download: http://www.infinity.cz/downloads/sms/SMS%20ConvRules%20M1%20Guide.zip.)

2. After reviewing the SMS ConvRules M1 Guide.doc, use the following links to download the files to your TEST SMS server (short registration required):

    a. Use http://www.infinity.cz/download.asp?soubor=SMS_CRM1.zip to download manufacturer information, and unzip the file to C:\temp\SMS_CRM1.

    b. Use http://www.infinity.cz/download.asp?soubor=SMS_CRP1.zip to download product information, and unzip the file to C:\temp\SMS_CRP1.

3. Execute C:\temp\SMS_CRM1\SMS_CRM1.01.exe /x. In the dialog, select all of the files, and click OK. Save all files to C:\temp\SMS_CRM1\Extract\, and then review readme.txt and HowToTraceImport.txt.

4. Execute C:\temp\SMS_CRP1\SMS_CRP1.exe /x. In the dialog, select all of the files, and click OK. Save all files to C:\temp\SMS_CRP1\Extract\, and then review readme.txt.

5. On your TEST SMS server, launch Microsoft SQL Query Analyzer.

6. In SQL Query Analyzer, click the Open icon, browse to C:\temp\SMS_CRM1\Extract\ConversionRulesM1.sql, and open it.

7. On the first line of the SQL script, replace SMS_??? with the proper database name (e.g., SMS_LAB).

8. Press F5 to execute the SQL script.

9. Repeat steps 6 through 8 using `C:\temp\SMS_CRP1\Extract\ConversionRulesP1.sql`.

10. Back in the SMS Administrator console, navigate to the software inventory Client Agent Settings, view properties, and select the Inventory Names tab to view the manufacturer and product information that was just imported.

Discussion

The purpose of this recipe is the same as Recipe 10-12, "Consolidating Manufacturer or Product Names." This is an example of how to group manufacturer and product information to simplify web reporting results for software inventory. For example, one of the modifications from the manufacturer script is to classify the manufacturer names "Sony," "Sony Corporation," and "Sony Electronics" as "Sony."

Caution The scripts in this recipe contain a lot of information—they consolidate a wide range of products. In fact, they may consolidate more than you prefer. Be sure to run these scripts in a test lab before implementing them in production.

Observe the SQL view named `v_SoftwareConversionRules` or the WMI class `SMS_SoftwareConversionRules` to view all conversion rules in your site. More than 1,000 rules are imported when you execute the scripts in this recipe.

See Also

- Recipe 10-12, "Consolidating Manufacturer or Product Names," describes how to manually insert SMS software inventory manufacturer and product conversion rules.

- Visit the Infinity web site (`http://www.infinity.cz/sms`), especially if you can read Czech, for a tool that helps with consolidation. (Note that you can click the British flag to view the site in English, but the SMS information disappears when you do this. Luckily for English speakers, the documentation for the SMS Conversion Rules scripts is in English.)

10-14. Preventing Software Inventory on a Single Client or Drive

Problem

You don't want software inventory to collect software information on a specific client or drive.

Solution

1. Create a hidden file, and name it `skpswi.dat`.

2. Copy the file to the root of the drive or drives on the system (or network drives on a file server) that you do not want software inventory to search.

3. Verify that software inventory is not collecting information from these systems or drives.

Discussion

A couple of good reasons why you might not want to inventory a specific drive follow:

Performance: You don't want the software inventory cycle to affect the performance of the system.

False positives: You don't want to inventory files on a network resource (e.g., server share) that is used as an installation source for an application. The software may be stored on the server but not actually installed.

Note Skpswi.dat also applies to file collection rules. SMS automatically excludes the Recycle Bin from inventory on all SMS clients.

See Also

- The Microsoft Knowledge Base article titled "SMS: Turning Off Software Inventory on a Single Client" (http://support.microsoft.com/default.aspx?scid=kb;en-us;255959) provides information on turning off software inventory.

- Chapter 2 of the *SMS 2003 Operations Guide* provides more information about how to properly use the skpswi.dat file.

CHAPTER 11

■ ■ ■

Hardware Inventory

Hardware inventory is the vehicle that retrieves most of the client data in SMS. Like the *Transformers* cartoon characters of the 1980s, it also is quite a bit "more than meets the eye." In addition to data on hardware components, it collects data on programs added and removed (according to data obtained from Add or Remove Programs), patch compliance, the operating system, and just about any other data that you would want to retrieve from an SMS client.

Hardware inventory is critical to the success of any SMS implementation. If anyone suggests that you don't need hardware inventory, you need to say, "Put down the mouse, and step away from the keyboard!" Then, give them a copy of this book, so that they can see the error of their ways.

Hardware inventory is by far the most customizable feature in SMS. It is amazing to see what SMS administrators have configured hardware inventory to retrieve from SMS clients. We'll highlight some of those methods and give you a few examples. Then, let your imagination run wild!

11-1. Enabling Hardware Inventory

Problem

You want to enable hardware inventory.

Solution

1. Open the SMS Administrator console.

2. From the SMS Administrator console, expand Site Database (*<Site Code>*), Site Hierarchy, *<Site Name>*, Site Settings, and Client Agents.

3. Right-click Hardware Inventory Client Agent, and select Properties.

4. Check the box next to "Enable hardware inventory on clients."

5. Click OK to apply the settings.

Discussion

Unless you have thousands of SMS clients deployed without hardware inventory enabled, you should be able to fire it up using the default schedule without any problems. If you happen to have deployed thousands of clients without enabling hardware inventory, you might need to be a little more cautious, as your first inventory cycle will be a full inventory and may drag down your SMS server or your network. You may use a similar strategy to that described in the previous chapter's sidebar titled "Enabling Software Inventory on a Site with Many Clients."

When you enable hardware inventory as described in this recipe, the SMS Inventory Agent will become enabled, and the hardware inventory cycle action will appear on the client and report the hardware inventory using the schedule you defined.

Caution The initial full hardware inventory will be approximately 88KB per client if using the default SMS_DEF.MOF file. Subsequent delta inventories are approximately 7KB per client.

As stated previously, if you have a large SMS site, use caution when enabling hardware inventory. Using the default SMS_DEF.MOF file, with no Management Information Format (MIF) files to retrieve, a full hardware inventory will occur on each client according to the schedule specified. The initial full inventory will be approximately 88KB per client. Subsequent delta inventories are approximately 7KB per client. Multiply this by the total number of systems that report to one SMS site, and you'll get an idea of the amount of data transferred for hardware inventory.

The hardware inventory cycle on the Advanced Client can be initiated outside of the schedule. We'll cover that in Recipe 16-3, "Initiating the Hardware Inventory Cycle."

See Also

- Recipe 2-20, "Configuring Hardware Inventory," demonstrates how to enable and configure hardware inventory.

- Recipe 11-2, "Modifying the Hardware Inventory Collection Schedule," describes how to modify the hardware inventory schedule.

- Recipe 11-5, "Creating a New Hardware Inventory Rule," describes how to create a new hardware inventory rule.

- Recipe 16-3, "Initiating the Hardware Inventory Cycle," demonstrates how to initiate hardware inventory for both local and remote systems.

- SMS Help within the SMS Administrator console provides additional information for properly configuring hardware inventory.

- The *Scenarios and Procedures for Microsoft SMS 2003: Planning and Deployment* guide provides detailed information about client inventory analysis, including examples for calculating load on an SMS server (http://www.microsoft.com/smsserver/techinfo/deployment).

- The SMS 2003 Capacity Planner tool helps you plan and verify your site configuration (http://www.microsoft.com/smsserver/techinfo/deployment).

- Chapter 2 of the *SMS 2003 Operations Guide* contains additional information about enabling hardware inventory.

- Chapter 9 of the *Microsoft Systems Management Server 2003 Administrator's Companion* by Steven Kaczmarek (Microsoft Press, 2004) also contains additional information about enabling hardware inventory.

HARDWARE VS. SOFTWARE INVENTORY—WHAT'S THE DIFFERENCE?

Asking the difference between hardware and software inventory is a loaded question. On the surface, it seems very basic. Hardware inventory is an inventory of hardware, and software inventory is an inventory of software. The true difference between the two has often confused both the novice and the seasoned SMS administrator.

Software inventory is a *file-based* inventory of a system. When software inventory is executed, it performs a Windows Management Instrumentation (WMI) query to obtain file information for files and file types you specified (e.g., `*.exe`, `dbcfg.dll`, etc.). The *SMS 2003 Operations Guide* suggests that you may think of software inventory as "file inventory." The *Operations Guide* also states, "Software inventory works by scanning the disks on each computer to find files and gather information about files. You can also configure software inventory to collect specific files when it finds them."

When you want to determine if a system has a specific file, and you're interested in file properties (version, creation date, modified date, etc.), software inventory is the way to go. Also, if you are interested in collecting a file, or multiple files, from all systems in your site, file collection (an option in software inventory) is your best friend.

Hardware inventory is a WMI-based inventory of a system. When hardware inventory is executed, it queries WMI for data in specified WMI classes. Some of the classes that are inventoried by default are operating system configuration, installed software (according to Add or Remove Programs), network configuration, BIOS information, patch information, other hardware components (such as hard drives, CD/DVD drives, the motherboard, and audio and video information). This is just a sample of the data collected with hardware inventory. This chapter will open your eyes to the amount of data that can be obtained with hardware inventory.

Notice we mentioned that hardware inventory contains Add or Remove Programs data. This data is actually obtained from the following registry:

`HKEY_LOCAL_MACHINE\SOFTWARE\Microsoft\Windows\CurrentVersion\Uninstall`

And now we come to one of the greatest abilities of hardware inventory: You can extend hardware inventory to capture additional data from the registry or WMI! That's right. If you can store it in the registry or in WMI, you can pick it up in a hardware inventory.

Which inventory, hardware or software, should you use to identify systems with a particular piece of software installed? We're glad you asked. And the answer is . . . it depends. (Yes, that's our favorite answer also.) It depends on what software you're attempting to query. Since software inventory is a file-based inventory, you can use software inventory to obtain all systems that have a specific file. Of course, there are some problems with querying for all systems with a specific file:

- The file name could be a name that is used by several different applications (a favorite among developers is `ui.exe`). This can cause very large discrepancies between actual data and SMS-inventoried data. You can help reduce the chance for error by using the software file path if the software is consistently installed in a specific location.

- File servers that have source files on a drive may be inventoried and would report having the file (or multiple versions and locations of the file). This can also be filtered out based on the software file path if the software is consistently installed in a specific location.

Hardware inventory may provide you with more exact data, provided the information is registered in Add or Remove Programs on the client. We prefer to use hardware inventory data (Add or Remove Programs data) whenever possible, but you will find instances when software is not registered in Add or Remove Programs. For example, the Windows Installer service is not registered there (possibly updates to it will be in Add or Remove Programs but not all versions). The easiest way to obtain Windows Installer version data is to enable software inventory and inventory for `msiexec.exe`, or for `*.exe` to return data for all executables on a system.

Both software and hardware inventory use WMI to query systems for inventory information. Watch the `InventoryAgent.log` file on the Advanced Client while software inventory, file collection, and hardware inventory are executed.

11-2. Modifying the Hardware Inventory Collection Schedule

Problem

You want to modify the collection schedule of hardware inventory.

Solution

1. Open the SMS Administrator console.

2. From the SMS Administrator console, expand Site Database (*<Site Code>*), Site Hierarchy, *<Site Name>*, Site Settings, and Client Agents.

3. Right-click Hardware Inventory Client Agent, and select Properties.

4. On the General tab, select the Simple Schedule radio button if you want to use an interval of hours, days, or weeks as your hardware inventory collection schedule.

5. If you want the collection to happen at specific times (e.g., only Tuesdays and Thursdays), select the Full Schedule radio button, and click the Schedule button to set the specific schedule for the collection.

6. Click OK to apply the settings.

Discussion

The hardware inventory collection schedule is a very real indicator of the responsiveness of your SMS infrastructure. If you need to have your inventory data refreshed every day, then you need to set your collection schedule to correspond to your needs. Also, if you need to limit hardware inventory from running during business hours, you can use the Full Schedule option to specify the times that hardware inventory collection can run. This schedule will put a bit of a strain on your SMS servers when all those inventories are returned at the same time, but if it solves daytime issues, then it may be the right solution for you. Thankfully, SMS 2003 sends delta updates of only the new hardware inventory changes after the first full inventory, which makes the process easier on your systems and network.

▮**Caution** The initial full hardware inventory will be approximately 88KB per client if you're using the default `SMS_DEF.MOF` file. Subsequent delta inventories are approximately 7KB per client.

See Also

- SMS Help within the SMS Administrator console provides additional information for properly configuring hardware inventory.

- The *Scenarios and Procedures for Microsoft SMS 2003: Planning and Deployment* guide provides detailed information about client inventory analysis, including examples for calculating load on an SMS server.

- The SMS 2003 Capacity Planner tool helps you plan and verify your site configuration (`http://www.microsoft.com/smserver/techinfo/deployment`).

- Chapter 2 of the *SMS 2003 Operations Guide* contains additional information about hardware inventory.

- Chapter 9 of the *Microsoft Systems Management Server 2003 Administrator's Companion* by Steven Kaczmarek (Microsoft Press, 2004) also contains additional information about hardware inventory.

11-3. Limiting the MIF File Size in Hardware Inventory

Problem

You want to limit the size of MIF files used for hardware inventory.

Solution

1. Open the SMS Administrator console.

2. From the SMS Administrator console, expand Site Database (*<Site Code>*), Site Hierarchy, *<Site Name>*, Site Settings, and Client Agents.

3. Right-click Hardware Inventory Client Agent, and select Properties.

4. On the bottom of the General tab, change the "Maximum custom MIF file size (kb)" to your desired size.

5. Click OK to apply the settings.

Discussion

You're thinking about collecting MIF files during hardware inventory, but you don't want to send massive MIF files to the SMS server and potentially cause a performance issue or worse. That's no problem. Simply specify the maximum size limit in kilobytes that you want SMS to use. All MIF files that are over that size limit will not be returned with hardware inventory. Keep in mind that this is a *per-MIF* file limit. For example, if you set the maximum MIF file size to 512KB, this limit would prevent a 600KB MIF from being forwarded to SMS. However, this maximum limit will not prevent 82 MIF files of 400KB each from being forwarded to your SMS site.

See Also

- Review the discussion in Recipe 11-4, "Enabling MIF Collection in Hardware Inventory," for risks to consider when using MIF files.

- Chapter 2 of the *SMS 2003 Operations Guide* contains additional information about MIF collection and hardware inventory.

- Chapter 9 of the *Microsoft Systems Management Server 2003 Administrator's Companion* by Steven Kaczmarek (Microsoft Press, 2004) also contains additional information about MIF collection and hardware inventory.

WHAT IS A MIF FILE?

MIF stands for Management Information Format. It is actually a standard for computer management data designed by the Distributed Management Task Force (http://www.dmtf.org). A MIF file is a text file containing information that can be collected by management systems, such as SMS.

In the context of this chapter, a MIF file is used to extend SMS hardware inventory. MIF files can be created by an application or manually. Applications such as Dell OpenManage Client Instrumentation (OMCI) and IBM Director can gather vendor-specific information from hardware and write to MIF files. These MIF files are then obtained by SMS during the next scheduled hardware inventory on the client.

You can also create your own program to write MIF files. For example, you may want to capture spending-code or department information, warranty expiration dates, and peripheral serial numbers (for printers, scanners, etc.). You can use any program that can create a text file (VBScript, Visual Basic, C++, Java, etc.). As long as it's a properly formatted file and is stored in the proper directory, SMS will pick these files up on the next hardware inventory. There are two kinds of MIF files:

- *NOIDMIF.* Think "No ID MIF," meaning that the MIF file has no unique ID. A NOIDMIF file is a MIF file that is associated with the system that the MIF file is located on. For example, when capturing peripheral information, you may want to use a NOIDMIF file, so that the data is associated with the computer (similar to other data obtained during hardware inventory, such as network card, BIOS information, etc.).

- *IDMIF:* Think "ID MIF," meaning that the MIF file has a unique ID. When inventoried, IDMIFs are not associated with the computer they are collected from. The computer is merely a vessel used to get the data into SMS. IDMIFs are appropriate for data that you do not want associated with a computer, such as the network printer down the hall or the company vehicle assigned to the Novell guy (maybe he has to travel a little more than you do to manage his systems). This information is still vital, but it isn't associated with a computer. By creating an IDMIF file, you're able to save this data in SMS.

MIF files for the Advanced Client are typically stored in %windir%\system32\ccm\Inventory under their respective subdirectory. Since IDMIFs are not associated with a particular computer system, you can drop them into \SMS\Inboxes\Inventry.box if you desire.

Review the discussion in Recipe 11-4, "Enabling MIF Collection in Hardware Inventory," for risks to consider when using MIF files. Also see Chapter 3 of the *SMS 2003 Operations Guide* for more information about how to create IDMIFs and NOIDMIFs.

11-4. Enabling MIF Collection in Hardware Inventory

Problem

You want to enable the collection of MIF files during hardware inventory.

Solution

1. Open the SMS Administrator console.

2. From the SMS Administrator console, expand Site Database (*<Site Code>*), Site Hierarchy, *<Site Name>*, Site Settings, and Client Agents.

3. Right-click Hardware Inventory Client Agent, and select Properties.

4. On the MIF Collection tab, check the boxes for the MIF file types that you want to collect for the Legacy Clients and Advanced Clients.

5. Click OK to apply the settings.

Discussion

Deciding whether or not to collect MIFs may take you longer than actually enabling their collection. Read the sidebars in this chapter about MIFs to see if they are something that you plan on using. Make sure to check with vendors of other management products that you use, as they may create MIF files that contain data that is valuable to you.

Be aware that collecting MIFs can be a security risk, since SMS does not check them for errors prior to processing them. This creates a possibility for MIFs to overwrite critical data with incorrect data. However, modifying the SMS_DEF.MOF file does not have the same security risks as collecting MIF files for hardware inventory, since server-side modifications are required and must be executed with the proper permissions, thus eliminating the risk of errant data being processed by SMS.

See Also

- Chapter 5 of the *SMS 2003 Concepts, Planning, and Deployment Guide* for more information about the security risk mentioned in this recipe.

- Chapter 2 of the *SMS 2003 Operations Guide* contains additional information about MIF collection and hardware inventory.

- Chapter 9 of the *Microsoft Systems Management Server 2003 Administrator's Companion* by Steven Kaczmarek (Microsoft Press, 2004) also contains additional information about MIF collection and hardware inventory.

WHAT IS A MOF FILE?

MOF, as far as SMS hardware inventory goes, stands for Managed Object Format. It is also a standard for computer management data designed by the Distributed Management Task Force (http://www.dmtf.org/education/mof). A MOF file is a manifest of management information that is to be collected from WMI. The MOF syntax is derived from the Interface Definition Language (IDL).

Similar to a MIF file, a MOF file is used to extend SMS hardware inventory. Think of MOF files as an upgrade of MIFs. See the sidebar in this chapter titled "Should I Use MOF or MIF?" for a brief comparison.

The primary inventory MOF file (and the only inventory MOF file by default) is SMS_DEF.MOF, which is located in \SMS\inboxes\clifiles.src\hinv on the SMS site. Open this file with a text editor (e.g., Windows Notepad) to get an idea of what an SMS-inventory MOF looks like. Don't worry; we'll describe how to make modifications to SMS_DEF.MOF later in this chapter and provide you with many references to help you learn how to safely manage your SMS_DEF.MOF file. The inventory MOF file uses WMI on the client to obtain information.

You can edit SMS_DEF.MOF to enable or disable inventorying of specific objects. You can also append MOF data to SMS_DEF.MOF to query for information that SMS is not configured to query by default (e.g., virus definitions updates, profile information, etc.). Instead of modifying the SMS_DEF.MOF file, you can also create a new inventory MOF if you prefer.

Note that if you add classes to or remove classes from the SMS_DEF.MOF file, you must recompile it on all systems using the following command line:

Mofcomp.exe SMS_DEF.MOF

When you make a change to SMS_DEF.MOF, a backup copy is stored in \SMS\data\hinvarchive on the SMS site.

There are other types of MOF files in SMS. When exporting a query or web report, the file format is a MOF file. Review Chapters 8 and 9 for more information on queries and web reports.

Chapter 3 of the *SMS 2003 Operations Guide* provides more information about how to modify the SMS_DEF.MOF file.

11-5. Creating a New Hardware Inventory Rule

Problem

You want to customize the SMS_DEF.MOF file to retrieve additional information.

Solution

1. Using a text editor (e.g., Window Notepad), edit the following file on your SMS test lab site: \sms\inboxes\clifiles.src\hinv\sms_def.mof.

2. Locate the desired data to inventory, and ensure the SMS_Report class qualifier for the desired class is set to True.

3. Locate the desired data properties, and ensure the SMS_Report property qualifier for the desired properties is set to True.

4. Save the SMS_DEF.MOF file.

5. Copy the updated SMS_DEF.MOF file to \sms\inboxes\clifiles.src\hinv\sms_def.mof on every primary site in your hierarchy.

Note Each time SMS_DEF.MOF is modified, SMS backs it up to the \SMS\data\hinvarchive folder. See Chapter 2 of the *SMS 2003 Operations Guide* for information about the location of backups.

Discussion

The discussion in this solution walks you through a scenario to enable inventory for boot configuration information. By default, this class is available in the SMS_DEF.MOF but not enabled to report in SMS hardware inventory.

As described in the solution steps, open \sms\inboxes\clifiles.src\hinv\sms_def.mof in your test lab. Now look for the phrase "Boot Configuration", and notice the line immediately above it. It reads SMS_Report(FALSE). This means that no data for this class will be forwarded to SMS. Replace that line with SMS_Report(TRUE), and this class will be ready to report.

A few lines below the words "Boot Configuration", observe the properties listed under class Win32_BootConfiguration. The available properties are BootDirectory, ConfigurationPath, Description, LastDrive, Name, ScratchDirectory, SettingID, and TempDirectory. For each property, notice SMS_Report(FALSE). Since all of the properties are set to False, no data would be inventoried for this class, even though we modified the class to SMS_Report(TRUE). We must also turn on the individual properties that we desire to inventory. The bold text in Example 11-1 demonstrates the modifications required to obtain the BootDirectory, Description, LastDrive, and Name properties from the Win32_BootConfiguration class.

Example 11-1. *Modified Boot Configuration Information from SMS_DEF.MOF*

```
[ SMS_Report      (TRUE),
  SMS_Group_Name ("Boot Configuration"),
  SMS_Class_ID("MICROSOFT|BOOT_CONFIGURATION|1.0") ]

class Win32_BootConfiguration : SMS_Class_Template
{
    [SMS_Report (TRUE)      ]
        string      BootDirectory;
    [SMS_Report (FALSE)     ]
        string      ConfigurationPath;
    [SMS_Report (TRUE)      ]
        string      Description;
    [SMS_Report (TRUE)      ]
        string      LastDrive;
    [SMS_Report (TRUE), key ]
        string      Name;
    [SMS_Report (FALSE)     ]
        string      ScratchDirectory;
    [SMS_Report (FALSE)     ]
        string      SettingID;
    [SMS_Report (FALSE)     ]
        string      TempDirectory;
};
```

As you may expect, if SMS_Report(FALSE) appears for boot configuration (Win32_BootConfiguration), no data will be inventoried for this class via SMS, even if properties within the class are configured to report with SMS_Report(TRUE).

Note If a class is already defined in the SMS_DEF.MOF (such as in our example), there is no need to recompile the SMS_DEF.MOF file on all systems.

In this example, we have simply enabled reporting for specific properties of the Win32_BootConfiguration class. Modifying SMS_DEF.MOF and installing it properly on all primary sites is all that's required.

See Also

- Recipe 11-6, "Collecting Registry Values from the SMS Client," describes how to collect data from the registry for hardware inventory.

* Recipe 11-7, "Collecting WMI Values from the SMS Client," describes how to collect additional WMI data from the client.

- Chapter 2 of the *SMS 2003 Operations Guide* contains additional information about modifying SMS_DEF.MOF.

- Chapter 3 of the *SMS 2003 Operations Guide* contains additional information about extending SMS_DEF.MOF, including a "Best Practices for MOF Extensions" section.

- Chapter 9 of the *Microsoft Systems Management Server 2003 Administrator's Companion* by Steven Kaczmarek (Microsoft Press, 2004) also contains additional information about modifying SMS_DEF.MOF.

SHOULD I USE MOF OR MIF?

As the SMS_DEF.MOF file is the basis for hardware inventory, it's not actually a question of whether you will use it, but whether or not to extend it. Since MOF extensions are a newer standard than MIF extensions, consider primarily using MOF extensions. A brief comparison of MOF and MIF follows.

The benefits of using MOF extensions are as follows:

- MOF is a newer technology and a newer standard than MIF.

- MOF files give you more control at the server level than MIF files. The server determines what data is forwarded to the SMS site with MOF files, so MOF files work better with dynamic data. For example, if you're inventorying a specific registry value with a MOF file, the updated value will be forwarded when hardware inventory runs.

- MOF files work just as well with dynamic data as they do with static data.

- With MOFs, it's easier to enumerate information in WMI and the registry.

- When you modify SMS_DEF.MOF on your SMS site so that it no longer inventories custom information, inventory will no longer forward that information.

The following are disadvantages to using MOF extensions:

- Using MOF extensions requires that you edit the SMS_DEF.MOF or manage a new MOF file.

- If you want to capture specific data on 20 systems, you can do this if that data exists *only* on those systems or if you compile the updated SMS_DEF.MOF file on only the systems of interest, which breaks the standards you want to maintain.

- Some data (such as custom data for Dell or IBM hardware) may be immediately available in a MIF file. You may have to do a bit of investigating to determine how to properly edit the SMS_DEF.MOF file to obtain the same information.

- You cannot create new architectures (as with IDMIFs). You can, however, create custom data discovery records (DDRs) to get this data into the SMS database.

MIF files offer the following advantages:

- If you want to capture specific data on a subset of systems, you can install the MIF file (and modify it) on each system desired, with no requirement to install it on all systems. Some data (such as custom data for Dell or IBM hardware) may automatically save MIF files to the proper location, allowing SMS to immediately pick up the additional information.

- You can create new architectures (using IDMIFs) to add data that is not associated with a specific system.

MIF files have disadvantages as well:

- MIF is an older technology and an older standard than MOF.

- MIF files give you less control at the server level. If your configuration allows inventory of MIF files, a malicious user could place a large number of MIF files on a system (or multiple systems), which may cause extra overhead on your SMS site. It may also cause inaccurate data to be stored in your SMS site. While this scenario is far-fetched, keep in mind that it is possible. Be aware that collecting MIFs can be a security risk.

- Custom data requires you to create the MIF by hand or programmatically. Saving a properly formatted MIF to a system can sometimes be a challenge.

- MIF files don't handle dynamic data as well as MOF files. Whatever application was used to create the MIF file will need to be rerun frequently on dynamic data, to ensure SMS is picking up accurate data.

- SMS will continue to query the information until every MIF file that has the information is removed from every system (or you could disable MIF inventory). With MIFs, the client is more in control than the server.

As you can see, there are many reasons for and against using either extension in hardware inventory. As a rule of thumb, we suggest using the MOF method as much as possible.

Use caution with either method; removing unwanted data from SMS can be painful and challenging. Before collecting additional information using MOF or MIF, test, test, and retest in your lab to ensure the data's accuracy.

11-6. Collecting Registry Values from the SMS Client

Problem

You want to capture registry values and include them in hardware inventory.

Solution

1. In your test lab, copy \sms\inboxes\clifiles.src\hinv\sms_def.mof to a workstation in the test lab.

2. Edit the SMS_DEF.MOF file using Windows Notepad, and append the information in Example 11-2 to the end of the SMS_DEF.MOF file.

Example 11-2. *Microsoft Data Access Components*

```
#pragma namespace("\\\\.\\root\\cimv2")
#pragma deleteclass("MDACVer", NOFAIL)


//Class info
[DYNPROPS]
class MDACVer
{
[key] string    KeyName="";
    string    FullInstallVer;
    string    Version;
};


// Instance info
[DYNPROPS]
instance of MDACVer
```

```
{
KeyName="MDAC Version";
[PropertyContext
("local|HKEY_LOCAL_MACHINE\\SOFTWARE\\Microsoft\\➡
DataAccess|FullInstallVer"),Dynamic, ➡
Provider("RegPropProv")] FullInstallVer;
[PropertyContext
("local|HKEY_LOCAL_MACHINE\\SOFTWARE\\Microsoft\\➡
DataAccess|version"),Dynamic, ➡
Provider("RegPropProv")] Version;
};


//Reporting Info
#pragma namespace("\\\\.\\root\\cimv2\\SMS")
    #pragma deleteclass("MDACVer", NOFAIL)
    [SMS_Report(TRUE), SMS_Group_Name("MDAC Version"), SMS_Class_ID("MDACVer")]
class MDACVer : SMS_Class_Template
{
[SMS_Report(TRUE),key]    string    KeyName;
[SMS_Report(TRUE) ]    string    FullInstallVer;
[SMS_Report(TRUE) ]    string    Version;
};
```

3. On the test workstation, compile SMS_DEF.MOF. The output should appear as follows:

```
C:\>mofcomp sms_def.mof
Microsoft (R) 32-bit MOF Compiler Version 5.1.2600.2180
Copyright (c) Microsoft Corp. 1997-2001. All rights reserved.
Parsing MOF file: sms_def.mof
MOF file has been successfully parsed
Storing data in the repository...
Done!
```

4. If your output appears similar to the output in step 3, your updated MOF was compiled successfully and doesn't appear to contain syntax errors. If errors were reported, go back to step 1, and try to figure out what went wrong.

5. Once you have a successful compile on your workstation, copy the updated SMS_DEF.MOF file to \sms\inboxes\clifiles.src\hinv\sms_def.mof on your test SMS server. Watch the \sms\logs\Dataldr.log file to see when the SMS server picks up this change and recompiles on the server. It should automatically recompile within ten minutes.

Discussion

Here is a brief overview of the data in Example 11-2. First, we declare the namespace that this example applies to:

```
#pragma namespace("\\\\.\\root\\cimv2")
```

Next, we delete the class. We use NOFAIL, so that the MOF compiler will continue even if the class doesn't already exist:

```
#pragma deleteclass("MDACVer", NOFAIL)
```

We then define the class with three strings (KeyName, FullInstallVer, and Version):

```
[DYNPROPS]
class MDACVer
{
[key] string    KeyName="";
    string    FullInstallVer;
    string    Version;
};
```

Next, we declare the instance information. As you can see, KeyName will always equal MDAC Version. FullInstallVer is obtained by querying the registry value FullInstallVer located at HKEY_LOCAL_MACHINE\SOFTWARE\Microsoft\DataAccess. Version is obtained by querying the registry value Version located at HKEY_LOCAL_MACHINE\SOFTWARE\Microsoft\DataAccess.

```
[DYNPROPS]
instance of MDACVer
{
KeyName="MDAC Version";
[PropertyContext
("local|HKEY_LOCAL_MACHINE\\SOFTWARE\\Microsoft\\➡
DataAccess|FullInstallVer"),Dynamic, ➡
Provider("RegPropProv")] FullInstallVer;
[PropertyContext
("local|HKEY_LOCAL_MACHINE\\SOFTWARE\\Microsoft\\➡
DataAccess|version"),Dynamic, ➡
Provider("RegPropProv")] Version;
};
```

The last section is the reporting section. Notice that SMS_Report(TRUE) appears for the class and all properties. The group name (SMS_Group_Name) is MDAC Version—this is the name you will look for inside Resource Explorer.

```
#pragma namespace("\\\\.\\root\\cimv2\\SMS")
    #pragma deleteclass("MDACVer", NOFAIL)
    [SMS_Report(TRUE), SMS_Group_Name("MDAC Version"), SMS_Class_ID("MDACVer")]
class MDACVer : SMS_Class_Template
{
[SMS_Report(TRUE),key]    string   KeyName;
[SMS_Report(TRUE) ]    string   FullInstallVer;
[SMS_Report(TRUE) ]    string   Version;
```

There are three types of modifications that you can make to a MOF file, and they each require the performance of different actions:

- If you are changing an existing class in your SMS_DEF.MOF file, you do not have to recompile the MOF file on the SMS client, but you still have to copy the updated file to the SMS site server.

- If you are adding a class that is supported by an existing provider, you must distribute and recompile the MOF file on the SMS client in addition to copying the updated file to the SMS site server.

- If you are adding a class that is not supported by an existing provider, you must install the new provider, distribute and recompile the MOF file, and copy the updated file to the SMS site server.

See Also

- Recipe 11-7, "Collecting WMI Values from the SMS Client," describes how to inventory data located in WMI on the client.

- The Microsoft Knowledge Base article titled "Systems Management Server 2003 Clients May Not Report New Hardware Inventory Data After You Modify or Extend the Sms_def.mof File" provides detailed information about recompiling the MOF (http://support.microsoft.com/?kbid=840679).

- Review the sidebar in this chapter titled "Registry Instance Provider and Registry Property Provider—What's the Difference?" to learn about the registry property provider (which was used in this recipe) and the registry instance provider.

- SMS Expert's *MOF Editing Guide* provides detailed information about editing and managing the SMS_DEF.MOF file (http://www.smsexpert.com/mof).

- Chapter 3 of the *SMS 2003 Operations Guide* contains additional information about extending the SMS_DEF.MOF, including a "Best Practices for MOF Extensions" section.

REGISTRY INSTANCE PROVIDER AND REGISTRY PROPERTY PROVIDER—WHAT'S THE DIFFERENCE?

Both the registry instance provider and the registry property provider enable SMS hardware inventory to retrieve data from the system registry. The provider you need depends on the type of data you are retrieving.

The *registry property provider* is used to retrieve values from a single registry location. For example, to obtain the PhysicalHostName value for a virtual PC, you would use the registry property provider to query HKEY_LOCAL_MACHINE\Software\Microsoft\Virtual Machine\Guest\Parameters for the name value of PhysicalHostName. In your test lab, edit \sms\inboxes\clifiles.src\hinv\sms_def.mof using Windows Notepad. Search for PhysicalHostName to see the MOF information related to querying this value.

The *registry instance provider* is used when the data you want is contained in several subkeys in a registry location. For example, say you want to obtain all information located in Add or Remove Programs. In your test lab, launch the registry editor (e.g., regedit.exe), and navigate to HKEY_LOCAL_MACHINE\SOFTWARE\Microsoft\Windows\CurrentVersion\Uninstall. Notice there are several subkeys to the Uninstall key. Some are global unique identifiers (GUIDs), and some have real names (e.g., NetMeeting, OutlookExpress, QuickTime, etc.). As you click each key, you may begin to notice that most of the keys have similar name values within them (e.g., DisplayName, UninstallString, etc.).

If we wanted to query for all information in Add or Remove Programs, we would need to know each key name to query, or be able to enumerate all subkeys under the . . . \Uninstall key. Knowing all the key names in advance would be a challenge. Fortunately, we can use the registry instance provider to enumerate all registry keys under the . . . \Uninstall key and report the desired information for known named values under each key. Once again, in your test lab, edit \sms\inboxes\clifiles.src\hinv\sms_def.mof using Windows Notepad. Search for "Add/Remove" to see the MOF information related to these values (i.e., DisplayName, InstallDate, Publisher, and DisplayVersion).

For more information, see the WMI SDK and the *SMS 2003 Operations Guide*.

11-7. Collecting WMI Values from the SMS Client

Problem

You want to capture WMI values and include them in hardware inventory.

Solution

1. Append the code from Example 11-3 to your SMS_DEF.MOF file, and save the result in \sms\inboxes\clifiles.src\hinv\sms_def.mof.

Example 11-3. *Win32_ServerConnection into SMS Hardware Inventory*

```
[ SMS_Report      (TRUE),
  SMS_Group_Name ("Server Connection"),
  SMS_Class_ID   ("MICROSOFT|Server_Connection|1.0"),
```

```
Namespace("\\\\\\\\.\\\\root\\\\cimv2") ]

class Win32_ServerConnection : SMS_Class_Template
{
    [SMS_Report (TRUE), key]    string ComputerName;
    [SMS_Report (TRUE)]         string ShareName;
    [SMS_Report (TRUE)]         string UserName;
    [SMS_Report (TRUE)]         uint32 ActiveTime;
    [SMS_Report (TRUE)]         uint32 NumberOfFiles;
    [SMS_Report (TRUE)]         uint32 NumberOfUsers;
};
```

   2. Recompile the MOF file on each SMS 2003 Advanced Client using `mofcomp sms_def.mof`.

Discussion

Example 11-3 demonstrates how to add existing WMI data to SMS hardware inventory. Simply create a reporting class and append it to your `SMS_DEF.MOF` file on all primary servers. There is no need to recompile the updated `SMS_DEF.MOF` on all clients, as the class `Win32_ServerConnection` already exists on the (XP and newer) client.

See Also

- Table 11-1 in Recipe 11-6, "Collecting Registry Values from the SMS Client," describes scenarios for when `SMS_DEF.MOF` is required to be recompiled on client systems.

- Recipe 11-6, "Collecting Registry Values from the SMS Client," describes how to inventory data located in the registry on the client.

- Review the sidebar in this chapter titled "Registry Instance Provider and Registry Property Provider—What's the Difference?" for more information on these two providers.

- SMS Expert's *MOF Editing Guide* provides detailed information about editing and managing the `SMS_DEF.MOF` file (`http://www.smsexpert.com/mof`).

- Chapter 3 of the *SMS 2003 Operations Guide* contains additional information about extending `SMS_DEF.MOF`, including a "Best Practices for MOF Extensions" section.

11-8. Collecting Logon Auditing Information

Problem

You want to collect audit information about who is logging on to your SMS clients.

Solution

   1. Download Steve Bobosky's User Security Logon auditing tool from `http://www.systemcentertools.com`.

   2. Unzip the files to your favorite location.

   3. Enable "Audit logon events" in Group Policy for all SMS clients.

   4. Create a package, program, and advertisement for the application that will be deployed to your SMS clients. A package definition file is available in the download to simplify this.

   5. Modify the `SMS_DEF.MOF` file with the changes included in `userlogoninfo.mof`.

6. Deploy the updated SMS_DEF.MOF file to all primary SMS sites, and recompile it on all Advanced Clients.

7. Wait for hardware inventory to return the logon data from the SMS client.

8. Import the custom web reports.

Discussion

SMS automatically retrieves user data with hardware inventory, but it isn't audit data. The user associated with the SMS client is whoever is logged on when the hardware inventory cycle runs, which creates a problem. This data is only accurate if the "real" user is logged on when the hardware inventory cycle runs.

To overcome that issue and allow for some user auditing, Steve Bobosky created the User Security Logon auditing tool. With this tool, you can leverage the hardware inventory cycle of SMS to retrieve logon audit data to gain a more realistic picture of who is using which PCs at any given time.

Steve Bobosky has been administering SMS for many years, and his experience shines through in the design of this tool. He has made it very easy to implement and manage. The tool has a /kick switch that will initiate a hardware inventory after it has completed. It also contains the /groupson switch to allow for collection of global groups that the user is a member of.

To understand what exactly we are trying to accomplish with this tool, let's look at the process that takes place. From a functional standpoint, you are deploying an executable that will collect and store logon audit information in WMI on every SMS client, which is retrieved by hardware inventory and stored in the SMS database for querying or reporting with web reports.

Let's look at the SMS_DEF.MOF file additions in Example 11-4, so we can understand what data is being retrieved. The User Security Logon auditing tool creates a class in WMI called UserLogonInfo and uses data from the 528 logon audit events to populate the eight data points that will be returned with hardware inventory.

Example 11-4. *userlogoninfo.mof*

```
/----------------------------------------
// UserLogonInfo - sbobosky@centerlogic.com
//----------------------------------------

#pragma namespace("\\\\.\\root\\cimv2\\sms")

[SMS_Report(TRUE),
SMS_Group_Name("User Logon Info"),
SMS_Class_ID("MCS|UserLogonInfo|1.0")]

class UserLogonInfo : SMS_Class_Template
{
    [SMS_Report(TRUE), Key]
    string FullUserName;

    [SMS_Report(TRUE)]
    string UserName;

    [SMS_Report(TRUE)]
    string UserDomain;

    [SMS_Report(TRUE)]
    string UserGroups[];
```

```
[SMS_Report(TRUE)]
sint32 LogonCount;

[SMS_Report(TRUE)]
sint32 UserRank;

[SMS_Report(TRUE)]
datetime LastUpdated;

[SMS_Report(TRUE)]
datetime MostRecentEventDate;
};
```

See Also

- Recipe 4-16, "Creating a Package from a Package Definition File," demonstrates how to import a package definition file (.pdf).

- Recipe 5-1, "Creating a Program," demonstrates how to create a program.

- Recipe 6-1, "Creating an Advertisement," demonstrates how to create an advertisement.

- Recipe 8-7, "Importing a Report," shows how to import a web report into your SMS environment.

- Recipe 11-5, "Creating a New Hardware Inventory Rule," provides information about modifying and testing modifications to the SMS_DEF.MOF file.

- Recipe 11-15, "Implementing a Customized SMS_DEF.MOF File," shows how to deploy SMS_DEF.MOF updates.

- Recipe 16-3, "Initiating the Hardware Inventory Cycle," demonstrates how to initiate hardware inventory for both local and remote systems.

- SMS Expert's *MOF Editing Guide* provides detailed information about editing and managing the SMS_DEF.MOF file (http://www.smsexpert.com/mof).

- Chapter 3 of the *SMS 2003 Operations Guide* contains additional information about extending the SMS_DEF.MOF, including a "Best Practices for MOF Extensions" section.

- Download the User Security Logon audit tool here: http://www.systemcentertools.com.

11-9. Collecting Local Administrator Group Membership Information

Problem

You want to collect the membership of the local administrator's group through hardware inventory.

Solution

1. Download the file MIFShift-LocalAdmin.zip from http://www.smsexpert.com/mof/scripts.asp.

2. Extract the .zip file to your favorite location. It will extract the MIFShift-LocalAdmin.vb_ file.

3. Rename the file MIFShift-LocalAdmin.vbs.

4. Create a package that includes the MIFShift-LocalAdmin.vbs file as a source file.

5. Create a program that uses the following command line:

    cscript.exe MIFShift-LocalAdmin.vbs

6. Advertise the program to your SMS clients.

7. Wait for hardware inventory to retrieve the MIF and populate the SMS database with the data contained in the MIF file (provided you have enabled MIF file collection).

8. Create appropriate reports or queries to leverage the new local-administrator data returned from your SMS clients.

Discussion

SMS Expert has several great tools for extending hardware inventory. In this recipe, we use the MIFShift script that creates a NOIDMIF, which is retrieved by hardware inventory. SMS Expert also has a DataShift script, which does nearly the same thing, except that it creates a class in WMI and populates it with data. Editing your SMS_DEF.MOF file to include the new class created by the DataShift script can retrieve that data.

SMS Expert has several MIFShift and DataShift scripts for various purposes, available in both MIF and MOF format. In this recipe, we use their MIFShift script for local administrators. See Example 11-5 for details.

The MIFShift script needs to be executed on the local SMS client, so that it can create the local MIF file. The easiest way to accomplish that is to have SMS deliver and execute the script. When the script is run, it will create the MIF file with the appropriate data included, so that the SMS database can be updated with the information. At the next hardware inventory cycle, the MIF will be collected and returned to the SMS site server for processing, and the data will be entered into the database. Once the data is in the database, it is formatted exactly the same way as any other SMS data, so it can be utilized by queries, collections, web reports, and so forth.

Example 11-5 displays the code required for MIFShift-LocalAdmins.vbs from SMS Expert.

Example 11-5. *MIFShift-LocalAdmin.vbs from SMS Expert*

```
option explicit
On Error Resume Next

'Constants for file I/O
CONST ForReading = 1, ForWriting = 2, ForAppending = 8

'Constants for WbemCIMTypes
Dim wbemCimtypeSint16
Dim wbemCimtypeSint32
Dim wbemCimtypeReal32
Dim wbemCimtypeReal64
Dim wbemCimtypeString
Dim wbemCimtypeBoolean
Dim wbemCimtypeObject
Dim wbemCimtypeSint8
Dim wbemCimtypeUint8
Dim wbemCimtypeUint16
Dim wbemCimtypeUint32
Dim wbemCimtypeSint64
Dim wbemCimtypeUint64
Dim wbemCimtypeDateTime
Dim wbemCimtypeReference
Dim wbemCimtypeChar16

wbemCimtypeSint16 = 2
wbemCimtypeSint32 = 3
wbemCimtypeReal32 = 4
```

```
wbemCimtypeReal64 = 5
wbemCimtypeString = 8
wbemCimtypeBoolean = 11
wbemCimtypeObject = 13
wbemCimtypeSint8 = 16
wbemCimtypeUint8 = 17
wbemCimtypeUint16 = 18
wbemCimtypeUint32 = 19
wbemCimtypeSint64 = 20
wbemCimtypeUint64 = 21
wbemCimtypeDateTime = 101
wbemCimtypeReference = 102
wbemCimtypeChar16 = 103

'Declare variables
Dim strTempDir, strWinDir, strComputer
Dim strOS, strWinVer
Dim StdOut, objWshShell, objFileSys, objRegistry
Dim strPrinterKeyPath, strServerKeyPath
Dim arrPrinters, Printer
Dim arrServers, Server
Dim strNoIDMifDir, strMifFile, objMifFile
Dim intRetVal, intErr, intID
Dim ClassID

ClassID = "Microsoft|SMXLocalAdminsMIF|1.0"

'Create some standard object references.
Set StdOut = WScript.StdOut
Set objWshShell = CreateObject("WScript.Shell")
Set objFileSys = CreateObject("Scripting.FileSystemObject")

strTempDir = objWshShell.ExpandEnvironmentStrings("%Temp%")
strWinDir = objWshShell.ExpandEnvironmentStrings("%WinDir%")

'This is the name of the .mif file that is created.
strMifFile = "\LocalAdmins.mif"

If objFileSys.FileExists(strTempDir & strMifFile) Then _
    objFileSys.DeleteFile(strTempDir & strMifFile)

'Create object reference to the .mif file. (This is a new file)
If NOT blnOpenFile(strTempDir & strMifFile, objMifFile, ForAppending) Then
    intErr = 1
    Call Cleanup
End If

objMifFile.Writeline "Start Component"
objMifFile.Writeline "  Name = " & Chr(34) & "WORKSTATION" & Chr(34)

Dim oLocation, oServices, oInstances, oObject, oDataObject, oNewObject, _
    oRptObject, sField
Set oLocation = CreateObject("WbemScripting.SWbemLocator")
Set oServices = oLocation.ConnectServer(, "root\cimv2")
'Add Instances to data class
Set oServices = oLocation.ConnectServer(, "root\cimv2")
```

```
Dim sComputerName
Dim sQuery
dim iColon

Set oInstances = oServices.ExecQuery("SELECT * FROM Win32_ComputerSystem")

FOR EACH oObject in oInstances
    sComputerName = oObject.Name
NEXT

sQuery = "select partcomponent from " & _
    "win32_groupuser where groupcomponent = ""\\\\" & _
    sComputerName & "\\root\\cimv2:Win32_Group.Domain=\""" & _
    sComputerName & "\"",Name=\""Administrators\"""""
Set oInstances = oServices.ExecQuery(sQuery)

intID = 1
FOR EACH oObject in oInstances
    objMifFile.Writeline "  Start Group"
    objMifFile.Writeline "     Name = " & Chr(34) & "Local Admins" & Chr(34)
    objMifFile.Writeline "     ID = " & intID
    objMifFile.Writeline "     Class = " & Chr(34) & ClassID & Chr(34)

    objMifFile.Writeline "      Start Attribute"
    objMifFile.Writeline "       Name = " & Chr(34) & "Account" & Chr(34)
    objMifFile.Writeline "       ID = 1"
    objMifFile.Writeline "       ACCESS = READ-ONLY"
    objMifFile.Writeline "       Storage = Specific"
    objMifFile.Writeline "       Type = String(100)"
    sField = oObject.PartComponent
    sfield = mid(sfield, instr(1, sfield, chr(58)) + 1)
    If Instr(1, sfield, Chr(92), 1) > 0 Then sfield = _
        Replace(sfield, Chr(92), Chr(92) & Chr(92), 1, -1, 1)
    If Instr(1, sfield, Chr(34), 1) > 0 Then sfield = _
        Replace(sfield, Chr(34), Chr(39), 1, -1, 1)
    objMifFile.Writeline "       Value = " & Chr(34) & sfield & Chr(34)
    objMifFile.Writeline "      End Attribute"

    objMifFile.Writeline "  End Group"

    intID = intID + 1

NEXT

objMifFile.Writeline "End Component"
objMifFile.Close

strNoIDMifDir = objWshShell.RegRead("HKEY_LOCAL_MACHINE\SOFTWARE\Microsoft\" & _
    "SMS\Client\Configuration\Client Properties\NOIDMIF Directory")

If intErr <> 1 Then
    If objFileSys.FileExists(strNoIDMifDir & strMifFile) Then _
        objFileSys.DeleteFile(strNoIDMifDir & strMifFile)

    If objFileSys.FileExists(strTempDir & strMifFile) Then _
        objFileSys.MoveFile strTempDir & strMifFile, _
        strNoIDMifDir & strMifFile
End If
```

```
Call Cleanup


'Open File Function
Private Function blnOpenFile(ByValstrFilename, ByRef objMifFile, ByVal intMode)

    blnOpenFile = False

    'Verify that a file name was passed

    If IsEmpty(strFilename) OR strFileName = "" Then
      blnOpenFile = False
      Exit Function
    End If

    'Verify objFileSys exists
    If Not IsObject(objFileSys) Then _
      Set objFileSys = CreateObject("Scripting.FileSystemObject")
    Err.Clear

    'Open the file for I/O
    Set objMifFile = objFileSys.OpenTextFile(strFileName, intMode, True)
    'Error check
    If blnErrorOccurred(" creating object reference to " & strFileName) Then
        blnOpenFile = False
        intErr = 1
        Exit Function
    End If

    blnOpenFile = True

End Function

'Error Occurred Function
Private Function blnErrorOccurred (strIn)

    If Err <> 0 Then

        'Set intermediate variables

        lngMyErr = Err.Number
        strMyErrDesc = Err.Description
        Call WriteLine( " ")
        Call WriteLine( "Error 0x" & CStr(Hex(lngMyErr)) &  " occurred " & strIn)
        Call WriteLine( " ")

        'See if it's a WBEM error
        If blnWBEM_ErrorCheck(lngMyErr) Then
            Call WriteLine( "WBEM error description: " & vbCrLf & strWBEMErrDesc)
            Call WriteLine( " ")
        Else
            If Err.Description <> "" Then _
                Call WriteLine( "Error description: " & vbCrLf & Err.Description)
                Call WriteLine( " ")
        End If
        Err.Clear
        blnErrorOccurred = True
        intErr = 1
```

```
    Else
        blnErrorOccurred = False
    End If

End Function

'Cleanup Sub
Sub Cleanup

    Set StdOut = Nothing
    Set objWshShell = Nothing
    Set objFileSys = Nothing
    Set objMifFile = Nothing
    Set objRegistry = Nothing

    Wscript.Quit(intErr)

End Sub
```

Example 11-5 queries the `Win32_GroupUser` class to identify all local administrators. Be aware of permission requirements for this script. When the advertisement runs for this program on the client, it must have Create and Delete permissions for the `%windir%\system32\ccm\inventory\noidmifs` directory.

See Also

- Recipe 11-5, "Creating a New Hardware Inventory Rule," contains information about modifying and testing modifications to the `SMS_DEF.MOF` file.

- Recipe 11-10, "Collecting Share Information," shows how to collect system share information.

- Recipe 11-11, "Collecting Printer Information," shows how to collect printer information.

- Recipe 11-15, "Implementing a Customized SMS_DEF.MOF File," contains information about deploying `SMS_DEF.MOF` updates.

- SMS Expert's *MOF Editing Guide* provides detailed information about editing and managing the `SMS_DEF.MOF` file (`http://www.smsexpert.com/mof`).

- Chapter 3 of the *SMS 2003 Operations Guide* contains additional information about extending the `SMS_DEF.MOF` file, including a "Best Practices for MOF Extensions" section.

11-10. Collecting Share Information

Problem

You want to inventory information on the shares of a system.

Solution

1. Download the `MIFShift-Shares.zip` file from `http://www.smsexpert.com/mof/scripts.asp`.

2. Extract the `.zip` file to your favorite location. It will extract the `MIFShift-Shares.vb_` file.

3. Rename the file to `MIFShift-Shares.vbs`.

4. Create a package that includes the `MIFShift-Shares.vbs` file as a source file.

5. Create a program that uses the following command line:

   ```
   cscript.exe MIFShift-Shares.vbs
   ```

6. Advertise the program to your SMS clients.

7. Wait for hardware inventory to retrieve the MIF file and populate the SMS database with the data contained in the MIF file.

8. Create appropriate reports or queries to leverage the new local administrator data returned from your SMS clients.

Discussion

This process is nearly the same as the one in Recipe 11-9, "Collecting Local Administrator Group Membership Information," but this time, it will collect file share information instead of data on members of the local administrator's security group. Example 11-6 displays the MIFShift-Shares.vbs script, which you could use as a model to create a script to generate a MIF that contains any type of data that you might need in your enterprise.

Example 11-6 displays the code required for MIFShift-Shares.vbs from SMS Expert.

Example 11-6. *MIFShift-Shares.vbs from SMS Expert*

```
option explicit
On Error Resume Next

'Constants for file I/O
CONST ForReading = 1, ForWriting = 2, ForAppending = 8

'Constants for WbemCIMTypes
Dim wbemCimtypeSint16
Dim wbemCimtypeSint32
Dim wbemCimtypeReal32
Dim wbemCimtypeReal64
Dim wbemCimtypeString
Dim wbemCimtypeBoolean
Dim wbemCimtypeObject
Dim wbemCimtypeSint8
Dim wbemCimtypeUint8
Dim wbemCimtypeUint16
Dim wbemCimtypeUint32
Dim wbemCimtypeSint64
Dim wbemCimtypeUint64
Dim wbemCimtypeDateTime
Dim wbemCimtypeReference
Dim wbemCimtypeChar16

wbemCimtypeSint16 = 2
wbemCimtypeSint32 = 3
wbemCimtypeReal32 = 4
wbemCimtypeReal64 = 5
wbemCimtypeString = 8
wbemCimtypeBoolean = 11
wbemCimtypeObject = 13
wbemCimtypeSint8 = 16
wbemCimtypeUint8 = 17
wbemCimtypeUint16 = 18
wbemCimtypeUint32 = 19
wbemCimtypeSint64 = 20
wbemCimtypeUint64 = 21
wbemCimtypeDateTime = 101
```

```
wbemCimtypeReference = 102
wbemCimtypeChar16 = 103

'Declare variables
Dim strTempDir, strWinDir, strComputer
Dim strOS, strWinVer
Dim StdOut, objWshShell, objFileSys, objRegistry
Dim strPrinterKeyPath, strServerKeyPath
Dim arrPrinters, Printer
Dim arrServers, Server
Dim strNoIDMifDir, strMifFile, objMifFile
Dim intRetVal, intErr, intID
Dim ClassID

ClassID = "Microsoft|SMXShareMIF|1.0"

'Create some standard object references.
Set StdOut = WScript.StdOut
Set objWshShell = CreateObject("WScript.Shell")
Set objFileSys = CreateObject("Scripting.FileSystemObject")

strTempDir = objWshShell.ExpandEnvironmentStrings("%Temp%")
strWinDir = objWshShell.ExpandEnvironmentStrings("%WinDir%")

'This is the name of the .mif file that is created.
strMifFile = "\Shares.mif"

If objFileSys.FileExists(strTempDir & strMifFile) Then _
    objFileSys.DeleteFile(strTempDir & strMifFile)

'Create object reference to the .mif file. (This is a new file)
If NOT blnOpenFile(strTempDir & strMifFile, objMifFile, ForAppending) Then
    intErr = 1
    Call Cleanup
End If

objMifFile.Writeline "Start Component"
objMifFile.Writeline "  Name = " & Chr(34) & "WORKSTATION" & Chr(34)

Dim oLocation, oServices, oInstances, oObject, oDataObject, _
    oNewObject, oRptObject, sField
Set oLocation = CreateObject("WbemScripting.SWbemLocator")
Set oServices = oLocation.ConnectServer(, "root\cimv2")
Set oInstances = oServices.InstancesOf("win32_Share")

intID = 1
FOR EACH oObject in oInstances
    objMifFile.Writeline "  Start Group"
    objMifFile.Writeline "    Name = " & Chr(34) & "Shares" & Chr(34)
    objMifFile.Writeline "    ID = " & intID
    objMifFile.Writeline "    Class = " & Chr(34) & ClassID & Chr(34)

    objMifFile.Writeline "    Start Attribute"
    objMifFile.Writeline "      Name = " & Chr(34) & "Allow Maximum" & Chr(34)
    objMifFile.Writeline "      ID = 1"
    objMifFile.Writeline "      ACCESS = READ-ONLY"
    objMifFile.Writeline "      Storage = Specific"
```

```
objMifFile.Writeline "      Type = String(100)"
sField = oObject.AllowMaximum
If Instr(1, sfield, Chr(92), 1) > 0 Then sfield = _
    Replace(sfield, Chr(92), Chr(92) & Chr(92), 1, -1, 1)
objMifFile.Writeline "      Value = " & Chr(34) & sfield & Chr(34)
objMifFile.Writeline "    End Attribute"

objMifFile.Writeline "    Start Attribute"
objMifFile.Writeline "      Name = " & Chr(34) & "Caption" & Chr(34)
objMifFile.Writeline "      ID = 3"
objMifFile.Writeline "      ACCESS = READ-ONLY"
objMifFile.Writeline "      Storage = Specific"
objMifFile.Writeline "      Type = String(100)"
sField = oObject.caption
If Instr(1, sfield, Chr(92), 1) > 0 Then sfield = _
    Replace(sfield, Chr(92), Chr(92) & Chr(92), 1, -1, 1)
objMifFile.Writeline "      Value = " & Chr(34) & sfield & Chr(34)
objMifFile.Writeline "    End Attribute"

objMifFile.Writeline "    Start Attribute"
objMifFile.Writeline "      Name = " & Chr(34) & "Description" & Chr(34)
objMifFile.Writeline "      ID = 4"
objMifFile.Writeline "      ACCESS = READ-ONLY"
objMifFile.Writeline "      Storage = Specific"
objMifFile.Writeline "      Type = String(100)"
sField = oObject.Description
If Instr(1, sfield, Chr(92), 1) > 0 Then sfield = _
    Replace(sfield, Chr(92), Chr(92) & Chr(92), 1, -1, 1)
objMifFile.Writeline "      Value = " & Chr(34) & sfield & Chr(34)
objMifFile.Writeline "    End Attribute"

objMifFile.Writeline "    Start Attribute"
objMifFile.Writeline "      Name = " & Chr(34) & "Name" & Chr(34)
objMifFile.Writeline "      ID = 5"
objMifFile.Writeline "      ACCESS = READ-ONLY"
objMifFile.Writeline "      Storage = Specific"
objMifFile.Writeline "      Type = String(100)"
sField = oObject.Name
If Instr(1, sfield, Chr(92), 1) > 0 Then sfield = _
    Replace(sfield, Chr(92), Chr(92) & Chr(92), 1, -1, 1)
objMifFile.Writeline "      Value = " & Chr(34) & sfield & Chr(34)
objMifFile.Writeline "    End Attribute"

objMifFile.Writeline "    Start Attribute"
objMifFile.Writeline "      Name = " & Chr(34) & "Path" & Chr(34)
objMifFile.Writeline "      ID = 6"
objMifFile.Writeline "      ACCESS = READ-ONLY"
objMifFile.Writeline "      Storage = Specific"
objMifFile.Writeline "      Type = String(100)"
sField = oObject.Path
If Instr(1, sfield, Chr(92), 1) > 0 Then sfield = _
    Replace(sfield, Chr(92), Chr(92) & Chr(92), 1, -1, 1)
objMifFile.Writeline "      Value = " & Chr(34) & sfield & Chr(34)
objMifFile.Writeline "    End Attribute"
```

```
        objMifFile.Writeline "    Start Attribute"
        objMifFile.Writeline "       Name = " & Chr(34) & "Status" & Chr(34)
        objMifFile.Writeline "       ID = 7"
        objMifFile.Writeline "       ACCESS = READ-ONLY"
        objMifFile.Writeline "       Storage = Specific"
        objMifFile.Writeline "       Type = String(100)"
        sField = oObject.Status
        If Instr(1, sfield, Chr(92), 1) > 0 Then sfield = _
            Replace(sfield, Chr(92), Chr(92) & Chr(92), 1, -1, 1)
        objMifFile.Writeline "       Value = " & Chr(34) & sfield & Chr(34)
        objMifFile.Writeline "    End Attribute"

        objMifFile.Writeline "  End Group"

        intID = intID + 1

NEXT

objMifFile.Writeline "End Component"
objMifFile.Close

strNoIDMifDir = objWshShell.RegRead("HKEY_LOCAL_MACHINE\SOFTWARE\Microsoft\" & _
    "SMS\Client\Configuration\Client Properties\NOIDMIF Directory")

If intErr <> 1 Then
    If objFileSys.FileExists(strNoIDMifDir & strMifFile) Then _
        objFileSys.DeleteFile(strNoIDMifDir & strMifFile)

    If objFileSys.FileExists(strTempDir & strMifFile) Then _
        objFileSys.MoveFile strTempDir & strMifFile, _
        strNoIDMifDir & strMifFile
End If

Call Cleanup


'Open File Function
Private Function blnOpenFile(ByVal strFileName, ByRef objMifFile, ByVal intMode)

    blnOpenFile = False

    'Verify that a file name was passed

    If IsEmpty(strFileName) OR strFileName = "" Then
      blnOpenFile = False
      Exit Function
    End If

    'Verify objFileSys exists
    If Not IsObject(objFileSys) Then _
      Set objFileSys = CreateObject("Scripting.FileSystemObject")
    Err.Clear

    'Open the file for I/O
    Set objMifFile = objFileSys.OpenTextFile(strFileName, intMode, True)
    'Error check
```

```
        If blnErrorOccurred(" creating object reference to " & strFileName) Then
            blnOpenFile = False
            intErr = 1
            Exit Function
        End If

        blnOpenFile = True

End Function

'Error Occurred Function
Private Function blnErrorOccurred (strIn)

    If Err <> 0 Then

        'Set intermediate variables

        lngMyErr = Err.Number
        strMyErrDesc = Err.Description
        Call WriteLine( " ")
        Call WriteLine( "Error 0x" & CStr(Hex(lngMyErr)) &  " occurred " & strIn)
        Call WriteLine( " ")

        'See if it's a WBEM error
        If blnWBEM_ErrorCheck(lngMyErr) Then
            Call WriteLine( "WBEM error description: " & vbCrLf & strWBEMErrDesc)
            Call WriteLine( " ")
        Else
            If Err.Description <> "" Then _
                Call WriteLine( "Error description: " & vbCrLf & Err.Description)
                Call WriteLine( " ")
        End If
        Err.Clear
        blnErrorOccurred = True
        intErr = 1
    Else
        blnErrorOccurred = False
    End If

End Function

'Cleanup Sub
Sub Cleanup

    Set StdOut = Nothing
    Set objWshShell = Nothing
    Set objFileSys = Nothing
    Set objMifFile = Nothing
    Set objRegistry = Nothing

    Wscript.Quit(intErr)

End Sub
```

The script in Example 11-6 enumerates the Win32_Share class and writes to the MIF file. Be aware of permissions requirements for this script. When the advertisement runs for this program on the client, it must have Create and Delete permissions for the %windir%\system32\ccm\inventory\noidmifs directory.

See Also

- Recipe 11-5, "Creating a New Hardware Inventory Rule," provides information about modifying and testing modifications to the SMS_DEF.MOF file.

- Recipe 11-9, "Collecting Local Administrator Group Membership Information," shows how to collect local administrator group membership information.

- Recipe 11-11, "Collecting Printer Information," shows how to collect printer information.

- Recipe 11-15, "Implementing a Customized SMS_DEF.MOF File," provides information about deploying SMS_DEF.MOF updates.

- Download free scripts from SMS Expert to extend hardware inventory here: http://www.smsexpert.com/mof/scripts.asp.

11-11. Collecting Printer Information

Problem

You want to collect printer information for each client in your organization.

Solution

1. Download the DataShift-Printer.zip from http://www.smsexpert.com/mof/scripts.asp.

2. Extract the .zip file to your favorite location. It will extract the DataShift-Printer.vb_ file.

3. Rename the file to DataShift-Printer.vbs.

4. Create a package that includes the DataShift-Printer.vbs file as a source file.

5. Create a program that uses the following command line:

   cscript.exe DataShift-Printer.vbs

6. Append Example 11-7 to the bottom of \sms\inboxes\clifiles.src\hinv\sms_def.mof.

7. Advertise the program to your SMS clients.

8. Wait for hardware inventory to retrieve the data and populate the SMS database.

9. Create appropriate reports or queries to leverage the new printer data returned from your SMS clients.

Example 11-7 displays the MOF file required for DataShift-Printer.vbs from SMS Expert.

Example 11-7. *MOF for DataShift-Printer.vbs from SMS Expert*

```
[SMS_Report(TRUE),
SMS_Group_Name("Printer Data"),
SMS_Class_ID("MICROSOFT|SMX_Printer|1.0"),
Namespace("\\\\\\\\.\\\\root\\\\cimv2")]

class SMX_Printer: SMS_Class_Template
{
    [SMS_Report(TRUE), Key]
    string DeviceID;

    [SMS_Report(TRUE)]
    string Comment;
```

```
        [SMS_Report(TRUE)]
        boolean Default;

        [SMS_Report(TRUE)]
        string DriverName;

        [SMS_Report(TRUE)]
        boolean local;

        [SMS_Report(TRUE)]
        string Location;

        [SMS_Report(TRUE)]
        string Name;

        [SMS_Report(TRUE)]
        boolean Network;

        [SMS_Report(TRUE)]
        string Portname;

        [SMS_Report(TRUE)]
        uint32 PrinterState;

        [SMS_Report(TRUE)]
        string Servername;

        [SMS_Report(TRUE)]
        boolean Shared;

        [SMS_Report(TRUE)]
        string ShareName;

};
```

Discussion

This solution uses nearly the same process as the previous two recipes, except that instead of writing to a MIF file, we're writing directly to WMI and then collecting the data using the SMS_DEF.MOF file. Example 11-8 displays the code required for DataShft-Printers.vbs script from SMS Expert.

Example 11-8. *DataShift-Printers.vbs from SMS Expert*

```
option explicit
On Error Resume Next

Dim wbemCimtypeSint16
Dim wbemCimtypeSint32
Dim wbemCimtypeReal32
Dim wbemCimtypeReal64
Dim wbemCimtypeString
Dim wbemCimtypeBoolean
Dim wbemCimtypeObject
Dim wbemCimtypeSint8
Dim wbemCimtypeUint8
Dim wbemCimtypeUint16
```

```
Dim wbemCimtypeUint32
Dim wbemCimtypeSint64
Dim wbemCimtypeUint64
Dim wbemCimtypeDateTime
Dim wbemCimtypeReference
Dim wbemCimtypeChar16

wbemCimtypeSint16 = 2
wbemCimtypeSint32 = 3
wbemCimtypeReal32 = 4
wbemCimtypeReal64 = 5
wbemCimtypeString = 8
wbemCimtypeBoolean = 11
wbemCimtypeObject = 13
wbemCimtypeSint8 = 16
wbemCimtypeUint8 = 17
wbemCimtypeUint16 = 18
wbemCimtypeUint32 = 19
wbemCimtypeSint64 = 20
wbemCimtypeUint64 = 21
wbemCimtypeDateTime = 101
wbemCimtypeReference = 102
wbemCimtypeChar16 = 103

Dim oLocation, oServices, oInstances, oObject, oDataObject, oNewObject, oRptObject

Set oLocation = CreateObject("WbemScripting.SWbemLocator")

'Remove classes
Set oServices = oLocation.ConnectServer(, "root\cimv2")
set oNewObject = oServices.Get("SMX_Printer")
oNewObject.Delete_

Set oServices = oLocation.ConnectServer(, "root\cimv2\SMS")
set oNewObject = oServices.Get("SMX_Printer")
oNewObject.Delete_

'Create data class structure
Set oServices = oLocation.ConnectServer(, "root\cimv2")

Set oDataObject = oServices.Get
oDataObject.Path_.Class = "SMX_Printer"
oDataObject.Properties_.add "Comment", wbemCimtypeString
oDataObject.Properties_.add "Default", wbemCimtypeBoolean
oDataObject.Properties_.add "DeviceID", wbemCimtypeString
oDataObject.Properties_.add "DriverName", wbemCimtypeString
oDataObject.Properties_.add "Local", wbemCimtypeBoolean
oDataObject.Properties_.add "Location", wbemCimtypeString
oDataObject.Properties_.add "Name", wbemCimtypeString
oDataObject.Properties_.add "Network", wbemCimtypeBoolean
oDataObject.Properties_.add "PortName", wbemCimtypeString
oDataObject.Properties_.add "PrinterState", wbemCimtypeUint32
oDataObject.Properties_.add "ServerName", wbemCimtypeString
oDataObject.Properties_.add "Shared", wbemCimtypeBoolean
oDataObject.Properties_.add "ShareName", wbemCimtypeString
oDataObject.Properties_("DeviceID").Qualifiers_.add "key", True
oDataObject.Put_
```

```
'Add Instances to data class
Set oServices = oLocation.ConnectServer(, "root\cimv2")
Set oInstances = oServices.InstancesOf("win32_Printer")

FOR EACH oObject in oInstances
    Set oNewObject = oServices.Get("SMX_Printer").SpawnInstance_
    oNewObject.Comment = oObject.Comment
    oNewObject.Default = oObject.Default
    oNewObject.DeviceID = oObject.DeviceID
    oNewObject.DriverName = oObject.DriverName
    oNewObject.Local = oObject.Local
    oNewObject.Location = oObject.Location
    oNewObject.Name = oObject.Name
    oNewObject.Network = oObject.Network
    oNewObject.PortName = oObject.PortName
    oNewObject.PrinterState = oObject.PrinterState
    oNewObject.ServerName = oObject.ServerName
    oNewObject.Shared = oObject.Shared
    oNewObject.ShareName = oObject.ShareName
    oNewObject.Put_
NEXT


'Create reporting class structure
Set oServices = oLocation.ConnectServer(, "root\cimv2\SMS")
Set oRptObject = oServices.Get("SMS_Class_Template").SpawnDerivedClass_

'Set Class Name and Qualifiers
oRptObject.Path_.Class = "SMX_Printer"
oRptObject.Qualifiers_.Add "SMS_Report", True
oRptObject.Qualifiers_.Add "SMS_Group_Name", "Printer Information"
oRptObject.Qualifiers_.Add "SMS_Class_ID", "MICROSOFT|SMXPrinterInfo|1.0"

'Add Reporting Class Properties
oRptObject.Properties_.Add("Comment", wbemCimtypeString). _
    Qualifiers_.Add "SMS_Report", True
oRptObject.Properties_.Add("Default",wbemCimtypeBoolean). _
    Qualifiers_.Add "SMS_Report", True
oRptObject.Properties_.Add("DeviceID", wbemCimtypeString). _
    Qualifiers_.Add "SMS_Report", True
oRptObject.Properties_("DeviceID").Qualifiers_.Add "key", True
oRptObject.Properties_.Add("DriverName", wbemCimtypeString). _
    Qualifiers_.Add "SMS_Report", True
oRptObject.Properties_.Add("Local", wbemCimtypeBoolean). _
    Qualifiers_.Add "SMS_Report", True
oRptObject.Properties_.Add("Location", wbemCimtypeString)._
    Qualifiers_.Add "SMS_Report", True
oRptObject.Properties_.Add("Name", wbemCimtypeString). _
    Qualifiers_.Add "SMS_Report", True
oRptObject.Properties_.Add("Network", wbemCimtypeBoolean). _
    Qualifiers_.Add "SMS_Report", True
oRptObject.Properties_.Add("PortName",wbemCimtypeString). _
    Qualifiers_.Add "SMS_Report", True
oRptObject.Properties_.Add("PrinterState", wbemCimtypeUint32). _
    Qualifiers_.Add "SMS_Report", True
oRptObject.Properties_.Add("ServerName", wbemCimtypeString). _
    Qualifiers_.Add "SMS_Report", True
```

```
oRptObject.Properties_.Add("Shared", wbemCimtypeBoolean)._
    Qualifiers_.Add "SMS_Report", True
oRptObject.Properties_.Add("ShareName", wbemCimtypeString). _
    Qualifiers_.Add "SMS_Report", True
oRptObject.Put_
```

The script in Example 11-8 enumerates the Win32_Printer class and writes to the MIF file. Be aware of permissions requirements for this script. When the SMS program runs this script on the client, it must have proper permissions to write to WMI. This gives us a bit of a catch-22: in order to write to WMI, we must have Administrator permissions, so the script must run in an administrative context. If we configure the SMS program to "Run with user's rights," it will work only for users who have administrative privileges on the client. The VBScript script will silently fail for users who do not have Delete and Create permissions in the root\cimv2 namespace of WMI. Therefore, for this script to run properly on every targeted system, we must configure the program to "Run with administrator's rights." When we configure the program in this manner, we limit the script to only report printers that can be queried under the Local System account. Effectively, only locally installed printers (not printers that are only visible while a user is logged on) can be identified with this VBScript script as it currently stands.

In order to inventory current user printers, you can choose among the following options:

- Reconfigure the script in Example 11-8 to create a class outside of the root\cimv2 namespace; modify permissions, so that authenticated users have Create and Delete permissions; and run the DataShift-Printer.vbs with users' rights.

- Modify Example 11-8 to write to a specified registry key in HKEY_LOCAL_MACHINE. You need to modify the key, so that authenticated users have Create and Delete permissions, and run the modified DataShift-Printer.vbs with users' rights. You also need to modify SMS_DEF.MOF to retrieve the new entries in the registry. This could be completed a little more dynamically on a user basis with the registry instance provider in a method similar to the one to obtain Add or Remove Programs data.

- SMS Expert also provides a MIFShift-Printers file that works similarly to the previous two recipes. You can modify permissions on the %windir%\system32\ccm\invetory\noidmifs directory, so that authenticated users have Create and Delete permissions, and run MIFShift-Printers.vbs with users' rights.

Note Each of the options listed in this section captures the data for the first user, but if the script runs for a second user in its current state, it overwrites the previous user's data.

See Also

- Recipe 11-5, "Creating a New Hardware Inventory Rule," provides information about modifying and testing modifications to the SMS_DEF.MOF file.

- Recipe 11-9, "Collecting Local Administrator Group Membership Information," shows how to collect local administrator group membership information.

- Recipe 11-10, "Collecting Share Information," shows how to collect information about shares on a system.

- Recipe 11-15, "Implementing a Customized SMS_DEF.MOF File," contains information about deploying SMS_DEF.MOF updates.

- Download free scripts from SMS Expert to extend hardware inventory here: http://www.smsexpert.com/mof/scripts.asp.

11-12. Viewing Hardware Inventory for an SMS Resource

Problem

You want to view the hardware inventory of a system.

Solution: Using a Graphical Interface

1. Open the SMS Administrator console.

2. From the SMS Administrator console, expand Site Database (*<Site Code>*) and Collections, and select a collection that contains the resource you want to review.

3. In the right pane, right-click the system, and select All Tasks ➤ Start Resource Explorer.

4. In Resource Explorer, expand Hardware, and click the hardware class that you would like to view the inventory information.

5. Close Resource Explorer when you are finished.

Solution: From the Command Line

1. Create a batch file called `ResExplorer.bat`, and save it in `%windir%\System32`.

2. Enter the following text into `ResExplorer.bat`:

```
set strSMSServer = <SMSServer>
set strSMSSiteCode = <SMSSiteCode>
rem ***The next three lines are actually one line!
start mmc C:\SMSAdmin\bin\i386\explore.msc -s -sms:ResExplrQuery=➥
"Select ResourceID From SMS_R_SYSTEM Where Name = ""%1""" -➥
sms:connection=\\%strSMSServer%\root\sms\site_%strSMSSiteCode%
```

3. Enter the appropriate site code and SMS server name, and verify the proper path to `explore.msc` for your environment.

4. Ensure that the last three lines in the example are all on the same line.

5. Save `ResExplorer.bat`.

6. Click Start ➤ Run, type **ResExplorer Computer1** (where **Computer1** is the name of the computer to observe), and click OK.

7. Resource Explorer will launch and display data for `Computer1`.

8. Close Resource Explorer when you are finished.

Discussion

Besides SMS web reporting, you can view hardware inventory for a specific SMS resource with Resource Explorer. This method is not the most efficient way to review inventory, but if you are looking for a specific piece of inventory information that you may not have included in a web report, this will get it done.

Note To determine the last hardware inventory scan that the SMS server received for a particular system, view Workstation Status under Hardware in Resource Explorer.

You will also find most of the standard hardware inventory information available in the default set of SMS web reports. To view similar data in SMS web reports, first select Computer Details from the left-hand pane. Next, enter a computer name into the Computer Name text box. Finally, expand any of the available nodes (e.g., Hardware, CD-ROM, Network, Operating System, etc.) to see data for the desired system.

See Also

- Recipe 11-14, "Viewing Hardware Inventory History for an SMS Resource," shows how to view hardware inventory history.
- Recipe 11-13, "Querying Hardware Inventory Data from the Command Line," shows how to display hardware inventory from the command line.
- Chapter 2 of the *SMS 2003 Operations Guide* describes how to use SMS Resource Explorer.
- Chapter 9 of the *Microsoft Systems Management Server 2003 Administrator's Companion* by Steven Kaczmarek (Microsoft Press, 2004) also describes how to use SMS Resource Explorer.

11-13. Querying Hardware Inventory Data from the Command Line

Problem

You want to query hardware inventory data in SMS from the command line.

Solution

Example 11-9 demonstrates how to query hardware inventory using VBScript.

Example 11-9. *HQInvQuery.vbs*

```
strSMSServer = "SMSVPC"
strComputer = "2KPRO"

Set objLoc = CreateObject("WbemScripting.SWbemLocator")
Set objSMS= objLoc.ConnectServer(strSMSServer, "root\sms")
Set Results = objSMS.ExecQuery _
    ("SELECT * From SMS_ProviderLocation WHERE ProviderForLocalSite = true")
For each Loc in Results
    If Loc.ProviderForLocalSite = True Then
        Set objSMS = objLoc.ConnectServer(Loc.Machine, "root\sms\site_" & _
            Loc.SiteCode)
    end if
Next

strWQL = "select arp.*, sys.Name from SMS_R_System sys " & _
    "inner join SMS_G_System_ADD_REMOVE_PROGRAMS arp on " & _
    "arp.ResourceID = sys.ResourceId where sys.Name = '" & _
    strComputer & "' order by arp.DisplayName"

Set colARPs = objSMS.ExecQuery(strWQL)

wscript.echo "Add/Remove Programs information for " & strComputer
for each objARP in colARPs
    wscript.echo objARP.arp.DisplayName & vbTAB & _
    objARP.arp.InstallDate & vbTAB & objARP.arp.Publisher
next
```

Discussion

In most instances, you will use SMS web reporting to obtain hardware inventory data. In other instances, you will use SMS queries to obtain the data. But there may be an occasion when you want to pull that data from SMS on a regular basis and do something magical with it. Example 11-9 is a basic script that displays the DisplayName, InstallDate, and Publisher for Add or Remove Programs information obtained from an SMS hardware inventory.

After connecting to the site, we build our WQL query (by the way, this same query could be used as an SMS query). We then use ExecQuery to execute the query. Finally, we use a basic for-each loop to display the information.

See Also

- Recipe 11-14, "Viewing Hardware Inventory History for an SMS Resource," shows how to view hardware inventory history using SMS Resource Explorer.

- The *SMS 2003 Scripting Guide* provides several examples of scripting queries in SMS.

11-14. Viewing Hardware Inventory History for an SMS Resource

Problem

You want to view the hardware inventory history of a system.

Solution

1. Open the SMS Administrator console.

2. From the SMS Administrator console, expand Site Database (*<Site Code>*) and Collections, and select a collection that contains the resource you want to review.

3. In the right pane, right-click the system, and select All Tasks ➤ Start Resource Explorer.

4. In Resource Explorer, expand Hardware History and the hardware class that you would like to view.

5. Click the current or specific past inventory to review the inventory that was returned at that time.

6. Close Resource Explorer when you are finished.

Discussion

Hardware inventory history isn't something that you will use every day, but in a pinch, it can be a lifesaver. We usually turn to it when someone complains about a problem with a system but can't tell you what has changed on it. A worse situation is when changes have been made to a server and it is no longer functioning. If your inventory is rather frequent, you can correlate changes that may not be logged with user security events. On many occasions, we have been able to identify exactly when the offending software or hardware was installed along with who might have initiated the change.

See Also

- Recipe 11-12, "Viewing Hardware Inventory for an SMS Resource," shows how to view hardware inventory.

- Chapter 2 of the *SMS 2003 Operations Guide* describes how to use SMS Resource Explorer.

- Chapter 9 of the *Microsoft Systems Management Server 2003 Administrator's Companion* by Steven Kaczmarek (Microsoft Press, 2004) also describes how to use SMS Resource Explorer.

11-15. Implementing a Customized SMS_DEF.MOF File

Problem

You want to implement a customized SMS_DEF.MOF file into your SMS environment.

Solution

Proceed with your initial implementation as follows:

1. Edit and test your SMS_DEF.MOF file to include the customizations that your require.

2. Copy the SMS_DEF.MOF file to the \SMS\inboxes\clifiles.src\hinv directory of your primary site server.

3. Create a package that uses the \SMS\inboxes\clifiles.src\hinv directory as the source location.

4. Create a program that uses the following command line:

   ```
   mofcomp.exe SMS_DEF.MOF
   ```

5. Advertise the package to all of your Advanced Clients.

Next, make updates using the following process:

1. Edit and test your SMS_DEF.MOF file to include the customizations that your require.

2. Copy the SMS_DEF.MOF file to the \SMS\inboxes\clifiles.src\hinv directory of your primary site server.

3. Update your distribution points.

4. Add a new mandatory assignment to the schedule of your advertisement.

Discussion

This is probably the easiest way to implement your custom SMS_DEF.MOF file to your SMS clients. Once you get this package and advertisement built, it should take you no longer than a couple of minutes to implement any new changes to your SMS_DEF.MOF file.

See Also

- Recipe 4-1, "Creating a Package," shows how to create a new SMS package.

- Recipe 4-11, "Adding a Package to Distribution Points," demonstrates how to add your newly created package to distribution points.

- Recipe 5-1, "Creating a Program," shows how to create a new program for the package.

- Recipe 6-1, "Creating an Advertisement," shows how to create a new advertisement.

- Recipe 11-5, "Creating a New Hardware Inventory Rule," provides information about how to modify and test the SMS_DEF.MOF file.

- Review the sidebar in this chapter titled "What Is a MOF File?" for more information about MOF files.

- Download free scripts from SMS Expert to extend hardware inventory here: http://www.smsexpert.com/mof/scripts.asp.

- SMS Expert's *MOF Editing Guide* provides detailed information about editing and managing the SMS_DEF.MOF file (http://www.smsexpert.com/mof).

- Chapters 2 and 3 of the *SMS 2003 Operations Guide* describe how to use SMS Resource Explorer.

11-16. Removing Hardware Inventory Extensions from SMS

Problem

You want to remove customized hardware inventory extensions from SMS.

Solution

1. If you're making SMS_DEF.MOF modifications, remove the desired data from SMS_DEF.MOF (or comment out using //). If the data is in the form of a MIF file, delete the MIF file from all systems.

2. Obtain DelGrp.exe from the SMS 2003 Toolkit.

3. On each SMS primary site, stop the SMS_EXECUTIVE service, and then execute the following command from the command line (the text in quotes is specific to the SMS class ID. See the discussion that follows for more information):

```
Delgrp.exe "MICROSOFT|Server_Connection|1.0"
```

Note You must have Database Owner permissions for the SMS database to remove a class.

---

4. Restart the SMS_EXECUTIVE service.

Discussion

Removing the data from the SMS_DEF.MOF file on the primary site(s) causes SMS to no longer request or accept the data. However, the data will remain in the SMS site until the Delete Aged Inventory task purges the old data from SMS. Use the delete group (DelGrp) command mentioned previously to remove the tables from your SMS SQL server(s) immediately. Notice the command line used in the solution:

```
Delgrp.exe "MICROSOFT|Server_Connection|1.0"
```

MICROSOFT|Server_Connection|1.0 is the MIFClass (or GroupClass) of the desired class. To obtain a list of all MIF classes, create an SMS web report using the following SQL query:

```
SELECT * FROM v_GroupMap
```

The WMI classes on the server *should* be automatically removed by SMS as soon as the SQL tables are removed. We say "should," because we have encountered instances where the WMI data isn't removed as cleanly as we would prefer. *This is why we stress the importance of triple-testing MOF and MIF changes before implementing them into production.*

Caution Removing classes that are created because of MIF files can be a challenge. One system with a MIF file on it is all it takes to keep the inventoried class in SMS. Often SMS administrators will use DelGrp to remove a group, and suddenly find it reappearing in SMS. This is because they have a client that still has the MIF file on it. As long as a client has a MIF file and is properly reporting hardware inventory, the class you want to remove will remain alive (unless, of course, you globally disable MIF inventory).

If you want to remove the WMI class from the client, add the following lines to your SMS_DEF.MOF file, and recompile on all clients:

```
#pragma namespace("\\\\.\\root\\cimv2")
#pragma deleteclass("MDACVer", NOFAIL)
```

Ensure the namespace specified is the proper namespace for the class you desire to delete. In this example, we're deleting the MDACVer class in the root\cimV2 namespace.

See Also

- The SMS 2003 Toolkit Help file provides detailed information about how to run DelGrp.exe.

- Download the latest SMS 2003 Toolkit here: http://www.microsoft.com/smserver/downloads/2003.

- SMS Expert's *MOF Editing Guide* provides detailed information about editing and managing the SMS_DEF.MOF file (http://www.smsexpert.com/mof).

- SMS Expert also sells a product called SiteSweeper 2005 that is used to automate the process of cleaning your site. It advertises that it will do a better job than using only DelGrp.

- Chapter 3 of the *SMS 2003 Operations Guide* contains additional information about removing hardware inventory extensions, including a "Best Practices for MOF Extensions" section.

CHAPTER 12

■ ■ ■

Remote Tools and Remote Assistance

Using a remote control application for the first time is like moving from a dial-up to a high-speed Internet connection. Before you use it, you don't know what you're missing, and afterward, you don't know how you got along without it. SMS 2003 supports three remote applications: Remote Tools, Remote Assistance, and Remote Desktop Connection.

Remote Tools is a carryover from SMS 2.0 and is installable on all systems that will support an SMS client. However, it lacks the more-integrated security of Remote Assistance or Remote Desktop Connection.

Remote Assistance is integrated into the operating system itself in XP and later operating systems. Both the initiating and remote systems must have XP or higher operating systems to use Remote Assistance.

Remote Desktop Connection is the new name for Terminal Services, which is included in the various flavors of Terminal Server with XP and later operating systems. Remote Desktop Connection is also available as a separate download for Windows 2000 systems. The SMS Administrator console allows you to establish a Remote Desktop Connection directly.

12-1. Enabling Remote Tools

Problem

You want to enable Remote Tools.

Solution

1. Open the SMS Administrator console.

2. From the SMS Administrator console, expand Site Database (*<Site Code>*), Site Hierarchy, *<Site Name>*, Site Settings, and Client Agents.

3. Right-click Remote Tools Client Agent, and select Properties.

4. On the General tab, select the "Enable remote tools on clients" check box.

5. Click OK to apply the settings.

Discussion

Remote Tools wasn't significantly updated with SMS 2003, but it still serves a vital role. Most importantly, it can provide an avenue for support personnel to assist users on a wide range of operating systems. Some companies have found such great value in Remote Tools that they have been able to justify their whole SMS implementation on just that feature alone!

Note Remember that when you use SMS Remote Control (or Remote Assistance), you are merely viewing the desktop of the user who is logged on, so you only have the level of permissions as the logged on user. However, you can use SMS Remote Control to log off the current user, and log in as yourself to perform administrative functions if you have administrative permissions. Also, membership in the Permitted Viewers list is not required for users who are members of the local administrators' group on the target system

---

See Also

- Recipe 2-22, "Configuring Remote Tools," demonstrates how to enable Remote Tools.

- Recipe 12-5, "Configuring Security for Remote Tools and Remote Assistance," demonstrates setting a list of permitted viewers for Remote Control.

- Chapter 10 of the *Microsoft Systems Management Server 2003 Administrator's Companion* by Steven Kaczmarek (Microsoft Press, 2004) provides additional information about the Remote Tools Client Agent.

- Chapter 9 of the *SMS 2003 Operations Guide* provides an in-depth look at Remote Tools.

COMPARING REMOTE TOOLS, REMOTE ASSISTANCE, AND REMOTE DESKTOP CONNECTION

In the Windows world, there are three options provided by Microsoft for accessing a user's desktop remotely: Remote Tools, Remote Assistance, and Remote Desktop Connection. All three of these options allow you to see and manage a remote computer (with proper permissions of course). Depending on how SMS is configured in your environment and on the operating system and configuration of the client you desire to control, multiple options may be available. The primary differences between the three technologies are as follows.

Remote Tools is the remote program that is installed and configured solely through SMS. Remote Control is the primary feature of Remote Tools. This feature can be enabled for all SMS clients, or only SMS clients that do not support Remote Assistance. Remote Control allows you to remotely connect to a system that is logged on or logged off. Remote Control can be configured to automatically allow control or to prompt before allowing control of a remote system. When you successfully remote control a system, you remotely operate the system with the same permissions as the user who is logged on to the system. One of the greatest features of SMS Remote Control (in our opinion) is that you can log a user off, see the login screen, and log in as yourself to perform administrative functions on the system (provided you have administrative access to that system). Another great feature of SMS Remote Control is that you will see console messages, such as "at least one service or device failed to start" or other administrative messages.

Remote Assistance is not installed using SMS 2003. SMS 2003 simply leverages the technology built into the operating system (Windows XP or newer). As this chapter demonstrates, you can use SMS 2003 to configure Remote Assistance in your environment. When initiating Remote Assistance with a system, the user logged in to the system will receive a prompt asking for permission to remotely connect. If the user grants permission, you have the ability to navigate the system as if you're the local user who is logged on to it. Unlike SMS Remote Control, Remote Assistance does not allow you to log a user off and log on as yourself. Also, there is no configuration in Remote Assistance to remotely connect to a system *without* user permission, so a user must be sitting in front of the remote system to accept the request to connect. If Remote Assistance provides all the functionality you need, use it (and not SMS Remote Control) to manage Windows XP and newer operating systems.

We strongly recommend that you leverage Remote Assistance or a Remote Desktop Connection on operating systems that have them incorporated, instead of Remote Tools. Remote Tools is not as secure as the other tools that are integrated with the operating system.

Remote Desktop Connection (previously called Terminal Services Connection) is also not installed or configured on SMS 2003 clients, with one exception. On computers running Windows 2000, the SMS Administrator console installation upgrades the Terminal Services client to the Windows Server 2003 version of Remote Desktop Connection. Remote Desktop Connection provides a remote avenue for you to log in to a remote system, without any need for a user on the remote system. You cannot use Remote Desktop Connection to *see* a user's desktop like you can with SMS Remote Control and Remote Assistance. Remote Desktop Connection loads your desktop at login time. Remote Desktop Connection works with Windows 2000 Server and Windows XP and newer operating systems. When connecting to Windows XP using Remote Desktop Connection, you will force the remote user to log off (if a user is logged on). Multiple users can connect simultaneously to Windows Server operating systems.

Spend some time in Windows Help and on `www.microsoft.com` for more information about Remote Desktop Connection and Terminal Services Administration mode.

12-2. Restricting Users from Changing Remote Tools Settings

Problem

You want to restrict end users from changing Remote Tools settings.

Solution

1. Open the SMS Administrator console.

2. From the SMS Administrator console, expand Site Database (*<Site Code>*), Site Hierarchy, *<Site Name>*, Site Settings, and Client Agents.

3. Right-click Remote Tools Client Agent, and select Properties.

4. On the General tab, enable the "Users cannot change Policy or Notification settings for SMS Remote Tools" check box.

5. Click OK to apply the settings.

Discussion

If you want to use Remote Tools effectively, limiting the changes to Remote Tools is important. Giving your end users the freedom to control the functionality of Remote Tools will limit its effectiveness, as many users may view it as a spying tool and disable it before they can fully understand how helpful it can be.

Note Ensure that your corporate policies support the use of Remote Tools.

See Also

- Chapter 10 of the *Microsoft Systems Management Server 2003 Administrator's Companion* by Steven Kaczmarek (Microsoft Press, 2004) provides additional information about the Remote Tools Client Agent.

- Chapter 9 of the *SMS 2003 Operations Guide* provides an in-depth look at Remote Tools.

12-3. Excluding Remote Tools in Operating Systems Supporting Remote Assistance

Problem

You want to exclude operating systems that currently support Remote Assistance from installing the Remote Tools components.

Solution

1. Open the SMS Administrator console.

2. From the SMS Administrator console, expand Site Database (*<Site Code>*), Site Hierarchy, *<Site Name>*, Site Settings, and Client Agents.

3. Right-click Remote Tools Client Agent, and select Properties.

4. On the General tab, enable the check box next to "Do not install Remote Control components for Advanced Clients running Windows XP, Windows Server 2003, or later."

5. Click OK to apply the settings.

Discussion

For security reasons, you may choose to use Remote Tools only on systems that don't support Remote Assistance or Remote Desktop Connection. If you are in this situation, this recipe is a perfect solution for you, as SMS will skip the installation of Remote Tools on systems that support the more secure, integrated technologies.

See Also

- The sidebar titled "Comparing Remote Tools, Remote Assistance, and Remote Desktop Connection" offers a comparison between SMS Remote Tools and Remote Assistance.

- Chapter 10 of the *Microsoft Systems Management Server 2003 Administrator's Companion* by Steven Kaczmarek (Microsoft Press, 2004) provides additional information about the Remote Tools Client Agent.

- Chapter 9 of the *SMS 2003 Operations Guide* provides an in-depth look at Remote Tools.

12-4. Enabling Remote Assistance Configuration Management

Problem

You want to enable SMS to manage or enforce the configuration of Remote Assistance.

Solution

1. Open the SMS Administrator console.

2. From the SMS Administrator console, expand Site Database (*<Site Code>*), Site Hierarchy, *<Site Name>*, Site Settings, and Client Agents.

3. Right-click Remote Tools Client Agent, and select Properties.

4. On the General tab, enable the "Manage Remote Assistance settings" check box for SMS to provide the Remote Assistance configuration to clients that support it.

5. Enable the check box next to "Override Remote Assistance user settings" if you want to enforce a Remote Assistance configuration.

6. Click OK to apply the settings.

Discussion

You would think that with multiple remote technologies available, it would be difficult to manage the settings of each of them. Nope, just check one or two boxes, and SMS does the rest. Remote Assistance settings managed by SMS are configured using local Group Policy. As with all local Group Policy, it will be overridden by domain Group Policy (when configured).

Note Remote Assistance settings configured through domain Group Policy override SMS settings for Remote Assistance.

See Also

- Recipe 12-5, "Configuring Security for Remote Tools and Remote Assistance," explains setting a list of permitted viewers for Remote Assistance.

- The sidebar titled "Comparing Remote Tools, Remote Assistance, and Remote Desktop Connection" offers a comparison between SMS Remote Tools and Remote Assistance.

- Chapter 10 of the *Microsoft Systems Management Server 2003 Administrator's Companion* by Steven Kaczmarek (Microsoft Press, 2004) provides additional information about the Remote Tools Client Agent.

- Chapter 9 of the *SMS 2003 Operations Guide* provides an in-depth look at Remote Tools.

12-5. Configuring Security for Remote Tools and Remote Assistance

Problem

You want to add or delete users or security groups from the list of permitted viewers.

Solution

1. Open the SMS Administrator console.

2. From the SMS Administrator console, expand Site Database (*<Site Code>*), Site Hierarchy, *<Site Name>*, Site Settings, and Client Agents.

3. Right-click Remote Tools Client Agent, and select Properties.

4. On the Security tab, click the New button (the yellow starburst icon) to open the New Viewer dialog box.

5. Enter a user or security group name in the box provided.

6. Click OK to close the New Viewer dialog box.

7. The new Viewer will be visible in the Permitted Viewer pane.

8. To delete a permitted viewer, highlight it and click the Delete button or press the Delete key on your keyboard.

9. Click OK to apply the settings.

Discussion

The permitted viewers list applies to both Remote Tools and Remote Assistance if you have selected to have SMS manage the Remote Assistance settings.

Caution A long permitted viewers list will degrade the performance of Remote Tools, as it increases the number of authentications that have to be made to the domain.

Remote Assistance settings managed by SMS are configured using local Group Policy. As with all local Group Policy, it will be overridden by domain Group Policy (when configured).

Note Remote Assistance settings configured through domain Group Policy override SMS settings for Remote Assistance.

See Also

- Recipe 12-6, "Configuring the Level of Access Provided by Remote Tools," provides instructions for configuring the proper level of access for SMS Remote Tools users.

- Recipe 12-7, "Configuring the Level of Access Provided by Remote Assistance," provides instructions for configuring the proper level of access for Remote Assistance.

- Chapter 10 of the *Microsoft Systems Management Server 2003 Administrator's Companion* by Steven Kaczmarek (Microsoft Press, 2004) provides additional information about the Remote Tools Client Agent.

- Chapter 9 of the *SMS 2003 Operations Guide* provides an in-depth look at Remote Tools.

12-6. Configuring the Level of Access Provided by Remote Tools

Problem

You want to configure the level of access that will be available during a Remote Tools session.

Solution

1. Open the SMS Administrator console.

2. From the SMS Administrator console, expand Site Database (*<Site Code>*), Site Hierarchy, *<Site Name>*, Site Settings, and Client Agents.

3. Right-click Remote Tools Client Agent, and select Properties.

4. On the Policy tab in the SMS Remote Tools section, choose Full, Limited, or None from the drop-down menu to reflect the level of access you want granted.

5. If you chose Limited, you need to click the Settings button and choose which of the six options to allow.

6. If you want to allow your end user to control the Remote Control sessions, enable the "Display a message to ask for permission" radio button.

7. Click OK to apply the settings.

Discussion

Far too much corporate wrangling has taken place over the Remote Tools settings, so prepare in advance to head off any controversy by having a solid plan explaining the purpose of every setting that controls the access level of Remote Tools.

As discussed in Chapter 2, the most debated configuration setting for Remote Tools is whether to ask the user for permission before initiating remote control of the system. Many end users feel that not asking for permission is an invasion of their privacy at work, while Help Desk personnel see it as a way to remotely touch that user's desktop to fix a problem even when the user is not available. Each environment is different, so be sure to work with management and security personnel before enabling remote control.

Note Remember that when you use SMS Remote Control (or Remote Assistance), you are merely viewing the desktop of the user who is logged on, so you only have the level of permissions as the logged on user. However, you can use SMS Remote Control to log off the current user and log in as yourself to perform administrative functions if you have administrative permissions. You can also use the Run As functionality to initiate applications and processes under a different security context than the current user.

See Also

- Recipe 12-5, "Configuring Security for Remote Tools and Remote Assistance," explains properly configuring the security for Remote Tools.

- Recipe 12-8, "Configuring Notifications for Remote Tools," shows how to configure notifications for SMS Remote Tools.

- Chapter 10 of the *Microsoft Systems Management Server 2003 Administrator's Companion* by Steven Kaczmarek (Microsoft Press, 2004) provides additional information about the Remote Tools Client Agent.

- Chapter 9 of the *SMS 2003 Operations Guide* provides an in-depth look at Remote Tools.

12-7. Configuring the Level of Access Provided by Remote Assistance

Problem

You want to configure the level of access that will be available during a Remote Assistance session.

Solution

1. Open the SMS Administrator console.

2. From the SMS Administrator console, expand Site Database (*<Site Code>*), Site Hierarchy, *<Site Name>*, Site Settings, and Client Agents.

3. Right-click Remote Tools Client Agent, and select Properties.

4. On the Policy tab in the Remote Assistance section, choose "Full control," "Remote viewing," or "None" from the drop-down menu to reflect the level of access you want granted.

5. Click OK to apply the settings.

Discussion

As in the previous recipe, choose your access levels in accordance with your corporate policies.

Note Remember that when you use SMS Remote Control (or Remote Assistance), you are merely viewing the desktop of the user who is logged on, so you only have the level of permissions as the logged on user. However, you can use SMS Remote Control to log off the current user and log in as yourself to perform administrative functions if you have administrative permissions.

See Also

- Recipe 12-5, "Configuring Security for Remote Tools and Remote Assistance," explains properly configuring the security for Remote Assistance.

- Chapter 10 of the *Microsoft Systems Management Server 2003 Administrator's Companion* by Steven Kaczmarek (Microsoft Press, 2004) provides additional information about the Remote Tools Client Agent.

- Chapter 9 of the *SMS 2003 Operations Guide* provides an in-depth look at Remote Tools.

12-8. Configuring Notifications for Remote Tools

Problem

You want to configure notifications that will alert end users that Remote Tools is being used on their system.

Solution

1. Open the SMS Administrator console.

2. From the SMS Administrator console, expand Site Database (*<Site Code>*), Site Hierarchy, *<Site Name>*, Site Settings, and Client Agents.

3. Right-click Remote Tools Client Agent, and select Properties.

4. On the Notification tab, choose to display a visual indicator, play a sound, or use both by checking the appropriate check box.

5. If you chose to display a visual indicator, select the type of indicator and whether you want it to be visible even when a session is not active.

6. If you chose to play a sound, select whether to play it at the beginning and end of the session or repeatedly during the session.

7. Click OK to apply the settings.

Discussion

Notifications can easily become annoyances if you take them too far, so make sure you test them all and choose the settings that work best in your environment. This is another area where users or managers may voice a strong preference in one notification method, so have a rock-solid justification before letting them throw in their two cents.

See Also

- SMS 2003 Service Pack 1 encountered an issue with the audible signal (the chime) repeatedly notifying the user of a remote session, when configured to signal only when the session begins. This issue is fixed in the SMS 2003 Service Pack 2, but if you're still on Service Pack 1, review Microsoft Knowledge Base article 897254: `http://support.microsoft.com/?kbid=897254`.

- Chapter 10 of the *Microsoft Systems Management Server 2003 Administrator's Companion* by Steven Kaczmarek (Microsoft Press, 2004) provides additional information about the Remote Tools Client Agent.

- Chapter 9 of the *SMS 2003 Operations Guide* provides an in-depth look at Remote Tools.

12-9. Configuring the Compression Level Used by Remote Control

Problem

You want to configure the compression level used by Remote Control.

Solution

1. Open the SMS Administrator console.
2. From the SMS Administrator console, expand Site Database (*<Site Code>*), Site Hierarchy, *<Site Name>*, Site Settings, and Client Agents.
3. Right-click Remote Tools Client Agent, and select Properties.
4. On the Advanced tab, select Low (RLE), High (LZ), or Automatically Select from the drop-down menu.
5. Click OK to apply the settings.

Discussion

If you are experiencing slow responses with Remote Control, adjust the compression level setting to see if that will resolve the problem. Otherwise, the default setting shouldn't need to be changed.

See Also

- Chapter 10 of the *Microsoft Systems Management Server 2003 Administrator's Companion* by Steven Kaczmarek (Microsoft Press, 2004) provides additional information about the Remote Tools Client Agent.

- Chapter 9 of the *SMS 2003 Operations Guide* provides an in-depth look at Remote Tools.

12-10. Enabling and Configuring Accelerated Screen Transfer

Problem

You want to enable and configure Accelerated Screen Transfer for Remote Control sessions.

Solution

1. Open the SMS Administrator console.

2. From the SMS Administrator console, expand Site Database (*<Site Code>*), Site Hierarchy, *<Site Name>*, Site Settings, and Client Agents.

3. Right-click Remote Tools Client Agent, and select Properties.

4. On the Advanced tab, enable the "Install accelerated screen transfer on Windows-based clients" check box.

5. Add additional compatible video drivers by clicking on the New button (the yellow starburst icon) to open the New Video Driver dialog box.

6. Enter the name of the new video driver in the space provided, and click OK to close the New Video Driver dialog box.

7. Click OK to apply the settings.

Discussion

Accelerated Screen Transfer allows SMS to pass the screen refreshes more effectively. Try the default settings first before making any changes.

Note The "Compatible video drivers" box is not used with Windows 2000 and above.

See Also

- Chapter 10 of the *Microsoft Systems Management Server 2003 Administrator's Companion* by Steven Kaczmarek (Microsoft Press, 2004) provides additional information about the Remote Tools Client Agent.

- Chapter 9 of the *SMS 2003 Operations Guide* provides an in-depth look at Remote Tools.

12-11. Launching Remote Tools from the SMS Administrator Console

Problem

You want to launch Remote Tools from within the SMS Administrator console.

Solution

1. Open the SMS Administrator console.

2. From the SMS Administrator console, expand Site Database (*<Site Code>*) and Collections.

3. Expand any collections that contain the system that you want to access with Remote Tools, and select that system in the right pane.

4. Right-click the system, and select All Tasks ➤ Start Remote Tools. The Remote Tools application will launch and attempt to connect with the system you selected.

5. Use the Remote Tools to accomplish the task at hand.

6. When the task is completed, select File ➤ Exit, or click the Close button to exit Remote Tools.

Discussion

This recipe and several following it highlight the various ways that you can launch Remote Tools. The method described in this recipe is the most obvious, since it is a part of the SMS Administrator console, but it may not be the best choice for everyone.

Remote Tools provides a connection status window (Figure 12-1), so that you can see what the tools are doing while they are attempting a connection. Once a connection is made, the Remote Tools console (Figure 12-2) gives you a jumping-off point for launching any of the Remote Tools.

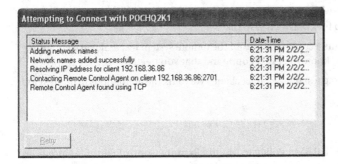

Figure 12-1. *Remote Tools connection status window*

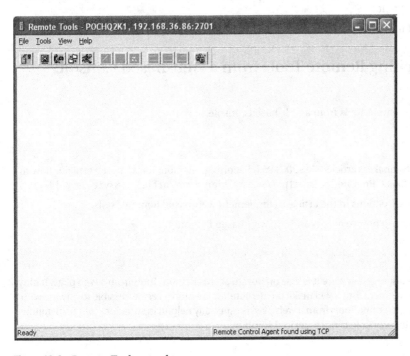

Figure 12-2. *Remote Tools console*

A list of the Remote Tools that are available to you follows:

Remote Control: This tool allows you to see exactly what a user is seeing on a system in real time. You also can control the mouse and keyboard just as if you were sitting there.

Reboot: This tool allows you to remotely shut down or restart the system that Remote Tools is connected to.

Chat: This tool pops up a basic two-pane chat window for you to communicate with the end user of the target system.

File Transfer: This tool creates a two-pane window with a file explorer of your system and the target system. You can drag and drop files between systems.

Remote Execute: This tool presents a command line for the remote system just as if you were sitting there. However, you do need to know the exact command that you need to run.

Ping Test: This tool executes a ping test on the target client. (We think the animations of this test are well worth watching!)

See Also

- Recipe 12-17, "Creating a Local SMS Policy to Modify Remote Control Settings," provides instructions for bypassing the user prompt for permission.

- Chapter 10 of the *Microsoft Systems Management Server 2003 Administrator's Companion* by Steven Kaczmarek (Microsoft Press, 2004) provides additional information about the Remote Tools Client Agent.

- Chapter 9 of the *SMS 2003 Operations Guide* provides an in-depth look at Remote Tools.

12-12. Launching Remote Tools from a Web-Based Console

Problem

You want to launch Remote Tools from a web-based console.

Solution

1. Read Ron Crumbaker's article "SMS 2003 Web Reporting—Remote Tools," which explains how to create web-based Remote Tools: `http://www.myitforum.com/articles/8/view.asp?id=7933`.

2. Follow the instructions in the article to implement web-based Remote Tools.

3. Instruct users on how to access and use web-based Remote Tools.

Discussion

Ron Crumbaker has put together a great article on how to access Remote Tools from a web page. It may take a few steps to implement, but it will make the Remote Tools features very accessible to anyone who needs them. Accessing Remote Tools from a web page is especially helpful in situations where installing the SMS Administrator console is not a desired solution.

See Also

- Recipe 12-17, "Creating a Local SMS Policy to Modify Remote Control Settings," provides instructions for bypassing the user prompt for permission.

- Chapter 10 of the *Microsoft Systems Management Server 2003 Administrator's Companion* by Steven Kaczmarek (Microsoft Press, 2004) provides additional information about the Remote Tools Client Agent.

- Chapter 9 of the *SMS 2003 Operations Guide* provides an in-depth look at Remote Tools.

12-13. Launching Remote Tools from an Accessory Program

Problem

You want to launch Remote Tools from an accessory program.

Solution

1. Read Heine Jeppesen's article "Remote Control Frontend," which shows how to install and use his Remote Frontend tool: http://www.myitforum.com/articles/1/view.asp?id=5250.

2. Download the accessory tool: http://www.creativeminds.dk/sms/remotecontrol.zip.

3. Install the tool on support team workstations.

Discussion

Heine Jeppesen's little gem of a program will significantly increase the use of Remote Tools in your support organization. It also allows you to sleep well at night, knowing that your support staff won't trip over something as they wade through the SMS Administrator console trying to use Remote Tools. This tool does require the SMS Administrator console to be installed on the local system.

See Also

- Recipe 12-17, "Creating a Local SMS Policy to Modify Remote Control Settings," provides instructions for bypassing the user prompt for permission.

- Chapter 10 of the *Microsoft Systems Management Server 2003 Administrator's Companion* by Steven Kaczmarek (Microsoft Press, 2004) provides additional information about the Remote Tools Client Agent.

- Chapter 9 of the *SMS 2003 Operations Guide* provides an in-depth look at Remote Tools.

12-14. Launching Remote Tools from the Command Line

Problem

You want to launch Remote Tools from the command line.

Solution: Using the Command Line to Launch the remote.exe GUI

1. Open a command window.

2. Type **C:\SMSADMIN\bin\i386\remote.exe**, and press Enter.

3. Choose an address type, enter the address of the system you are targeting, and click OK.

4. Remote Tools will attempt to contact the system.

Solution: Using the Command-Line Parameters with remote.exe

1. Open a command window.

2. Type **C:\SMSADMIN\bin\i386\remote.exe** along with a protocol type, an address, and a site server name (e.g., remote.exe 3 mypc \\mysmsserver), and press Enter.

3. Remote Tools will attempt to contact the system.

Discussion

Both of the methods given in this recipe can be used as shortcuts to launching Remote Tools, especially if you are launching Remote Tools from another application or script. Here are the three protocol types that can be used.

- 1: IPX address

- 2: IP address

- 3: NetBIOS address

See Also

- Recipe 12-16, "Launching Remote Control from the Remote Tools Console," shows how to launch Remote Tools from the SMS Administrator console.

- Recipe 12-11, "Launching Remote Tools from the SMS Administrator Console," shows how to launch Remote Tools from the SMS Administrator console.

- Chapter 10 of the *Microsoft Systems Management Server 2003 Administrator's Companion* by Steven Kaczmarek (Microsoft Press, 2004) provides additional information about the Remote Tools Client Agent.

- Chapter 9 of the *SMS 2003 Operations Guide* provides an in-depth look at Remote Tools.

12-15. Launching Remote Assistance

Problem

You want to launch Remote Assistance.

Solution

1. Open the SMS Administrator console.

2. From the SMS Administrator console, expand Site Database (*<Site Code>*) and Collections.

3. Expand any collections that contain the system that you want to access with Remote Assistance, and select that system in the right pane.

4. Right-click the system, and select All Tasks ➤ Start Remote Assistance. The Remote Assistance application will launch.

5. Use Remote Assistance to complete the tasks at hand after the user has accepted the invitation.

6. When you've finished, exit the Remote Assistance application.

Discussion

Remote Assistance is very slick and integrated, but it lacks some key components found in Remote Tools. Remote Assistance is limited by the operating system requirement of Windows XP or newer for both systems. Also, a user must be logged in and must accept the offer for assistance before you can access a system remotely.

See Also

- Chapter 10 of the *Microsoft Systems Management Server 2003 Administrator's Companion* by Steven Kaczmarek (Microsoft Press, 2004) provides additional information about the Remote Tools Client Agent.

- Chapter 9 of the *SMS 2003 Operations Guide* provides an in-depth look at Remote Tools.

12-16. Launching Remote Control from the Remote Tools Console

Problem

You want to launch Remote Control from the Remote Tools console.

Solution

1. Launch Remote Tools using one of the methods mentioned in the previous recipes.
2. Click the Remote Control button (the leftmost button), or choose Tools ➤ Remote Control from the menu bar.
3. After the Remote Control window opens, you have remote control of the target system.
4. If the system is locked or not logged in, click the button displaying the key icon in the top-right corner of the window. It will initiate a Ctrl+Alt+Delete key sequence, so you can enter proper credentials to access the system.
5. Close the Remote Control window to close your session.
6. Close the Remote Tools window, or select another tool to use from the Remote Tools console.

Discussion

Remote Control is the most widely used tool in the Remote Tools console, but the least secure. The Remote Control window (Figure 12-3), with its barbershop pole border, is very easy to navigate. The following buttons are available to you (from left to right):

Start button: This has the same functionality as the Start button and will launch the Start Menu.

Alt+Tab button: This button will bring up the window picker that will let you choose between the windows that are currently open.

Ctrl+Alt+Delete button: This button initiates a Ctrl+Alt+Delete key sequence and exposes the logon dialog box or the shutdown/logoff dialog box.

System key pass-through button: This button allows system-key actions on the keyboard, like Alt, to be passed to the target system.

Area button: This button will create a small window of the entire desktop area of the target system for quick navigation. This small window is extremely helpful when the target system has a very high screen resolution and your Remote Control window does not. The scroll bars on the side of the window are very small, so using the area button makes it much easier to navigate.

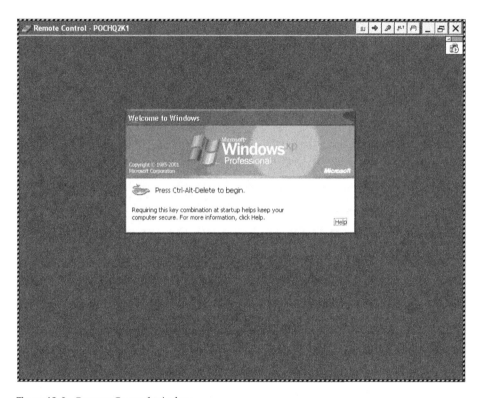

Figure 12-3. *Remote Control window*

See Also

- Recipe 12-14, "Launching Remote Tools from the Command Line," shows how to launch Remote Tools from the command line.

- Recipe 12-17, "Creating a Local SMS Policy to Modify Remote Control Settings," provides information on bypassing the user prompt for permission.

- Chapter 10 of the *Microsoft Systems Management Server 2003 Administrator's Companion* by Steven Kaczmarek (Microsoft Press, 2004) provides additional information about the Remote Tools Client Agent.

- Chapter 9 of the *SMS 2003 Operations Guide* provides an in-depth look at Remote Tools.

12-17. Creating a Local SMS Policy to Modify Remote Control Settings

Problem

You want to disable the PermissionRequired property for Remote Control on one Advanced Client system in your environment.

Solution

1. On the local client, paste the contents of Example 12-1 into a text file, and save the file as C:\TurnOffPermissionsRequired.mof.

2. From a command line, execute the following command:

   mofcomp TurnOffPermissionsRequired.mof

3. Delete C:\TurnOffPermissionsRequired.mof.

Example 12-1 demonstrates how to create a local policy to set the PermissionRequired property to False.

Example 12-1. *TurnOffPermissionsRequired.mof*

```
#pragma namespace("\\\\.\\root\\ccm\\policy\\machine\\requestedconfig")

[CCM_Policy_PartialPolicy(true)]
instance of CCM_RemoteToolsConfig

{
PolicySource = "local";
Type = 1;
[ccm_policy_override(TRUE)]
PermissionRequired = false;
};
```

Discussion

As you know, Remote Tools configuration is a sitewide setting. Using the MOF file in Example 12-1, you can make exceptions to the sitewide rule on a per-client basis. You can see that Example 12-1 connects to the \\.\root\ccm\policy\machine\requestedconfig namespace and creates a partial policy in the CCM_RemoteToolsConfig class. By using a partial policy, only the specified settings are modified, and all other settings from the SMS site server will apply. You can also see that the PolicySource property is set to local. The process in this recipe could also be used to modify the PermittedViewers property if desired.

Once you have a policy in place, you may someday decide to remove it. Example 12-2 demonstrates how to remove all local polices in the CCM_RemoteToolsConfig class under the \Root\CCM\Policy\Machine\RequestedConfig namespace.

Example 12-2. *RemoveLocalRemoteToolsPolicies.vbs*

```
strComputer = "."
Set objWMIService = GetObject _
    ("winmgmts:{impersonationLevel=impersonate}!\\" & _
        strComputer & "\root\ccm\Policy\Machine\RequestedConfig")
Set colLocalPolicy = objWMIService.ExecQuery _
    ("Select * from CCM_RemoteToolsConfig " & _
        "where policysource = 'local'")

for each objPolicy in colLocalPolicy
    objPolicy.Delete_
next
```

Caution Example 12-2 removes *all* local policies for the class CCM_RemoteToolsConfig.

Consider the following WMI Query Language (WQL) statement:

```
Select * from CCM_RemoteToolsConfig where PolicySource = 'local'
```

This statement will return all local polices for Remote Tools. If you have more than one (or if you want to be more precise), you may consider modifying the WQL to find the exact setting that has been modified, for example:

```
Select * from CCM_RemoteToolsConfig where PolicySource = 'local' AND
PermissionRequired = 'false'
```

Disabling the PermissionRequired property can also be accomplished by configuring the registry entry HKEY_LOCAL_MACHINE\SOFTWARE\Microsoft\SMS\Client\Client Components\Remote Control | Permission Required to 0. However, this modification is only temporary, as this setting will be reset at the next client configuration refresh interval.

See Also

- The SMS 2003 SDK provides the example MOF used to create the local policy for Remote Control.
- The SMS 2003 SDK also provides more information about the CCM_RemoteToolsConfig class.

■ ■ ■

CHAPTER 13

Software Distribution

Software distribution challenges come in every shape and size. We cannot address every one of those challenges in this chapter, but we will provide examples for applying SMS to some of the common ones. We'll look at installation tasks, such as installing shortcuts, modifying registry information in the HKEY_CURRENT_USER profile, and replacing a file on a workstation, and we'll cover the SMS 2003 Elevated Rights Deployment Tool. In addition to examples, we provide several links to resources for installing Windows Installer–based applications, as well as InstallShield-based applications.

There isn't currently a book devoted to software distribution in SMS 2003, but that doesn't mean that good information isn't available. Microsoft has white papers on deploying their applications, and http://appdeploy.com is a great place to start looking for deployment help. Also, if you're banging your head against the wall, don't forget the online forums, e-mail lists, and local user groups. You will always find someone who is willing to help you out.

13-1. Creating a Shortcut on the All Users Desktop

Problem

You want to create a shortcut on the desktop that is available to every user who logs into a system.

Solution

1. Using SMS Installer, query HKEY_LOCAL_MACHINE\Software\Microsoft\Windows\CurrentVersion\ Explorer\Shell Folders\Common Desktop using the Get Registry Key Value action to obtain the Common Desktop (e.g., All Users) path.

2. Use the Create Shortcut action to create a shortcut with the following properties:

   - *Source path*: The path to the Internet browser executable (e.g., C:\Program Files\ Internet Explorer\iexplore.exe).

   - *Destination path*: The path and file name of the shortcut to create (e.g., C:\Documents and Settings\All Users\Desktop\Launch TechNet.lnk).

   - *Command options*: The argument(s) to pass to the executable. In this example, we're passing the URL to Microsoft TechNet (http://www.microsoft.com/technet).

   - *Description*: Information to be displayed when the user holds the mouse over the icon (e.g., Launch Microsoft TechNet).

Discussion

From time to time, you may run into a situation in which you need to add a shortcut to the desktop. To make that shortcut available to each user and keep your environment standard, consider saving it to the All Users profile. In Windows 2000 and Windows XP, by default, the All Users profile is located in C:\Documents and Settings\All Users. To ensure that you're installing the icon to the proper location, query the registry mentioned in step 1 of this recipe. This registry key also contains other common paths, such as Common Desktop and Common Favorites.

Figure 13-1 is an example SMS Installer script in script editor mode. In this script, we create three variables that will allow us to more easily modify the script in the future if needed. We declare a fourth variable called ALLUSERSDSKTP. The value of this variable is determined at the runtime (installation time) of the script. It will query the HKEY_LOCAL_MACHINE\Software\Microsoft\Windows\CurrentVersion\Explorer\Shell Folders key to obtain the value for Common Desktop. This will give us the path to the All Users desktop for the local system. Figure 13-2 shows an example of the Get Registry Key Value action. Figure 13-3 shows an example of the Create Shortcut action. Notice that in this action we use all four variables that have been defined in the script. The Create Shortcut action will automatically overwrite a shortcut if it already exists by that name in the Destination path.

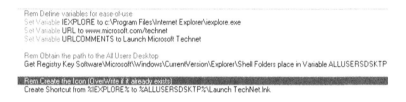

Figure 13-1. *CreateShortcutOnAllUsersDesktop.ipf code within SMS Installer*

Figure 13-2 shows the Get Registry Key Value action dialog box. Create a new variable named ALLUSERSDSKTP and set its value to HKEY_LOCAL_MACHINE\Software\Microsoft\Windows\CurrentVersion\Explorer\Shell Folders\Common Desktop. Select the root to query (e.g., HKEY_LOCAL_MACHINE), and enter the registry key path (**Software\Microsoft\Windows\CurrentVersion\Explorer\Shell Folders**) and the value name to query (**Common Desktop**).

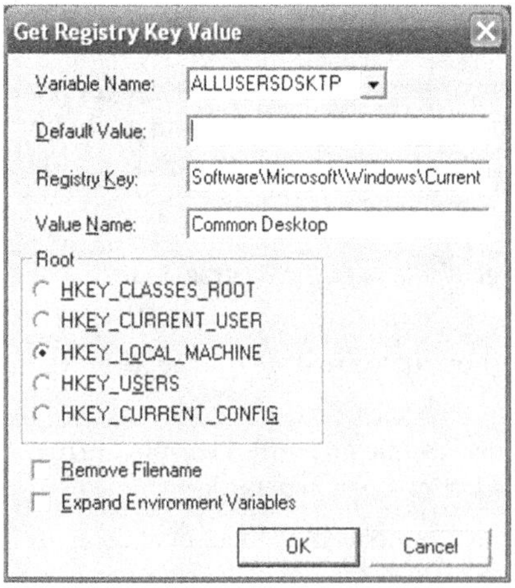

Figure 13-2. *Use the Get Registry Key Value action dialog box to obtain the Common Desktop value.*

At this point, you have the full path to the All Users desktop. For example, with a default installation of Windows XP, ALLUSERSDSKTP would be equal to C:\Documents And Settings\All Users\Desktop. See Figure 13-3 for the Create Shortcut action.

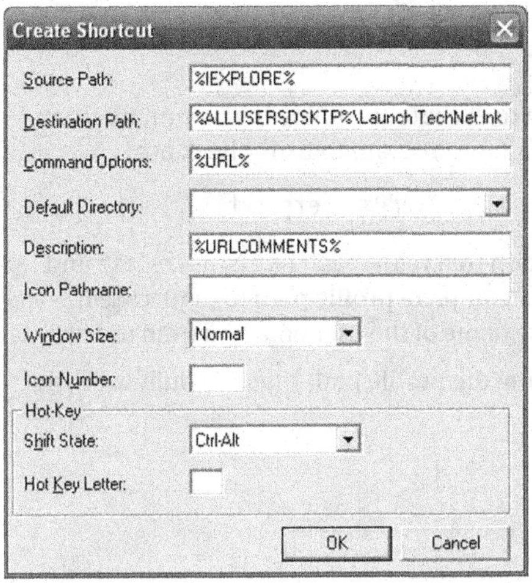

Figure 13-3. *The Create Shortcut action within SMS Installer*

As you can see, in the Create Shortcut action dialog box (Figure 13-3), you use all the variables from the installation script in the Get Registry Key Value action. You could hard-code the information into this action, but the method we use may make the installation script more flexible for future use.

A considerable amount of dynamic help is available for SMS Installer. Even though you don't see a Help button on any of the figures in this recipe, simply press the F1 key to display Help for the desired action.

Note Don't be afraid to press the F1 key when using SMS Installer. You may be surprised by the amount of information available at your fingertips.

You can obtain this sample script (CreateShortcutOnAllUsersDesktop.ipf) from the *SMS Recipes* source code site and modify it to fit the needs of your environment.

See Also

- Recipe 13-2, "Creating a Shortcut on Every User's Desktop," demonstrates how to create a shortcut on every user's desktop.

- Recipe 13-3, "Creating a Shortcut on the Quick Launch Toolbar," demonstrates how to create a shortcut on every user's Quick Launch toolbar.

- SMS Installer Help provides detailed information for each action mentioned in this recipe.

- Download the latest version of SMS Installer from the SMS downloads site (http://www. microsoft.com/smserver/downloads/20/tools/installer.mspx).

- Chapter 5 of *Microsoft SMS Installer* by Rod Trent (McGraw-Hill, 2000) provides detailed information for most of the actions available in SMS Installer.

13-2. Creating a Shortcut on Every User's Desktop

Problem

You want to create a shortcut on each user's desktop.

Solution

1. In SMS Installer, use the Execute Program action to execute the following command from the SMS Installer executable (and enable the "Wait for Program to Exit" check box):

   ```
   cmd.exe /c dir /b /ad "C:\Documents and Settings">%TEMP%\users.txt
   ```

2. Use the Read/Update Text File action to start a loop that reads each line of users.txt and uses those lines of data from users.txt to build a complete profile path to C:\Documents and Settings\username\Desktop, where username is the name of the user obtained from users.txt.

3. During the loop in step 2, create the shortcut using the profile path that you built using the data from users.txt.

4. Delete %temp%\users.txt.

Discussion

Recipe 13-1, "Creating a Shortcut on the All Users desktop," describes how to create an icon on the All Users desktop, so that each user can use the icon but cannot modify or delete it (in a locked-down environment). In our opinion, managing one icon in the All Users desktop is much easier than managing the *same* icon in each user's profile. That being said, you may have a situation where you want the user to be able to modify the icon. You may even want the user to have the ability to delete the icon. The easiest way to do this is to install the icon on the user's desktop for them.

Figure 13-4 shows an example SMS Installer script in script editor mode. First, we perform a registry query to obtain the All Users desktop profile path, and then we use the Parse String action to obtain the path to the root of the profiles directory. Next, we install the icon file into the predefined variable %SYSWIN% (which is equivalent to %WINDIR% in DOS). We then run a command to obtain the user name for each profile on the system. Next, we enumerate each profile on the system and create the shortcut for each user *except* for the Administrator and All Users profiles. Finally, we delete the temporary list of user profiles on the system.

```
Rem Obtain the path to the All Users Desktop
Get Registry Key Software\Microsoft\Windows\CurrentVersion\Explorer\Shell Folders place in Varia

Rem Parse string ALLUSERSDSKTP to extract Profile Paths
Parse String "%ALLUSERSDSKTP%" into PROFILEPATH and TMPJUNK

Rem Get the TEMP environement variable
Get Environment Variable TEMP into Variable SYSTEMP

Rem Install the icon file locally
Install File \\MySMSServer\SourceFiles\GoogleLaunch\GoogleLocal.ico to %SYSWIN%\GoogleLo

Rem Execute Command to create %temp%\users.txt, and wait...
Execute cmd.exe /c dir /b /ad "%PROFILEPATH%">%SYSTEMP%\users.txt (Wait)

Rem Read each line of users.txt, and use the username to comlete the path
Rem    to the user's desktop
Read lines of file %SYSTEMP%\users.txt into variable USERNAME Start Block
   If USERNAME Not Equal (Ignore Case) "Administrator" then
      If USERNAME Not Equal (Ignore Case) "All Users" then
         Create Shortcut from c:\Program Files\Internet Explorer\iexplore.exe to %PROFILEPATH%\%L
      End Block
   End Block
End Block

Delete File(s) %SYSTEMP%\users.txt
```

Figure 13-4. *CreateShortcutOnEachUsersDesktop.ipf code within SMS Installer*

In Figure 13-4, you can see that we first obtain the path to the All Users desktop. We don't actually need the All Users desktop; we just used it to obtain the path of the profiles on the system. For example, with a default installation of Windows XP, ALLUSERSDSKTP would be equal to C:\Documents And Settings\All Users\Desktop. The only part of this string that we care about (at least for this example) is the C:\Documents and Settings. We use the Parse String action to accomplish this task; the Parse String dialog box is shown in Figure 13-5.

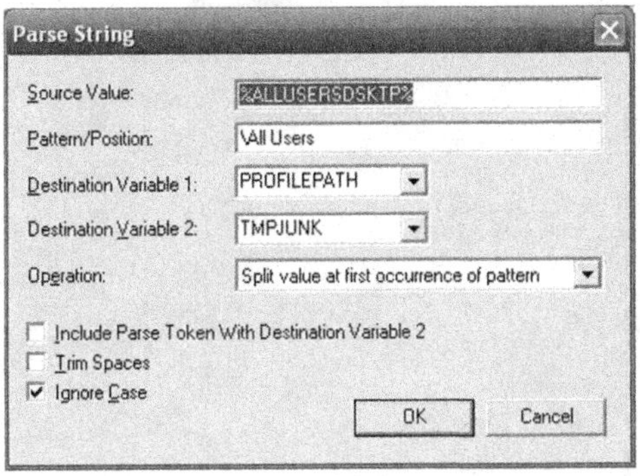

Figure 13-5. *Using the Parse String action to obtain the path to the profiles directory*

In Figure 13-5, you can see we're using the ALLUSERSDSKTP variable and looking for a Pattern/ Position equal to **\All Users** (notice we enabled the Ignore Case option). Assuming the path to the All Users desktop is C:\Documents And Settings\All Users\Desktop (which is the default for Windows XP), upon completion of the Parse String action, the variable PROFILEPATH would be equal to C:\Documents and Settings, and the variable TMPJUNK would be equal to \Desktop. As you can see in Figure 13-8, the PROFILEPATH variable is helpful in determining the users on this system.

Figure 13-6 illustrates the Get Environment Variable dialog box used to obtain the value of an environment variable. In our example, we're setting the SMS Installer variable %SYSTEMP% to the environment variable %TEMP%. The Get Environment Variable action can be used to obtain the value for any system variable.

Note To list the environment variables available on a system from a command prompt, use the Set command and press the Enter key.

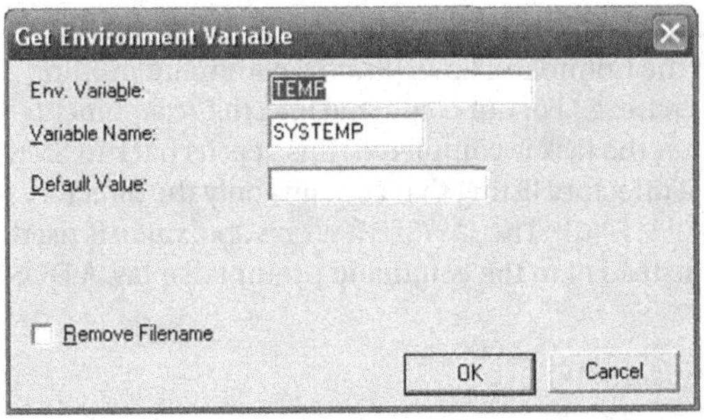

Figure 13-6. *Using the Get Environment Variable action to obtain the environment variable %TEMP%*

Figure 13-7 demonstrates basic use of the Install File(s) action. In this action, we specify the Source Pathname to be \\MySMSServer\SourceFiles\GoogleLaunch\GoogleLocal.ico, and the Destination Pathname to be %SYSWIN%\GoogleLocal.ico. This action will install the icon to the Windows directory, so that it can be referenced in the Create Shortcut action. As you can see, many more options are available in the Install File(s) action. SMS Installer Help (press F1 while the window shown in Figure 13-7 is in focus) and *Microsoft SMS Installer* by Rod Trent (McGraw-Hill, 2000) can help you understand each of these options.

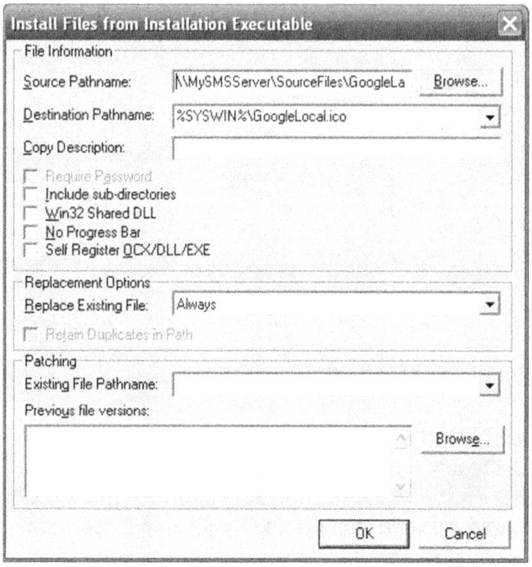

Figure 13-7. *Using the Install File(s) action*

Figure 13-8 shows the Execute Program action dialog box. In our example, we are simply creating a file named users.txt, which contains a listing of user names for the system. For the EXE Path, simply enter the path and executable name. Again in our example, cmd.exe is in the %WinDir%\System32 directory. Since this directory is included in the Windows path statement, there is no need to specify the path. Notice that the Execute Program action splits the EXE Path and the Command Line. If you were to run this command from a command prompt, you would execute the following:

```
cmd.exe /c dir /b /ad "%PROFILEPATH%">%SYSTEMP%\users.txt
```

In the Execute Program action, you enter **cmd.exe** for the EXE Path, and **/c dir /b /ad "%PROFILEPATH%">%SYSTEMP%\users.txt** for the Command Line. (From a command prompt, you enter **cmd.exe /?** for all available arguments for cmd.exe.) For our command line, the /c argument for cmd.exe means to exit the command prompt after the task is completed (this gets us back to SMS Installer installation). We use dir /b /ad to obtain a directory listing that contains only the directory name(s) of each subdirectory under the variable PROFILEPATH. The >%SYSTEM%\users.txt value is used to redirect the output results to the file users.txt instead of to the command prompt display. A DOS equivalent to this line follows:

```
dir /b /ad "C:\Documents and Settings">%TEMP%\users.txt
```

Notice in Figure 13-8 that we also enabled the Wait for Program to Exit check box. Without this check box enabled, SMS Installer would continue through its script even before the task has completed. Continuing this script without the Wait for Program to Exit check box enabled can cause problems sometimes, because as in our example, the very next step is to read the text file. If the text file hasn't yet been completely written, you may encounter an error.

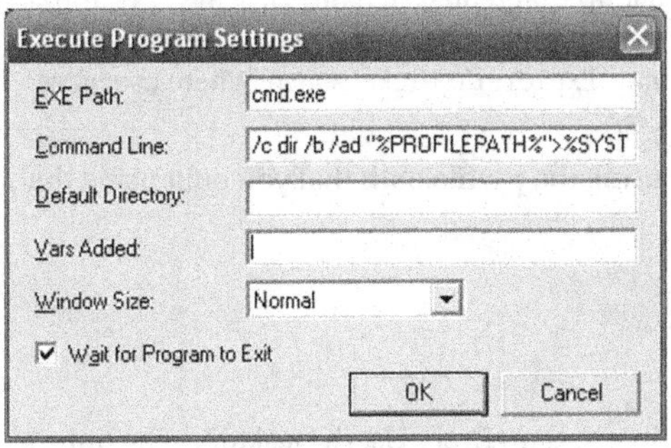

Figure 13-8. *The Execute Program action used to obtain a list of all profiles on the system*

A considerable amount of dynamic help is available for SMS Installer. Even though you don't see a Help button on any of the figures in this recipe, simply press the F1 key to display Help for the desired action.

Note Don't be afraid to press the F1 key when using SMS Installer. You may be surprised by the amount of information available at your fingertips.

Download CreateShortcutOnEachUsersDesktop.ipf from the *SMS Recipes* source code site.

See Also

- Recipe 13-1, "Creating a Shortcut on the All Users Desktop," demonstrates how to create a shortcut on the All Users desktop.

- Recipe 13-3, "Creating a Shortcut on the Quick Launch Toolbar," demonstrates how to create a shortcut on each user's Quick Launch Toolbar.

- SMS Installer Help provides detailed information for each action mentioned in this recipe.

- Chapter 5 of *Microsoft SMS Installer* by Rod Trent (McGraw-Hill, 2000) provides detailed information for most of the actions available in SMS Installer.

- Microsoft's Hey, Scripting Guy! web page demonstrates an alternate method you can use to enumerate user profiles on a system (http://www.microsoft.com/technet/scriptcenter/resources/qanda/jun05/hey0603.msp).

13-3. Creating a Shortcut on the Quick Launch Toolbar

Problem

You want to create a shortcut on each user's Quick Launch toolbar.

Solution

1. Use the Execute Program action to execute the following command from the SMS Installer executable:

```
cmd.exe /c dir /b /ad "C:\Documents and Settings">%TEMP%\users.txt
```

2. Use the Read/Update Text File action to start a loop that reads each line of users.txt and uses those lines of data to build a complete profile path to C:\Documents and Settings\ username\Application Data\Microsoft\Internet Explorer\Quick Launch, where username is the name of the user obtained from users.txt.

3. During the loop in step 2, create the shortcut using the profile path that you built using the data from users.txt.

4. Delete %temp%\users.txt.

Discussion

This recipe is very similar to Recipe 13-2, "Creating a Shortcut on Every User's Desktop." The only difference is the target directory for the shortcut.

Figure 13-9 demonstrates the same process as Recipe 13-2. We obtain the path to the user profiles and enumerate each one, adding a shortcut to each of their Quick Launch toolbars.

```
Set Variable QLAUNCH to Application Data\Microsoft\Internet Explorer\Quick Launch
Rem Obtain the path to the All Users Desktop
Get Registry Key Software\Microsoft\Windows\CurrentVersion\Explorer\Shell Folders place in Variable A

Rem Parse string ALLUSERSDSKTP to extract Profile Paths
Parse String "%ALLUSERSDSKTP%" into PROFILEPATH and TMPJUNK

Rem Get the TEMP environement variable
Get Environment Variable TEMP into Variable SYSTEMP

Rem Install the icon file locally
Install File \\MySMSServer\SourceFiles\GoogleLaunch\GoogleLocal.ico to %SYSWIN%\GoogleLocal.ic

Rem Execute Command to create %temp%\users.txt, and wait...
Execute cmd.exe /c dir /b /ad "%PROFILEPATH%">%SYSTEMP%\users.txt (Wait)

Rem Read each line of users.txt, and use the username to comlete the path
Rem    to the user's quick Launch
Read lines of file %SYSTEMP%\users.txt into variable USERNAME Start Block
  If USERNAME Not Equal (Ignore Case) "Administrator" then
    If USERNAME Not Equal (Ignore Case) "All Users" then
      Create Shortcut from c:\Program Files\Internet Explorer\iexplore.exe to %PROFILEPATH%\%USER
    End Block
  End Block
End Block

Delete File(s) %SYSTEMP%\users.txt
```

Figure 13-9. *CreateShortcutOnEachUsersQuickLaunch.ipf code within SMS Installer*

Note There is no All Users Quick Launch toolbar. However, you could create a common Toolbar (built into your desktop image, configured in your Default User profile) that could provide the same functionality as an All Users Quick Launch toolbar.

See Also

- Recipe 13-1, "Creating a Shortcut on the All Users Desktop," demonstrates how to create a shortcut on the All Users desktop.

- Recipe 13-2, "Creating a Shortcut on Every User's Desktop," demonstrates how to create a shortcut on each user's desktop.

- SMS Installer Help provides detailed information for each action mentioned in this recipe.

- Chapter 5 of *Microsoft SMS Installer* by Rod Trent (McGraw-Hill, 2000) provides detailed information for most of the actions available in SMS Installer.

- Microsoft's Hey, Scripting Guy! web page demonstrate an alternate method you can use to enumerate user profiles on a system (http://www.microsoft.com/technet/scriptcenter/resources/qanda/jun05/hey0603.mspx).

13-4. Modifying Shortcut Target Paths

Problem

You need to modify the target path of a shortcut without losing additional shortcut properties.

Solution

Example 13-1 demonstrates how to change the target shortcuts for Microsoft Access (msaccess.exe) from Office XP to Office 2003.

Example 13-1. *ModifyShorcuts.vbs*

```
strNewAccess = ucase("c:\program Files\microsoft " & _
    "office\office11\msaccess.EXE")

strComputer = "." 'connecting to local computer

Set objWMIService = GetObject _
    ("winmgmts:\\" & strComputer & "\root\cimv2")
Set colFiles = objWMIService. _
    ExecQuery("Select * from CIM_DataFile where Extension = 'lnk'")
    For Each objFile in colFiles
        CheckShortcut(objFile.Name)
    Next

Sub CheckShortcut(strName)
    wscript.echo strName
    'this actually looks inside the shortcut and modifies
    '    "targetpath" as needed. This only affects the target,
    '    not the arguments after the target.
    Set WshShell = wscript.CreateObject("WScript.Shell")
    'using create is a bit confusing.  If it already exists,
    '    CreateShortcut edits instead of creates.
    Set oShellLink = WshShell.CreateShortcut(strName)

    If InStr(1, UCase(oShellLink.TargetPath), _
        UCase("MSACCESS.EXE")) Then
        oShellLink.TargetPath = strNewAccess
        oShellLink.IconLocation = strNewAccess
    End If
    oShellLink.Save
end sub
```

Discussion

Consider the following scenario: You're *finally* upgrading from Office XP Professional to Office 2003 Professional. The applications department in your company has a small team dedicated to Microsoft

Access development and maintenance. They have done an outstanding job of making users' lives easier, because they created custom shortcuts for each database that would launch the msaccess.exe executable, followed by command lines for user names, target databases, blood types, and . . . well, you get the picture.

Unfortunately, when you upgrade to Office 2003, the target path for these icons will not update to reflect the new target path to msaccess.exe in Office 2003. In fact, you may lose the icons completely unless you modify the target for them first (review the references in this recipe's "See Also" section for more information). To complicate this issue even further, these shortcuts could be anywhere on the system. They may be on the user's desktop or Quick Launch toolbar. They could also be in the All Users desktop or maybe even on the Start menu! Changing each of these shortcuts could be challenging enough, but now we have to locate them, too. Luckily, VBScript comes to the rescue!

Example 13-1 demonstrates how to modify the target path for all Microsoft Access shortcuts. First, we define strNewAccess as the target path of the new version of Office. Next, we perform a WMI query on the CIM_DataFile class to collect all shortcuts on the system (all files with a .lnk extension). Next, we enumerate each shortcut and call the CheckShortcut method to check the Target property of each shortcut to see if the string msaccess.exe is in the target path. If so, we modify the TargetPath and IconLocation properties and call the Save method.

Note The CreateShortcut method is used to *create* a new shortcut if the shortcut doesn't currently exist. If the shortcut does exist, CreateShortcut is used to *modify* the existing shortcut.

See Also

- Greg Ramsey provided a script similar to the example in this recipe, but also with logging, in the article titled "Office 2003 Lessons Learned—Part I" on myITforum.com (http://www.myitforum.com/articles/6/view.asp?id=6984).

- The MSDN Library provides additional information about the Win32_ShortcutFile class: http://msdn.microsoft.com/library/default.asp?url=/library/en-us/wmisdk/wmi/win32_shortcutfile.asp.

- The MSDN Library also provides additional information about the CreateShortcut method.

13-5. Listing Predefined Variables for SMS Installer

Problem

You want to identify the predefined variables available in SMS Installer.

Solution

A list of Predefined Variables available during installation execution follows; this list was obtained from SMS Installer Help (search for **Predefined Variables**), with additional comments from us:

RESTART: This variable contains the restart status of the installation. If during your installation, a file to be replaced is in use, the RESTART flag will be set, prompting for a restart of the system (if run in attended mode) or automatically restarting without user warning (if run in unattended mode). Typically, when we run into a situation where a reboot may be forced, we use the Set Variable action at the end of the installation script and set the RESTART flag to blank (no quotes, no numbers, no spaces—just blank). This will prevent SMS Installer from prompting for or forcing a reboot. You could then set the SMS program to SMS Restarts the Computer, to give the user a countdown warning before rebooting.

WIN: This variable contains the path of the Windows directory (usually C:\Windows). On a multiuser system, such as Windows 2000 with Terminal Services enabled, this path may be the user-specific Windows directory on a computer with multiple user directories. This variable has gotten us into trouble once or twice—we had been using it so long, we forgot about this characteristic of the WIN variable. If you never install software on Terminal Services–enabled servers, the WIN variable will work consistently for you, but we suggest using SYSWIN all of the time, unless you have a reason for files to be installed into the user-specific WIN variable on Terminal Services.

SYS: This variable contains the path of the Windows System directory (usually C:\Windows\System).

SYS32: This variable contains the system directory for Win32 files under Windows (usually C:\Windows\System32).

SYSWIN: This variable contains the Windows directory. On a multiuser system, such as Windows 2000 with Terminal Services enabled, this variable returns a listing of the root system directory (not the user-defined Windows directory).

TEMP: This variable contains the directory in which temporary files can be placed. This variable is useful for placing DLLs before you call their functions. Keep in mind that the TEMP variable will point to the location under which the system runs the installation. If the installation is run under a user context, the TEMP variable will point to the user's temp directory (e.g., C:\Documents and Settings\UserName\Local Settings\Temp). If it's run using administrative privileges, you may find the TEMP variable pointing to the C:\Windows\Temp directory.

INST: This variable contains the directory that contains the SMS Installer–generated executable file that is running. We have found this variable to be very useful over the years. The INST variable can be useful when you want to display a Readme.txt file that is located on the same disk as the Installer-generated executable file. The INST variable contains the full path to wherever the executable is executed, which is very helpful in situations where you want to launch a second executable from the first executable. In this situation, simply create an Execute Program action where the EXE Path points to %INST%\2ndExecutable.exe, where 2ndExecutable.exe resides in the same directory as the first installation executable.

CMDLINE: This variable contains the command-line options that were passed to the Installer-generated executable file. It is also very handy if you want to pass options to your installation executable. For example, you could parse a value from the CMDLINE to modify a registry value.

LANG: This variable contains the language that users selected in a multilanguage installation.

FONTS: This variable contains the directory containing the fonts installed on the client computer.

PROCEXITCODE: This variable contains the exit code of the last process called using the Execute Program script item with the Wait for Program to Exit option selected. This variable can also be very handy. If, for example, you use the Execute Program action to launch a second installation, you can use PROCEXITCODE to determine if (or how) the installation continues from this point.

Discussion

Spend some time getting familiar with the predefined variables. They will come in very handy someday!

See Also

- Review the SMS Installer Help; search for **Predefined Variables** for information.

13-6. Modifying a Registry Entry in HKEY_CURRENT_USER for Each User

Problem

You need to modify registry information in HKEY_CURRENT_USER for each user that logs into a system.

Solution

1. Install the installation file that contains the current user registry settings to the target system.

2. On the target system, launch regedit.exe, and navigate to the following registry key:

   HKEY_LOCAL_MACHINE\SOFTWARE\Microsoft\Active Setup\Installed Components\

3. Create a new unique registry key (e.g., CLAIM_HKCUMOD).

4. Create the following two values, both of type REG_SZ:

   StubPath=<local path>\CLAIM_HKCUMOD.exe
   Version=1

Discussion

You may occasionally receive requests to modify a registry key in the user's profile. You can use one of the following approaches to accomplish this task:

- Create an SMS installation package to modify the HKEY_CURRENT_USER registry, and send it via SMS to run with the user's permissions. But when you send this installation via SMS, by default, it will run for the first user only. If a second user (including a new user) logs on to the system, the registry modification will not appear, unless you configure SMS to run this program "For every user who logs on." By keeping the current user registry updated in this fashion, you will have to keep this SMS advertisement available to systems *forever*.

- Use a Windows program called reg.exe. With this program, you can perform REG LOAD and REG UNLOAD to temporarily load a user registry, merge registry information, and then unload the user registry. This program has to be run while no user is logged on, because you will not be able to mount the profile of any user that *is* logged on. You would have to repeat the process for each user on the system (including the default user). We have used this process in the past (before we were aware of the Active Setup feature), and it worked fairly well for us, but we always ran into a couple systems that were unable to unload the registry, causing problems for the user (and for us) the next day. This unload-and-load process is commonly used, though, and you will probably find more documentation on this approach than on the others mentioned in this recipe. To find out more about the reg.exe process, spend some time searching http://www.myITforum.com.

- Create a startup script that runs in the user's environment. Active Directory, Logon Scripts, or even adding a process to the Startup program group on the client can accomplish the task.

- Use Active Setup as described in this recipe.

Active Setup is a process that runs every time a user logs on to the system. When a user logs on, Active Setup checks the current user registry key HKEY_CURRENT_USER\SOFTWARE\Microsoft\Active Setup\Installed Components to verify that it matches HKEY_LOCAL_MACHINE\SOFTWARE\Microsoft\Active Setup\Installed Components. Each key in HKEY_LOCAL_MACHINE (HKLM) that has values for StubPath and Version is compared with HKEY_CURRENT_USER (HKCU) to verify that both values exist and that the values match identically. If either of these verifications tests negative, Active Setup executes the command value for StubPath and duplicates the key from HKLM to HKCU. Once HKCU has Version and StubPath values matching the values in HKLM, the program will not be executed for that user again unless the version changes.

Before we walk through the script in Figure 13-10, consider the following scenario: You have an in-house application called Claim. The developers of Claim need to point the client application to a different server. Unfortunately, the server settings for the Claim application are configured on a per-user basis (so the settings are stored in HKEY_CURRENT_USER). By creating two executables, you will be able to modify HKEY_CURRENT_USER for every user that logs on to the system.

First, make an installation that will modify the HKEY_CURRENT_USER registry settings, and call the installation CLAIM_HKCUMOD.exe. When you run this installation manually while a user is logged on, the client settings are correctly modified. Now that you know you have an installation that takes care of the settings, you'll create the wrapper around it to get it to install for each user.

Figure 13-10 demonstrates the installation wrapper executable (called HKCU_RegMod.exe) created by SMS Installer. This installation doesn't make the changes required for the Claim application; it merely enables the Windows client to configure the settings upon the next user logon. Think of it as a Run Once key for HKEY_CURRENT_USER, which is applied to each user at their next login.

First, we install CLAIM_HKCUMOD.exe to the local system. Next, we create the unique registry key CLAIM_HKCUMOD and place the two registry values within that key, as described earlier in this recipe. At this point, the HKCU_RegMod.exe installation is complete, and will return a "Successful Installation" status message to SMS. At this point, the first time each user logs on to the system, CLAIM_HKCUMOD.exe will run and modify the registry as previously configured.

```
Rem Install the File to be Run when the user logs in
Install File \\MySMSServer\Sources\CLAIM_HKCUMOD.exe to %SYSWIN%\CLAIM_HKCUMOD.exe

Rem Add/Update Registry keys in ActiveSetup
Registry Key SOFTWARE\Microsoft\Active Setup\Installed Components\CLAIM_HKCUMOD = %SYSWIN%\CLAIM_
Registry Key SOFTWARE\Microsoft\Active Setup\Installed Components\CLAIM_HKCUMOD = 1
```

Figure 13-10. *HKCU_RegMod.ipf code within SMS Installer*

See Also

- The WindowsITPro web page contains an example of modifying the current user registry using REG LOAD written by John Savill: http://www.windowsitpro.com/WindowsScripting/Article/ArticleID/48506/48506.html.

- Ed Tippelt provides additional information about the Active Setup method on the ETL Engineering Limited web site: http://www.etlengineering.com/installer/activesetup.txt.

13-7. Replacing All Instances of One File with Another

Problem

You want to replace all instances of one file with another on the local system. For example, you might want to replace all instances of Foo.Doc with Foo2.Doc.

Solution: Using SMS Installer

1. Use the Search for File action to search the local hard drive for instances of the desired file, combined with a while loop to identify multiple locations for the same file name on the system.

2. Use the Rename File/Directory action to make the original file a backup file.

3. Use the Install File(s) action to install the updated file.

Solution: Using VBScript

Example 13-2 demonstrates how to use VBScript to search drive `C:\` for one file and replace it with a new file.

Example 13-2. *FindAndReplace.vbs*

```
Const OverwriteExisting = TRUE
strComputer = "."
'Because of CIM_DataFile, split File Name and Extension into
' two variables
strFileName = "Foo"
strFileExt = "doc"
strNewFileName = "Foo2.doc"

'use this to obtain the current path to the VBScript
Set objFso= createobject("Scripting.FileSystemObject")
strScriptPath = objFso.GetParentFolderName(WScript.ScriptFullName)

Set objWMIService = GetObject("winmgmts:" _
    & "{impersonationLevel=impersonate}!\\" & _
    strComputer & "\root\cimv2")

'WQL query - notice we're only looking for files on C:
Set colFiles = objWMIService.ExecQuery _
    ("Select * from CIM_Datafile where FileName = '" & _
    strFileName & "' and Extension = '" & strFileExt & _
    "' and drive = 'C:'")

For Each objFile in colFiles
    'rename file
    objFile.Rename(objFile.Name & ".bak")
    'copy the new file
    objFSO.CopyFile strScriptPath & "\" & strNewFileName,_
        objFile.Drive & objFile.Path, OverwriteExisting
Next
```

Discussion

On occasion, you may be asked to "search and destroy" a file on every workstation in your environment. You may also be asked to replace that file with an updated file. The process can be a challenge, but hopefully, Example 13-2 and the following SMS Installer example (see Figure 13-11) will give you ideas for how to accomplish this task. Both of these scripts can also be modified to simply *remove* the desired file as well.

Example 13-2 shows how to accomplish the task or replace file A with file B using a VBScript script. After declaring the required variables, we use `objFso.GetParentFolderName(WScript.ScriptFullName)` to obtain the path to the VBScript script during script execution time (just like the variable %INST% in SMS Installer). This path will be used later in the script to copy the new file from the SMS distribution point to the local system. Next, we connect to the `\root\cimv2` namespace and perform a WQL query on the `CIM_DataFile` class to locate all files with the specified name (Foo.Doc) on the C: drive. Once we have the collection of files, we perform a for-each loop to append a .bak (a backup, for safety purposes) to the current file and then copy the new file from the distribution point (strScriptPath) to the file name and path of the file we just renamed.

Figure 13-11 demonstrates how to replace file A with file B for all instances on the local hard drive. First, we set the variable FindFile to Foo.doc and the variable FOUNDFILE to "" (null). Next, we create a while loop to continue searching for Foo.doc until the file no longer exists on the local drive. Once we find the file, we append a .bak to the end of it. Then we install the new file (Foo2.doc) in the same directory location as the original file (Foo.doc).

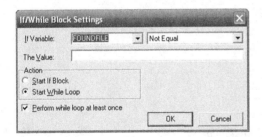

```
Rem File to find
Set Variable FINDFILE to Foo.doc
Set Variable FOUNDFILE to

Rem While Loop (perform loop at least once)
While FOUNDFILE Not Equal "" do

   Search for file %FINDFILE% place in Variable FOUNDFILE

   If FOUNDFILE Not Equal "" then
      Rename %FOUNDFILE%\%FINDFILE% to %FINDFILE%.Bak
      Install File \\smsserver\sources\FooDoc\Foo2.doc to %FOUNDFILE%\Foo2.doc
   End Block

End Block
```

Figure 13-11. *FindfileAndReplace.ipf code within SMS Installer*

Figure 13-12 demonstrates how to start a while loop in SMS Installer. Just before this while loop statement, we set the variable FOUNDFILE equal to "", which is exactly what causes this while loop to exit. Select the "Perform while loop at least once" check box, so that loop will operate at least one time.

Figure 13-12. *An If/While block action demonstrating a while loop*

Note Every If/While block must also use an End Block action. These blocks also give the installation script proper indentation, making the code easier for you to read. Refer to Figure 13-11 for an example.

As simple as it appears, Figure 13-13 is the focus of this example. Instead of entering the file name in this action, we use the predefined variable %FINDFILE%, which is equal to Foo.Doc in our example. If the file is found, the variable FOUNDFILE will contain the path to the file. If no file by the specified name is found, FOUNDFILE will be null (or ""). Also, we configure the action to search Local Hard Drives Only with a Search Depth of **0** (which causes the search of the entire drive). If we set the Search Depth to **3**, for example, the action will only search three levels deep in the directory structure.

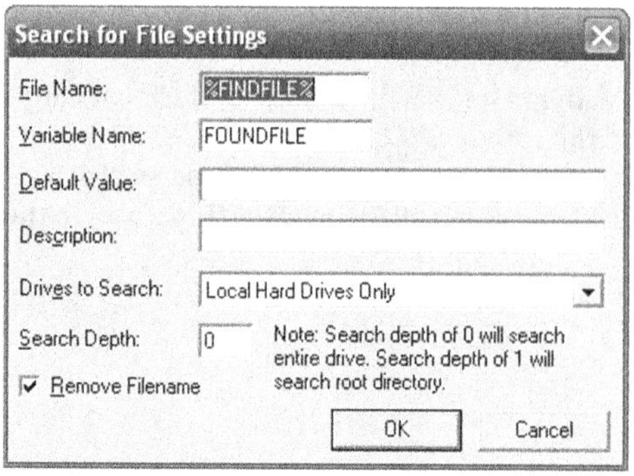

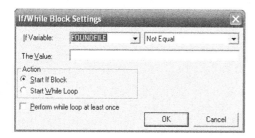

Figure 13-13. *The Search for File action*

Note In SMS Installer, do not use percent symbols when declaring a variable. Only use percent symbols when referring to an existing variable.

Figure 13-14 is fairly simple. As long as FOUNDFILE contains something other than "" (null), start the If block. This will cause the loop to continue until there are no more files of that name.

Figure 13-14. *An If/While block action demonstrating an if loop*

Figure 13-15 illustrates the Rename File/Directory action in SMS Installer. As you can see, we use two variables to obtain the path and file name, and then simply append .Bak to the end of the file.

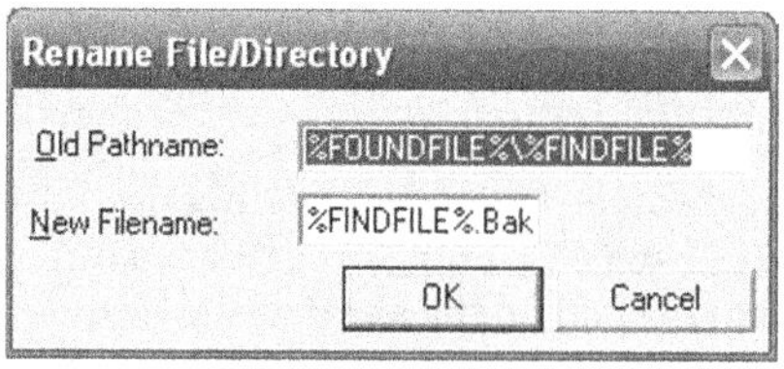

Figure 13-15. *Rename File/Directory action*

Note that we cannot use the Search for File Settings dialog box shown in Figure 13-11 to install a brand-new Foo.doc, since the while loop will continue to run until no Foo.Doc files exist on the system. To perform a one-for-one replacement using SMS Installer, you need some additional magic.

One alternative would be to create two `while` loops. The first loop renames the file you're looking for, and the second loop uses the renamed file name from the first loop to install the new file (using the original name). Figure 13-16 demonstrates how to use two loops to complete this task.

```
Rem File to find
Set Variable FINDFILE to Foo.doc
Set Variable FOUNDFILE to

Rem While Loop (perform loop at least once)
While FOUNDFILE Not Equal "" do

    Search for file %FINDFILE% place in Variable FOUNDFILE

    If FOUNDFILE Not Equal "" then
        Rename %FOUNDFILE%\%FINDFILE% to %FINDFILE%.Bak
    End Block

End Block

Set Variable FOUNDFILE to
Rem While Loop (perform loop at least once)
While FOUNDFILE Not Equal "" do

    Search for file %FINDFILE%.bak place in Variable FOUNDFILE

    If FOUNDFILE Not Equal "" then
    Rename %FOUNDFILE%\%FINDFILE%.Bak to %FINDFILE%.Bak.Old
    Install File C:\scripts\sms\swdist\Foo2.doc to %FOUNDFILE%\Foo.doc
    End Block

End Block
```

Figure 13-16. *FindFileAndReplace_II.ipf code within SMS Installer*

See Also

- Review the WMI SDK (located in the MSDN Library) for more information about the properties and methods (such as `Rename`) available in the `CIM_DataFile` class: `http://msdn.microsoft.com/library/default.asp?url=/library/en-us/wmisdk/wmi/cim_datafile.asp`.

13-8. Launching an Installation Program Interactively

Problem

You want to use SMS to launch an installation program that allows the user to select options and/or see installation progress.

Solution

1. In the SMS Administrator console, navigate to the desired SMS package.
2. From the desired SMS package, navigate to the appropriate program.
3. Right-click the program, and select Properties.
4. In the Program Properties dialog box, select the Environment tab.
5. Enable the "Allow users to interact with this program" check box.
6. Click OK to save your changes to the program.

Discussion

Enabling a user to interact with an installation program in SMS is fairly simple. On the Environment tab for the program, you simply enable the "Allow users to interact with this program" check box. To enable this check box, the program must be configured to run "Only when a user is logged on" or "Whether or not a user is logged on."

Enabling the check box is the easy part of allowing a user to interact with a program, but there is more to consider. The level of interaction in your installation program depends on the installation software package (e.g., SMS Installer, InstallShield, Windows Installer, etc.) and the command line used to install that software. Each application you deploy may use different command-line switches during installation.

Remember, Microsoft SMS is a delivery mechanism. SMS can *hide* installation dialogs and progress bars from the user's view at installation time, but SMS cannot display dialogs if the installation program is not configured to display them. Spend some time researching the proper command-line switches for each application you desire to install. Refer to the "See Also" section of this recipe for additional resources.

In our environment, we avoid (like the plague) installing software that requires user intervention during the installation process. Relying on users to select the correct options can sometimes be a challenge and can delay consistent software deployment in your environment. Also, depending on the configuration of the software installation, the process used by the installer may run with more rights than the user, increasing opportunities for mischief.

We do, however, attempt to display progress windows whenever possible. We deploy as many unattended installations as possible during the evening, when most users are not at their desks. But when new systems are brought on to the network or laptops connect back to the network, we want them to be able to *see* that something is being installed and, hopefully, reduce the chances of a user rebooting a system because the computer is running slowly.

See Also

- Recipe 13-9, "Finding Information for Deploying Windows Installer–Based Applications," provides deployment information of Windows Installer–based (.msi-based) applications.

- Recipe 13-10, "Finding Information for Deploying InstallShield-Based Applications," provides deployment information of InstallShield-based applications.

13-9. Finding Information on Deploying Windows Installer–Based Applications

Problem

You want to find more information about deploying Windows Installer–based (.msi-based) applications.

Solution

Here's a partial list (in no particular order) of free information about Windows Installer:

- "Windows Installer Error Messages": http://msdn.microsoft.com/library/en-us/msi/setup/windows_installer_error_messages.asp

- "Windows Installer Error Codes": http://msdn.microsoft.com/library/en-us/msi/setup/error_codes.asp

- "Standard Installer Command-Line Options (Windows Installer 3.0 and newer)": http://msdn.microsoft.com/library/default.asp?url=/library/en-us/msi/setup/standard_installer_command_line_options.asp

- "Windows Installer Command-Line Options (All Versions)": http://msdn.microsoft.com/library/default.asp?url=/library/en-us/msi/setup/command_line_options.asp and http://support.microsoft.com/kb/314881

- "How to Use Property Reference Command-Line Parameters with Msiexec.exe": http://support.microsoft.com/?kbid=230781

- Windows Installer start page: http://msdn.microsoft.com/library/en-us/msi/setup/windows_installer_start_page.asp

- "Windows Installer Scripting Examples": http://msdn.microsoft.com/library/en-us/msi/setup/windows_installer_scripting_examples.asp

- "Overview of the Windows Installer Technology": http://support.microsoft.com/?kbid=310598

- InstallSite (for several links to additional information about the Windows Installer and InstallShield products): http://www.installsite.org

- "MSI 101: Introduction to Windows Installer" at DesktopEngineer.com: http://desktopengineer.com/msiintro

- "MSI 110: The Definitive Guide to Windows Installer Technology for Administrators" at DesktopEngineer.com: http://desktopengineer.com/msiebook

- "Windows Installer: Benefits and Implementation for System Administrators": http://www.microsoft.com/technet/prodtechnol/windows2000serv/maintain/featusability/winmsi.mspx

- Wise Solutions System Administrator Resource Center (for additional information about using Windows Installer and other unattended installation methods): http://www.wise.com/sysadmin_resources.asp

- SourceForge.net (for a project with a lot of information about unattended installations and command-line switches): http://unattended.sourceforge.net/installers.php.\

Discussion

Windows Installer is the wave of the future. We haven't seen that mentioned anywhere else on the Web yet, so we thought we would take this opportunity to say it ourselves. One of the SMS administrator's greatest challenges can be deploying software. A *properly created* Windows Installer file in conjunction with good documentation can make software deployment much easier, so spend some time getting to know Windows Installer.

Not all Windows Installer applications are alike. While the majority that we have dealt with follow Microsoft's standards, we have run across a few bad apples that we still spend a lot of time working on during a deployment. Before spending too much time on a crazy installation, visit the web sites mentioned in the following "See Also" section to help ease your pain. And don't forget to ease someone else's pain by submitting your installation solutions to web sites like http://www.appdeploy.com.

See Also

- Recipe 13-10, "Finding Information for Deploying InstallShield-Based Applications," provides information about InstallShield-based applications.

- Learn from others! Spend some time at http://www.appdeploy.com and http://www.myITforum.com to obtain information about deploying specific Windows Installer applications. Search the articles, and post questions to user forums. You will find a lot of administrators like you who are willing to help.

13-10. Finding Information on Deploying InstallShield-Based Applications

Problem

You want to find more information about deploying InstallShield-based applications (InstallScript scripts).

Solution

This solution refers to *older* InstallShield installations that use the InstallScript language. For InstallShield installations that use Windows Installer technology, see the previous recipe.

A partial list (in no particular order) of free information about InstallScript installations follows:

- The Macrovision web site offers the very detailed article "HOWTO: Authoring a Silent Installation" about InstallShield silent installations and error codes at `http://support.installshield.com/kb/view.asp?pcode=ALL&articleid=Q101901`.

- AppDeploy.com has an article titled "InstallShield Setup Silent Installation Switches" at `http://appdeploy.com/tips/detail.asp?id=18`.

- AppDeploy.com also offers the article "InstallShield Error Codes (Setup.log)" at `http://www.appdeploy.com/tips/detail.asp?id=20`.

- The InstallShield web site has an article titled "INFO: What Command-Line Parameters Are Available for Setup.exe?" at `http://support.installshield.com/kb/view.asp?articleid=Q102894`.

- The InstallShield web site also offers the article "INFO: Setup.exe Command-Line Parameters" at `http://support.installshield.com/kb/view.asp?articleid=Q105473`.

- SourceForge.net has a project with a lot of information about unattended installations and command-line switches at `http://unattended.sourceforge.net/installers.php`.

Discussion

In our experience, InstallScript unattended installations can be a bit more temperamental than other unattended installations (e.g., Windows Installer, Wise, etc.). As with all installations, be sure to test the installation in as many situations as you can. On several occasions, we have run into difficulties when a system that has never had the software installed reacts differently than a system that once had the software installed (even if it was a previous version). You will also find that the installation log and exit codes are a bit more cryptic than Windows Installer information.

See Also

- Recipe 13-9, "Finding Information for Deploying Windows Installer–Based Applications," provides information about Windows Installer–based (`.msi`-based) applications.

- Learn from others! Spend some time at `http://www.appdeploy.com` and `http://www.myITforum.com` to obtain information about deploying specific Windows Installer applications. Search the articles, and post questions to user forums. You will find a lot of administrators like you who are willing to help.

13-11. Repackaging Software

Problem

You want to find more information about repackaging software.

Solution

The following web resources (in no particular order) can help you with your software repackaging endeavors:

- Several white papers are available at the Wise Solutions web site. Of particular interest to this recipe are "The Case for Quality Assurance in Enterprise Software Packaging," "Enterprise Software Packaging," "Repackaging Basics," and "Disadvantages of Repackaging Applications" (http://www.wise.com/sysadmin_resources_page.asp).

- InstallShield (Macrovision) published a book titled *Administrator's Introduction to Application Repackaging and Software Deployment Using Windows Installer* by Bob Baker and Robert Dickau (2002) (http://www.macrovision.com/services/education/publications/repackaging/index.shtml).

- The Macrovision web site offers the article "The Pros and Cons of Repackaging Applications" (http://www.installshield.com/news/newsletter/0508-articles/pro_con.asp).

- Microsoft has downloads of white papers provided by InstallShield (Macrovision); those most relevant to this recipe are "MSI Repackaging and Customization Best Practices Guide" and "The 20 Commandments of Software Packaging" (http://www.microsoft.com/technet/desktopdeployment/bdd/enterprise/abstract.mspx).

- Michael Drummond (of Wise Solutions) posted a few articles on myITforum.com about repackaging best practices (http://www.myitforum.com/contrib/default.asp?nm=Michael%20Drummond&cid=5395).

Discussion

Many seasoned SMS administrators consider repackaging software an art more than a science. Five years ago, we would have totally agreed with this. Today, however, we only partially agree. With repackaging products from vendors like Wise Solutions and InstallShield, repackaging has become more consistent. Features such as virtual capture, conflict management, automated testing, application isolation, and package validation have greatly improved the software repackaging process.

WHAT IS SOFTWARE REPACKAGING?

When you repackage software, you take a preinstallation snapshot of a clean model system, install the desired software by selecting the appropriate installation options, and then take a postinstallation snapshot. You create an installation package based on the differences between the two snapshots.

Inevitably, you will capture extra garbage while following this process, and this is where the seasoned SMS administrators' "form of art" idea comes into play. Depending on your application repackager, the "normal" garbage may be removed automatically. For successful repackaging, further analysis will always be required by the administrator repacking the software to ensure that excess data is not included in the new installation.

The advantage to software repackaging is that you will know exactly what modifications will be done to your clients at installation time. One disadvantage is that you may lose functionality of the program in mixed environments (e.g., multiple-hardware or multiple-operating-systems configurations). For example, a specific application may install one set of components for Windows XP systems and a separate (or partially separate) set for Windows Vista. Another disadvantage is that you may not be able to apply vendor-supplied patches to your repackaged installation, requiring you to repackage patches to apply to the installation.

Caution Repackage applications as a last resort only! When possible, use the vendor-supplied unattended installation method.

If an application vendor provides a method to install and configure the software in an unattended fashion, use all your strength to follow that method before considering repackaging the application—especially if the application is a Windows Installer–based application. Many Windows Installer applications use a feature called *self-healing*, which will fail (or at least function differently than the vendor's version) if self-healing is initiated in the future.

Adhere to the following basic rules when repackaging software:

- Repackage only as a last resort.

- Keep your environment as standard as possible.

- Always use a clean model workstation when creating snapshots.

- Try to be conservative when repackaging. Often when repackaging, files and registry entries that are not part of the actual installation will be captured, because other services and processes are running on the model system. Take the time to clean up the repackaged installation to ensure that you're not going to accidentally install configurations and files for anything other than the desired application. Cleaning up a repackaged installation can be the most difficult part of repackaging, and this is where the seasoned packager will shine.

- Consider using virtual computer systems (e.g., Microsoft Virtual PC, VMware, etc.) for repackaging, unless the application you're repackaging affects system hardware.

- Test, test, test. Extra time spent testing now will reduce the chances of spending time in front of your CIO explaining what happened.

- Test as an average user. Hopefully, not everyone in your environment is an administrator. You want to test with the lowest possible rights for the application.

- Get the requestor involved. Work with the experts on the software. Have them perform full function tests on your software. Have them sign off on it to confirm that it's working properly (which will encourage them to perform full function tests).

- Test some more—trust us.

- Keep your repackaging source file(s) handy, along with the installation media used to create the capture, in case it's needed in the future.

- Even if you return to your original package to update it someday, don't delete that original repackage. You may have thousands of clients that were installed using the original installation. You'll want to keep that around for future testing. For example, if you deployed the original package to 2,000 systems, and 3,000 other systems received the second revision, always keep the original around, so that you can avoid application compatibility problems with future installations

---

Note Software repackaging is most successful in a standardized environment.

13-12. Selecting Repackaging Software

Problem

You want to select the best repackaging software for your environment.

Solution

Which software repackaging application should you purchase? Unfortunately, this is a difficult question to answer, but we will attempt to give you some guidance in this decision.

If you are new to repackaging, we suggest that you get your feet wet first; some ideas for places to start follow:

Microsoft SMS Installer: True, this product is becoming an antique, but it's a great place to start learning about application repackaging and new application packaging. SMS Installer is very lightweight; you have the ability to create an installation executable (.exe) or a Windows Installer (.msi) installation in some cases. We suggest using SMS Installer to create executables. SMS Installer is free to companies that are licensed to use SMS (http://www.microsoft.com/smserver/downloads/20/tools/installer.mspx).

FLEXnet AdminSutdio 7 SMS Edition: FLEXnet AdminStudio 7 SMS Edition is another tool available from the Microsoft SMS download site. This tool allows you to repackage installations into true Windows Installer (.msi) installations. It also converts SMS, Novel ZENworks, Veritas WinINSTALL, and Wise WSE software packages directly into Windows Installer files. The SMS edition also includes the InstallShield Tuner, used for creating Windows Installer transforms (.mst). The biggest limitation we see (as far as a repackager) is that you can only *exclude* files and registry settings from the package capture; you cannot *add* additional files or registry information. This product also includes a limited SMS 2003 web console that "provides Web-based access to key settings and configuration capabilities including server connection settings, package selection, package configuration, distribution points, and package summary" (http://www.microsoft.com/smserver/downloads/2003/featurepacks/adminstudio/default.mspx).

Once you've become familiar with these tools, if you feel they do not provide you with the features you require, consider more powerful (and more expensive) packaging suites, two of which follow:

Wise Package Studio: Wise Package Studio is a very powerful packaging suite. Two versions are currently available: Standard and Professional. The Standard Edition is a very powerful product and is considered a stand-alone packaging tool. The Professional Edition adds a considerable number of enterprise features to the program, including the two main features: the Quality Assurance Module and the Enterprise Management Server. The Enterprise Management Server gives you the ability to store packages in a repository, promoting collaboration in a packaging team environment. Visit the Wise Package Studio web site for detailed information on the latest version (http://www.wise.com/wps.asp).

FLEXnet AdminStudio: FLEXnet AdminStudio is a complete packaging solution from Macrovision (InstallShield), and it has three editions available currently. The Standard Edition is similar in features to the Wise Package Studio Standard Edition, with the addition of a limited-feature web-based console for SMS. The Professional Edition adds ConflictSolver and QualityManager testing features. The Enterprise Edition includes security management inside of AdminStudio, a web-based Report Center, and a patch impact manager. Visit the web site for detailed information on the latest version (http://www.macrovision.com/products/flexnet_adminstudio/adminstudio/index.shtml).

These two products boast too many features to accurately compare in this recipe. The information provided here is merely to spark your interest in the abilities of these two packaging suites. We highly recommend taking the time to evaluate each product and to download and test the evaluation copies. Also, don't be afraid to contact your nearest SMS users' group to see about bringing each product in at future meetings for a demonstration.

Full-featured suites are very expensive, so evaluate them to see which best fits your needs. It may also be to your benefit to post the question to online forums (e.g., SMS newsgroups, http://www.myITforum.com, etc.).

See Also

- Check out http://www.appdeploy.com and http://www.myITforum.com for updated product reviews and comparisons of software packaging and repackaging suites.

- Review Chapter 1 for more information about online forums and SMS newsgroups.

WHAT IS A WRAPPER?

A *wrapper* is an executable that is used to wrap multiple tasks into one task during software distribution. For example, assume your company just purchased a new application from Acme Corporation called Widget 2.0. The installation program is rather basic; you simply add a /s to the end of the execution line to install the program. But for your environment, management wants to have a shortcut created on the desktop to launch the application, and unfortunately, this feature isn't included in the Widget installation program. You have multiple options for installing this shortcut:

- Repackage the Widget 2.0 installation, and include the code to install the shortcut. This is not our recommended method; we suggest using the vendor-supplied silent installation whenever possible.

- Create a separate installation executable (we'll call it Widget_Customize.exe), and within SMS, leverage the Run Another Program First feature in the Program Properties dialog box. By setting this option, every time SMS installs Widget 2.0, Widget_Customize.exe will also be installed. This method will work well when installing software via SMS. But when your desktop team installs the Widget application manually, they will have to remember to install the Widget 2.0 installation, followed by Widget_Customize.exe. This manual process will only be as consistent as the user who runs it manually.

- Create a wrapper installation executable that first executes the Widget 2.0 installation, waits for the executable process to terminate, and then installs the shortcut on the desktop. SMS can use this wrapper program to install the software, and your desktop team can use the same wrapper program to ensure a consistent installation.

As you can see from this example, wrappers can provide added flexibility. Wrappers can be used to make those one-off configuration changes (without modifying the original install) and allow you to bundle multiple installations into one.

Wrapper programs can hide secondary application failures. Remember that when you launch an executable with SMS during software distribution, SMS returns the exit code of that process. If your wrapper launches a secondary program that fails, unless you have coded the wrapper properly, the wrapper may still return a success code.

13-13. Using the Elevated Rights Deployment Tool

Problem

You want to use the SMS Elevated Rights Deployment Tool to deploy software.

Solution

The following solution shows how to use the Elevated Rights Deployment Tool to install the latest version of Microsoft Data Access Components (MDAC). On rare occasions, you may find an application that requires a reboot prior to registering DLLs, OCXs, and so on. If someone who is not an administrator logs on to a system that needs to register these files, the registration process may fail, and the application may not work as expected. MDAC is a fine example of this situation.

1. Download the latest version of MDAC (http://msdn.microsoft.com/data/mdac), and save it to a location to be used as your package source for the SMS package (e.g., C:\Source\MDAC on your primary site server).

2. Download the SMS 2003 Administration Feature Pack (http://www.microsoft.com/smserver/downloads/2003/adminpack.mspx), and save it to a temporary location.

3. Extract the zipped file to your SMS primary site server (e.g., C:\SMSTools\AdminFP).

4. On your primary site server, execute RunOnce_Setup.exe (located in the AdminFP\RunOnce directory) and accept the license agreement.

5. In the Select Destination Directory dialog box, enter the path to your MDAC installation executable (**C:\Source\MDAC**), and click Next.

6. In the Distribution Settings dialog box, clear the check boxes for creating a collection, creating an advertisement, and assigning to all distribution points. For Package Name, enter an accurate name (e.g., **MDAC 2.8 SP1 Installation**), and click Next.

7. Move the MDAC installation executable (MDAC_TYP.EXE) into the newly created package directory (e.g., C:\source\MDAC\Package).

8. In the Command Line dialog box, enter the following command and click Next:

   ```
   mdac_typ /Q:A /C:"dasetup /Q /N"
   ```

9. Click Next to complete the package preparation, and click Finish to exit the installation wizard.

Discussion

The use of the Elevated Rights Deployment Tool is applicable if all of the following tests are true:

- A setup program, application, or script places entries into the RunOnce or RunOnceEx registry.
- Those entries require administrative credentials when the setup program, application, or script runs.
- You are using SMS to deploy the setup program, application, or script.

Consider our example deployment of MDAC 2.8 SP1 to workstations used by those with limited rights (typically, nonadministrators or non–power users). If you install this application manually and check the registry before rebooting the system, you will probably see information in the HKEY_LOCAL_MACHINE\SOFTWARE\Microsoft\Windows\CurrentVersion\RunOnce and HKEY_LOCAL_MACHINE\SOFTWARE\Microsoft\Windows\CurrentVersion\Run keys. When MDAC is installed, several DLLs and other files may not be able to be installed and registered before the system is rebooted. Data in the Run and RunOnce keys specified previously will be executed at the next login by any user. For MDAC, the data that appears in the Run and RunOnce keys is used to register new DLLs that were replaced at system restart. Administrative privileges are required to register these new DLLs with the operating system. If a low-rights user is the first to log in to a system after the initial install and reboot of MDAC (but before the Run and RunOnce data has been executed), the low-rights user will automatically attempt to register the files at login time, which will generate an error and prevent the successful installation of MDAC. Eliminate these issues by using the Elevated Rights Deployment Tool.

The Elevated Rights Deployment Tool actually performs a little differently than the name of the tool implies. Technically, it doesn't elevate rights during deployment. When you run the Elevated Rights Deployment Tool Wizard (RunOnce_Setup.exe), you create a new package to deploy the desired software (in this example, MDAC). The Elevated Rights Deployment Tool Wizard creates two programs within the package, linked together by the SMS program advanced property "Run another program first." The first program to run is the `MDAC_TYP.EXE` installation, with a wrapper around this executable. At installation time, the wrapper is executed, which calls the actual executable and waits for the actual installation to exit. When complete, the wrapper program moves registry information from the standard `RunOnce` and `RunOnceEx` registry keys to registry keys inside of the SMS section of the registry.

After the data has been successfully moved to the temporary location within the SMS section of the registry (which means it no longer exists in the actual `RunOnce` and `RunOnceEx` keys), the system is rebooted.

After the reboot, the second part of the installation is run, which takes the `RunOnce` and `RunOnceEx` registry keys located in the temporary location within the SMS section of the registry and performs the actions defined by them (in administrative context).

See Also

- Download the Elevated Rights Deployment Tool from the SMS web site (`http://www.microsoft.com/smserver/downloads/2003/adminpack.mspx`).

- At the time of this writing, the hotfix referenced in the Microsoft Knowledge Base article titled "The Elevated Rights Deployment Utility in the Systems Management Server 2003 Service Pack 1 Administration Feature Pack Does Not Move Registry Entries" supersedes the Elevated Rights Deployment Tool located in the preceding SMS Downloads link. Compare file information between the two to ensure that you have the latest version (`http://support.microsoft.com/?kbid=893174`).

CHAPTER 14

■ ■ ■

Software Updates

Almost overnight, managing software updates has gone from an afterthought to a full-time job. Thankfully, SMS 2003 is perfectly suited to help limit the effort involved in maintaining a fully patched environment. The Distribute Software Updates Wizard (DSUW) is fully integrated into SMS 2003 and is your one-stop shopping experience for managing Microsoft software updates in your environment.

In this chapter, we focus on the Inventory Tool for Microsoft Updates (ITMU) and the Extended Software Updates Inventory Tool (ESUIT), which were released with Service Pack 2 for SMS 2003. Two other scanners were released with SMS 2003, but they will be out of support soon.

The software update process in SMS is a bit cumbersome, yet very powerful. Spend the time (in your test lab, of course) learning more about the software update process. Before you dig in, here are a few handy references for you:

- Review the *Scenarios and Procedures for Microsoft Systems Management Server 2003: Software Distribution and Patch Management* guide and the "Best Practices: Security Patch Management Solution Accelerator" white paper, both of which are available from the SMS downloads site (http://www.microsoft.com/smserver/downloads/2003).

- Visit http://www.learnsms.com. In addition to the large amount of training materials available for purchase, a demonstration training session for the DSUW is also available for immediate viewing.

- Visit the Blogcast Repository web page (http://www.blogcastrepository.com) to download free training videos for SMS, including a few videos about patch management and SMS.

- Review the Microsoft white paper titled "SMS 2003 Software Update Management to Mobile Computers" for an in-depth discussion about patching mobile systems. Some of the screens displayed for the DSUW are now out of date, but the figures describing the process and the considerations when managing mobile or low-bandwidth clients are very accurate and helpful.

14-1. Understanding the Software Update Process

Problem

You want to have a general understanding of the requirements for deploying software updates with SMS 2003.

Discussion

The software update features of SMS 2003 have made patching your environment easier, but the process to accomplish that is still difficult to understand. This recipe provides an overview of all of the process components needed to accurately deploy software updates in your environment and points you to other recipes for further details:

Installing the scan tools: With the arrival of Service Pack 2 for SMS 2003, you might assume that the scan tools are incorporated into the install—that's not so. You still need to download the latest versions of the tools and install them. For further information, see Recipe 14-2, "Downloading the Scanning Tools"; Recipe 14-3, "Installing the Inventory Tool for Microsoft Updates (ITMU)"; and Recipe 14-4, "Installing the Extended Software Updates Inventory Tool (ESUIT)."

Configuring the scan tools: Before a patch can be applied, the patch installation engine needs to know what patches are required. This is accomplished by the scan tools and must be done prior to deploying a patch. Since each scan tool creates packages, programs, collections, and advertisements by default, you might think that you are all set. Well, you are almost right. You still need to link collections to the collections that were created by the scan tools, so that your clients will get scanned. Also, you may want to adjust the schedule of the advertisement to match your needs; it is set to "weekly" by default. See Recipe 14-5, "Configuring the Scan Tools to Scan SMS Clients for Security Patches," for further information.

Synchronizing the scan tool to detect the latest software updates: This needs to be accomplished every time new patches are available, or your clients will not know whether or not the newest patches are applicable. You have lots of flexibility in how and when this gets accomplished, so choose the method that works for you. See Recipe 14-6, "Synchronizing the Scan Tools to Detect the Latest Software Updates," for more information.

Reviewing the scan data: After your clients have returned their scan information via the hardware inventory, you should review the latest software updates applicable in your environment, so that you can accurately assess the vulnerabilities that exist there. For more information, see Recipe 14-7, "Viewing Patch Status for a System"; Recipe 14-9, "Displaying Systems That Are Missing Security Patches"; and Recipe 14-10, "Displaying Systems That Have Not Run a Security Scan Recently."

Creating the DSUW package: Now that you have the scan tools installed and have scan information from all your clients regarding the latest released patches, the only thing left to do is create and deploy a package that contains the latest software updates. The DSUW installation process will create the package for you when you perform the installation. If you need to use both the ITMU and the extended scan tool to identify and patch the latest vulnerabilities, then you will have to create at least two packages. However, you do not have to create packages for every operating system that you have in your environment. That would invalidate the purpose of the scan tool—it takes care of that process for you. You should have more than one package for each scanner only to accommodate scheduling and reboot requirements for different groups of systems. See Recipe 14-8, "Creating a Distribute Software Updates Wizard (DSUW) Package," for more information.

Verifying the patch deployments: SMS does an excellent job of deploying patches, but you still need to verify that all of your systems have installed them correctly and in a timely manner. The web reports provided in SMS will make this job easy. For further information, see Recipe 14-7, "Viewing the Patch Status for a System"; Recipe 14-9, "Displaying Systems That Are Missing Security Patches"; and Recipe 14-10, "Displaying Systems That Have Not Run a Security Scan Recently."

See Also

- Chapter 13 of the *Microsoft Systems Management Server 2003 Administrator's Companion* by Steven Kaczmarek (Microsoft Press, 2004) provides additional information about software updates.

- Chapter 6 of the *SMS 2003 Operations Guide* also provides an in-depth look at software updates.

- Review the *SMS Inventory Tool for Microsoft Updates Deployment Guide*, which is part of the ITMU download.

- Review the *Scenarios and Procedures for Microsoft Systems Management Server 2003: Software Distribution and Patch Management* guide, available from the SMS downloads site (http://www.microsoft.com/smserver/downloads/2003).

- Review the white paper titled "Best Practices: Security Patch Management Solution Accelerator," also available from the SMS downloads site (http://www.microsoft.com/smserver/downloads/2003).

- Review the Microsoft white paper titled "SMS 2003 Software Update Management to Mobile Computers" for additional considerations for managing mobile or remote computers.

WHICH SCANNING TOOL DO I NEED?

The ITMU is the latest scanning engine for identifying patch status in your SMS-managed environment. The ITMU detects the same critical security updates, update rollups, and service packs as Microsoft Update, Windows Server Update Services (WSUS), and the Microsoft Baseline Security Analyzer (MBSA) 2.0, since they are all based on the same scanning technology.

As technology advances, we sometimes have growing pains. The ITMU is the replacement for the Software Update Inventory Tool (SUIT), which is based on MBSA 1.2 scanning technologies. It is also considered a replacement for the Office Inventory Tool for Updates (OITU) and the Extended Security Update Inventory Tool (ESUIT). However, the ITMU is not currently a complete replacement for these products. This sidebar and the web references listed here will help you determine which scanning tools you need for your environment.

While we would like to tell you which inventory tools you need for your environment, we're going to have to go with the all too well-known answer of "It depends." This information is changing too fast to give you a definitive answer in this book. We do, however, want to direct you to where you can find the answers:

- See the Microsoft Knowledge Base article titled "Microsoft Baseline Security Analyzer (MBSA) 2.0 is available" (http://support.microsoft.com/?scid=kb;en-us;895660). Although this article does not discuss SMS scanning tools directly, keep in mind that the scanning technology for the MBSA 2.0 and the SMS ITMU is the same. Similarly, the article refers to the Enterprise Scanning Tool, which is the same as the SMS ESUIT. This article provides a nice (and frequently updated) table to help you determine which scanning tools you need.

- If you have installed (or have considered installing) Microsoft Office products in your environment using patched administrative installation points, the Microsoft Knowledge Base article titled "No Microsoft Office updates are displayed when you use Microsoft Update or Windows Server Update Services" is a must read (http://support.microsoft.com/kb/903773). It will probably also convince you to consider not installing Office with patched administrative installation points in the future. For Office 2003 and newer, consider using a chained installation, as described in "How to perform a chain installation of Office 2003 and Office 2003 updates" (http://support.microsoft.com/kb/902988).

- The Ohio SMS Users Group's web log also keeps an updated article concerning issues and considerations with the ITMU (http://myitforum.com/cs2/blogs/osug/archive/2005/08/08/12442.aspx).

As the ITMU matures (and older products go out of support), we'll see more complete coverage in the ITMU. The key to successful patch detection with the SMS scanning tools is knowing what products you have in your environment. For example, are all SQL 2000 instances running SQL 2000 SP4? If not, the ITMU will not detect an issue. Do you have Office 2000 in your environment? If so, you will need the OITU. Review the articles mentioned previously for more information.

Also, a custom scanning tool is to be released this year in SMS 2003 R2. You will be able to create your own criteria for identifying systems that are not in compliance with your standards as well as receive updates from Microsoft's partners to receive patches, such as updates from Adobe to receive patches for Adobe Flash.

Take the time to understand your environment, and make sure that you are using the proper scanning tools to provide the high level of service to your enterprise of which SMS is capable.

14-2. Downloading the Scanning Tools

Problem

You want to download the software updates scanning tools for SMS 2003.

Solution

1. Open the SMS Administrator console.

2. From the SMS Administrator console, expand Site Database (*<Site Code>*) and Software Updates.

3. Right-click Software Updates, and select All Tasks ➤ Download Inventory Scanning Programs.

4. Your browser will open to the SMS 2003 downloads page. Click Scanning Tools to be directed to the links to download them.

5. Click the link to SMS 2003 Inventory Tool for Microsoft Updates or to SMS Extended Security Update Inventory Tool to open the downloads page for the specified scan tool.

6. Click the link for the language version that you want to download.

7. Select a location to save the download.

Discussion

Microsoft built the SMS 2003 software updates feature to accommodate several scanners. The ITMU is already a third-generation scanning tool, and the ESUIT is updated frequently to support the identification of patches that cannot be detected with the ITMU.

See Also

- Chapter 13 of the *Microsoft Systems Management Server 2003 Administrator's Companion* by Steven Kaczmarek (Microsoft Press, 2004) provides additional information about software updates.

- Chapter 6 of the *SMS 2003 Operations Guide* also provides an in-depth look at software updates.

- Review the *Scenarios and Procedures for Microsoft Systems Management Server 2003: Software Distribution and Patch Management* guide, available from the SMS downloads site (http://www.microsoft.com/smserver/downloads/2003).

- Review the white paper titled "Best Practices: Security Patch Management Solution Accelerator," also available from the SMS downloads site.

14-3. Installing the Inventory Tool for Microsoft Updates (ITMU)

Problem

You want to install the ITMU.

Solution

1. Extract the ITMU download to your favorite location.

2. On the SMS site server, browse to the location of the ITMU files.

3. Double-click `SMSITMU.msi` to launch the installation.

4. Read the Welcome screen, and click Next to continue. See Figure 14-1.

5. Read and choose to accept the license agreement. Click Next to continue. See Figure 14-2.

6. Choose the destination folder for the installation, and click Next to continue. See Figure 14-3.

7. Enter a synchronization host computer name, and specify the download method for the catalog. See Figure 14-4.

8. If the synchronization host is not available, provide an alternative method for obtaining the latest catalog. Click Next to continue. See Figure 14-5.

9. Specify the name to be used for the ITMU objects (collections, packages, etc.). Also, determine your distribution options and a test system. Click Next to continue. See Figure 14-6.

10. Specify whether or not SMS will create objects to deploy the Windows Update Agent and distribution settings for the package and program. Click Next to continue. See Figure 14-7.

11. Click Next to begin the installation. See Figure 14-8.

12. Click Finish when the setup completes. See Figure 14-9.

13. Open the SMS Administrator console, and verify that the collections, advertisements, packages, and programs have been created for the ITMU.

Discussion

Installing the ITMU is not a function that you will likely have to do over and over, so we are including screenshots of what you will encounter to help familiarize you with the process prior to installing it. Figure 14-1 shows the Welcome screen for the ITMU.

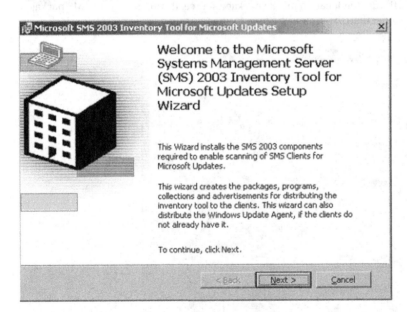

Figure 14-1. *The ITMU Welcome screen*

Figure 14-2 is the license agreement (everyone's favorite screen).

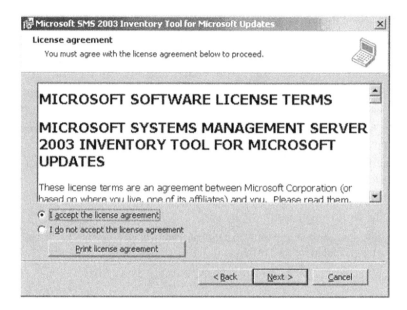

Figure 14-2. *The ITMU license agreement*

Figure 14-3 shows the default location for the package source. If you prefer your SMS package source to be on a drive other than C:\, now is the time to change it.

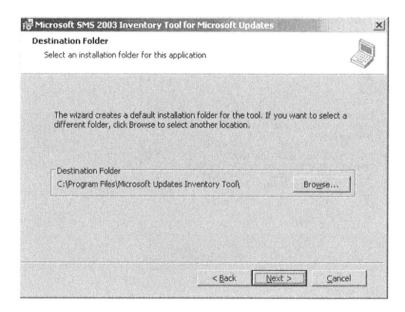

Figure 14-3. *The ITMU destination folder*

Figure 14-4 is used to specify the computer for your synchronization host. This host will be used to download the latest update catalog.

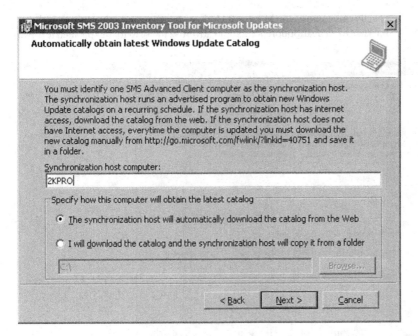

Figure 14-4. *The ITMU synchronozation host*

Figure 14-5 prompts you for the method to obtain the initial Microsoft Updates catalog. You must obtain the initial catalog before you can complete the ITMU installation.

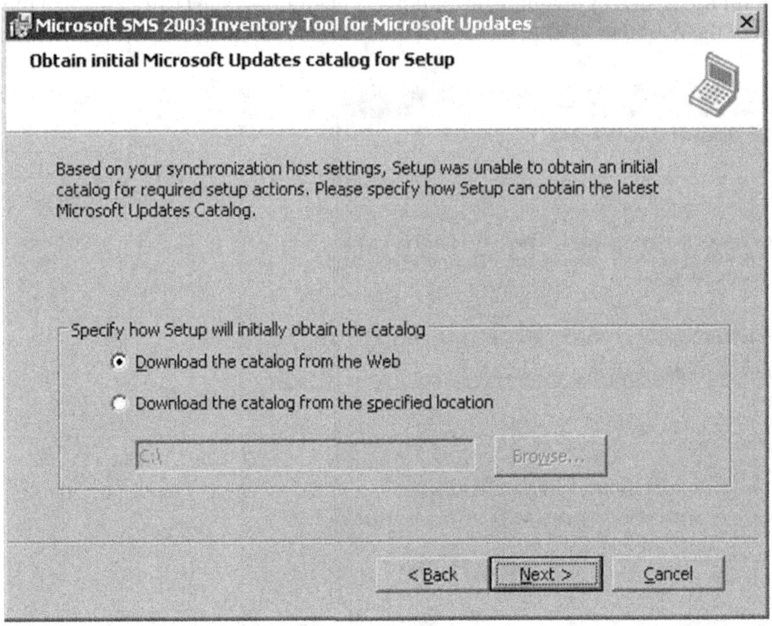

Figure 14-5. *The ITMU setup catalog download*

In Figure 14-6, you specify the name of the Microsoft Updates package and other initial settings, such as copying the scan package to all distribution points, and advertise the scan to the specified test PC.

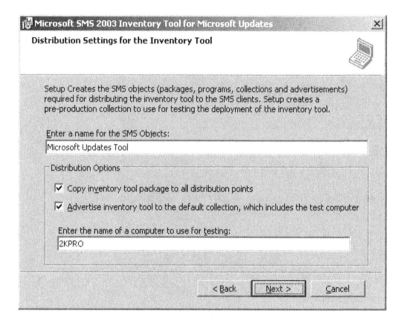

Figure 14-6. *The ITMU scan tool distribution settings*

The data in Figure 14-7 is used to create the Windows Update Agent package. The Windows Update Agent is a requirement for the ITMU. By enabling the options in Figure 14-7, the ITMU will force the upgrade or installation of the Windows Update Agent before the first ITMU scan runs.

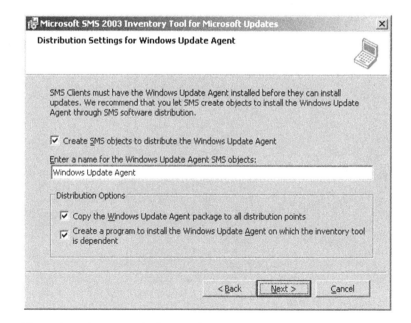

Figure 14-7. *The ITMU Windows Update Agent settings*

In Figure 14-8, you're finally ready to begin the installation of the ITMU. Click Next to install the ITMU files, along with the package, programs, new collections, and advertisement to the test system. Also, if selected, the Windows Update Agent package and program will be created.

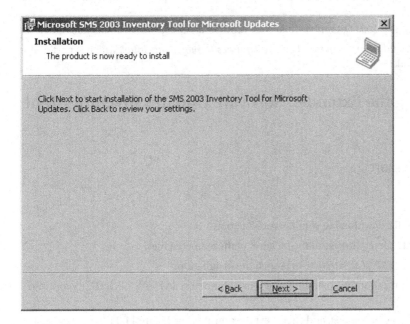

Figure 14-8. *ITMU installation*

Figure 14-9 displays after setup is complete.

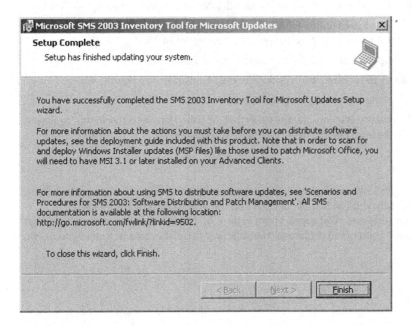

Figure 14-9. *ITMU setup is complete.*

See Also

- Chapter 13 of the *Microsoft Systems Management Server 2003 Administrator's Companion* by Steven Kaczmarek (Microsoft Press, 2004) provides additional information about software updates.

- Chapter 6 of the *SMS 2003 Operations Guide* also provides an in-depth look at software updates.

- Review the *SMS Inventory Tool for Microsoft Updates Deployment Guide*, which is part of the ITMU download.

14-4. Installing the Extended Software Updates Inventory Tool (ESUIT)

Problem

You want to install the ESUIT.

Solution

1. Extract the ESUIT download to your favorite location.

2. On the SMS site server, browse to the location of the extracted files.

3. Double-click SMSEXT_SCAN-ENU.EXE to launch the installation.

4. Read the warning about uninstalling previous extended scan tools. Click OK to continue. See Figure 14-10.

5. Read the Welcome dialog box, and click Next to continue. See Figure 14-11.

6. Read and accept the license agreement, and click Next to continue. See Figure 14-12.

7. Choose a destination directory for the installation, and click Next to continue. See Figure 14-13.

8. The extended scan tool is ready to be installed. Click Next to continue. See Figure 14-14.

9. Specify the name to be used for the ESUIT objects (collections, packages, etc.), and determine your distribution options. Click Next to continue. See Figure 14-15.

10. Specify a test computer, and click Next to continue. See Figure 14-16.

11. Click Next to apply the configuration options to the installation. See Figure 14-17.

12. Click Finish when the setup completes. See Figure 14-18.

13. Open the SMS Administrator console, and verify that the collections, advertisements, packages, and programs have been created using the name you specified.

Discussion

The ESUIT will be updated whenever the ITMU cannot conclusively identify the applicability of a software update. Typically, you can install the ESUIT on top of your existing installation.

Figure 14-10 displays the screen that appears prior to the ESUIT Welcome screen to remind you that ESUIT replaces two older scanners and to uninstall the older scanners if they exist in your environment.

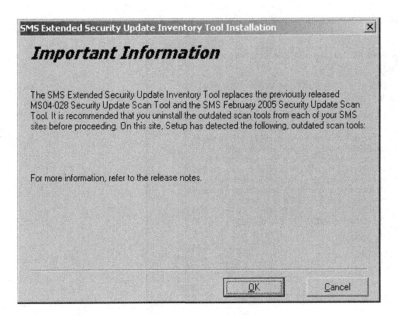

Figure 14-10. *The ESUIT uninstallation warning*

Figure 14-11 displays the Welcome screen for the ESUIT.

Figure 14-11. *The ESUIT Welcome screen*

Figure 14-12 shows your favorite license agreement. Accept the license agreement in order to continue.

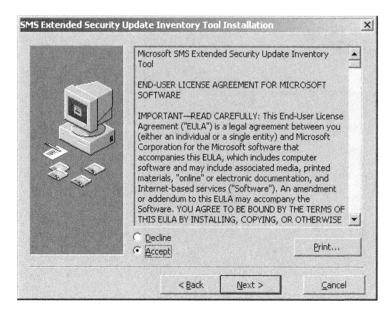

Figure 14-12. *The ESUIT license agreement*

In Figure 14-13, choose your source file destination path, and click Next to continue.

Figure 14-13. *The ESUIT destination directory*

In Figure 14-14, click Next to begin the installation. Initial files will be copied to the selected destination directory.

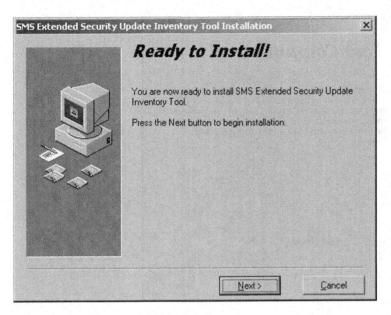

Figure 14-14. *ESUIT scan tool installation*

In Figure 14-15, select your desired distribution settings. As you can see, you can create the package, program, test collection, and advertisement during the ESUIT installation.

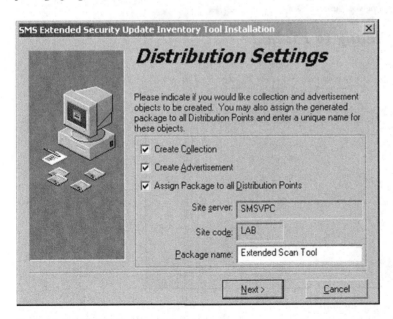

Figure 14-15. *ESUIT distribution settings*

In Figure 14-16, enter the test computer name, which will be added to the test collection.

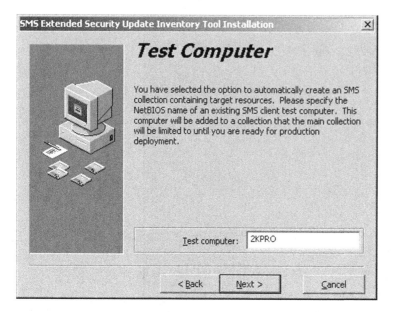

Figure 14-16. *ESUIT test computer entry*

In Figure 14-17, click Next to create the SMS objects that you selected.

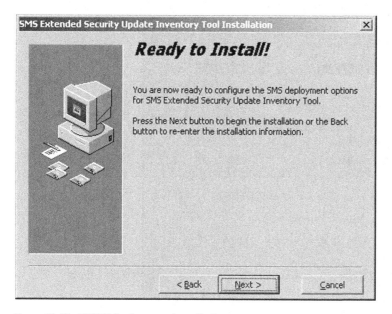

Figure 14-17. *ESUIT deployment installation*

In Figure 14-18, click Finish to complete the installation.

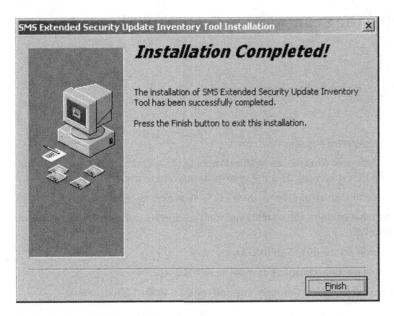

Figure 14-18. *ESUIT installation complete*

See Also

- Review the *Scenarios and Procedures for Microsoft Systems Management Server 2003: Software Distribution and Patch Management* guide, available from the SMS downloads site (http://www.microsoft.com/smserver/downloads/2003).

- Review the white paper titled "Best Practices: Security Patch Management Solution Accelerator," also available from the SMS downloads site.

- The Microsoft Knowledge Base article titled "Microsoft Baseline Security Analyzer (MBSA) 2.0 is available" provides a detailed list of security vulnerabilities that can only be detected with the ESUIT. The stand-alone equivalent to the ESUIT is the Enterprise Scanning Tool (EST), which is how this article refers to the tools (http://support.microsoft.com/?scid=kb;en-us;895660).

PATCHING MICROSOFT OFFICE PRODUCTS

The ITMU is the primary patching tool for Microsoft Office products, but the following caveats apply when using the ITMU:

- The ITMU does not support Microsoft Office 2000. To successfully identify security patch vulnerabilities for Office 2000, you must use the OITU, available from the SMS 2003 downloads page.

- If you have installed (or have considered installing) Microsoft Office products in your environment using patched administrative installation points, the ITMU will not be your best friend. Review the Microsoft Knowledge Base article titled "No Microsoft Office updates are displayed when you use Microsoft Update or Windows Server Update Services" for more information (http://support.microsoft.com/kb/903773). It will probably also convince you to consider not installing Office with patched administrative installation points in the future. For Office 2003 and newer, consider using a chained installation, as described in "How to perform a chain installation of Office 2003 and Office 2003 updates" (http://support.microsoft.com/kb/902988).

Review the previous sidebar in this chapter titled "Which Scanning Tool Do I Need?" for more information.

14-5. Configuring the Scan Tools to Scan SMS Clients for Security Patches

Problem

You want to scan SMS clients for applicable security patches.

Solution

1. Open the SMS Administrator console.

2. From the SMS Administrator console, expand Site Database (<*Site Code*>) and Collections, and select the collection that was created for the scan tool you want to use.

3. Right-click the collection, and from the menu select New ➤ Link to collection.

4. Select the collection that contains the systems you want scanned to link it under the scan tool collection, and click OK.

5. Initiate a policy refresh on the linked collection.

6. Monitor the scan tool package completion with the web reports.

7. Initiate a hardware scan to collect the scan data and return it to the SMS database.

Discussion

When you installed the scan tool, the default action was to create packages, programs, collections, and advertisements for the scan tool. However, the only system that is a member of the collection is the test system you indicated during the installation of the scan tool.

To begin scanning other systems, you need to add them to the collection or link an existing collection to the scan tool collection. The scan tool advertisements have a default recurring schedule of one week. You should review this schedule and adjust it to your needs.

Note The results from the scan tool are returned with hardware inventory. If you need the results returned more quickly, you can add the /kick switch to the command line of the scan tool program to initiate a hardware inventory cycle immediately after the scan.

See Also

- Recipe 3-5, "Creating a Linked Collection," describes how to create a linked collection.

- Recipe 16-3, "Initiating the Hardware Inventory Cycle," demonstrates how to initiate a hardware inventory cycle, both locally and to a remote system.

- Recipe 16-5, "Initiating the Machine Policy Retrieval and Evaluation Cycle," demonstrates how to refresh machine policy on both local and remote systems.

- Chapter 13 of the *Microsoft Systems Management Server 2003 Administrator's Companion* by Steven Kaczmarek (Microsoft Press, 2004) provides additional information about software updates.

- Chapter 6 of the *SMS 2003 Operations Guide* also provides an in-depth look at software updates.

- Review the *Scenarios and Procedures for Microsoft Systems Management Server 2003: Software Distribution and Patch Management* guide, available from the SMS downloads site (http://www.microsoft.com/smserver/downloads/2003).

- Review the white paper titled "Best Practices: Security Patch Management Solution Accelerator," also available from the SMS downloads site.

14-6. Synchronizing the Scan Tools to Detect the Latest Software Updates

Problem

You want to synchronize the scan tools to detect the latest released patches.

Discussion

Synchronizing your scan tools is the first thing that you will do when new patches are released. You can configure the SMS Sync Host advertisement to run on a schedule that is similar to Microsoft's patch release date or set the schedule manually, so that you can initiate the synchronization as soon as the patches are released. Since patches are time sensitive, most administrators tend to use the latter method, instead of waiting for a scheduled time.

Note The extended scan tool does not have a synchronizing process. It is updated as a whole when you install the new scanner on top of the older version.

The synchronization process will update the scanner package with the updated catalog from Microsoft and redistribute it to your distribution points.

Now that your distribution points have been updated with the new update catalog, you need to initiate a scan on all your clients and decide on one of the following options for returning the scan data to SMS:

- Wait for the next scheduled scan, followed by the regular hardware inventory cycle. This wait is probably too long if critical patches are released.

- Force a new scan by creating a new schedule item in the advertisement, and wait for the next hardware inventory cycle to run. This option is helpful if you are concerned about negatively affecting your network.

- Force a new scan and immediate hardware inventory cycle. This is the fastest way to return the new patch data and can be accomplished with a separate advertisement that uses the /kick switch on the scan tools. If your network (and SMS infrastructure) is able to handle the onslaught of hardware inventories from all systems in a short amount of time, then this option will get you all the new patch applicability information just a few minutes after the patches are released.

See Also

- Chapter 13 of the *Microsoft Systems Management Server 2003 Administrator's Companion* by Steven Kaczmarek (Microsoft Press, 2004) provides additional information about software updates.

- Chapter 6 of the *SMS 2003 Operations Guide* also provides an in-depth look at software updates.

- Review the *Scenarios and Procedures for Microsoft Systems Management Server 2003: Software Distribution and Patch Management* guide, available from the SMS downloads site (http://www.microsoft.com/smserver/downloads/2003).

- Review the white paper titled "Best Practices: Security Patch Management Solution Accelerator," also available from the SMS downloads site.

14-7. Viewing Patch Status for a System

Problem

You want to view the patch status for a specific system.

Solution: Using Resource Explorer

1. Open the SMS Administrator console.
2. From the SMS Administrator console, expand Site Database (*<Site Code>*) and Collections, and select a collection that contains the resource for which you want to review the patch status.
3. In the right pane, right-click the system, and select All Tasks ➤ Start Resource Explorer.
4. In Resource Explorer, expand Hardware, and click Software Updates.
5. The right pane will list all applicable software updates and their current statuses.
6. Close Resource Explorer when you are finished.

Solution: Using a Web Report

1. Browse to your SMS web reporting site.
2. Expand the Software Update–Compliance node.
3. Select the "Software Updates for a specific computer" report.
4. Enter a computer name in the Values field, and click the Display button to launch the report.
5. The report will give you plenty of information on the applicable patches, and the Compliance column will indicate whether it has been patched.

Discussion

Some of the most important SMS information that you will reference regularly is software update compliance data. With the time between vulnerability identification and exploitation shrinking very rapidly, you need to have accurate information about which systems are patched and which need to be addressed. The web reports are probably your best option for information on several systems. If you're looking for patch status of a specific system, web reports or Resource Explorer will work just fine.

Note Providing a report link to IT managers (so they can review software updates information themselves) can make your job of updating systems much easier, because you have given them a clear picture of what needs to be accomplished. See Chapter 8 for more information about granting rights to a web report for a specific user.

See Also

- Recipe 8-5, "Running a Report," demonstrates how to run and view an SMS web report.
- Recipe 8-9, "Exporting a Report," describes how to export a report.
- Chapter 13 of the *Microsoft Systems Management Server 2003 Administrator's Companion* by Steven Kaczmarek (Microsoft Press, 2004) provides additional information about software updates.

- Chapter 6 of the *SMS 2003 Operations Guide* also provides an in-depth look at software updates.

- Review the *Scenarios and Procedures for Microsoft Systems Management Server 2003: Software Distribution and Patch Management* guide, available from the SMS downloads site (`http://www.microsoft.com/smserver/downloads/2003`).

- Review the white paper titled "Best Practices: Security Patch Management Solution Accelerator," also available from the SMS downloads site.

14-8. Creating a Distribute Software Updates Wizard (DSUW) Package

Problem

You want to create a package using the DSUW.

Solution

1. Open the SMS Administrator console.

2. From the SMS Administrator console, expand Site Database (*<Site Code>*) and Software Updates.

3. Right-click Software Updates, and select All Tasks ➤ Distribute Software Updates to open the DSUW.

4. Click Next after reading the Welcome dialog box. See Figure 14-19.

5. Select the type of scanner that you would like to use in this package from the drop-down menu, and click Next. See Figure 14-20.

6. Select whether you are creating a new package or adding updates to an existing package, and click Next. See Figure 14-21.

7. Enter the name of the package in the space provided; you will notice that the scanner name is added as a prefix to the name you chose. Then click Next. See Figure 14-22.

8. Edit the text that will be used in the notifications to the end users, or you can import an `.rtf` file instead. Then click Next. See Figure 14-23.

9. Select the program that you would like to run from the drop-down menu, and click Next. See Figure 14-24.

10. Select the check box next to each update that you would like to include in the package, and click Next. See Figure 14-25.

11. Specify where the package source files will be stored. Give a priority to the package, and specify whether you want to automatically download the updates or manually download them later. Then click Next. See Figure 14-26.

12. Review the Ready column to make sure that all of your selected updates read Yes. If not, double-click the update to resolve the issue. See Figure 14-27.

13. If you double-click an update, you will have the option to manually download the update and make changes to the command-line switches. You can also change the authorization date for the update. Click OK to return to the previous screen. See Figure 14-28.

14. Now your package is ready to be placed on the distribution points. Select the distribution points you would like to use by enabling the check box next to each of them, and click Next. See Figure 14-29.

15. Choose whether you want to initiate a hardware inventory cycle after the program has run and whether you want to create a client template to reference. Also, select how you would like to handle reboots. Then click Next. See Figure 14-30.

16. Choose whether the installation will be unattended or whether the user will be able to interact with it. Also, select whether you will have a maximum runtime for the program on Advanced Clients. Then click Next. See Figure 14-31.

17. Choose whether or not to notify your users and allow them to postpone the updates, and click Next. See Figure 14-32.

18. Choose to automatically configure and create an advertisement now or to create one manually later, and click Next. See Figure 14-33.

19. Click Finish to close the DSUW. See Figure 14-34.

Discussion

The DSUW does a very good job of giving you a single point of input for managing Microsoft software updates. Even though you may feel that you need a wrist brace after clicking through 16 or so screens, it is actually a pretty efficient way to deploy patches. After a few tries, you will be able to deploy new patches in just a few minutes.

Figure 14-19 shows the DSUW Welcome screen, and Figure 14-20 shows one of the nice features of the DSUW. It doesn't matter which scan tools you may be using—they all use the DSUW as their entry point.

Figure 14-19. *The DSUW Welcome screen*

In Figure 14-20, you specify the software update type. The ITMU appears as Microsoft Updates, and the ESUIT appears as Extended MBSA.

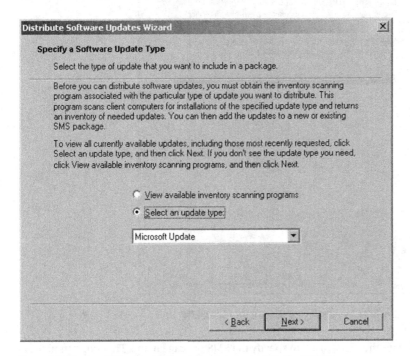

Figure 14-20. *Specifying the software update type with the DSUW*

Figure 14-21 shows that you don't have to create a new package for every patch that comes out; that would defeat the purpose of the DSUW. Instead, you have the capability to select an existing package and add new updates to it. If that existing package is currently being advertised with a recurring schedule, then you're finished! Just wait for the client to run the package again, and the client will then scan and install the newly added updates.

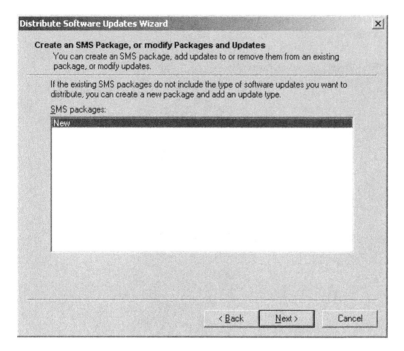

Figure 14-21. *Choosing a new or an existing package with the DSUW*

Figure 14-22 displays the dialog used to specify the SMS package name. The program name is automatically generated.

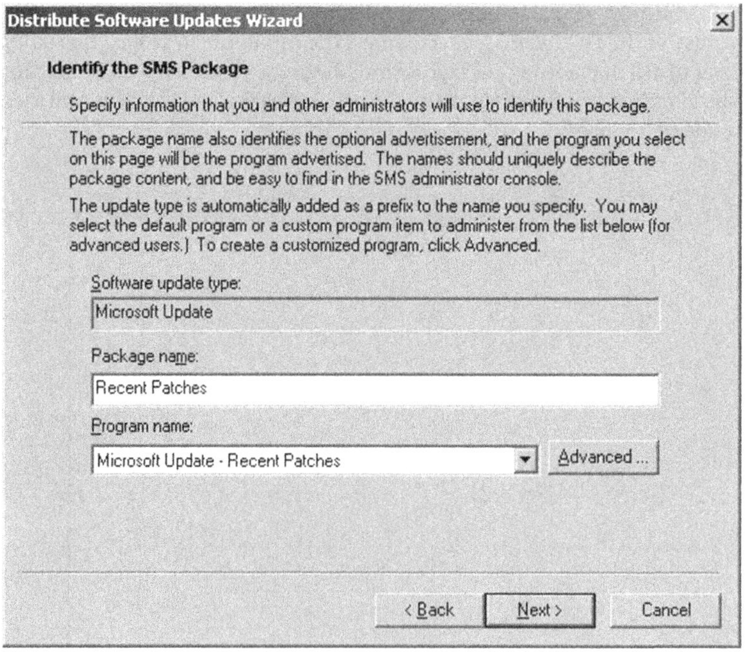

Figure 14-22. *Identifying the DSUW package name*

It's not always fun to be the person forcing patches down the throats of the end users. If you don't want all of those complaints to come to you, simply change the Organization to point to someone more appropriate, like the Help Desk, using the dialog shown in Figure 14-23. If you really want to get fancy, you can include a Rich Text document customized for your company that explains in detail what information your end users need.

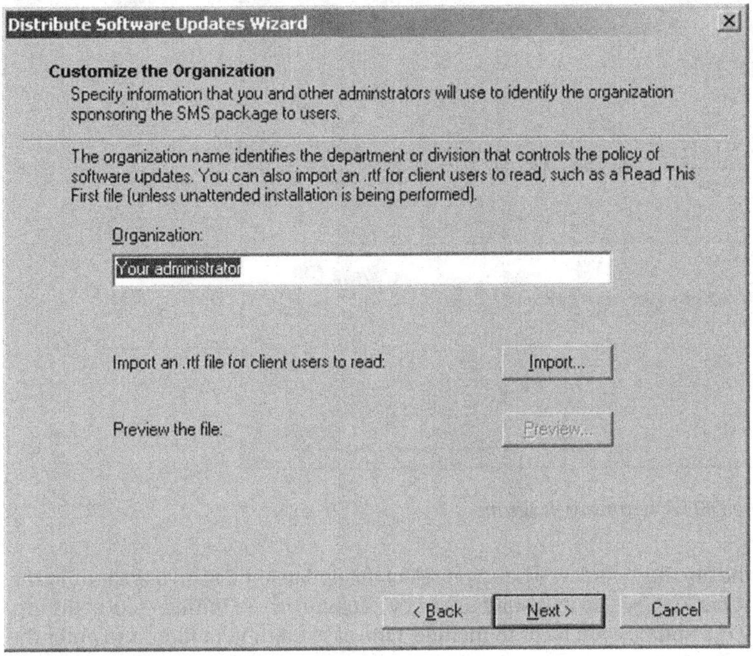

Figure 14-23. *DSUW customizations*

Figure 14-24 allows you to select the inventory scanning program. For example, the Microsoft Updates Tool scanning program is used for the ITMU. This selection will be the primary scanning program you use for Microsoft security patches. The scanning tool that is selected in this dialog box will determine the patches that you can select for this package.

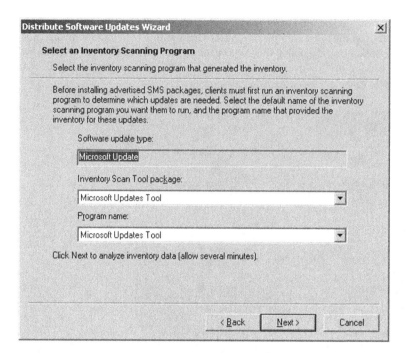

Figure 14-24. *Choosing the DSUW scanning program*

Figure 14-25 shows the fun little window where you select the updates you want to include in the package. The list can get rather long, so you may want to sort by a column or use the filter tool at the top of the column to identify the updates you want to include. One easy method to filter is to enter the beginning numbers for QNumber.

A default package source directory should be present in the screen shown in Figure 14-26, but if you don't like the location, you can change it. If you are throttling bandwidth by using package priority, you will want to make sure that you are setting the correct priority to your patch packages.

If you happen to have your SMS site server in a data center that does not allow Internet traffic directly to the server, then you can download the packages separately and provide the location to the wizard later.

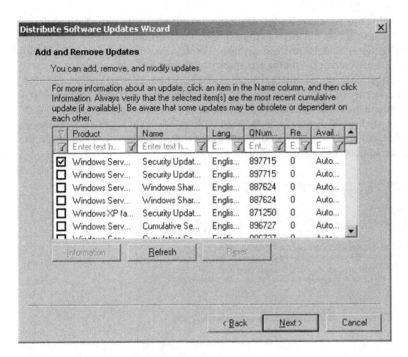

Figure 14-25. *DSUW update selections*

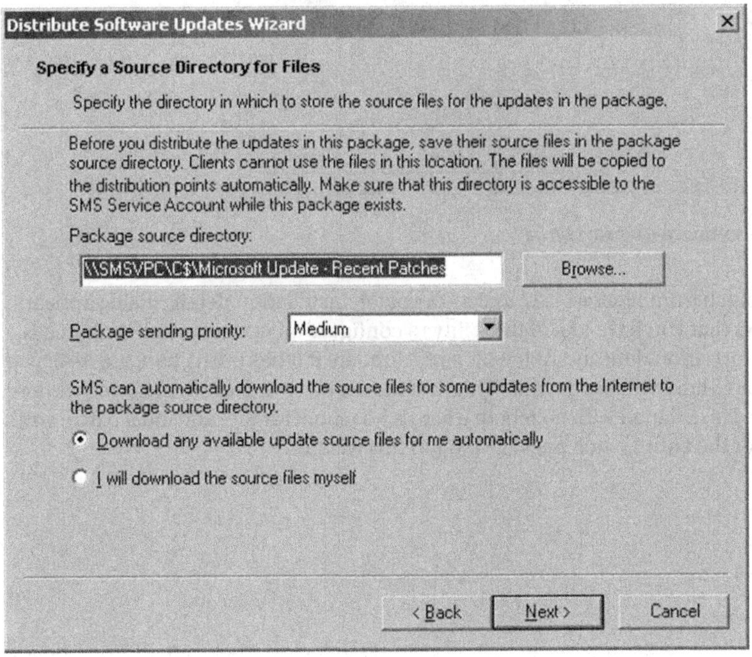

Figure 14-26. *The DSUW package source*

Click Next in the dialog box in Figure 14-26 to use the default option to download updates automatically. If you are able to access the Internet from this system, the hotfixes will be downloaded automatically. Be advised, however, that this process may take a considerable amount of time, depending on how many patches were selected in the dialog box shown in Figure 14-25.

Figure 14-27 displays the summary information for all patches you have selected and downloaded. The DSUW and ITMU take care of most of the configuration in this stage (DSUW took care of downloading the patches, and the ITMU contains the command-line switches for proper unattended installation). Generally, all patches will display Yes in the Ready column shown in Figure 14-27. However, if you have an update that isn't ready or if you need to modify the default settings, you can review the options for that particular update by double-clicking it.

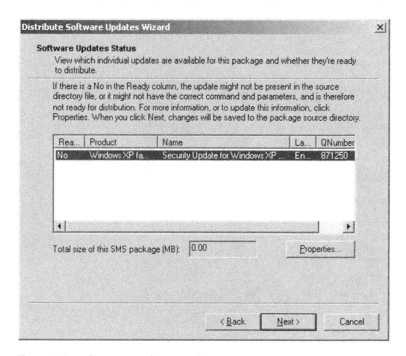

Figure 14-27. *The DSUW software update status*

Double-clicking a patch from Figure 14-27 makes the patch installation details dialog appear; see Figure 14-28. It shows that you have lots of flexibility to configure an update to suit your needs. You can change the authorization date and redownload the update if it has been changed. Also, you can configure the command-line switches to your liking, but the default switches are preferred, as they create a silent, unattended installation with no reboot (there is no reboot for the individual patch; you still control the reboot for the entire patch package later in this wizard).

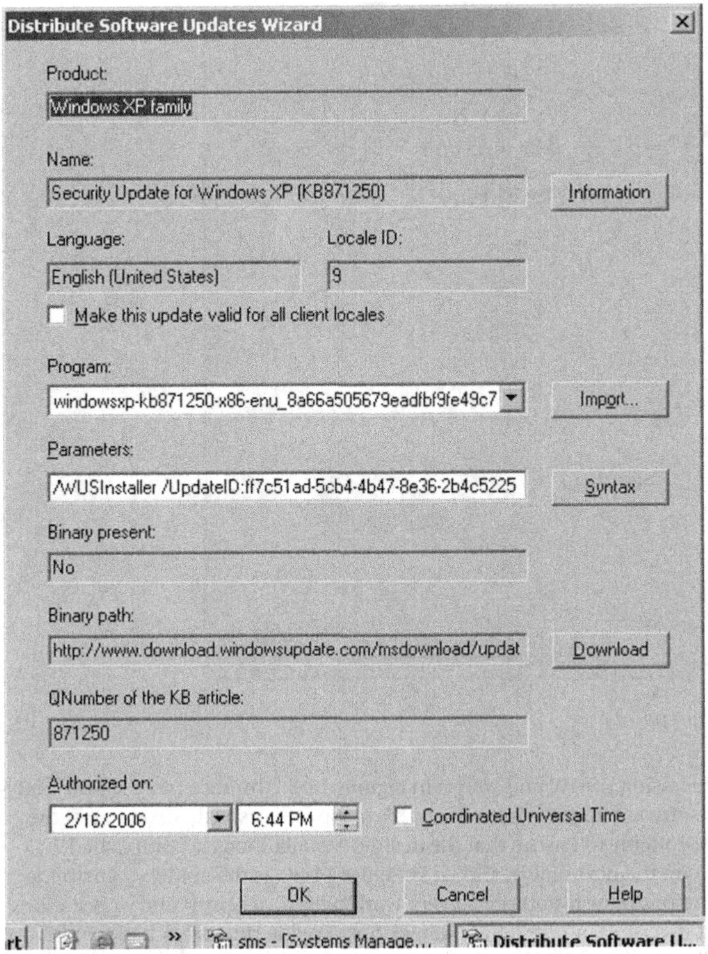

Figure 14-28. *DSUW update configuration*

With a normal package, you have to manage the distribution points after you build the package. With the DSUW, as shown in Figure 14-29, you are able to finish that task as a part of the wizard.

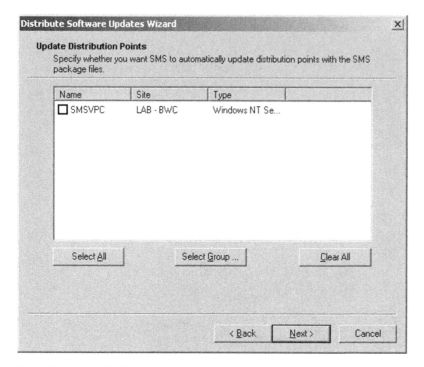

Figure 14-29. *DSUW distribution points*

The configurations created using DSUW and shown in Figures 14-30 through 14-32 significantly affect the look and feel of the software updates from the user's perspective, so you need to test the software updates packages thoroughly to ensure that the desired installation is accomplished.

The most important item on the next dialog, shown in Figure 14-30, is the ability to postpone restarts. You have the flexibility to postpone restarts for servers, workstations, or servers and workstations. Also notice the "Collect client inventory immediately" check box. Enable this check box to initiate a hardware inventory immediately after patch installation.

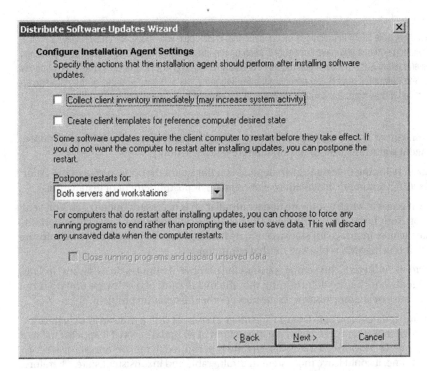

Figure 14-30. *DSUW installation settings*

The options shown in Figures 14-31 and 14-32 have significant impact on the patching installation process for the target systems and users. The following options apply to the dialog in Figure 14-31:

Perform unattended installation of software updates (recommended): This check box determines whether or not notifications are displayed to the end user when software updates are available for installation or are being installed. Restricting users' awareness of system activity can increase security.

When this box is empty, end users can receive notifications. The nature of the notifications and the actions that are available to the end user depend on the type of client (Legacy Client or Advanced Client) that is running on the user's computer and the other software update installation settings you specify in the wizard.

When this box is checked, end users are not notified of impending or in-progress software update installations, and the software updates are silently installed, subject to the default actions you have defined on this page of the wizard. If the installation requires a system restart, the user interface that appears is the operating system's progress dialog box that indicates that a system restart is being initiated. It will also show when patches are installed, but they are not effective until a reboot is performed if you do not specify a reboot in the job.

Note If you choose to enable silent installations by enabling this check box, you should carefully review the other software update installation settings you have configured, such as the installation grace period and restart behavior, to make sure that the end result is the behavior you require. For example, if you enable this check box but then specify that the software update computer restart can be postponed indefinitely, the software updates in the package are never completely installed if they need a computer restart and the computer is not restarted.

Countdown (minutes): This setting specifies the amount of time, if any, the Software Updates Installation Agent waits for a user to respond before it takes action.

The action taken following the countdown depends on the action that you specify in the "After countdown" setting: automatic installation of the update or postponement of installation.

This countdown is useful when a software update installation is necessary, but no user is present to provide input. Note, however, that the delays that could be caused by such cases are important, because while the user interface for software update installation is displayed, all other software distribution that is using SMS is blocked for that computer.

Maximum runtime (minutes): This setting specifies the number of minutes the Software Updates Installation Agent waits before determining that the installation of a software update is not progressing because of an unresponsive computer or other installation problem.

Because software updates can come from a wide range of sources with a wide array of behaviors, it is recommended that you proceed with the installation of an update even if it appears to have become unresponsive. However, if a software update is permitted to remain unresponsive for a long period of time, it could leave the system in a vulnerable and inconsistent state. Therefore, it is necessary to set the time-out value to allow an unresponsive update to be disabled. The default setting is 30 minutes. If you enter a value of zero in this setting, the software update is not given any time to be installed. To avoid this problem, you should provide at least 10 minutes for this time-out value.

Enforce start time and maximum installation time (Advanced Client only): SMS uses the mandatory advertisement start time and the maximum installation time to enforce an installation time window to install the software updates. For example, to take your servers offline for maintenance every Friday from 2:00 a.m. to 4:00 a.m., select this option and set the maximum installation time to 120 minutes. If you select this option, the DSUW does not create the advertisement for this update. When you finish the wizard, the final text reminds you to create your advertisement.

Figure 14-31 is the second dialog box for Software Updates Installation Agent settings.

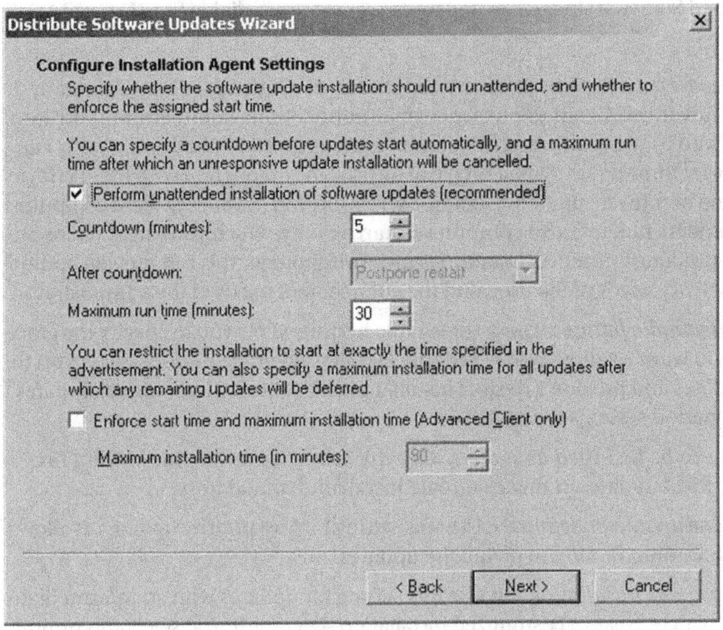

Figure 14-31. *DSUW installation settings continued*

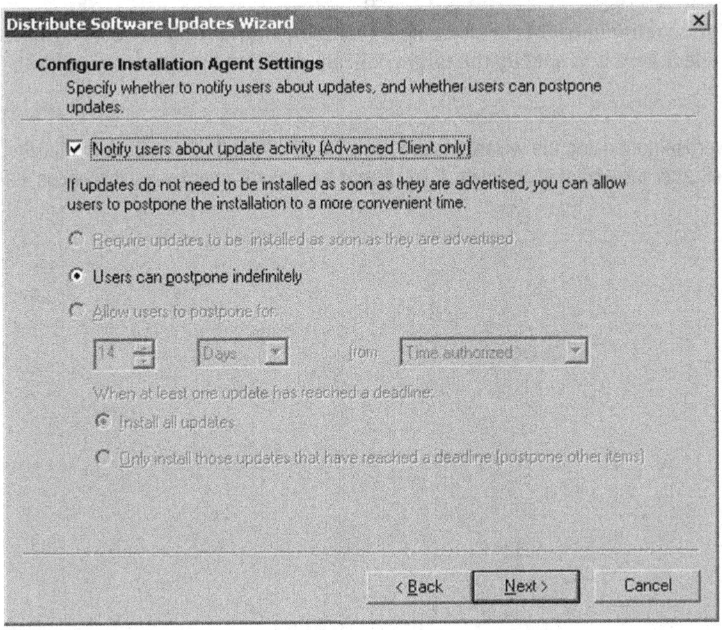

Figure 14-32. *Further DSUW installation settings*

The options in the second Software Updates Installation Agent settings dialog box (Figure 14-31) are as follows:

- *Notify users about update activity*: This check box applies to the SMS Advanced Client only. It enables users of the Advanced Client to receive regular notifications of impending software update installations and to postpone or schedule software update installations locally. The notifications occur every three hours. This setting can be used in conjunction with the "Perform unattended installation of software updates" setting, so users of SMS Advanced Client computers will receive only reminders that relate to computer restart activity, which you might choose to enforce after a future deadline is reached. In more secure environments, this can provide optimal balance of the productivity needs of the user, and the enforcement needs of the administrator.

- *Installation grace period radio buttons*: These three radio buttons allow you to specify the grace period, if any, that you want to allow users. Variable installation grace periods allow you to prioritize critical updates and provide a flexible installation schedule for less-critical updates. Three types of grace period settings are available:

  - *Require updates to be installed as soon as they are advertised*: Use this setting for high-priority, critical updates. It makes update installation mandatory.

  - *Users can postpone updates indefinitely*: Use this setting for low-priority updates. It allows users an infinite amount of time to install the updates.

  - *Allow users to postpone installation for*: Use this setting for updates with an intermediate priority. It allows you to create a customized installation schedule. If you select this option, you can set the basis for the grace period according to the time the update is detected as applicable to the computer or according to the time it was authorized. The grace period can be enforced per update or for an entire package of updates, which allows you to include critical and noncritical updates in the same package.

Configure the options shown in Figure 14-33 to create a recurring mandatory advertisement. Simply select the Advertise check box, and specify the target collection and the recurrence interval.

Note When creating an advertisement using the wizard (as in Figure 14-33), the effective start time for the advertisement will be immediately after the wizard is complete. If you create the advertisement using this option, be sure to target a test collection.

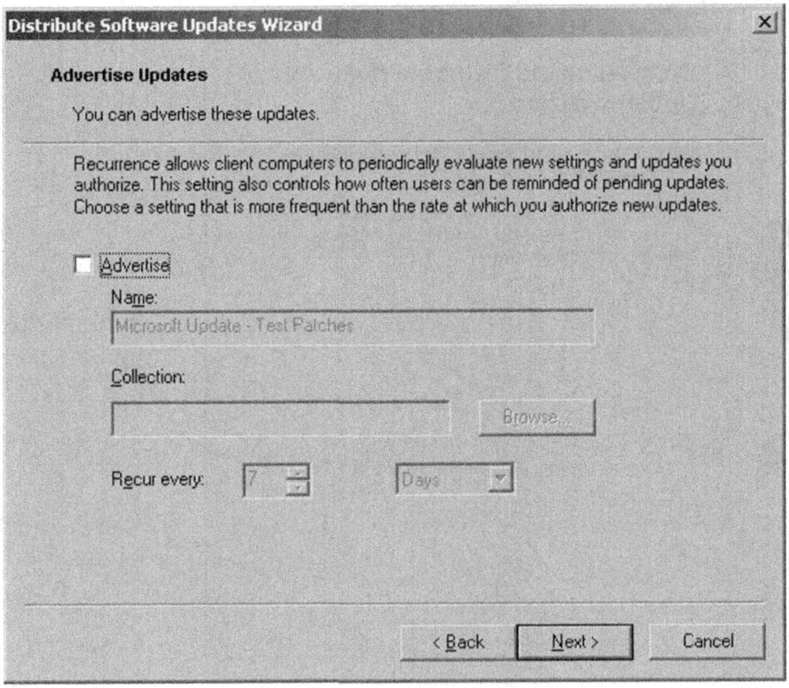

Figure 14-33. *DSUW advertisement settings*

Figure 14-34 displays the final dialog box in the DSUW. Click Finish to automatically create the package and program. The program command line will be configured based on the selected options. Also, the optional configuration you selected during installation will be executed (selected distribution points will be updated, advertisements created, etc.).

Figure 14-34. *The final DSUW dialog box*

See Also

- Chapter 13 of the *Microsoft Systems Management Server 2003 Administrator's Companion* by Steven Kaczmarek (Microsoft Press, 2004) provides additional information about software updates.

- Chapter 6 of the *SMS 2003 Operations Guide* also provides an in-depth look at software updates.

- Review the *Scenarios and Procedures for Microsoft Systems Management Server 2003: Software Distribution and Patch Management* guide, available from the SMS downloads site (http://www.microsoft.com/smserver/downloads/2003).

- Review the white paper titled "Best Practices: Security Patch Management Solution Accelerator," also available from the SMS downloads site.

- Visit http://www.learnsms.com. In addition to the large amount of training material available for purchase, a demonstration training session for the DSUW is also available for immediate viewing.

- Visit the Blogcast Repository web page (http://www.blogcastrepository.com) to download free training videos for SMS, including a few videos about patch management and SMS.

PATCHING STRATEGIES FOR MOBILE CLIENTS OR CLIENTS OVER SLOW NETWORKS

Patching mobile clients has come a long way since the good old days of SMS 2.0, but the process is still far from perfect. Using the SMS 2003 Advanced Client and Background Intelligent Transfer Service (BITS) technology, you can perform a Download and Execute for a patch installation package, which has helped out many SMS administrators. We want to ensure that you're also aware of other mobile client (and slow network) issues: security patch planning and security patch deployment.

Regardless of how you configure the security patch scanning tool packages, all SMS scanning tools will be cached locally on the system in the %windir%\system32\VPCache directory. After the tool is cached locally, the CAB file (if required for the scanner) is extracted, and the scan is performed. Therefore, you must consider that every time you update a scanning tool, that data will be transferred to the client at the next advertisement start time. For some scanners, this is minimal, but other scanners carry a little more weight with them. For example, the MSSECURE.CAB for the SUIT is approximately 307KB, but the WSUSSCAN.CAB for the new and improved ITMU is currently larger than 5,100KB. Sometimes you have to pay a price for progress.

With security patch deployment, you have more control over whether the advertisement is run from a distribution point or is set to Download and Execute using the advertisement properties. You, as the SMS administrator, can also control the size of the package. The following two methodologies are used by SMS administrators for setting the size of the security patch package:

- *Large Patch Package*: One of the best features of SMS patch management (using the DSUW) is that you can include multiple security patches for multiple operating systems in one SMS package. At patch-installation time, the patch installation engine is smart enough to determine which patches apply to the system (based on previous security scan data). Some SMS administrators have one very large (100MB or more) patch installation package that they update each time new patches are released, and then they simply readvertise this installation to the desired systems. This approach works best for well-connected systems. If you use this approach for a not-so-well-connected system and configure the advertisement to Download and Execute, that system would have to download the large package before applying the few updates applicable to it. This process leaves the remote system vulnerable for a longer time period, because it may take days (or weeks) to download the package, depending on bandwidth available and the amount of time connected to the network. Adding to this complexity, if the SMS administrator updates the package before the client downloads and installs it, the download process starts over again.

- *Small Patch Package*: After reading about the previous method, you can probably see the benefit in creating a smaller patch package for a Download and Execute scenario for remote systems. The more standardized your fleet of remote systems (e.g., operating system, Office, media player, standard Service Pack levels), the smaller the installation package required.

Many SMS administrators use a hybrid of these two methods. For example, when new patches are released, consider creating a small patch installation package to target your remote systems using a Download and Execute advertisement, followed by updating your large patch package (which isn't configured to Download and Execute) and targeting all systems that need the applicable patches.

The SMS documentation team has provided some guidance with patching remote systems in the *SMS 2003 Operations Guide*, the *Scenarios and Procedures for Microsoft Systems Management Server 2003: Software Distribution and Patch Management* guide, and a white paper titled "SMS 2003 Software Update Management to Mobile Computers."

14-9. Displaying Systems That Are Missing Security Patches

Problem

You want to display systems that are missing security patches.

Solution: Using Web Reports

1. Open the SMS Administrator console.

2. From the SMS Administrator console, expand Site Database (*<Site Code>*), Reporting, and Reports.

3. Select the "Software Updates with count of Applicable and Installed computers" report.

4. Right-click the report, and select All Tasks ➤ Run ➤ *<Reporting Point Server>* from the menu to open the report in a web browser.

5. Select the scanner type from the drop-down menu, and click Display.

6. After you review the data, close your browser to close the report.

Solution: Using the Administrator Console

1. Open the SMS Administrator console.

2. From the SMS Administrator console, expand Site Database (*<Site Code>*) and Software Updates.

3. In the right pane, scroll over until you see the Requested and Compliant columns. These will give you a count of the systems that need the update, but you cannot get the additional detail that is available in the web reports.

Solution: Using the DSUW

1. Open the SMS Administrator console.

2. From the SMS Administrator console, expand Site Database (*<Site Code>*) and Software Updates.

3. Right-click Software Updates, and select All Tasks ➤ Distribute Software Updates to open the DSUW.

4. Click Next after reading the Welcome dialog box. Figure 14-19 shows this dialog.

5. Select the type of scanner that you would like to use in this package from the drop-down menu; Figure 14-20 shows the dialog used to select the udpate type. Click Next.

6. Select whether you are creating a new package or adding updates to an existing one, and click Next. See Figure 14-21.

7. Enter the name of the package in the space provided. You will notice that the scanner name is added as a prefix to the name you chose; see Figure 14-22. Click Next.

8. Edit the text that will be used in the notifications to the end users, or you can import an .rtf file instead. Click Next. See Figure 14-23.

9. Select the program that you would like to run from the drop-down menu; see Figure 14-24. Click Next.

10. Enable the check box next to each update that you would like to include in the package, and click Next. See Figure 14-25. The Requested column will give you a count of systems that require the individual update. There is no additional detail as to which systems require it. Reference the web reports for specific information on which systems require a specific update.

Discussion

You can stay informed of applicable updates in several ways. However, the most efficient and detailed way is through web reports. The report we referenced in the solution is just one of many that is installed by default with the scanning tools.

■ Note Spend some extra time becoming familiar with all of the web reports in the Software Update node. You may not need all of them initially, but if you are familiar with them from the beginning, you will know what data is readily available when you get the call from your manager to provide more software update information.

See Also

- Recipe 8-5, "Running a Report," demonstrates how to run and view an SMS web report.

- Chapter 13 of the *Microsoft Systems Management Server 2003 Administrator's Companion* by Steven Kaczmarek (Microsoft Press, 2004) provides additional information about software updates.

- Chapter 6 of the *SMS 2003 Operations Guide* also provides an in-depth look at software updates.

- Review the *Scenarios and Procedures for Microsoft Systems Management Server 2003: Software Distribution and Patch Management* guide, available from the SMS downloads site (http://www.microsoft.com/smserver/downloads/2003).

- Review the white paper titled "Best Practices: Security Patch Management Solution Accelerator," also available from the SMS downloads site.

14-10. Displaying Systems That Have Not Run a Security Scan Recently

Problem

You want to display systems that have not run a security scan recently.

Solution

1. Open the SMS Administrator console.

2. From the SMS Administrator console, expand Site Database (*<Site Code>*), Reporting, and Reports.

3. Select the "List of computers that have not scanned with the latest synchronized catalog" report.

4. Right-click the report, and select All Tasks ➤ Run ➤ *<Reporting Point Server>* from the menu to open the report in a web browser.

5. Select a collection and a scanner type from the drop-down menus, and click Display.

6. After you review the data, close your browser to close the report.

Discussion

SMS 2003 approaches software updates by following the tenet "innocent until proven guilty." The client indicates from its scan data whether it needs an update and then shares that information with SMS. If the client has not run a scan recently, SMS will not report it as needing additional patches. This approach puts a tremendous amount of importance on getting timely scans from all of your systems. With this report, the job of tracking those systems that are not reporting scan data is easy.

See Also

- Chapter 13 of the *Microsoft Systems Management Server 2003 Administrator's Companion* by Steven Kaczmarek (Microsoft Press, 2004) provides additional information about software updates.

- Chapter 6 of the *SMS 2003 Operations Guide* also provides an in-depth look at software updates.

- Review the *Scenarios and Procedures for Microsoft Systems Management Server 2003: Software Distribution and Patch Management* guide, available from the SMS downloads site (`http://www.microsoft.com/smserver/downloads/2003`).

- Review the white paper titled "Best Practices: Security Patch Management Solution Accelerator," also available from the SMS downloads site.

14-11. Viewing the Command-Line Switches for DSUW Packages

Problem

You want to view the available command-line switches for DSUW packages.

Solution

1. Open the SMS Administrator console.
2. Press the F1 key to open SMS Help.
3. Click the Search tab, enter **agent syntax** into the box, and click List Topics.
4. Double-click the first entry to open the Software Updates Installation Agent Syntax page.
5. Close SMS Help when you finish.

Discussion

When you need to make a change to a DSUW package, there are two ways of doing it: you can run through all the pages of the wizard again, or you can edit the command line of the package directly. Familiarizing yourself with the command-line switches will allow you to make those changes quickly and troubleshoot any potential problems with a DSUW package.

The following list details the uses of command-line switches and their correlations to the DSUW options:

- /g:hhh: This switch sets the grace period (in hours) and dictates whether the installation is mandatory (/g:0) or can be postponed by the end user. The grace period is affected by the /d switch. The grace period switch corresponds with the following DSUW options (see Figure 14-32):
    - "Require updates to be installed as soon as they are advertised" (/g:0)
    - "Users can postpone updates indefinitely" (no /g switch)
    - "Allow users to postpone installation for" (/g:xxx where xxx represents the hours specified)

- /d: This switch works in conjunction with the /g:xxx switch and indicates that the grace period starts when the SMS client determines that the update is applicable. If the /d switch is not specified (the default), the grace period will begin when the update was authorized. This option is set in the DSUW using the From drop-down option that is available if you select the "Allow users to postpone installation for" radio button (see Figure 14-32).

- /s: If you want to suppress the immediate initiation of a hardware inventory cycle after the installation of the updates, the /s switch accomplishes that for you. Microsoft uses the /s switch as the default setting to eliminate unnecessary inventory cycles. If you need an immediate inventory, you can remove this switch manually from the command line or by enabling the "Collect client inventory immediately (may increase system activity)" check box (see Figure 14-30).

- /p: Use the /p switch to postpone the installation of the software updates after the countdown timer (the /c switch) has expired. The /p switch is not specified by default and corresponds to the "After countdown" field in Figure 14-31. If you don't use the /p switch (the default), all updates are automatically installed for unresponsive users after the countdown period parameter (specified using the /c switch) expires.

- /i: Use the /i switch to force installation of required updates only. This switch corresponds to the check box "Only install those updates that have reached a deadline (postpone other items)" in Figure 14-32. It forces the patch installation to use the per-patch configuration instead of the per-package one. Without the /i switch, all updates will be considered mandatory.

- /z:s|w|sw: Use the /z switch to force postponement of automated system restarts after patches are installed. The /z switch must be followed by s, w, or sw: /z:s postpones restarts for servers, /z:w for workstations, and /z:sw for both servers and workstations. This switch corresponds to the "Postpone restarts for" option box in Figure 14-30. The default setting has no /z switch, which forces a restart (if required) for both workstations and servers.

- /f: Use the /f switch to force client programs to close and discard any unsaved data. This switch corresponds to the "Close running programs and discard unsaved data" check box in Figure 14-30.

- /c:mm: Use the /c switch to specify (in minutes) when the installation will take action on behalf of an unresponsive user. This value is used before both the patch installation and the system reboot. For example, if you use /c:30, the SMS advertisement will begin at the specified mandatory time, and the DSUW executable will count down for 30 minutes before beginning the patch installation process. After the patching process is complete, the DSUW will wait another 30 minutes before restarting the system. In effect, the SMS advertisement runs for a little over one hour, depending on the number and size of patches installed. This switch corresponds to the "Countdown (minutes)" switch in Figure 14-31. Note that during this countdown process, all other SMS software installation is suspended.

- /t:mm: Use the /t switch to specify the maximum execution time (in minutes) for a specific update in the installation package. For each update that is executed in the package, this maximum runtime will be monitored, and if the maximum runtime is exceeded, the installation will terminate the current update, allowing the next update to begin. This switch corresponds to the "Maximum runtime (minutes)" switch in Figure 14-31.

- /q : Use the /q switch to install the software updates with no user interface or interaction. This option is not available through the wizard. Append this switch to the end of the command line for the program if desired.

- /x: Use this switch to create a software updates authorization list reference file that you can use to expedite software updates distribution to your enterprise. You use this switch when you use a reference computer for expedited approval processing. This switch corresponds to the "Create client templates for reference computer desired state" check box in Figure 14-30.

- /l:mmm: Use this switch to create a change window based on mmm minutes (maximum of 480) after the mandatory installation time. This switch corresponds to the "Enforce start time and maximum installation time" check box and the "Maximum installation time (in minutes)" list box in Figure 14-31.

See Also

- Chapter 13 of the *Microsoft Systems Management Server 2003 Administrator's Companion* by Steven Kaczmarek (Microsoft Press, 2004) provides additional information about software updates.

- Chapter 6 of the *SMS 2003 Operations Guide* also provides an in-depth look at software updates.

- Review the *Scenarios and Procedures for Microsoft Systems Management Server 2003: Software Distribution and Patch Management* guide, available from the SMS downloads site (http://www.microsoft.com/smserver/downloads/2003).

- Review the white paper titled "Best Practices: Security Patch Management Solution Accelerator," also available from the SMS downloads site.

CHAPTER 15

■ ■ ■

SMS Status Messages and Logs

A thorough understanding of status messaging and logging in SMS is one of the traits that define an SMS expert. Even if you aren't endeavoring to become an expert, a basic understanding of status messages and logs will help you track issues in SMS. In many cases, status message information and logs provide the only methods for identifying issues.

15-1. Viewing Advertisement Status

Problem

You want to view the status of advertisements.

Solution

1. Open the SMS Administrator console.

2. In the SMS Administrator console, expand Site Database (*<Site Code>*), System Status, and Advertisement Status.

3. The right pane displays advertisement status for all advertisements.

4. Double-click an advertisement to view the status by site server.

Discussion

In addition to using web reports for tracking advertisements, the Advertisement Status node in the SMS Administrator console adds two dimensions to status reporting: You can view the status messages based on a broader range of time intervals and based on your hierarchy. The latter option is extremely helpful when identifying an issue surrounding a specific site server.

See Also

- Chapter 5 of the *Microsoft Systems Management Server 2003 Administrator's Companion* by Steven Kaczmarek (Microsoft Press, 2004) provides additional information on viewing status messages.

- Chapter 14 of the *SMS 2003 Operations Guide* provides an overview of the SMS status system.

15-2. Viewing Package Status

Problem

You want to view the status of packages.

Solution

1. Open the SMS Administrator console.
2. From the SMS Administrator console, expand Site Database (*<Site Code>*), System Status, and Package Status.
3. The right pane displays the package status on all packages.
4. Double-click a package to view the status by distribution point.

Discussion

SMS 2003 does an excellent job of maintaining distribution points, so you won't need to monitor package status on a daily basis. However, the extreme importance of proper package versions on distribution points makes the package status messages very important.

See Also

- Chapter 5 of the *Microsoft Systems Management Server 2003 Administrator's Companion* by Steven Kaczmarek (Microsoft Press, 2004) provides additional information on viewing a package's status.
- Chapter 14 of the *SMS 2003 Operations Guide* provides an overview of the SMS status system.

15-3. Viewing Site System Status

Problem

You want to view the status of a site system.

Solution

1. Open the SMS Administrator console.
2. From the SMS Administrator console, expand Site Database (*<Site Code>*), System Status, and Site Status.
3. The right pane displays the site status of all sites with a summary of the status message types.
4. Double-click a site to choose whether to view Component Status or Site System Status.
5. Double-click Component Status to view the current status of the individual site-server components.
6. Double-click Site System Status to view the current status of the site-system roles on that server.

Discussion

When a site server is having problems, you want to turn to the site system status messages. You will be able to quickly evaluate all of the SMS components on the site server and decide which steps need to be taken to fix the problem.

Note In many cases, the details of an SMS site system status message will provide the resolution steps to take to resolve the issue that triggered the message in the first place.

See Also

- Chapter 5 of the *Microsoft Systems Management Server 2003 Administrator's Companion* by Steven Kaczmarek (Microsoft Press, 2004) provides additional information on site system status messaging.
- Chapter 14 of the *SMS 2003 Operations Guide* provides an overview of the SMS status system.

15-4. Viewing Status Message Queries

Problem

You want to view a status message query.

Solution

1. Open the SMS Administrator console.
2. From the SMS Administrator console, expand Site Database (*<Site Code>*), System Status, and Status Message Queries.
3. The right pane displays status message queries for you to choose from.
4. Right-click a status message query, and select Show Messages to open the Status Message Viewer.
5. Enter any requested variables, and click OK to initiate the query.
6. Close the Status Message Viewer.

Discussion

SMS web reports offer many handy status message reports, but they don't include all of the queries that are available to you. Many of the default queries look for errors with site systems and advertisements. These are important to monitor, so that you can keep your SMS environment running smoothly.

Within the SMS Administrator console, you have access to more than 60 status message queries. You can query for client status messages; site status messages; specific advertisements, collections, packages, or Remote Tools activity by user, site, or system; and more.

See Also

- Chapter 5 of the *Microsoft Systems Management Server 2003 Administrator's Companion* by Steven Kaczmarek (Microsoft Press, 2004) provides additional information on status message queries.
- Chapter 14 of the *SMS 2003 Operations Guide* provides an overview of the SMS status system.

15-5. Listing the Properties of a Specific Status Message Query

Problem

You want to list the properties of a specified SMS status message query.

Solution

Example 15-1 demonstrates how to display query properties for a specific SMS status message query.

Example 15-1. *DisplayStatusMessageQuery.vbs*

```
strQueryID = "LAB0023"
strSMSServer = <SMSServer>

Set objLoc =  CreateObject("WbemScripting.SWbemLocator")
Set objSMS= objLoc.ConnectServer(strSMSServer, "root\sms")
Set Results = objSMS.ExecQuery _
    ("SELECT * From SMS_ProviderLocation WHERE ProviderForLocalSite = true")
For each Loc in Results
    If Loc.ProviderForLocalSite = True Then
        Set objSMS = objLoc.ConnectServer(Loc.Machine, "root\sms\site_" & _
            Loc.SiteCode)
    end if
Next

Set objQuery = objSMS.Get("SMS_Query.QueryID='" & _
    strQueryID & "'")
wscript.echo objQuery.Expression
wscript.echo objQuery.GetObjectText_
wscript.echo objQuery.GetText_(2)
```

Discussion

In Example 15-1, after connecting to the site, we use the Get method to obtain the instance of the status message query. Next, we display the query Name, QueryID, and Expression properties. Then, we use the GetObjectText_ method to display all objects in the instance, in MOF format. Finally, we use the GetText_(2) method to display the data in XML format.

█**Note** The GetText_(2) method is only available in Windows operating systems released *after* Windows 2000 (i.e., Windows XP and Server 2003 and newer).

See Also

- Recipe 15-6, "Listing All Status Message Queries," demonstrates how to list all status message queries programmatically.

- The SMS 2003 SDK provides more information about the SMS_Query class.

- The "WMI Scripting Primer: Part 2" by Greg Stemp, Dean Tsaltas, Bob Wells, and Ethan Wilansky demonstrates the use of GetObjectText and GetText_(2) (http://msdn.microsoft.com/library/en-us/dnclinic/html/scripting08132002.asp).

- The "Representing Objects in XML" section of the WMI SDK provides further information about SMS status message queries.

15-6. Listing All Status Message Queries

Problem

You want to list all SMS status message queries from the command line.

Solution: Using VBScript

Example 15-2 demonstrates how to display the query name and WMI Query Language (WQL) expression for each status message query.

Example 15-2. *DisplayStatusMessageQueries.vbs*

```
strSMSServer = <SMSServer>

Set objLoc =  CreateObject("WbemScripting.SWbemLocator")
Set objSMS= objLoc.ConnectServer(strSMSServer, "root\sms")
Set Results = objSMS.ExecQuery _
    ("SELECT * From SMS_ProviderLocation WHERE ProviderForLocalSite = true")
For each Loc in Results
    If Loc.ProviderForLocalSite = True Then
        Set objSMS = objLoc.ConnectServer(Loc.Machine, "root\sms\site_" & _
            Loc.SiteCode)
    end if
Next

Set colQueries = objSMS.ExecQuery _
    ("select * from SMS_Query where TargetClassName = " & _
    "'SMS_StatusMessage' order by Name")
for each objQuery in colQueries
    wscript.echo objQuery.Name & "(" & _
        objQuery.QueryID & ")" & vbTAB & objQuery.Expression
next
```

Discussion

Example 15-2 demonstrates how to list SMS status message queries from the command line. After connecting to the SMS site, we perform a WQL query of the SMS_Query class to obtain all queries that have a TargetClassName of SMS_StatusMessage. Instances in this class that do not meet these criteria are *normal* SMS queries, which appear in the Query node of the SMS Administrator console. Finally, we perform a for-each loop to display the status message query Name, QueryID, and Expression properties.

Also notice in Example 15-2 that canned SMS status message queries have a QueryID that begins with SMS. Any query created by an SMS administrator will have a QueryID that begins with the SMS site code.

See Also

- The SMS 2003 SDK provides more information about the SMS_Query class.

15-7. Creating a Status Message Query

Problem

You want to create a status message query.

Solution

1. Open the SMS Administrator console.

2. From the SMS Administrator console, expand Site Database (*<Site Code>*), System Status, and Status Message Queries.

3. Right-click Status Message Queries, and select New ➤ Status Message Query to open the Status Message Query Properties dialog box.

4. Enter a name and any comments.

5. Choose to import an existing query or create your own by clicking the appropriate button.

6. Edit your query statement properties to your specifications, and click OK.

7. Click OK to close the Status Message Query Properties dialog box.

8. Your new query will be listed in the right pane.

9. Close the Status Message Viewer.

Discussion

If you didn't think that you had enough ways to get data out of SMS with the web reports, WMI queries, SQL queries, and so on, then the status message queries will round out the arsenal. The query-building interface is similar to the regular queries, so you should be able to jump in with both feet.

See Also

- Chapter 5 of the *Microsoft Systems Management Server 2003 Administrator's Companion* by Steven Kaczmarek (Microsoft Press, 2004) provides additional information on status message queries.

- Chapter 14 of the *SMS 2003 Operations Guide* also provides an overview of the SMS status system.

15-8. Exporting Multiple SMS Status Message Queries

Problem

You want to export custom SMS status message queries from the command line to a file.

Solution

Example 15-3 demonstrates how to export multiple SMS status message queries using VBScript.

Example 15-3. *ExportStatusMessagesToMOF.vbs*

```
Const ForWriting = 2
Set fso = CreateObject("Scripting.FileSystemObject")
strSMSServer = <SMSServer>
strNEWSMSServer = "SMSVPC"
strNewSMSSiteCode = "LAB"
strFileLoc = "C:\scripts\"
```

```
Set objLoc =  CreateObject("WbemScripting.SWbemLocator")
Set objSMS= objLoc.ConnectServer(strSMSServer, "root\sms")
Set Results = objSMS.ExecQuery _
    ("SELECT * From SMS_ProviderLocation WHERE ProviderForLocalSite = true")
For each Loc in Results
    If Loc.ProviderForLocalSite = True Then
        Set objSMS = objLoc.ConnectServer(Loc.Machine, "root\sms\site_" & _
            Loc.SiteCode)
    end if
Next

Set colStatQueries = objSMS.ExecQuery _
("select * from SMS_Query where TargetClassName = '" & _
"SMS_StatusMessage' and QueryID not like 'SMS%'")

for each objStatQuery in colStatQueries
    wscript.echo "Exporting " & objStatQuery.Name & vbTAB & _
        objStatQuery.QueryID
    Set fout = fso.OpenTextFile(strfileLoc & _
        objStatQuery.QueryID & ".MOF", ForWriting, True)
    fout.writeline "//*******************************"
    fout.writeline "//Created by SMS Recipes Exporter"
    fout.writeline "//*******************************"
    fout.writeline vbCRLF
    'only use the following line if planning to import MOF
    'from the command line
    fout.writeline "#pragma namespace(" & chr(34) & "\\\\" & _
        strNEWSMSServer & "\\root\\SMS\\site_" & _
        strnewSMSSiteCode & chr(34) & ")"
    fout.writeline vbCRLF
    fout.writeline "// **** Class : SMS_Query ****"
    fout.writeline "[SecurityVerbs(140551)]"
    for each strLine in split(objStatQuery.GetObjectText_, chr(10))
        if instr(strLine, "QueryID =") then
            fout.writeline(vbTAB & "QueryID = " & chr(34) & _
                chr(34)) & ";"
        else
            fout.writeline cstr(strLine)
        end if
    next
    fout.writeline "// **** End ****"
    fout.close
next
```

Discussion

Example 15-3 may become a very handy utility for you. This script demonstrates how to export all noncanned SMS status messages into individual MOF files using VBScript. At the beginning of the script, we use a couple new variables: strNEWSMSServer and strNewSMSSiteCode. These variables should be set to the new SMS server and site code that you plan to import the reports to.

After connecting to the SMS site, we perform a query to obtain all query objects that are not status message queries and do not start with SMS% (canned SMS queries). Next, we begin the for-each loop, where all the action happens.

The for-each loop enumerates all noncanned SMS queries. First, we display the query Name and QueryID. Next, we create (or overwrite) a text file named the same as the QueryID with a .mof extension.

We then write a few comment lines (lines that start with // are comments). Next, we add the namespace line.

Note If you plan to import queries using the Import Object Wizard, change the three lines of code that are used to write the #pragma namespace line into comment lines.

After writing a couple more lines of information, we use the split function in a for-each loop to split data obtained from GetObjectText_, which contains the query instance information that we need to save. Unfortunately, the formatting is a little off for what we need. We use the split function to split the instance information into an array of strings (one string represents one line of instance data). Notice that we split the information on chr(10), which is a linefeed character (*usually* we split on a carriage-return linefeed [vbCRLF] combination). Finally, we write each line to the MOF file, using a carriage-return linefeed at the end of each line. When writing the instance information to the MOF file, we modify the line that contains QueryID. In the MOF file, we want the QueryID to be equal to "", so that a new query is created when it is imported into a site. See Example 9-16 for a sample MOF file.

See Also

- Recipe 9-21, "Importing a Query from the Command Line," demonstrates how to import a query (in MOF format) from the command line. The same process could be applied to import a status message MOF file.

- The SMS_Query class is described in the SMS 2003 SDK.

- The topic titled "How to Run an SMS Scripting Query" in the *SMS 2003 Scripting Guide* explains how to run SMS scripting queries.

- The "Representing Objects in XML" section of the WMI SDK provides further information about exporting WMI data to XML and MOF format.

15-9. Viewing SMS Logs

Problem

You want to view SMS logs.

Solution

1. Download the latest SMS 2003 Toolkit from Microsoft's web site.
2. Install the SMS 2003 Toolkit.
3. Launch the SMS Trace utility (Trace32.exe).
4. Choose to use the SMS Trace utility as the default viewer for all log files.
5. Close the SMS Trace utility.
6. Browse for an SMS log file, and double-click it to open it in the SMS Trace utility.

Discussion

Without the SMS Trace utility, SMS administrators would very quickly go cross-eyed trying to decipher an SMS log using Notepad. Don't try it—it's not a pretty picture. Thankfully, this wonderful utility was created, and it is one of the best log viewers available.

Note Don't forget to check out the Highlight and Filter features that are available with the SMS Trace utility. It is more than just a cute log viewer.

See Also

- Review the section in this book's appendix titled "SMS Toolkit" for more information about using the SMS Trace utility.
- The Microsoft Knowledge Base article titled "A list of log files that are created in Systems Management Server 2003" gives an overview of the SMS Trace utility (`http://support.microsoft.com/default.aspx?scid=kb;en-us;867490`).

15-10. Identifying Site Server Logs

Problem

You want to locate and identify SMS logs for the SMS site server.

Solution

The SMS site server logs can be found in the `\\<siteserver>\SMS_<sitecode>\Logs` directory.

Discussion

The following list of all the site server logs offers a brief description of each:

`Adminui.log` logs the connection actions of the local SMS Administrator console.

`Ccm.log` logs the Client Push Installation process. Go here first when you can't remotely install the SMS client on a system.

`Cidm.log` logs the activity of the Client Install Data Manager (CIDM), which maintains client settings.

`Colleval.log` logs all modifications to collections and the evaluation cycle.

`Compsumm.log` logs the activity of the Component Status Summarizer.

`Cscnfsvc.log` logs the Courier Sender confirmation service activity.

`Dataldr.log` logs the processing of MIF files and hardware inventory.

`Ddm.log` logs the Discovery Data Manger when processing discovery data records (DDRs).

`Despool.log` logs communications between site servers.

`Distmgr.log` logs the package distribution process from site server to distribution point.

`Hman.log` logs changes to the hierarchy and monitors site control file changes.

`Inboxast.log` logs site server inbox activity.

`Inboxmgr.log` logs client access point (CAP) file maintenance.

`Invproc.log` logs inventory processing of delta inventories in MIF format.

`Mpcontrol.log` logs the WINS registration of the management point (MP) and checks the MP availability every ten minutes.

`Mpfdm.log` logs the transfer of client files from the MP to the inboxes.

`MPMSI.log` is the Windows Installer log for the MP installation.

MPSetup.log logs the MP installation.

Ntsvrdis.log logs the SMS server discovery process.

Offermgr.log logs changes to advertisements.

Offersum.log logs the advertisement status summarizer.

Policypv.log logs changes to the Advanced Client policies.

Replmgr.log logs file transfers between site server components.

Rsetup.log logs the initialization of the reporting point installation.

Sched.log logs site-to-site transfers of packages.

Sender.log keeps a manifest of what files were transferred between sites.

Sinvproc.log logs software inventory processing.

Sitecomp.log logs changes to the site components.

Sitectrl.log logs changes to the site control file.

Sitestat.log logs the status monitoring of site systems.

Smsdbmon.log logs changes to the SMS database.

Smsexec.log logs the status of all site components.

Smsprov.log logs WMI connectivity with the SMS database.

SMSReportingInstall.log logs the reporting point installation.

Srvacct.log logs any changes to the SMS accounts.

Statmgr.log logs the processing of status messages.

Swmproc.log logs the processing of software metering files.

See Also

- The Microsoft Knowledge Base article titled "A list of log files that are created in Systems Management Server 2003" outlines all of the SMS log files (http://support.microsoft.com/default.aspx?scid=kb;en-us;867490).

- Chapter 3 of the *Microsoft Systems Management Server 2003 Administrator's Companion* by Steven Kaczmarek (Microsoft Press, 2004) provides additional information about SMS logging.

- Chapter 13 of the *SMS 2003 Operations Guide* provides an overview of maintenance tasks and logging.

- Chapter 10 of the *SMS 2003 Concepts, Deployment, and Planning Guide* provides information on logging.

15-11. Identifying Management Point (MP) Logs

Problem

You want to locate and identify the various MP logs.

Solution

The SMS management point logs can be found in the <drive>:\SMS_CCM\Logs directory.

Discussion

A list of the SMS management point logs and a brief description of each follows:

MP_Ddr.log logs the processing of DDRs from clients and their transfers to the site server.

MP_Framework.log logs the security exchanges between the MP and site server.

MP_GetAuth.log logs the status of the MP.

MP_GetPolicy.log logs new policy information.

MP_Hinv.log logs the processing of hardware inventory files.

MP_Location.log logs the activity of the MP location manager.

MP_Policy.log logs the activity of the MP policy manager.

MP_Relay.log logs the copying of files that are collected from the SMS clients.

MP_Retry.log logs the hardware inventory retry process.

MP_Sinv.log logs the processing of software inventory files collected from SMS clients.

MP_Status.log logs the processing of SMS client status messages.

Note If you installed the SMS client on your management point after the MP install, the SMS client logs will also be in the same directory.

See Also

- The Microsoft Knowledge Base article titled "A list of log files that are created in Systems Management Server 2003" outlines all of the SMS log files (http://support.microsoft.com/default.aspx?scid=kb;en-us;867490).

- Chapter 3 of the *Microsoft Systems Management Server 2003 Administrator's Companion* by Steven Kaczmarek (Microsoft Press, 2004) provides additional information about SMS logging.

- Chapter 13 of the *SMS 2003 Operations Guide* provides an overview of maintenance tasks and logging.

- Chapter 10 of the *SMS 2003 Concepts, Deployment, and Planning Guide* provides information on logging.

15-12. Identifying Advanced Client Logs

Problem

You want to locate and identify the various Advanced Client logs.

Solution

The Advanced Client logs are typically located in the %WinDir%\System32\CCM\Logs directory.

Discussion

A list of the Advanced Client logs and a brief description of each follows:

CAS.log is the log for the content access service that manages the local cache. Issues arising when the local cache is out of space will be noted here.

CCMExec.log is the log for the SMS agent host service. It tracks the initialization of the SMS agent host service and connections with the MP.

CertificateMaintenance.log stores information related to the MP certificate. The MP certificate is verified and logged periodically. Issues with communication with either the MP or Active Directory will be noted here.

ClientIDManagerStartup.log logs the process of maintaining the SMS GUID. If a new global unique identifier (GUID) is required, you will be able to track that change in this log.

ClientLocation.log logs information about issues with site assignments by the Advanced Client. Also, if you want to verify the functionality of your server locator point (SLP) and MP, it will be reflected in this log.

ContentTransferManager.log allows you to monitor the download jobs that are created for transferring packages from the distribution point to the client cache. It logs both Background Intelligent Transfer Service (BITS) and Server Message Block (SMB) transfers.

DataTransferService.log logs communication between the client and the MP. If you are having issues because policies are not getting to the client, look here.

ExecMgr.log records Execution Manager data. The Execution Manager is responsible for building the command lines for launching the software distribution requests. If you want to watch software being deployed in real time, then this is the log for you.

FileBITS.log tracks packages that are being accessed with SMB but not BITS.

FileSystemFile.log logs software inventory actions, specifically software collections.

InventoryAgent.log logs DDRs and both hardware and software inventory cycles.

LocationServices.log logs the identification process for MPs and distribution points.

Mifprovider.log logs MIF file collections.

Mtrmgr.log is the log for software metering process activity.

PolicyAgent.log logs policy request actions.

PolicyAgentProvider.log logs policy changes.

PolicyEvaluator.log logs new policy settings.

Scheduler.log logs any client tasks that are scheduled.

Smscliui.log logs all actions that are initiated in the Systems Management Control Panel applet.

StatusAgent.log logs all status messages that are created by the client.

SWMTRReportGen.log logs the creation event for the software metering usage data report.

Remctrl.log logs the Remote Control component.

See Also

- The Microsoft Knowledge Base article titled "A list of log files that are created in Systems Management Server 2003" outlines all of the SMS log files (`http://support.microsoft.com/default.aspx?scid=kb;en-us;867490`).

- Chapter 3 of the *Microsoft Systems Management Server 2003 Administrator's Companion* by Steven Kaczmarek (Microsoft Press, 2004) provides additional information about SMS logging.

- Chapter 13 of the *SMS 2003 Operations Guide* provides an overview of maintenance tasks and logging.

- Chapter 10 of the *SMS 2003 Concepts, Deployment, and Planning Guide* provides information on logging.

CHAPTER 16

■ ■ ■

SMS Advanced Client

Any seasoned SMS administrator can tell you about the significant performance and reliability increases in the SMS 2003 Advanced Client. In our opinion, performance and reliability are two of the best improvements in SMS 2003. This chapter explains, in detail, how to perform various Advanced Client tasks both locally and remotely. We describe initiating a policy refresh, kicking a hardware inventory, forcing SMS site assignment, displaying current SMS advertisements, displaying SMS advertisement history, and more!

This chapter also provides a lot of detail about scripting the Advanced Client. When SMS 2003 was in its beta release, one of the Microsoft marketing sound bytes was that "SMS 2003 will have a scriptable client." We recall talking to other SMS administrators, and we all thought, "Yeah, right." Then we got our hands on the SMS 2003 beta code, and— sure enough—the SMS 2003 Advanced Client has "Script me!" written all over it.

This chapter provides solutions using the native SMS 2003 Advanced Client graphical interface, the SMS 2003 Toolkit, and VBScript. Be sure to check out this book's appendix, as you will find tools (both free and at a nominal cost) that complement the solutions in this chapter.

16-1. Viewing SMS Client Components' Installed and Current Status

Problem

You want to view the status of SMS client components on an Advanced Client.

Solution: Using a Graphical Interface

1. From the system Control Panel, launch the Systems Management applet.

2. Select the Components tab.

3. Review the Components; click the sort bar to sort by Component, Version, or Status if desired.

4. Click OK to exit.

Solution: Using VBScript

Example 16-1 demonstrates how to display the Advanced Client component status using COM objects.

Example 16-1. *GetClientComponents_COM.vbs*

```
Set oCPAppletMgr=CreateObject("CPApplet.CPAppletMgr")
Set oClientComponents=oCPAppletMgr.GetClientComponents

For Each oClientComponent In oClientComponents

    strInfo = oClientComponent.DisplayName

     Select Case oClientComponent.State
     Case 0
         strInfo = strInfo & vbTAB & "(Installed)"
     Case 1
          strInfo = strInfo & vbTAB & "(Enabled)"
     Case 2
          strInfo = strInfo & vbTAB & "(Disabled)"
     End Select
         strinfo = strInfo & vbTAB & oClientcomponent.Version

    wscript.echo strInfo
Next
```

Example 16-2 demonstrates how to display the Advanced Client component status using WMI.

Example 16-2. *GetClientComponents.vbs*

```
strComputerName = "2KPro"
Set objSMS = GetObject("winmgmts://" & strComputerName & _
    "/root/ccm")
                            .
Set objSMSComponents = objSMS.ExecQuery _
    ("Select * from CCM_InstalledComponent")

for each objComponent in objSMSComponents
    wscript.echo objComponent.Name & vbTAB & objComponent.Version
next
```

Discussion

Knowing the status of the SMS components on a client can be very valuable when troubleshooting client issues. The status information may help you determine if you have a healthy client. Keep in mind, though, that some components will never display as enabled. Verify with *known, healthy* clients to verify correct status information for your environment.

The component versions on the client can help you with troubleshooting. For example, consider a component version of 2.50.3174.1115. The 2.50 represents SMS 2003; 3174 represents Service Pack 1 for SMS 2003; and the last set of numbers represents a patch or hotfix. The third set of numbers in the component version is the easiest way to determine the service pack level for the SMS 2003 Advanced Client.

Example 16-1 demonstrates how to display the SMS Advanced Client status locally on a client. We use the Advanced Client COM Automation Control Panel (CPAppletMgr) object to call the method GetClientComponents. We then perform a for-each loop to obtain the DisplayName, State, and Version of each component. To make this script more readable to humans, we add a case statement to transpose the numerical values for State into the English-word equivalents. Finally, we display the data for the component.

Example 16-1 can be a very handy script to use when you have the ability to execute the VBScript script on the local system. Sometimes, however, you need the ability to execute these types of scripts remotely.

Example 16-2 demonstrates how to obtain the component Name and Version remotely. Unfortunately, we are unable to locate a Status value in WMI. Notice the variable strComputerName. In our example, we're connecting to the computer 2KPro. You can replace 2KPro with any computer that you have remote access to (i.e., for which you have administrative privileges or custom permissions configured on the client). To connect to the local system using this script, simply replace 2KPro with a period (.), which represents the local system in WMI. After connecting to the SMS client namespace root/ccm, perform a WQL query to obtain all information from the CCM_InstalledComponent class. Finally, perform a for-each loop to display the component name and version.

See Also

- Review the sidebar in Chapter 9 titled "What Is WMI?" for more information about WMI.

- The SMS 2003 SDK provides additional information about the CCM_InstalledComponent class and the CPAppletMgr COM object.

- Chapter 9 of the *SMS 2003 Operations Guide* provides additional information about scripting client operations.

- The *SMS 2003 Scripting Guide* provides examples of how to use the CPAppletMgr COM object.

16-2. Initiating Advanced Tasks Using SendSched.vbs

Problem

You want to use SendSched.vbs, which is part of the SMS 2003 Toolkit.

Discussion

The Send Schedule tool (SendSched.vbs) is a VBScript script that is part of the SMS 2003 Toolkit. It is used to trigger a schedule on the SMS 2003 Advanced Client. This script can be run locally or remotely. To run this script, open a command prompt, and navigate to the Toolkit directory (currently the default location is C:\Program Files\SMS 2003 Toolkit 2). From the Toolkit directory, execute a command similar to the following:

```
Cscript SendSched.vbs ScheduleID [machine name]
```

Replace SheduleID with the proper schedule ID. The argument [machine name] is an optional argument. If executing against the local machine, simply execute Cscript SendSched.vbs ScheduleID. If executing against a remote machine, add the proper machine name as the last argument to the command line. By running this command line, you are *triggering* the schedule to run at that moment. For example, you can trigger hardware inventory or software inventory using this process as well, but if the node is not online at the time of triggering, nothing will be executed on the client (i.e., the action you're attempting to initiate will not be queued to run on the client when it comes online). Table 16-1 provides the most popular schedules to trigger when using SendSched.vbs.

Table 16-1. *Sample Schedules for Common Administrator Tasks*

Description	ScheduleID˄
Hardware inventory	{00000000-0000-0000-0000-000000000001}
Software inventory	{00000000-0000-0000-0000-000000000002}
Discovery data record (DDR)	{00000000-0000-0000-0000-000000000003}
Machine policy assignment request	{00000000-0000-0000-0000-000000000021}
File collection	{00000000-0000-0000-0000-000000000010}
Software metering usage report cycle	{00000000-0000-0000-0000-000000000022}
MSI product source update cycle	{00000000-0000-0000-0000-000000000032}

For example, to trigger hardware inventory on the remote computer 2KPRO, execute the following command:

```
Cscript SendSched.vbs {00000000-0000-0000-0000-000000000001} 2KPRO
```

Using this process, you can trigger all schedules that appear in the root\ccm\policy\machine namespace in the CCM_Scheduler_ScheduledMessage class. The easiest way to review this data is to launch SMS Policy Spy (also part of the SMS 2003 Toolkit), and on the Actual tab, expand Machine and CCM_Scheduler_ScheduledMessage. Each of the ScheduledMessageIDs listed there represents a task that can be initiated using SendSched.vbs. In SMS Policy Spy, highlight the ScheduledMessageID, and review the Details pane to get an idea of what each schedule does. You will notice each advertisement that is currently advertised to the client will also appear as an instance in this class. Another recipe in this chapter will discuss how to rerun an advertisement.

SendSched.vbs is a great tool for triggering schedules. Subsequent recipes will demonstrate scripts to trigger specific schedules, which will assist you when you are creating a custom script.

See Also

- Review the SMS 2003 Toolkit Help for more information about how to use the Send Schedule tool.

- Appendix C of the *SMS 2003 Operations Guide* demonstrates several client actions using a VBScript script, which can be run on the local system to perform various operations. This script, Advclient.vbs, uses COM objects such as Microsoft.SMS.Client, UIResource.UIResourceMgr, and CPApplet.CPAppletMgr.

16-3. Initiating the Hardware Inventory Cycle

Problem

You want to initiate the hardware inventory cycle on an Advanced Client.

Solution: Using a Graphical Interface

1. From the system Control Panel, launch the Systems Management applet.

2. Select the Actions tab.

3. Highlight the Hardware Inventory Cycle action, and click the Initiate Action button.

4. Click OK to close the informational pop-up dialog box, and click OK to exit.

Solution: Using VBScript

Example 16-3 demonstrates how to force a hardware inventory cycle on a local or remote client using WMI.

Example 16-3. *ForceHardwareInv.vbs*

```
Const HWINV = "{00000000-0000-0000-0000-000000000001}"
strComputer = "2kPro"

FullInv = Msgbox("Full Inventory?", vbYesNo)

If FullInv = vbYes then
    Set objSMS = GetObject("winmgmts://" & strComputer & _
        "/root/ccm/invagt")
    objSMS.Delete "InventoryActionStatus.InventoryActionID=" _
        & Chr(34) & HWINV & Chr(34)
End If

Set objCCM = GetObject("winmgmts://" & strComputer & "/root/ccm")
Set objClient = objCCM.Get("SMS_Client")
Set objSched = objClient.Methods_("TriggerSchedule"). _
    inParameters.SpawnInstance_()
objSched.sScheduleID = HWINV
objCCM.ExecMethod "SMS_Client", "TriggerSchedule", objSched
```

Alternately, to use the COM object, execute the VBScript code in Example 16-4 to initiate a hardware inventory cycle on the local system.

Example 16-4. *ForceHardwareInv_COM.vbs*

```
set mgr = CreateObject("CPApplet.CPAppletMgr")
set actions=mgr.GetClientActions
for each action in actions
    if action.name="Hardware Inventory Collection Cycle" then
        action.PerformAction
        wscript.echo action.Name & " Initiated"
    end if
next
```

Discussion

If you have hardware inventory configured in your SMS site, it will run automatically on a regular basis (defined by you). On occasion, you may need to expedite the hardware inventory process. Hardware inventory generally completes in less than 20 seconds. As you can see from the Actions tab in the Systems Management applet on the SMS Advanced Client, you can initiate any of the listed actions manually at any time.

Note Update the Hardware Inventory Client Agent to modify the hardware inventory schedule. See Recipe 2-20, "Configuring Hardware Inventory," for more information.

Example 16-3 demonstrates how to initiate the hardware inventory collection cycle action using VBScript scripts on the local client or on a remote client. As you can see, we give the user the option to select a standard delta hardware inventory or a full hardware inventory. Forcing a full hardware inventory is one of the first steps we usually do when troubleshooting hardware inventory issues on a client.

If the user selects to initiate a full hardware inventory, we connect to the root/ccm/invagt namespace and delete the hardware InventoryActionID instance. Since this instance no longer exists,

SMS will perform a full hardware inventory the next time hardware inventory is initiated. And, conveniently, the remainder of this example is used to initiate hardware inventory. First, we connect to the root/ccm namespace and then connect to the SMS_Client class. Next, we create a new instance of the TriggerSchedule method and add the hardware inventory ScheduleID to the properties of the schedule we just created. Finally, we initiate the ExecMethod method to execute the TriggerSchedule method.

Note Review the %windir%\system32\ccm\logs\InventoryAgent.log file to monitor hardware inventory, software inventory, and file collection actions.

Example 16-4 demonstrates how to initiate hardware inventory on the local SMS Advanced Client. We use the Advanced Client COM Automation Control Panel (CPAppletMgr) object to call the method GetClientActions. We then use a for-each loop to enumerate each available action. When we find "Hardware Inventory Collection Cycle", we call the PerformAction method to initiate hardware inventory.

See Also

- Recipe 16-2, "Initiating Advanced Tasks Using SendSched.vbs," explains how to use SendSched.vbs, a VBScript tool included with the SMS 2003 Toolkit.

- This book's appendix demonstrates how to initiate the hardware inventory collection cycle action on one system or on an entire collection from within the SMS Administrator console.

- Chapter 13 discusses hardware inventory in detail.

- This book's appendix provides resources for additional tools to initiate schedules locally and remotely.

- The SMS 2003 SDK provides additional information about the SMS_Client class.

- The *SMS 2003 Scripting Guide* demonstrates how to resynchronize hardware inventory on the SMS 2003 Advanced Client.

- Appendix C of the *SMS 2003 Operations Guide* demonstrates several client actions using a VBScript script that can be run on the local system to perform various operations. This script, Advclient.vbs, uses COM objects such as Microsoft.SMS.Client, UIResource.UIResourceMgr, and CPApplet.CPAppletMgr.

16-4. Initiating the Software Inventory Cycle

Problem

You want to initiate the software inventory cycle on an Advanced Client.

Solution: Using a Graphical Interface

1. From the client PC's system Control Panel, launch the Systems Management applet.

2. Select the Actions tab.

3. Highlight the Software Inventory Cycle action, and click the Initiate Action button.

4. Click OK to close the informational pop-up dialog box, and click OK to exit.

Solution: Using VBScript

Example 16-5 demonstrates how to initiate software inventory on a local or remote Advanced Client using WMI.

Example 16-5. *ForceSoftwareInv.vbs*

```
Const SWINV = "{00000000-0000-0000-0000-000000000002}"
strComputer = "2kPro"

FullInv = Msgbox("Full Inventory?", vbYesNo)

If FullInv = vbYes then
    Set objSMS = GetObject("winmgmts://" & strComputer & _
        "/root/ccm/invagt")
    objSMS.Delete "InventoryActionStatus.InventoryActionID=" _
        & Chr(34) & SWINV & Chr(34)
End If

Set objCCM = GetObject("winmgmts://" & strComputer & "/root/ccm")
Set objClient = objCCM.Get("SMS_Client")
Set objSched = objClient.Methods_("TriggerSchedule"). _
    inParameters.SpawnInstance_()
objSched.sScheduleID = SWINV
objCCM.ExecMethod "SMS_Client", "TriggerSchedule", objSched
```

Alternatively, to use the COM object, execute the VBScript code in Example 16-6 to initiate a software inventory cycle on the local system.

Example 16-6. *SoftwareInv_COM.vbs*

```
set mgr = CreateObject("CPApplet.CPAppletMgr")
set actions=mgr.GetClientActions
for each action in actions
    if action.name="Software Inventory Collection Cycle" then
        action.PerformAction
        wscript.echo action.Name & " Initiated"
    end if
next
```

Discussion

Like hardware inventory, if you have software inventory configured in your SMS site, it will run automatically on a regular basis (defined by you). On occasion, you may need to expedite the software inventory process. As you can see from the Actions tab in the Systems Management applet on the SMS Advanced Client, you can initiate any of the listed actions manually at any time.

Note Update the Software Inventory Client Agent to modify the software inventory schedule. See Recipe 2-21, "Configuring Software Inventory," for more information.

In our experience, default software inventory generally takes approximately 15 minutes to complete on a system with 35GB of used hard disk space. This number can vary greatly depending on additional files and file types being inventoried in your environment.

Note Review the %windir%\system32\ccm\logs\InventoryAgent.log file to monitor hardware inventory, software inventory, and file collection actions.

Example 16-5 demonstrates how to force the software inventory cycle action using VBScript on the local client or a remote client. Review the "Discussion" section for Example 16-3 in Recipe 16-3, "Initiating the Hardware Inventory Cycle," for more information on the script process.

Example 16-6 demonstrates how to initiate the software inventory cycle on the local SMS Advanced Client; it is very similar to Example 16-4 in Recipe 16-3, "Initiating the Hardware Inventory Cycle." In Example 16-6, we are simply initiating the PerformAction method on the software inventory collection cycle action instead.

See Also

- Recipe 16-2, "Initiating Advanced Tasks Using SendSched.vbs," explains how to use SendSched.vbs, a VBScript tool included with the SMS 2003 Toolkit.

- Chapter 10 discusses software inventory in detail.

- This book's appendix demonstrates how to initiate the software inventory cycle on one system or on an entire collection from within the SMS Administrator console.

- This book's appendix also provides resources for additional tools to initiate schedules locally and remotely.

- The *SMS 2003 Scripting Guide* also demonstrates how to resynchronize software inventory on the SMS 2003 Advanced Client.

- The SMS 2003 SDK provides additional information about the SMS_Client class.

- Appendix C of the *SMS 2003 Operations Guide* demonstrates several client actions using a VBScript script that can be run on the local system to perform various operations. This script, Advclient.vbs, uses COM objects such as Microsoft.SMS.Client, UIResource.UIResourceMgr, and CPApplet.CPAppletMgr.

16-5. Initiating the Machine Policy Retrieval and Evaluation Cycle

Problem

You want to initiate a Machine Policy Retrieval and Evaluation Cycle on an Advanced Client.

Solution: Using a Graphical Interface

To initiate a Machine Policy Retrieval and Evaluation Cycle using the Systems Management applet in the Control Panel, perform the following steps:

1. From the system Control Panel, launch the Systems Management applet.

2. Select the Actions tab.

3. Highlight the Machine Policy Retrieval & Evaluation Cycle action, and click the Initiate Action button.

4. Click OK to close the informational pop-up dialog box, and click OK to exit.

To initiate the cycle using SMS Policy Spy, perform the following steps:

1. From the SMS 2003 Toolkit, launch SMS Policy Spy.

2. To connect to a remote system, from the Tools menu in Policy Spy, select Open Remote, and enter a remote computer name.

3. From the Tools menu, select Request Machine Assignments.

Solution: Using VBScript

Example 16-7 demonstrates how to refresh the machine policy on a local or remote Advanced Client using WMI.

Example 16-7. *RefreshMachinePolicy.vbs*

```
Const MachinePol = "{00000000-0000-0000-0000-000000000021}"
strComputer = "2kPro"

Set objCCM = GetObject("winmgmts://" & strComputer & "/root/ccm")
Set objClient = objCCM.Get("SMS_Client")
Set objSched = objClient.Methods_("TriggerSchedule"). _
    inParameters.SpawnInstance_()
objSched.sScheduleID = MachinePol
objCCM.ExecMethod "SMS_Client", "TriggerSchedule", objSched
```

To use the COM object, execute the VBScript code in Example 16-8 to refresh the machine policy on the local system.

Example 16-8. *RefreshAndEvalMachinePolicy_COM.vbs*

```
set mgr = CreateObject("CPApplet.CPAppletMgr")
set actions=mgr.GetClientActions
for each action in actions
    if action.name="Request & Evaluate Machine Policy" then
        action.PerformAction
        wscript.echo action.Name & " Initiated"
    end if
next
```

Discussion

Your SMS site has a configured polling interval for refreshing machine policy. By default, that interval is 60 minutes. Some SMS administrators lengthen the polling interval, and some shorten it. You may find on occasion that you need to install software faster than the normal interval in your environment. The scripts in this recipe will help you kick off that polling interval immediately, instead of minutes, hours, or days later.

Note Review `%windir%\system32\ccm\logs\StatusAgent.log` to monitor SMS policy retrieval and evaluation actions.

Example 16-7 demonstrates how to initiate the Machine Policy Retrieval and Evaluation Cycle action using VBScript on the local client or on a remote client. Review the "Discussion" section for Example 16-3 in Recipe 16-3, "Initiating the Hardware Inventory Cycle," for more information on the script process.

Example 16-8 demonstrates how to initiate a Machine Policy Retrieval and Evaluation Cycle action on the local SMS Advanced Client. It is very similar to Example 16-4 in Recipe 16-3, "Initiating the Hardware Inventory Cycle." In Example 16-8, we are simply initiating the PerformAction method on the Request and Evaluate Machine Policy action instead.

Note Modify the Advertised Programs Client Agent properties to modify the polling interval for your SMS environment. See Recipe 2-23, "Configuring the Advertised Program Client Agent," for more information.

See Also

- Recipe 16-2, "Initiating Advanced Tasks Using SendSched.vbs," explains how to use SendSched.vbs, a VBScript tool included with the SMS 2003 Toolkit.

- This book's appendix demonstrates how to initiate a machine policy refresh on one system or on an entire collection from within the SMS Administrator console.

- Obtain SMS Policy Spy and SMS Advanced Client Spy from the SMS 2003 Toolkit (http://www. microsoft.com/smserver/downloads/2003/tools/toolkit.mspx).

- The SMS 2003 SDK provides additional information about the SMS_Client class.

- Appendix C of the *SMS 2003 Operations Guide* demonstrates several client actions using a VBScript script that can be run on the local system to perform various operations. This script, Advclient.vbs, uses COM objects such as Microsoft.SMS.Client, UIResource.UIResourceMgr, and CPApplet.CPAppletMgr.

16-6. Initiating the Discovery Data Collection Cycle

Problem

You want to initiate a discovery data collection cycle on an Advanced Client.

Solution: Using a Graphical Interface

1. From the system Control Panel, launch the Systems Management applet.

2. Select the Actions tab.

3. Highlight the Discovery Data Collection Cycle action, and click the Initiate Action button.

4. Click OK to close the informational pop-up dialog box, and click OK to exit.

Solution: Using VBScript

Example 16-9 demonstrates how to initiate a discovery data record (DDR) collection cycle action on a local or remote Advanced Client using WMI.

Example 16-9. *InitiateDDRs.vbs*

```
Const DDR = "{00000000-0000-0000-0000-000000000003}"
strComputer = "2kPro"

Set objCCM = GetObject("winmgmts://" & strComputer & "/root/ccm")
Set objClient = objCCM.Get("SMS_Client")
Set objSched = objClient.Methods_("TriggerSchedule"). _
    inParameters.SpawnInstance_()
objSched.sScheduleID = DDR
objCCM.ExecMethod "SMS_Client", "TriggerSchedule", objSched
```

To use the COM object, execute the VBScript code in Example 16-10 to initiate a Discovery Data Collection Cycle action on the local system.

Example 16-10. *InitiateDDR_COM.vbs*

```
set mgr = CreateObject("CPApplet.CPAppletMgr")
set actions=mgr.GetClientActions
for each action in actions
    if action.name="Discovery Data Collection Cycle" then
        action.PerformAction
        wscript.echo action.Name & " Initiated"
    end if
next
```

Discussion

Each client automatically reports a DDR at the interval specified by Heartbeat Discovery, when enabled. If you have made significant changes to the system (e.g., changes to the IP address, operating system version, AD site name, etc.) and you want SMS to receive this information faster than the scheduled DDR collection cycle, this recipe will help you.

Note Update the Heartbeat Discovery method to modify the discovery data collection schedule. See Recipe 2-40, "Configuring Heartbeat Discovery," for more information.

Example 16-9 demonstrates how to initiate the discovery data collection cycle action using VBScript on the local client or on a remote client. Review the "Discussion" section for Example 16-3 in Recipe 16-3, "Initiating the Hardware Inventory Cycle," for more information on the script process.

Example 16-10 demonstrates how to initiate the discovery data collection cycle action on the local SMS Advanced Client. It is very similar to Example 16-4 in Recipe 16-3, "Initiating the Hardware Inventory Cycle." In Example 16-10, we are simply initiating the PerformAction method on the discovery data collection cycle action instead.

Note Review the %windir%\system32\ccm\logs\SMSClientMethodProvider.log file to monitor the discovery data collection cycle action.

See Also

- Recipe 2-40, "Configuring Heartbeat Discovery," for information about configuring heartbeat discovery.

- Recipe 16-2, "Initiating Advanced Tasks Using SendSched.vbs," explains how to use SendSched.vbs, a VBScript tool included with the SMS 2003 Toolkit.

- This book's appendix demonstrates how to initiate the DDR cycle action on one system or on an entire collection from within the SMS Administrator console.

- The SMS 2003 SDK provides additional information about the SMS_Client class.

- Appendix C of the *SMS 2003 Operations Guide* demonstrates several client actions using a VBScript script that can be run on the local system to perform various operations. This script, Advclient.vbs, uses COM objects such as Microsoft.SMS.Client, UIResource.UIResourceMgr, and CPApplet.CPAppletMgr.

16-7. Initiating the File Collection Cycle

Problem

You want to initiate the file collection cycle on an Advanced Client.

Solution: Using a Graphical Interface

1. From the system Control Panel, launch the Systems Management applet.

2. Select the Actions tab.

3. Highlight the File Collection Cycle action, and click the Initiate Action button.

4. Click OK to close the informational pop-up dialog box, and click OK to exit.

Solution: Using VBScript

Example 16-11 demonstrates how to initiate the file collection cycle action on the local or remote Advanced Client using WMI.

Example 16-11. *InitiateFileCOLL.vbs*

```
Const FILECOLL = "{00000000-0000-0000-0000-000000000010}"
strComputer = "2kPro"

Set objCCM = GetObject("winmgmts://" & strComputer & "/root/ccm")
Set objClient = objCCM.Get("SMS_Client")
Set objSched = objClient.Methods_("TriggerSchedule"). _
    inParameters.SpawnInstance_()
objSched.sScheduleID = FILECOLL
objCCM.ExecMethod "SMS_Client", "TriggerSchedule", objSched
```

To use the COM object, execute the VBScript code in Example 16-12 to initiate a file collection cycle action on the local system.

Example 16-12. *InitiateFileCOLL_COM.vbs*

```
set mgr = CreateObject("CPApplet.CPAppletMgr")
set actions=mgr.GetClientActions
for each action in actions
    if action.name="Standard File Collection Cycle" then
        action.PerformAction
        wscript.echo action.Name & " Initiated"
    end if
next
```

Discussion

Each client automatically initiates a file collection cycle at the interval specified by the Software Inventory Client Agent, when enabled. If you want SMS to receive updated file collection information faster than the scheduled file collection cycle indicates, this recipe will help you.

Note Update the Software Inventory Client Agent to modify the file collection cycle schedule. See Recipe 2-21, "Configuring Software Inventory," for more information.

Example 16-11 demonstrates how to initiate the file collection cycle action using VBScript on the local client or on a remote client. Review the "Discussion" section for Example 16-3 in Recipe 16-3, "Initiating the Hardware Inventory Cycle," for more information on the script process.

Example 16-12 demonstrates how to initiate the file collection cycle on the local SMS Advanced Client. It is very similar to Example 16-3 in Recipe 16-3, "Initiating the Hardware Inventory Cycle." In Example 16-12, we are simply initiating the file collection cycle action instead.

Note Review %windir%\system32\ccm\logs\InventoryAgent.log to monitor the file collection cycle action.

See Also

- Recipe 16-2, "Initiating Advanced Tasks Using SendSched.vbs," explains how to use SendSched.vbs, a VBScript tool included with the SMS 2003 Toolkit.

- Chapter 10 discusses software inventory and file collection in detail.

- This book's appendix demonstrates how to initiate a file collection cycle on one system or on an entire collection from within the SMS Administrator console.

- The SMS 2003 SDK provides additional information about the SMS_Client class.

- Appendix C of the *SMS 2003 Operations Guide* demonstrates several client actions using a VBScript script that can be run on the local system to perform various operations. This script, Advclient.vbs, uses COM objects such as Microsoft.SMS.Client, UIResource.UIResourceMgr, and CPApplet.CPAppletMgr.

16-8. Initiating the Software Metering Usage Report Cycle

Problem

You want to initiate a software metering usage report cycle on an Advanced Client.

Solution: Using a Graphical Interface

1. From the system Control Panel, launch the Systems Management applet.

2. Select the Actions tab.

3. Highlight the Software Metering Usage Report Cycle action, and click the Initiate Action button.

4. Click OK to close the informational pop-up dialog box, and click OK to exit.

Solution: Using VBScript

Example 16-13 demonstrates how to initiate a software metering usage report cycle on a local or remote Advanced Client using WMI.

Example 16-13. *InitiateSWM.vbs*

```
Const SWM = "{00000000-0000-0000-0000-000000000022}"
strComputer = "2kPro"

Set objCCM = GetObject("winmgmts://" & strComputer & "/root/ccm")
Set objClient = objCCM.Get("SMS_Client")
Set objSched = objClient.Methods_("TriggerSchedule"). _
```

```
    inParameters.SpawnInstance_()
objSched.sScheduleID = SWM
objCCM.ExecMethod "SMS_Client", "TriggerSchedule", objSched
```

Alternatively, to use the COM object, execute the VBScript code in Example 16-14 to initiate a software metering usage report cycle action on the local system.

Example 16-14. *InitiateSWM_COM.vbs*

```
set mgr = CreateObject("CPApplet.CPAppletMgr")
set actions=mgr.GetClientActions
for each action in actions
    if action.name="Software Metering Usage Report Cycle" then
        action.PerformAction
        wscript.echo action.Name & " Initiated"
    end if
next
```

Discussion

Each client automatically initiates a software metering usage report cycle at the interval specified by the Software Metering Client Agent, when enabled. If you want SMS to receive updated software metering information faster than the scheduled software metering usage report cycle, use the examples in this recipe.

Note Update the Software Metering Client Agent to modify the software metering usage report schedule. See Recipe 2-24, "Configuring the Software Metering Client Agent," for more information.

Example 16-13 demonstrates how to initiate the software metering usage report cycle action using VBScript on the local client or on a remote client. Review the "Discussion" section for Example 16-3 in Recipe 16-3, "Initiating the Hardware Inventory Cycle," for more information on the script process.

Example 16-14 demonstrates how to initiate a software metering usage report cycle action on the local SMS Advanced Client. It is very similar to Example 16-3 in Recipe 16-3, "Initiating the Hardware Inventory Cycle." In Example 16-14, we are simply initiating the software metering usage report cycle action instead.

See Also

- Recipe 16-2, "Initiating Advanced Tasks Using SendSched.vbs," explains how to use SendSched.vbs, a VBScript tool included with the SMS 2003 Toolkit.

- Chapter 7 discusses software metering in detail.

- The SMS 2003 SDK provides additional information about the SMS_Client class.

- Appendix C of the *SMS 2003 Operations Guide* demonstrates several client actions using a VBScript script that can be run on the local system to perform various operations. This script, Advclient.vbs, uses COM objects such as Microsoft.SMS.Client, UIResource.UIResourceMgr, and CPApplet.CPAppletMgr.

16-9. Initiating the User Policy Retrieval and Evaluation Cycle

Problem

You want to initiate the user policy retrieval and evaluation cycle on an Advanced Client.

Solution: Using a Graphical Interface

To initiate the user policy retrieval and evaluation cycle on an Advanced Client using the Systems Management applet in the Control Panel, use the following steps:

1. From the system Control Panel, launch the Systems Management applet.

2. Select the Actions tab.

3. Highlight the User Policy Retrieval & Evaluation Cycle action, and click the Initiate Action button.

4. Click OK to close the informational pop-up dialog box, and click OK to exit.

Initiate the cycle using SMS Policy Spy as follows:

1. From the SMS 2003 Toolkit, launch SMS Policy Spy.

2. From the Tools Menu, select Request User Assignments.

Solution: Using VBScript

Example 16-15 demonstrates how to initiate a user policy refresh on the Advanced Client for the user that is currently logged on.

Example 16-15. *InitiateUserPol_COM.vbs*

```
set mgr = CreateObject("CPApplet.CPAppletMgr")
set actions=mgr.GetClientActions
for each action in actions
    if action.name="Request & Evaluate User Policy" then
        action.PerformAction
        wscript.echo action.Name & " Initiated"
    end if
next
```

Discussion

By default, the polling interval for policy refresh is 60 minutes. Some SMS administrators lengthen the polling interval, and some shorten it. You may find on occasion that you need to install software faster than the normal interval in your environment allows. The scripts in this recipe will help you kick off that polling interval immediately, instead of several minutes, hours, or days from now.

▓**Note** Review %windir%\system32\ccm\logs\StatusAgent.log to monitor SMS user policy retrieval and evaluation actions.

Example 16-15 demonstrates how to initiate the user policy retrieval and evaluation cycle action on the local SMS Advanced Client. It is very similar to Example 16-3 in Recipe 16-3, "Initiating the Hardware Inventory Cycle." In Example 16-15, we are simply initiating the PerformAction method on the Request and Evaluate User Policy action instead.

Note The user policy retrieval and evaluation cycle action can only be initiated locally (you have no remote access to this policy refresh).

Modify the Advertised Programs Client Agent properties to change the polling interval for your SMS environment. See Recipe 2-23, "Configuring the Advertised Programs Client Agent," for more information.

See Also

- Obtain SMS Policy Spy and SMS Advanced Client Spy from the SMS 2003 Toolkit (http://www.microsoft.com/smserver/downloads/2003/tools/toolkit.mspx).

- Appendix C of the *SMS 2003 Operations Guide* demonstrates several client actions using a VBScript script that can be run on the local system to perform various operations. This script, Advclient.vbs, uses COM objects such as Microsoft.SMS.Client, UIResource.UIResourceMgr, and CPApplet.CPAppletMgr.

16-10. Initiating the Windows Installer Source List Update Cycle

Problem

You want to initiate the Windows Installer source list update cycle on an Advanced Client.

Using a Graphical Interface

1. From the system Control Panel, launch the Systems Management applet.

2. Select the Actions tab.

3. Highlight the Windows Installer Source List Update Cycle action, and click the Initiate Action button.

4. Click OK to close the informational pop-up dialog box, and click OK to exit.

Using VBScript

Example 16-16 demonstrates how to initiate a Windows Installer source list update cycle on a local or remote SMS Advanced Client using WMI.

Example 16-16. *InitiateWIUpdate.vbs*

```
Const WIU = "{00000000-0000-0000-0000-000000000032}"
strComputer = "2kPro"

Set objCCM = GetObject("winmgmts://" & strComputer & "/root/ccm")
Set objClient = objCCM.Get("SMS_Client")
Set objSched = objClient.Methods_("TriggerSchedule"). _
    inParameters.SpawnInstance_()
objSched.sScheduleID = WIU
objCCM.ExecMethod "SMS_Client", "TriggerSchedule", objSched
```

To use the COM object, execute the VBScript code in Example 16-17 to initiate a Windows Installer Source List Update Cycle action on the local system.

Example 16-17. *InitiateWIUpdate_COM.vbs*

```
set mgr = CreateObject("CPApplet.CPAppletMgr")
set actions=mgr.GetClientActions
for each action in actions
    if action.name="MSI Product Source Update Cycle" then
        action.PerformAction
        wscript.echo action.Name & " Initiated"
    end if
next
```

Discussion

Windows Installer is a wonderful feature when used properly. Many applications that are installed using Windows Installer (those with the file extension .msi) have self-healing capabilities—if a component in the application becomes corrupt or is accidentally removed, Windows Installer can automatically detect the problem and initiate a repair. In many situations, the installation source files are required for the application to heal itself. You can use SMS to manage the source files for your Windows Installer products, provided you keep the installation source on one or more distribution points.

There are several triggers to initiate a Windows Installer source list update cycle (also known as an MSI product source update cycle). A brief overview of these triggers follows:

Management point (MP) change: Whenever an Advanced Client's MP, or proxy management point (PMP), changes, a full MSI product source update cycle will be run.

Network change: If a client changes from one network subnet to another, a full MSI product source update cycle will be run. If the client has multiple network addresses (e.g., built-in NIC, wireless PC card, etc.), as long as one network subnet remains the same, an MSI product source update cycle will not be triggered. Computers that use a dial-up or VPN connection to a corporate network will also trigger an MSI product source update cycle.

Installing a program with associated Windows Installer information: When a Windows Installer application is installed on the client, the MSI product source update cycle will be triggered once installation is complete.

Refresh interval: An MSI product source update cycle will be triggered automatically at each refresh interval as described in the SMS site control file.

User logon/logoff: Per-user Windows Installer installations are updated by the MSI product source update cycle when a user logs on. When a user logs off, a flag is toggled to indicate that only per-machine installations should be evaluated at that time.

Manual methods: Using either the manual or scripting methods mentioned earlier in this recipe can trigger an MSI product source update cycle.

Example 16-17 demonstrates how to initiate the MSI product source update cycle action using VBScript on the local client or on a remote client. Review the "Discussion" section for Example 16-3 in Recipe 16-3, "Initiating the Hardware Inventory Cycle," for more information on the script process.

Example 16-18 demonstrates how to initiate an MSI product source update cycle action on the local SMS Advanced Client. It is very similar to Example 16-4 in Recipe 16-3, "Initiating the Hardware Inventory Cycle." In Example 16-18, we are simply initiating an MSI product source update cycle action instead.

Note Review %windir%\system32\ccm\logs\SrcUpdateMgr.log to monitor the Windows Installer source list update cycle.

See Also

- Recipe 16-2, "Initiating Advanced Tasks Using SendSched.vbs," explains how to use SendSched.vbs, a VBScript tool included with the SMS 2003 Toolkit.

- This book's appendix demonstrates how to initiate an MSI product source update cycle action on one system or on an entire collection from within the SMS Administrator console.

- Review the "Windows Installer Source Location Manager" white paper for a detailed description of the MSI product source update cycle (http://www.microsoft.com/smsserver/techinfo/productdoc/default.mspx).

- The SMS 2003 SDK provides additional information about the SMS_Client class.

- Appendix C of the *SMS 2003 Operations Guide* demonstrates several client actions using a VBScript script that can be run on the local system to perform various operations. This script, Advclient.vbs, uses COM objects such as Microsoft.SMS.Client, UIResource.UIResourceMgr, and CPApplet.CPAppletMgr.

16-11. Initiating a Client Repair

Problem

You want to initiate the repair of an Advanced Client.

Solution: Using a Graphical Interface

1. From the system Control Panel, launch the Systems Management applet.

2. Select the Components tab.

3. Click the Repair button.

4. Step away from the keyboard, and allow SMS to perform the repair.

Solution: Using VBScript

Example 16-18 demonstrates how to initiate a client repair action on a local or remote Advanced Client using WMI.

Example 16-18. *InitiateClientRepair.vbs*

```
strComputer = "2kPro"
Set smsClient = GetObject("winmgmts://" & strComputer & _
 "/root/ccm:SMS_Client")
Set result = smsClient.ExecMethod_("RepairClient")
wscript.echo "Repair Initiated on " & strComputer
```

Discussion

Occasionally, you may encounter a client that is no longer receiving updated policies or has stopped sending inventory. If your client is otherwise healthy, consider initiating a client repair as one of your first steps in troubleshooting.

Note Review %windir%\system32\ccm\logs\CCMRepair.log to monitor the Windows Installer source list update cycle.

Example 16-18 can be used to initiate a client repair on the local system or on a remote system by simply changing the value of strComputerName. To make the script in Example 16-18 more SMS administrator–friendly, use the Arguments property, as in Example 16-19.

Example 16-19. *InitiateClientRepair_CommandLine.vbs*

```
Set objArgs = WScript.Arguments
StrComputer = objArgs(0)
Set smsClient = GetObject("winmgmts://" & strComputer & _
 "/root/ccm:SMS_Client")
Set result = smsClient.ExecMethod_("RepairClient")
wscript.echo "Repair Initiated on " & strComputerName
```

Now, use the command line to specify the desired computer to force client repair (in our example, 2kPro):

```
InitiateClientRepair_CommandLine.vbs 2kPro
```

The Client Push Installation Wizard can also be used to initiate a client repair. See Recipe 2-25, "Configuring Client Push Installation," for more information about the Client Push Installation Wizard.

See Also

- The SMS 2003 SDK provides additional information about the SMS_Client class.

16-12. Displaying the SMS Assigned Site

Problem

You want to display the assigned site code for the SMS Advanced Client.

Solution: Using a Graphical Interface

1. From the system Control Panel, launch the Systems Management applet.

2. Select the Advanced tab.

3. View the current SMS site code in the SMS Site frame.

4. Click OK to exit.

Solution: Using VBScript

Example 16-20 demonstrates how to obtain the assigned site for the SMS Advanced Client using WMI.

Example 16-20. *GetAssignedSite.vbs*

```
strComputerName = "2kPro"
Set smsClient = GetObject("winmgmts://" & strComputerName & _
    "/root/ccm:SMS_Client")
Set result = smsClient.ExecMethod_("GetAssignedSite")
WScript.Echo "Client is currently assigned to site " & _
    result.sSiteCode
```

To use the COM object, execute the VBScript code in Example 16-21 to display the SMS assigned site for the local system.

Example 16-21. *GetAssignedSite_COM.vbs*

```
Set smsClient = CreateObject("Microsoft.SMS.Client")
WScript.Echo "Client is currently assigned to site " & _
    smsClient.GetAssignedSite
```

Discussion

Example 16-20 demonstrates how display the SMS assigned site using VBScript on the local client or on a remote client. We execute the GetAssignedSite method from the SMS_Client class.

Example 16-21 demonstrates how to display the SMS assigned site using VBScript on the local client using COM. We use the GetAssignedSite method.

See Also

- Recipe 16-13, "Discovering the SMS Site Assignment," demonstrates how to discover (or rediscover) the SMS assigned site for the Advanced Client.

- Recipe 16-14, "Forcing the SMS Assigned Site," demonstrates how to force the SMS Advanced Client to report to a specific SMS site.

- The SMS 2003 SDK provides additional information about the SMS_Client class.

- Appendix C of the *SMS 2003 Operations Guide* demonstrates several client actions using a VBScript script that can be run on the local system to perform various operations. This script, Advclient.vbs, uses COM objects such as Microsoft.SMS.Client, UIResource.UIResourceMgr, and CPApplet.CPAppletMgr.

16-13. Discovering the SMS Site Assignment

Problem

You want to trigger a discovery or rediscovery of the SMS site assignment on an Advanced Client.

Solution: Using a Graphical Interface

1. From the system Control Panel, launch the Systems Management applet.

2. Select the Advanced tab.

3. Click the Discover button.

4. Click OK to close the informational pop-up dialog box, and click OK to exit.

Solution: Using VBScript

Example 16-22 demonstrates how to force the client to rediscover the assigned site.

Example 16-22. *DiscoverAssignedSite.vbs*

```
'Requires a restart of the SMS Agent Host Service
strComputer = "2kPro"
Set objSMS = GetObject("winmgmts://" & _
    strComputer & "/root/ccm")
Set objSMSClient = objSMS.ExecQuery _
    ("Select * from SMS_Client")

for each objClient in objSMSClient
    objClient.EnableAutoAssignment = 1
    objClient.Put_ 0
next
```

To use the COM object, execute the VBScript code in Example 16-23 to discover the SMS assigned site for the local system.

Example 16-23. *DiscoverAssignedSite_COM.vbs*

```
Set SMSClient = CreateObject("Microsoft.SMS.Client")
WScript.Echo "Client is now assigned to " & _
    SMSClient.ReAssignSite
```

Discussion

Depending on how the SMS Advanced Client was installed, you may not be able to select the Discover button on the Advanced tab. Either script in this recipe can be used locally on the system to programmatically discover the assigned site.

Example 16-22 demonstrates how to initiate a client discovery of the SMS assigned site for a local or remote client using VBScript. After connecting to the SMS_Client class in the root/ccm namespace, we set the EnableAutoAssignment property and save the setting using the Put_ method.

Note When enabling site assignment with Example 16-22, you must restart the SMS Agent Host service.

Example 16-23 demonstrates how to initiate a client discovery using VBScript on the local client using COM. We use the ReAssignSite method.

See Also

- Recipe 16-12, "Displaying the SMS Assigned Site," demonstrates how to display the current SMS assigned site for the Advanced Client.

- Recipe 16-14, "Forcing the SMS Assigned Site," demonstrates how to force the SMS Advanced Client to report to a specific SMS site.

- The SMS 2003 SDK provides additional information about the SMS_Client class.

- Appendix C of the *SMS 2003 Operations Guide* demonstrates several client actions using a VBScript script that can be run on the local system to perform various operations. This script, Advclient.vbs, uses COM objects such as Microsoft.SMS.Client, UIResource.UIResourceMgr, and CPApplet.CPAppletMgr.

16-14. Forcing the SMS Assigned Site

Problem

You want to force the SMS Advanced Client to a specific SMS site.

Solution: Using a Graphical Interface

1. From the system Control Panel, launch the Systems Management applet.

2. Select the Advanced tab.

3. In the SMS Site frame, enter the desired site code, and click Apply.

4. Click OK to close the informational pop-up dialog box, and click OK to exit.

Solution: Using VBScript

Example 16-24 demonstrates how to force the assignment of the Advanced Client to a specific SMS site.

Example 16-24. *SetAssignedSite.vbs*

```
strComputer = "2kPro"
strSMSSite = "XXX"
Set objSMS = GetObject("winmgmts://" & strComputer & _
    "/root/ccm")
Set objSMSClient = objSMS.Get("SMS_Client")
set objParams = objSMSClient.Methods_("SetAssignedSite"). _
    inParameters.SpawnInstance_()
objParams.sSiteCode = strSMSSite
objSMS.ExecMethod _
    "SMS_Client", "SetAssignedSite", objParams
```

To use the COM object, execute the VBScript code in Example 16-25 to set the SMS assigned site for the local system.

Example 16-25. *SetAssignedSite_COM.vbs*

```
Set SMSClient = CreateObject("Microsoft.SMS.Client")
WScript.Echo "Client is currently assigned to site " & _
    SMSClient.GetAssignedSite
SMSClient.SetAssignedSite "XXX", 0
WScript.Echo "Client is now assigned to " & _
    SMSClient.GetAssignedSite
```

Discussion

Depending on how the SMS Advanced Client was installed, you may not be able to modify the SMS assigned site using the graphical user interface. Either script in this recipe can be used locally on the system to set the assigned site.

Example 16-24 demonstrates how to set the SMS assigned site on the local or remote client using VBScript. After connecting to the SMS_Client class in the root/ccm namespace, we create a new instance for the parameters to set the assigned site. Next, we execute the method SetAssignedSite.

Example 16-25 demonstrates how to set the SMS assigned site using VBScript on the local client using COM. First, we call the GetAssignedSite method to display the current site. Next, we call the SetAssignedSite method to set the client to the new site (in our example, XXX). Finally, we call GetAssignedSite again to display the updated site code for the client.

Note Using these scripts, you are able to set the site to an invalid site code. Use caution when setting the Advanced Client's assigned site programmatically.

See Also

- Recipe 16-12, "Displaying the SMS Assigned Site," demonstrates how to display the current SMS assigned site for the Advanced Client.

- Recipe 16-13, "Discovering the SMS Site Assignment," demonstrates how to discover or rediscover the assigned site for the Advanced Client.

- This book's appendix demonstrates how to set SMS client assignment on one system or on an entire collection from within the SMS Administrator console.

- The SMS 2003 SDK provides additional information about the SMS_Client class.

- Appendix C of the *SMS 2003 Operations Guide* demonstrates several client actions using a VBScript script that can be run on the local system to perform various operations. This script, Advclient.vbs, uses COM objects such as Microsoft.SMS.Client, UIResource.UIResourceMgr, and CPApplet.CPAppletMgr.

16-15. Displaying the SMS Client Cache Size

Problem

You want to display the SMS Advanced Client cache size.

Solution: Using a Graphical Interface

There are two graphical interface solutions. The first uses the Systems Management applet in the Control Panel:

1. From the system Control Panel, launch the Systems Management applet.

2. Select the Advanced tab.

3. View the cache size in the Temporary Program Download Folder frame.

4. Click OK to exit.

The second graphical interface solution uses SMS Advanced Client Spy:

1. From the SMS 2003 Toolkit, launch SMS Advanced Client Spy.

2. To connect to a remote system, select Connect from the Tools menu, and enter a remote computer name.

3. Select the Software Distribution Cache Information tab.

4. Expand the Cache Config node to display the cache location, its size, and whether the cache is currently in use.

5. Expand the Cached Items node to display and drill down into each item currently in the SMS client cache.

6. Expand the Downloading Items node to display items that are currently being downloaded.

Solution: Using VBScript

Example 16-26 demonstrates how to obtain the cache size of the Advanced Client using WMI.

Example 16-26. *GetCacheSize.vbs*

```
strComputer = "2kpro"
Set objSMS = _
    GetObject("winmgmts:{impersonationLevel=impersonate}!//" & _
    strComputer & "/root/ccm/SoftMgmtAgent")
Set objCacheConfig = objSMS.ExecQuery _
    ("Select * from CacheConfig")
for each objCache in objCacheConfig
    wscript.echo objCache.Size
next
```

Alternatively, to use the COM object, execute the VBScript code in Example 16-27 to display the size of the cache for the local system.

Example 16-27. *GetCacheSize_COM.vbs*

```
Set oUIResource = CreateObject("UIResource.UIResourceMgr")
Set objCacheInfo = oUIResource.GetCacheInfo
wscript.echo objCacheInfo.TotalSize
```

Discussion

Example 16-26 demonstrates how to display the SMS Advanced Client cache size on the local client or on a remote client using VBScript. After connecting to the CacheConfig class in the root/ccm/SoftMgmtAgent namespace, we display the value for the Size property, which is in megabytes.

Example 16-27 demonstrates how to display the SMS Advanced Client cache size using VBScript on the local client using COM. First, we call the GetCacheInfo method to obtain the client cache information. We then display the value for the TotalSize property, which is in megabytes.

See Also

- Recipe 16-16, "Changing the SMS Client Cache Size," demonstrates how to change the Advanced Client cache size.

- This book's appendix demonstrates how to set SMS client cache size on one system or on an entire collection from within the SMS Administrator console.

- Obtain SMS Policy Spy and SMS Advanced Client Spy from the SMS 2003 Toolkit (http://www.microsoft.com/smserver/downloads/2003/tools/toolkit.mspx).

- The SMS 2003 SDK provides additional information about the CacheConfig class.

- Appendix C of the *SMS 2003 Operations Guide* demonstrates several client actions using a VBScript script that can be run on the local system to perform various operations. This script, Advclient.vbs, uses COM objects such as Microsoft.SMS.Client, UIResource.UIResourceMgr, and CPApplet.CPAppletMgr.

16-16. Changing the SMS Client Cache Size

Problem

You want to change the size of the cache on an Advanced Client.

Solution: Using a Graphical Interface

1. From the system Control Panel, launch the Systems Management applet.

2. Select the Advanced tab.

3. In the Temporary Program Download Folder frame, move the slider, or enter the desired size (in megabytes), and click Apply.

4. Click OK to exit.

Solution: Using VBScript

Example 16-28 demonstrates how to set the cache size on the Advanced Client using WMI.

Example 16-28. *SetCacheSize.vbs*

```
'Requires a restart of the SMS Agent Host Service
strComputer = "2kpro"
Set objSMS = _
    GetObject("winmgmts:{impersonationLevel=impersonate}!//" & _
    strComputer & "/root/ccm/SoftMgmtAgent")
Set objCacheConfig = objSMS.ExecQuery _
    ("Select * from CacheConfig")
for each objCache in objCacheConfig
        objCache.Size = 800
        objCache.Put_ 0
next
```

Alternatively, to use the COM object, execute the VBScript code in Example 16-29 to set the cache size for the local system.

Example 16-29. *SetCacheSize_COM.vbs*

```
Set oUIResource = CreateObject("UIResource.UIResourceMgr")
Set objCacheInfo = oUIResource.GetCacheInfo
objCacheInfo.TotalSize = 800
```

Discussion

Depending on how the SMS Advanced Client was installed, you may not be able to modify this setting using the graphical user interface. Either script in this recipe can be used locally on the system to set the client cache size.

Example 16-28 demonstrates how to set the SMS Advanced Client cache size on the local client or on a remote client using VBScript. After connecting to the CacheConfig class in the root/ccm/SoftMgmtAgent namespace, we set the Size property to 800 (MB). We then use the Put_ method to save the change.

Note When setting the cache size with Example 16-28, you must restart the SMS Agent Host service.

Example 16-29 demonstrates how to set the SMS Advanced Client cache size using VBScript on the local client using COM. First, we call the GetCacheInfo method to obtain the client cache information. We then set the TotalSize to 800 (MB).

See Also

- Recipe 16-15, "Displaying the SMS Client Cache Size," demonstrates how to display the Advanced Client cache size.

- The SMS 2003 SDK provides additional information about the CacheConfig class.

- Appendix C of the *SMS 2003 Operations Guide* demonstrates several client actions using a VBScript script that can be run on the local system to perform various operations. This script, Advclient.vbs, uses COM objects such as Microsoft.SMS.Client, UIResource.UIResourceMgr, and CPApplet.CPAppletMgr.

16-17. Rerunning an SMS Advertisement

Problem

You want to rerun an SMS advertisement on an Advanced Client.

Solution: Using a Graphical Interface

You can only rerun an advertisement using the graphical user interface if the user has been granted the ability to run the advertisement. See the "Discussion" section of this recipe for more information.

1. From the system Control Panel, launch the Run Advertised Programs applet.

2. Highlight the desired advertisement, and click the Run button.

3. Click the Close button to exit the Run Advertised Programs applet.

Solution: Using VBScript

Example 16-30 demonstrates how to rerun an advertisement on a local or remote client using WMI.

Example 16-30. *RerunAdvert.vbs*

```
strComputerName = "2KPro"
strAdvID = "LAB20025"
set objSMS = GetObject("winmgmts://" & _
    strComputerName & _
    "/root/ccm/policy/machine/actualconfig")
Set objScheds = objSMS.ExecQuery _
    ("select * from CCM_Scheduler_ScheduledMessage")
For each objSched in objScheds
    'locate ScheduleMessageID that contains strAdvID
```

```
    If Instr(objSched.ScheduledMessageID, strAdvID) > 0 then
        strMsgID = objSched.ScheduledMessageID
        exit for
    End If
Next
'strMsgID now contains proper Advertisement

Set objSWDs = objSMS.ExecQuery _
("select * from CCM_SoftwareDistribution where " & _
    "ADV_AdvertisementID = '" & strAdvID & "'" )
for each objSWD in objSWDs
    strOrigBehavior = objSWD.ADV_RepeatRunBehavior
    'strOrigBehavior now contains original Repeat Behavior
    'Now temporarily set RepeatRunBehavior to RerunAlways
    objSWD.ADV_RepeatRunBehavior = "RerunAlways"
    objSWD.Put_ 0
Next

set objCCM = GetObject("winmgmts://" & strComputerName & _
    "/root/ccm")
Set objSMSClient = objCCM.Get("SMS_Client")
objSMSClient.TriggerSchedule strMsgID

'sleep for 5 seconds, for advert to start
wscript.sleep 5000

Set objScheds = objSMS.ExecQuery _
("select * from CCM_SoftwareDistribution where " & _
    "ADV_AdvertisementID = '" & strAdvID & "'" )
for each objSched in objScheds
    'Set RepeatRunBehavior back to original config
    objSched.ADV_RepeatRunBehavior = strOrigBehavior
    objSched.Put_ 0
Next
```

It's also possible to rerun an advertisement via the COM object, provided the advertisement is nonmandatory or is configured to allow the advertisement to be executed independently of mandatory assignments. To do that, you must have been granted the ability to run the advertisement. Example 16-31 works through the COM object to rerun the advertisement named SMS 2003 SDK V3.

Example 16-31. *RerunAdvert_COM.vbs*

```
Set uiResource = CreateObject("UIResource.UIResourceMgr")
Set programList = uiResource.GetAvailableApplications
For each p in programList
    wscript.echo p.Name
    If p.Name = "SMS 2003 SDK V3" then
        uiResource.ExecuteProgram p.ID, p.PackageID, True
        Exit For
    End if
Next
```

Discussion

Example 16-30 demonstrates how to rerun an SMS advertisement on the local client or on a remote client using VBScript (provided you have sufficient permissions to trigger the schedule in WMI). After connecting to the root/ccm/policy/machine/actualconfig namespace, we enumerate all instances of the CCM_Scheduler_ScheduledMessage class to find a ScheduledMessageID that contains the advertisement ID strAdvID. Once it is found, we keep that ScheduledMessageID in strMsgID to be used later in the script.

Next, we query the CCM_SoftwareDistribution class to obtain the instance of the AdvertisementID. We then save the repeat run behavior (ADV_RepeatRunBehavior) to strOrigBehavior, temporarily set the repeat run behavior to RerunAlways, and then save the change.

Next, we trigger the schedule (just as we did for hardware inventory in Example 16-3) and instruct the VBScript script to sleep for five seconds to allow the program execution to begin.

Finally, we reset the repeat run behavior (ADV_RepeatRunBehavior) to strOrigBehavior and save the change.

Note Example 16-30 works for all programs (both mandatory and nonmandatory) that do not have a program dependency in SMS (which occurs when the advanced properties of a program have the Run Another Program First option enabled).

Example 16-31 demonstrates how to rerun a voluntary advertisement using COM and VBScript on the local client. First, we connect to the UIResource.UIResourceMgr COM object. Next, we enumerate all voluntary advertisements using the GetAvailableApplications method. Once we find the desired program name (in our example, SMS 2003 SDK V3), we initiate the ExecuteProgram method.

Note Using the COM example in Example 16-31, programs with program dependencies will automatically run (if configured) before the desired program. The disadvantages to the COM example are that it can only be run locally and that it can only run nonmandatory advertisements and advertisements configured to "Allow users to run the program independently of assignments".

See Also

- In this book's appendix, the section titled "Right-Click Tools" demonstrates how to rerun an advertisement on one system or on an entire collection from within the SMS Administrator console.

- This book's appendix also contains information about additional tools for rerunning advertisements.

- The SMS 2003 SDK provides additional information about the CCM_Scheduler_ScheduledMessage, CCM_SoftwareDistribution, and SMS_Client classes.

- Appendix C of the *SMS 2003 Operations Guide* demonstrates several client actions using a VBScript script that can be run on the local system to perform various operations. This script, Advclient.vbs, uses COM objects such as Microsoft.SMS.Client, UIResource.UIResourceMgr, and CPApplet.CPAppletMgr.

16-18. Displaying the Current SMS Site Code, Management Point, and Proxy Management Point

Problem

You want to identify the current MP and PMP (if the client is connected to a PMP).

Solution: Using VBScript

Example 16-32 demonstrates how to query the local or remote Advanced Client for the current MP (or PMP, if it exists).

Example 16-32. *GetCurrentMP_PMP.vbs*

```
strComputerName = "2kPro"
Set objSMS = GetObject("winmgmts://" & strComputerName & _
    "/root/ccm")
Set objAuthority = objSMS.ExecQuery _
    ("Select * from SMS_Authority")

For Each authority In objAuthority
    wscript.echo "SMS Site: " & _
        Replace(authority.Name, "SMS:", "")
    wscript.echo "MP: " & authority.CurrentManagementPoint
Next

Set colProxyMPs = objSMS.ExecQuery _
    ("Select * from SMS_MPProxyInformation")
For Each objProxyMP in colProxyMPs
    wscript.echo "Proxy MP: " & objProxyMP.Name
Next
```

Discussion

Example 16-32 demonstrates how to display the current SMS site code, MP, and PMP (if it exists) for a local or remote system. After connecting to the root/ccm namespace, we query the SMS_Authority class to display the SMS site code (Name) and MP (CurrentManagementPoint). Next, we query the SMS_MPProxyInformation class to display the PMP (Name), if it exists.

See Also

- Recipe 16-12, "Displaying the SMS Assigned Site," demonstrates how to display the SMS assigned site code.

- Recipe 16-3, "Discovering the SMS Site Assignment," demonstrates how to perform a discovery to obtain the proper SMS site assignment.

- Recipe 16-14, "Forcing the SMS Assigned Site," demonstrates how to force SMS site assignment.

- The SMS 2003 SDK provides additional information about the SMS_Authority and SMS_MPProxyInformation classes.

16-19. Determining the Last Hardware and Software Inventories

Problem

You want to determine the last time hardware and software inventories were run on the client.

Solution: Using a Graphical User Interface

Two graphical approaches are possible. The first uses SMS Policy Spy:

1. From the SMS 2003 Toolkit, launch SMS Policy Spy.

2. To connect to a remote system, from the Tools menu of Policy Spy, select Open Remote, and enter a remote computer name.

3. Select the Actual tab.

4. Expand Machine and Inventory Action.

5. Drill down into the InventoryAction class, and select an InventoryActionID. Then view the instance details for the selected InventoryActionID. The Description property of the InventoryAction will display the type of inventory action (e.g., hardware, software, etc.).

The second graphical approach uses SMS Advanced Client Spy:

1. From the SMS 2003 Toolkit, launch SMS Advanced Client Spy.

2. To connect to a remote system, select Connect from the Tools menu, and enter a remote computer name.

3. From the Tools menu, select Inventory.

4. Expand the desired inventory type, and observe the Date Last Cycle Started property.

Solution: Using VBScript

Example 16-33 demonstrates how to display the last start time for the enabled inventory actions (hardware, software, file collection, and DDR).

Example 16-33. *DisplayLastHWSWInvDates.vbs*

```
strComputerName = "2kPro"

'first, get the time zone bias
Set objWMIService = GetObject("winmgmts://" & strComputerName & _
    "/root/cimv2")
Set colTimeZone = objWMIService.ExecQuery _
    ("Select * from Win32_TimeZone")
For Each objTimeZone in colTimeZone
    intBias = cint(objTimeZone.Bias )
Next

'now query data from SMS
Set objSMS = GetObject("winmgmts://" & strComputerName & _
    "/root/ccm/invagt")
Set colInvInfo = objSMS.ExecQuery _
    ("Select * from InventoryActionStatus")
```

```
for each objInvInfo in colInvInfo
    select case objInvInfo.InventoryActionID
        case "{00000000-0000-0000-0000-000000000001}"
            strInv = "Hardware Inventory"
        case "{00000000-0000-0000-0000-000000000002}"
            strInv = "Software Inventory"
        case "{00000000-0000-0000-0000-000000000010}"
            strInv = "File Collection"
        case "{00000000-0000-0000-0000-000000000003}"
            strInv = "Discovery Data Record"
    end select
    wscript.echo strInv & vbTAB & _
        convDate(objInvInfo.LastCycleStartedDate, intBias) & _
        vbTAB & convDate(objInvInfo.LastReportDate, intBias)
next

Function convDate(dtmInstallDate, intBias)
    convDate = CDate(Mid(dtmInstallDate, 5, 2) & "/" & _
    Mid(dtmInstallDate, 7, 2) & "/" & Left(dtmInstallDate, 4) _
    & " " & Mid (dtmInstallDate, 9, 2) & ":" & _
    Mid(dtmInstallDate, 11, 2) & ":" & Mid(dtmInstallDate, 13, 2))
    convDate = DateAdd("N",intBias,convDate)
End Function
```

Discussion

Example 16-33 demonstrates how to display information for the last hardware, software, file collection, and DDR inventory that was reported from the SMS client. Since the dates obtained from the InventoryActionStatus class are in Greenwich Mean Time (GMT), we obtain the TimeZone Bias from the system to display the inventory timestamp in local system time.

After obtaining the TimeZone Bias, we connect to the root/ccm/invagt class and enumerate all members of the class. We use a Select Case statement to modify the displayed data based on InventoryActionIDs. We also use the utility function convDate to convert the WMI date-time string to a standard date-time stamp, including the TimeZone Bias offset from GMT.

In this example, we display the LastCycledStartedDate and the LastReportDate. You may notice little difference between these two properties, because, unfortunately, both properties report exactly the same date-time stamp in most situations. They report the time that the action was initiated, not the actual time it was reported (as you might otherwise expect for LastReportDate). The only time you see a discrepancy between the two is when the inventory is run but an action does not report data. For example, file collection inventory is enabled as long as software inventory is enabled, but file collection inventory will only report if a rule has been created for file collection inventory.

See Also

- Recipe 16-3, "Initiating the Hardware Inventory Cycle," demonstrates how to initiate a hardware inventory cycle.

- Recipe 16-4, "Initiating the Software Inventory Cycle," demonstrates how to initiate a software inventory cycle.

- Obtain SMS Policy Spy and SMS Advanced Client Spy from the SMS 2003 Toolkit (http://www.microsoft.com/smserver/downloads/2003/tools/toolkit.mspx).

- The SMS 2003 SDK provides additional information about the SMS_Authority and SMS_MPProxyInformation classes.

16-20. Displaying All Advertisements for the Advanced Client

Problem

You want to display all advertisements that are advertised to an Advanced Client.

Solution: Using a Graphical User Interface

From the graphical interface, you can use either SMS Policy Spy or SMS Advanced Client Spy. The following procedure uses SMS Policy Spy:

1. From the SMS 2003 Toolkit, launch SMS Policy Spy.
2. To connect to a remote system from the Tools menu of Policy Spy, select Open Remote, and enter a remote computer name.
3. Select the Actual tab; expand Machine and CCM_SoftwareDistribution.
4. Review each instance of CCM_SoftwareDistribution. By clicking on a specific instance, you can view additional advertisement, package, and program properties (e.g., CommandLine, InstallFromLocalDPOptions, etc.).

The following procedure uses SMS Advanced Client Spy:

1. From the SMS 2003 Toolkit, launch SMS Advanced Client Spy.
2. To connect to a remote system, select Connect from the Tools menu, and enter a remote computer name.
3. Select the Software Distribution Pending Execution tab.
4. Expand Machine (or user SID if desired) to display mandatory, optional, and past mandatory advertisements.

Solution: Using VBScript

Example 16-34 demonstrates how to display all advertisements assigned to the local or remote Advanced Client.

Example 16-34. *DisplayAdverts.vbs*

```
strComputer = "2kPro"
Set objSMS = GetObject("winmgmts://" & strComputer & _
    "/root/ccm/Policy/Machine/ActualConfig")
Set colSW = objSMS.ExecQuery _
    ("Select * from CCM_SoftwareDistribution")
wscript.echo colSW.count & " Advertisements"
for each oSW in colSW
    wscript.echo oSW.PRG_HistoryLocation & vbTAB & _
        oSW.ADV_AdvertisementID & vbTAB & oSW.PKG_PackageID & _
        vbTAB & oSW.PRG_ProgramID & vbTAB & _
        oSW.ADV_ActiveTime & vbTAB & oSW.ADV_ExpirationTime & _
        vbTAB & oSW.ADV_MandatoryAssignments & vbTAB & _
        oSW.PKG_Name & vbTAB & oSW.PRG_ProgramName & vbTAB & _
        oSW.PRG_PRF_AfterRunning & vbTAB & _
        oSW.PRG_CustomLogoffReturnCodes & vbTAB & _
        oSW.PRG_MaxDuration & vbTAB & _
        oSW.PRG_PRF_UserLogonRequirement
next
```

You can accomplish a similar task as in Example 16-34 using the COM object. To use the COM object, execute the VBScript code in Example 16-35 to display voluntary advertisements. This code will only show advertisements with no mandatory assignments and advertisements that are configured to "Allow users to run the program independently of assignments".

Example 16-35. *DisplayAdverts_COM.vbs*

```
Set UI = CreateObject("UIResource.UIResourceMgr")
Set programList = UI.GetAvailableApplications
For each program in programList
    wscript.echo program.PackageID & vbTAB & program.ID & _
        vbTAB & program.Name & vbTAB & program.PackageName & _
        vbTAB & program.Version
Next
```

Discussion

Example 16-34 demonstrates how to display all advertisements for the desired system. After connecting to the root/ccm/Policy/Machine/ActualConfig namespace, we perform a WQL query to the CCM_SoftwareDistribution class. Next, we display the count of items returned in the WQL query. Finally, we perform a for-each loop to display various advertisement properties. The CCM_SoftwareDistribution class stores information specific to a software distribution. This information includes data about the advertisement, package, and program being advertised. The following properties are among those that we use on a regular basis:

- ADV_AdvertisementID: The ID of the advertisement.
- PKG_PackageID: The ID of the package of which this program is a child.
- PRG_ProgramID: The ID of the program associated with this advertisement.
- ADV_ADF_Published: Determines whether the program should be presented to the user in one of the execution user interfaces. If this value is True, users can see this program. If the program has no assignments, this value is True. If the program has assignments and the administrator has selected the option to run the program independently of assignments, this value is True. Otherwise, this value is False.
- ADV_ActiveTime: The date and time the advertisement becomes available to targets. Another property, ADV_ActiveTimeIsGMT, tells you if the ADV_ActiveTime is in local time or GMT.
- ADV_ExpirationTime: The date and time at which the advertisement expires. This property is only required if there is an expiration time. Another property, ADV_ExpirationTimeIsGMT, tells you if the ADV_ExpirationTime is in local time or GMT.
- ADV_RepeatRunBehavior: Determines how the client should respond when a program is run more than once on a computer. Possible values are RerunAlways, RerunIfFail, RerunIfSuccess, and RerunNever.
- PRG_PRF_RunNotification: Determines whether the program notification dialog box is displayed. If the program notification dialog box is displayed, the value is True. If the program notification dialog box is suppressed (not displayed), the value is False, which is the equivalent of enabling the "Suppress program notifications" check box in the program's advanced properties.
- ADV_RunNotificationCountdownDuration: Specifies the duration, in seconds, of the run notification countdown. If the value is Null, the site setting is used.
- PKG_Name: The name of the package.

- PRG_ProgramName: The name of the program associated with this advertisement.

- PRG_PRF_Disabled: The flag to determine if the program is disabled. The program is disabled when this value is True.

- PRG_CommandLine: The command line to be executed.

- PRG_WorkingDirectory: The working directory that the program uses when it runs.

- PRG_PRF_AfterRunning: Specifies whether the computer restarts or the user is logged off after the program completes. Possible values are NoAction, SMSReboots, ProgramReboots, SMSLogsOffUser, and ProgramLogsOffUser.

- PRG_PRF_UserLogonRequirement: Determines whether a user needs to be logged on when this program runs. Possible values are NoUserLoggedOn, UserLoggedOn, and None.

- PRG_PRF_RunWithAdminRights: Determines whether the program should run with user rights or administrative rights. When this value is True, the program should run in the administrator's context. When this value is False, the program should run in the user's context.

- PRG_DependentProgramProgramID: The program ID of the program on which this program is dependent.

- PRG_DependentProgramPackageID: The package ID of the program on which this program is dependent.

As you can see, CCM_SoftwareDistribution contains a plethora of invaluable information. Notice that each property in this class begins with PRG_, PKG_, or ADV_. This gives you an indication of where the property resides on the SMS site (SMS_Program, SMS_Package, or SMS_Advertisement). Review the SMS 2003 SDK for full details on the CCM_SoftwareDistribution class, where you will find additional valuable properties such as ADV_RCF_InstallFromLocalDPOptions and ADV_RCF_InstallFromRemoteDPOptions, which help you see how the client will install the software (from a local/remote DP or local client cache).

Example 16-35 demonstrates how to display voluntary advertisements. After calling the GetAvailableApplications method, we perform a for-each loop to display properties of the advertisement. The program object in our example has several properties that are similar to those found in Example 16-34. You may need the following properties on a regular basis:

- AdditionalRequirements: Any additional requirements specified by the administrator

- Comments: Program comments entered by the administrator

- DependentPackageID: The package ID of the program on which this program is dependent

- DependentProgramID: The program ID of the program on which this program is dependent

- PackageID: The ID of the package of which this program is a child

- Name: The ID of the program associated with this advertisement

- LastRunTime: The last time the application was run

- LastExitCode: The exit code from the last time the application was run

---

▪**Note** The disadvantages to the COM example are that it can be run only locally, and it can run only nonmandatory advertisements and advertisements configured to "Allow users to run the program independently of assignments".

See Also

- Recipe 3-17, "Viewing Advertisements Assigned to a Collection," demonstrates how to display all advertisements assigned to a collection.

- Recipe 16-17, "Rerunning an SMS Advertisement," demonstrates how to rerun an SMS advertisement.

- Appendix C of the *SMS 2003 Operations Guide* provides additional scripts for listing voluntary advertisements using the COM object.

- Obtain SMS Policy Spy and SMS Advanced Client Spy from the SMS 2003 Toolkit (`http://www.microsoft.com/smserver/downloads/2003/tools/toolkit.mspx`).

- The SMS 2003 SDK provides additional information about the `CCM_SoftwareDistribution` class.

16-21. Determining If an Advertisement Is Currently Running

Problem

You want to determine if an advertisement is currently running on the SMS Advanced Client.

Solution: Using VBScript

Example 16-36 demonstrates how to display running advertisements.

Example 16-36. *DisplayRunningAdverts.vbs*

```
strComputer = "2kPro"
Set objSMS = GetObject("winmgmts://" & strComputer & _
    "/root/ccm/SoftMgmtAgent")
Set colER = objSMS.ExecQuery _
    ("Select * from CCM_ExecutionRequest")
for each oER in colER
    wscript.echo oER.ProgramID & vbTAB & oER.State & vbTAB & _
        oER.ProcessID & vbTAB & oER.AdvertID & vbTAB & _
        oER.IsAdminContext
next
```

Discussion

Example 16-36 demonstrates how to display SMS advertisements that are currently running or that are preparing to run. After connecting to the `root/ccm/SoftMgmtAgent` namespace, we perform a WQL query to obtain all instances in the `CCM_ExecutionRequest` class. We then enumerate all instances, displaying the program name (`ProgramID`), state (e.g., `Running`, `WaitingEnvironment`, etc.), process ID (`ProcessID`), advertisement ID (`AdvertID`); and showing whether the advertisement is running in an Administrative Context (`IsAdminContext`).

See Also

- Recipe 16-17, "Rerunning an SMS Advertisement," demonstrates how to rerun an advertisement.

- At the time of this writing, `CCM_ExecutionRequest` is not documented in the SMS 2003 SDK. A request to include it has been submitted to and acknowledged by Microsoft.

16-22. Displaying Advertisement History on a Client

Problem

You want to display SMS advertisement history on a client.

Solution: Using a Graphical User Interface

1. From the SMS 2003 Toolkit, launch SMS Advanced Client Spy.

2. To connect to a remote system, select Connect from the Tools menu, and enter a remote computer name.

3. Select the Software Distribution History tab.

4. Expand the System node to display each advertisement history, listed by PackageID. Expand a PackageID to display program names that have been executed, as well as their execution states and last run times.

Solution: Using VBScript

Example 16-37 demonstrates how to display advertisement history for a local or remote Advanced Client.

Example 16-37. *DisplayAdvertHistory.vbs*

```
Const HKEY_LOCAL_MACHINE = &H80000002
' Only show adverts that have occurred within the last 90 days
Const intMaxDays = 90
strComputer = "2kPro"

'this is the base key path
strKeyPath = "SOFTWARE\Microsoft\SMS\Mobile Client\" & _
    "Software Distribution\Execution History\System"
'connect to the registry provider
Set oReg=GetObject _
    ("winmgmts:{impersonationLevel=impersonate}!\\" & _
    strComputer & "\root\default:StdRegProv")

oReg.EnumKey HKEY_LOCAL_MACHINE, strKeyPath, arrSubKeys

'this first for-each loop is used to enumerate each package
'   key
For Each PackageID In arrSubKeys
    oReg.EnumKey HKEY_LOCAL_MACHINE, strKeyPath & "\" & _
    PackageID, arrSubKeys2
    'the second for-each loop is used to enumerate each
    '  GUID key within a package key
    For Each GUID in arrSubKeys2
        SearchStrKeyPath = strKeyPath & "\" & PackageID & _
            "\" & GUID
        oReg.GetStringValue HKEY_LOCAL_MACHINE, _
            SearchStrKeyPath, "_ProgramID", strProgramID
        oReg.GetStringValue HKEY_LOCAL_MACHINE, _
            SearchStrKeyPath, "_RunStartTime", strRunStartTime
        oReg.GetStringValue HKEY_LOCAL_MACHINE, _
            SearchStrKeyPath, "_State", strState
        oReg.GetStringValue HKEY_LOCAL_MACHINE, _
            SearchStrKeyPath, "SuccessOrFailureCode", _
```

```
            strSuccessOrFailure
    oReg.GetStringValue HKEY_LOCAL_MACHINE, _
        SearchStrKeyPath, "SuccessOrFailureReason", _
            strSuccessOrFailureReason

    'Only display data for advert starts < 90 days
    If not DateDiff _
        ("d",strRunStartTime, now())    > intMaxDays Then
    wscript.echo strProgramID & vbTAB & _
        strRunStartTime & vbTAB & strState & vbTAB & _
        strSuccessOrFailure & vbTAB & _
        strSuccessOrFailureReason
    End If
  Next
Next
```

Solution: Using an HTML Application

HTML applications (sometimes called HTAs) can also be very handy in your daily SMS tasks. An HTML application is basically an HTML page (with a few custom formatting and execution tags) that is run from your local system or a shared network location. By using an HTML application, you may use VBScript (or JavaScript) to do the work and still be able to display and manipulate data without using the command line. An example HTML application is provided with the sample code available for download from this book. FIGURE 16-1 shows the HTML sample application titled AdvertHistory.hta.

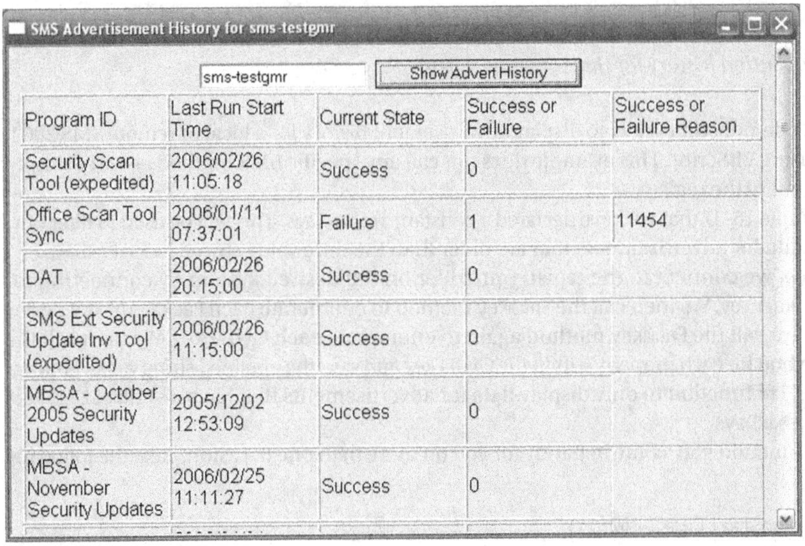

Figure 16-1. *An advertisement history HTML application*

As you can see in Figure 16-1, the HTML application displays the same information as Example 16-37, except that it is in a more human-readable format. You can also query remote systems (provided you have remote registry permissions to the registry key) by entering the computer name into the text box and then clicking the Show Advert History button.

Discussion

Advertisement history is stored in the registry of the SMS 2003 Advanced Client. On a healthy Advanced Client, launch regedit.exe to edit the registry. Navigate to the following key:

HKEY_LOCAL_MACHINE\SOFTWARE\Microsoft\SMS\Mobile Client\➥

Software Distribution\Execution History\System

From this key, you will see a subkey that is named the PackageID for each package that has been deployed to this client. Expand a PackageID key to display one or more global unique identifier (GUID) keys, which contain advertisement history. Each unique program name (_ProgramID) for the PackageID will be listed under a different GUID. From this location, you can see the last time the program started (_RunStartTime), whether it started successfully or failed (_State), the exit code, and any comments (SuccessOrFailureCode and SuccessOrFailureReason). See Figure 16-2 as an example of the execution history provided by Registry Editor.

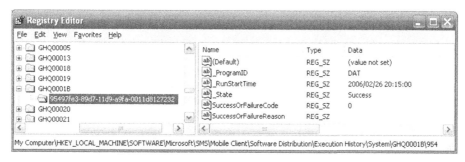

Figure 16-2. *SMS execution history for the Advanced Client*

Example 16-37 demonstrates how to display advertisement history for a local or remote SMS 2003 Advanced Client using VBScript. This example does not call any specific SMS methods—we're simply using VBScript to query the registry.

Notice in Example 16-37 that we have declared a constant intMaxDays. This will be used to filter out (not display) any data for advertisements that are older than the time value stored in intMaxDays.

As you can see, we connect to the registry provider on the desired system by connecting to \root\default:StdRegProv. We then call the EnumKey method to enumerate each PackageID key under strKeyPath. Next, we call the EnumKey method again to enumerate each GUID key. We then call the GetStringValue method for each property within the GUID key and save the obtained string value. Finally, we perform a DateDiff function to only display data for advertisements that have a strRunStartTime that is less than intMaxDays.

The DateDiff function may come in handy for you on more than one occasion. Take the following code sample:

```
DateDiff ("d",strRunStartTime, now())
```

The "d" tells the DateDiff function to return the difference in days between the current date-time on the system (now()) and strRunStartTime, which is also a properly formatted date.

See Also

- Obtain SMS Policy Spy and SMS Advanced Client Spy from the SMS 2003 Toolkit (http://www. microsoft.com/smserver/downloads/2003/tools/toolkit.mspx).

- The WMI SDK provides information about the WMI System Registry Provider (http://msdn. microsoft.com/library/default.asp?url=/library/en-us/wmisdk/wmi/stdregprov.asp).

- The MSDN library provides an overview of HTAs (http://msdn.microsoft.com/library/ default.asp?url=/workshop/author/hta/overview/htaoverview.asp).

- Search the Microsoft Downloads site for the HTA Helpomatic (hta_helpomatic.exe), an HTA that you can use to help you build HTAs.

■■■

CHAPTER 17

Building a Virtual SMS Lab

In this chapter, we provide instructions for building an SMS test environment using evaluation software that you can download for free. We will use Microsoft Virtual PC to create the virtual lab. If you haven't used Virtual PC, this chapter will give you a look into the wonderful world of virtualized computing. If you don't have a couple hours to set up an SMS lab using Virtual PC, check out the online Virtual Labs that are available through Microsoft TechNet (http://www.microsoft.com/technet/traincert/virtuallab/sms.mspx).

Downloading Trial Software

First, you need to download trial versions of the software. It would be very difficult to download all of this software over a dial-up connection, so make sure you have a high-speed one. The downloaded files will total over 1GB of data. You'll want to download all of the following:

- *Virtual PC*: Download the 45-day trial version of Microsoft's Virtual PC 2004 at http://www.microsoft.com/windows/virtualpc/default.mspx.

- *Windows Server 2003 Release 2 (R2)*: Download a copy of the Windows Server 2003 R2 trial software at http://www.microsoft.com/windowsserver2003/evaluation/trial/default.mspx. You need to complete the registration. The registration will ask for billing information, but you will not be charged to download the 180-day trial version.

- *SQL Server 2005*: Download a trial copy of SQL Server 2005 at http://www.microsoft.com/windowsserver2003/evaluation/trial/default.mspx. Choose the DVD-image format when you download it. You will be able to launch the ISO file directly in Virtual PC.

- *SMS 2003 with Service Pack 2 (SP2)*: Download a trial copy of SMS 2003 SP2 at http://www.microsoft.com/smserver/evaluation/default.mspx.

Installing Virtual PC

Installing Virtual PC is a snap. Open the downloaded files, and double-click setup.exe. Select the defaults for any prompts while installing Virtual PC.

Creating a Virtual Machine

Creating the virtual machine is pretty easy also, but you have to perform a few important steps to succeed. We include screenshots in the following instructions, so you can follow along.

1. Launch Virtual PC, and click OK on the Welcome screen displayed in Figure 17-1.

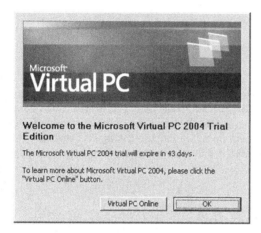

Figure 17-1. *The Virtual PC Welcome screen*

2. Click Next to start the New Virtual Machine Wizard shown in Figure 17-2.

Figure 17-2. *The New Virtual Machine Wizard*

3. Click Next to create a new virtual machine by selecting the "Create a virtual machine" radio button, as shown in Figure 17-3.

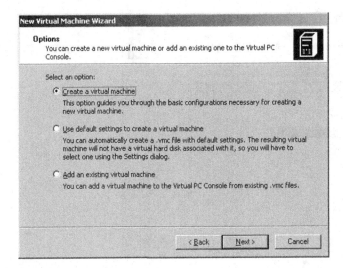

Figure 17-3. *Creating a new virtual machine*

4. Enter a name for your new virtual machine in the space provided, as shown in Figure 17-4.

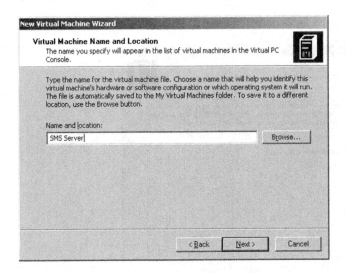

Figure 17-4. *Naming a virtual machine*

5. Select the operating system that will be installed, as shown in Figure 17-5; use Windows Server 2003 for this exercise. Click Next.

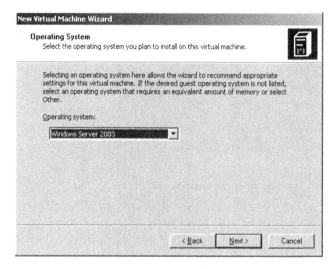

Figure 17-5. *Selecting the operating system*

6. In the screen shown in Figure 17-6, you can adjust the memory that you want to allocate to this machine. The default should be fine for now, and you can easily change it later if it isn't enough.

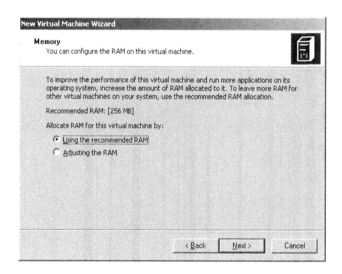

Figure 17-6. *Allocating memory usage*

7. As shown in Figure 17-7, leave the default "A new virtual hard disk" option selected, and click Next.

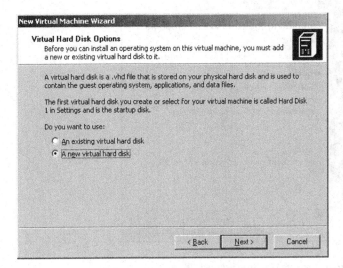

Figure 17-7. *Configuring the virtual hard disk*

8. In the screen shown in Figure 17-8, leave the default location for the virtual hard disk, or specify one that you like better. Click Next.

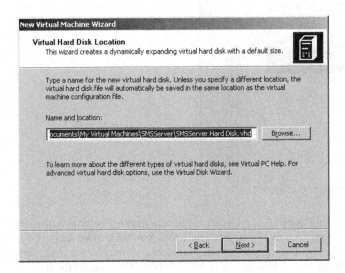

Figure 17-8. *Setting the virtual hard disk location*

9. Click Finish to close the Virtual Machine Wizard, as shown in Figure 17-9.

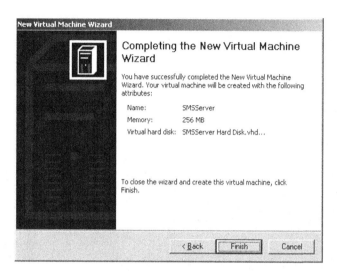

Figure 17-9. *Closing the Virtual Machine Wizard*

10. In your Virtual PC console, you can see that your new virtual machine is listed. Highlight the new machine, and click Settings, as shown in Figure 17-10.

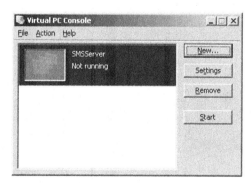

Figure 17-10. *The Virtual PC console*

11. In the window shown in Figure 17-11, you can modify the network settings of the virtual machine. For the best protection of your other networks, you want to set Adapter 1 to "Local only." This setting allows you to copy files from your local system onto the virtual machine, but the virtual machine doesn't have any network connectivity outside of its virtual world. The "Local only" setting also allows you to connect to other virtual systems on the local host, depending on the network properties you configure. If you need to access the Internet, choose the "Shared networking (NAT)" option. You can also adjust any of the other virtual machine settings here.

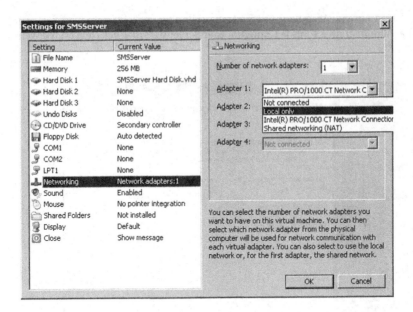

Figure 17-11. *Virtual machine settings*

Installing Windows Server 2003 R2

Now that your virtual machine is built, you need to load an operating system on it. You will be surprised how easy this is. Here are the steps to follow:

1. From your Virtual PC console, double-click the virtual machine you just created. It opens in a new window and begins a boot cycle.

2. Quickly select Action ➤ Pause to suspend the boot cycle. Click the CD menu item at the top of the virtual machine, and choose Capture ISO Image.

3. Browse to the first Windows 2003 Server R2 download (e.g., x11-03905.iso), and click Open.

4. Select Action ➤ Resume to continue the boot cycle.

5. The virtual machine will boot into the Windows Server 2003 setup from the ISO file you just captured.

6. Complete the Windows Server setup to your liking. Don't join it to a domain, as we will create our own domain in a little bit. You can add the additional R2 features by selecting Release CD from the CD menu and then selecting Capture ISO Image and loading the second Windows Server 2003 R2 download (the one with the very long name).

Configuring the Server for AD, DNS, and DHCP

Before you configure your virtual server, make sure you have configured the virtual machine to use only local networking. The following configuration steps install Dynamic Host Configuration Protocol (DHCP) on the server, which will cause havoc on your network if you have not isolated this virtual machine:

1. Launch the Configure Your Server Wizard (shown in Figure 17-12) from Start ➤ Control Panel ➤ Administrative Tools ➤ Configure Your Server Wizard. Click Next on the Welcome screen.

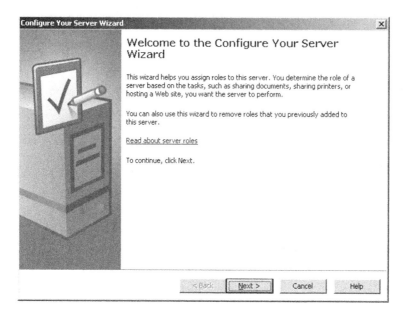

Figure 17-12. *The Configure Your Server Wizard Welcome screen*

2. Review the preliminary steps shown in Figure 17-13, and click Next.

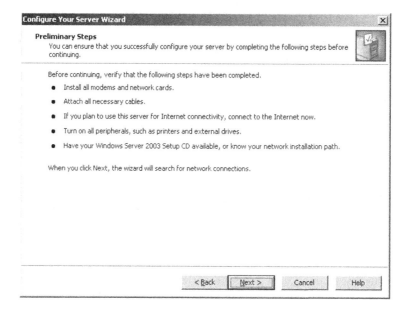

Figure 17-13. *Preliminary steps*

3. In the screen shown in Figure 17-14, choose the "Typical configuration for a first server" radio button, and click Next.

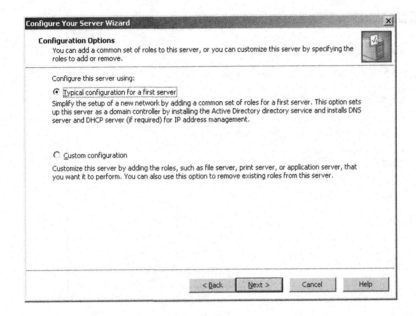

Figure 17-14. *Choosing a configuration*

4. In the screen shown in Figure 17-15, type in the full Domain Name Service (DNS) name for the domain to be created. We used SMSVLab.local in the example.

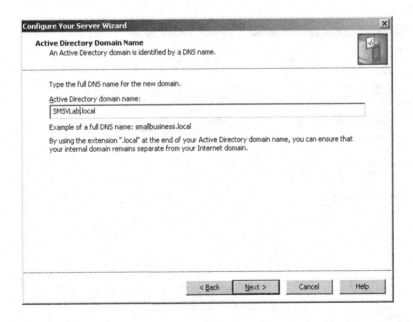

Figure 17-15. *Setting the domain DNS name*

5. As shown in Figure 17-16, the wizard will suggest a Network Basic Input/Output System (Net-BIOS) name for the domain. If you don't like the suggested name, change it before clicking Next.

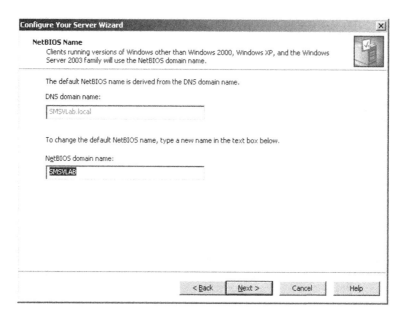

Figure 17-16. *Setting the NetBIOS name*

6. Since you have isolated the virtual machine from the network, there isn't any reason to forward DNS queries. You can change this setting later if you wish, but for now choose not to forward DNS queries and click Next as shown in Figure 17-17.

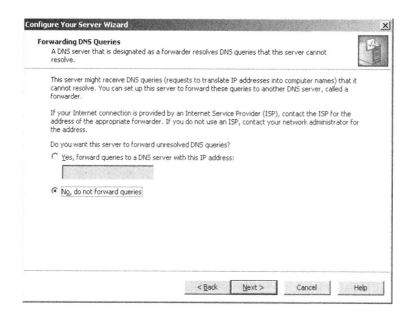

Figure 17-17. *Setting DNS forwarding options*

7. Review the summary shown in Figure 17-18, and click Next.

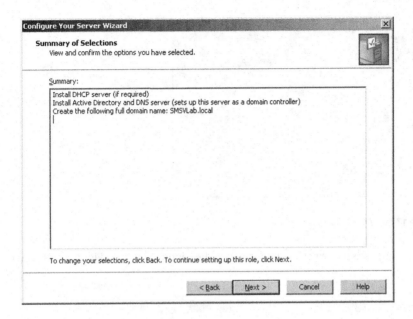

Figure 17-18. *The configuration summary*

8. The installation of the selected components will begin, as shown in Figure 17-19.

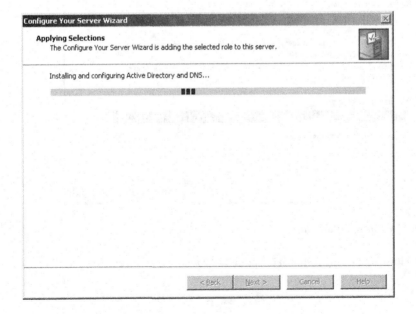

Figure 17-19. *Component installations*

9. The Active Directory Promotion (DCPROMO) process will be initiated, as shown in Figure 17-20.

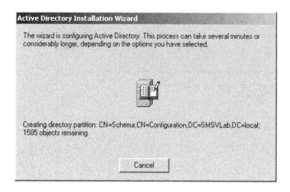

Figure 17-20. *DCPROMO process*

10. Review the status of the actions performed in the window shown in Figure 17-21, and click Next.

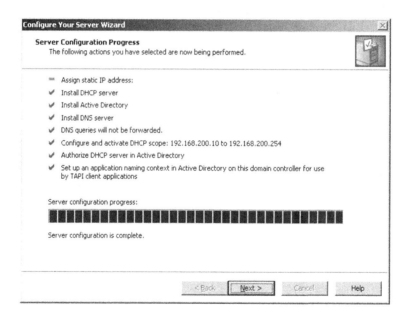

Figure 17-21. *Installation status*

11. Click Finish in the screen shown in Figure 17-22 to close the wizard.

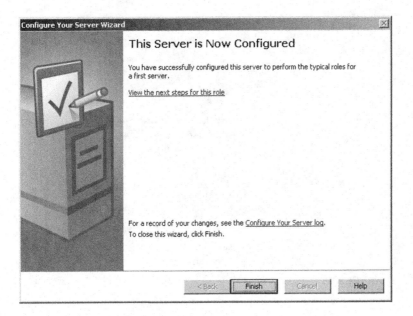

Figure 17-22. *Successful configuration*

Caution DHCP is now enabled on your virtual machine. This isn't a problem if you keep the virtual server isolated from the network, as it is currently configured. But to be on the safe side, disable the DHCP Server service.

Installing SQL Server 2005

SMS 2003 with SP2 includes support for SQL Server 2005. If you plan to use SQL Server 2005 with your SMS installation, you must install SQL Server before installing SMS. The following steps will help you install and configure SQL Server 2005 for your virtual test environment:

1. Capture the SQLEVAL.iso CD image on your virtual machine. It should automatically start and present you with the screen shown in Figure 17-23. Click the "Server components, tools, Books Online, and samples" option.

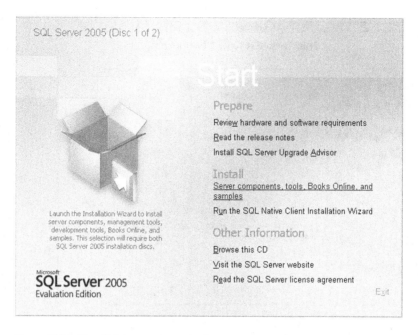

Figure 17-23. *The SQL Server 2005 splash screen*

2. Accept the license agreement shown in Figure 17-24, and click Next.

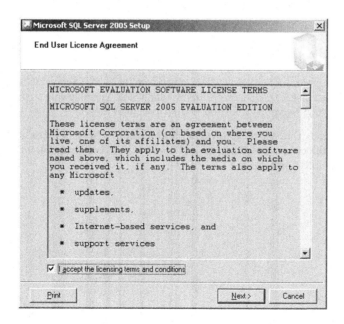

Figure 17-24. *The end user license agreement*

3. A check will be made for prerequisites. If any are missing, click Install to have them loaded, as shown in Figure 17-25.

Figure 17-25. *Installing prerequisites*

4. Once the prerequisites have been installed, click Next as shown in Figure 17-26 to continue with the component installation.

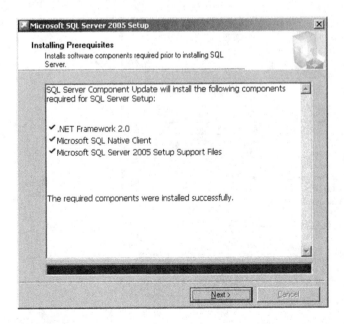

Figure 17-26. *Prerequisites installed*

5. Click Next on the Welcome screen shown in Figure 17-27.

Figure 17-27. *The SQL Server Welcome screen*

6. Review the system configuration shown in Figure 17-28, and check and address any errors. Click Next to continue. You may notice a warning on the Internet Information Services (IIS) feature. You can disregard this warning for now, as we will configure IIS following the installation of SQL.

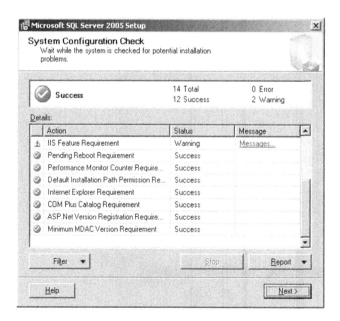

Figure 17-28. *Checking the system configuration*

7. Edit the Name and Company fields, shown in Figure 17-29, as desired, and click Next.

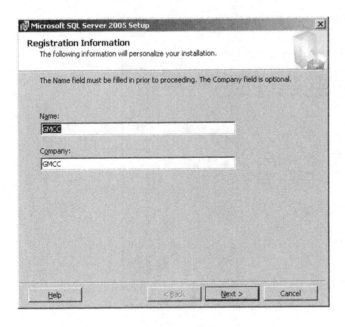

Figure 17-29. *Editing registration information*

8. In the Components to Install dialog box shown in Figure 17-30, select at least SQL Server Database Services, and click Next (you can also include Analysis Services, Notification Services, Integration Services, and Workstation components if desired).

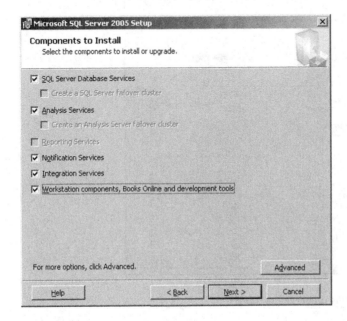

Figure 17-30. *Selecting components*

9. In Figure 17-31, leave the "Default instance" radio button selected, and click Next.

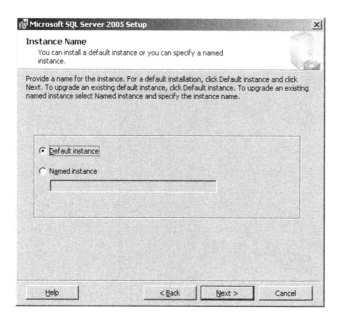

Figure 17-31. *Selecting the instance name*

10. As shown in Figure 17-32, select the built-in local system account for your service account.

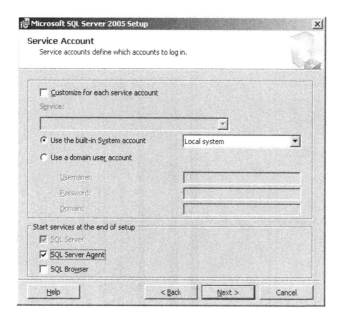

Figure 17-32. *Selecting the service account*

11. Select the Windows Authentication Mode radio button, as shown in Figure 17-33, and click Next.

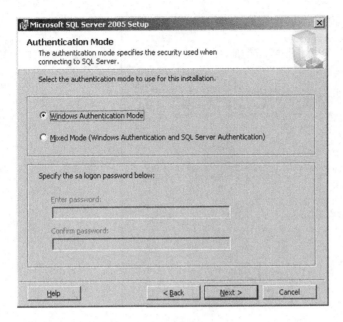

Figure 17-33. *Selecting the authentication mode*

12. Click Next in the screen shown in Figure 17-34 to choose the default collation settings.

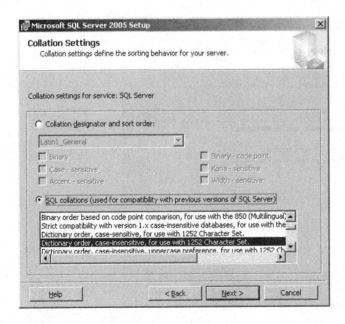

Figure 17-34. *Choosing the collation settings*

13. In the screen shown in Figure 17-35, choose whether or not to send data to Microsoft. Click Next to continue.

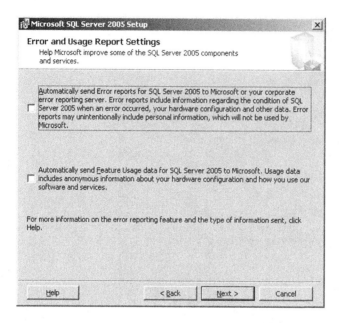

Figure 17-35. *Choosing to report data to Microsoft*

14. Click Install in the screen shown in Figure 17-36 to begin the component installation.

Figure 17-36. *Installing the components*

15. In the screen shown Figure 17-37, review the setup progress, and click Next when you finish.

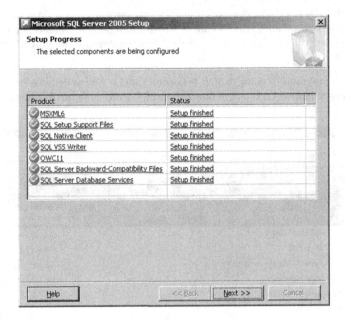

Figure 17-37. *Reviwing the setup progress*

16. Click Finish once you have reviewed the installation, as shown in Figure 17-38.

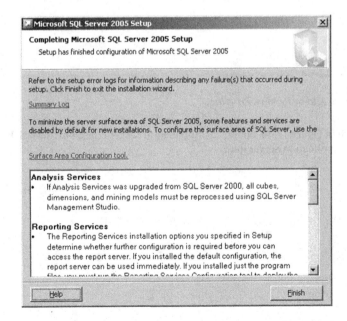

Figure 17-38. *Finishing the setup*

Installing IIS

IIS is a required component if you plan to have a reporting point, management point (MP), or Background Intelligent Transfer Service–enabled (BITS-enabled) distribution point on the site server. In this virtual lab environment, we will do exactly that, using the following steps to configure IIS on the SMS site server virtual machine:

1. Open Add or Remove Programs by going to Start ➤ Control Panel ➤ Add or Remove Programs. Click the Add/Remove Windows Component button in the left pane, as shown in Figure 17-39.

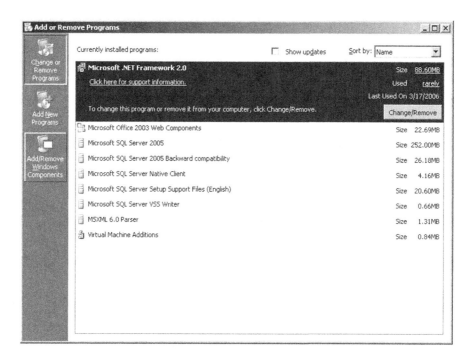

Figure 17-39. *Selecting Add or Remove Programs*

2. In the screen shown in Figure 17-40, enable the Application Server check box, and click Details to open the Application Server item.

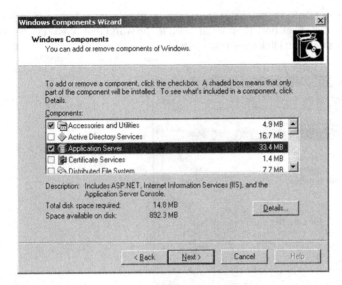

Figure 17-40. *Adding and removing Windows components*

3. As shown in Figure 17-41, select the "Enable network DTC access" check box. Next highlight the Internet Information Services (IIS) item, and click Details to open it.

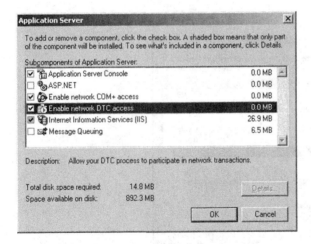

Figure 17-41. *Setting application server details*

4. In the screen shown in Figure 17-42, enable the Background Intelligent Transfer Service (BITS) Server Extensions check box. Then scroll down to the World Wide Web Service item (the last one), highlight it, and click Details to open it.

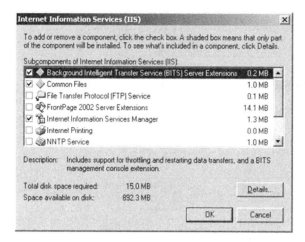

Figure 17-42. *Setting IIS details*

5. As shown in Figure 17-43, enable the Active Server Pages and WebDAV Publishing check boxes.

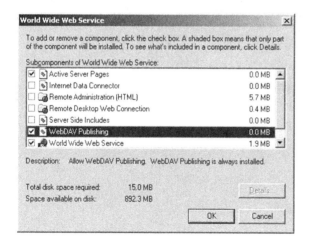

Figure 17-43. *Setting web service details*

Note Before you begin the installation, make sure you have captured the CD image for the Windows Server 2003 CD, or you will be prompted to do so.

---

6. Click the OK button three times to initiate the installation of IIS. Click Finish when the installation is complete, as shown in Figure 17-44.

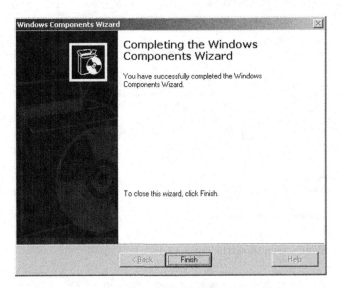

Figure 17-44. *Completing the IIS installation*

7. Close the Add or Remove Programs applet.

Installing SMS 2003 with SP2

Finally, we get to the real reason for setting up this lab: SMS 2003. Let's get busy! The following list provides the steps required to install SMS 2003 in your virtual test environment:

1. Drag and drop the SMS2003_SP2_Eval.exe file onto your SMS site server virtual machine. It will be copied to the desktop.

2. Double-click the file to extract it to a location of your choice.

3. Inside the extracted folder is a CD.Eval folder. Open it, and double-click the autorun.exe file to launch the install.

4. In the dialog box shown in Figure 17-45, click SMS 2003 Service Pack 2.

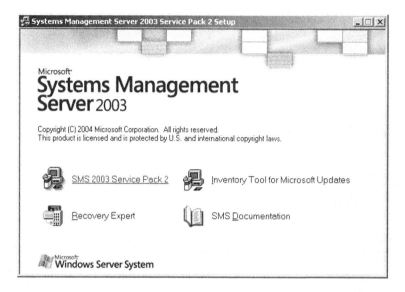

Figure 17-45. *The installation splash screen*

5. Click Next on the Welcome screen shown in Figure 17-46.

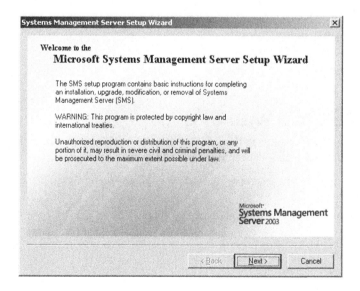

Figure 17-46. *The SMS 2003 Welcome screen*

6. Click Next on the screen shown in Figure 17-47 to continue the installation.

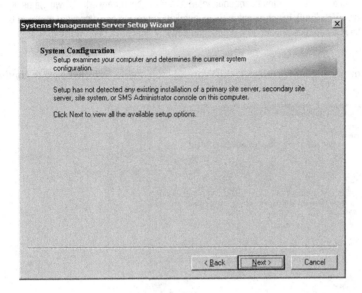

Figure 17-47. *The System Configuration screen*

7. As shown in Figure 17-48, choose the "Install an SMS primary site" option, and click Next.

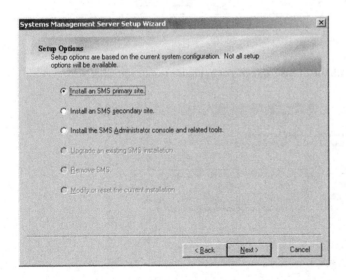

Figure 17-48. *Choosing setup options*

■Caution Make sure that your virtual machine is not connected to a production network. We will be using the Express Setup option to install SMS 2003, which enables client installation options and discovery methods by default. This option would have a negative impact on a production network. You have been warned!

8. In the screen shown in Figure 17-49, select the Express Setup option, and click Next to continue.

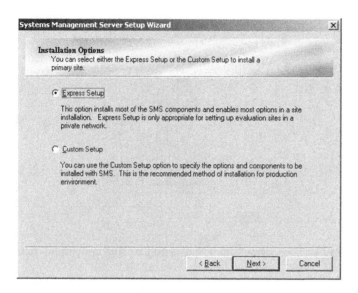

Figure 17-49. *Selecting express or custom setup*

9. Choose to agree with the license agreement in Figure 17-50, and click Next.

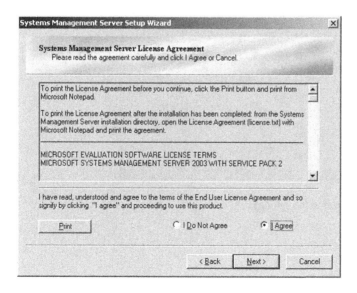

Figure 17-50. *Accepting the end user license agreement*

10. As shown in Figure 17-51, provide a Name and Organization; the evaluation CD product key should be present. Click Next.

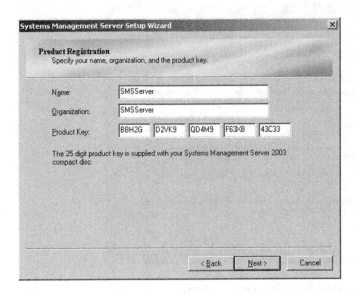

Figure 17-51. *Registering the product*

11. In the screen shown in Figure 17-52, enter a three-letter site code, and click Next.

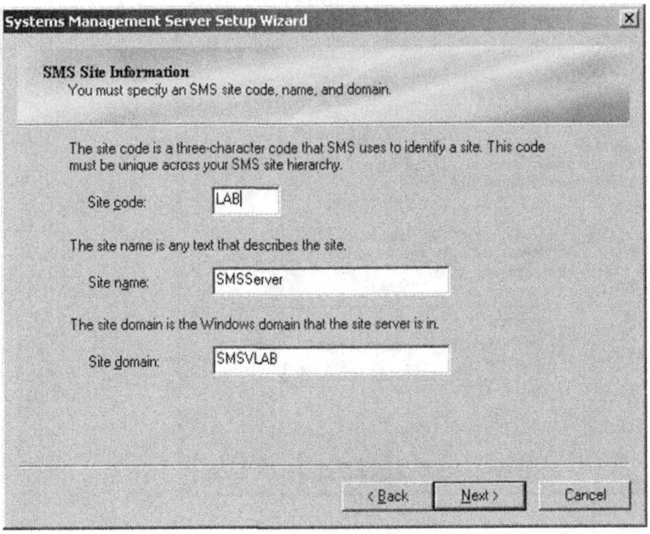

Figure 17-52. *Providing SMS site information*

12. Enable the "Extend the Active Directory schema" check box, as shown in Figure 17-53.

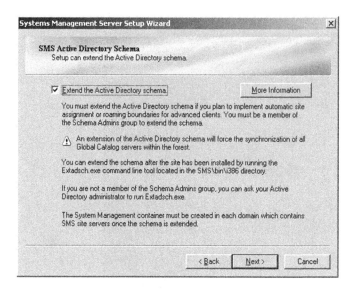

Figure 17-53. *Extending the Active Directory schema*

13. In the screen shown in Figure 17-54, choose Advanced security, and click Next.

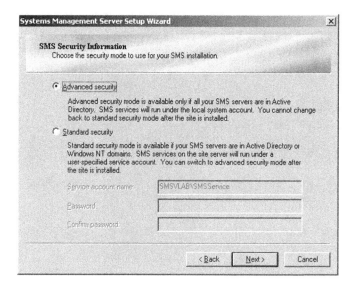

Figure 17-54. *Choosing SMS security*

14. As shown in Figure 17-55, the default value for the number of SMS clients should be fine for this virtual lab. Click Next.

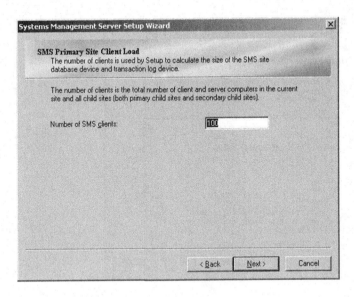

Figure 17-55. *Setting the client load*

15. The default value for the "Number of SMS Administrator consoles" in Figure 17-56 should be fine for this virtual lab. Click Next.

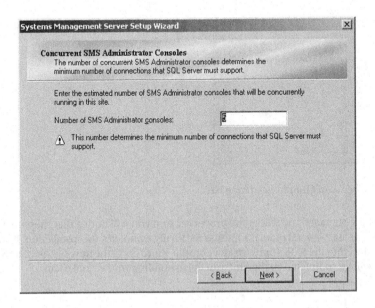

Figure 17-56. *Setting the number of Administrator consoles*

16. In the screen shown in Figure 17-57, review your information, and click Finish to initiate the installation.

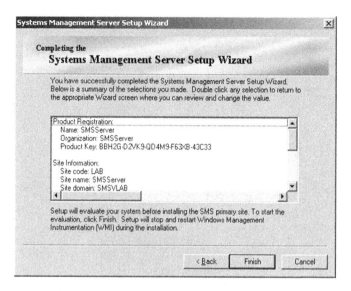

Figure 17-57. *Completing the SMS setup*

17. When the completion dialog box shown in Figure 17-58 is displayed, click OK, but don't believe it—additional setup processes will proceed for approximately 20 minutes.

Figure 17-58. *The Setup Completion dialog box*

18. Open your Task Manager and watch the processes, and you will notice that they will be quite busy for at least several more minutes as SMS truly completes the installation. If you are eager to dive into the SMS Administrator console, move on to the next section. The SMS installation will be completed by the time you finish building your virtual client.

Creating a Virtual Client

In this section, we will create a second virtual system. This system will be used as an SMS client. You can use any currently supported Windows operating system. For our demonstration purposes, we are creating a new Windows Server 2003 R2 system to be used as the client system.

1. Follow the steps in the section of this chapter titled "Creating a Virtual Machine" to create another virtual machine.

2. Follow the steps in the section of this chapter titled "Installing Windows Server 2003 R2" to install the operating system on the new virtual machine.

3. Configure the virtual machine to use only local networking, and set the Network setting in the virtual machine to be compatible with the SMS server.

4. Join the virtual machine to the domain that you created on your virtual SMS server.

Having Fun with the Virtual Lab

Now that you have a virtual lab set up, you can go back to previous chapters and run through any of the recipes that interest you. If you are new to SMS 2003, start with Chapter 2 to get comfortable with the many SMS configuration options.

A few items follow that the Express Setup installation didn't address:

- You need to enable the SMS server as a reporting point if you plan on testing web reporting.

- The network access account is not set. You need this if you will be using Client Push Installation in your testing.

- Containers aren't added to any of the Active Directory Discovery methods.

- You need to install the SMS client on your virtual client.

- You need to install the Inventory Tool for Microsoft Updates (ITMU) to test Microsoft patch deployment with SMS.

APPENDIX

■■■

Additional SMS Tools

The more you use SMS, the more you will see opportunities for growth with the product. Microsoft provides several additional tools for SMS; many third-party vendors and contributions from SMS administrators around the world also provide additional tools. Chapter 1 identifies many other available resources (most of them free) that will help make your job easier.

SMS 2003 is extremely functional right out of the box, but don't let that prevent you from using other tools that complement SMS. In this appendix, we try to highlight as many of those additional tools as possible.

Microsoft Tools

Microsoft has a number of additional tools for SMS 2003. They can be downloaded at http://www.microsoft.com/smserver/downloads/2003/default.mspx.

SMS 2003 Toolkit

The SMS 2003 Toolkit (currently in its second revision) includes 22 tools that help you better leverage SMS. Some of the tools are task specific, while others are for general use. We highlight some of the tools in the toolkit that should be helpful for everyone. You can download the toolkit at http://www.microsoft.com/smserver/downloads/2003/tools/toolkit.mspx. The following list briefly describes many of the tools available in the current version of the SMS 2003 Toolkit:

SMS Trace (Trace32.exe): You will use this tool every day for viewing the passel of log files that SMS creates. You can also view and actively monitor other log files, such as Windows Installer log files. Logs can be viewed with this tool even when the file is being modified, allowing you to watch an installation progress.

Advanced Client Spy (Clispy.exe): Use this tool for troubleshooting software distribution, inventory, and software metering on computers running an Advanced Client.

URLScan Template (URLScan.ini): SMS uses the URLScan version 2.5 security tool for implementing an Internet Information Services (IIS) lockdown on SMS 2003 site systems that use IIS 6.0 running on Windows Server 2003.

Policy Spy (PolicySpy.exe): Use this tool for viewing and troubleshooting the policy system on SMS Advanced Clients. This tool can also be used to refresh machine policy both locally and remotely. User policy can be refreshed locally.

Advanced Client and Management Point Cleaner (CCMClean.exe): Removing the Advanced Client or a management point (MP) requires manipulating Windows Installer, services, WMI, the registry, and the file system. Because of the difficulty in removing these roles, especially if they are not functioning properly and a successful uninstall might be impossible, this tool is required to automate the removal process.

Policy Verifier (PolicyVerifier.exe): Policy Verifier is a troubleshooting tool used to verify advertisement targeting problems. You can also troubleshoot connectivity problems on computers running SQL Server that host the SMS site database and SMS MPs.

Send Schedule (SendSched.vbs): The Send Schedule tool is used to trigger a schedule on an Advanced Client. You can run the script locally or remotely. For example, you can use the tool to trigger an inventory schedule. If a number of Advanced Clients have not reported inventory recently, you can run the tool to initiate the necessary schedule for each client.

Management Point Spy (MPGetPolicy.exe): The Management Point Spy connects with the SMS site database, retrieves all policies, and displays them with their policy versions. The tool also sends HTTP requests to the MP to view the actual policy. The MP can also be queried for the management point certificate.

Delete Certificate (CCMDelCert.exe): Delete Certificate removes certificates used by an SMS 2003 Advanced Client from a computer. Computer certificate removal is helpful when you want to capture a system image from a computer that will later be deployed to other computers.

Delete Group Class (DelGrp.exe): Creating an inventory group with hardware inventory permanently changes the schema of the SMS database. Occasionally, you may need or want to remove inventory group definitions when you need to reduce the amount of space being used by inventory, when an inventory group is no longer being collected, or when it was collected by accident. Use the Delete Group Class tool (DelGrp.exe) carefully.

Caution Even if you use the Delete Group Class (DelGrp.exe) tool, the class will reappear if the class is picked up again via hardware inventory. You may need to modify SMS_DEF.MOF or remove MIF files to prevent re-collection and schema extension in SMS.

Transfer SMS ID (TranGUID.exe): To use SMS effectively for asset management, a client computer's identity in the SMS site database must remain constant. If the client's identity changes, three problems will emerge: historical data from hardware inventory and software metering will be lost; the previous record will remain as an inactive record; and the new record will not be part of any direct membership collections that previously included the client. Use TranGUID.exe to preserve data when you move the SMS client GUID from one system to another.

Package Loader (Preloadpkgonsite.exe): The Package Loader tool is used to manually load a package on a site. This prevents a central site from sending a package to a child site by a sender. The tool is useful for organizations that must add a large number of packages to distribution points on primary or secondary sites that are connected by slow network links.

MP Troubleshooter (MPTroubleshooter.exe): The MP Troubleshooter tool checks a computer system before and after MP installation to ensure that the installation meets the requirements for MPs.

Client Assignment Verifier (ClientAssignment.exe): The Client Site Assignment Verifier tool is a troubleshooting resource to help you deploy and support SMS 2003 by verifying that clients can become assigned to a site.

Site Boundary (`SiteBoun.exe`): This tool imports and exports an array of SMS site boundary addresses in a text file, importing a text file to replace the array or appending a text file to the end of the array.

Create Secondary Site (`CrScndry.exe`): The Create Secondary Site tool creates a secondary site on the computer where you run the tool.

Create SMS Address (`CrAddr.exe`): The Create SMS Address tool creates or modifies addresses. Using the Create SMS Address tool is a convenient way to configure many addresses for numerous parent or child sites at the same time.

Note Consider the SMS 2003 Toolkit an "as-is, no-warranty" product. Microsoft does not offer any support for these tools.

Review the SMS 2003 Toolkit help file for a complete description of each available tool in the SMS 2003 Toolkit.

SMS Client Health Monitoring Tool

The Client Health Monitoring tool was introduced with SP1 and does an excellent job of identifying systems in your environment that may need remediation or have been offline for a significant amount of time. Use this tool to help predict and increase software distribution success rates.

SMS Operating System Deployment (OSD) Feature Pack

We haven't really touched on the OSD Feature Pack, but that doesn't mean it's not worth implementing. On the contrary, it could easily be the most valuable part of SMS for your organization. It does have a bit of a learning curve, and implementing it properly can take a while but is well worth it. The main features of the current version of the SMS 2003 OSD Feature Pack follow:

- *Image capture management*: You create a model system with the desired software installations and configurations, and use the OSD image capture process to capture the image (this process uses Microsoft Sysprep). The image is captured into Windows Image (WIM) format.

- *OS package management*: Once the image has been captured, you create an OS installation package in SMS. Within the operating system (OS) package, you can manage additional settings for the package, such as user notification, distribution settings, and network settings. Within the package, you are also able to configure multiple programs to install additional SMS packages. The ability to customize the image deployment to contain additional software gives you the flexibility to use the image for groups requiring different requirements.

- *User state migration*: The OSD Feature Pack integrates with the current version of the User State Migration tool to migrate and preserve user profiles when installing new OSs.

- *Image deployment*: Deploys OS images using the highly customizable, task-based SMS 2003 infrastructure. You can deploy the images using standard SMS software distribution methods, using a bootable CD, or by booting to the network. In all deployment methods, the SMS distribution points will be leveraged to minimize the impact on your network.

- *Reporting*: The OSD Feature Pack uses SMS advertisement status reporting for each deployment to help troubleshoot and demonstrate deployment success.

The OSD Feature Pack is used to deploy a new image of a system. This image can be deployed using SMS, a CD-based installation, and even Microsoft Remote Installation Services (RIS). When deploying with SMS, you can transfer user settings and documents from the *old* operating system to the *new* operating system (user state migration). The OSD leverages SMS software distribution, as well as SMS distribution points to target systems. Before you decide to purchase another imaging solution, consider the OSD Feature Pack. You will find a lot of power and extensibility, as well as a great support group at `http://www.myITforum.com`, the Microsoft SMS Newsgroups page (`microsoft.public.sms.tools`), and from the Microsoft SMS list (`http://www.myitforum.com/Lists.asp`). You can obtain the latest OSD information from the Microsoft downloads page (`http://www.microsoft.com/smserver/downloads/2003/osdfp.mspx`).

Also check out `http://support.microsoft.com/webcasts` for previous and future webcasts. Past Systems Management Webcasts may be viewed from here: `http://support.microsoft.com/pwebcst?cid=C_7953`.

SMS 2003 SP1 Administration Feature Pack

The Administration Feature Pack has three tools that you should be aware of:

- *Manage Site Accounts tool*: This tool allows you to centrally update the accounts that SMS uses to operate, without having to touch all of the SMS servers in your environment.

- *Transfer Site Settings Wizard*: If you create multiple SMS site servers at one time, this tool helps you clone the setting of one site server onto the rest of the site servers that you want to have a similar configuration.

- *Elevated Rights Deployment Tool (ERDT)*: This tool can be a lifesaver when you have an application that has to execute additional actions in an administrative context after a reboot.

Download these tools at `http://www.microsoft.com/smserver/downloads/2003/adminpack.mspx`.

SMS 2003 Device Management Feature Pack

If you have to manage Pocket PC devices in your enterprise, you may want to check out the Device Management Feature Pack. The SMS 2003 Device Management Feature Pack allows you to manage mobile devices running Windows CE (version 3.0 or later) and Windows Mobile software for Pocket PCs (version 2002 or later). The Device Management Feature Pack allows you to configure settings and security policies, deploy and update software, and obtain asset information from the device.

The Device Management Feature Pack provides the following capabilities:

- Hardware inventory
- Software inventory
- File collection
- Software distribution
- Settings management
- Password policy management

Review the Device Management Feature Pack web site for more information (`http://www.microsoft.com/smserver/downloads/2003/dmfp.mspx`). Also check out `http://support.microsoft.com/webcasts` for previous and future webcasts. Past systems management webcasts may be viewed at `http://support.microsoft.com/pwebcst?cid=C_7953`.

SMS 2003 SDK Version 3.1

For those who desire the ultimate in SMS knowledge, delving into the SDK should suit you just right. The SDK will provide all the information on extending all aspects of SMS, as well as give you a better understanding of what's under the hood. As you have read in previous chapters in this book, the SDK has a plethora of information. The SDK is a great starting point for learning how to extend SMS. Many examples are included for both managed and nonmanaged code.

The Help file that's included with the SDK is easily searchable and very detailed. Download the SDK from the main SMS 2003 downloads site (http://www.microsoft.com/smserver/downloads/2003).

SMS 2003 Scripting Guide

In addition to the many examples provided in this book, you will find over 40 example scripts in the *SMS 2003 Scripting Guide* (http://go.microsoft.com/fwlink/?LinkId=45570). This guide also provides a little more detail about WMI. Another up-and-coming link is the SMS 2003 Script Center (http://www.microsoft.com/technet/scriptcenter/hubs/sms.mspx).

SMS 2003 Capacity Planner

The Capacity Planner tool allows you to perform scenario-based analysis on your existing and proposed SMS 2003 hierarchy. The tool analyzes the input you provide and suggests site topology configurations and hardware configurations for SMS site servers and site systems. Download the tool from the SMS 2003 downloads site (http://www.microsoft.com/smserver/downloads/2003/default.mspx).

SMS 2003 Inventory Tool for Dell Updates

This tool currently supports Dell servers (contact your Dell representative for workstation support—we would like to see that too). This tool allows you to determine compliance and deploy the necessary updates for Dell BIOS, firmware, and drivers using the same process utilized to deploy security updates with SMS 2003. Similar to the Inventory Tool for Microsoft Updates (ITMU), you have a Sync tool, a Scan tool, and a new option in the Distribute Software Updates Wizard (DSUW) for deploying Dell server updates. Download the tool from the SMS 2003 downloads site (http://www.microsoft.com/smserver/downloads/2003/tools/dellupdates.mspx).

IBM Systems Update Tool for Microsoft SMS

The IBM Systems Update Tool for Microsoft SMS helps enable Microsoft SMS to manage IBM firmware and driver updates. This tool helps simplify the process of identifying needed IBM firmware and driver updates for IBM eServer and IBM eServer xSeries servers.

The IBM Systems Update Tool for SMS can leverage IBM UpdateXpress Server as a source for IBM updates. UpdateXpress Server is a web-based program for managing multiple versions of IBM device drivers and firmware updates from a central repository within your network. Download the tool from the IBM web site (http://www-03.ibm.com/servers/eserver/xseries/systems_management/utsms/).

SMS Installer

Microsoft SMS Installer is a free tool SMS administrators can use to create installations, repackage installations, and more. On the surface, it may appear to be a basic (and outdated) tool. But as some of the examples in this book demonstrate, you can use SMS Installer to accomplish difficult tasks SMS administrators encounter often. Because SMS Installer is free (with the purchase of SMS, of course) and fairly intuitive, it is a nice tool for beginners. And as many SMS experts will tell you, SMS Installer is very handy to have around to take care of smaller tasks. SMS Installer also has uninstall support. Download the SMS Installer from the SMS 2003 downloads site (http://www.microsoft.com/smserver/downloads/ 20/tools/installer.mspx).

SMS 2003 Desired Configuration Monitoring

Desired Configuration Monitoring (DCM) is one of the more recent additions to the SMS family. Use DCM to monitor hardware and software changes on systems where you need to be able to identify change. For example, you could write specific rules for your human resources (HR) application servers, and use the DCM tool to verify that development, user-acceptance test, and production systems maintain a specific set of software and/or hardware configurations. Download the DCM at http://www.microsoft.com/technet/itsolutions/cits/mo/sman/dcm.mspx.

SMS 2003 Account Review Tool

Are you using too many SMS accounts? Use the SMS 2003 Account Review tool to audit your SMS accounts and help identify risky account settings in your environment. Download the Account Review tool from the SMS 2003 downloads site (http://www.microsoft.com/smserver/downloads/ 2003/default.mspx).

Systems Management Server 2003 R2

The most recent feature available for SMS 2003 is SMS 2003 Release 2 (R2). SMS 2003 R2 builds on SMS 2003 SP2. The need for more efficient change and configuration management processes is one of the driving forces behind SMS 2003 R2. One of the primary features of SMS 2003 R2 is the Inventory Tool for Custom Updates (ITCU).

The ITCU gives you the ability to perform scans on targeted systems, as well as use the DSUW to deploy software based on custom catalogs. These custom catalogs can be catalogs that you create or catalogs that are provided by independent software vendors. For example, you could create a custom catalog that contains the minimum file versions for your line of business applications and their dependent applications.

Independent software vendors are also starting to catch on to the idea of the ITCU. Currently, Adobe, Citrix, and 1E provide ITCU catalogs that you can use to detect application version or patch issues, so you can use the DSUW to pull the installation application(s) to distribute the updates.

To create your own custom catalogs for the ITCU, use the Custom Updates Publishing Tool. Don't be alarmed by the requirement of SQL Server 2005 for the Custom Updates Publishing Tool. This doesn't mean that your SMS site needs to be using SQL 2005. You only need SQL 2005 components on the system that has the Custom Updates Publishing Tool installed.

As you can see, SMS is really pushing into the desired configuration realm. Spend some time getting to know these tools—desired configuration is adding a whole new dimension to SMS.

Another feature of SMS 2003 R2 is the Scan Tool for Vulnerability Assessment (STVA). The STVA uses MBSA 2.0 technology to perform checks for vulnerabilities that may exist because of improper system configuration. STVA checks for unnecessary services, file share permissions, Windows Firewall, unsecured guest accounts, and more. Use the STVA to help make your environment more secure.

The SMS 2003 R2 tools are available from the SMS downloads site (http://www.microsoft.com/ smserver/downloads/2003/default.mspx).

Right-click Tools

If you have spent much time in the SMS Administrator console, you know that right-clicking a node provides you with several options for managing the selected node, depending on the node type. For example, when you right-click a collection and select All Tasks, you can select Install Client (to install the client via Client Push), Distribute Software, Update Collection Membership, and more. Speaking of collections in particular, there are many other actions you may wish to perform against a collection, or a member of a collection. Right-click tools provide this functionality. Figure A-1 displays an SMS Administrator console with additional context menu integration.

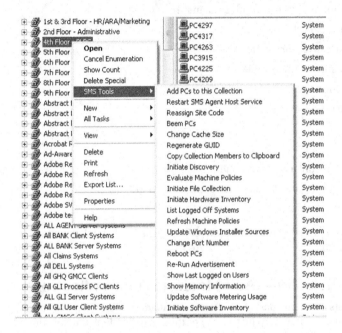

Figure A-1. *Context Menu Integration*

As you can see in Figure A-1, additional actions are available under the SMS Tools menu. By selecting one of these options, that action will be performed on all systems in the collection. For example, to refresh SMS machine policy on all systems in this collection, simply select Refresh Machine Policies.

■**Caution** Most actions that appear under the SMS Tools context menu require the SMS client to be on the network (at the time the action is initiated) and remotely accessible. Also, the user initiating the action must have proper permissions to the client. Many of the examples in Figure A-1 require administrative access to the targeted systems, as they are touching WMI in the root/ccm namespace for the Advanced Client.

The following sections describe a few of our favorite *free* right-click tools available for download from http://www.myitforum.com.

Cory Becht's Right-click Tools

Almost all of the client actions you would like to perform on a system, or a collection of systems, can be accomplished using Cory Becht's set of tools. For example, you can use these tools to perform the following tasks:

- Reassign the site code
- Restart the SMS Agent Host service
- Regenerate the SMS client GUID
- Rerun advertisements without modifying the advertisement
- Initiate the Heartbeat Discovery cycle
- Initiate a delta or full software inventory cycle
- Initiate a delta or full hardware inventory cycle
- Initiate a software file collection cycle
- Initiate a software metering usage report cycle
- Refresh machine policy
- Evaluate machine policies
- Initiate the Update Windows Installer Sources cycle
- Change the port number that the SMS client uses to connect to its MP
- Change the Advanced Client cache size

Cory Becht's right-click tools are probably the most used SMS tools in our arsenal; download them at http://www.myitforum.com/articles/8/view.asp?id=7099.

Greg Ramsey's Right-click Tool—Add Machines to a Collection

If you're like us, you receive requests on a daily basis for software installations. Some requests may be to thousands of systems, while others may be to just a few. For those smaller deployments, this tool may help make your job easier. You may have standard installations of software that are already advertised, and all you need to do is add the requested systems to a collection to receive the desired software. By using Greg Ramsey's tool, you are able to right-click a collection and select Add PCs to this Collection. A dialog box will appear that allows you to enter (or paste) multiple computer names, one per line. Next click OK, and the desired systems will be added to the selected collection, using a direct membership rule. It's written as an HTML application, so modify it to fit your needs. Download this tool at http://www.myitforum.com/articles/1/view.asp?id=7609.

Brian Tucker's Custom Tools to View Site and Client Information

Brian Tucker has compiled a nice set of tools to help you troubleshoot a remote client from your Administrator console. You can perform the following actions from Brian's Context Menu integration:

- Assign a client to an SMS site
- Launch SMS Service Manager
- Launch SMS Trace
- Launch an SMS web reporting server
- Launch MP Troubleshooter
- Connect to C$ on a remote system

- Connect to `ADMIN$` on a remote system
- Ping a workstation
- Reboot a workstation
- Start Event Viewer
- Open a client cache folder
- Restart Remote Control
- Launch Client Spy
- Open a remote client log folder
- Open 24 individual client log files with SMS Trace

Download Brian's Tools at `http://www.myitforum.com/articles/8/view.asp?id=8342`.

Creating Your Own Context Menu Integration

As you can see from the previous sections, SMS administrators have been very creative in expanding the SMS Administrator console to help make their jobs easier. You can take a look at the examples and learn from them to create your own integration. Here are a couple web resources that will help get you started with adding your own context menu integration for the SMS Administrator console:

- The SMS 2003 SDK (`http://msdn.microsoft.com/library/en-us/smssdk03/hh/sms/usingsms_8ipa.asp`)
- An article titled "Create Your Own Custom Tools in SMS 2003" by Brian Tucker (`http://www.myitforum.com/articles/8/view.asp?id=8354`)

Recipe 3-20, "Adding a Right-click Option to Affect a Member of a Collection," also discusses how to extend context menu integration.

Keep in mind that context menu integration in the SMS console doesn't actually have to be related to SMS. You can use context menu integration to simply launch your favorite application or web site. Keep an eye on the myITforum.com downloads page (`http://www.myitforum.com/downloads`); handy utilities are posted there frequently.

Wake-On-LAN (WOL) Tools

Wake-On-LAN (WOL) is a feature that allows you to turn on a computer from another location over a network connection. Many businesses use WOL with SMS to wake up systems during the night for software (or patch) installations. Installing software during nonworking hours reduces frustrations for end users, as well as for SMS administrators.

WOL Overview

We can't take the time in this book to explain how WOL works, but the following web links may help you understand the process a little better:

- `http://www.depicus.com/wake-on-lan/what-is-wake-on-lan.aspx`
- `http://www.activexperts.com/activsocket/tutorials/wol/`
- `http://www.annoyances.org/exec/show/article04-101`
- `http://www.solarwinds.net/Toolsets/Content/Wake-On-LAN.htm`

The first two links provide more detail about how WOL works. The last two links describe how to enable WOL on a client. According to information on the Annoyances.org web site, your client must meet the following requirements to be WOL-capable:

- You must have a power supply that is complaint with ATX 2.01 (or above) and an ATX motherboard with a WOL connector.

- You must have a WOL-compliant network card with a WOL connector. An example is the 3Com Fast Etherlink XL PCI 3C905B-TX but not the 3Com Fast Etherlink XL PCI 3C905B-TX-NM (nonmanaged).

- Compare the WOL pin descriptions for your network card and for your motherboard. They must be identical; otherwise, your motherboard or power supply may be damaged.

- Your BIOS must support WOL, and the WOL option in your BIOS setup must be enabled. If you don't see a WOL option, check with the manufacturer of your motherboard for an updated BIOS.

- Your network card drivers must also support WOL; check with your network card manufacturer for the latest drivers.

As you can see from the configuration points, WOL may take some time and planning to implement. The best place to start this configuration process is in your standard images, so that all new clients receive proper configuration. One of the biggest issues we've experienced in our environments is that the network card driver doesn't support WOL, typically because the installed driver is a generic Windows plug-and-play driver and not a driver from the manufacturer. Another issue we see frequently is that the BIOS is not properly configured.

Configuring all of your clients manually would be difficult and time-consuming. Depending on your hardware manufacturers, both motherboard and network interface card (NIC), you may be able to apply these updates using SMS. For example, Dell has a client configuration utility that you can use to update and configure the BIOS for WOL. Dell also provides the proper drivers for the installed network card, which can (generally) be installed using SMS. HP/COMPAQ and Lenovo also provide similar functionality. Contact your PC manufacturer for additional details. For an example of managing a Dell BIOS using VBScript, review Dan Thomson's article titled "Managing Dell BIOS Settings" (http://www.myitforum.com/articles/11/view.asp?id=5494).

Note When purchasing new systems, you may want to take these configuration options into consideration. When managing large environments (as SMS usually does), the ability to update and reconfigure the BIOS in an unattended fashion could be considered priceless. You may also want to consider working with the hardware vendor to have the BIOS settings configured to your standards when the systems are purchased.

One of the biggest challenges for WOL is the difficulty in waking up a system on a network other than your local network (or from wherever the WOL utility is run). When a program initiates a WOL packet, the packet is usually a broadcast to the local network. For security reasons, broadcasts are typically confined to the local network. There are two work-arounds to wake up systems on a remote network:

- Enable directed broadcasts. Enabling directed broadcasts is a configuration in your network hardware that allows a system to broadcast to predefined networks. This solution is the *easiest*, but not necessarily the most secure (just ask your network administrator—you'll get an ear full).

- Use a (powered-on) client (sometimes called a "slave" or "helper" system) on the remote network to wake up the systems on its network. This work-around requires at least one system on each network to be powered on and able to communicate with the system that requests the WOL for the remote network.

SMS Tools for WOL

You can use any WOL tool to wake up systems, but the following tools are specifically configured to function with SMS—in fact, most are integrated into the SMS Administrator console:

- *SMS Companion 2006*: SMS Expert's SMS Companion 2006 suite includes a WOL feature that can be used to wake up clients for advertisements and inventory processes through the SMS Administrator console. For more information on SMS Companion 2006 and other tools from SMS Expert, see `http://www.smsexpert.com/products/companion.asp`.

- *SMSWakeUp*: 1E's SMSWakeUp also provides WOL functionality from the SMS Administrator console. You have the ability to right-click a collection (or single system) and initiate a wake-up. You can also configure SMSWakeUp to automatically wake up systems prior to a mandatory advertisement time. With logging enabled, you can identify systems that failed to wake up. SMSWakeUp can be used with directed broadcast or with single or multiple slaves (running a slave service) on each network. SMSWakeUp is sold as a stand-alone product, as well as with the SMS Patch Management Pack, which includes SMSWakeUp and NightWatchman, a product used to intelligently shut down systems while safely closing applications and saving application data (e.g., Microsoft Word documents). For more information on SMSWakeUp and NightWatchman, visit the 1E web page (`http://www.1e.com/SoftwareProducts/SMSWakeUp`).

- *WakeonLanSMS*: Similar to the other products previously mentioned, SMSUtils's WakeonLanSMS provides WOL functionality that automatically wakes up client systems prior to a mandatory advertisement start time. For more information on WakeonLanSMS, visit the SMSUtils web page (`http://www.smsutils.com/Default.aspx?tabid=61`).

- *WOL.NET*: Top Technologies Consulting's WOL.NET is a web-based solution that enables you to initiate WOL on one or multiple SMS collections. The WOL initiation can be scheduled in advance as well. WOL.NET requires directed broadcast enabled network routers. For more information on WOL.NET, visit the Top Technologies Consulting web page (`http://www.toptechnologies.de/prod_wol.aspx?displaylang=en`).

Shopping Cart Technology and Software License Management

Shopping cart technology allows end users to shop for software to be installed on their computers. Think of this shopping as a mostly self-service process. Depending on your individual processes, the SMS administrator may not have any involvement at all on the day-to-day installations of software that uses a shopping cart. Both of the shopping carts described in this section also provide for an approval process for software to be deployed.

Software license management helps you keep track of how many licenses you have for a specific product and compare them with how many are installed (according to SMS). Here are the three most popular SMS add-ons for license management:

Enterprise Service Desk 2006 (ESD 2006): According to SMS Expert's ESD 2006 product web page (`http://www.smsexpert.com/products/esd.asp`), "ESD 2006 provides users with a familiar and easy-to-use storefront to request any type of IT assets like software, hardware, and active directory user accounts. Publish any type of request including OSD images, service packs, computers, laptop bags, and office supplies. ESD 2006 uses approval and inventory management policies to ensure requests are secure and receive the proper approval."

Shopping: According to 1E's Shopping product web page (http://www.1e.com/SoftwareProducts/ Shopping),"Shopping from 1E is a simple, self-service, shopping cart solution that enables your users to select the applications they need from the applications available for installation in your organization. Shopping automates the approval workflow, software delivery and license control, ensuring your users get their applications as quickly and effortlessly as possible."

Systems Audit Manager (SAM): ExtendedTool's SAM is a reasonably priced auditing tool to help you track license compliance in your environment. With SAM, you can add license counts, group multiple products into one (for license tracking), and even track on a "per SMS site" basis. For more information on SAM, visit ExtendedTool's SAM product web site (http://www.extendedtools. com/sam/sam.htm).

In addition to license management, ESD 2006 and 1E's Shopping provide shopping cart technologies, which allow the end-user to shop for and order software.

Software Packaging/Repackaging and Windows Installer Transform Creation Tools

Software packaging is what an SMS administrator does for in-house applications (applications for which a developer has given you the files and configuration information). You create a software installation package, so that you can deploy this software using SMS. Generally speaking, the software is deployed in an unattended fashion, meaning no input is required from the user. Your abilities as a software packager (and the abilities of the packaging application) may not be needed daily, but you should always be well prepared for them to be called upon.

Software repackaging is an *art*, not a science. We're not exactly sure who said that first, but we're certain more than one SMS administrator has said it on occasion. In our own words, when you repackage software, you are creating a new installation that conforms to the standards of your enterprise. Often (but not always), this standard will include the ability to install the software in an unattended fashion. After all, you are the SMS administrator—part of your job is to deliver software to the end user in the most efficient (and least painful) way possible. In our practice, software repackaging is a last resort. Always attempt to configure your installation using the vendor's installation first. After you've attempted all avenues of approach (including those suggested by newsgroups like http://www. myITforum.com and http://www.appdeploy.com), proceed cautiously with software repackaging. The end result of a software package/repackage is typically an installation executable or a Windows Installer file with the data files and configurations either compressed inside the file or required as source files for installation.

Windows Installer Transforms can be handy tools to help you create preconfigured and unattended installations of Window Installer (.msi) files. Without going into detail about Windows Installer and Transforms, think of Windows Installer Files as a database that contains all installation details for the application—custom setup, default setup, all other installation options, and even application configuration can be included in a Windows Installer File. You can use a Windows Installer Transform (.mst) to modify the installation to your desired parameters.

The following list provides basic details of a few of the primary software packaging/repackaging applications; spend some time determining your needs and evaluating the products before cutting a check:

- *Microsoft SMS Installer*: Although this tool is starting to show its age, the SMS Installer is a very popular packager/repackager among SMS administrators. If you're looking to install a shortcut, perform a basic software installation, or modify an installation that's not Windows Installer–based, this tool can probably handle it. It's very lightweight (under 50MB) and is provided free of charge to licensed SMS users (http://www.microsoft.com/smserver/downloads/ 20/tools/installer.mspx).

- *Macrovision FLEXnet AdminStudio, SMS Edition*: The SMS edition of AdminStudio is a scaled-back version of their full product (mentioned later). With the SMS Edition, you can repackage software and create custom Windows Installer Transforms. You cannot *add* configuration changes and/or files to a product that has been repackaged with AdminStudio, SMS Edition. This product is also provided free of charge to licensed SMS users (`http://www.microsoft.com/smserver/downloads/2003/featurepacks/adminstudio/default.mspx`).

- *Macrovision FLEXnet AdminStudio*: Formerly called InstallShield AdminStudio, this very powerful suite contains all features of the AdminStudio SMS Edition product mentioned previously, with a higher price tag of course. Many additional features are also included. Research and evaluate AdminStudio on the Macrovision web site (`http://www.macrovision.com/products/flexnet_adminstudio`).

- *Wise Package Studio (WPS)*: WPS is also a very powerful suite. Features like Conflict Manager and Preflight Deployment will help you succeed in packaging/repackaging software. WPS includes a program called InstallTailor, which helps you create Windows Installer Transforms. InstallTailor is also available as a free, stand-alone product (`http://www.wise.com/wps.asp`).

- *Caphyon Advanced Installer*: This product is new to us, but we feel it's well worth mentioning. From the product description, the free version of the product allows you to create fairly complex Windows Installer–based packages (no repackaging). It's probably worth a few minutes of your time to evaluate (`http://www.advancedinstaller.com`).

Which packager/repackager is best for you? That's for you to evaluate. If you are new to software packaging and repackaging, we strongly recommend you begin with the free tools mentioned in this section. Once you've truly experienced their limitations, consider moving into the more powerful, full-featured suites of Macrovision FLEXnet AdminStudio or Wise Package Studio. Chapter 1 contains a sidebar that compares SMS Installer and Macrovision's InstallShield SMS Edition. Also, consider reviewing Recipe 13-11, "Repackaging Software," which provides additional information about repackaging software.

SMS Remote Tools and Other Client Management Tools

If you use SMS Remote Control, you may find it painful to expand the Collections node in the SMS Administrator console *just* to initiate Remote Control on a system. In this section, we'll provide examples of how to launch Remote Control without navigating the SMS Administrator console (the console must be installed on the system but does not need to be open).

We will also discuss other client management tools in this section. All tools mentioned in this section (and its subsections) are *free*!

We also feel that right-click utilities are worth mentioning again, in case you haven't read the "Right-click Tools" section earlier in this appendix. Be sure to look at the "Right-click Tools" section for more ways to make your job easier.

Remote Control from the Command Line

Many SMS administrators (especially those in large environments) avoid using Remote Control through the SMS Administrator console, because enumerating a collection with a large number of resources can be time consuming. If you know the IP address of the desired system, open a command prompt, and navigate to the SMS Administrator console installation directory (e.g., c:\smsadmin\bin\i386\). Enter **remote 2 192.168.25.21**, where 192.168.25.21 is the IP of the desired system.

Remote Control Using a VBScript Script by Dave Kindness

While launching Remote Control using an IP address is useful (and sometimes necessary because of DNS or WINS issues in your environment), end users may be more familiar with the computer name. You will find a few examples on myITforum.com that demonstrate how to use a computer name to query the SMS database to obtain the IP address. You can then extend that example to then initiate a Remote Control session. For an example, obtain the VBScript source script written by Dave Kindness from myITforum.com (`http://www.myitforum.com/articles/11/view.asp?id=431`), and follow the directions on the web page.

Heine Jeppesen's Remote Control FrontEnd Tool

Heine Jeppesen's Remote Control tool is our personal favorite. As you can see from Figure A-2, after launching the program you are prompted for either a computer name *or* a user name. Simply select the desired type, enter the name, and click Search. Remote Control FrontEnd will query the SMS database and return all records that match the criteria. Next, select the desired system, and click Remote Control. Download this very handy utility from myITforum.com (`http://www.myitforum.com/articles/1/view.asp?id=5250`).

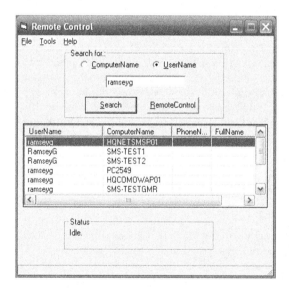

Figure A-2. *Remote Control FrontEnd by Heine Jeppesen*

Using Ron Crumbaker's Remote Tools Page for Multiple Remote Operations

Ron Crumbaker developed an ASP page that is used to perform multiple remote operations on a client. For example, you can perform any of the following operations:

- Initiate Remote Control
- Display the current user name
- Launch Computer Management
- Launch a Remote Desktop Connection

- Refresh SMS machine policy
- Display system resources
- Display Add or Remove Programs information
- Launch SMS Resource Explorer
- Launch Remote Assistance
- Initiate client repair
- Find a machine name based on the last logon user name
- Push an SMS advertisement to a system (add a member to a collection that currently has the advertisement)

Figure A-3 displays the main functionality area of the Remote Tools Page. Download Ron's Remote Tools Page at http://www.myitforum.com/articles/19/view.asp?id=8662.

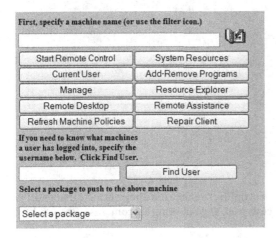

Figure A-3. *The Remote Tools Page by Ron Crumbaker*

Using Greg Ramsey's SMSView for Multiple Remote Client Operations

Greg Ramsey created a Visual Basic .NET application called SMSView that can be used to manage the SMS Advanced Client on the local system or on a remote system. SMSView has the following highlights:

- Display mandatory assignments, nonmandatory assignments, and current advertisement status (e.g., running, success, waiting for logoff, etc.)
- View advertisement history (past 60 days)
- Rerun advertisements
- Display hardware and/or software inventory status
- Display the current MP (or PMP)
- Initiate client repair
- Refresh machine policy

The best feature of SMSView is that it can be used to manage remote systems as well as the local system. Visit `http://www.smsview.com` to obtain the latest version of this tool. Figure A-4 shows the main page of SMSView.

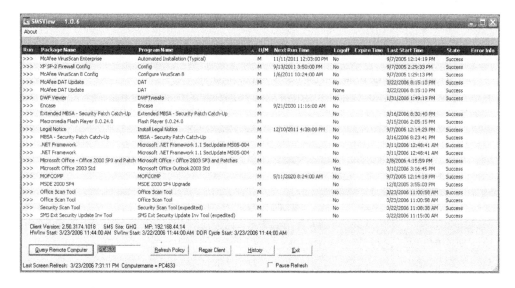

Figure A-4. *SMSView by Greg Ramsey*

Scripting Resources

Throughout this book you find many references to scripting resources. We hope by now that you consider this book as a valuable scripting resource as well. The following list contains a few worth mentioning one more time:

- *The TechNet Script Center*: The TechNet Script Center is a very large site that's full of script examples and tutorials to help you become a better scripter. This site is good for both the novice and the expert (`http://www.microsoft.com/technet/scriptcenter`).

- *SMS 2003 Scripting Guide*: With over 40 example SMS scripts for both the SMS Advanced Client and SMS Server, this is a great resource to get you started with scripting in SMS. Visit the SMS Product Documentation web page, and search for **SMS Scripting Guide**. It's available through a web interface as well as a downloadable help (.chm) file (`http://www.microsoft.com/smsserver/techinfo/productdoc`).

- *The myITforum.com Code Repository*: Instead of reinventing the wheel, take some time to analyze the resources available to you. The myITforum.com Code Repository contains more than 1,200 scripts for your scripting pleasure. In the Code Repository, you can search by author, name, description, source, or code. Figure A-5 displays the main page of the Code Repository. From within the application, you can run code, save code to file, import, and more! Visit the following web page to see more views of the Code Repository and to download it for yourself: `http://www.myitforum.com/articles/11/view.asp?id=6298`.

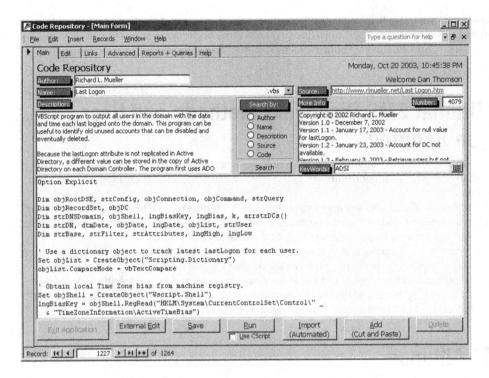

Figure A-5. *The myITforum.com Code Repository*

Managing Non-Windows Platforms with SMS 2003

Who says SMS can't manage non-Windows platforms? Not Quest Software, that's for sure. If you have UNIX, Linux, or Mac OS X, you can manage those platforms through Quest's Vintela Management Extensions (VMX). VMX allows you to natively manage these systems through the SMS Administrator console. So yes, you can centralize and standardize systems management across heterogeneous environments. In addition to all of these great benefits, first-level support for VMX is provided directly from Microsoft Product Support Services (PSS).

Most of the features for standard Windows clients are available to the non-Windows systems mentioned previously—features such as software distribution, software inventory, software metering, Remote Tools, file collection, and more. Before purchasing another management tool to handle non-Windows systems, take some time to evaluate VMX (http://www.vintela.com/products/vmx). The Blogcast Repository also has a great blogcast that shows VMX in action (http://blogcastrepository.com/blogcasts/37/sms/entry348.aspx).

Consolidating Manufacturer and Product Names en Masse for Software Inventory

SMS software inventory can be a very powerful (and often necessary) feature for your organization. Software inventory's *weakest link* is that software manufacturer and software product names for a specific piece of software often change from version to version. As detailed in Chapter 10, you can customize software inventory to consolidate product and manufacturer names to increase the accuracy (and readability) of software inventory data. A Czech company named Infinity has two scripts available for download to help you consolidate these manufacturer and product names. Run these scripts in a test environment first to ensure products don't become *too* consolidated. Review Recipe 10-13, "Consolidating Manufacturer and Product Names en Masse," for download and installation information.

Additional SMS Discovery Methods and User Logon Auditing

If you're looking to discover additional devices or include additional Active Directory data in SMS (e.g., e-mail addresses, telephone numbers, etc.), review the additional discovery methods described in Chapter 2.

As an SMS administrator, you may receive requests from time to time to identify the computer a user logs into or even to identify all the systems a user has logged into. Steve Bobosky from Centerlogic created the User Security Login auditing tool (often abbreviated SLAT).

According to the Centerlogic web site, you can "use the User Security Login auditing tool to track where users are logging in. Some sample web reports are included which allow you to: identify all systems a specific user has logged onto, list all users who have logged onto a specific system, identify the top users of systems, and identify systems where the top user is not the last logged on user."

Download the SLAT from `http://www.systemcentertools.com/`.

SMS Alliance

The SMS Alliance was formed in 2004. It is a group of companies that address SMS customers' needs that fall outside the basic scope of SMS. These six companies provide applications that extend SMS and consulting services to help implement a total solution for SMS customers. If you are looking for someone to provide an end-to-end SMS implementation, look to the SMS Alliance. They have a web site at `http://www.sms-alliance.com`.

An overview of the Alliance members follows:

- *1E*: This London-based company has an arsenal of SMS-enhancing tools. They also consult on systems management implementations.

- *Intrinsic*: This Chicago-based consulting company has probably assisted with more implementations of SMS than any other consulting company. They also have some applications that interface with SMS.

- *PS'SOFT*: They specialize in asset management and service management. Their products tie into SMS to extend the capabilities for managing IT assets.

- *iAnywhere*: iAnywhere provides the capability to manage all your various handheld devices.

- *Quest (Vintela)*: Quest's Vintela products are designed to allow SMS to extend to non-Windows platforms.

- *Macrovision (InstallShield)*: They provide repackaging and installation building through their AdminStudio product. They also offer an SMS Edition of the product that has limited functionality but can be downloaded for free.

Index